Government and Politics in Britain

Fourth Edition

4TH EDITION

GOVERNMENT AND POLITICS

IN BRITAIN

BY JOHN KINGDOM
WITH PAUL FAIRCLOUGH

polity

To the memory of my father, John Henry Kingdom

First edition published in 1991 by Polity Press

This edition first published in 2014 by Polity Press

Polity Press
65 Bridge Street
Cambridge CB2 1UR, UK

Polity Press
350 Main Street
Malden, MA 02148, USA

ISBN-13: 978-0-7456-3889-8(pb)

A catalogue record for this book is available from the British Library.

Typeset in 10 on 14 pt Utopia by
Servis Filmsetting Ltd, Stockport, Cheshire
Printed and bound in China by 1010 Printing International Ltd., China

The publisher has used its best endeavours to ensure that the URLs for external websites referred to in this book are correct and active at the time of going to press. However, the publisher has no responsibility for the websites and can make no guarantee that a site will remain live or that the content is or will remain appropriate.

Every effort has been made to trace all copyright holders, but if any have been inadvertently overlooked the publisher will be pleased to include any necessary credits in any subsequent reprint or edition.

For further information on Polity, visit our website: www.politybooks.com

Contents

Preface

The chapters of this book represent a wide-ranging introduction to British politics. The expectation is that it will be studied over some time (one or two years) and the chapters generally reflect a sense of cumulative development so that, for example, chapter 4 is written on the assumption that chapters 1, 2 and 3 have been mastered. However, it is also the case that each has a clearly discernible focus and assumes no detailed prior knowledge of the topic. Hence the chapters can (under the direction of the teacher/tutor) be studied in a different order without major conceptual difficulty. Each chapter concludes with a summary of main points, a list of key terms and concepts, questions for discussion and debate and a guide to further reading.

The summaries and key terms and concepts

The summary of key points is intended to highlight the essential thrust of the discussion in the chapter, providing a means of quick recapitulation and a revision aid. The lists of key terms and concepts are intended as a form of self-testing upon completion of each chapter. One should feel able to give concise definitions of all these before proceeding. Usually they are explained fully in the chapter.

The Glossary and Chronology

The Glossary can be used variously as an aid to revision, in essay writing and to provide speedy clarification of a meaning during the course of reading. The definitions offered are necessarily brief and greater clarification should be sought in that part of the text where the topic is dealt with most fully (as indicated in the Index). New terms appear in **bold** type when they are first discussed.

The Chronology will enable you to see at a glance the sequence of the major events in British politics and their relationship to world history. It is often surprising to discover what happened when.

Further reading

The study of politics at an introductory level is essentially concerned with reading and thinking. We are not able to study our subject in a laboratory and we cannot manipulate the real world to conduct experiments. There is of course a real world of political activity, and it is profoundly dangerous to forget this fact, but the amount any individual can find out by direct observation is minuscule. In the early stages of study, we must rely on accounts from various sources, including the mass media, historians, and academics from the range of disciplines discussed in chapter 1.

The further reading suggested at the end of each chapter cannot pretend to be comprehensive and students should feel free to explore the literature of the discipline according to their particular interests. The sources listed are chosen for various reasons: sometimes the work is a classic, sometimes it is controversial, and sometimes unusual. Generally the suggestions are made because they are regarded as of an intrinsically high quality as well as being stimulating.

The suggestions for reading around the subject include material that does not always appear to be political. However, much literature and drama, both light and serious, addresses the big questions of life and politics. It is important to remember that politics is not something outside normal social experience, unable to explain everyday problems; on the contrary, it lies at the very root of our social condition.

Journal articles are not included in the further reading because there are so many, though of course references can be found throughout the text. However, students new to the subject will find *Politics Review* a useful way of keeping up to date. Other accessible journals are *Parliamentary Affairs* and *Political Quarterly*. There is also, of course, some excellent political reporting and analysis in the quality press.

Since the first edition of this book was published, the expansion of the internet has given students another source of information. Several websites are mentioned at the end of most chapters; by using a search engine and following hypertext links you will find countless others. Although government websites provide much useful information, remember that they are also purveying the 'official' line. Similarly, some of the more outlandish sources must be approached with caution.

Discussion

Mere width of reading and acquisition of information does not constitute good study practice; it must be accompanied by thought and a search for understanding. It is better to study a limited number of sources thoroughly, so that they are understood, than to try to cover a wider range in order to commit things to memory 'parrot fashion'. The subject requires thought as much as factual knowledge, and we develop this through argument and discussion with others. This was the essence of the method employed by Plato in the Grove of Academos (hence 'academic') in Ancient Greece, and in spite of the breathtaking advances in modern information technology, it cannot be bettered. Talking seriously about politics is more than an academic enterprise, it is part of the process of being a citizen; it is itself an element of the good life (the prohibition of such talk is a sign of oppression). It can also lead to self-revelation: we can better understand the way we are by recognizing the greater political forces that govern our environment. You will see throughout this book that much in politics is about power, and the tension between the powerful and the powerless.

Questions for discussion and debate

The questions included at the end of each chapter are integral to the study of politics. Sometimes controversial, they should be used to stimulate sustained argument. They may be discussed in groups, made the subject of a debating session, or used as the basis for an essay or for examination practice. They are posed to encourage you to address certain issues of fundamental importance. Even so, the more you study the more you will realize that they have many variants and teachers and tutors will provide a never-ending supply! The process of taking part in academic argument and debate can stimulate thought in a way that lone contemplation may not. Of course discussion and debate are empty and sterile if one does not read and think by way of preparation. If people attend your debates without having done this, you are entitled to shred their egos with your knowledge and wit.

Acknowledgements

Previous editions of this book have benefited from comments and suggestions from professors Anthony Giddens, David Held, John Dearlove, John Greenwood, Howard Elcock and Andrew Gamble, and these continue to be valued. In addition, various anonymous reviewers have made suggestions which have materially enhanced the book. In the case of this edition, five anonymous readers considered the whole draft meticulously and their helpful and encouraging comments have been much appreciated. Paul Fairclough has also brought enthusiasm and (relative) youth to the undertaking, his contribution going well beyond the research and analysis he has provided.

Louise Knight, as commissioning editor, has provided support and encouragement over a long gestation period and has contributed many valuable suggestions over its structure, content and appearance (including the cover). David Winters and Neil de Cort have dealt with all day-to-day production matters with unfailing courtesy. As proofreader, Jane Robertson has gone through the text with her finest tooth comb and has saved us from many a solecism and banana skin. As copy-editor, Ann Kingdom has worked tirelessly on the complex structure of the book, including the finding and presentation of various pictures, obtaining permissions, preparing many diagrams and tables and generally providing research assistance. In addition, she has produced a detailed index, which greatly enhances the value of a book of this kind. For all inconsistencies, solecisms and errors of judgement, however, Paul and I must take responsibility.

I am grateful to the following for permission to reproduce material. Corbis Images for the photographs on pp. 102, 118, 204, 382 and 507; the European Parliament for the photograph on p. 178; Express Newspapers and the British Cartoon Archive, University of Kent (www.cartoons.ac.uk) for the cartoon by Paul Thomas, published in the *Daily Express* (5 Oct 1998) on p. 324; Noel Ford for the cartoons on pp. 307 and 374; Getty Images for the photographs on pp. 242, 311, 468, 687 and 735; Greenpeace for the photograph on p. 62; the Mary Evans Picture Library for the pictures on pp. 86, 215, 270 and 700; the National Archives for the images of cabinet minutes on pp. 480–1; Not the Nine O'Clock News and R. W. Newstead for the extract on p. 721; Parliament for the photographs on pp. 134 and 413 (by Catherine Bebbington) and 441 (all parliamentary copyright); Punch Ltd for the cartoons on pp. 14, 527, 690 and 746; Albert Rusling for the cartoon on p. 669; the Telegraph Media Group for the photograph on p. 334; Bill Tidy for the cartoon on p. 720.

The photographs on the following pages are reproduced under the terms of Creative Commons licences CC-BY-2.0 (http://creativecommons.org/licenses/by/2.0/), CC-BY-SA-2.0 (http://creativecommons.org/licenses/by-sa/2.0) or CC-BY-SA-3.0 (http://creativecommons.org/licenses/by/3.0/) via Wikimedia Commons: p. 3 © David Hunt (CC-BY-2.0); p. 42 © user: Burn_the_asylum (CC-By-SA-3.0); p. 155 © user: ArcCan (CC-BY-SA-3.0); p. 205 © Alan Stanton (CC-BY-SA-2.0); 235 © user: Birdy10 (CC-BY-SA-3.0); p. 398 ©Aurelien Guichard (CC-BY-SA-2.0); p. 485 © Ronnie Macdonald (CC-BY-2.0); p. 569 © Alex Gunningham (CC-BY-2.0); p. 581 © Garry Knight (CC-BY-SA-2.0); p. 652 © Mark Andrew (CC-BY-2.0).

Every effort has been made by the publishers to trace the copyright holders. If any have been inadvertently overlooked, appropriate arrangements will be made at the earliest opportunity.

INTRODUCTION: STUDYING POLITICS

Contents

No one is unaffected by politics. Speaking very broadly, it is about the way people organize their lives together in a community. The important collective decisions shaping the very quality of life – concerning wealth, health, education, morality – are all essentially political in their nature. Studying and talking about politics is a necessary part of the good life which we seek. To be denied the right to do this is one of the first symptoms of oppression. This chapter considers the essential nature of the subject and the terms and concepts associated with its study. Finally we address the actual study of politics.

What is Politics?

Encountering politics

People will say with pride 'I'm not interested in politics.' They might as well say, 'I'm not interested in my standard of living, my health, my job, my rights, my freedoms, my future or any future.'
Martha Gellhorn (American novelist, journalist and war correspondent), 1984

Human social life is not a tranquil experience. People seem able to argue and disagree over most things – education, nuclear weapons, the National Health Service, race, gender, the European Union, genetic engineering, climate change, the north–south divide, terrorism, and so on *ad infinitum*. Differences are voiced in arguments in pubs and clubs and MPs are elected to continue the arguments in Parliament. Even religious leaders may enter the fray; the Church of England's 1985 report, *Faith in the City*, was a damning indictment of inner-city decay and neglect. In June 2012 the Archbishop of Canterbury described the Prime Minister's concept of 'the big society' as 'aspirational waffle'.

Not only do people argue, they resort to violence. Today we see demonstrations, race riots, attacks on the police, attacks by the police and bitter strikes. We see blood and death as people fight for their rights, the rights of others or even the rights of animals. Some are prepared to die. In 1913 Emily Wilding Davison was fatally injured under the hooves of the King's horse in the Derby and other women threatened to starve themselves to death in Britain's prisons because they wanted the right to vote. People will also kill for their beliefs; in July 2005 suicide bombers killed and maimed London commuters. Even the state will take lives; in the same month Jean Charles de Menezes was shot in the head seven times by the police on the (mistaken) suspicion of being a terrorist. Throughout all, the unblinking eye of the mass media watches, reports and incites.

These widely disparate patterns of behaviour, involving matters great and small, serious and trivial, originating at home or abroad, affecting ordinary people and the high and the mighty, which may be enacted within the great state institutions of

Westminster, Whitehall and the Inns of Court, or in streets and factories, share little in common except for one thing: along with countless other such examples they would be recognized as events in politics. It is clear that if we are to study this subject seriously it is necessary to make some order of a world of bewildering complexity, to try to distil the essence of the activity known as politics. This is by no means easy; scholars continue to dispute its definition.

Politics arises from certain basic facts of human existence: that people generally choose (indeed, find it necessary for survival) to live together and that they differ in myriad ways in their opinions as to how the community should be organized and the nature of the decisions it makes. The source of conflict may either be the simple fact that individuals are self-interested and greedy, never able to feel content with their lot, or that they hold differing views on big moral questions. Disputes are inevitable because the world's resources are finite (no one can have all he or she wants) and the range of opinion on moral questions is limitless.

However, when we come to address directly the fundamental question 'What is politics?' we find it impossible to give a simple answer. Politics can be seen variously as concerned with the art of compromise, the exercise of authority, the acquisition of power and as a form of devious deception. It is a many-sided concept, only to be understood if viewed from various angles.

I hope I will not destroy faith in the omniscience of professors entirely if I now confess that I do not really know what my subject is.
F. E. Ridley (professor of politics), 'The importance of constitutions', *Parliamentary Affairs* (1966: 312)

'Troops out': anti-war march through London in 2007

Politics as compromise: the 'art of the possible'

Politics as **'the art of the possible'** is a well-known but enigmatic definition (authorship of which is attributed variously) that remains relevant because it encapsulates a particular view of politics as a process of participating and finding agreement. This has been attractive to western minds since the time of the Ancient Greek philosopher Aristotle (384–322 BC). Amongst modern thinkers it was eloquently expressed by Bernard Crick (1964: 141):

> Politics is not just a necessary evil; it is a realistic good. Political activity is a type of moral activity; it is a free activity, and it is inventive, flexible, enjoyable, and human.

However, adhering rigidly to such a view would leave little material for political scientists to study in the real world of violence, murder, duplicity and self-interest. Yet this definition remains important for several reasons.

- It defines the pure essence of politics.
- It stands as an ethical ideal.
- It provides a measure against which real-world systems may be judged.

The view of politics as a compromising and conciliatory activity might suggest that it is opposed to the idea of sovereignty and rule by a central authority. This is wrong because differences cannot be reconciled without some overarching authority, even if this is no more than the idea of agreement (or contract) reached between the parties. This leads to a second definition.

Politics as authority

David Easton, an influential American political scientist, argued that politics was concerned with the **'authoritative allocation of values'** (1953: 129). **Authority** is the right of some person or institution (king or government) to make decisions affecting the community. A woman with a gun, or a man with a large wallet, may be able to get their own way but will not have authority if those obeying do so with a sense of grievance. Such rule is unstable; those subjected may be expected to revolt when they glimpse their chance. Authority is derived from legitimacy.

Legitimacy

When a government enjoys **legitimacy**, people will obey because they believe it right to be ruled in this way. This is a key to the success of any political system, and explains why military dictatorships taking power by force are soon seeking the appearance of democratic civilian rule.

The strongest is never strong enough to be always the master, unless he transforms strength into right, and obedience into duty.

Jean Jacques Rousseau (1712–78; French philosopher and writer), *The Social Contract* (1762: ch. 3)

Forms of authority

The great sociologist Max Weber (1864–1920) distinguished three kinds of authority: rational legal (bestowed by normative rules, such as constitutions and elections); traditional (conferred by history, habit and custom – like a hereditary monarchy); and charismatic (where the personal qualities of the leader inspire the confidence, and even adulation, of the masses).

> The erosion of public confidence in the holders of public office is a serious matter. In so far as a culture of moral vagueness, a culture of sleaze has developed, we seek to put an end to it.
>
> Nolan Committee on Standards in Public Life (1994), quoted in the *Guardian* (12 May 1995)

Of course, to say that a government enjoys legitimacy does not necessarily imply that it is a *good* government; legitimacy merely resides in popular consciousness. Hence political regimes will devote considerable time and energy not to making policies for the people's education, welfare and so on, but to the shaping of attitudes – the process of **legitimation**. This was recognized in the addition to the political lexicon in the 1980s of two new terms: 'news management' and 'spin doctor'. We shall see that a great deal of British political life serves the process of legitimation. For example, when Elizabeth II was crowned by the Archbishop of Canterbury the British people witnessed a tradition whereby the monarchs of old sought to present their earthly power as a manifestation of the will of God.

While it is clear that the exercise of authority is part of politics, this presents a rather legalistic and simplistic picture. Governments cannot always expect to possess legitimacy; in a complex society there will be elements opposed to the government of the day, questioning and challenging it and even seeking to destroy it. This leads to an analysis of one of the most central concepts in politics – power.

Politics as power

American political scientist Harold Lasswell (1936) gave the discipline a memorable catch-phrase in the title of his book *Politics: Who Gets What, When, How?* Here the essence of politics is **power**, and those who get most of what is going are the powerful. Power can be defined as the ability to achieve some desired effect, regardless of the opposition. Authority is one form of power, but a glance at the world today quickly reveals that many regimes are based on cruder forms such as wealth, gender, physical might and violence.

Concentration on pure power takes us beyond the trappings of government into shadowy corners behind the throne. The authority of the government is often nothing more than an empty legal (**de jure**) title; the real (**de facto**) power to get what is wanted, when it is wanted, lies elsewhere. Although some are content to study only the outward trappings of the state, it should be a central task of political analysis to track down the real source of power, to find the constitutional Mr Big, though the trail can often resemble the Yellow Brick Road to the elusive end of the rainbow.

We will discover later in this book that the most important approaches to the study of politics centre around hypotheses about where real power lies. Does it lie with the people, some of the people, a particular race, the male sex, the armed forces, the talented, the wealthy, the aristocracy, Parliament, the Cabinet, the prime minister, the civil service, the mass media, the professional classes, the managers of industry, the controllers of capital, and so on? Alternatively, does it lie outside the state territory altogether with superpowers like the USA, international groupings like NATO, or mighty transnational corporations with budgets dwarfing those of many nations? We shall find that power (like wealth) is unevenly distributed; some people have much while others have little.

Politics as deception

A popular use of the term 'political' denotes devious, shifty behaviour generally aimed at securing personal advantage – usually position or office. Political scientist Colin Hay (2007: 153) argues that 'politics' has become a 'dirty word', synonymous with terms such as sleaze, corruption, duplicity, self-interest and self-importance. Perhaps it was ever thus. Many of Shakespeare's plays dwell on the intrigue in politics, so that politician Enoch Powell could say in a 1950s BBC series: 'The stage used to be called the Court, now they call it a Cabinet, but all the characters are in Shakespeare . . . Only the costumes date.' As King Lear says:

> Get thee glass eyes;
> And, like a scurvy politician, seem
> To see the things thou dost not.

Deception can take place at the micro level (within government organizations), as well as the macro level (between rulers and the ruled).

I put for a general inclination of all mankind, a perpetual and restless desire for power after power, that ceaseth only in death.
Thomas Hobbes (1588–1659; English philosopher), Leviathan (1651: ch. 11)

One has to be a bit of a lowbrow, a bit of a murderer, to be a politician, ready and willing to see people sacrificed, slaughtered for the sake of an idea.
Henry Miller (1891–1980; American writer), Writers at Work

Deception in micro-politics

It was probably in this sense that the word 'politics' first appeared in English, as a term of disapproval applied to the activities of those engaged in faction, intrigue and opposition to established governments. People who are 'politicking' are usually understood to be plotting against rivals. The term is often applied to the behaviour of individuals in large organizations, where those engaged in politics (from planning to oust the chairman to gaining a larger desk) are unlikely to be contributing to the organization's collective goal. Much activity of this kind takes place within the corridors, bars and tea rooms of the Palace of Westminster, and in the clubs and hotels nearby. Indeed, the British Cabinet itself was originally a secretive group of ministers scheming together as a cabal. Alan Clark's *Diaries* (1 Feb. 1991) record such ministerial rivalries:

> I have lots of enemies. . . . Hurd has always been against me, told the lady [Margaret Thatcher] not to make me Minister for Trade – which she very splendidly repeated to me on the evening of my appointment. Arsehole.

This view of politics is often linked with the ideas of the Italian Renaissance thinker Niccolò Machiavelli; to be labelled 'Machiavellian' is usually taken as insulting. However, Machiavelli's essential point was that intrigue and plotting were justified, enabling his 'prince' to gain office and rule for the good of all. In other words, he believed that the ends justify the means: 'when the act accuses, the end excuses'. This leads to deception at the level of macro-politics.

Deception in macro-politics

The Ancient Greek philosopher Plato argued in his *Republic* that it would sometimes be right for a ruler to tell a 'noble lie' to a people in order to maintain social harmony.

From the great nineteenth-century prime minister Benjamin Disraeli came the aphorism that politics was 'the art of governing mankind through deceiving them'. Legitimation itself can be seen as a form of deception. The perceptive English political essayist Walter Bagehot (1826–77) placed particular stress on deception of the masses as a key to successful government (see p. 401). Today spin doctors can generate a great mist of deceptive activity (including official secrecy). The attempt to shine a searchlight through this is one of the principal duties of the political scientist.

It should be apparent by now that all our definitions are inextricably interwoven. There is no doubt that society harbours many conflicting interests which must be reconciled, often by the exercise of authority, and the process is clouded by evidence of great inequality of power and much devious behaviour.

Politics is the art of preventing people from taking part in affairs which properly concern them.
Paul Valèry (1871–1945; French writer), *Tel quell*

Politics and the fate of mankind are shaped by men without ideals and without greatness. Men who have greatness within them don't go in for politics.
Albert Camus (1913–60; French philosopher and writer), *Notebooks* (1935–42)

Political Science

What do political scientists study?

Individuals and groups disagree over ends and means in most walks of life. There are countless institutions that can resolve such conflict, including religious groups, trade unions, clubs, schools, universities, business firms, families and so on. Does this mean that these are political institutions? Although some academics do study the politics of small communities, usually taking a psychological perspective, the particular focus of attention for the political scientist is the **state** – a very special, unique and profoundly important social formation – and how it is governed.

The state

A state is a community formed for the purpose of government. The Ancient Greeks talked of the **city-state** (sometimes termed the **polity**, from the Greek *polis*) and today we speak of the **nation-state**, a relatively recent formation. Philosophers have disputed the nature of the state, with Georg Hegel giving it a particularly metaphysical significance as the highest expression of ethics: only through allegiance to, and service in, the state could individuals fully realize themselves. Generally the state is taken to be a community with the following characteristics (Lasswell and Kaplan 1950: 181).

- A clearly defined territory.
- A legitimate government.
- Sovereignty within its territory.
- An existence recognized by other states in international law.
- A 'persona', in which name it is able to make treaties and have obligations and rights independent of any actual person. Thus we speak of the state doing this and that: prosecuting people (state prosecution), providing welfare (welfare state), being sinned against (crimes against the state), keeping secrets (state secrets), educating citizens (state education) and so on.
- Perpetual succession – rulers may change but the state continues to exist, with no alteration to its commitments and responsibilities.
- Universality – all those living within the jurisdiction of the state (there are some exceptions for diplomats) are subject to its rules. Unlike other associations (say, sports clubs or churches), members do not have the right to opt out of state jurisdiction (unless they emigrate, though in this case they would soon come under some other state).
- The right to use force and coercion against members. Max Weber saw this as

the most singular characteristic of the state, distinguishing it from all other organizations. If other agencies (say bouncers outside a disco, teachers, or even parents) use force, they may find themselves subject to the law, but the state can legally imprison, harass, and sometimes kill. Operating the state apparatus thus confers great and threatening power.

Today some argue that a process of globalization through economics and technology and the horror of modern weaponry make the concept of the nation-state dangerously outmoded. With the increasing role of international associations and transnational groupings, the borders of modern states are certainly becoming softened (Giddens 1998: 130). Moreover, human rights and security concerns lead states or groups of states to demand rights of inspection over others, thereby compromising their sovereignty.

The state and society

The notion of the state may be differentiated from that of society; the former is constructed and based upon law, while the latter arises naturally from the free association of people (often termed **civil society**). In the state, individual members stand as **citizens** with legally prescribed rights and obligations, but no such conditions attach to them as members of society, where they are constrained more by economic and ethical norms. A similar distinction was made by German sociologist Ferdinand Tönnies (1855–1936), who spoke of *Gesellschaft* (a community formed by artificial, human contract) and *Gemeinschaft* (a community arising naturally from bonds of affection or kinship). The national community is both state *and* society, a fact that is a source of friction. While all citizens are legally equal, as members of society they can be decidedly unequal. When the legal equality of citizenship is markedly at variance with the real level of societal equality, there will be the potential for political tension.

Government

The idea of **government** lies at the heart of political science. Indeed, no society has ever been found that did not have some kind of government (Mair 1970). It can take various forms: it may be constitutional (limited by laws, see pp. 94–8), absolutist (unlimited by laws), primitive (a chieftain's rule over a tribe), or pluralist (consisting of several institutions sharing the role). Following Aristotle, it is customary to group forms of government in terms of the number of rulers, thus distinguishing **monarchy** (rule by one person), **aristocracy** (rule by an enlightened few) and **democracy** (rule by all the people – the *demos*). However, each of these may be said to tend in practice towards a corrupt variant: **tyranny**, **oligarchy** and **mob rule** (figure 1.1).

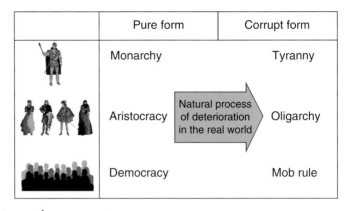

Figure 1.1 Forms of government

Government and self-interest

The fatal deterioration of the forms of government is usually attributed to the corrupting influences of power, which may lead those holding it to act in their own interests rather than those of the community. As the historian Lord Acton (1834–1902) observed memorably:

> Power tends to corrupt, and absolute power corrupts absolutely. Great men are almost always bad men.

The selfish tendency of human beings is a hard truth that forms the starting point for much political thought. The key issue is reconciling the common good with the need for government. Scottish philosopher David Hume (1711–76) believed that 'every man ought to be supposed a knave and to have no end other than private interest', arguing that it was crucial for a state to devise a form of government that would inhibit the corrupting tendencies.

> A republican and free government would be an obvious absurdity, if the particular checks and controuls [sic], provided by the constitution, had really no influence, and made it not in the interest, even of bad men, to act for the public good. (Hume 1882 edn: 6–7)

The philosophical radicals of the nineteenth century took the individual pursuit of self-interest as the key to understanding human behaviour, an idea that was very influential in shaping many of our modern institutions.

Government and politics

Government will necessarily entail politics, even in primitive societies where institutions have taken only the most rudimentary form. In developed societies, politics is often seen as being about the formal working of the **machinery of government** – taking control of it, influencing its decisions, reforming it, changing those in office, and so on. However, as we shall see in this book, politics does not belong exclusively to the world of institutions. From the boardrooms of industry to clubs, pubs and family get-togethers – politics is found wherever people meet and express their anger, hopes and anxieties, and assess their potential to influence events.

The state and the government

The state and the government are conceptually distinct. In the UK, the position of the monarch, who plays no effective part in government yet is head of state, underlines the distinction. For practical purposes the British government is usually regarded as the collection of around a hundred secretaries of state, ministers, junior ministers and their various assistants drawn from Parliament. In contrast, the state can be seen to comprise a much wider set of institutions (the civil service, the Bank of England, local authorities, health authorities, various quasi-autonomous bodies, the judiciary, the military and the police). Some, such as Middlemas (1979), would go further and include the mass media, the institutions of the capitalist economy and trade unions.

The political and the non-political

It will be apparent that if politics is about reconciling diverse interests it must have many manifestations; indeed, no area of life can be seen as intrinsically non-political. Some people find this thought peculiarly disturbing and it is common to hear calls to 'take education (or health, or the siting of power stations, and so on) out of politics'. If something is to be taken out of politics, where is it to go? We have seen that politics is a process whereby differences and conflicts are resolved through conciliation, the exercise of authority and power. However, politics is by no means the only way of resolving such differences; there are three particularly important alternatives. All these are present in Britain today, though each has limitations.

The market

The economic market place allows the forces of supply and demand to set prices and determine who gets what. The eighteenth- and nineteenth-century classical economists believed the **market** to be a wondrous mechanism for bringing buyers and sellers together at a mutually acceptable price, resulting in the optimum allocation of resources within society. However, this raises difficult ethical problems. Not only is it undemocratic, favouring the economically strong against the weak because it does not *redistribute* resources, but it also gives only unto him or her that

Market sovereignty is not a complement to liberal democracy: it is an alternative to it.
Eric Hobsbawm (1917–2012; historian) in the *New Statesman* (5 March 2001)

already hath (that is, can afford the price). Thus, rather than taking matters out of politics, it creates a new basis for dissatisfaction and conflict.

Furthermore, some issues cannot be determined by the laws of supply and demand. Matters such as the level of sex and violence on television, the decision whether to send troops to Iraq, the degree of religious toleration to be allowed within society, or the right of homosexuals to marry, lie in a territory of value-judgement and morality where the market is quite silent. When governments try to bring the market into areas such as education and health care many people are deeply disturbed. Indeed, because the human capacity to disagree over value-judgements is potentially limitless, there are infinitely more areas of dispute to be settled by politics than by the market.

Rational decision-making

The idea of making communal decisions on the basis of rational criteria seems very attractive; it is the argument for the use of experts (town planners, scientists, and the like) to weigh up the pros and cons of a case to arrive at the 'best' solution. Organizational theorist Herbert Simon (1947) believed that state decision-makers should arm themselves with all the available information, calculate the outcomes of all possible courses of action, and choose the best policy for the community. However, in practice certain intractable problems beset such processes.

- The principle is essentially elitist and paternalistic, based on the notion that certain people know what is best for the masses.
- It is difficult to decide who the experts should be; obviously election cannot be the answer.
- In reality, experts can never be sure that they have all the information necessary to make the 'right' decisions.
- Experts may be tempted to place their own personal interests before those of the community.
- Experts frequently disagree with each other.

The idea of **rational decision-making** also carries with it connotations of a threatening 'Big Brother' style of bureaucratic rule as depicted in George Orwell's novel *Nineteen Eighty-Four*. Both fascist and communist governments can be accused of trying to govern by putting experts in charge, while the call to replace politics with managerialism is ever-present in Britain.

Violence

Violence enables the unsatisfied, dispossessed or greedy to attempt to take what they want by physical force. In the real world there can be little doubt that making

War is nothing more than the continuation of politics by other means.
Karl von Clausewitz (1780–1831); German military expert), *Vom Kriege*

and enacting collective decisions for communities is often accomplished by various forms of physical force and **state violence**. Two world wars, the Holocaust, the treatment of blacks in South Africa, the silencing of dissidents in Eastern Europe, the brutality of the Tiananmen Square massacre or the ethnic cleansing in Croatia or Rwanda can leave no one in any doubt of this harsh reality. Historically Britain has been a very violent nation and the Northern Ireland situation, the Falklands war and the invasion of Iraq have revealed modern politicians willing to seek violent solutions to political problems. After the Falklands war, Mrs Thatcher employed the language of force on the home front, speaking of the 'enemy within'. The miners were to find themselves embroiled in a physical confrontation with the police and security services.

As an alternative to participating in conventional political processes, guerrilla warfare is increasingly chosen by groups wishing to gain their ends or make their voices heard. Today nobody is immune; several thousand civilians have been killed over Northern Ireland, hijacks and atrocities such as the Lockerbie air disaster can occur anywhere, and in 1989 the Ayatollah Khomeini set a chilling precedent with his fatwa on author Salman Rushdie because his novel *The Satanic Verses* gave religious offence. Most dramatically of all, the events of 11 September 2001 (9/11) sent reverberations throughout the world and the response from the USA was to declare a 'war of terror'. It was said that things could never be the same again. However, like the market and the rational decision-making model, violence is not very effective at resolving problems. The issue was known to the Ancient Greeks. In Plato's dialogues Thrasymachus argues that might is right but Socrates dismantles his case. Violence breeds more violence and, when the fighting is over, the parties must sit around the table to seek a durable solution. This has been the case in both the Northern Ireland and Arab–Israeli conflicts, despite the high price paid in blood.

Is there really a world beyond politics?

It will become apparent throughout this book that when reformers believe they are taking an issue out of the sordid world of politics by handing it over to the market or the experts, they delude themselves. Similarly, the idea that violence is not part of politics is unrealistic. Hence, in defining what is political we must be guided not by the nature of the issue but by the way people react to it. If we accept that politics is about reconciling diverse interests then it follows that anything can become political. The world that some believe to exist outside politics is a fantasy land, as inaccessible as that discovered by Alice when she went through the looking-glass.

Man is by nature a political animal.
Aristotle (Ancient Greek philosopher),
Politics

"Maurice has always been politically active."

Reproduced by permission of *Punch*

Political Science as the Master Science?

Every intellectual attitude is latently political.
Thomas Mann (1875–1955; German writer), quoted in the *Observer* (11 Aug. 1974)

Throughout the history of western civilization there runs a great tradition of **political thought**, with a pantheon of giant figures who have applied their minds to profound questions. The subject is also the stuff of much great drama, literature and art. Aristotle described politics as the 'Master Science' and it is not difficult to see what he meant. All we do in our lives, in society, the sciences and arts, will be influenced by politics; it is through politics that the totality of social existence is orchestrated.

Political scientists do not wear white coats, peer through microscopes or fill up test tubes. Is **political science** really a science? Can it produce the systematic, ordered, predictive propositions associated with a subject such as physics? This is not a new question. The work of Aristotle, which involved him in a famous classification of the constitutions of the many Greek city-states, was just as systematic and 'scientific' as his work in the natural sciences. However, the advent of Galileo and Newton in physics led to developments that seemed to transport the physical sciences into new realms of precision, uniformity and prediction.

Yet some social scientists have tried to build a body of **political theory** – laws of society and politics resembling those of the physical sciences. Thomas Hobbes (1588–1679) aimed to be scientific in breaking society down into its smallest atom, the self-preserving individual. Karl Marx (1818–83) sought scientific-type laws governing the operation of the capitalist economy. Another influence was logical-positivism (a school of philosophy holding that only statements capable of being disproved can be meaningful) and the post-war era saw renewed efforts by political scientists to steer the discipline towards rigorous theoretical propositions by the use of careful techniques and methods of empirical observation. In this effort to ape the objective observational methods of the 'hard' sciences they sought to ally the discipline more closely with anthropology and psychology. This movement was termed **behaviouralism** and one of its results was a preoccupation with the observable, or more particularly, the quantifiable. The problem with this was that many of the studies (from attitude surveys to voting statistics) were often tedious and sometimes essentially trite. They did not address the really big questions of politics, such as: what is power? where does it really lie? why do states go to war? why do people die of starvation amidst abundance?

Others, including Max Weber, were sceptical of the idea that people and organizations could be studied in this way. Human beings reason and interpret the world, and the proposition that they are best treated as unthinking molecules in a test tube is dubious, if not ludicrous. He argued that the study of human affairs should take account of reason, motives and emotions in order to afford a deeper level of understanding, which he termed *verstehen*.

Today few would deny Weber's argument, and some political scientists apply approaches derived from hermeneutics, placing value on how we interpret events. There are also the rational-choice theorists who construct abstract models in which individuals pursue self-interest. Ironically, as the hard sciences push further into the unknown they encounter less rather than more precision and are obliged to construct 'uncertainty principles', 'fuzzy logic' and 'chaos theories', reflecting the vagaries that have long confronted the social scientist. Yet behaviouralism has left a beneficial legacy in that political scientists can no longer allow their minds to dwell for too long in the stratosphere of abstraction and metaphysics, like medieval scholastics who disputed how many angels could balance on the point of a needle. Hence, the modern discipline of political science combines many approaches and includes a number of interrelated subdisciplines with various focuses and methodologies.

- *Political theory* examines theories of political institutions, including the law, the state, systems of representation, forms of government, and so on.
- *Political philosophy* searches for highly generalized answers to major questions such as the meaning of freedom, justice, equality and rights. Ultimately **political**

Politics is not a science but an art.
Otto von Bismarck (1815–98; Prusso-German statesman), speech, Reichstag (15 March 1884)

philosophy addresses the biggest questions of all: what is the nature of the 'good life' and what must the state do to promote this?

- *Political ideology* is concerned with ideas about the way the state should be organized.
- *Political economy* examines the state in the economic system. It leads us to the power of economic forces and the working of the global economy.
- *Political sociology* looks more towards the social world for an understanding of politics. It is concerned with how political attitudes are formed and how they are influenced by those with power. It also studies social stratification, including class formation and elites.
- *Political institutionalism* focuses on the formal machinery of the state, a key site of much political activity.
- *Policy studies* focus on the policy-making process of government and are centrally concerned with the analysis of power.
- *Comparative government* searches for generalizations about politics derived from widespread examination of groups of countries. Conceptually straightforward, it can be immensely daunting in practical terms.
- *International relations* studies the ways in which states relate to each other in war and in peace.
- *Political geography* embraces the spatial dimension of politics, considering such issues as territoriality, ethnicity and voting behaviour.

The interdisciplinary perspective

Not only does political science comprise the subdisciplines outlined above, it is itself multidisciplinary; magpie-like, it draws upon a wide range of other disciplines. The social sciences study one single, complex reality and the different disciplines are artificial territories staked out to facilitate microscopic study of particular aspects. However, this can hinder understanding if we adopt a blinkered view.

Hence, while this book is rooted in the territory of political science, it is open to other perspectives. It is, for example, an inescapable fact that many of the forces acting upon the political system are economic in origin, whether originating from the stock exchange or the plight of the homeless. To understand the British constitution we require a legal perspective, although this must be seasoned with an understanding of the balance of power, which breathes life into the formal constitution. The discipline of sociology, concerned with education, culture, class, racism and gender – all of which fuel much political activity – must also have a central place. Underlying all is the historical dimension. It is almost impossible to comprehend the present without understanding patterns of development. We do not take an historical perspective by way of neat chronological introduction; we do so because the politics of today are only an ephemeral bloom on the tree of the past.

The multi-level-governance perspective

Governance is the act of governing and is not always the preserve of state governments. The existence of inter-state groupings, particularly the development of the European Union (EU), has led some scholars to focus on the concept of multi-level governance. In the case of the UK, bodies such as NATO, the World Bank and the EU imply a level of governance above the state. In addition there are transnational corporations (TNCs), which are themselves virtual institutions of governance, and international non-government organizations (NGOs) pursuing social goals such as the relief of child poverty, peace or environmental protection. Globalization means that it no longer makes sense (if it ever did) to study state governments in isolation, as if they were in complete command of their destinies.

In this world, state boundaries become blurred and hierarchical relationships slacken or disappear entirely, to be replaced by more subtle processes of negotiation, bargaining, exchange and compromise. Thus the EU does not necessarily command state governments and state governments do not necessarily command local governments. Regional and local authorities, or even private companies, can bypass nation-states to treat directly with international bodies.

Peering behind the facade

Believing in the neutrality of the state, writers in the orthodox liberal-democratic tradition have betrayed a tendency to describe what they see as a beautiful stately home. Like overawed paying visitors, they have been content to admire the ornate outer facade and the fine draperies and furniture inside but remain too timid to push beyond the red ropes into the living quarters. However, the political scientist must be attentive to the real world before all else and, like Machiavelli, seek to peel away the layers in search of a deeper reality for, as observed above, much in politics is about deception. A central concern of this book is to encourage the habit of enquiry, of looking beneath the surface or, where we are not permitted (and we are talking about one of the most secretive systems in the world), to remain conscious of the limitations of conventional accounts.

Key points

- A common definition of politics is the resolution by compromise and conciliation of the inevitable conflicts in any community.

- Politics is also about power and the concept of authority.

- 'Politics' can also be used as a term of abuse – a 'dirty word'.

- It is possible to speak of the politics of any organization but political scientists mainly study the state.

- The state is a community with a territory within which it enjoys legal sovereignty.

- A government may be in control of the state but is conceptually distinct from it.

- The decisions made through politics can be made by other means, such as the economic market, but the idea that politics can be removed from life is an illusion.

- The study of politics should be concerned with where power lies; to understand who gets what, when and how.

Review your understanding of the following terms and concepts

aristocracy
art of the possible
authoritative allocation
  of values
authority
behaviouralism
citizen
democracy
demos

Gemeinschaft
Gesellschaft
governance
legitimacy
machinery of
  government
market
mob rule
monarchy

nation-state
oligarchy
polis
political science
polity
power
rational decision-making
tyranny

Questions for discussion and debate

Consider these propositions and be prepared to present the cases for and against. Try to produce debating propositions of your own.

1   Politics is about who gets what, when, how.
2   Politics is the art of the possible.
3   Power without authority cannot be sustained.
4   A state is not a society.
5   Violence is the abrogation of politics.
6   Power corrupts.
7   Education should be taken out of politics.
8   Politics is the means whereby the powerful delude the mass.
9   Politics is the art of preventing people from taking part in affairs which properly concern them.
10   The study of politics is the 'master science'.

Further reading

Briscoe, S. (2006) *Britain in Numbers*.
Facts and figures to help the political scientist.

Butler, D. and Butler, G. (2010) *British Political Facts*, 10th edn.
Well-established classic reference work on British politics.

Cornford, E. M. (ed. and translator) (1941) *The Republic of Plato*.
Accessible edition of the great masterwork, raising many of the questions and conundrums of the study of politics today.

Crick, B. (2000) *In Defence of Politics*, 5th edn.
Classic essay on the idea of politics as a peaceful and highly desirable process of conciliation.

Duverger, M. (1966) *The Idea of Politics*.
Classic text by French scholar. Analyses political conflict from its roots in primitive societies to modern times.

Flinders, M. (2013) *Defending Politics: Why Democracy Matters in the 21st Century*.
Reappraises and updates the arguments of Crick's classic defence.

Hay, C. (2007) *Why we Hate Politics.*
Thought-provoking study of contemporary politics.

Lasswell, H. (1936) *Politics: Who Gets What When, How?*
Seminal statement of the power view of politics.

Leftwich, A. (1984) *What is Politics? The Activity and its Study.*
Accessible and engaging introduction.

Mackenzie, W. J. M. (1969) *Politics and Social Science.*
A 'Cook's Tour' of a wide range of approaches to the study of politics.

Marsh, D. and Stoker, G. (2010) *Theory and Methods of Political Science*, 3rd edn.
Wide-ranging survey of methods of contemporary political analysis.

Ryan, A. (2013) *On Politics: A History of Political Thought from Herodotus to the Present.*
Written on an epic scale, this study addresses the ways in which thinkers have, throughout history, sought to solve the problems arising from our propensity to live communally.

For reading around the subject and some light relief

The fact that so many plays, novels and films deal with essentially political themes underlines how politics shapes all aspects of our lives. These are but a few examples; there are countless others.

Jean Anouilh, *Antigone.*
Highlights conflicts between personal morality and the hypocrisy of a corrupt society, the main character preferring death to compromise.

Anthony Arblaster, *Viva la Libertà: Politics in Opera.*
Uncovers the political dimension and the ideals of freedom in a vast range of operas, from *The Marriage of Figaro* to *Nixon in China.*

Bertolt Brecht, *The Caucasian Chalk Circle.*
Who owns what? What is the moral authority for ownership? Brecht's play makes brilliant use of analogy to explore these questions.

Kevin Jefferys, *Sport and Politics in Modern Britain.*
If you doubt that politics intrudes into all aspects of life, read this.

Thomas More, *Utopia* (first published 1516).
Mysterious traveller Raphael Hythloday describes a pagan state governed by reason. Addressing issues such as religion, feminism, state control, colonialism and warfare, the work remains a key text in political theory.

Jeremy Paxman, *The Political Animal.*
Does power corrupt? A forensic examination of people in power in Britain by one of their scourges.

William Shakespeare, *Macbeth.*
Intrigue of politics and the corrupting effects of high-vaulting political ambition.

L. Neil Smith, *The Venus Belt.*
A sci-fi story about two parallel universes, one with and one without a government.

Anthony Trollope, *The Pallisers.*
The world of the nineteenth-century political establishment, with its intrigue, romance and arrogant power.

Graham Wallas, *Human Nature in Politics.*
Criticizes the idea that people act rationally in politics.

PART I
POLITICS IN CONTEXT

A central tenet of this book is that politics does not take place in a vacuum; it is enacted against a larger world canvas as well as being inextricably interwoven into the domestic social and economic fabric. Hence Part I of this book aims to set the scene by examining the framework that shapes the space in which domestic politics is enacted. This includes ideas about how people should live together (ideologies), the legal framework in which political actions take place (the constitution) and the country's wider geographical setting.

Much political debate and action is derived from beliefs about how we should live, what is fair and what is unfair, and chapters 2 and 3 explore the world of ideas and ideology. Chapter 4 considers the constitution, which lays down the rules of political engagement and protects the political rights people need to be able to participate. Increasingly domestic politics is influenced by events taking place thousands of miles away in a compelling contemporary development termed globalization, which is examined in chapter 5. Chapters 6 and 7 centre on that sector of the world into which Britain is becoming ever more closely integrated – the European Union.

CHAPTER 2

IDEOLOGY: THE WESTERN TRADITION

Contents

Ideologies are beliefs about how people should live together in society. As such they provide a central motive force in politics, associated not only with party politics but also with great revolutions and wars. Ideologies are the product of rational thought and of ideas, and at the heart of such thinking lie fundamental concepts such as justice, freedom, equality, community, sovereignty, the character of human nature, happiness and fulfilment: the good life as sought from the time of the Ancient Greeks. People do not easily agree on such big questions, and centuries of debate have generated a body of profound thought, perhaps more important to human survival than any other. Ideologies cannot be studied in vacuo like insects under glass; they are the products of particular times and bound in political struggle and conflict. This chapter aims to introduce not only the classic ideologies in the western tradition, but also some of the great thinkers and times with which they are associated.

Does Ideology Matter?

The extent to which ideas influence events can be disputed; sometimes events influence the ideas. Only rarely do thinkers have the joy of seeing their words directly translated into action. Although **ideologies** are regularly associated with political parties, even to the extent of bestowing their names, there is no consistent one-to-one identification. Members of communist parties can espouse values that can only be termed conservative, while nominally conservative parties can support a dominant state. Under Tony Blair Labour moved onto the territory staked out by the Conservative Margaret Thatcher in the 1980s, and when David Cameron took over the Conservative leadership he moved the party towards the left. Thus, in practical politics, parties tend to be pragmatic rather than ideologically driven. They will adopt policies on the basis of 'what works' (or what wins votes) rather than in accordance with ideological principle. Yet ideas permeate the cultural air-shaping our attitudes on what is right and what is wrong. When 'men of action' renounce the abstract world of thinkers they delude themselves. When despots hear voices they are often receiving echoes of some cloistered academic ringing down through the ages. Furthermore, ideologies are not the exclusive property of parties; they inspire individuals, movements and pressure groups fired with ambitions to change the way we live.

(Those) who believe themselves to be quite exempt from any intellectual influences are usually the slaves of some defunct economist.
J. M. Keynes (1883–1946; economist), *The General Theory of Employment, Interest and Money* (1936)

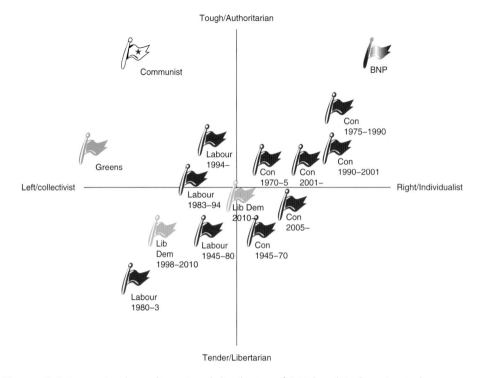

Figure 2.1 A notational two-dimensional distribution of British political parties in the post-war era

A common basis for distinguishing ideologies is in terms of a left–right dichotomy. The distinction originated in the seating arrangements of the French Estates General in 1789, when the nobility (opposing change) sat on the king's right and those calling for change on his left. Never used with academic precision, modern usage tends to parallel the distinction between **collectivism** (members of society work together) and **individualism** (people live competitively, each acting self-interestedly). A more realistic conceptualization is in terms of a continuum, with an infinite range of intermediate positions, although it is generally believed that most members of the British public are nearer the centre than either extreme. Even this model is simplistic; in addition to substantive policy outcomes there are ideological questions related to means. It is possible to take a tough (authoritarian, secretive, centralist) or tender (libertarian, open, decentralized) attitude towards government, and these preferences may not coincide with the left–right divide (see Eysenck 1951). Fascists, with extreme right-wing views, have taken tough attitudes, but so have communists. This addition creates a two-dimensional matrix (figure 2.1). More recently psychologists have sought a genetic explanation of the two broad political types. However, critics regard this as a rather 'sloppy' branch of science, arguing that character traits cannot be measured with the same accuracy as, say, height or eye colour (Giles 2008) Moreover, genetic explanations would not account for the fact that an individual's ideological position can change during a lifetime.

If you are not a socialist by the time you are 25, you have no heart. If you are still a socialist by the time you are 35, you have no head.
Attributed to Winston Churchill (and others)

In the real world, ideology cannot be divorced from sectional self-interest. Indeed, Karl Marx saw ideology as a prevalent body of ideas shaping mass political consciousness and largely controlled by a dominant class to consolidate its power and privileges. Accordingly, in considering ideologies we shall pay some attention to the way they can serve particular interests. The 'haves' in society tend to view life rather differently from the 'have nots'.

Ideology and the Western Tradition

Ideas, like commodities, can travel. In Britain they have evolved not only from developments within domestic society but also from the wider western world. The modern western ideological tradition emerged through a dramatic break with the intellectual habits of past ages. Certain momentous events stand as milestones along an evolutionary road, influencing and influenced by new ways of thinking.

The Renaissance

An intellectual rebirth in the arts and literature of the fifteenth and sixteenth centuries was associated with such great figures as Leonardo da Vinci, Michelangelo and Erasmus. Centring on Italy, it entailed a rediscovery of classical learning (buried away in the monasteries during the Dark Ages when free thought was stifled by religious dogma) and a challenge to medieval doctrine and authority. A key political thinker of the period was Niccolò Machiavelli (1469–1527), perhaps the first theorist of the modern nation-state, who rejected religion and superstition as a basis for government.

The Reformation

The medieval church under the Pope had held society in a stranglehold with power and corruption. This dominance was challenged by Martin Luther. In a reform movement sweeping Europe in the sixteenth century he asserted the right of individuals to defy authority and worship in their own way. The ground was being prepared for the idea of individual political rights.

The Enlightenment

A seismic intellectual shift raised the curtain on the modern era. Seventeenth-century Europe saw spectacular advances in scientific thinking which spread to other areas, including politics and religion. The consequences of the **Enlightenment** were to be revolutionary. Although the French Enlightenment (which between 1751 and 1772 saw publication of a famous *Encyclopédie*) is the most feted, the movement enveloped Europe as an intellectual forest fire. At its heart was **rationalism** – a new confidence in human reason – and a conviction that people had both a right and the ability to improve how they lived.

The liberation of man from his self-caused state of minority.
Immanuel Kant, German philosopher, in *What is Enlightenment?* (1784)

Metaphysical thinking and superstition were challenged, as were traditional forms of authority, including the church, aristocracy and monarchy. The very term 'ideology' was coined at this time by French philosopher Destutt de Tracy as the science of ideas.

The western tradition

This awakening of ideas and the great events they promoted altered the fundamental nature of western civilization and constituted the 'western tradition'. Two ideologies of change were to achieve supremacy in the West – liberalism and socialism – which in turn promoted a powerful reaction under the name of conservatism. More recent challenges have come through feminism and environmentalism (chapter 3). Ideologies are seen as the products of reason and the reasoning starts from a basic premise or building block: a view of human nature itself. We shall see that each ideology begins with a particular stance on this.

Liberalism

Necessity is the plea for every infringement of human freedom. It is the argument of tyrants; it is the creed of slaves.
William Pitt (1759–1806; prime minister), House of Commons speech (18 Nov. 1783)

It is hardly possible to overestimate the significance of **liberalism** in modern western history. The word implies freedom. But we must ask what we mean by freedom, and from whom or what we are to be free. Contrasting answers to these questions result in various strands within a broad liberal tradition. Early thinking opposed autocratic regimes based on royal power, aristocratic privilege, religion and the divine right of kings. It spawned the major revolutions that transformed the world from the ancient to the modern. Later thinking emphasized freedom from social deprivation.

Human nature

Early liberal thinkers stressed the essential individuality of people, who are seen as separate entities, driven by egotistical desires aiming to maximize their own well-being. However, later liberals modified this view.

The form of government

For classical liberals, the state is not virtuous in itself (as it was for the Ancient Greeks). It is a necessary evil; it exists to enable individuals to pursue their private ends but it must not be allowed to become over-powerful. Liberty is paramount and good government is minimal government. This is the essence of **liberal democracy**. Later liberals saw a role for the state in acting positively to actually promote freedom, but would still term the form of government liberal democracy.

The pattern of development: *liberté, egalité, fraternité*

Two key figures in the emergence of this tradition were Thomas Hobbes and John Locke, writing against the background of the English civil war when the rights of the people against the Crown were hotly and violently debated. Their method of reasoning was to imagine life in a **state of nature** (without society or government) and logically deduce the character of the good state. This early thinking produced what may be termed classical liberalism.

Thomas Hobbes

Probably England's greatest political thinker, Hobbes (1588–1679) wrote in the spirit of the Enlightenment, seeking to harness the methods of science to the study of politics. In analysing society he saw the individual as the basic atom, driven by a fundamental instinct of self-preservation. In a state of nature this egoism would prove fatal; it would lead to an unrelenting war of all against all. This could hardly be seen as freedom. Therefore people must place themselves under an all-powerful hereditary sovereign (hereditary to prevent fighting over the succession) – a **Leviathan** (the title of his greatest work, published in 1651). This is hardly a liberal conclusion; indeed, it could be seen as a defence of monarchy in the civil war. However, although government is absolute it is not arbitrary; the people enter into a compact with each other to create a sovereign for their common good.

> *Solitary, poore, nasty, brutish and short.*
> Hobbes's description of life in a state of nature, *Leviathan* (1651)

John Locke

Another English philosopher has a clearer claim as the founder of modern liberalism. In the second of his *Two Treatises of Government* (1690), John Locke (1632–1704) took a less bleak view of human nature. In a state of nature people would cooperate rather than fight; government should be minimal in order to maximize the freedom and rights to life which he believed were bestowed by nature. The state cannot *create* rights; it merely protects those present in nature (**natural rights**). Once government exists there is an ever-present threat that it will break its part of the contract and operate in its own interests rather than those of the governed. Constitutional provisions are needed to prevent this. Hence, Locke approved of the 1689 settlement limiting royal authority (see pp. 97–8) and advocated certain key principles that lie at the heart of the liberal constitution, including:

- a minimal state;
- representative government with regular elections;
- majority rule;
- separation of powers;
- constitutional monarchy.

Montesquieu

Abhorring the absolutist reign of Louis XVI, French scholar Baron de Montesquieu (1689–1755) became an admirer of what he saw as freedom and toleration following the 1689 settlement. In his *L'Esprit des Lois* (1748) he developed Locke's ideas, laying particular stress on the separation of powers and distinguishing more clearly between the executive, legislative and judicial organs of government. Liberty is best protected when checks and balances in the constitution render tyranny impossible – ideals embraced by America's founding fathers.

Jean Jacques Rousseau

More than any other thinker Rousseau (1712–78) is identified with the French Revolution. He was concerned with individual freedom, the role of the state, the basis for political obedience, the nature of sovereignty and the idea of contract. Like Hobbes and Locke, he imagined a state of nature but placed a quite different construction on liberty. Submission to a Leviathan 'is to suppose a people of madmen' (1913: 7), while a 'natural' freedom to pursue selfish ends was bondage to the appetites. For Rousseau, people in nature are not selfish egoists but 'noble savages' with compassion for one another. Civilization corrupts this with private property, generating greed, vanity, inequality, privilege and envy. The liberal contract is really a trick; the poor are offered protection but what is protected is the wealth of the rich. True freedom in society can only be realized through a communal life where all are equal.

Rousseau pioneered a new conception of popular sovereignty – a social contract whereby people do not forfeit freedom in return for state protection; rather they forfeit rights unconditionally to the community. Because all do so equally, each recovers all they lose. Natural freedom is exchanged for social freedom. Individual wills are unified into a *volonté generale* (**General Will**), something greater than the sum of 'petty self-interest' and the only legitimate sovereign force. It is difficult to underestimate Rousseau's influence, which spread to the arts, literature and education. In replacing the atomized theories with an organic view of the state, he inspired much moral philosophy, his ideas leading to the New Liberalism (see p. 33) that was to lay the foundations of the modern social democratic state.

Tom Paine

An Englishman who emigrated to America, Paine (1737–1809) has a legendary fame as a champion of the oppressed. A passionate exponent of Enlightenment thinking, he held much in common with Locke, arguing in his pamphlet *Common Sense* (published in 1776 on the eve of the American War of Independence) that government was a necessary evil and advocating America's independence from Britain. The only grounds for obedience were that it was fulfilling its obligations. However, unlike Locke he was a radical. His *Rights of Man* (1791) used natural rights reasoning to defend the French Revolution.

James Madison

The American constitution, drafted after independence, reflected much of Paine's sentiment. One of the founding fathers, James Madison (1751–1836), developed liberal thinking into a more coherent theory and political strategy. Like many liberals he feared that advancing democracy would replace one form of tyranny with another, a 'tyranny of the majority'. In *The Federalist* (1788) he argued for strong republican government of enlightened rulers regularly called to account through elections. He saw virtue in the large state, which increased the possibility of finding good rulers and allowed for political pluralism (see chapter 19), preventing domination by any single interest.

The liberal revolutions

Post-Enlightenment liberal thinking gave new meaning to the idea of revolution. For the Ancient Greeks (particularly the Stoics) it had meant a cyclical process of decay and renewal beyond human control: monarchy, tyranny, aristocracy, oligarchy, democracy and 'mobocracy'. Christianity had strengthened the attitude; life was to be endured as a better existence would come beyond the grave. However, the new thinking asserted that the revolving wheel could be turned but then made to stop in a new position. Major liberal revolutions, in the new meaning of the term, were to usher in the modern age of politics.

The English civil wars and the Glorious Revolution

In the 1640s a conflict began within the English landowning classes, with one section rebelling against royal authority and the other supporting it. Following the defeat of the Royalists and the beheading of Charles I a short-lived republic was proclaimed. But on the restoration of the monarchy things were fundamentally different; there had indeed been a 'Glorious Revolution'. In the 1689 constitutional settlement the traditional belief that kings enjoyed absolute power by divine right was destroyed.

The American Revolution

Using the Whigs' language of rights and freedom, the American colonists cast off the British imperialist yoke in the American Declaration of Independence of 1776:

> Men are endowed by their creator with certain inalienable rights; that among them are life, liberty and the pursuit of happiness . . . whenever any form of government becomes destructive of these ends, it is the right of the people to alter or abolish it.

The French Revolution

> It was the best of times, it was the worst of times, it was the age of wisdom, it was the age of foolishness, it was the epoch of belief, it was the epoch of incredulity, it was the season of light, it was the season of darkness.
>
> Opening lines of Charles Dickens's novel on the French Revolution,
> *A Tale of Two Cities*

That this nation, under God, shall have a new birth of freedom, and that the government of the people, by the people, for the people, shall not perish from the earth.
Abraham Lincoln (US president), Gettysburgh Address (19 Nov. 1863)

In the history of modern politics the great revolution in France, beginning in 1789, stands as an indelible landmark. The supreme manifestation of Enlightenment ideals, it influenced all modern ideologies. Initially the revolutionaries held the sentiments of their English and American counterparts: opposing royal absolutism and ancient privilege. The 1789 Declaration of Rights established people as citizens rather than subjects. In 1791 a new constitution enfranchised a large section of the male population and a democratic spirit began to permeate the cultural air. Political clubs blossomed (the largest being the Jacobins) and popular debate was extended through newspapers and pamphleteering. The momentum was to carry things beyond the middle classes. Government fell under the radical wing of the Jacobins, the Republic replaced the monarchy and the country became more democratic than any previous state. Laws provided for the radical redistribution of property and a bloody Reign of Terror saw thousands of high-born heads roll from the guillotine.

However, opposition forces began to regain the initiative. The Jacobins and revolutionary statesman Robespierre were overthrown in 1794 and the nation subjected to a military dictatorship under Napoleon. Yet the wheel had turned and could never go back. The new *Code Napoléon* accepted that sovereignty rested with the people. In Europe it was recognized that a road had been opened that others could follow.

Liberalism in Evolution

From its early classical development the ideology of liberalism was to take other forms, partly in response to changing political circumstances.

Economic liberalism

A different strand in the liberal tradition came from the new discipline of political economy. Here the justification for limited government lay not in natural rights but in the quest for economic prosperity. Freedom was allied to the word 'market'.

Adam Smith and laissez-faire

An important aspect of the new thinking was the Scottish Enlightenment and one of its leading figures was Adam Smith (1723–90). He argued in *An Inquiry into the Nature and Causes of the Wealth of Nations* (1776) that in a free market, where individuals pursued economic self-interest, every transaction made all parties better off; otherwise it would not take place. A '**hidden hand**' would guide the economy towards the best possible result. This ***laissez-faire*** principle extended to international dealings, where free trade became a liberal rallying cry. Though it might appear cruel it was still right. Other classical economists, David Ricardo (1772–1823) and Thomas Malthus (1776–1834), saw poverty, famine and death as a natural prevention of overpopulation. This approach was supported by **social Darwinists**, such as Herbert Spencer (1820–1903). Reasoning from the principle of the survival of the fittest, they saw in the competitive economy a means of improving the species, while government intervention would weaken it. This thinking influenced Charles Darwin in developing his view of evolution. The ideas appealed to the rising bourgeoisie, who could add to accumulating wealth a conviction of their own superiority.

The industrial revolution

Economic liberalism spawned its own revolution, less bloody than previous ones but no less profound in its political effects. Emerging first in Britain between 1760 and 1860, as new scientific thinking was applied to production, it was to create a new kind of civilization – an industrial one. Driving the new order was a thrusting entrepreneurial class, which used the freedoms gained in 1689 and the thinking of the classical economists to make the *laissez-faire* economy a reality. Their escalating wealth was to rival that of the landed class and they were to transform economic strength into political power, with far-reaching consequences. It was this, rather than the astonishing application of technology, that justified the term 'revolution'.

Jeremy Bentham and the Utilitarians

A further strand of liberalism, with much in common with free-market reasoning, was led by Jeremy Bentham (1748–1832). The moral guide for life, law and government was to be not natural rights but the promotion of 'the greatest happiness for the greatest number' – **utilitarianism**. Although individuals can generally best judge their own happiness and should be free to do so, the legal and political systems should set patterns of reward and punishment so that the self-interested behaviour of individuals and governments produces the maximum public benefit or *utility*. Together with the philosopher James Mill (1773–1836), Bentham founded the philosophical radical movement, which advocated a wide range of constitutional reforms, including frequent elections, a wide franchise, secret ballots, competition between candidates, a free press, freedom of speech, freedom of association and a separation of powers.

However, utilitarianism contained paradoxical implications. Dispensing with natural rights undermined the liberal argument for minimum state interference, clearing the intellectual path for paternalistic state action. Indeed, Bentham supported intervention in areas such as education, wage levels, guaranteed employment and sickness benefits. The reasoning was to be taken much further by J. S. Mill.

It is not from the benevolence of the butcher, the brewer or the baker that we expect our dinner, but from their regard to their own interest.
Adam Smith, An Inquiry into the Nature and Causes of the Wealth of Nations (1776)

Nonsense on stilts.
Jeremy Bentham's view of natural rights

J. S. Mill

With the good fortune, or otherwise, to be the son of James, John Stuart Mill (1806–73) was subjected by his father and Bentham to an intense utilitarian education which gave him a prodigious intellect. However, this came with emotional costs and, after a period of acute depression, he resolved to change his life and in doing so changed utilitarianism. Influenced by French thinker Alexis de Tocqueville (1805–59), he saw Bentham's approach as narrowly materialistic, arguing that the freedoms seen mainly in terms of the economy should extend to other walks of life. This interpretation had radical implications for wider emancipation and a generally more permissive society. Mill's most influential work, *On Liberty* (1859), gave a moral view of freedom.

Mill's arguments for democracy go beyond preventing corruption or maximizing utility. Like the Ancient Greeks he saw political participation as a good in itself, necessary for human dignity. Nevertheless, in his *Considerations on Representative Government* (1861) he echoed de Tocqueville's fear of the 'tyranny of the majority'. Hence, while supporting representative democracy he favoured plural voting, the 'wiser' having more (up to six) votes than others (with property the measure of wisdom!). Political equality should be withheld until the populace was fully educated in civic virtue. Mill's more sophisticated thinking on individualism, freedom and the role of the state was to prove hugely influential and lead to yet another strain of liberalism.

New Liberalism

Persistent poverty, inequality and unemployment mocked the free market's claim to promote the common good. Some liberals began to feel that freedom in modern society was more complex than their classical forebears had believed. In this they were influenced by the German philosopher Hegel, one of the intellectual giants of the modern age.

Georg Hegel

Sharing Rousseau's view that the state was not an infringement of freedom but its highest expression, Hegel (1770–1831) rejected the idea of a pre-social state of nature. He believed that rights could only have meaning in a social context and that human nature was a product of social interaction. In *The Philosophy of Right* (1821) he asserted that true freedom lay not in a life lived away from the state but in its service. Such an idea could be seen as dangerous; it could lead to a crushing of the individual in totalitarianism. However, in late-nineteenth-century England a group of thinkers leavened this extreme collectivism with a radical form of individualism. They formed the school of English Idealists, under their most notable member, T. H. Green.

T. H. Green

An Oxford classicist, Thomas Hill Green (1836–82) believed in the goodness of human instinct. Although not the all-consuming ideal of Hegel, the state did exist to secure the 'common good', something greater than the sum of individual happiness sought by utilitarians. Others extended this thinking. L. T. Hobhouse argued that, whereas classical liberalism had sought to protect individuals from the state, New Liberalism used the state to liberate individuals from social and economic restrictions. J. A. Hobson viewed society as a living organism, each part promoting the well-being of the whole. In these terms, *laissez-faire* could be seen as a disease requiring treatment.

John Maynard Keynes

A radical economic thinker, Keynes (1883–1946) refuted the classical economists' view that the market would necessarily allocate resources in the best way. The state could not stand aside; it should take on the job of managing the market, increasing demand through public borrowing and expenditure to maintain full employment. This is the essence of **Keynesianism** (see p. 562).

Essentially New Liberalism saw freedom not as a product of nature but as a creation of the state. Its influence was seen in practical terms with the Liberal governments of 1905–15, which helped to lay the foundations of the welfare state. Indeed, for critics it was socialism rather than liberalism. However, in principle, the individual is given only the *means* to pursue fulfilment; self-help remains central (see Simhony 1991).

Defining freedom

While most ideologies claim to cherish freedom, their interpretations of the term can vary and produce conflicting policy conclusions.

Negative: Classical liberal thinkers saw freedom as the absence of restriction. This negative concept of freedom is achieved by minimum state intervention in people's lives.

Positive: New Liberal thinkers argued that the freedom offered by the absence of state interference was bogus. Poverty, ignorance, illness, unemployment, bullying by the rich and so on left the mass of people quite unfree. They advocated positive state action, through social policies, to release people from their social fetters. In his great report of 1942, which laid the foundations of the post-war welfare state, William Beveridge used the language of New Liberalism when he spoke of the state freeing people from what he termed the 'evil giants' of ignorance, disease, squalor, poverty and idleness.

Neoliberalism

Amidst the transformations within liberalism there remained critics who clung to the earlier classical formulation. Isaiah Berlin (1970) saw in the new idea of freedom the foundation of oppression, but perhaps the most tenacious critic was Friedrich von Hayek.

Friedrich von Hayek

During a long lifetime Hayek (1899–1992) witnessed both fascism and Stalinism and most of his work was preoccupied with the threat posed by the state. He perpetuated a body of neoclassical economic thought originated by Carl Menger (1840–1921), known as the Austrian School, which admitted only a limited role for the state in offsetting social hardship. A fellow member, Ludwig Von Mises (1881–1973), stressed the impossibility of state planning. Hayek's mission was to show modern **capitalism** as an essential element of the free society, asserting that the market resolves social problems, producing a 'spontaneous order', the outcome of human action but not of human design. Hayek's work was frequently coupled with that of US economist Milton Friedman (1912–2006) and the Chicago School, which again associated the market with freedom and democracy and, in opposition to Keynesianism, advocated an economic policy known as monetarism (see p. 564).

From the 1980s **neoliberalism** seized the heart of the British polity in a new consensus. First it became associated with those thinkers and politicians, including Enoch Powell and Margaret Thatcher, who labelled themselves Conservative. They formed the '**New Right**' and the term **Thatcherism** entered the ideological lexicon. After an initially sceptical response, the Labour Party was to reinvent itself as New Labour and don much of the new garb (see p. 370). However, the worldwide economic crisis of 2008 saw the governments of the USA and other states intervening in the market to shore up failing economies in what many saw as a return to the discredited doctrines of Keynes (see chapter 18).

Whose interest?

Early liberalism used rationalism and the value of freedom to undermine the claims of monarchy, aristocracy and religion, clearing the way for lasting democratic and egalitarian reforms. However, the principle that governments keep out of private affairs was very much in the interests of those becoming economically powerful through capitalism. The liberal claim that all people were of equal worth sounded a hollow ring in an economic system that created poverty as well as riches (Arblaster 1984: 84–91). While New Liberalism recognized the harsh effects of capitalism, it

The system of private property is the most important guarantee of freedom, not only for those who own property but scarcely less for those who do not.
Friedrich von Hayek, The Road to Serfdom (1944)

There's no such thing as a free lunch.
Americanism, sometimes attributed to neoliberal economist Milton Friedman

sought to save rather than to replace it. However, alternative views of the nature of freedom and society spawned two more western ideologies. First came conservatism, opposing the reforms of the liberals, and then came socialism, with an even more radical collectivist agenda.

Conservatism

Initially **conservatism** aimed to provide a rationale for resisting the changes called for by liberals; it is a doctrine of reaction. Indeed, the first political use of the term came with English opposition to the Enlightenment and French Revolution. Later conservatives have resisted variously republicanism, industrialism, liberalism, utilitarianism and socialism. Leading conservative thinker Michael Oakeshott (1962) argued that although conservatives accept that reform may sometimes be necessary, it should not arise from abstract principles, which will inevitably distort and oversimplify. There is also a certain pragmatism in their thinking; if something works it is accepted, with little theory of why it does so.

If it ain't broke, don't fix it.
An Americanism

Human nature

Conservatives aim to see people as they actually are. Hence they reject individualistic theories as simplistic; real people are always part of society, surrounded by cultural accretions – language, histories, customs, literature and so on. Human reason is limited; wisdom is not the product of rational thought but of feelings, instincts and prejudices evolved over the generations. The sense of realism leads to an acceptance of the Christian idea of original sin; people are not perfect and cannot be made so. Life and politics are about making the best of a bad job.

The form of government

> I believe it to be of the utmost importance that a territorial aristocracy should be maintained. I believe that in no country is it more important than in this, with its ancient constitution, ancient habits and mixed form of government.
>
> Sir Robert Peel (1788–1850; Conservative PM), House of Commons speech (4 May 1846)

Political equality is not merely a folly, – it is a chimera . . . the multitude will always have leaders among them.
Marquis of Salisbury (1830–1903; Conservative leader), in *How Conservatives Think*

Conservatism does not lay down a blueprint; constitutions are not designed, they evolve. Each nation will have its own uniquely fitted system of government and countries should not import alien practices. Conservatives characteristically value good order, social hierarchy and religion. The particular features British conservatives have seen as *their* tradition include an aristocracy, the monarchy, the House of Lords, the patriarchal family, property and a natural ruling class. Opposition to membership of the EU is a more recent manifestation. Social inequality is seen as both natural and socially necessary; it cannot be eradicated. Consequently poverty, while nothing to be ashamed of, must be borne with stoicism.

The pattern of development: the retreat from rationalism

Its anti-rationalism suggests conservatism will produce fewer thinkers than most ideologies. On the other hand, the argument that it is a natural cast of mind allows it to claim a long tradition, exponents not realizing they were talking conservative prose. Thus, 'conservative' thinking can be traced to the Ancient Greeks, including Plato (Auerbach 1959: 26), through a range of thinkers, including those of a religious persuasion, who have challenged rationalism in one way or other.

Classical conservatism

Society is a partnership not only between those who are living, but between those who are living, those who are dead and those who are yet to be born.
Edmund Burke,
Reflections on the Revolution in France (1790)

Ironically, the father of modern 'conservatism' was a Whig. An opponent of the Enlightenment, Irish-born writer and politician Edmund Burke (1729–97) outlined the rationale for resisting change in his *Reflections on the Revolution in France* (1790). Generally he argued for a presumption in favour of the status quo; virtue should be assumed in existing institutions – this explained their survival. Burke was not against revolution as such but he argued that it should reassert the natural order rather than destroy it. Hence he welcomed the outcome of the Glorious Revolution of 1688, believing it restored the ancient rights of the aristocracy against encroaching royal authority. Similarly, he supported the colonists in the American War of Independence, whom he believed to be demanding traditional English liberties. However, the French affair was a different matter. Here, an ancient order was being challenged – an affront to God, its creator. He saw the enterprise as doomed, predicting the rise of a military dictatorship (he was of course partly right in this). However, Burke's conservatism was augmented with other strains.

Romantic conservatism

Bliss was it in that dawn to be alive.
William Wordsworth (1770–1850) on the French Revolution, in *The Prelude* (xi: 108)

Industrialization destroyed old patterns of life. Its critics saw gross ugliness that was disfiguring the landscape with factories and urban squalor and undermining the social fabric by replacing the harmonious feudal order with exploitative relationships. In response to this, writers such as Coleridge, Carlyle, Wordsworth and Sir Walter Scott began to express nostalgia for the more simple way of life. Unlike classical conservatives, the romantics were not necessarily opposed to rationalism;

indeed, Wordsworth wrote enthusiastically of the French Revolution. A romantic strain was also evident within the New Right during the Thatcher premiership, with figures such as Enoch Powell, Roger Scruton and Maurice Cowling advocating traditional conservative values, from monarchy to foxhunting (Scruton 1980: 34).

Paternalist conservatism

With property as the basis of power, the aristocracy was seen by early conservatives as the only group that could be trusted to govern, its interest being identical with the common good. There was no case for limiting government; state intervention was recognized as a necessity of the industrial age well before the reforms of the Liberals. This was a form of paternalism which continued the feudal doctrine of *noblesse oblige*. Perhaps the most important representative of this strain was Benjamin Disraeli (1804–81), astute Tory Party leader who, in 1854, expressed the sentiment in a novel, *Sybil, or: the Two Nations*. The 'two nations' of rich and poor must be united if the whole is to be maintained (see chapter 9). From this comes the term 'one-nation conservatism'. However, conservatives have taken a Janus-like stance over the one-nation principle, some looking more fondly towards the liberal free market.

Power has only one duty – to secure the social welfare of the people.
Benjamin Disraeli, Sybil, or: the Two Nations (1854: book IV, ch. XIV)

Liberal conservatism

State intervention in welfare had, for both principled and political reasons, certain limitations: too much social reform would resemble a rationalist blueprint and paternalism could weaken the nation's moral fabric. Moreover, state interference could threaten property-ownership, the traditional basis of aristocratic power. As a Whig, Burke had himself favoured free trade because it weakened monarchy (Hampsher-Monk 1987: 20), and believed that industrialization, as a natural development, should not be hindered. Furthermore, in the early stages of industrialization the aristocracy had shared some interests with the bourgeoisie as the railways scored the surface of their land and the mines burrowed beneath. This version of conservatism was to come to the fore in the 1980s as part of the New Right (see chapter 13). Indeed, the term 'liberal conservatism' was even used to describe the ideology of New Labour (see Driver and Martell 1998).

Whose interest?

The conservative position is seductive; it can be said that we are all conservative at heart (Cecil 1912: 9), and many speak nostalgically of a 'golden age' of, say, football or theatre or popular music. Moreover, the world is littered with examples of failed rationalist reforms, including the socialist 'utopias' of Eastern Europe. In the arts much is made of wisdom built up over centuries. The great Bolshoi Ballet of Russia,

Conservatives know there are books to read, pictures to look at, music to listen to – and grouse to shoot.
Harold Macmillan (1894–1986; Conservative PM), quoted by Nigel Nicolson in Thames TV's The Day Before Yesterday (1970)

A democracy of the dead.

G. K. Chesterton (1874–1936; British writer) on conservative respect for the wisdom of the past, in *Orthodoxy* (1908)

for example, prides itself on a tradition of over two hundred years and the result is unrivalled artistry, while the National Gallery in Trafalgar Square preserves the work of great masters. Yet there is a fundamental paradox. In arguing for tradition and prejudice over rationalism, conservatism uses reason to attack reason; it is an ideology not to be ideological (Vincent 1992: 82). Moreover, there is much evidence (cannibalism, witch-burning, female circumcision, racism, religious fundamentalism) to show that a blind adherence to tradition can be dangerous. In many walks of life we do not slight reason; most would prefer a trained physician to the ministrations of a witch doctor and the products of scientific thinking dominate modern life. When religious extremists plot attacks on secular society they often do so on mobile phones. In practice, many conservative thinkers allow some place for rationalism but stress its limitations. However, in the world of politics, conservatism as an ideology must by definition serve the interests of the 'haves' rather than the 'have-nots'. It also serves the interest of religious leaders, historically linked with political leaders, who deny rationality at various points, sometimes to the extent, most bizarrely, of denying evolution.

Modern conservatism as a defined ideology arose as a response to liberalism and the French Revolution, an event striking fear into English aristocratic hearts and providing a strong motive for resisting change. The newer ideology of socialism was also something to resist.

Socialism

Socialism stands as the antithesis of liberalism, repudiating its central precepts of individualism, the free market and private property. However, the two share a common core of western assumptions and values: faith in science, belief in industrialization and confidence in the possibility of rationalist improvement. In this respect, both stand in opposition to conservative values.

Human nature

Socialism reasons from an optimistic view of people. They are not isolated individuals but part of a larger society, with a sense of moral responsibility towards one another. Human nature cannot be found in some imaginary state of nature; it is a product of society. Socialism argues that the individualism of liberal thought encourages people's worst characteristics. In contrast, the collectivism of socialism fosters values such as altruism and fraternity.

The form of government

A major misconception about socialism is that it entails a dominant state. On the contrary, some early socialists were libertarians and associated with anarchy.

However, such thinking was undermined by industrialization, and socialism was forced to advocate either a particular form of government within the liberal tradition or an alternative to it. Both models featured in subsequent developments.

The pattern of development: in search of Utopia

Initially seen as cranks and eccentrics, the early socialists established the environment for new thinking. Central to this was the value of a sense of community, as opposed to competitive individualism. Many of these ideas evolved in France, an important pioneer being the aristocrat Claude Saint-Simon (1760–1825), whose views were spread by his secretary, the philosopher and sociologist Auguste Comte (1798–1857). He envisioned a centrally planned industrialized economy administered for the common good, but, with liberal instincts, he had no wish to abolish private property. François Fourier (1772–1837) saw in large-scale industrialization not progress but impoverishment. Like Rousseau, he valued a simple, unsophisticated life, arguing for industry based on small craftsmen and farmers living in cooperatives (*phalanstères*) of fewer than 2,000. Though rejecting these as rustic fantasies, Pierre-Joseph Proudhon (1809–65) argued that industrialization led only to exploitation, inequality and oppression.

Property is theft. Proudhon's memorable indictment of capitalism in *Qu'est-ce que la Propriété?* (1840)

   The harsh logic of individualism was not applauded by all capitalists. Self-made English industrialist Robert Owen (1771–1858) thought the workplace could be a socialist community. His New Lanark Mills were run paternalistically, providing workers' families with housing, health care and education. The experiment aroused considerable interest at home and in the USA.

Forms of socialism

Marx and Marxism

The rural peasantry and the disorganized urban poor of the early nineteenth century could hardly transform society. Hence a key circumstance in the development of socialism was industrialization and the new class structure. This inspired a strand of thought intended to revolutionize the modern world – **Marxism**. It came from liberalism's most trenchant critic, the German polymath Karl Marx (1818–83). Influenced variously – by the Enlightenment, the French Revolution, English liberalism, classical economics, Hegel, Darwin and the earlier socialists, as well as European literature and classical philosophy – Marx identified the most compelling question of the modern era: how can a just community exist in the context of modern industrial society? No modern thinker has a greater claim to have placed his stamp on the intellectual climate of the twentieth century and on the course of world events.

The father of socialism: the tomb of Karl Marx in Highgate Cemetery, London

Marx aimed to portray political development rather like natural history as a process obeying scientific laws. His theory was one of **historical materialism**: the key lay in the way work, a necessity imposed by nature, was organized. This 'mode of production' shaped laws, arts, politics, state institutions and the dominant ideology. This simple though little-appreciated fact of survival unlocked a Pandora's box. In the new industrial society the vital tools, factories and land necessary for survival were not owned by those who did the work, but by relatively few private individuals – the **bourgeoisie** or capitalists.

> Capital is reckless of the health or length of life of the labourer unless under compulsion from society. To the outcry as to the physical and mental degradation, the premature death, the torture of overwork, it answers: Ought these to trouble us since they increase our profits?
>
> Karl Marx, *Capital* (1867: ch. 10)

Although liberalism made citizens legally free, in reality they were bound to the capitalists who purchased their labour, just like any other commodity (the commodification of labour). While labour was purchased in one market, the workers' products were sold in another, so that prices were unrelated to wages. Employers would seek to widen the gap between the two by keeping wages down and retaining a surplus for themselves. Although Locke had asserted that everyone had a right to the product of their labour, that of the modern worker was being expropriated (stolen). This exploitative relationship was inescapable under capitalism, for without it no one would invest in capital.

Moreover, domination went beyond the workplace to penetrate the state itself. Marx disputed the claim that the liberal state had broken free from class domination. Capitalism is not possible unless the state operates in the bourgeois interest, ensuring the conditions for maximizing profit (maintaining order, protecting property, limiting trade union activity and fostering an ideology of inequality). The bourgeoisie becomes, in effect, a ruling class.

Marx's socialism

Because the system of government was a function of the mode of production, it was here that the fundamental change should be made. Marx's socialism followed a broadly Fourierist vision of a workers' state, which was but a transitory stage leading to an even greater transformation: a society without a wages system, with no division between manual and intellectual labour, and no private property or classes. Far from being totalitarian, this was to be a communal society in which the state would wither away.

How could such change come about? Here lies the secret of Marx's extraordinary appeal to oppressed peoples the world over. He believed revolution was not only necessary but, owing to the tensions and contradictions within capitalism, inevitable. Such an idea deeply unnerved those living behind the bastions of privilege, making Marx a hated figure within the liberal establishment. The French Revolution had demonstrated what a united people could achieve and Marx saw the new working class as a Frankenstein's monster that would destroy its capitalist creators. He identified a two-stage process: a bourgeois revolution with the liberal overthrow of the aristocratic order, followed by a proletarian revolution with the workers' overthrow of the bourgeoisie. In Britain, the first had already taken place; the second was predestined. The possibility of this dramatic challenge preoccupied a growing socialist movement and parties formed to prepare for the revolution. However, differing interpretations and circumstances led to tension between those favouring violent action (**voluntarism**) and the moderates prepared to wait for the inevitable collapse of capitalism (**determinism**).

Revolutionary socialism

In Russia, the revolutionary leader Lenin (1870–1924) began in a determinist position. However, the backward development of Russian capitalism led him towards

A committee for managing the affairs of the bourgeoisie. Karl Marx's view of democratic government under capitalism

On 14 July 2005, in a ballot conducted for the BBC Radio 4 programme In Our Time, *listeners overwhelming voted Karl Marx 'the world's greatest philosopher'.*

voluntarism. He developed a theory of the party as an intellectual vanguard spearheading the revolution. The Czarist regime was weakened by its inability to manage the world war, the government was divided and the country in chaos. In the great revolutions of 1917 the Czar was overthrown and in July 1918 the first Soviet Constitution was proclaimed. Whether or not this model was applicable to the special conditions of Russia, its subsequent export led to the inflexible and ruthless imposition of a theory that abandoned Marx's vision. In Russia itself the subsequent reign of Stalinist terror was a mockery of the liberty the revolution had promised.

Reformist socialism

The majestic egalitarianism of the law, which forbids rich and poor alike to sleep under bridges, to beg in the streets, and to steal bread.

Anatole France (1844–1924; French writer), *The Red Lily*

In the light of Italian conditions, Antonio Gramsci (1891–1937) advocated more subtle means of reform. He argued that the ruling class could avert the predicted crisis of capitalism because they exercised continuing dominance (**hegemony**) by holding influential positions throughout the state and shaping the prevailing common sense of society to legitimize their role. Hence the task of the revolutionary was to infiltrate these establishment bastions, ultimately to unleash the social forces below.

A leading revisionist, the German Eduard Bernstein (1850–1932) believed socialism could be pursued through liberal constitutional structures. This was an attractive idea in those West European nations where such systems were relatively well established. Moreover, the goals were also more moderate – **social democracy**, with welfare policies rather than **communism**. Such an approach was advanced in Britain by the Fabian Society, a group of intellectuals influential at the turn of the twentieth century and instrumental in the formation of the Labour Party (see chapter 13).

The anarchistic tradition

Although mainstream socialism after Marx tended towards either the radical or parliamentary forms, other strains continued the ideology's more **anarchic** tendencies. This was not the political disorder, violence and lawlessness of popular imagination. They envisaged a socialist society working harmoniously through workers' associations rather than the state. A movement began in France in the 1890s known as Syndicalism, while in England guild socialism in the early twentieth century sought to incorporate into workers' associations the fraternal spirit of the ancient guilds.

Others have argued for market socialism whereby a free market functions with citizens' assemblies, trade unions and workers' councils rather than a capitalist state. Production is by private cooperatives operating competitively but without profit accumulation. The theory aroused interest in the 1930s though it had many critics. There are those who argue that, with the collapse of Soviet-style socialism and the failure of nationalization, some form of market socialism could still have a future.

Whose interest?

Although attracting intellectuals and altruistic members of the middle classes, socialist doctrines make a broadly sectional appeal to the poorer members of society and were particularly attractive to the rising labour movements. It can also be seen as in the interests of party machines and large powerful state bureaucracies. The principal objection from liberals concerned the threat to freedom, high taxation and totalitarianism, while Conservatives saw socialism as a class-based threat to the natural order of society.

A Third Way?

> By three methods we may learn wisdom: first, by reflection, which is noblest; second, by imitation, which is easiest; and third, by experience, which is the most bitter.
>
> Confucius (551–479 BC; Chinese philosopher and political theorist)

For some critics, the three traditional ideologies are unable to meet the challenge of the modern age. The problems of the twenty-first century are multifaceted, with increasing cultural and economic globalization, the dominance of free markets and corporate wealth, a state of permanent technological revolution in communications and production, omnipresent ecological threats, the collapse of communism and growing levels of inequality and international terrorism in an unstable multipolar world.

One response has been to search for a new position that can draw upon the traditional ideologies while rejecting their more fundamentalist versions. The idea that there is a viable position between right and left is seductive and by no means new. New Liberalism in the early twentieth century had tempered individualism with collectivism and the fledgling Labour Party sought a moderate position between Marxism and capitalism. In the early post-war decades the social democracies of Western Europe took a stance between unbridled capitalism and communism by adopting Keynesianism. By the end of the 1990s some thinkers were again charting what they saw as a '**third way**'. To a considerable extent this was spearheaded by the British scholar Anthony Giddens (1998), who gave his ideas wider audience in the

BBC Reith Lectures in 2000. Popularly described as Tony Blair's 'favourite academic', Giddens influenced New Labour and also US President Bill Clinton.

> Third way politics emerged against a backdrop of a double political crisis. . . the revolutions of 1989 revealed that socialism was not a viable approach to economic organization, yet unchecked enthusiasm for the free market . . . was also flawed.
>
> Anthony Giddens, *Sociology* (2006: 866)

Broadly a revision of social democracy, the third way recognized the necessity and power of markets but aimed to modify them with strategies for promoting equality, sustainable development and social inclusion. While classical social democracy was concerned to mitigate suffering resulting from capitalism, the third way saw welfare policies as a means of investing in human resources to benefit an entrepreneurial culture. Hence, for example, 'unemployment benefits . . . should carry an obligation to look actively for work' (Giddens 1998: 65). At the same time businesses must accept social responsibilities. Neo-Keynesian economist Will Hutton (1996) suggested that British shareholders were too demanding of quick returns so that companies could not take a long-term view of development and growth. He argued for 'stakeholder capitalism' in which businesses look beyond shareholders: to communities, the environment, employees and customers. When investors unload their shares for short-term profit, government should levy a high capital gains tax.

However, globalization limits the opportunity for political control over social and economic life in any detail (see chapter 5). The operations of transnational corporations, global finance, terrorism, international crime and ecological threats lie largely beyond the arm of national governments. Hence, the third way also calls for a cosmopolitan orientation, promoting a sense of world citizenship, and for global governance to regulate this global society. Attempts to adopt third-way nostrums were apparent in the USA under President Clinton but less so under George W. Bush. They were part of the early New Labour agenda and also in evidence throughout Europe, albeit to a more limited extent. In Germany in 2006 and France in 2007, the elections of Angela Merkel and Nicolas Sarkozy signalled moves in this direction.

A radically meritocratic society would create deep inequalities of outcome, which would threaten social cohesion . . . A top tennis player or opera singer earns vastly more than one who isn't quite so good.
Anthony Giddens, *The Third Way* (1998: 101)

Whose interest?

On the face of it, the ideal version of the third way seeks synergy by harmonizing many interests. Indeed, one criticism is that it tries to 'take the politics out of politics'. However, as with all ideologies, the ideals become distorted in government policies. Thus, for example, Tony Blair's commitment to social justice meant equality of opportunity, while Giddens's vision emphasized equality of outcome, a requirement calling for redistributive measures to protect society's inevitable 'losers' (Giddens 1998: 101–2; 1999). Again, by fostering an entrepreneurial culture and mistrusting the public sector, New Labour was seen by critics to be favouring the interests of capital beneath a cloak of third-way rhetoric.

The reality of corporate power and self-interest became starkly clear in the 'credit crunch' triggered by the September 2008 collapse of US giant Lehman Brothers. Governments felt compelled to fund huge bailouts of the banks which had indulged in injudicious lending and casino-style investment. Inequality rose as the bankers insisted on continuing to pay themselves million-pound bonuses while limiting their lending to struggling businesses. While the voice of Karl Marx was drowned out by the triumph of neoliberalism, his diagnoses began to appear more compelling.

Beyond Traditional Thinking

In this chapter we have examined three great ideologies that have done much to shape the modern western world. However, they are not the only basis for thinking about how people should live together in society. People's expectations have changed since these ideologies were established. The ideologies of feminism and environmentalism reflect new areas of concern. Dissatisfaction with the pattern of contemporary life also sees people turning to alternatives such as religion or more extreme ideologies such as fascism. All these colour modern political debate and we turn to them in the next chapter.

Key points

- Ideologies are nothing more than beliefs about how people should live together.

- Although ideologies are reflected in the names of political parties, pragmatism often guides their actions.

- The western ideological tradition emerged from a dramatic break with the thinking of past ages – the Enlightenment.

- Liberalism cherishes freedom from political oppression. It spawned major revolutions which opened the modern era.

- Economic liberalism influenced the new discipline of political economy, in which the justification for limited government lay in the quest for prosperity through a free market.

- New Liberalism perceived freedom as liberation from poverty, rather than from dominant rulers.

- Neoliberalism rose in the late 1970s to reassert individualism, competition and the free market as the *sine qua non* of the free society.

- Conservatism values tradition and provides a rationale for resisting rationalist change.

- Socialism rejects individualism for collectivism, viewing people as part of a greater whole – society.

- The so-called 'third way' remains a goal of some thinkers to reconcile conflicting traditions in a moderate consensus within capitalist society.

Review your understanding of the following terms and concepts

anarchy	Leviathan	Reformation
collectivism	Marxism	Renaissance
communism	natural rights	revolutionary socialism
Enlightenment	neoliberalism	social democracy
General Will	New Liberalism	state of nature
historical materialism	pragmatism	third way
individualism	rationalism	utilitarianism

Questions for discussion and debate

Consider these propositions and be prepared to present the cases for and against. Try to produce debating propositions of your own.

1 The actions of political parties are better explained by pragmatism than ideology.

2 Classical liberalism is the only version of liberalism that cherishes true liberty.

3   The view of freedom implicit in New Liberalism owes more to Marx than Locke.

4   Marx's critique of liberalism cannot be described as 'scientific'.

5   Reformist socialism can never produce real social change.

6   Conservatism presents a rationalist case against rationalism.

7   Ideologies always serve the interests of one section of society against those of another.

8   The socialist view of human nature is idealistic and unreal.

9   In today's world the 'third way' is the only way.

10   Ideologies are of little concern to the parties that bear their names.

Further reading

Benn, T. (1979) *Arguments for Socialism.*
A stimulating essay, written on the eve of the New Labour era, but with ideas that continue to engage.

Bernstein, E. (1961) *Evolutionary Socialism.*
A classic defence of gradualist reform.

Crick, B. (1987) *Socialism.*
Leading figure of the intellectual left charts growth of various variants of socialism.

Gamble, A. (1981) *An Introduction to Modern Social and Political Thought.*
Places ideas in their historical contexts.

Giddens, A. (1998) *The Third Way: The Renewal of Social Democracy.*
Presented not as an 'end to politics' but as a strategy to renew the left.

Gray, J. (1995) *Enlightenment's Wake: Politics and Culture at the Close of the Modern Age.*
Stimulating set of essays placing major ideologies in their contemporary context.

Hayek, F. von (1976) *The Road to Serfdom* (first published 1944).
Classic and profound critique of the concept of the social state. The starting point of much of the New Right thought of the 1970s and 1980s.

Held, D. (1987) *Models of Democracy*.
The nature, application and importance of democracy, from classical Athens to modern times.

Hobbes, T. (1985) *Leviathan*, Penguin Classics version edited by C. B. Macpherson (first published 1651).
One of the great works in the English language. Editor's introduction makes the ideas crystal clear.

Jones, T. (2011) *The Revival of British Liberalism: From Grimond to Clegg*.
A history of the development of thinking within Liberal and Liberal Democrat parties.

Nozick, R. (1974) *Anarchy, State and Utopia*.
Challenging polemic arguing compellingly for the minimal state.

Oakeshott, M. (1962) *Rationalism in Politics and Other Essays*.
Classic by a post-war conservative.

Putnam, R. (2000) *Bowling Alone*.
Argues that individualism erodes the sense of community to the impoverishment of all. A study of US society that may resonate in Britain.

Scruton, R. (1980) *The Meaning of Conservatism*.
Essays by controversial contemporary thinker.

Smith, A. (1982) *The Wealth of Nations*, Penguin edition (first published 1776).
Classic statement of *laissez-faire* theory.

White, S. (ed.) (2001) *New Labour: The Progressive Future?*
Examines the dilemmas of social democracy in the contemporary world. Critique of the third way.

For reading around the subject and some light relief

In addition to telling a story, many writers aim to alter the way we think about life and society.

Bertolt Brecht, *The Good Person of Szechwan*.
Brilliant Marxist satire. The 'good person' is made bad when she tries to run a shop under the constraints of capitalism.

Terry Christensen, *Reel Politics: American Political Movies from* Birth of a Nation *to* Platoon.
Studies over 200 films. Argues that Hollywood films are suffused with conservative values.

Charles Dickens, *A Tale of Two Cities*.
Novel on the French Revolution by one of England's greatest writers.

Arthur Koestler, *Darkness at Noon*.
Hungarian-born British novelist tells a nightmare tale of Rubashov, a Bolshevik revolutionary imprisoned and tried for treason by the Soviet government he had helped to create.

J. B. Priestley, *An Inspector Calls*.
Makes the case for collectivism against individualism with ingenious theatricality.

Robert Tressell, *The Ragged-Trousered Philanthropists*.
Working-class protagonists ruminate on life. They are 'philanthropists' because it is their willingness to be poor that allows the rich to stay rich.

On the net

The political parties bearing the names of ideologies all have websites. In addition, the world of ideas sees a substantial number of think-tanks promoting some version of an ideology, with the aim of influencing the views of politicians and public, and the translation of ideas into policy. For example:

http://www.adamsmith.org/
Named after the legendary thinker, the Adam Smith Institute is an independent think-tank aiming to promote libertarian and free-market ideas.

http://www.smith-institute.org.uk/
The Smith Institute is an independent think-tank founded in memory of the late John Smith MP, once leader of the Labour Party. With socialistic leanings, its proclaimed goal is the promotion of a 'fairer society'.

CHAPTER 3

IDEOLOGY: BEYOND THE WESTERN TRADITION

Contents

It is difficult to overestimate the impact of the western tradition in political life. However, it is increasingly revealed as unable to fully address compelling questions of contemporary life. This chapter expands our consideration of ideology by examining feminism and environmentalism. It also looks at fascism, an ideology that raises new concerns and cannot be ignored. Finally we consider ideas on how we should live that come from a mode of thought based on faith rather than reason, which the Enlightenment undermined, but which is still very much with us – religion. We end with the question: can we ever reach an end of ideology?

A Changing Climate

In the contemporary world new assumptions arising from new conditions and new social norms colour political debate. A new uncertainty gives rise to philosophical searching in various directions, some of which are described as postmodern – a vaguely defined concept denoting a stage, or epoch, beyond that ushered in by the Enlightenment (see Harvey 1989). Prominent within the new thinking is the conviction that the rights accorded through the western tradition cannot be confined to only one half of humankind, but should be extended to the other half: the women.

Feminism

You cannot entrust the interests of one class entirely to another class, and you cannot entrust the interests of one sex entirely to another sex.

David Lloyd George (1863–1945; Liberal statesman), speech (1911)

Political thinkers refer variously to man, his rights, his liberation, his equality, his nobility *ad infinitum*. This is no accident; for many the intention is deliberately to exclude women on the grounds that the territory of politics is beyond bounds. Even Rousseau, champion of freedom and equality, made this exclusion. Sometimes the sexist language merely reflects convention, but such usage shrouds deeper forces at the level of the subconscious. In the same way that Gramsci saw patterns of class hegemony woven into a 'common sense' of life, so male domination is built into common consciousness through language, family life, personal relationships and work patterns. Hence, many people, including some political scientists, have regarded it as 'natural' that women are not political (Randall 1982: 1–5). The body of ideological thought termed **feminism** arose as a reaction to this position. Feminism seeks sexual justice. While not presenting an alternative to liberalism or socialism, it meets the requirements of an ideology in its own right, being concerned with human nature and the social arrangements whereby people conduct their lives.

Human nature

The key issue revolves around the idea of difference in the natures of men and women. This is of central importance because difference implies distinct male and female roles. Differences can be considered in physiological and psychological terms. Physiologically the prime feature concerns childbirth and child-rearing. Women are indeed designated by nature as the child-bearers. Yet while such physiological differences are obvious, some researchers have gone further to suggest that men have different brains, bestowing superior ability in various fields. Arguments based in psychology have asserted that boys tend to be more assertive, so that when, for example, confronted with an obstacle they will seek to find an alternative route while girls will merely sit and cry (Wilson 1994: 60).

All these arguments can be refuted. Observed differences may lie not in people's natures but in the way genders are treated; parents tend to socialize children into stereotypal gender roles. While there may be debate over the degree of real difference between the natures of men and women, all strains of feminism argue that this is far less than has been assumed. Debate continues as to the extent of the real (as opposed to socially conditioned) differences between the sexes.

The form of government

In the view of feminists, a gender-based division of labour has permeated societies, and in terms of politics this has meant male domination – **patriarchy**. Empirically speaking, there can be little doubt that politics has been a man's game (see McCormack 2007). This may of course mean that men are more interested in acquiring power than are women. However, feminists attack male dominance in the state territory, calling for more women in government. It can be argued that women are naturally more caring and compassionate, making them eminently suitable for the public sphere, promising a more ethical and compassionate society (see Elshtain 1981). The entry of over a hundred women into Parliament after the 1997 and 2001 general elections helped to soften policy on certain fronts, although in other areas, such as benefits to single mothers and the invasion of Iraq, there was disappointment (see p. 426).

The pattern of development: *liberté, egalité* and sisterhood

In plotting the development of feminism one must remember that history has largely been written by men. A key early feminist was Christina de Pizan, who wrote

The emotional, sexual, and psychological stereotyping of females begins when the doctor says, 'It's a girl.'
Shirley Chisholm (1924–2005; black American politician, educator and author)

Instead of getting hard ourselves and trying to compete, women should try and give their best qualities to men – bring them softness, teach them how to cry.
Joan Baez (b. 1941; American folk singer)

The City of the Ladies in 1405. There was also the exotic Aphra Behn (1640–89), who spied for the court of Charles II and was a prolific author of plays and novels ridiculing prevailing patterns of sexual inequality. However, the birth of modern feminism lies, like other major ideologies, in the Enlightenment. In *A Vindication of the Rights of Man* (1790) Mary Wollstonecraft (1759–97), the greatest of the early feminists, countered Burke's attack on the French Revolution (in which women were active). Two years later she applied the same reasoning to argue for equality for her own sex in *A Vindication of the Rights of Woman*, a major feminist landmark. In America, women were active in another great cause, the fight against slavery. However, after the American civil war, when political rights were extended to black men, but not women (black or white), they mobilized as a specifically feminist force. Indeed, the USA has always provided a major spearhead of the movement.

Added impetus came from industrialization, which brought poor women into the new workplaces, while giving their bourgeois sisters issues to ponder and the leisure to do so. The movement saw them active in charitable work, education, propaganda and a sustained fight for the right to vote, which was achieved partly as a result of their efforts in the Great War (chapter 8). However, with the franchise secured the movement fell dormant, submerged by economic depression, the second world war and subsequent reconstruction.

The 1960s saw feminism's renaissance as an international civil rights movement sought emancipation for various oppressed groups. Changing attitudes towards sex, marriage, divorce and the family, coupled with the availability of the contraceptive pill and easier access to abortion, altered women's perceptions. In 1961, Simone de Beauvoir's influential 1949 classic, *The Second Sex*, reappeared in paperback, while in 1970 Germaine Greer's *The Female Eunuch* sent tremors through university campuses and suburbia. The movement continued to grow, with new journals, books and plays, and a rediscovery of earlier writers, such as Virginia Woolf. Specialist publishers, such as Virago (1977) and The Women's Press (1978), emerged and universities mounted courses in Women's Studies. The ideology also permeated certain academic disciplines, offering courses in areas such as feminist geography, feminist sociology, feminist literature and feminist history. A third stage of the movement became apparent from the early 1990s, with some reaction against what was seen as the movement's predominantly white middle-class orientation (see Krøløkke and Sørensen 2006).

The worldwide credit crunch beginning during the first decade of the twenty-first century created fears that women's newly won rights might be eroded. The threat reinvigorated the movement. In Britain, and elsewhere, seminars and conferences organized by groups such as Fawcett, Object!, and Million Women Rise discussed contemporary issues, including sex trafficking, the pay gap, 'workaholic cultures' and childcare. Bloggers, tweeters, authors and magazines began to gain the attention of a younger generation. There was also direct action such as the 5,000-strong London demonstration in March 2009 by the women's coalition against male violence.

Another wave has been broadly characterized as neo-feminist. A younger generation emerged recognizing a need to work *with* rather than against men (van der Gaag 1995). The think-tank Demos discerned an historic shift in the relations between the sexes, an 'unravelling of not only 200 years of industrial society, but millennia of traditions and beliefs' (Wilkenson 1995). In bringing about a more fully egalitarian society, reform can be seen to be in men's interest as much as that of women.

Forms of feminism

As with most ideologies, there is no single version of feminism and approaches range from moderate to extreme. A wide and fluid variety of movements describe themselves variously as black feminism, postcolonial feminism, third-world feminism, multiracial feminism, libertarian feminism, postmodern feminism and eco-feminism. They can also be broadly seen in terms of the classical ideologies.

Liberal feminism

One could logically expect classical liberalism to be hospitable to feminism. The idea of natural freedoms should surely include women. Similarly, the utilitarian principle of maximum happiness might be expected to endorse sex equality. Moreover, rationalism should be suspicious of ancient patriarchal customs. Yet this has not proved so. The resounding calls for emancipation largely expressed male aspirations. Indeed, it was a Liberal government that held out against the suffragettes, falling into the very conservatism they castigated.

As a liberal feminist Mary Wollstonecraft was a lone swallow and J. S. Mill, as a male thinker deeply concerned with women's rights, was a rare bird indeed. To Wollstonecraft sexual imbalance was a social creation and harmful to society at large. Mill noted how the liberal distinction between state and civil society confined women to the latter. In *The Subjection of Women* (1869), he saw their position as a relic of slavery, grounded ultimately in force. Such conclusions were deeply disturbing to a male establishment and, compared with his other writings, were to languish in obscurity (Held 1987: 80). However, his prescriptions, including reforming the marriage laws, equal educational opportunities and female enfranchisement, were limited to freeing women to help themselves (Pateman 1983). Today liberal feminists continue to be distinguished by a moderate agenda framed in terms of equal legal, social and political rights. The goal is *freedom* to pursue their own advancement for the benefit of all society. Men, although called to change attitudes, are not seen as the enemy and the heterosexual family remains the norm.

The divine right of husbands may . . . , it is hoped in this enlightened age, be contested without danger.
Mary Wollstonecraft, *A Vindication of the Rights of Woman* (1792: ch.3)

Socialist feminism

Socialists find liberal (and radical) feminists blind to the economic basis of patriarchy. The basic premise of early socialist feminism was that women's plight was rooted in class oppression. Some saw sexual equality as integral to a broader socialist vision entailing alternative lifestyles. Fourier borders on eroticism in advocating free love, bisexuality and lesbianism. Owen believed patriarchal marriage sustained the competitive economy lying at the heart of much misery. Marx himself was rather unsympathetic but his collaborator, Friedrich Engels (1820–95), recognized women's oppression, arguing in *The Origin of the Family, Private Property and the State* (1884) that it was rooted in capitalism and the role of women in the maintenance and reproduction of labour (without payment). The demands of socialist feminists include free and widespread birth control, abortion on demand, state payment for domestic work, state child care and full equality in the workplace. Heterosexual families are not necessarily seen as the norm, though where they exist, they should be restructured to share the domestic burden. Activism takes place largely within established parties of the left.

Radical feminism

Radicals are those adopting an aggressive stance towards men, accusing liberal feminists of accepting patriarchal values. The free market, for example, glorifies competitiveness, seen as a male characteristic. Partly a breakaway from the socialists, the radical variant sees Marxism as 'sex blind'. The most fundamental basis for discrimination in society is sexual difference. The problem lies in the attitudes of men and their tendency towards aggression, violence and even rape. Yet the natural differences between the sexes are seen as minimal; conditioning is the key. This leads to calls for androgyny, both sexes playing identical roles, not only in rearing children but in work and even (with medical intervention) nurturing foetuses. Where radicals do concede difference they argue for female superiority, women's life-giving qualities making them more peaceable, caring and intuitive.

The movement has attracted overtly sexual lesbians, but in addition a form of political lesbianism emerged advocating separatism (living in sisterhood communities), sperm banks (to facilitate birth without direct male participation) and lesbian marriages. It is difficult to discern in radical feminism an underlying theory. Drawing more from **postmodernism**, it embraces aspects of eastern philosophy and mysticism, seeing rationalism itself as a male characteristic. Action can take direct forms outside mainstream politics and peaked in the 1960s, when passions inflamed brassieres as well as debate. This is the arm of the movement that gained its notoriety and 'women's lib' moniker and moderates fear that it alienates public opinion.

Conservative feminism?

It is unusual to speak of conservative feminism; indeed, the term may be an oxymoron. The subjugation of women is historic reality sanctified by ancient custom, the very thing conservatives venerate. Indeed, anti-feminism is often a hallmark of the far right. **Nazism** stressed women's role in rearing children, outlawed birth control and denounced women in politics. Similar calls have come from a self-proclaimed Moral Majority in the USA and right-wing think-tanks in Britain. This conservatism often takes religious forms, revering sacred texts which tend to be anti-feminist. Muslim fundamentalism limits women in various ways, while in the USA the Christian Right, with millions of active supporters, campaigns for the restoration of 'family values' and pursues strenuous anti-abortion crusades. The Anglican Church long opposed women priests, a stance still maintained by the Catholic Church.

Yet despite all, groups bearing names such as 'conservative pro-family feminism' view traditional roles like male-supporting and child-rearing, as valid female roles. This can be seen as radicalism in a different guise, according the family, and the woman's role within it, greater value. Such thinking is not entirely foreign to mainstream feminists when they advocate a wage for parenting and housework.

Whose interest?

Superficially, feminism could be said to promote an unashamedly sectional interest: women calling for a better deal for women. However, not all women share the same interests and the movement is fragmented into various groups. British examples have included the National Women's Network, Change, Womankind, Women against Fundamentalism and the Women's Environmental Network. Some organize around specific issues, such as reproductive rights, lesbian rights, welfare, violence, sexist advertising, children and professional career development. Further divisions reflect class, race, nationality and sexuality. Moreover, many women do not support any version of the movement. A *YouGov* poll reported in the *Sunday Telegraph* (16 Nov. 2008) that only 38 per cent of British women would describe themselves as feminists while 78 per cent would rather have a male boss.

Yet feminism has permeated political culture, its global nature underlined in high-profile UN Women's Conferences. More women are now found in boardrooms and government. A new consciousness permeates the language; those once known as 'actresses' are now 'actors' and 'batsmen' are 'batters'. Although feminists generally believe they have further to go, the ideology is woven into the fabric of contemporary life, with many seeing greater equality as in the interest of society in general.

Nobody will ever win the Battle of the Sexes. There's just too much fraternizing with the enemy.
Henry Kissinger (b. 1923; political scientist, diplomat, and former US Secretary of State)

Environmentalism

In the twenty-first century a view is consolidating that the western ideological tradition is dangerously myopic. Under a broadly liberal banner, the post-war era has seen industrial growth raising material standards beyond imagination. Yet its costs are becoming increasingly apparent, not only to scientists but in everyday life. In towns, polluted air causes childhood asthma; in the countryside, rivers and lakes turn brown and lifeless. Supermarket shoppers worry about contaminated meat, pesticides and whether the hygienic packaging is wasting limited resources. At the macro level there are problems of over-fishing, deforestation and the green-house effect. There seems no escape; those opting out of the rat race for a place in the sun expose their bodies to ultraviolet radiation seeping through the depleted ozone layer. Modern science and rationalist ideologies may have brought humanity to a 'multifaceted global crisis' (Spretnack and Capra 1986: xv) that prompts new ideological thinking – **environmentalism**. This is an ideology with a scientific basis: ecology, the study of the relationship of living organisms to their environment. This discipline was founded in the late nineteenth century by German biologist Ernst Haeckel. Its essential view is holistic: a single species cannot be understood without reference to its interactions with other species.

There are two distinctive perspectives.

- *Anthropocentric*. Human life remains the principal criterion of value; nature must be respected because it serves us. The depletion of fish stocks, for example, is bad because species may die out and humans will suffer food loss.
- *Ecocentric*. Value is judged in terms of the ecosystem as a whole; this is the more controversial position (sometimes termed 'deep ecology'). A popular version is the **Gaia** theory of James Lovelock (1979), which sees the earth as an organism, worthy of surviving with or without the human species.

Human nature

To environmentalists human nature *is* the problem. Driven by the egotistical desire to survive, it drives people to use natural resources for their own purposes, with little thought for other species or future generations. Whether anthropocentric or ecocentric, these natural urges must be curbed.

The form of government

While moderates believe that environmental goals can be met through existing forms of democratic government, radicals demand more extreme changes. For them the nation-state with powerful centralized government is seen as outmoded. The call is for more localism and a return to small, self-sufficient communities living in sustainable 'bioregions' in a form of peaceable anarchy. However, many environmental problems are global and solutions must come at the supranational level, often at the expense of national sovereignty.

The pattern of development: industrialism in question

Environmentalists see in ancient pre-industrial societies a greater ecological awareness than is found in modern industrialized society. In 1661, diarist John Evelyn's tract *Fumifugium: the Inconveniencie of the Aer and Smoak of London Dissipated* argued for more trees to purify the city air. In the nineteenth century, the great public health movement, spearheaded by arch-Benthamite Edwin Chadwick, did more to eradicate diseases such as typhoid and cholera than would an army of physicians. The threat of resource depletion was also recognized. Malthus's grim late-eighteenth-century warning that population would outstrip food supply coloured much thinking, as did Darwin's theory of evolution, which underlined the close integration of the human species with nature. Romantic conservatism, with its belief that industrialism despoiled nature, was also influential. For some, including Haeckel himself, nature acquired a spiritual significance, a pantheistic substitute for the God Darwin had questioned.

Contemporary environmentalism took off in the 1960s with Rachel Carson's influential *Silent Spring* (1962) – silent because the birds no longer sang, their reproductive cycles disrupted by pesticides. In 1968 Paul Ehrlich's *The Population Bomb* heightened the sense of alarm by reviving the Malthusian nightmare of over-population, and in similar vein the Club of Rome produced *The Limits to Growth* (Meadows et al. 1972). In the USA, the Carter administration commissioned the *Global 2000 Report* (1980), which concluded

> If present trends continue, the world in 2000 will be more crowded, and more vulnerable to disruption than the world we live in now. Serious stresses involving population, resources, and environment are clearly visible ahead. Despite greater material output, the world's people will be poorer in many ways than they are today. (Council on Environmental Quality 1980)

While some issues appeared to be within the scope of national governments to solve (Goodin 1992: 3), problems moved onto an entirely new plane as acid rain, the depletion of the ozone layer and global warming revealed that actions by single countries (curbing emissions, cleaning up rivers) could never meet the challenge. Traditional ideologies, premised upon a world of competitive, industrialized nation-states, began to look more like the problem than the solution.

More heterogeneous than most, the environmental movement began to appear in four broad manifestations: individuals pursuing green lifestyles, propagandists working through traditional institutions (political parties, media, churches),

The emergence of intelligence, I am convinced, tends to unbalance the ecology . . . It is not until a creature begins to manage its environment that nature is thrown into disorder.
Clifford D. Simak (1904–88; US science fiction writer), *Shakespeare's Planet* (1976)

Flag of protest: Greenpeace protesters on the roof of the Palace of Westminster
Photo: Cobbing/Greenpeace

green pressure groups and green parties (Parkin 1988: 168). The pressure groups, notably Friends of the Earth and Greenpeace, emerged at the end of the 1960s, often taking a high-profile, headline-catching stance. In some audacious oceanic encounters, *Rainbow Warrior*, literally the Greenpeace flagship, featured dramatically on television screens around the world. Political parties followed, with fully fledged agendas embracing foreign policy, the economy, education and so on. In 1983 Die Grünen (the Greens) seized the public imagination with a breakthrough into the West German Bundestag, the psychedelic garb of their twenty-seven members contrasting symbolically with the serried ranks of establishment grey. Greens also penetrated the European Parliament, forming a separate group in their own right.

In December 1997 a highly significant step came with an international agreement adopted in Kyoto, Japan. As part of the United Nations (UN) Framework Convention on Climate Change, the Kyoto Protocol set binding targets for thirty-seven industrialized countries and the EU for reducing greenhouse gas emissions over the five-year period 2008–2012 (later extended to 2020). Significantly, the USA had refused to ratify it and it was not until the 2012 UN climate conference (in Doha) that the rich nations accepted their responsibility for damage caused by climate change elsewhere. Although critics continued to bemoan the slow rate of progress towards emissions reduction, by 2013 UN Secretary General Ban Ki-Moon was highlighting climate change as one of his top priorities, a sentiment echoed by US President Barack Obama in his inaugural address.

In addition to the UN, the role of the EU has become increasingly significant. Although the Rome Treaty was silent on environmental policy, the Single European Act (SEA) of 1987 introduced the environment as one of its Titles (VII). The Maastricht Treaty enlarged the environmental provisions, promising financial assistance to states where disproportionate costs were imposed. Central to the strategy was an emissions trading system, introduced in 2005.

In 2006 a film was made by former US Democrat Vice-President Al Gore, urging his country to accept the global nature of the ecological threat. *An Inconvenient Truth* encouraged Arnold Schwarzenegger, as Republican governor of California, to cap carbon dioxide emissions and set targets for greener cars. In January 2007, US President George W. Bush used his annual State of the Union address to a Congress newly captured by the Democrats to call for a reduction in petrol consumption by 2013. In Britain, Gordon Brown recruited Al Gore as an environment adviser and commissioned an environmental review by Sir Nicholas Stern, former chief economist of the World Bank. Published in 2006, this was the first major contribution to the environmental debate by an economist rather than a scientist and it included dire predictions regarding millions made homeless through rising sea levels and the extinction of various species. Stern confirmed the view that the major share of responsibility for reducing the impact of climate change should be shouldered by the rich countries. Two years later, the 2008 Climate Change Act introduced the world's first legally binding framework for implementing emission reductions, while the 2011 Energy Act was seen as the main vehicle for implementing the coalition government's 'Green Deal'.

> *We have the time and knowledge to act. But only if we act internationally, strongly and urgently.*
> Sir Nicholas Stern, *The Economics of Climate Change: The Stern Review* (2006)

Forms of environmentalism

Posing challenges quite beyond the contemplation of traditional politicians, the movement takes two broad forms: the anthropocentric favouring moderate action while the ecocentric is more radical. The moderate approaches can exist within a framework of the classical ideologies.

Conservative environmentalism

Paradoxically, although many environmentalists betray socialist leanings, the ideology follows a conservative logic in questioning progress. Rationalist meddling can be dangerous; life has a logic beyond our understanding. Environmentalism also reflects the conservative conviction that we inhabit the planet for but a limited time, with a responsibility to future generations. Bodies such as the

Council for the Preservation of Rural England enjoy support amongst the middle classes.

Liberal environmentalism

For liberals, environmentalism can keep faith with the free market; if green products are demanded, competition will ensure their supply. In this 'New Age Capitalism' firms will use alternative energy sources, cleaner technology and biodegradable materials and practise recycling. Although the car remains supreme, emissions standards grow more stringent. For liberals, growth is not sacrificed but becomes sustainable and the mainstream parties continue to green their manifestos on this principle.

Socialist environmentalism

Environment-alism intensely illuminates the need to confront the corporate domain at its most powerful and guarded point – the exclusive right to govern the systems of production.
Barry Commoner (1917–2012; renowned US biologist and environmental activist)

Eco-socialists see capitalism as a serious problem, but one that can be met by government using state power to take on multinational corporations with regulative regimes. The use of certain pesticides has been banned and road traffic reduction has been a policy goal. In 2004 London Mayor Ken Livingstone introduced a congestion charge. Indeed, the call for regulation is by no means confined to the left. The London congestion charged was continued by Conservative Boris Johnson and the 2010 coalition produced a substantial list of environmental policies, including abandoning plans for a third runway at Heathrow airport and introducing incentives for the development of green technology.

Radical environmentalism

Within this category come the 'eco-warriors'. For radicals, the belief that the crisis can be met within existing political frameworks is delusion. Traditional politics is about compromise but, for the issues environmentalists address, there can be no halfway solutions (Goodin 1992: 12). The crisis demands seismic shifts in lifestyles, economies and politics.

- *Lifestyle.* Generally life must be less materialistic, with more emphasis on spiritual values (often of a Buddhist character). Many contemporary shibboleths (the supremacy of the car, foreign holidays) are challenged. People would live more frugally and populations would be stabilized through immigration control, abortion and sterilization.
- *Economics.* A 'new economics' questions both left and right. The talisman of growth is unnatural; the goal is a steady-state economy. Gross national product (GNP) should be replaced with adjusted GNP (AGNP), reflecting non-economic quality-of-life indicators. Energy would come mainly from renewable sources, with consumption drastically cut. The global economy must be shut down, the liberal orthodoxy of free trade replaced by autarky (national self-sufficiency).

- *Politics.* The system of centralized nation-states undermines the ecological community and is no longer viable. Democratic governments, ever seeking popularity through rising material standards, have worked hand in glove with large corporations, legitimating their activities and restricting information on pollution and harmful effects upon food.

Whose interest?

Although claiming to serve humanity as a whole, environmentalism is sometimes characterized as the self-indulgence of a middle-class intelligentsia. Lowe and Goyder (1983: 25) noted how peaks of activity follow expansionary phases of the business cycle (the 1890s, late 1920s, late 1950s and the 1970s), when affluence affords a leisured class the luxury of self-criticism.

Many in the general population may see their interests threatened rather than served. Parties will not gain votes by offering, say, to outlaw the car. Having discovered Benidorm, who will forsake the Mediterranean sun for the Blackpool pleasure beach of their grandparents? There are other bigger interests threatened. Multinational corporations masterminding global expansion, and sometimes funding politicians and parties, may not sit back while economies are radically recast. At their head is the oil industry. This awesome power was underlined at the Kyoto Summit in 1997, where progress was held back by US obstructionism. Bill Clinton's successor in 2001, the Republican George W. Bush, was bankrolled by US energy companies (the coal industry alone contributing $4 million to his election campaign in 1999/2000: *Guardian*, 16 March 2001) when he trumped his Democrat opponent, Al Gore.

Other parties have literally copied parts of our programme. But they don't implement them. They only do it cosmetically.
Petra Kelly (1947–92; Die Grünen MP, whose sudden death was shrouded in mystery), interview in *Living Marxism* (4 Feb. 1989)

> According to data collected by the US Department of Energy's Carbon Dioxide Information Analysis Center, in 2008 the USA (with less than 5% of the world's population) was responsible for 18% of the world's carbon dioxide emissions, while China, with almost 20% of the world's population, was responsible for 24%.

Developing nations must also doubt that the environmental agenda will be in their interest. In Eastern Europe environmentalists initially played a significant role in the overthrow of communism, the movement often providing a focus for anti-Soviet sentiments. However, as western values gained ascendancy they became marginalized. China, with some of the most polluted cities on the planet, is now the world's largest producer of greenhouse gases and produces more coal than any other nation. As a developing nation it was not required to reduce emissions under the Kyoto protocol. While its government promises to do more for the environment,

> On the eve of the 2012 Rio Earth Summit, 'business as usual' projections in the WWF *Living Planet Report* suggested that the Earth's natural resources were being depleted at such a rate that by 2030 even two extra planets would not be enough to meet humanity's annual demand on nature.

the economy, with the middle class replacing bicycles with cars, appears the main priority. Hence, while concerned with the very survival of the human race, the ideology can appear to offend more interests than it serves.

Fascism

As an ideology **fascism** came into prominence in the 1920s but it did not disappear with military defeat in 1945. Although indelibly tarnished by its association with the Holocaust, it has proved resilient. The rise of nationalist parties in Eastern Europe, the Bosnian war in the 1990s and 'ethnic cleansing' by Serbs show that it remains potent. There are also movements that can be termed fascist existing in Russia, France, the USA, Germany and Britain. Many of its principles have long ancestry and today the term is used loosely to embrace all far-right movements, such as Falangism, National Socialism, Nazism, Front National and the British National Party (BNP). It is also used as a term of abuse for any association seen as rightist, totalitarian or dictatorial, evoking terms such as 'eco-fascism' and 'food-fascism'. Channel Four TV presenter Jon Snow even labelled his critics 'poppy fascists' when he refused to wear the emblem.

Human nature

Fascists see human nature characterized by deep-seated unconscious feelings, with behaviour based not on reason (as liberals and socialists would claim) but on instinct and emotion. This links people with nature, their land and the environment. Violence is a natural human instinct, to be glorified in art as well as in politics. People are not to be seen as individuals; they are social by nature and part of a collectivity – the *Volk*. Biology determines that the races are not equal; some are genetically superior and interbreeding will weaken the species. Karl Popper used a socio-psychological concept which he termed 'the strain of civilization' to explain a popular desire for a strong ruler. Most people do not want freedom, which imposes burdens of responsibility (Magee 1973: 88). The concept of a god can fulfil a similar need.

For many fascists the Aryan race has been seen as the most superior, while the Semitic races, personified by the Jews, stand in the lowest position. Wars are won by the superior side, and as a result the species is improved. Driven by greed and

Make the lie big, make it simple, keep saying it, and eventually they will believe it.
Attributed to Adolf Hitler (1889–1945)

envy, the masses are regarded as selfish and weak. Despite certain differences, both Italian and German fascism shared a conviction that human nature was something to be improved, to be made more collectivist, heroic and genetically pure.

The form of government

It is difficult to outline a fascistic form of government because the term can embrace a wide range of far-right systems. The German and Italian variants have been seen as the most definitive but movements that can be termed fascist have been seen in various countries, including Belgium, Portugal, Argentina, Hungary, Japan, France and Britain. The characteristic form of government they advocate entails features such as the following, not all of which are present in every movement.

- *Heroic leadership.* Popular democracy is seen as weak government. The leader must be a heroic figure, a superman or *Übermensch*, standing above the herd.
- *Collectivism.* The state is the supreme ethical end, to which individuals are subordinate. It can legitimately use brutality and violence.
- *Corporatism.* Trade unions and employers would work in harmony. With functional (rather than geographical) representation, parliament should contain all sections of the national workforce, showing the primacy of politics over economics.
- *Totalitarianism.* There is no aspect of economic, political and social life beyond state control.
- *Autarky.* Economic self-sufficiency provides a foundation for war against other nations.

Racism, anti-Semitism and violence, although popularly seen as hallmarks of the ideology, have not always been present to the extent that they were in Germany under the Nazis. Also peculiar to Germany was the concept of *Lebensraum*, the militaristic quest for territory through expansion into Eastern Europe.

The pattern of development

The rise of fascism is often regarded as a consequence of the first world war (see Trevor-Roper 1981) but, with its eclectic nature, it can be said to have various intellectual precursors. It is possible to argue that collective folk consciousness has been present from the beginning of civilization. Plato's 'philosopher king' can be likened to the heroic leader, while his 'noble lie' is mirrored in the legitimacy of state deception to secure mass acquiescence. Many features appear in Hegel, including **nationalism**, the state as a natural enemy of other states, the idea of a superior race, an absence of moral obligation on the part of the state, service to the state as the sole ethical principle, propaganda and the leadership of the 'Great Man' (Popper 1962: 62).

Philosophers such as Nietzsche and Schopenhauer have, arguably, been said to

Fascism should rightly be called Corporatism, as it is the merger of corporate and government power.
Benito Mussolini
(1883–1945; Italian fascist president)

have inspired fascist leaders. Friedrich Nietzsche (1844–1900) railed against what he saw as the commonplace and smugness of human life. He viewed socialism, democracy, Christianity and egalitarianism as enfeebling principles and celebrated the values of virility, courage and resolution. The duty of a man was to transcend the herd instinct, rejecting popular morality to become the *Übermensch*. Passion was to be elevated above reason. Although fascist leaders could not so easily draw upon Nietzsche for nationalism and anti-Semitism, they were not averse to being seen as supermen.

Although often portrayed as a reaction against reason, fascism can, in its Italian variant, be related to the Renaissance and Enlightenment, with Machiavelli and the elitist Michels as thinkers. Fascist ideas also reflect nineteenth-century influences, from racial theory and social Darwinism to the anti-industrial conservative romanticism. Inspiration could also come from the arts. Some saw the germ of fascism in Futurism, a radical Italian literary and artistic movement, while the operas of German composer Richard Wagner, a disillusioned socialist (and, in the eyes of some, an anti-Semite), celebrated heroic figures such as Siegfried and Lohengrin.

All within the state, nothing outside the state, nothing against the state.
Benito Mussolini

The most significant manifestations of fascism were of course in Italy under Benito Mussolini and Germany under Adolf Hitler in the 1920s. In the late nineteenth century there had been revolutionary groups in Italy styling themselves *fasci* and the term was chosen by Mussolini for the movement that carried him to power. From ancient Rome he found the legend for his movement: a bundle of rods, a *fasces*, symbolizing the spirit of community, beneath an axe-head representing the state's authority, that was carried before consuls. Post-first-world-war Europe proved fertile ground for an ideology that promised economic regeneration and a restoration of national pride. Italy, with heavy debts and high unemployment, had gained a disappointing territorial settlement. Germany was a defeated nation burdened with heavy reparation payments imposed under the Treaty of Versailles. Hitler's National Socialists (Nazis) promised national rebirth. The nation's problems were blamed on those who were *not* of Aryan stock, particularly Jews. Arrogating to himself supreme power, Hitler instigated a programme to deal with the 'Jewish problem' that was to enter history as the Holocaust.

In Britain various small organizations terming themselves fascist arose in the interwar years, some, such as the British Fascists formed in 1923 by Rotha Lintorn-Orman, wearing Italian-style black uniforms. The most significant movement began in the 1930s under charismatic aristocrat Sir Oswald Mosley. Elected as a Conservative MP in 1918, he made a long political journey, becoming an independent and then Independent Labour Party MP for Smethwick in 1926. Finally, in 1932, he founded his own party, the British Union of Fascists (BUF). Once an energetic member of the Fabian Society, Mosley was impressed by Mussolini. His agenda was a corporatist one, with an added emphasis on the British empire, which would become protectionist and economically self-sufficient. Despite enjoying significant support within establishment circles and the press, the party became increasingly extreme and authoritarian. Its meetings and marches provoked disruptive action from Jewish and communist groups, and a core of militaristic 'Blackshirts' was formed to resist them. In the infamous 'Battle of Cable Street' in east London in October 1936, a BUF march through a predominantly Jewish area was disrupted despite police efforts to facilitate it. Yet despite economic depression fascism did not take hold within the British political culture, and the subsequent 1936 Public Order Act banned the wearing of militaristic uniforms.

New tensions arose in the 1960s. Inflammatory speeches on immigration by Conservative politician Enoch Powell gained considerable popular support. Although sacked from the shadow cabinet by party leader Edward Heath, it was said that he had contributed to the unexpected Conservative victory in the 1970 general election. In 1976 a party styling itself the National Front formed, advocating the repatriation of black Britons. It suffered a decline when Margaret Thatcher, a professed admirer of Powell, became Conservative leader. However, by 1983 it had re-emerged as the BNP under John Tyndall, whose zeal led to his imprisonment in 1986 for inciting racial hatred. From 1999, under Cambridge graduate Nick Griffin, the party began to appear more media savvy, seeking a softer image by modifying some policy positions, including that on Holocaust denial.

A measure of support for this way of thinking came when the BNP gained a significant proportion of the popular vote in white working-class areas where people feared immigration and unemployment. In 2002 it secured three council seats in Burnley, increasing the number to eight the following year and a total of thirteen nationwide. In 2008 it gained one of the London Assembly's twenty-five seats and finished fifth in the mayoral election, with 5.2 per cent of the vote. The Euro elections of 2009 produced two seats, one for Griffin. In the same year, amidst controversy, he gained some degree of establishment acceptance with an invitation to join the panel of the BBC's mass-audience *Question Time* TV programme. The party fielded over 300 candidates in the 2010 general election but, with 1.9 per cent of the vote, failed to win any seats. Griffin placed himself before the electors of Barking, coming third with 6,620 votes.

Maybe now it's time to start listening to the BNP.
BNP slogan after the 7/7 London bombing by Muslim extremists

Whose interest?

Formally fascism sought the interest not of classes or people but of nation. The fascist goal of expansion by war can be seen as an 'adventurer's philosophy' (Sabine 1963: 888) where the benefits come more in terms of a psychic national greatness than of tangible benefit. In economic terms, corporatism would reduce strife between employers and workers so that neither would gain the relative benefit they would under socialism or liberalism. However, Marxists criticize fascism as a tool of monopoly capitalism and the beneficiaries of its economic controls have tended to be right-wing interests (Milward 1979: 409), yet much fascist writing is anti-capitalist. Leaders, including Mussolini and Mosley, were often socialists at some point in their careers and Hitler's party termed itself National Socialist. The ideology can offer some hope to the poor and unemployed and it has tended to gain ground where working-class hopes of socialism have been disappointed (Goodwin 2007: 188). This appeared in the context of the 1920s depression and today fascist-type parties can gain support in areas of high unemployment and low morale.

Many fascist principles reveal affinities with mainstream ideologies. In the era of British imperialism, territorial expansion and notions of racial superiority were clearly evident. There is also veneration of heroic figures such as Churchill and de Gaulle. The ideal of putting country before self is lauded as patriotism. Its values of nationalism, inequality, anti-liberalism and anti-socialism are essentially conservative. Neither should it be forgotten that concentration camps were used by the British in the Boer war. Yet fascism manages to combine some acceptable ideas with a level of extremism, emotion, brutality and totalitarianism that mark it out as a deviation from the western tradition.

Religion

Ideologies have played an important part in shaping government and politics in the West. However, they are not the only source of ideas about how people should live. Before the Enlightenment, the medieval power structures of western nations were dominated by Christianity and, although the emergence of ideologies presented a challenge, they have by no means supplanted religion (see Burleigh 2005). Globalization adds to the complications by increasing the possibilities for religious conflict. The force behind the fateful 9/11 attack was religious extremism, and the rhetoric of its Muslim adherents expressed a rejection of western values. For philosopher John Gray (2003) it 'destroyed the West's ruling myth'. In 2005, the 7/7 London suicide bombings by British Muslims brought the threat closer. Such events raise compelling questions about the ideas that drive politics. Must religions be considered in a discussion of ideology?

Religion and ideology

> If somebody votes for a party you don't agree with, you're free to argue about it as much as you like. . . . But on the other hand if somebody says 'I mustn't move a light switch on a Saturday', you say, 'I *respect that*'.
>
> Douglas Adams (1952–2001; British writer), *The Salmon of Doubt* (2003)

Studies of ideology rarely consider religion. Certainly there remain fundamental differences between religion and ideology, most notably the basis for belief. An ideology is a product of reason, while religion is held to be the word of a supreme being communicated through an earthly prophet. Whilst rationalists must, by definition, be prepared to subject their views to debate, religious believers accept the divine word as an act of faith. At the most extreme level the way to counter unbelievers (infidels) is death, as is indeed sometimes demanded in the scriptures. In medieval times, those refuting the doctrines of the Catholic Church could be burned at the stake. The fatwa placed upon author Salman Rushdie in 1988, after the publication of his *The Satanic Verses*, remains a chilling threat. A second and related difference concerns the respect they command. Religion tends to enjoy a favoured status in discourse. While people may freely attack each other's ideologies, the questioning of someone's faith is often regarded as off-limits. The result can be that otherwise-unacceptable behaviour is tolerated, such as genital mutilation, the ritualistic killing of animals and the subjugation of women. A third difference lies in the degree of institutionalization. Adherents to ideologies do not create hierarchies of archbishops, priests, rabbis and imams; they do not normally congregate on a regular basis to proclaim their beliefs; neither do they wear distinctive dress or mark the landscape with awe-inspiring places of worship. Finally, ideologies make no promise of life beyond the grave, thereby offering little incentive to martyrdom.

Amongst the general public religion is more widely appreciated than ideology. A MORI poll for the BBC's *Heaven and Earth* show in 2003 found that 60 per cent believed in a god. In the USA the degree of religious belief is even greater. While a copy of the Bible or Quran may be found in many homes, it is rather less probable that the shelves will house the works of Locke, Marx or Darwin. Religion offers a far more intuitive system of thought than ideology or science. Handed down from pre-scientific ages, it can be understood by children from infancy. The mystery of where we come from is more easily explained by the idea of a creator than a complex account of evolution.

Of course it should be recognized that ideologies themselves are not always held rationally. Adherents can sometimes display a fervour suggesting faith rather than reason. The Jacobins of the French Revolution, the anarchists of late-nineteenth-century Russia, Leninists and Nazis all acted with a religious zeal, sometimes aiming to replace orthodox religion (see Burleigh 2005). Even martyrdom is not unique to religious believers: the Marxist-Leninist Tamil Tigers of South Asia engaged in suicide bombing. One could even argue that, for some, nationalism takes the form of faith, and those making the 'supreme sacrifice' are honoured.

Religion as ideology

It could be argued that religion is not to be considered in a study of ideology because its concerns are spiritual, and not about politics or government. However, in practice religions have much to say about earthly matters. In the view of Max Weber, much of the driving force in liberal capitalism came from a work ethic embedded in Protestantism. Religions lay down ethical legal codes prescribing behaviour and these can have much in common with state laws. Several of Christianity's Ten Commandments find an echo in the laws of the land, and it can be argued that the western ideological tradition itself rests upon a bedrock of Judaeo-Christian ethics. (Indeed, its Muslim culture has been adduced by some, including Pope Benedict XVI, as an argument against Turkey's admission into the EU.) Religious views and affiliations can influence political action in much the same way as ideology. While ideologies have lain at the heart of great revolutions that have changed the course of history, religion too is associated with major conflicts.

Throughout the world religion continues to influence government and politics. The British monarch, as head of state, is also the head of the established (Anglican) church and 'Defender of the Faith'. Bishops sit in the legislature and the parliamentary day begins with prayers. Many politicians claim religious affiliation. In the nineteenth century the austere Gladstone brought low-church ideals into his liberal economics. New Liberalism reflected the Christian beliefs of thinkers such as T. H. Green. Although Winston Churchill went no further than describing himself as an 'optimistic agnostic', politicians have generally professed a respect for religion. Margaret Thatcher's move from non-conformism to Anglicanism appeared more pragmatic than doctrinal, but it indicated the importance her party placed on religion.

In the post-9/11 era religion assumed a renewed salience in the West when two of its principal leaders clearly linked their politics with religious convictions. George W. Bush enjoyed the wholehearted support of Tony Blair, a prime minister who openly rejected ideology, claiming it was religion that had led him to the Labour Party. It was under Blair that the government supported the expansion of faith schools. His piety led the satirical magazine *Private Eye* to feature a regular 'Parish News Letter' from the 'Rev. Anthony Blair', Vicar of St Albions. Following Blair, Gordon Brown also stressed the religious basis of his political thinking, attributing his values to a childhood as a 'son of the manse'. Appreciating the need to engage with London's religious communities, the three main contenders in the 2008 mayoral campaign appeared to place religion high in their campaign strategies, with statements and walkabouts to temples, mosques and churches. Conversely, in 2010 two of the main party leaders, Nick Clegg and Ed Miliband, may have been taking an electoral risk when they declared themselves to be atheists.

At the same time, while politicians proclaim religious motivation, church leaders make regular pronouncements on government policy. While these can relate to moral matters (such as abortion, medical use of genetics, homosexuality and gambling) they also address social policy, the economy and foreign policy. Examples are numerous. Margaret Thatcher, as prime minister, endured continuing criticism of her free-market policies from the bishops. Chief Rabbi Jonathan Sachs published a book in 2007 criticizing the New Labour government's policy of multiculturalism. In September 2007, the Archbishop of York, John Sentamu, called for tougher sanctions against Zimbabwe.

The pattern of development

It is not possible to view the evolution of religion as one would an ideology, with a specific point of origin and a body of seminal thinkers. From the dawn of civilization people have sought to explain the puzzle of existence with forms of worship, choosing variously from the sun and moon to the extremely active gods of the Ancient Greeks and Romans. The great religions of Judaism, Christianity and Islam share a common ancestry and owe their beliefs to a succession of prophets who have brought the word to believers. In addition, there are philosophers in the modern age who have advanced, or been influenced by, theological thinking. Prior to the Enlightenment government and politics were dominated by pope and priests and, although monarchs ruled, they did so on the basis of divine right. However, while questioning its primacy, the Enlightenment did not see the end of religion.

Human nature

Religions tend to portray humans as imperfect and prone to stray from the path of righteousness. Some Christians recognize the concept of 'original sin'. Adherents speak of being 'saved' or 'forgiven' and some routinely confess their sins before a priest in order to gain absolution. In some religions the reward for goodness is eternal life. Such a view of human nature implies a need for strict limits on behaviour.

The form of government

Discussion on this point is of particular significance in the case of religion. A form of government based upon religion is a **theocracy**.

Theocracy

In a theocracy, power lies with priests, agents of a supreme being. This is obviously not a democracy, and the God of the Abrahamic line claims dictatorial power. Theocracies have long existed and do so today. After the revolution in 1979, Iran became a theocracy under the Ayatollah Khomeini. In 1996 Afghanistan fell under the religious rule of the fundamentalist Islamist movement, the Taliban. Religion also leads to patriarchy, and its rise in the post 9/11 decades can be seen as a threat to women's rights as well as their involvement in government (see Jeffreys 2011).

Despite the message of peace and love expressed in most religions, the form of rule is largely totalitarian and by no mean universally peaceable. In the ancient world the belief that gods would intervene in battle on the side of believers was common (today, armies continue to pray for divine assistance). The Old Testament records conflicts in which Jehovah, the god of the Israelites, instructs his chosen people to deal severely with infidels. Christians also fought Muslims in the thirteenth- and fourteenth-century crusades. There is also violence within faiths. The Reformation of the sixteenth and seventeenth centuries, and the following Inquisition, saw Protestants pitted against Catholics in a feud that has continued in various forms to the present, including the UK's own troubles in Northern Ireland (see chapter 20). In Iraq, after the ill-fated western invasion, Muslim Sunnis fought Muslim Shias. Sometimes a seemingly political conflict has an underlying religious basis. Richard Dawkins (2006: 43) argues that 'ethnic cleansing can be used as a cloak for what is really religious cleansing', while Martin Amis's trenchant critique of Islamism (2007), sees it as an ideology of violence superimposed upon a religion.

The rejection of theocracy

> The Senators and Representatives . . . shall be bound by Oath or Affirmation, to support this Constitution; but no religious Test shall ever be required as a Qualification to any Office or public Trust under the United States.
>
> Article 6 of the US Constitution

The care of each man's salvation belongs only to himself.

John Locke, *Letter concerning Toleration* (1689)

Enlightenment thinking produced a conviction that religion should not be part of government. Reason rather than faith should guide politics; the state should be secular. In the West the separation of church and state became a defining principle of government, receiving its most authoritative enunciation in the American constitution of 1789. Thomas Jefferson, one of the Founding Fathers, avowed that a wall should be built between the two (see Hitchens 2007: 33). After the revolution of

1789 the French constitution laid down the same principle. The Soviet Union went further in seeking to establish an atheistic state. In Britain there is no codified constitution to establish a separation between church and state but few would disagree that the state is effectively secular.

Yet any idea that secularism is established remains questionable. Some argue that the age of reason has not yet dawned (Gray 2003), and despite the astounding advances in science, religious influence may be on the increase. There are fundamentalists who see secularism as dangerous, if not evil, and believe that religion *should* inform government. In an address to the UN in 2005, Iranian president Mahmoud Ahmadinejad spoke fervently of the return of religion as a major goal in world politics, stating 'faith will prove to be the solution to many of today's problems'. In the USA George W. Bush reportedly claimed that God had told him to invade Iraq (MacAskill 2005). In December 2007 Pope Benedict XVI, in his second Encylical, launched an attack on atheists, accusing them of some of 'the greatest form of cruelty and violation of justice'. He urged Christians to put their hope for the future in God and not technology, wealth or political ideologies (*Daily Telegraph*, 1 Dec. 2007). Within Islam there are Islamists who declare their religion to be an ideology, while Christian fundamentalists in the USA also see their faith in ideological terms. The self-styled 'Muslim Parliament' notes in its manifesto that certain British laws stand in direct conflict with Sharia law and, in February 2008, the Archbishop of Canterbury aroused considerable controversy when, in a learned address, he predicted that elements of Sharia law would enter the UK statute book. The advance of globalization brings together democracies, non-democratic regimes and theocracies or quasi-theocracies. The study of the ideas that shape contemporary politics cannot therefore ignore religion.

> *Christianity neither is, nor ever was, a part of the common law.*
> Thomas Jefferson (1743–1826; third US president), *Whether Christianity is Part of the Common Law* (1764)

Whose interest?

> The rich man in his castle,
> The poor man at his gate,
> He made them high and lowly,
> And ordered their estate.
>
> Verse from the hymn 'All Things Bright and Beautiful' (usually omitted today)

Whose interest does religion serve? In some religions, those who gain are the faithful who ascend to heaven. Religion can also bring comfort and consolation to the distressed. Many religious charities work strenuously to aid the poor. However, in socio-political terms religion is closely linked with power. It has served the rich and powerful, legitimizing their authority. Before the Enlightenment, popes were supreme and kings legitimized their rule on the basis of divine right. With regard to the relationship between the sexes, religions have generally advocated male privilege and dominance. There is also domination in terms of class. During the industrial revolution the value of meekness, and the acceptance of inequality as God's will, served the capitalist bourgeoisie. For Marx it became the 'opium of the people', enabling them to bear inequality and exploitation. Today it can justify harsh dictatorships in theocracies around the world.

An End of Ideology?

Some writers have envisaged an age when ideological debate would cease. Marx's vision of a communist future in which the state would wither away did this. More recently, Daniel Bell's *End of Ideology* (1960) captured the post-war spirit when western political parties converged around a Keynesian social democratic consensus. With the collapse of East European communism and the neoliberal ascendancy in the West, US academic Francis Fukuyama's *End of History* (1992) proclaimed a final triumph of liberalism. In the idea of the 'third way', critics again saw an implication that there was only 'one way' – in other words, yet another attempt to find an end of ideology.

Yet such theories proved fanciful. States did not wither under communism and the emergence of the New Right exposed the frailty of the western post-war consensus. The neoliberal triumph itself soon looked insecure. In Russia and Eastern Europe, people generally used to full employment soon learned that the gods of capitalism demand sacrificial offerings in the form of losers as well as winners, and some communist leaders found themselves back in favour. The rise of feminism and ecology further challenge the classical ideologies. Moreover, the 9/11 attacks came as a stark reminder that, with many millions inhabiting a globalizing but culturally diverse world, the western tradition did not enjoy an ideological monopoly.

Today we inhabit a world of increasing inequality, where the twenty-six most developed countries, with under 15 per cent of the world's population, live in comfort while another 3,000 million live in abject poverty, suffering disease and even starvation. Such conditions can provide fertile soil for those preaching fascistic doctrines. This is hardly a stable world with no room for ideological debate.

Key points

- Ideologies and movements beyond those that constitute the western tradition are of increasing importance.

- Feminism seeks sexual justice and an end to male domination of the public sphere.

- Environmentalism judges value in terms of the ecosystem as a whole. To adherents it goes beyond politics to address the very survival of the human species.

- Although called an ideology, fascism reflects an emotional rather than a reasoned basis for thinking.

- The principal post-Enlightenment ideologies have been essentially rational and secular.

- Yet they have not eliminated religion and faith as a guide to how people should live together.

- Despite theories proclaiming an end to ideological politics, the potential for disagreement over social life remains limitless.

Review your understanding of the following terms and concepts

anthropocentrism	Islamism	secularism
ecocentrism	nationalism	social Darwinism
environmentalism	Nazism	theocracy
fascism	patriarchy	*Übermensch*
feminism	postmodernism	
Gaia theory	religion	

Questions for discussion and debate

Consider these propositions and be prepared to present the cases for and against. Try to produce debating propositions of your own.

1   The western ideological tradition does not provide adequate answers to contemporary problems.

2   Feminism does not challenge liberalism or socialism, it extends them.

3   Women are not political animals.

4   Moderate environmentalism cannot meet the challenge facing today's world.

5   Environmentalism is a preoccupation of the affluent middle classes.

6   All ideologies serve one interest over others.

7   Humans are motivated more by emotion and faith than by reason.

8   In an unequal society, fascism can always find support.

9   Religion and politics should not mix.

10   There can never be an end of ideology.

Further reading

Arneil, B. (1999) *Politics and Feminism*.
Considers the theoretical and historical underpinnings of women's exclusion from politics.

Barker, R. (1994) *Politics, Peoples and Government*.
Shows how the main lines of ideological debate have shifted during the twentieth century.

Burleigh, M. (2005) *Earthly Powers: Religion and Politics in Europe from the French Revolution to the Great War*.
Wide-ranging account of religion in the history of modern Europe. Puts religion clearly into political history.

Burleigh, M. (2006) *Sacred Causes*.
Critique of the secular state, stressing the centrality of religion in European politics from the interwar years. Aims to exonerate Christianity from charges of a violent history and links with fascism.

Carter, J. (2006) *Our Endangered Values: America's Moral Crisis*.
Former US president evaluates the increasing intersection between religious and political arenas and the danger of religious extremism.

Dawkins, R. (2006) *The God Delusion*.
Influential polemic by a scientist portraying religions as scientifically unfounded and dangerous.

Farrar, M. et al. (eds) (2012) *Islam in the West.*
Considers the tensions in the idea of multiculturalism and the assertion that it has failed.

Goodin, R. (1992) *Green Political Theory.*
Philosophical discussion of the green political programme, developing the 'green theory of value'.

Goodwin, B. (2007) *Using Political Ideas.*
Scholarly but not scary. Considers ideologies as political movements and the implications of the ideas they embody.

Goodwin, M. (2011) *New British Fascism: Rise of the British National Party,*
Argues that wider trends in society have created a favourable climate for the far right.

Gray, J. (2003) *Al Qaeda and What it Means to be Modern.*
Argues that the belief that we are becoming modern and rational is a myth. Al Qaeda is itself a product of modernity and globalization.

Greer, G. (1970) *The Female Eunuch.*
An influential and challenging book, which set the tone of much British debate about feminism.

Heywood, A. (2012) *Political Ideologies: An introduction,* 5th edn.
Well-established introduction includes major ideological traditions and the emergence of 'new' ideologies.

Hitchens, C. (2007) *God is Not Great.*
Argues for a society without religion.

Hitler, A. (1969) *Mein Kampf* (Hutchinson edn).
The dictator's views, written while imprisoned in the early 1920s.

Jaggar, A. (1983) *Feminist Politics and Human Nature.*
Influence of feminist thinking on political philosophy and political thought.

Jeffreys, S. (2011) *Man's Dominion: The Rise of Religion and the Eclipse of Women's Rights.*
Argues that religion is the founding ideology of patriarchy.

Lawson, N. (2008) *An Appeal to Reason: A Cool Look at Global Warming.*
Ex-Chancellor of the Exchequer antagonizes the global-warming lobby with a critique of their science and politics.

Leach, R. (2009) *Political Ideology in Britain,* 2nd edn.
Introduces a wide range of newer ideologies.

Lovenduski, J. and Randall, V. (1993) *Contemporary Feminist Politics.*

Detailed analysis of British feminism.

McCormack, M. (ed.) (2007) *Public Men: Masculinity and Politics in Modern Britain.*
From electioneering to the Westminster bear garden. Why is politics a man's world?

Vincent, A. (2009) *Modern Political Ideologies.*
Notes the ideological significance of the rise of religious fundamentalism and the
global influence on ideologies. Contains a useful glossary.

Wentz, R. E. (1993) *Why People do Bad Things in the Name of Religion.*
Political and economic needs of people determine the way in which they use religion.

For reading around the subject and some light relief

A surprising number of novels involve fascistic, religious and feminist themes.

Deborah Cartmell, I. Q. Hunter, Heidi Kaye and Imelda Whelehan (eds)
Sisterhoods.
Female relationships as portrayed in the (patriarchal) media, particularly
Hollywood.

Margaret Cook, *Lords of Creation: the Demented World of Men in Power.*
Critique of male politicians by the ex-wife of one of them.

Ben Elton, *Gridlock.*
A surreal vision of corporate power and the environment.

The Diary of Anne Frank.
Moving record by a young girl of her family's two-year struggle to survive in
hiding from the Nazis.

Graham Greene, *Brighton Rock.*
A prolific writer of gripping and exciting plots, many of Greene's novels have
religious themes. This is but one of them (also a film).

E. Hussain, *The Islamist.*
Memoir telling how a young London Muslim became a fundamentalist and
Islamist before returning to the gentle Sufi Islam of his family.

Henrik Ibsen, *A Doll's House.*
Powerful drama about women's oppression.

Margaret Kirkham, *Jane Austen, Feminism and Fiction.*
Analysis of Jane Austen in the context of feminist ideas past and present.

On the net

The 'newer' ideologies often spawn political parties with websites, and are also promoted by enthusiastic societies and think-tanks aiming to spread their ideas.

http://www.fawcettsociety.org.uk/
The Fawcett Society has continued in existence since its successful campaign for the women's vote and calls for women's equality and rights – at home, at work and in public life.

http://www.green-alliance.org.uk/home/
An environmental think-tank publishing papers and lobbying political leaders on global environmental issues.

http://bigthink.com/think-tank/atheism
Website arguing the case for atheism and inviting visitors to 'take the Dawkins test'.
http://www.muslimparliament.org.uk/
The self-styled Muslim Parliament aims for 'an informed, caring and morally upright Muslim community ready to engage with its environment.'

http://www.bnp.org.uk/manifesto
Far-right party sets out its manifesto, which includes a warning that democracy is under threat from the EU and mass immigration.

CHAPTER 4

THE CONSTITUTION: THE UNWRITTEN AND THE UNKNOWABLE

Contents

In this chapter we discuss the British constitution as a set of rules and prescriptions establishing the legal framework in which governments operate. This is not a simple matter; what is and is not part of the constitution is not always clear, and the opinions of experts can vary. Moreover, the constitution does not stand above politics; its content, the way it changes, and the criticisms people make of it are themselves manifestations of the political process. The chapter falls into four main sections. The first is concerned with the concept of a constitution, examining the importance of its study, identifying its sources and understanding its evolution. The second and third sections focus on two key constitutional principles – the limitation of government and the protection of individual rights. The final section addresses the important debate on constitutional reform.

Seeking the Constitution

Defining the constitution

All kinds of organizations (from sports clubs and hamster societies to trade unions and political parties) may have **constitutions**. They usually do two things: define the powers of those holding office and guarantee the rights of ordinary members. At the level of the state the principle remains the same. Hood Phillips (1987: 5) describes a constitution as

> the system of laws, customs and conventions which define the composition and powers of organs of the state, and regulate the relations of the various state organs to one another and to the private citizen.

However, another meaning of the term portrays the state constitution as a *description* of everything that takes place on a regularized basis in the process of government. This is a *behavioural* definition; found by discovery rather than laid down by prescription, it was the way in which the political essayist Walter Bagehot (1867) approached the study in his famous work *The English Constitution*.

 For the most part, this chapter adopts the first definition – the constitution as a set of rules regularizing behaviour in the process of government. However, this focus does not mean that the distinction between the prescriptive and descriptive aspects of political life is ignored. Indeed, it is particularly important to observe the dissonance between the two, for the belief that they coincide (that the prescriptive rules *describe* actual behaviour) has given the study of constitutions a bad name. Two games of cricket, although played according to the same rules, will be quite different. Although for the English politics might lack the nuances of the revered game, its reality reflects a myriad factors of personality and environment upon which the constitution can only remain silent.

Why study the constitution?

The inevitable discrepancy between prescribed and actual behaviour can render the study of formal constitutions a limited approach. This has led to another tradition of writing on British politics (following the 'behavioural revolution') which ignores the constitution altogether (see Bellamy and Castiglione 1996: 413). However, this has as many dangers as an excessive constitutionalism; there are three good reasons for studying the rules of the game.

The constitution bestows authority

Chapter 1 showed that politics is about power. In prescribing a framework the constitution bestows legitimacy on certain players. Thus, for example, the prime minister can send people to war and generals can discipline them if they refuse to fight, the police can arrest citizens and judges can send them to prison.

The constitution represents a political prize

It is itself *part of* the political process. Many of those engaged in historic struggles have seen constitutional change as their ultimate goal. Thus, for example, after humbling King John, the barons insisted that the new order be enshrined in the Magna Carta at Runnymede in 1215. The Glorious Revolution of 1688 led to the Act of Settlement in 1701, and the rising nineteenth-century bourgeoisie, the working class and the suffragettes all sought the constitutional goal of the right to vote. Many of today's most heated political debates – over Parliament, the monarchy, civil liberties, secrecy, police powers, the electoral system, EU membership, devolution, local government and so on – are essentially constitutional. In fact, the particular features of the British constitution make it more a part of the political process than most.

The constitution shapes political consciousness

Finally, even if the political analyst wishes to dismiss the constitution as a facade masking the reality of power, it remains important because of what people believe it to be. Thus, for example, even if people did not really possess effective freedom of speech (perhaps because of libel laws or access to the media), it interests political

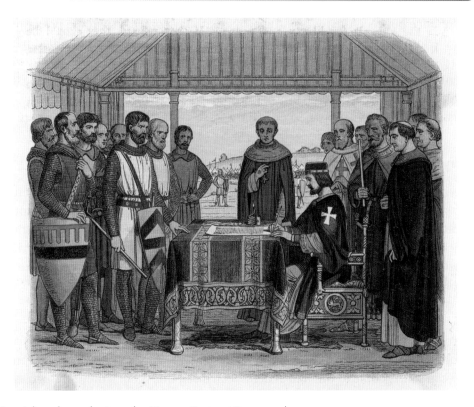

King John reluctantly signs the Magna Carta at Runnymede

Source: Mary Evans Picture Library

scientists that they *believe* themselves to have it; their consciousness shapes the political culture (see chapter 9).

Britain's elusive constitution

An American citizen can spend an edifying half-hour perusing the constitution on the bus or as a bedside companion. In contrast, the British constitution – the 'Great Ghost' – is notorious for its mysteriously unwritten manifestation. This is not strictly true because most of it certainly can be found in written form. However, the provisions are *uncodified*; they have not been drawn together in a single document grandly entitled 'The Constitution'. This is just as well, for if all the material was bound together, the British counterpart of the American patriot would be faced with something approaching the seven labours of Hercules.

The constitution takes this form because, unlike many other polities, including great ones such as France, Russia and the USA, Britain has never experienced a popular revolution in which a new class of rulers has wanted to erase all trace of the *ancien régime* and make a fresh start. There has been no defining moment comparable to the great Philadelphia convention of 1787, which established the US constitution, or the debates that led to West Germany's Basic Law in 1949.

Efficient and dignified elements

In looking at constitutions all may not be as it seems. In 1785 William Paley noted how in 'the actual exercise of royal authority in England we see these formidable prerogatives dwindled into mere ceremonies', and in the nineteenth century Jeremy Bentham and the great constitutional authority Dicey both charged the eighteenth-century constitutional chronicler Blackstone with being beguiled by what were no more than fictions. The passage of time has much to do with this; Bagehot likened the constitution to an elderly gentleman wearing the fashions of his youth, the outward finery belying the changes taking place beneath.

However, unlike the reforming radicals, Bagehot did not want to consign the outmoded garb to the shelves of the political curiosity shop. He discerned a special significance in empty 'ceremonies', arguing that all well-established constitutions required both **'dignified'** and **'efficient' elements**. The latter regulated those getting on with the job of ruling, defining what actually happens in the process of government. The dignified constitution fulfilled a vital function in generating authority. Bagehot believed it useless to expect the masses to understand the arcane mysteries of government but they could be kept happy if given pageantry at which to gawp and wonder. Modern political scientists agree with Bagehot that a political system must incorporate some mechanism for securing legitimacy.

The notion of dignified elements in a constitution means that we cannot ignore things that on the surface seem irrelevant to policy-making; they may be important in shaping mass attitudes. We must also be alert to the possibility that various state institutions may no longer play the part formally assigned to them. Indeed, we see throughout this book that imperceptible shifts from its efficient to its dignified pages leave the constitution in a state of permanent flux. Since 1970 Britain has seen a period of dramatic constitutional change, greater than that of any time since the eighteenth century.

The lower orders, the middle orders, are still, when tried by what is the standard of the educated, narrow-minded, unintelligent, incurious.
Walter Bagehot, *The English Constitution* (1963 edn: 63)

Sources of the constitution

The constitution has traditionally been seen to flow from five sources: royal prerogative, statutes, common law, convention and authoritative opinion (figure 4.1). However, more recent developments have seen it affected by Britain's relationship with mainland Europe.

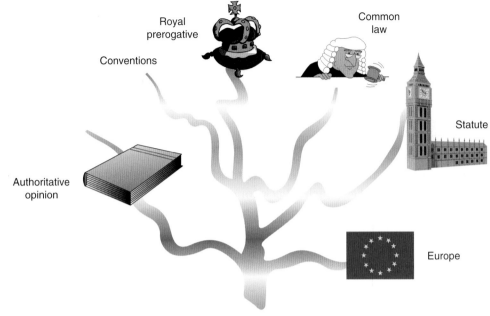

The British constitution

Figure 4.1 The British constitution flows from a number of sources

The royal prerogative

This is a set of privileges enjoyed exclusively by monarchs since medieval times. *Personal* prerogatives are held by the monarch in person and political prerogatives as head of state. The latter are the more important to the efficient constitution and include the rights to declare war or make peace, pardon criminals, dissolve Parliament and appoint ministers. These, like the Crown Jewels, have been carefully preserved. However, with the gradual erosion of the powers of the monarchy, today the **royal prerogative** is in effect exercised by the Cabinet and prime minister.

Statutes

These are no more than ordinary laws passed by Parliament. It is a rather unnerving fact that a **statute** changing the constitution is not required to undergo any special procedures, as is usually the case under written constitutions. Thus the monumentally important extensions of the franchise were all made by politically motivated governments with little elevated thought of democratic or constitutional principle. Similarly, in 1986 the government was able to erase from the political map part of the local government system (see chapter 21) to do little more than settle a political score. Again, the devolution reforms of 1998 flowed from no more than the normal legislative process, although referendums were held.

Statutes override all other domestic constitutional sources. Some, such as the 1689 Bill of Rights (defining the relationship between Crown and Parliament and ratifying the 1688 Glorious Revolution) and the 1701 Act of Settlement (determining the succession), are extremely venerable. More recently, there have been the Parliament Acts of 1911 and 1949 (determining the relationship between the two Houses of Parliament), the 1963 Peerage Act (enabling peers to renounce their titles) and the 1998 Human Rights Act (incorporating the European Convention on Human Rights into British law). In addition to statutes, and having much the same character and force, are certain revered historical documents, the most notable of which is the Magna Carta, sometimes seen as Britain's first statute.

Common law

Sometimes referred to as case law or judge-made law, this is based on precedent, from an accumulation of court decisions in specific legal cases throughout history. **Common law** is particularly useful for resolving ambiguities in other constitutional sources. It has proved a vital tool in the development of capitalism by protecting property and contracts. The two great virtues claimed for the common-law element are that it reflects past wisdom and is independent of politics. On the other hand, it can be very untidy, leaving judges to wrestle with a bewildering mass of precedents. Recent governments have sought to rationalize much common law into new statutes. Although important in developing the constitution, this source is not confined to great cases of the past; the duty of confidentiality owed to NHS patients, for example, comes from common law.

Common law has developed many civil liberties. Examples from hundreds of important cases include the *Case of Proclamations* in 1610 (the king could not create new offences by proclamation), *Anderson* v. *Gorrie* in 1895 (the immunity of judges) and *Bradlaugh* v. *Gossett* in 1884 (the supremacy of Parliament over its internal affairs). As recently as 1999, in *DPP* v. *Jones*, the House of Lords, in reversing a conviction by the Salisbury magistrates under recent public order legislation, decided that a peaceful assembly on the verge of the A344 at Stonehenge did not constitute trespass.

Conventions

These are regularly observed practices, having no legal basis and not enforceable in the courts. All states must evolve **constitutional conventions** to breathe life into their constitutions if they are to be flexible enough to survive. (The conventional elements of the constitution are the most easily changed.) However, in no other country have conventions been as important as in Britain, where they regulate the key processes of government. Democracy itself is based on conventions limiting the prerogative powers of the Crown and enabling them to be exercised by elected leaders. Many of the rules concerning the operation of the Cabinet, the epicentre of government, are known only through convention.

In addition, there are many lesser conventions. For example, MPs never tell lies to the House of Commons or, to be more precise, no MP ever accuses another of having done so. In 1987, Labour MP Tam Dalyell broke with this, accusing Margaret Thatcher of lying over the Westland scandal. Consequently, he was 'named' by the Speaker; that is, barred from the chamber. There can be disagreement as to whether or not a convention actually exists. Thus, for example, John Major argued that there was a convention that prime ministers did not appear before parliamentary select committees.

Excuse my parliamentary language

MPs are not supposed to accuse fellow members of lying or of being drunk, or to use unparliamentary language, but according to ex-MP Matthew Parris (1996) some insults have managed to slip past the Speaker's ear, including the following:

- 'devoid of any truth'
- 'cooking the figures'
- 'shameless lack of candour'
- 'the attention span of a gerbil'

- 'the hamster from Bolsover'
- 'a sex-starved boa constrictor'
- 'shut up, you old windbag'

Although conventions are the most obviously 'unwritten' part of the constitution, they are probably the most *written about* because there is more need for guidance where the formal law is silent. This leads to the next source.

Authoritative opinion

It is considered appropriate that learned works of great authority and wisdom be regarded as legitimate constitutional sources, though they may be said to possess only a persuasive authority. Great age is taken as important because it may be presumed that ancient texts distilled wisdom otherwise lost. Examples of such treasures include, among others, Fitzherbert's *Abridgement* of 1516, Hawkins's *Pleas of the Crown* (1716) and Foster's *Crown Cases* (1762). Of course not all authorities agree; it is often in their nature to be disputatious. The very belief that one can discover the constitution from the authorities of the past is itself open to question and was challenged by the philosophical radicals. An oft-quoted authority is Walter Bagehot, perhaps the one who first 'discovered' the constitution. Peter Hennessy

(1994), one of his modern counterparts, argues that, before Bagehot wrote, there was no constitution that could be recognized or apprehended as a living and working thing.

Though rather different in style from many of those works commonly cited as authoritative works, the draft *Cabinet Manual*, produced by the Cabinet Office under the direction of Cabinet Secretary Gus O'Donnell in 2010, none-theless went some way towards providing a codified overview of the main laws, conventions and rules pertaining to the operation of government. Chapter 2 of this document, 'Elections and Government formation' (O'Donnell 2010: 22–34), was published in draft form ahead of the 2010 general election and was said to have provided the framework for the negotiations that resulted in the forma-tion of the Liberal Democrat–Conservative coalition. Of particular interest in this context was the section on the procedures that would come into play in the wake of a 'hung' or 'balanced' parliament (paras 48–53, pp. 26–7) and a passage detailing the kinds of restrictions that should apply to government activity at such times (para. 70: p. 22). These guidelines went some way towards clarify-ing the role of the monarch in the wake of an inconclusive election, as well as detailing the responsibilities of party leaders and civil servants in facilitating and supporting negotiations that might lead to the formation of a government that could command the confidence of the Commons. It also set out how govern-ment and civil service relate to the devolved administrations and international institutions.

The European factor

The EU can also be seen as a source of the modern constitution, the scale of which was perhaps not fully recognized when Britain entered the EEC in 1973. It affects the powers of all domestic institutions since the EU comprises supranational institutions with law-making powers. If a legal dispute containing a European element reaches the UK Supreme Court (the final Court of Appeal), there must be an application to the European Court of Justice (ECJ, the EU court) for a final determination. Lower courts may also seek ECJ guidance. Moreover, the courts assume that in all domestic legislation it was Parliament's intention to be consist-ent with EU law (unless an expressed statement to the contrary is made). Hence, in *Pickstone* v. *Freemans PLC* (1987), regulations amending the Equal Pay Act were interpreted in a manner different from their literal meaning, to comply with EU law. A further constitutional strand comes from the European Convention on Human Rights (ECHR), which originated with the Council of Europe (as opposed to the EU) and was incorporated into British law under the 1998 Human Rights Act (see p. 683).

Change and development

> ### Amending a written constitution
> Amendments to the US constitution must be first proposed and then ratified. Proposals may be made by two-thirds majorities in both houses of Congress voting separately, or by a national convention called by Congress at the request of two-thirds of the state legislatures. Ratification requires a vote of three-quarters of the state legislatures or state conventions in three-quarters of the states. However, written constitutions need not be inflexible. Since 1809 Sweden's has been amended over 200 times – like the workshop hammer, with several new heads and shafts, one wonders whether it is any longer the same thing.

All constitutions are political but Britain's is particularly so because it may be changed as part of the normal process of politics. This is potentially threatening because, following the game metaphor, it is impossible to play if the rules keep changing. On the other hand, a constitution cannot work if it is entirely inflexible and, even in the USA where its veneration rouses religious fervour (there have been only twenty-seven formal **constitutional amendments**), small changes occur continually through judicial decisions and the establishment of conventions. However, written constitutions are usually given a propensity to resist change; they are **entrenched** through deliberately cumbersome processes of amendment. Does this mean the British constitution is unstable and but a flimsy defence of citizens' rights? There is some truth in this, though it contains both conservative and flexible elements.

Art or Nature: are constitutions machines or organisms?

There are two broad theoretical views on constitutional change: the mechanistic and the organic. The former sees constitutions as machines designed to give people the kind of government they desire. Thomas Hobbes and John Locke belong within this tradition, though it was the philosophical radicals who really addressed the issue of *rational* constitutional reform. The essence of their position was that, if a constitution was to serve the needs of a people at any particular time, they should deduce it from first principles. The principle was utilitarianism (see p. 33). For this school of thought statute law is the obvious constitutional source.

In contrast, the **organic** view argues that a constitution grows and develops naturally like a living organism; for thinkers of this school it is a thing of untouchable beauty. Frequent references liken the British constitution to a great tree:

> While the mechanical contrivance of political inventors has died away... the goodly tree of British freedom selecting from the kindly soil and assimilating its fit nutriment still increases its stately bulk... Outliving the storms and vicissitudes of

centuries, deeply rooted in the habits and affections of the people, it spreads far and wide its hospitable shade. (Hearn 1867)

Blackstone's view of the constitution, with its veneration of the past, would belong in this category, and the cover of Sir Ivor Jennings's *The British Constitution* (1966) was actually adorned with a picture of a spreading oak.

The organic view has a distinguished pedigree, extending from the Ancient Greeks. Hegel and T. H. Green also conceived the state in organic terms, while Edmund Burke suggested that the constitution should be treated with awe as a repository of the collective wisdom of the ages. He argued for 'a presumption in favour of any settled scheme of government against any untried project, that a nation has long existed and flourished under it' (Burke 1782: 146).

This distinction is related to the question of the moral justification for constitutions, leading into an important area of philosophical debate centring on a distinction drawn between positive law and natural law.

Positive law is laid down by human agency, say a government or a monarch, or through the accumulation of customs. Prominent among the positivists was the philosophical radical John Austin (1790–1859), who saw law as nothing more than the commands of the sovereign. Bentham was himself influenced by Austin. Some find this approach (legal positivism) unsatisfactory because it lacks a deeper justification.

Natural law is supposedly derived from something more fundamental than the dictates of any earthly sovereign. This idea can be traced back to the Ancient Greek philosophers, particularly the Stoics, whose ideas were adopted by the Romans when seeking a legal system that could extend over their empire independently of the customary laws of different lands. Natural law can be said to derive from an expression of the will of God, though some philosophers, including Hugo Grotius (1583–1645) and Immanuel Kant (1724–1804), argued that this is virtually a special kind of positive law with God as the sovereign. Others argue that it is derived from the idea of certain 'natural rights'. However, this introduces the problem of what these rights actually are. For Locke they included security of life, limb and property, and the US constitution begins by speaking grandiloquently of certain 'inalienable rights'.

Development and change in the British constitution have shown both organic and mechanistic characteristics. Common law and conventions have evolved gradually, while statute law has facilitated some great leaps, such as the extensions of the franchise. The two contrasting views are marked by more than a dispassionate search for the truth; they have been used to support political positions. For Burke's followers (the landowners), the organic and mystical view provided a basis for resisting the forces threatening to erode their privileges, while for the rising industrial bourgeoisie, attempting to shape the constitution in their own interests, the radical mechanistic view was irresistible.

Limiting Government

The essence of **constitutional government** is **limited government**. This is held to be necessary because there can never be any guarantee that rulers will not exercise power in their own self-interest. Most political thinkers have agreed that power tends to corrupt. This limitation can be secured by other institutions, through the law, or through popular control, and is sought through three fundamental principles: the **separation of powers**, the **rule of law** and **parliamentary sovereignty**. The first was regarded by the French jurist Montesquieu, in his *L'Esprit des Lois* (1748), as the key to British liberty. The last two were seen by Dicey (1959: xvii) as the twin pillars of the constitution, a view that has continued to colour much constitutional writing (Harden and Lewis 1986: 4).

The separation of powers

The accommodation of all powers in the same hands may justly be pronounced the very definition of tyranny.
James Madison (1751–1836; one of America's 'founding fathers'), in *The Federalist* (1788)

The idea of dispersing or separating power between various institutions so that they will curtail each other's actions is based on the theory that there are distinct functions of government, each of which can be entrusted to a different institution. Montesquieu followed Locke in arguing that the best safeguard of freedom was to ensure that those making the laws (the **legislature**) should not also be those responsible for their implementation (the **executive**). Similarly, those enforcing the laws (the **judiciary**) should be independent (see p. 691). The founding fathers of the American constitution were deeply impressed by the doctrine and today the executive (president), legislature (Congress) and judiciary are not only separate but have extensive power over each other; the constitution imposes 'checks and balances'. It is not unusual for the president to be thwarted in his policy ambitions by both Congress and the Supreme Court; indeed, at times the system seems in danger of grinding to a complete standstill as vetoes are exercised like power-assisted brakes. George W. Bush found himself with a Republican House and a Democrat Senate. In December 2001 this divided Congress killed off his recovery package in the wake of the 9/11 terrorist attack. Further separation is inherent in the US constitution through its federal structure, apportioning jurisdiction between the federal government and the states. In Britain the judiciary has only limited powers to check the executive, which come from the principle of *ultra vires* and, since 1998, the ability to issue a declaration of incompatibility where legislation is judged to be at variance with the Human Rights Act.

In fact Montesquieu was wrong about the British constitution. Bagehot was to stress that its 'efficient secret' was not a separation but a fusion of powers (figure 4.2) through the Cabinet – heading both the executive and the legislature. To add to this fusion, the House of Lords, as part of the legislature, was traditionally the final Court of Appeal. Furthermore, the Lord Chancellor was, by tradition, head

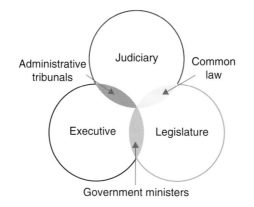

Figure 4.2 A fusion rather than a separation of powers

of the judiciary (responsible for senior judicial appointments) and a member of the Cabinet and of the legislature, where he sat on the 'Woolsack' as the Speaker of the House of Lords. The appointment of Derry Irvine in 1997 threw the anomalies of the position into stark relief. As head of the chambers in which Tony Blair had worked as a fledgling barrister, Lord Irvine was closer to the Prime Minister than any previous incumbent, and a number of reforms followed which increased the separation of the judiciary from the legislature and executive.

The 1998 Human Rights Act gives the judiciary the power to consider whether legislation complies with the provisions of the ECHR. If it does not then a declaration of incompatibility may be issued. This does not strike down the legislation but the legislators are enjoined to think again. Existing legislation, new legislation, administrative practice and common law in breach of the ECHR may all now be challenged in British courts.

Further measures came with the Constitutional Reform Act 2005. This replaced the Lord Chancellor's role in the House of Lords with a Lords' Speaker elected by the peers. The Lord Chancellor also lost responsibility for judicial appointments to an independent Judicial Appointments Commission (JAC). In addition, the act transferred the function of final court of appeal from the House of Lords to a new Supreme Court, physically and constitutionally separate from the other two arms of government, which opened for business opposite the Palace of Westminster in Middlesex Guildhall in October 2009.

Further judicial restrictions on sovereignty arise with devolution, which has given the UK a more federal character. The Westminster and provincial bodies must now accept judicial ruling in any conflict over their respective powers. In addition, the courts retain the power to consider the legality of an executive action (on grounds such as *ultra vires*) through a judicial review process, used increasingly from the 1980s (see pp. 695–6).

However, it remains the case that the judiciary does not have equality with the other arms of government. It cannot strike down legislation and Parliament is free to pass any new law in order to reverse a judgement with which it is unhappy. Hence, Bagehot's assertion that Britain has a fusion of powers largely stands, although there may be political constraints. Where home secretaries have tried to influence sentencing policy, the principle of the separation of powers has been tellingly adduced by Lord Chief Justices in defence of judicial independence.

The rule of law

This principle holds that the law is above the whims of any individual ruler. Lying at the heart of the idea of constitutional government, it can be traced back to the Ancient Greeks. It has been brought to bear throughout history wherever people have sought to resist arbitrary rule or despotism; in the Middle Ages the notion that the monarch was subject to God and the law provided a fundamental rationale for challenging royal absolutism. Dicey (1959) expressed the rule of law in terms of three precepts.

- No person can be punished except for a distinct breach of the law.
- No person, of whatever rank, is above the ordinary law.
- The general provisions of the constitution are the result of decisions made by an independent judiciary in deciding particular cases, rather than of declarations by rulers.

Various other principles may be added to these, such as the following.

- Laws should be made through an accepted, open and known process (the legislative process).
- They should be largely stable so that all can be sure what they are.
- Laws cannot be made retrospectively to try someone for an act that was legal when it took place.
- In disputes, all sides should have an opportunity to put their cases and the courts should be accessible to all.
- The judiciary must be independent.

There are various ways in which the rule of law breaks down in practice.

- Innocent people may be detained on the basis of police suspicion that they might commit a crime.
- There are various categories subject to different laws. For example: judges, MPs and diplomats are accorded extra privileges; the police have special powers, and members of the armed forces are subject to martial law.
- In certain Muslim communities in British cities systems of religious (Islamic) law are applied by Sharia courts. On a strict interpretation this is held to be the word of God, so that adherents will place it above the secular law. A BBC *Panorama* investigation (22 April 2013) revealed that this denied certain rights to women.

In Britain, the practical meaning of the rule of law has varied throughout history (Harden and Lewis 1986: 8) but today it largely holds that the government will operate within the law. This is not to say that it, or its agents, such as the secret services, do not sail close to the wind. In July 1993, the House of Lords in its appeal capacity ruled Home Secretary Kenneth Baker in contempt of court over the deportation of an asylum seeker in 1991 in defiance of a court order. The government had claimed that the law had no power by injunction or contempt proceedings against a minister acting in an official capacity, but the Court asserted that such a proposition would reverse the result of the Civil War! However, the rule of law is logically coupled with the second of Dicey's great twin 'pillars' of the constitution – the doctrine of the sovereignty of Parliament.

Parliamentary sovereignty

This doctrine enshrines the outcome of the prolonged constitutional struggle culminating in the Glorious Revolution of 1688, when the Bill of Rights (1689) set out the supremacy that Parliament had gained over the king through a succession of common-law decisions dating from the fourteenth century. However, not until the nineteenth century, following the great Reform Acts that changed the political system beyond recognition, was the principle formally enunciated by Dicey as the one fundamental (or entrenched) element in the British constitution. Parliamentary sovereignty entailed

> . . . the right to make or unmake any law whatever; and . . . that no person or body is recognized by the law of England as having a right to override or set aside the legislation of Parliament. (Dicey 1959: 39–40)

From this follow two principles: that the courts have no power to veto legislation and that no Parliament is bound by existing laws. As Bill Walker MP told the Commons in February 1993: 'If we get something wrong, as we often do, we can rectify it the following year' (quoted in Klug et al. 1996: 537).

At the time Dicey wrote, the generally accepted doctrine of **sovereignty** was that of Austin, that every state must contain some body with ultimate power. This carried no particular moral justification, but Dicey distinguished between two forms of sovereignty – legal and political – asserting the moral supremacy of the latter. Thus the sovereignty of Parliament was derived not from its inheritance of the absolute powers of the monarch, nor from God, but from the people.

Today, membership of the EU poses questions for the doctrine. British courts must give effect to laws emanating from Brussels and, in any conflict, these take precedence over those of Westminster. Although such conflict has generally been over technical matters, fundamental questions were raised in 1988 when the British government passed an Act to prevent foreigners from registering ships as British (permitted under the 1894 Merchant Shipping Act) in order to use British fishing quotas. In *R* v. *Secretary of State for Transport ex parte Factortame* (1990) this was challenged by Spanish fishermen as contrary to Community law. A decision of the European Court of Justice (ECJ) (now routinely referred to as the Factortame Case) effectively suspended part of a British statute. Crucially, this ruling also granted British courts the power to effectively 'suspend' a British statute where such disputes arose in the future – at least until the ECJ was able to make a final determination.

Incorporation of the ECHR into British law under the 1998 Human Rights Act also limits parliamentary sovereignty with the right of the courts to issue a 'declaration of incompatibility'. Parliament's Human Rights Committee scrutinizes new bills and the ministers introducing them are required to produce human rights statements; any breaches must be debated. Should these occur, a special fast-track procedure is available to amend the legislation. Judgments of the European Court of Human Rights must also be considered. Thus, in 2005 the court ruled that legislation barring most prisoners from voting violated the guarantee of free and fair elections enshrined in Article 3, Protocol 1 of the ECHR.

However, we shall see in chapter 16 that the greatest challenge to parliamentary sovereignty comes not from judges, power-hungry Eurocrats or a dissident Celtic fringe but from the political dominance of the British executive.

Protecting Individual Rights

In addition to regulating government, a constitution also guarantees **civil rights** – freedoms and protections for citizens. The two functions are not really distinct; the quantity and quality of personal freedom offered is related to the nature and degree of the state's authority. Of course, under certain circumstances people may be quite happy to relinquish freedom. Hobbes argued that we should all submit to the Leviathan in order to be safe from each other (see p. 29), and in his *Essay on Liberty*, J. S. Mill argued that one person's freedom should be curtailed only when it inflicted harm upon others. Much modern legislation (e.g. libel laws limiting freedom of expression) reflects this principle.

Written constitutions usually include positive guarantees of fundamental freedoms. In 1787, the framers of the US constitution neglected this and ten amendments were ratified subsequently as the Bill of Rights (1791). These ten amendments guaranteed freedom of worship, speech, assembly and to petition for redress of grievances; freedom from deprivation of life, liberty or property by unlawful means; freedom from cruel or unusual punishments; and security from unreasonable search of persons or houses and private papers and effects.

The aftermath of the second world war saw much talk of constructing a bulwark

> **The Glorious Revolution**
> The Bill of Rights following the Glorious Revolution is not like those of France or the USA. Conferring various privileges upon MPs, it is concerned with the rights of Parliament in relation to the monarch, rather than those of citizens in relation to the state.

against fascism, with Britain's prime minister Winston Churchill a prominent contributor. One outcome of this movement was the Council of Europe, created in May 1949 by the Treaty of London. This international association produced a European Convention on Human Rights and a European Court of Human Rights to adjudicate. With some irony, although British judges had played a part in drawing up the convention, the government declined to incorporate it into British law. Hence, in Britain, laws protecting basic freedoms were nothing more than the ordinary laws of the land. Granted only *negatively*, rights were not conferred by the constitution, they were merely not withheld. People could do anything not expressly prohibited; the freedoms were *residual* and governments were free to impose any restrictions they wished. Aggrieved citizens could petition the European Court of Human Rights at Strasbourg, but this was a journey that proved long and costly (though the Court had found British governments of left and right in violation of the Convention more often than any other signatory state; Klug et al. 1996: 538).

Dissatisfaction led to calls from libertarian groups and leading lawyers such as Lords Scarman and Lestor for an entrenched US-style **Bill of Rights**. This came a step closer with the Labour government's 1998 Human Rights Act, although the ECHR was incorporated in modified form. While not always making any new rights available, it gave existing ones constitutional status and made them much easier to claim at all levels of the judicial system.

Rights and politics

The significance of the new Human Rights Act in a state that had resisted such a move for centuries cannot be underestimated (Klug 2000). Many rights in the ECHR are relevant to politics and arouse controversy. The right to a fair trial (Article 6) means that the use of public interest immunity certificates (as in the Matrix Churchill case) would be outlawed. The right to 'private and family life' (Article 8) means that deportation decisions made by politicians can be reviewed by the courts. As in the case of the US Bill of Rights, even those rights that appear fundamental cannot be considered truly absolute. They must instead be weighed against other conflicting rights and the legitimate interests of the state.

Perhaps the most significant rights bearing on politics concern freedom of the *person*, of *speech*, and of *association* and *assembly*.

Freedom of the person

The right to go about one's business has long been regarded as a central pillar of the temple of liberty. In the eighteenth-century case of *Leach* v. *Money and Others* (1765) it was held that a general warrant for the arrest of unnamed persons was illegal and void. In *Liversidge* v. *Anderson and Another* (1942) it was held that 'every imprisonment is *prima facie* unlawful, and that it is for a person directing imprisonment to justify his act'. People who have been wrongfully imprisoned have a range of remedies available in civil and common law, on grounds such as malicious prosecution, false imprisonment, assault and battery. In addition there is the classic guarantee of individual liberty in Britain – the writ of habeas corpus – enabling anyone confined to demand a just trial before a court. This has served a variety of purposes, including removing apprentices from harsh masters, freeing slaves and establishing that a husband has no right to detain his wife against her will. To these may now be added freedom of life and personal liberty in Articles 2 and 5 of the ECHR.

However, the executive has the authority to limit freedom of the person by taking on unrestrained powers of arrest on the basis of great national emergency. The 1939 Emergency Powers (Defence) Act allowed the home secretary to detain anyone whom he 'has reasonable cause to believe' may be of 'hostile origin or association'. All ministers must show is that they acted in good faith. Under emergencies, even habeas corpus can be suspended, as was the case, for example, in the fight against the Chartists (see p. 272). The policy of internment in Northern Ireland, the operation of the 'sus' law against young blacks and the detention of asylum-seekers have all represented further serious infringements of freedom of the person. In a matter of a few days before Easter 1996, the Home Secretary, fearful of IRA activity, was able to give the police new stop-and-search powers under the Prevention of Terrorism Act. The police also have powers to stop and search under such legislation as the 1984 Police and Criminal Evidence Act, the 1991 Emergency Provisions Act and the 1994 Criminal Justice and Public Order Act. Moreover, the protection afforded by the Human Rights Act looks more flimsy still when one considers the measures implemented by the UK government in response to the terrorist attacks of 11 September 2001 and 7 July 2005. In 2005 the government brought in a Terrorism Act that allowed a home secretary to imprison suspected terrorists without a trial.

Freedom of speech

It is clear that in a democracy the freedom to express political opinion is fundamental; throughout the world the absence of such a right is held to be one of the most visible symptoms of oppression. Various cases have given this freedom to those such as political speakers, publishers, newspaper editors and pamphleteers.

Freedom of expression is guaranteed in the ECHR (Article 10). Yet in Britain the freedom has been restricted in various ways. Individuals are protected from verbal and written assault through the laws of slander and libel, while in the wake of the 9/11 attack, Home Secretary David Blunkett proposed enacting legislation that would have made incitement to religious hatred a criminal offence. There are also laws on obscenity, though the impossibility of deciding what exactly is obscene often produces ludicrous scenarios, as in the *Lady Chatterley's Lover* trial. In 2012 the widespread use of so-called super-injunctions saw celebrities endeavouring to protect their 'private and family life' (Article 8) against newspapers seeking to exercise their 'freedom of expression' (Article 10).

Attempts to limit the freedom of speech in this way are not, of course, limited to the UK. Even in the USA, which benefits from a codified constitution incorporating an explicit right to free expression under the First Amendment, the Supreme Court has accepted that freedom of speech cannot be regarded as absolute. The most serious restrictions on freedom of speech, however, tend to come from the agencies of the state. The repressive apparatus, though often lying dormant, carries a formidable potential, which is thrown into starkest relief in the reporting of politics by the media and the vexed question of government secrecy (see chapter 17).

Freedom of association and assembly

Politics is essentially about collective action through associations such as parties, trade unions and pressure groups. However, the constitution has placed considerable restrictions on this. There have been, for example, the crimes of conspiracy and public nuisance, and the common-law offences of riot, rout and unlawful assembly, later codified in the 1936 Public Order Act. Further restrictions were enacted in the 1986 Public Order Act, the 1994 Criminal Justice and Public Order Act and the 1998 Crime and Disorder Act. The police hold extensive powers in the event of a breach of the peace, or even the suspicion that such a breach might occur. Under normal circumstances the authorities claim to exercise their discretion in a liberal manner, but within this velvet glove is the clenched fist of state repression (see chapter 23). People can be bound over to keep the peace, road blocks can stop movement (as in the miners' strike of 1984/5) and powers to disperse crowds can curtail rights of assembly, including events such as rock festivals. In 1988, workers at the Government Communications Headquarters at Cheltenham lost their right to trade union membership (restored nine years later). Indeed, trade unions have been particular victims, with Combination Acts and various nineteenth-century common-law decisions restricting their growth. Not until the 1875 Conspiracy and Protection of Property Act were strikes effectively legalized and the 1906 Trade Disputes Act reversed the anti-union Taff Vale Judgment. In 1994 the Criminal

A right to use violence: policing student protests in 2010

Justice and Public Order Act aroused controversy by giving the police the power to order people to leave an area if they were believed to be preparing to hold a rave or waiting for a rave to start.

However, freedom of assembly becomes a positive right under Article 11 of the ECHR, with widespread implications for police and local authority powers to ban marches and demonstrations under the Public Order Acts. It also questions the imposition of bail conditions that prevent people awaiting trial from attending meetings and demonstrations.

Towards a rights culture?

> A citizen's person or property may not be interfered with – unless it may. A person is not liable for what he speaks or writes – unless he is. No liability attaches to one who takes part in a public meeting – unless it does.
>
> O. Hood Phillips, *Constitutional and Administrative Law* (1987: 39–40)

In Britain, individual rights have been so hedged with qualifications, ambiguities and what has been praised as the 'glorious uncertainty of the law' that it was difficult to know what one may actually do without impediment. In 1995, the UN Human Rights Committee, following its fourth periodic review, concluded that Britain failed to secure basic civil and political rights and provided inadequate remedy where rights were violated (Klug et al. 1996: 537). The government's defence was that the report failed to appreciate the subtle glories of the system (Weir and Boyle 1997).

Britain, it was argued, had not developed a rights culture. As part of the pattern of deference, strong government and public order have been elevated over individual liberties and the rights of minorities (Weir and Boyle 1997: 129). Such views are buoyed up by much tabloid journalism. Attitude surveys penetrating beyond the drawing rooms of Hampstead and Islington reveal greater interest in *social rights* (education, health care) than *civil and political* ones. In one poll, fewer than a third of respondents supported the principle of a defendant's right to silence (Weir and Boyle 1997: 132–3). A MORI poll for the *News of the World* (24 Sept. 2001) after the 9/11 attack showed 85 per cent in favour of tougher measures on all fronts. Moreover, a degree of xenophobia produces resistance to 'foreign' notions of rights. This may be stimulated by tabloid jingoism and a revolt against 'meddling judges'.

The incorporation of the ECHR under the Human Rights Act – in effect a Bill of Rights (though one not benefiting from the degree of entrenchment afforded to its American namesake) – offered the possibility of a cultural sea change. The feeling was that it could lead to the establishment of a 'rights' culture in Britain. Whether or not this has in fact been the case remains open to question. Some outcomes have undoubtedly proven unpopular with both government and the people. For example, in 1999 the European Court ruled that the length of time Thompson and Venables (the youths who murdered toddler Jamie Bulger) could be detained at Her Majesty's pleasure should not be determined by the home secretary. In October 2000, Lord Chief Justice Lord Woolf recommended their early release, resulting in tabloid outrage and fears that it could lead to the release of 'Moors Murderer' Myra Hindley.

Although New Labour ushered in the Human Rights Act, its strongly centralized style, tabloid sensitivity and neoliberal agenda gave cause for apprehension. Even 'old Labour' had been ambivalent in government. It could be argued that it was the influence of John Smith rather than Blair that set the 1998 reforms in motion and New Labour's 'tough on crime' mantra supported many Conservative measures that violated the ECHR. Moreover, the espousal of US 'communitarian' thinking emphasized *duties* of citizenship at the expense of *rights* and carried strongly authoritarian overtones (see Klug 1997). This was exemplified by, for example, anti-social-behaviour orders (or 'ASBOs'), curfews on the young.

The response to the 9/11 terrorist attack demonstrated how easily freedoms could be removed. Within days Parliament was debating a draconian list of anti-terrorism measures, including: the power to monitor emails, the admission as court evidence of transcripts of phone conversations bugged by MI5, rules compelling banks to release customers' details, the power to seize the assets of suspected terrorists, a fast-track extradition system, and the scrapping of certain appeal rights of people refused entry into Britain. Longer-term plans included proposals for identity cards, euphemistically named 'entitlement cards' – an initiative that was later watered down in the face of parliamentary opposition and ultimately abandoned by the 2010 coalition.

The sheer number and scope of measures passed onto the statute books in the wake of 9/11, and the subsequent attack on London on 7 July 2005, raised serious

---

Towards a police state?

2001 Anti-terrorism, Crime and Security Act: allowed the indefinite detention of foreign terrorist suspects.

2002 Proceeds of Crime Act: provided for the confiscation, without prior prosecution, of assets believed to be the product of criminal activity.

2002 Regulation of Investigatory Powers Act: permitted the use of a wide range of surveillance techniques.

2003 Criminal Justice Act: allowed for trial without jury in some complex cases and removed protection against double jeopardy.

2003 Anti-social Behaviour Act: allowed the imposition of anti-social-behaviour orders and curfews.

2005 Prevention of Terrorism Act: replaced the indefinite detention of foreign terror suspects, allowed under the 2005 Anti-terrorism, Crime and Security Act, with control orders. The Act came in the wake of the case of *A and others* v. *Secretary of State for the Home Department* (2004), where the Lords ruled that the provisions of the 2001 Act were incompatible with the Human Rights Act.

2005 Serious Organised Crime and Police Act: amongst other provisions, restricted protests in the vicinity of Parliament.

2006 Race and Religious Hatred Act: serves to limit expression that might incite religious hatred.

2006 Prevention of Terrorism Act: allowed detention of terrorist suspects for up to twenty-eight days as well as creating a new offence of 'glorifying terrorism'.

2008 Counter-Terrorism Act: increased the penalties for terrorist offences, relaxed rules on police gathering documentary evidence and restricted photography involving subjects likely to be of use to terrorists.

questions over the government's commitment to civil liberties. Although the coalition's 2012 Protection of Freedoms Act sought to withdraw (or at least limit) the use of some of the powers given to the authorities under these earlier Acts – not least reducing the period of pre-charge detention from twenty-eight days to fourteen (Almandras 2011: 32) – the first decade of the twenty-first century could hardly be said to have been a 'golden age' for civil liberties in the UK.

Despite developments, the issue of human rights has remained controversial. Many on the right were unhappy with the operation of the 1998 Act and the coalition government set up a commission of judges to consider replacing it with a very British Bill of Rights. However, to the disappointment of Conservative rebels, the recommendations in December 2012 were to incorporate and build on the existing Act rather than replace it with a watered-down version.

It is perhaps unsurprising that continuing debate on this topic centres on the delicate executive–judicial balance. Although New Labour established the UK Supreme Court, the party, buoyed as it was by massive Commons majorities in 1997 and 2001 (and a comfortable one in 2005), never appeared particularly keen to bow to a bewigged superior authority in areas such as sentencing policy or its anti-terror legislation. An issue arose in 2013, when politicians felt frustrated by judges interpreting Article 8 of the ECHR (right to a family life) to allow foreign criminals to avoid deportation. Conservative Home Secretary Theresa May announced plans for an Immigration Bill to compel them to take account of the fact that Article 8 did allow deportations to prevent 'disorder or crime'.

Hence, despite the enormous potential for cultural change from incorporation of the ECHR, the full impact may not be known until the dust finally settles in that uncertain constitutional territory between what is written and what actually happens. Far from emancipating citizens it may prove an exercise in gesture politics. For reformers, only constitutional earth movements will produce the soil for a rights culture. At the heart of this is a written constitution.

It is elected representatives who are held to account by the electorate, and it is they who should be the prime protectors of our rights rather than having to rely on the judicial system.
Home Secretary David Blunkett, quoted in the *Guardian* (24 Sept. 2001)

A Written Constitution? The Debate

Despite the praises sung to the mysterious virtues of the British constitution, its unwritten – or more properly, uncodified – manifestation is not universally acclaimed. Some argue that the twin guarantees of limited government and individual rights would be far safer if placed beyond the hand of the government of the day through entrenchment. A fully written and codified constitution would mean the end of parliamentary supremacy because certain laws would be so fundamental that they could no longer be changed by normal legislative means and parliaments would be bound by any constitutional amendments made under their predecessors. Moreover, new laws would be subject to judicial scrutiny to ensure their constitutionality. In addition, the executive could be made subject to effective checks by Parliament under a formal separation of powers.

Various other provisions could be made, covering any aspect of government, such as fixing the powers of local government to reduce meddling by the centre, setting out rules for the cabinet system and limiting the use of political patronage. An unrestricted Freedom of Information Act, wider in scope and more effectively entrenched than that which came into force in 2005 (see p. 529), could guarantee people's right to know and a home-grown Bill of Rights could meet British needs more fittingly than did incorporation of the ECHR. Reformers argue that such changes would release people from the grip of their monarchical past. No longer subjects claiming privileges from the powerful, they would become citizens, legally entitled to demand rights.

However, there is a case for the uncodified constitution. It has served Britain for centuries and evolved with the political culture. Any attempt to codify all the relevant material into a document of manageable size would rob it of its subtlety. Moreover, the virtue of flexibility would be sacrificed; no longer could changes take place imperceptibly to accommodate social developments. With the loss of parliamentary sovereignty would go the sovereignty of the people; non-elected organs of the state – particularly the judiciary – could become over-powerful, the fingers of judges and lawyers stained by the acrid alchemy of politics as they thwart the designs of elected politicians.

Numerous practical questions are posed. Do people really express any desire for a change? How much would the process of codification cost? How long would it take? Who could be entrusted with the task? Moreover, throughout the world evidence suggests that written constitutions do not work with anything like the precision implied by the legalists. Serious abuses of freedom take place in the name of countries that boast model bills of rights – witness the US government's use of 'enhanced interrogation techniques' and indefinite detention without trial in the wake of the 9/11 attack. Finally, it can be argued that the entire exercise would be futile because the reality of politics is shaped by the economic power structure, which would be little affected by any redrawing of the constitutional architecture. Thus, for example, the so-called Nolan rules, designed to place constitutional reins on public appointments, did little to remove the charge of cronyism under New Labour (see p. 517).

Towards codification

Yet while debate takes place, the constitution evolves. A growing body of statute law replaces conventions and judicial judgments. Incorporating the ECHR by means of the 1998 Human Rights Act has given Britain something resembling a bill of rights. Many of its provisions effectively replace much common law with respect to various freedoms, such as freedom of speech and assembly, and freedom from arrest without trial. There are also implications arising from the 2005 Constitutional Reform Act, which formalizes a separation of powers. Membership of the EU also has constitutional elements, including its Social Chapter. Despite its limitations (see chapter 17) it may be argued that the Freedom of Information Act represents a further codifying of the constitution. In addition, the devolution legislation, much of which has the character of fundamental law, limiting the legal powers of Westminster, establishes a quasi-federal constitution. The 2011 Fixed-Term Parliament Act removed a prime minister's freedom to dissolve Parliament and the 2013 Succession to the Crown Act proposed ending the succession rights of a first-born male and removing the bar on a potential monarch marrying a Catholic.

Furthermore, an enlarging corpus of authoritative documentation has a constitutional flavour. The *Ministerial Code*, first published as *Questions of Procedure for Ministers* in 1992 lays down 'rules' for ministers. *The Duties and Responsibilities of Civil Servants in Relation to Ministers*, produced by the head of the Civil Service in 1985, has become the *Civil Service Code*. The prospect of a coalition government in 2010 added urgency for clear constitutional clarification and led to the May 2010 *Coalition Agreement for Stability and Reform* and the *Cabinet Manual*, drafted by the Cabinet Office under Cabinet Secretary Gus O'Donnell (2010).

Unwritten and Unknowable?

The fact that the constitution is unwritten, or at least uncodified, means that it can never be entirely known; it must forever be subject to interpretation and dispute. Moreover, there is more to a constitution than what is written in the lawyers' books. The real constitution is the living constitution – what is actually happening in the process of government. In this sense it is for ever in flux (see King 2001; Hazell 2008).

Hence, the constitution is only part of the political landscape, the full extent of which we shall explore in the following chapters. This will sometimes take us into parts of the constitution that have passed from the 'efficient' into the 'dignified' realm and sometimes into areas where it remains silent. Underlying all is the distribution of power within society, which overrides all else. Yet the constitution remains central to political life, a crucial element in legitimization and an obscure object of desire for all actors, whether radicals or conservatives.

Key points

- The term 'constitution' can refer either to all that happens in the process of government, or to a legal framework within which governments must operate.

- Constitutions aim to prescribe and limit the powers of rulers and safeguard the rights of citizens.

- The British constitution is not written in the form of a single document.

- Although unwritten, many documents are involved and it is much written about.

- The constitution has traditionally been said to flow from five sources: the royal prerogative, statute, common law, convention and authoritative opinion, to which may now be added the EU.

- The role of convention is far greater in the British constitution than is the case in other countries.

- A constitution does not stand above the process of politics; it is subject to constant challenge, interpretation and change.

- Reformers call for a codified constitution, for both political and rational reasons.

- As a mechanism for the protection of rights the British constitution can be seen as fragile, requiring government willingness to impose self-restraint.

- A growing body of recent legislation gives the British constitution an increasingly written and codified character.

Review your understanding of the following terms and concepts

authoritative opinion	dignified and efficient	natural law
Bill of Rights	elements	parliamentary
civil rights	ECHR	sovereignty
common law	entrenchment	positive law
constitutional	judicial review	royal prerogative
amendment	judiciary	rule of law
constitutional	legislature	separation of powers
convention	limited government	statute

Questions for discussion and debate

Consider these propositions and be prepared to present the cases for and against. Try to produce debating propositions of your own.

1   The sources of the British constitution give it both flexibility and stability.

2   The first principle of good government is the rule of law.

3   The existence of a constitution does not guarantee constitutional government.

4   Only a fully codified constitution will bring Britain into the twenty-first century.

5   The British constitution is more dignified than real.

6   Constitutions cannot be designed, they form through evolution.

7   In a democracy judges should never be able to overrule politicians.

8   Human rights are no more than political claims made by individuals on the state.

9   Britain's membership of the EU has dangerous constitutional implications.

10   The Human Rights Act 1998 has given new and dangerous powers to the judiciary.

Further reading

Alder, J. (2011) *Constitutional and Administrative Law.*
Owners' manual for the nuts and bolts of the system, including changes following the coalition government.

Bagehot, W. (1963) *The English Constitution* (first published 1867).
A classic and immensely readable account of politics during the fleeting period of genuine parliamentary government before the 1867 Reform Act.

Bogdanor, V. (1996) *Politics and the Constitution: Essays on British Government.*
Collection of essays aiming to show how the struggle over the constitution is essentially political.

Bogdanor, V. (2009) *The New British Constitution*.
An authoritative yet accessible overview of recent constitutional developments from one of the leading academic authors in the field.

Bogdanor, V. (2011) *The Coalition and the Constitution*.
Considers the significance of coalition government for the constitution.

Chrimes, S. B. (first published 1967) *English Constitutional History*.
This slim volume is concise yet erudite on the subject.

Dicey, A. V. (first published 1885) *An Introduction to the Study of the Law and the Constitution*, 10th edn.
Classic account of the theory of liberal democracy, though author's heart is perhaps more with liberalism than democracy. (Digitized version freely available.)

Ewing, K. D. and Gearty, C. A. (1990) *Freedom under Thatcher: Civil Liberties in Modern Britain*.
Essay by leading authorities on civil liberties. Argues that Thatcher government eroded freedoms by pushing back the frontiers of the common law, the traditional guardian of the people.

Hailsham, Lord (1978) *The Dilemma of Democracy*.
The views of Lord Hailsham, a prominent and rumbustious Conservative politician and lawyer (and Lord Chancellor), must be read with due caution. His 'dilemma' is perhaps felt more acutely under Labour governments.

Harden, I. and Lewis, N. (1986) *The Noble Lie*.
Adopting a US-style approach (critical legal studies), explores gulf between orthodox constitutional theory (deriving largely from Dicey) and the reality of political power today.

Hazell, R. (ed.) (2008) *Constitutional Futures Revisited: Britain's Constitution to 2020*.
Thoughtful constitutional crystal-gazing by leading political scientists and lawyers.

Hennessy, P. (1995) *The Hidden Wiring: Unearthing the British Constitution*.
'Health check' on the British constitution assesses its response to changing circumstances.

Holme, R. and Elliot, M. (eds) (1988) *1688–1988: Time for a New Constitution*.
Critical and reformist essays marking tercentenary of the Glorious Revolution.

Jowell, J. and Oliver, D. (eds) (2011) *The Changing Constitution*, 7th edn.
Scholarly and thought-provoking essays on the key issues surrounding the UK's
constitutional development. Includes consideration of the effects of the formation
of the 2010 coalition.

King, A. (2001) *Does the United Kingdom Still Have a Constitution*?
Text of the Hamlyn Lectures. A critical microscope placed on the modern
constitution in a stimulating and erudite yet accessible essay. Makes an
illuminating comparison with the Netherlands.

Klug, F. (2000) *Values for a Godless Age: The Story of the United Kingdom's New Bill
of Rights*.
Written as a layperson's guide to the Human Rights Act, it is authoritative and
stimulating.

McLean, I. (2012) *What's Wrong with the British Constitution?* 2nd edn.
A sharp critique of much of the conventional wisdom surrounding our
understanding of the constitution.

For reading around the subject and some light relief

William Golding, *Lord of the Flies*.
Public schoolboys go feral. Allegory exploring mayhem when constitutional
rule breaks down.

George Orwell, *Animal Farm*.
Modern fable satirizing Russian revolution and, by extension, all revolutions.
New tyranny replaces old.

William Shakespeare, *Coriolanus*.
One of the most political of Shakespeare's plays. Deals with the relationship
between governors and the governed – Coriolanus and the common
people.

On the net

http://www.unlockdemocracy.org.uk/
Unlock Democracy's website contains a wealth of information on constitutional reform and links to other relevant sites.

http://www.ucl.ac.uk/constitution-unit/
The UCL Constitution Unit's website provides an overview of the unit's work and links to many of their online publications, including the excellent *Monitor* newsletter, which offers up-to-date coverage of developments across a range of themes in the field of constitutional reform.

CHAPTER 5

THE GLOBAL CONTEXT: THIS SCEPTRED ISLE

Contents

Any idea promoted in political rhetoric, and some traditional textbooks, that the government charts its own course with political compass and sextant is illusory; the ship of state is tossed on a stormy sea of world affairs. Today's world is encircled with electronic communications networks, trading and financial flows, production patterns, labour movements, military operations, media output and cultural exchanges. Giant corporations inhabit a political space bearing little relation to traditional state boundaries. This is all part of what is termed 'globalization' – a defining feature of the age. The chapter addresses Britain's evolving place on the global stage, the global economy, globalized violence, and the ideal of global governance.

On 28 February 2007 the Chinese government threatened to place a capital gains tax on profits from shares. The unsurprising result was a fall in share prices in Singapore – a problem for the Chinese. Yet it was rather more than this. As the sun rose in countries around the globe, first Asia, then Europe and finally the USA saw their own stock markets falling in an alarming domino effect. Such events have become all-too familiar with the global banking crisis that began in 2008 (see p. 120).

Critics of government have alleged failures in economic and social policy over previous decades. While there may have been substance in such criticism there were much more powerful forces at work. On many fronts government policies were little more than reactions to conditions beyond their control. The domestic crisis could only be understood in a global context. In the way that a butterfly can set in train a chain of events resulting in a storm on the other side of the planet, so the world economies are concatenated. A domestic event in one sends shock waves around the world to shape the quality of life of millions.

Defining Globalization

And what should they know of England who only England know.
Rudyard Kipling (1865–1936; Indian-born British writer), 'The English Flag'

Globalization can be seen as a phenomenon defining the age in which we live. Essentially it is the intensification of worldwide social relations that link distant localities in such a way that what happens locally is shaped by events occurring thousands of miles away (Giddens 1990: 64). At its heart are changes to the relationship between time and space: time–space distanciation. Distances travelled to conduct business or transport commodities are defined in terms of journey time. From the horse to supersonic travel, from the penny post to email, technology compresses space, so that today we can speak of a 'global village'. The phenomenon of globalization extends beyond economics to most areas of modern life and politicians recognize it as a key factor in debate. More than any previous prime ministers, Tony Blair and David Cameron embraced its reality, making it central in much rhetoric and political strategy.

While an analysis of the complexities of globalization is beyond the scope of this book, it is crucially important to recognize its significance in domestic politics. Much traditional writing has assumed a high degree of state **autonomy** and government control. If the economy does well it is to our credit, and if it fails we look for culprits at home (from trade unions and scroungers to the civil service, banks or business leaders). Explanations looking only inwards are termed **endogenous** and are essentially short-sighted. They arise from various factors, including a degree of arrogance, a 'Rule Britannia' conviction that we control world events, the egotistical rhetoric of politicians and intellectual laziness. In reality, few countries have been more closely enmeshed in the economy and politics of the world than Britain; any study ignoring this is incomplete. When we do direct our attention at *external* forces we are adopting an **exogenous** perspective.

Britain Entering the Global Stage

Many writers have dwelt with pride on the idea of Britain's insularity (physical and metaphorical) and a conviction, implicit or explicit, of political superiority. A much-vaunted factor is the country's geographical setting, shielding it from physical and cultural invasion or other forms of contamination. As it was for Shakespeare's John of Gaunt, it has been

> This fortress built by Nature for herself
> Against infection and the hand of war.
>
> (William Shakespeare, *Richard II*: Act 2, Scene 1)

The last invasion took place in 1066, and the defeat of the Spanish Armada in 1588 encapsulated in a legendary way this island advantage. Yet despite its protective 'moat', Britain's world position has for long shaped its politics. Central to developments has been the emergence and rapacious growth of a capitalist **world economy**. Nothing preoccupied the political elite or influenced political affairs as much as this. Indeed, Britain played an early role in its formation and has continued as a key actor.

The era of colonialism and mercantilism

The British Empire is one of the greatest enslavers of human beings in the world.
Paul Robeson (1898–1976; black American singer, victim of colour prejudice), quoted in *News Review* (3 Oct. 1946)

The great 'age of discovery' beginning in the fifteenth century opened up a New World and a new world economy. Developing from the mid-sixteenth century and traversing the Atlantic, it was to be shared by Portugal, Spain, Holland, France and Britain. This sea-borne trading network was based on **imperialism**, its emphasis on protecting colonies and trading with them. The **colonial** period was characterized by competitive struggle for territory, raw materials and people. As a sea-going nation, with enough farmland for self-sufficiency and safe from land attack, Britain was uniquely fitted to survive. While rivals warred on land, Britain could develop a strategy of oceanic domination of a world trade in commodities and slaves. In this the state willingly assumed a **mercantilist** role, protecting the commercial endeavours of its traders and settlers; trade wars were fought and Navigation Acts granted monopolies. Ultimately, with the gaining of India and Canada and the defeat of France in the Napoleonic wars, Britain emerged as the supreme world power. This dominance was to be increased through industrialization, although the role of the state would change.

The era of free trade

Beginning in the eighteenth century, the **industrial revolution** was further good fortune for the British. The first country to industrialize, its domination could be increased through superior productivity, feeding on raw materials from the colonies and disgorging manufactured goods to the world. **Free trade**, rather than mercantilism, became the rallying cry of the new bourgeoisie. Following Adam Smith's principle of **comparative advantage** (that each country should specialize in what it could do best), Britain abandoned protection and threw open its doors to all-comers, urging others to do likewise. The country produced a third of the world's manufactured goods and half its iron, steel, coal and cotton goods. The cost of this policy was to expose British agriculture (through the relaxing and ultimate repeal of the Corn Laws in 1846) to destructive competition, with an ensuing loss of national self-sufficiency. The industrial bourgeoisie were fully prepared to put at risk the future of the whole of society; it was perhaps the most decisive event in modern British history (Gamble 1990: 52).

The state was brought under the control of the newly enriched bourgeoisie through far-reaching constitutional reforms, and policy acquired an international outlook. Britain pledged itself to a world policing role to secure the vital trade routes. The pound (sterling), fixed to the gold standard, became the universal currency, with a financial, trading and communications network centred on London. Britain's economic empire was to extend even beyond the bounds of its political one. Yet there were risks involved; the dependency on food, raw materials and markets around the world contained the seeds of decline.

Decline

After so exhilarating a start in the industrial race some relative decline was inevitable as rivals penetrated the new markets. However, Britain's eclipse by Germany and the USA was accomplished not by following the free-trade doctrines of Adam Smith, which were seen as a pseudo-theory designed to perpetuate British domination, but by erecting tariff barriers. In response, a tariff reform movement led by Joseph Chamberlain grew up, but was killed in 1905 with the election of a Liberal government. Britain remained the world policeman, the system continued to centre on sterling and British capitalists continued to invest vast sums abroad. The burden was to take its toll; intense European competition culminating in two world wars left Britain gravely disabled. The USA was now the world leader, to which Britain looked for succour. The post-war era saw a burgeoning growth of economic players in a world drama in which Britain was to be but one of the cast.

> *Englishmen know instinctively that what the world needs most is whatever is best for Great Britain.*
> Ogden Nash (1902–71; US poet), *England Expects*

The future was one in which the country would be influenced by world events, including the rise and fall of the Bretton Woods system (see p. 120), crises in the oil-producing regions, serious decline in the US economy, the collapse of communism, the rise of the newly industrializing countries (NICs) in South-East Asia and the increasing significance of the BRIC (Brazil, Russia, India and China) economies. China in particular promised to supplant the USA as the world economic superpower (see Jacques 2009).

The Global Economy Today

On Boxing Day 1999, when the Chelsea football team took to the field not a single player was from that London borough. Indeed, none of them were even British, as Chelsea fans became the first in the country to support an entirely foreign team. According to Leicester University's Sir Norman Chester Centre for Football Research, during the 1999 season more than half the players in the Premier League were foreign. Not only is Britain's national game a global economic business, the contents of our fridges, the cars we drive, the television programmes and films we watch and the machines on which we play computer games – all provide daily reminders of the astonishing reach of **global capitalism**. The growing mobility of

Every sustained wave of technological progress and economic development everywhere has been fuelled by greed, profiteering, special privileges, and megalomania.

Theodore Levitt (Professor at Harvard Business School, credited with coining the term 'economic globalization')

capital, and cheaper communications and transportation, have taken globalization to quite a new plane. One key measure is the scale of direct foreign investment made by capitalists in countries other than their own. This rose from US$54.6 million in 1980 to reach a peak of US$2.3 trillion in 2005, falling back to US$1.3 trillion in 2009 (World Bank, *World Development Indicators*, 24 Jan. 2012). However, this global economy does not distribute its largesse equally; the world is marked by inequality (see Held and Kaya 2006) in which some are powerful and some are weak. We can begin to understand this by identifying the players in this global drama.

The *dramatis personae*

States are not alone on this global stage. Other major players are huge private companies (transnational corporations), financial institutions and a variety of international organizations.

Transnational corporations

A defining feature of modern globalization, the **transnational corporations** (TNCs) are commercial companies registered in multiple locations around the world. Their range is astonishing. The production and distribution most of the world's

Better known than national flags, multinational logos decorate developing countries

petroleum, vehicles, aeroplanes, foodstuffs, computers, electronic entertainment, chemicals and pharmaceuticals all lie within their control. Their logos, to be seen at many sporting occasions, are better known than national flags. They magnify their reach over many thousands of smaller companies in complex supply chains. In the eyes of their many critics they pose nothing less than a threat to democracy (see Hertz 2002).

Operating in more than one country and owing allegiance to none, their wealth is greater than that of many countries in the less developed world. They can fund political parties, threaten regimes and determine what people think through their media conglomerates. They can influence social policies everywhere as governments seek to attract them in order to increase employment levels.

The TNCs are owned and controlled by an international capitalist elite which, in the quest for profit, works to maintain a global economic environment beyond the regulation of any state. By the 1990s, a mere 500 corporations controlled some 70 per cent of all world trade (*Ecologist* 1992), with just ten controlling virtually every aspect of the worldwide food chain (Vidal 1997). There is much ethical debate around their practices. Some create employment, providing training and bringing in skills, others seek out low-wage economies with passive, non-unionized workforces, unsafe working conditions and repressive and sexist regimes, such as South Korea and the Philippines. The dramatic collapse of a garment factory in Bangladesh with the loss of eighty-seven lives in 2013 brought home to western consumers the human cost of readily available cheap clothing. Although economies like China's are growing, much production here also lies in the hands of the western-based giants (see Hutton 2002).

The financial institutions

Matching the TNCs are the financial and banking institutions monitoring market movements in Tokyo, London and New York through advanced computerized networks. In the City of London is the august Bank of England and the futuristic glass and metal stock exchange; currencies, stocks and shares, and 'futures' can speed around the globe at the click of a mouse button. A few streets away, overlooking the Thames, is the London International Financial Futures and Options Exchange (LIFFE), opened in 1982 to take advantage of the 1979 removal of currency controls in Britain. Here the action was manic as the 'open outcry traders', young men clad in psychedelic blazers (and professing 'balls of steel'), competed for enormous bonuses in a frenzy of shouting and waving, gambling on future prices and exchange rates around the world. Today the frenzy is concealed by electronic trading but the process continues. In 2002 LIFFE joined the exchanges of Amsterdam, Brussels, Paris and Lisbon to become Euronext.liffe.

Capitalism is to the market what cancer is to our bodies. We get cancer when a genetic defect causes a cell to forget that it is part of our body.
David Korten (US economist), speech to the 1999 AGM of the World Development Movement

Money has no motherland; financiers are without patriotism and without decency; their sole object is gain.
Napoleon Bonaparte (1761–1821; French Emperor)

What we know about the global financial crisis is that we don't know very much.
Paul Samuelson
(1915–2009; US economist)

The centrality of globalized finance was to be starkly revealed in 2008 when huge high-profile US financial institutions (including the mighty Lehman Brothers, which went bankrupt) began to collapse, largely as a result of lending in what was termed a sub-prime market. Tectonic after-shocks were to reverberate around the world and financial links became chaotic. Iceland actually went bankrupt and there was a run on banks as footloose capital fled any territory deemed to be at risk. With beleaguered national economies, governments moved desperately to bail out their own banks. In Europe the Eurozone was thrown into crisis as its weaker economies struggled to cope with their debt levels.

In Britain the Bank of England lowered interest rates to unprecedented levels in an effort to resuscitate the economy. The implications went well beyond financial policy as the government sought to reduce a record level of sovereign debt with public spending cuts. Paradoxically, the gap between rich and poor had grown larger, with bankers and directors of companies claiming huge bonuses on the grounds of the need for parity with those in other countries. In response students, public-sector workers, benefits claimants and the unemployed displayed a growing sense of outrage. Demonstrations and strikes were compounded by riots which saw rampaging and looting in the streets. A worldwide 'Occupy' movement spread to British cities and, to the consternation of both police and clergy, a village of tents sprang up on the forecourt of St Paul's Cathedral (see p. 594).

International associations

Governments do not always act alone in the global economy. **International associations** form to oil the wheels of production and trade. A defining moment in post-war reconstruction was the July 1944 conference at Bretton Woods, New Hampshire, where forty-four capitalist nations agreed a grand plan for rebuilding the world economy. Britain played a central role, a key figure being economist John Maynard Keynes. The conference sought a new order based on cooperation, cohesion and free trade. However, central to the arrangement was the domination (hegemony) of the one nation that had emerged from the war in a strengthened state. The world capitalist economy would centre on the US dollar, to which other currencies would be tied (and through the dollar to gold) at fixed **exchange rates**. There would be an International Monetary Fund (IMF), largely administered by the USA, and a World Bank (the International Bank for Reconstruction and Development), financed by borrowing and donations from member states in proportion to their wealth, to make loans and grants to weak economies. (The entry of the former communist bloc enlarged the IMF so that by 2012 there were some 187 members.) By convention, the managing director of the IMF is a European while the president of the World Bank is from the USA and chosen by the US president. The regime was cemented by a General Agreement on Tariffs and Trade (GATT) drawn up in 1947.

Global lenders and borrowers

Top ten lenders	Top ten borrowers
USA	India
Japan	China
Germany	Mexico
France	Brazil
UK	Indonesia
Canada	Turkey
Italy	Argentina
Netherlands	Pakistan
Belgium	South Korea
Spain	Russia

Intended to be temporary, the negotiations to remove tariffs taking place in 'rounds' became central. Following the conclusion of the Uruguay Round, GATT was succeeded in 1995 by the even more powerful World Trade Organization (WTO).

The World Bank, able to make enormous loans and grants to countries, has backed infrastructure projects bringing clean water and electricity to millions of the world's poor and stimulating local economies. However, these often come with strings attached. Countries can be told to deflate, reduce taxes, privatize, deregulate and cut public services in order to compete globally – a package termed the Washington Consensus. Some critics describe this as **neocolonialism**, viewing the tradition of appointing a US citizen as president of the Bank as an arm of American foreign policy. The appointment in 2005 of Paul Wolfowitz, a neo-conservative advocate of the invasion of Iraq, strengthened this impression. His policy of withholding aid to 'corrupt' governments appeared to place the USA in a policing role. Charitable bodies such as Christian Aid and War on Want claim that some policies exacerbate the suffering of the very poorest. Critics also allege that the Bank's support for mining projects, while producing profits for the western companies doing the work, has damaging environmental consequences and does little to enrich local populations.

The WTO gained an even wider mandate than its predecessor (GATT). It can facilitate trade negotiations, administer agreements, monitor trade policies, give technical assistance to developing countries and liaise with other international organizations. Unlike other international bodies it has teeth, able to adjudicate in trade disputes and authorize sanctions against countries stepping out of line. Although each of its 150-plus members has a vote, in practice the rich have dominated. Many states cannot even afford a full-time staff at the Geneva headquarters. Critics allege that import duties, quotas, non-tariff barriers and the regulation of intellectual property all favour the developed countries

We are writing the constitution of a single global economy.
Renato Ruggerio (Director General of the WTO), quoted in Rowan (1998)

Another body is the Organization for Economic Cooperation and Development (OECD), founded in 1961 by the world's twenty-nine richest countries to promote their economic interests. Its lobbying resulted in the creation by the WTO of the General Agreement on Trade in Services (GATS), which extended the GATT regime into *services* such as water supply, and health and tourism. Critics argue that this gives a country's obligations to free trade precedence over domestic regulatory laws aimed at protecting citizens.

Heads of state can also come together on a less formal basis. The Group of Eight (G8) was a loose association of eight highly industrialized non-communist and democratic nations: France, Germany, Italy, Britain, Japan, the USA, Canada and Russia. Originating in 1975 as the G6, it provided a forum to address economic concerns. A decrease in the combined economic muscle of its members, and the exclusion of major developing economies, has reduced its impact and it was effectively supplanted with the formation of the G20, comprising nineteen of the world's largest economies plus the EU. Meeting for the first time in December 1999, the G20 became particularly significant in addressing the 2008 global financial crisis, with British Prime Minister Gordon Brown playing a leading role.

Davos Man

[One who has] little need for national loyalty, views national boundaries as obstacles that thankfully are vanishing, and sees national governments as residues from the past whose only useful function is to facilitate the élite's global operations.

Samuel P. Huntington (1928–2007; influential US political scientist,) in *The National Interest* (2004)

Another high-profile and controversial organization is the World Economic Forum, a Swiss foundation based in Geneva and best known for its annual summits in Davos, a ski resort in the eastern Alps. Here the world's economic elite, comprising business leaders, politicians, intellectuals and journalists, exchange ideas on business, the world economy and other social issues. Its meetings often occasion violent demonstrations from anti-capitalist and anti-globalization campaigners.

Non-governmental organizations (NGOs)

However, economic associations do not entirely dominate the global landscape. There are several hundred international non-governmental organizations (NGOs), the most rapid growth having taken place since the early 1970s (Held 1989: 196). Charities and pressure groups such as Save the Children, the Red Cross and Oxfam organize internationally to mitigate the social effects of governments and profit-hungry companies.

Globalized Violence

Violence has from the earliest times been central to globalization. Britain's economic empire was founded by military means; not only were the colonies themselves captured by force, European rivals fought fierce battles over them. Britain established military bases throughout the world to defend its empire and trade routes. Today, countries and terrorist organizations have the capability to unleash awesome destructive power across vast distances at the touch of a button or the click of a mouse.

Militarism. . . is one of the chief bulwarks of capitalism, and the day that militarism is undermined, capitalism will fail. Helen Keller (1880–1968; blind and deaf US writer and lecturer), *The Story of My Life* (1947)

Arms bazaar

Militarism is an important stimulant to the global economy; the arms trade ships the merchandise of violence from the developed world, sometimes into the hands of dictators and megalomaniacs. The quest for profit can make light of arms embargoes, the 1992 arms-for-Iraq scandal revealing the extent of official involvement. Britain has always been a major arms producer, hosting glitzy arms fairs where manufacturers show off their wares, often in the delicate hands of super-models, and with enticing displays, rather like an ideal-homes exhibition. Although New Labour promised an 'ethical foreign policy', an Oxfam report of 1998 found business to be very much as usual, with a secret trade worth some £660 million to over a hundred countries, many with citizens in abject poverty. Refuting claims that few British companies were involved, the report listed 120, all encouraged with tax-payers' money in the form of export credit guarantees.

Military associations

Not only does militarism drive the process of globalization, it has itself become globalized, with an expanding network of military ties embracing a single geostrategic space. The Western European Union (WEU), a joint defence association of Britain, France and the Benelux states, emerged from the Brussels Treaty of 1948, but before the ink was dry it was superseded as Western Europe allied with the USA to form the North Atlantic Treaty Organization (NATO) in 1949, after the Russian blockade of Berlin. The USA was to be the biggest contributor to the NATO budget and, with its vast armoury, offered the protection of a 'nuclear umbrella'. In mirror image, the communist bloc allied under the banner of the Warsaw Pact.

The end of the cold war (see below) cast doubts over NATO's future but a defining moment was reached in the 1991 Gulf war. This showed that 'mid-intensity conflicts' could flare up at any time and provided a rationale for continuing strategic alliances (see K1are 1992); a November 1991 summit erected a 'business as usual' sign. Some eastern bloc countries were keen to join and by 2009 the association's twenty-eight members included the Czech Republic, Hungary, Poland, Bulgaria, Estonia, Latvia, Lithuania, Romania, Slovakia, Slovenia, Albania and Croatia. In addition, fears of instability in Eastern Europe saw a revival of the WEU (relaunched in Rome in 1984 in response to the US 'Star Wars' programme). The 1992 Maastricht Treaty made it central to the common foreign and security policy pillar of the EU.

A world at war

Nothing could better symbolize the reality of military globalization than the twentieth century, an age of violent struggle that could accurately be termed world war. In the 1914–18 conflict the imperial possessions were quickly drawn in and hostilities spread to Africa and the Middle East. The concept of the battlefield was extended to engulf continents and civil populations. The second world war, with its unprecedented impact on civilian populations, became even more global in its reach, with only Latin America and southern Africa escaping. And far from ending global conflict, the cessation of hostilities signalled the opening of a new era of tension – the **cold war** between East and West.

War in a cold climate

From Stettin in the Baltic to Trieste in the Adriatic an Iron Curtain has descended upon the Continent.
Winston Churchill, public speech, Fulton, Missouri (March 1946)

Although the term was coined in America, the cold war grew from early British warnings of the Soviet threat. A bipolar global divide entailing tense psychology, it was directly related to the world economy, being a clash of economic ideologies. In this bizarre confrontation the capitalist and communist blocs on either side of the **Iron Curtain** each acted as if at war (manufacturing weapons and conducting espionage and economic and political subversion), while generally avoiding actual combat.

For capitalist interests, the cold war had the advantage of keeping populations permanently hostile to left-wing policies. 'Reds under the beds' scares were fanned by the media, the hysteria reaching epic proportions in the USA with the medieval-style witch-hunts of McCarthyism that pilloried prominent figures for left-wing sympathies and sometimes hounded them from the country. In Britain, the climate helped the Conservatives maintain their badge as the party of patriotism. When Labour adopted an anti-nuclear stance it proved electorally suicidal. An entrenched feature was arms manufacture, insistently demanding resources and exerting a heavy economic toll on both blocs. In the communist bloc, citizens were subject to harsh totalitarian state regimes.

The chill was also felt in the supposedly **non-aligned world**, with the USA bolstering up a motley collection of oppressive anti-socialist regimes (including the Taliban in Afghanistan) in accordance with a 'domino theory'. An anti-communist war was fought in Korea, the democratically elected socialist government of Chile was brought down by an American-backed insurrection, and the fatal involvement in Vietnam dragged on inconclusively to ignominious withdrawal.

British governments of all shades maintained full commitment to the cold-war spirit. It was Labour Prime Minister Clement Attlee who agreed to an independent nuclear deterrent despite the US 'nuclear umbrella'.

Our scientific power has outrun our spiritual power. We have guided missiles and misguided men.
Martin Luther King (assassinated 1968; US civil rights campaigner), *Strength to Love* (1963)

The thaw

In the 1980s, the unthinkable began to happen as the accession of Mikhail Gorbachev in the USSR began a process of **détente**. His programme of reform (*perestroika* and *glasnost*) set off reverberations throughout the eastern bloc and a permanent thaw set in as one by one hard-line Stalinist regimes were popularly rejected. On 9 November 1989, with profound symbolism, the Berlin Wall dividing the city between East and West began to crumble, physically dismantled by the ordinary people who had lived in its shadow. This unexpected end to the cold war appeared to mean victory for the West.

From cold war to hot peace

Yet there was a paradox: although few could mourn the passing of a tense era, the **new world order** brought new uncertainties. Disillusion with the free market in former communist countries saw them react variously: in some, old leaders returned to favour; in others, communism was replaced not by liberalism but by rampant nationalism, territorial conflict, civil war, religious fundamentalism and the fascistic horrors of ethnic cleansing. Moreover, the Russian bear remained a mighty military force, while the dragon of China promised to become a new superpower. Bipolarity had given way to **multipolarity**, with potential flashpoints that could be ignited by unbalanced dictators. Many leaders of developing states were keen to acquire weapons and economic growth had done little to remove provocative disparities of wealth. Moreover, in the new era fear of war between nations was supplemented by fear of individually driven religious fanaticism threatening acts of terrorism.

Global terror: the day the world changed

On the morning of 11 September 2001, three US airliners, hijacked by Islamist terrorists, swooped from the sky into the twin towers of New York's World Trade Center and the heart of the US defence establishment, the Pentagon (a fourth crashed before reaching its target in Washington, DC). Close to 3,000 died. Some saw this as the day the USA, previously considered impregnable, entered the real world. For others it was variously the ripening of a harvest sown by years of violent US foreign policy, an act of religious extremism or a result of global fragmentation into rich and poor worlds. The outrage united the Americans with Western Europe, Eastern Europe and much of the Islamic world. The attack was masterminded by Osama bin Laden, believed to be operating his worldwide al-Qaeda terrorist network from the unsignposted caves of Afghanistan. The event revealed an unsuspected inability of highly developed states to protect both the vast achievements of their culture and the lives of their citizens. The year 2001 was to see more deaths from terrorism than any before.

President Bush declared a 'war on terror', but this was a war with no clearly defined enemy or strategy. The rhetoric of war was soon to give way to its reality. Early attention focused on Afghanistan which, under the fundamentalist Taliban regime, was believed to be providing a safe haven for al-Qaeda. Led mainly by the USA and Britain but supported by other NATO forces, military operations began in October 2001 with the objective of regime change. Despite some protests, there was much sympathy for the action, which was supported by the UN. However, it was to be almost ten years before bin Laden was discovered, not in Afghanistan but in Pakistan (in May 2011), where he was summarily killed rather than captured and tried. Despite this, the ill-focused action in Afghanistan continued.

Buoyed by general approval of the Afghanistan adventure attention turned to Iraq, but this was to be a different story. The US-led invasion in March 2003 was initially justified on the grounds that President Saddam Hussain possessed weapons of mass destruction and posed an imminent threat to his neighbours and the rest of the world. Prime Minister Tony Blair made an impassioned speech in the Commons in which he appeared to convince MPs that the country was indeed in imminent danger.

> This is not the time to falter. This is the time for this house, not just this government or indeed this prime minister, but for this house to give a lead, to show that we will stand up for what we know to be right, to show that we will confront the tyrannies and dictatorships and terrorists who put our way of life at risk. (Tony Blair, speech to the Commons in the Iraq debate, 18 March 2003)

While the military might of the USA secured a relatively easy victory, with Saddam captured in December 2003, the aftermath was to prove tragic. Sunni and Shia Iraqis fought a violent civil war with suicide bombings, kidnappings and assassinations, while al-Qaeda found in the unsettled country a convenient place to conduct business. Criticism abounded from many quarters, suggesting variously that Bush had intended to invade even before 9/11, that oil was at the heart of the action and that Tony Blair had lied to the House of Commons. Few would argue that the invasion had made the world a safer place.

We believe that military intervention would be the worse solution.
Dominique de Villepin (French Foreign Minister), speaking in the Iraq debate in the UN (20 Jan. 2003)

A clash of civilizations?

In the final decade of the twentieth century, Samuel Huntington (1996) saw a conflict deeper than that between nations and territories; it was between civilizations or civilizational identities. More enduring than the divides of the cold war, these identities were distinguished by ethnicity, religion and moral codes. The western identity, grounded in a pattern of thought emanating from the Ancient Greeks, included Christianity and liberalism. Beyond this were the Chinese identity (reflecting Confucian values), the Hindu, Latin American, Slavic orthodox, African and finally the Islamic. The power of such identities is demonstrated in the rise of forms of fundamentalism which, based on faith rather than reason and understanding, transcends national boundaries, divides nations and challenges capitalism's most cherished assumptions. Such faith offers moral certainties in a relativistic world and cannot compromise.

This is a world in which a suicidal pilot, car driver, tube passenger or a woman passing through customs with a suitcase of anthrax can be as menacing as a guided missile. Instability is increased by an underground global economy of laundered money, drugs trading and government corruption. The implications of these developments are not only that citizens live in uncertainty and fear, but that their governments will take measures, ostensibly to safeguard against terrorism, that will erode traditional freedoms. These can include imprisonment without trial, invasive forms of surveillance and the monitoring of internet communications. In post-9/11 Britain, governments found themselves at loggerheads with the human rights lobby on various fronts.

The Arab East still sees the West as a natural enemy . . . any hostile action – be it political, military or based on oil – is considered no more than legitimate vengeance.
Amin Maalouf (Lebanese novelist), The Crusades through Eastern Eyes (2001)

Globalized Governance: the Missing Dimension?

The mixtures of the modern world are marked 'highly inflammable'. Although driven by economics, globalization is political and a form of world politics has evolved in arenas formed around issue areas, policy sectors and geographical regions. States, intergovernmental associations, bureaucracies, TNCs and international NGOs are locked in a complex process of negotiation, bargaining, brinksmanship and sometimes violence. Although a world of politics, this is not a world of government. There is no overarching authority to exercise control. Yet at the same time the power and authority of the traditional state is seriously weakened.

Who governs?

While state authority is weakened, other institutions emerge to fill a governance vacuum. So great is the might of the TNCs, they have from the mid-1970s transformed international relations (Hobsbawm 1995: 403). Virtually units of governance, governments must negotiate with them much as they conduct diplomacy with other states. Many are indeed richer than states: of the world's hundred largest economies, over fifty are companies rather than countries.

The economic associations provide further units of virtual governance. Conflict between the duty of states to protect citizens and the demands of the Washington Consensus make the WTO an important political cockpit. Thousands of meetings take place each year with armies of corporate lobbyists dominating its numerous technical committees. Trade ministers assemble every two years at high-profile WTO 'Ministerials'. Additional settings are the annual World Economic Forum in Davos and the EU summits two or three times a year.

Not surprisingly, NGOs pursuing political goals such as child welfare, food aid, environmentalism, human rights and anti-capitalism often bypass state governments to set their sights on the TNCs and economic organizations.

Hegemonic rule

For Bush and Blair to go into Iraq together was like a bunch of white vigilantes going into Brixton to stop drug dealing. . . . they are not credible people to deal with it.
Tom Wright (Bishop of Durham), quoted in the *Guardian* (30 Dec. 2003)

Another way in which the power vacuum at global level may be filled is through the dominance, or hegemony, of one single state. This may be seen as a source of stability and preferable to global anarchy. Britain was such a hegemon during the eighteenth and nineteenth centuries but its position was fatally undermined by economic rivalry and two great European wars. After the collapse of the Soviet empire one country stood out, with vastly superior economic and military power over the rest. In the neoliberal climate the USA was to occupy a position of unparalleled dominance. Indeed, for some commentators, the term 'globalization' should be replaced with 'Americanization'. Even in the bipolar days, US influence in the West was enormous, the Bretton Woods system reflecting a US vision of a liberal world. Much US Washington Consensus rhetoric speaks of a new world order and of the need to maintain stability, peace and freedom. However, for critics, the economic consequences of the unfettered market can include inequality and instability.

When the USA intervenes in the politics of other states, ostensibly to protect free markets, liberty and human rights, critics see the actions as mainly promoting US interests. US policy towards the Arab–Israeli conflict has created profound doubt that any single nation can successfully police the world. Critics fear bullying. An opinion poll for the *Guardian* (3 Nov. 2006) revealed that 75 per cent of a sample of UK citizens saw George W. Bush as a greater threat to world peace than North Korean leader Kim Jong-il and Iranian president Mahmoud Ahmadinejad.

Clearly global governance by the economically powerful does not mean global stability or democracy. The system remains one of potential anarchy, containing enormous risks and justifying the call for an overarching political authority – a world polity with a world government (Gray 1998; Monbiot 2002). Despite seeing their independence eroded, states have jealously sought to protect their autonomy, or some illusion of it. Yet notwithstanding the problems, there has been one serious step along the road to a world authority: the United Nations Organization.

Uniting the nations

The precursor of the United Nations was the League of Nations, established after the first world war through the 1919 Treaty of Versailles. Here was a forum where diplomats could upstage the generals. However, the enterprise collapsed into the tragedy of the second world war and the UN was a second attempt to pick up the pieces. In 1941, Britain and the USA had signed an Atlantic Charter and the following year twenty-nine other countries signed an agreement (the Declaration of United Nations) to work together to defeat Germany, Japan and Italy. At the Yalta conference in February 1945 it was agreed that a permanent organization for world peace would be established. Membership has continued to grow, reaching 192 by 2007.

The United Nations

With its headquarters in New York, the main UN institutions are:

- *The Security Council*: comprising the five permanent founder members (Britain, France, the USA, Russia and China) and ten others serving two-year terms. Members can veto decisions, often inhibiting action.
- *The General Assembly*: the main forum containing delegations from all member states. Each has one vote regardless of size, giving a prominence to weak countries not always welcomed by the strong. It meets regularly and may be summoned in emergencies (e.g. the Suez Crisis, the Cuban Missile Crisis, the Gulf war, 9/11).
- *The Secretariat*: a 4,000-strong bureaucracy servicing the assembly, drawn from all states and headed by a secretary general, whose role includes monitoring world events and negotiating with disputants. The holder invariably becomes a world figure. In Jan 2007 Ban Ki-moon of South Korea replaced Kofi Annan of Ghana.
- *The International Court of Justice*: located at The Hague and presided over by judges (serving limited terms) from member countries, to uphold international law.
- *Specialized organizations*: fulfilling a large range of social and cultural functions. This extensive network of specialized and largely autonomous agencies includes UNICEF (children), WHO (health) and UNESCO (education).

The UN is an international association but not a world government; it neither passes laws nor imposes taxes. Member states retain full sovereignty and can withhold contributions (the USA has been a major offender). During the 1980s it came close to bankruptcy and in 1992 Secretary General Boutros Boutros-Ghali talked of organizational paralysis. By 1995, member states owed $2.6 billion.

Although it sends peacekeeping forces to trouble-spots, the UN's essential purpose is dialogue, the value of its resolutions lying mainly in influencing opinion. Generally countries are loath to accept restrictions: Israel has ignored UN resolutions in its conflict with Palestine, as did Iraq over the inspection of its weapons. In early 1982 Argentina invaded the Falklands (or Malvinas), seeking to repossess the islands, one of the few tiny jewels remaining in the British imperial crown. As Britain's task force set sail, the UN Secretary General shuttled between London and Buenos Aires, seeking a diplomatic solution. However, the controversial sinking of the Argentinian warship the *General Belgrano* put paid to such hopes. British troops landed on the islands and, amidst orgasms of jingoism in the English press, quickly secured an Argentinian surrender.

It was not in conformity with the UN Charter. ...from the Charter point of view, it was illegal.

UN Secretary General Kofi Annan on the invasion of Iraq, quoted in the *Guardian* (16 Sept. 2004)

While the post-9/11 action against the Taliban in Afghanistan enjoyed UN support, the US-led invasion of Iraq in 2003 did not, taking place without a UN resolution. In 2013, the Security Council was split over the situation in Syria, with Russia and China supporting the Assad regime, while the USA, the UK and France argued that they could take military action without a UN resolution under the doctrine of 'humanitarian intervention'. But for critics this would seriously undermine the UN's authority.

The end of the cold war coincided with a revival of chauvinistic nationalism and terrorism. Increasingly UN forces have found themselves in dangerous intra-state, ethnic, tribal and religious conflicts (as in Bosnia and Rwanda) but, with confusion over their role, leaving the organization largely ineffective. With no resources of its own and no power of independent action, perhaps the best that could be said for the UN was that it survived the twentieth century (Hobsbawm 1995: 430). In the twenty-first it faced the challenge of reforming its structure, culture and decision-making processes to cope with the post-cold-war world.

The permanent membership of Security Council still comprises the victors of the second world war. This is now outdated in geopolitical terms and there are calls for the inclusion of Asian, South American and African countries. There is also a case for removing the power of veto to enable more positive action and less compromise and prevarication. The UN bureaucracy does not escape censure either, being accused of inefficiency and corruption. There is also a need for attitudinal changes. Central to success is international respect. This cannot be achieved when powerful nations ignore its resolutions.

Britain and the World: Three Spheres of Influence

There are other groupings and relationships in the world, encompassing regions rather than the entire globe. Britain, historically an outward-looking state, has developed its world location in terms of three spheres: the empire, a so-called 'special relationship' with the USA, and mainland Europe.

Retreating from empire: the Commonwealth of Nations

Seriously weakened by the second world war, Britain's empire imposed unrealistic burdens on the 'mother country' and could not be sustained. A process of retreat was painfully negotiated, virtually completed in 1967 when troops withdrew from east of Suez. The bitter pill of vanishing splendour was sugared by the idea of the British Commonwealth, an echo of empire. Initially consisting of the 'white' dominions of Canada, Australia, South Africa and New Zealand, these were joined from 1945 by the 'New Commonwealth' countries in Asia, Africa and the West Indies. No longer an imperial layer of governance, the Commonwealth today is a loose family of fifty-four nations with no formal rules, treaty or constitution. Not all ex-colonies have chosen to be members. Although many are republics, all unite under Queen Elizabeth II rather than her government and 'British' has been dropped from its title. The Queen's position is purely symbolic although she stands as the head of state of sixteen members. The others have their own heads of state and some are monarchies. Each state remains sovereign, with the right to secede (as did South Africa, Pakistan and the Republic of Ireland). Countries can be suspended, as happened to Zimbabwe under Robert Mugabe in 2002. (The country subsequently withdrew from membership.) France, under the leadership of Prime Minister Guy Mollet, secretly considered the possibility of Commonwealth membership in the 1950s.

A London-based Secretariat handles day-to-day administration and its executive head is the secretary general. Kamalesh Sharma, an Indian diplomat, took up the position in 2008. The flags of the member states can be seen flying in Horse Guards Parade, next to the Foreign and Commonwealth Office. Heads of Government Meetings, jamborees where leaders come together to discuss major policy over several days, take place every two years.

The Commonwealth embraces a wider cultural, political and economic range than most other groupings, giving it potential as a force for cooperation and understanding. With a membership including four with advanced economies, economic development, democratization and the alleviation of poverty are among its central concerns. In terms of economics, the empire had been an enormous

I have not become the King's First Minister in order to preside over the liquidation of the British Empire.
Winston Churchill, speech at Lord Mayor's Banquet (10 Nov. 1942)

trading bloc and the early Commonwealth preserved these links with a system of 'Commonwealth Preferences'. Although these were eroded by world markets and EU membership, echoes remain, with consumers in Commonwealth countries preferring goods from other members. In addition, the Lomé Convention preserved certain preferential access rights of Commonwealth goods to Britain after European Community membership.

The four-year suspension of Nigeria in 1996, and the suspension of Zimbabwe, showed the association as an active force for democracy and human rights. More significantly, the Commonwealth stand against apartheid finally bore fruit when South Africa's first democratic elections in 1994 made Nelson Mandela its heroic president and the country rejoined the Commonwealth. However, the legacy of empire inhibits equality of partnership, Britain often disdaining Commonwealth support when making important foreign policy decisions (Suez, the Falklands, supporting the USA). In 1996, the House of Commons Foreign Affairs Committee called for a more positive approach to the Commonwealth and emphasized its business advantages.

Special relations

One alliance that was to prove central to Britain's relationship with the outside world was based not on treaties but on an understanding. Unlike its relationships with any other country, that with the USA was termed, at least by the British, 'special'. To the political elite it was perhaps more important than the relationships with the Commonwealth and the rest of Western Europe. Although America had spurned British rule in 1776 and a festering legacy of hostility towards the British establishment lingered, cultural links remained. The language that took root in that polyglot society was English and White Anglo-Saxon Protestants (WASPs) formed an elite class. There was also hard necessity. Whether or not the Americans were special relations, they were certainly rich ones. Winston Churchill had worked assiduously to secure US aid and participation in the war and their support was just as necessary in the aftermath. It was no small irony that in working to defeat one rival Britain was obliged to succumb to the hegemony of the other. British economic interests, as well as a continued world role for its political class, were seen to lie in two conditions: maintaining the international trading network for British capital and securing liberal ideology against communism. Hence the cold war was a key circumstance in sustaining the **special relationship**. The USA was the only state with the resources to restore political and economic order to the world, and Britain sought to involve it through the Bretton Woods agreement.

Yet securing US aid was not easy. Initially Americans were loath to support a continuing British empire, seen as a serious trade threat. In addition, with Labour's

You see, Mr President, I have nothing to conceal from you.
Winston Churchill to Franklin Roosevelt, when found dictating a letter stark naked in his White House bedroom in 1941, quoted in *The Economist* (7 Feb. 1998)

1945 election victory they had no desire to finance socialism. However, Foreign Office courtship continued ardently until the British view of the Soviet threat prevailed (Gamble 1990: 108). From July 1948 funds to refurbish West European capitalism as a buttress against communism flowed through the generous Marshall Aid programme, marking 'the *peacetime* assumption of superpower responsibilities by the United States and their *de facto* relinquishment by Britain' (Hennessy 1992: 286). Britain generally supported the USA in its foreign policy and military adventurism, as well as shouldering the burden of a costly world military presence. In return, the USA enabled Britain to retain some semblance of world leadership, not pressing it to dismantle the empire and preserving an international role for sterling. The view of Britain's elite was that, while the USA was rich, the British had the know-how and experience for world leadership. To many US statesmen this was self-delusion.

Waxing and waning during the post-war era (see Louis and Bull 1986), the relationship seemed stronger when their leaders were ideologically congruent. Macmillan courted the Americans adroitly after the Suez crisis but the relationship weakened under Wilson. Thatcher and Reagan were simpatico, both personally and in terms of economic philosophy, but relations between Major and Clinton became strained (not least because Major's government tried to assist Clinton's presidential opponents by unearthing information on his Oxford student days). However, Labour's return to office in May 1997 was greeted warmly by Bill Clinton, who even played a part in Blair's peace efforts in Northern Ireland. The similarities between the two were obvious: young, personable, telegenic leaders of the centre-left, repackaging the neoliberal policies of their predecessors with 'third way' rhetoric.

When the Republican George W. Bush entered the White House in 2001, there was expectation that the relationship would again cool. Bush did not endear himself to the British left, refusing to honour the Kyoto protocol on environmental protection and reneging on the nuclear non-proliferation treaty. However, Blair courted the new president with complete loyalty after the 9/11 terrorist attacks, appearing, in the eyes of some, a roving ambassador for the USA. With impassioned speeches in Congress he was lionized in America and, like Bush, he professed deeply religious views. Ten years later, David Cameron, the leader of the British right, found himself paired with the talisman of the global left, Barack Obama, but he acted promptly to establish his US-friendly credentials. Becoming the first world leader to board Air Force One, the presidential plane, he was soon watching basketball with the President. As the chemical weapons crisis in Syria unfolded in 2013, he and his deputy, Nick Clegg, held talks with their US counterparts. However, the Commons' rejection of an emergency motion to support the USA in military action came as a severe embarrassment, prompting some alarmist critics to proclaim a crisis in the special relationship.

Diplomatic language!
We want you to get up the arse of the White House and stay there.
Instruction from Blair's chief of staff to Christopher Meyer on his appointment as Britain's ambassador to Washington, quoted in *DC Confidential* (2005: 1)

Special relationship: Commons Speaker John Bercow directs US President Barack Obama, under the watchful gaze of Margaret Thatcher

Photo: Catherine Bebbington/parliamentary copyright

Great Britain has lost an Empire and has not yet found a role.
Dean Acheson (US Secretary of State), speech at Military Academy, West Point (5 Dec. 1962)

The idea that Britain can influence US policy may be a delusion. When asked whether Whitehall had ever changed Washington's mind on any issues of substance, Robert Cecil, First Secretary at the British Embassy at Washington during the immediate post-war years, could recall no such occasion (Hennessy 1992: 365). As the US train moved towards an attack on Iraq, Britain appeared merely a passenger with no place on the footplate. For previous leaders, Britain's role had been seen as counselling and sometimes curbing the ambitions of the superpower. In the Suez crisis the USA had counselled against aggression and even in the Falklands war its support was not unreserved. Yet Blair's support for the USA appeared unconditional and came in the face of EU opposition. In May 2002, European Commission President Romano Prodi chided the British government for cherishing the special relationship at the expense of European integration. Economist Will Hutton (2002) saw the relationship giving the USA a wide-ranging domination over Britain, extending beyond the military and political to embrace areas such as finance, academic life, culture, film, music, television and fashion.

Britain and mainland Europe

The third sphere is where much British history since (and even before) 1066 has been enacted. Dynastic intrigues, strategic alliances, imperial struggles and two world wars testify to a European heritage. Yet separated by its defensive moat, Britain's position towards the continent has remained ambiguous. Even the establishment of FIFA to organize international football (in Paris in 1904) met with British hostility. While domination by the global economy and the USA is largely accepted, the idea of sacrificing any sovereignty to the European Union is viewed as a constitutional catastrophe. This increasingly important issue calls for more detailed consideration and is the subject of the next two chapters.

British Politics and Globalization: an End of Sovereignty?

Those questioning the real extent of globalization are able to see a continuing role for modern governments in shaping social and economic policies. However, although the legal and political sovereignty of states is technically unimpaired by globalization, their powers are seriously compromised (Held et al. 1999: 50). More than ever before, governments sit, Canute-like, at the mercy of the global tides. Whether it be the economy, welfare, foreign affairs, law and order, the environment, the very political culture and even the constitution, there are few areas of policy where the power of governments is unconstrained.

The economy

It is the economic system that lies at the heart of all globalization. This reveals a declining ability of governments to manage the national economy. Indeed, the dominant neoliberal doctrine argues for *laissez-faire* policies, leaving the market free to allocate resources. For Britain, the harsh reality of an economy beyond control was marked indelibly in the textbooks as Black Wednesday in September 1992 (see p. 565). The worldwide banking crisis from 2007 underlined the point. Beyond these stark examples lie numerous ways in which domestic economies are subject to global influence. The footloose movements of the multinationals can leave deserts of unemployment, and cheap goods from newly industrializing states can exert downward pressure on wages, as can increased immigration from low-wage economies.

Welfare

The Bretton Woods system was founded upon free trade, but with a sense of social responsibility. With the collapse of the system came the discrediting of Keynesian management of the economy in pursuit of social objectives. The willingness of corporations to seek out favourable tax and employment regimes limits a government's ability to raise the tax upon which welfare programmes depend. The option of single-country socialism is foreclosed (Dunleavy 1993: 144) and IMF bailouts frequently demand welfare cuts.

Foreign affairs

Foreign policy has for long been central to British governments, making the Foreign and Commonwealth Office one of the great departments of state. However, military alliances remove strategic autonomy from governments.

The global context is changing. The world is more complex, more uncertain, and foreign and domestic policy are increasingly linked. Sir Michael Jay (head of British diplomatic service), in the *Guardian* (4 March 2006)

Law and order

Once a largely domestic affair, the creation of a Home Affairs and Justice pillar in the EU gave a global dimension to law-and-order policy. Moreover, illegal immigration, large-scale asylum-seeking, human slavery, drugs trafficking and terrorism take the scope of global influences beyond the EU. The result is a questioning of a range of liberties fought for over centuries as successive home secretaries have sought to toughen up laws, such as those on detaining terrorism suspects.

Policy and morality

The moral right of nations to act in their own immediate interest is called into question by the concatenated nature of globalization. A country cannot justify a right to an energy policy producing acid rain that will harm another. Moreover, problems such as global warming and marine pollution are beyond the scope of any single state to solve. The issue becomes more urgent as developing states, such as China and India, claim a right to western lifestyles. Even the USA was by 2006 coming to accept some need for constraints. Within Britain, the 2011 Energy Act set out a wide range of measures regulating households and companies.

Political culture

British culture itself cannot escape global penetration. The communications revolution has made possible the formation of virtual communities, bearing no relation to state boundaries and spreading attitudes and ideas. Many young people in Britain speak with traces of an accent resulting from their devotion to antipodean soap operas. In the way that lifestyle, dress and aspirations can be influenced, so can political attitudes.

In the same way that a community of football fans can unite across the world to support the same teams, so can political movements exchange ideas, plan strategies and coordinate their activities. At the click of a mouse ideas can be disseminated through social media, leading populations to demand the rights and liberties they discover in other states. The free passage of people between countries also influences political culture. Growing British secularism and attitudes towards women are challenged by communities where faith remains a dominant influence.

The constitution

Although a product of hundreds of years of history, even the British constitution cannot remain immutable before global forces. Elections to the European Parliament could not continue on the first-past-the-post principle when the other partners used proportional representation and the habit spread to the new provincial assemblies. The referendum on the Alternative Vote system, although lost, pointed to a new climate. The incorporation of the ECHR has helped to foster a 'rights culture' and judicial activism has increased. Membership of international associations and of the EU pose questions over the sovereignty of Parliament.

Britain's self image – still a 'sceptred isle'?

Finally, Britain's view of itself is greatly influenced by its global setting. When considered in a world context the most striking feature since the late nineteenth century is that, while remaining amongst the wealthy core of nations, Britain has experienced relative economic and political decline. The search for an explanation from both left and right has attached blame variously to most political, social and economic institutions, but the historical links with the world order are frequently ignored. However, the remarkable overseas expansion of the state and its location at the very epicentre of the developing world economy, while serving capitalist interests, were to bequeath damaging obsessions with free trade and world leadership.

A free trade idée fixe

The commitment to free trade meant that as world conditions changed, Britain's markets were penetrated and many home industries destroyed. At the same time its global orientation saw capital exploring the world for profitable locations, putting the number of British-based multinationals second only to that of the USA. For the domestic economy this meant persistent under-investment (generally about half that of rivals such as the USA, Japan and West Germany) and restricted productivity (Gamble 1990: 17), while more recently the emerging economies of Asia have cut a swathe through world markets.

Folie de grandeur

Although imperialism and free trade made Britain open to the world, this was a world to be dominated and led rather than joined on equal terms. Consequently it has not been easy for the political class to come to terms with the new reality. Although the delusion of grandeur was exposed in the humiliating Suez crisis, a defining moment of the new era, it was not eliminated. As prime minister, Tony Blair took the country into five 'wars': air strikes in Iraq (1998), the Kosovo war (1999), the dispatch of troops to Sierra Leone (2000), the action against the Taliban in Afghanistan (2001) and the invasion of Iraq (Kampfner 2003). In 2007 Parliament voted to renew Britain's nuclear deterrent, the US-built Trident missile system, at an estimated cost of at least £25 billion. A continuing desire to punch beyond the country's weight in the global arena places heavy burdens on the domestic economy.

> **The Suez crisis**
> In July 1956, Colonel Nasser of Egypt, generally suspected of anti-westernism, nationalized the Suez Canal Company. An ill-fated military action ensued with the intention of toppling him. It was based on the bogus pretext of separating the warring factions in the Arab–Israeli conflict, the Israelis advancing upon the canal with RAF cover. The disclosure of the true facts produced world outrage. The greatest humiliation was the USA's chilly response. Not only did the 'special relation' openly disapprove, it refused to intervene to halt a run on sterling until an ignominious withdrawal was effected.

I am not an Athenian or a Greek, but a citizen of the world.
Socrates (470–399 BC; Greek philosopher), in Plutarch, *Of Banishment*

However, this *folie de grandeur* could serve the political class, gilding the Establishment with status in the eyes of citizens. Thus, when the Falklands war allowed the decrepit lion again to yawn its arthritic jaws, the government, amidst triumphalism and jingoism, was able to surmount previous unpopularity.

* * *

The essential message of this chapter is that the globalization process is a reality no country can escape or master; territorial boundaries and government authority continue to dissolve before a battery of economic, social and technological forces.

The British polity has been conditioned by this world context to a greater extent than most. Today, perhaps the most significant of these groupings is the European Union, membership of which continues as a burning controversy within the political class. It is the subject of the next two chapters.

Key points

- Globalization is the intensification of worldwide linkages so that local events are influenced by things occurring thousands of miles away.

- Domestic politics can no longer be seen as an autonomous activity.

- Britain, with an early lead in industrialization, played a crucial role in developing a world economy based on free trade.

- Globalization exposes uneven development, with exploitative relationships between richer and poorer countries.

- Globalization can result in cultural clashes between civilizations, leading to violence and terrorism.

- Rich transnational corporations operate within the global space, wielding power over governments.

- Within the global system there is no world authority; states are generally loath to give up legal sovereignty.

- Britain's approach to its world relationships has been a factor in explaining its relative decline.

Review your understanding of the following terms and concepts

bipolarity	free trade	national autonomy
Bretton Woods system	globalization	neo-colonialism
colonialism	imperialism	New World Order
comparative advantage	international association	non-aligned world
exchange rate	Iron Curtain	special relationship
exogenous and endogenous	mercantilism	transnational corporation
	multipolarity	

Questions for discussion and debate

Consider these propositions and be prepared to present the cases for and against. Try to produce debating propositions of your own. Some of these issues may be easier to consider when further chapters have been studied.

1 An exogenous perspective is essential for a full understanding of contemporary British politics.

2 The impact of globalization on British politics can be overstated.

3 Britain is open to the world, yet politically insular.

4 The relationship between states today is neo-colonialism.

5 The 'special relationship' gives Britain enhanced global status.

6 9/11 had far-reaching implications for British politics.

7 Britain's relative post-war decline is a result of delusions of grandeur.

8 The end of the cold war has not seen the removal of threats to Britain.

9 The nation-state still has a central role in modern politics.

10 National sovereignty is a delusion in today's world.

Further reading

Axford, B (1995) *The Global System: Economics, Politics and Culture*.
Stresses how globalization takes place along various dimensions, including that of culture.

Bauman, Z. (2000) *Community: Seeking Security in an Insecure World*.
Argues that globalization reduces security and freedom.

Bronstein, J. and Harris, A. (2012) *Empire, State, and Society: Britain since 1830*.
Analysis of Britain's transformation from global superpower to its position in the twenty-first century.

Callaghan, J. (1997) *Great Power Complex*.
Shows how ideas of supremacy within Britain's elites led to costly attempts to maintain a world role in the post-war era.

Chomsky, N. (1997) *World Orders, Old and New.*
Critique of the 'new world order', as ingenious 'historical engineering' whereby old pretexts for cold war have been replaced by new.

Deane, P. (1963) *The First Industrial Revolution.*
Detailed account of the industrial revolution in Britain. Critical of the minimal role played by the government.

George, S. (1991) *The Debt Boomerang.*
Critique of World Bank and IMF policies, which accelerate deforestation, mass migration, the drugs trade, third-world debt and global instability.

Gray, J. (1999) *False Dawn: The Delusions of Global Capitalism.*
Critique of unregulated global capitalism by leading thinker who discarded earlier free-market advocacy.

Hale, T. and Held, D. (2011) *Handbook of Transnational Governance: Institutions and Innovations.*
Notes how globalization creates new centres of power and forms of transnational governance beyond the nation-states.

Held, D. and Kaya, A. (eds) (2006) *Global Inequality: Patterns and Explanations.*
Notes major trends and patterns in global inequality and its implications for global governance.

Held, D. and McGrew, A. (2007) *Globalization Theory: Approaches and Controversies.*
Explains leading theoretical approaches to the study of globalization and considers prescriptions for the future.

Hennessy, P. (1992) *Never Again: Britain 1945–1951.*
Rich account of British politics in a crucial stage of reappraising its world position.

Hertz, N. (2002) *The Silent Takeover: Global Capitalism and the Death of Democracy.*
Argues persuasively that transnational corporations are threatening the very basis of our democracy.

Hirst, P. and Thompson, G. (1996) *Globalization in Question.*
Argues against the more extreme versions of the globalization thesis.

Hobsbawm, E. (1995) *Age of Extremes.*
Marxist perspective on the evolving world economy.

Hutton, W. (2002) *The World We're In.*
Sequel to *The State We're In*, argues that Britain has more in common with Europe than the USA and should place less importance on the 'special relationship'.

Jacques, M. (2009) *When China Rules the World.*
Prophesies that the economic rise of China will transform, and dominate, the world in the way that first Britain and then the USA did.

MacGillivray, A. (2006) *A Brief History of Globalization.*
A lively read which gives an historical context to the process of globalization.

Stiglitz, J. (2002) *Globalization and its Discontents.*
Stinging critique of the IMF by Nobel Prize winner and one-time chief economist at the World Bank.

Weiss, T. G. and Urquhart, B. (2012) *What's Wrong with the United Nations and How to Fix it*, 2nd edn.
Detailed analysis argues that today's UN is ill equipped to deal with contemporary challenges and suggests reforms.

For reading around the subject and some light relief

Globalization stimulates considerable thought, much of it sceptical.

Sharon Beder, *Suiting Themselves: How Corporations Drive the Global Agenda.*
Argues that an international corporate elite dictate global politics for their own benefit.

Tom Clancy, *Debt of Honour.*
Thriller set within the international economy. Political intrigue and military threat in the context of trade conflict between the USA and Japan.

Ben Elton, *Stark.*
Surreal novel about global capitalist power.

Franklin Foer, *How Soccer Explains the World: An Unlikely Theory of Globalization.*
Football is seen as the medium for explaining the effects globalization has on society as a whole.

A Fistful of Dollars.
Sergio Leone Film which broke the mould for the American western. Depicting corrupt capitalism, culture clashes, fake branding, labour exploitation and dubious multinationals. Starring Clint Eastwood.

Naomi Klein, *No Logo.*
Globalization as branded capitalism.

Christopher Meyer, *DC Confidential.*
Entertaining and alarming exposé of the human side of the special
relationship by Britain's one-time ambassador to Washington.

V. S. Naipaul, *Among the Believers: An Islamic Journey.*
The journey is through a number of Islamic countries, noting tensions
between globalization and tradition.

John Pilger, *The New Rulers of the World.*
Exposé of the secrets that lie behind corporate and state power by a radical
journalist committed to getting behind the propaganda.

Peter Preston, *51st State.*
Former *Guardian* editor imagines Britain as the 51st State of the US.
Uncomfortably feasible.

G. Ritzer, *The McDonaldization of Society.*
Globalization as Americanization.

John Ralston Saul, *The Collapse of Globalism.*
Readable challenge to the conventional wisdom on the irresistible rise of
globalization.

On the net

https://www.gov.uk/government/organisations/foreign-commonwealth-office
https://www.gov.uk/government/organisations/department-for-international-
development
The Foreign Office and the Department for International Development sites
include a wide range of information on foreign policy and current international
issues, together with links to related organizations.

www.newint.org
The *New Internationalist* site deals with issues of world poverty and inequality,
and the relationship between rich and poor nations. Also includes a
comprehensive guide to relevant organizations and resources.

http://wdm.org.uk
The World Development Movement is just one of many organizations
campaigning for justice for the world's poor.

http://www.un.org
For a truly international flavour, try the United Nations site.

http://www.makepovertyhistory.org
Make Poverty History is a campaign to relieve world poverty and suffering, with organizations existing in many countries. It highlights what are seen as inequities in the global economy.

CHAPTER 6

BRITAIN AND EUROPE: AWKWARD PARTNERS?

Contents

One aspect of Britain's international setting is of particular and increasing importance – its membership of the European Union. This has wide-ranging and often controversial implications for domestic politics. In this chapter we begin by examining the association's origins and the protracted process of Britain's entry. Beyond this we focus on certain important aspects of the process of EU evolution, noting the key landmarks through its various treaties. Finally we address some of the central areas of debate, including the concept of a single currency, the development of a social dimension, enlargement, and the question of national sovereignty.

We are part of the community of Europe and we must do our duty as such.
Marquis of Salisbury (1830–1903; Conservative statesman), speech (11 April 1888)

Notwithstanding the legacy of the British Empire, the special relationship with the USA and a long history of European rivalry and warfare, Britain remains an offshore island of Western Europe, sharing much of its history and culture. Geographical logic has exerted an inexorable pressure towards integration, which became more compelling during the post-war era. Of all Britain's relationships none has generated more internal political heat than that with what was to become the European Union (EU) – an association of twenty-eight member states by 2013. As will be seen throughout this book, EU membership sends ripples throughout the political system (see Bache and Jordan 2008). No other association penetrates so deeply into the state and the lives of its citizens. While other groupings between nations are international, the EU is supranational. Members are expected to submerge national sovereignty beneath a superior power in a form of federalism.

The British Entry Process

The origins of a West European integrationist movement lay partly in the economic need to repair the devastation wrought by the second world war but also with an ambition to end a history of destructive conflict that had brought the continent to its knees. During the second world war these thoughts occupied the minds of thinkers and statesmen. Winston Churchill had enthused over the idea of a United States of Europe, envisaging the Great Powers accepting government through a joint council backed by a court and an army. However, the moves to establish a Council of Europe exposed a fundamental difference between Britain and its continental neighbours.

As developments proceeded, Britain began a kind of square dance with the continent: advancing, pausing before the promised embrace, only to turn aside to another partner, the USA or the Commonwealth. An early move came in 1948 with the Brussels Treaty, aiming to promote collective defence, and in 1949 a Council of Europe was formed to facilitate wider cooperation. Perhaps its greatest achievement was the European Convention on Human Rights, intended to outlaw fascistic tendencies (see p. 99). British lawyers played a leading role in this but, although ratifying the Convention, Britain declined to incorporate it into domestic law. Another important development in 1948 came when sixteen West European countries established an Organisation for European Economic Cooperation (OEEC – later the Organisation for European Co-operation and Development (OECD)) to coordinate post-war recovery and administer the US Marshall Aid programme. However, hopes that it might develop into a permanent supranational institution were dashed by British and Scandinavian opposition. Even so, the **federalist** movement gathered pace. A key mover was the French economist and international administrator Jean Monnet. Even as war raged, he was warning that a post-war reconstruction reflecting nationalistic pride and protectionism would never guarantee peace.

A major event came in 1951 with the establishment of the European Coal and Steel Community (ECSC). Monnet's reasoning was that cooperation in key functional areas of production would render war impossible. This was a functionalist rather than a federalist approach to integration, but the one could lead to the other through a 'spillover' effect if more functions were combined. Yet as Italy, France, West Germany and the Benelux (Belgium, the Netherlands and Luxembourg) countries joined the dance, the UK again chose to remain a wallflower. Wishing to drive things further, Monnet resigned the ECSC presidency in November 1954 to help found an Action Committee for a United States of Europe. This led to the establishment of a European Atomic Energy Community (Euratom) and, rather more significantly, the European Economic Community (EEC) or Common Market, soon to be known as the European Community (EC). Formally the EC was to be a trading bloc with a common external tariff barrier and no internal barriers, but it could also be an embryonic political union.

Based on the ECSC model, the EEC would be headed by a Council of Ministers from member states making decisions on the basis of voting. It would be served by a Commission – a bureaucracy of national civil servants and headed by a team of commissioners appointed by state governments. In addition there was to be an assembly with members nominated by governments from national parliaments, leaving each with a dual mandate.

Unsurprisingly there was to be no British signature on the 1957 Treaty of Rome establishing the EEC. This decision to stay out was intriguing. Why did a state that had captained a huge empire, pioneered the development of the world economy,

The political unity of tomorrow will depend on making the economic union effective in everyday activities. Jean Monnet (1888–1979), Memoirs (1978)

Critics might see as symbolic the fact that the Rome Treaty, signed in 1957, was actually a blank document owing to printing problems in Italy.

been a devoted worshipper at the altar of free trade, taken a prominent role within NATO, with a seat on the UN Security Council and a credible claim to have 'won the war' for the allies, relinquish all claim to a leadership role in this major arena? The reasons may lie in its past success. Despite the ravages of war Britain believed in its world leadership destiny. The political class looked beyond Europe for status on the world stage: to the special relationship with US brawn and to the Commonwealth, with its echoes of empire. Britain had flexed its diplomatic biceps in 1952 by becoming a nuclear power.

However, the economies of the EEC members soon began to prosper and Britain sought an alternative means of economic survival. In 1959 a regional grouping was formed with Britain, Norway, Denmark, Sweden, Switzerland, Austria and Portugal – the European Free Trade Association (EFTA). This was to be merely a trading bloc, without political overtones. Yet EFTA proved no rival to the EEC. Relative to West Germany and France, Britain experienced economic decline, suggesting that the earlier decision had been misguided. Moreover, a cold US response to the Suez crisis revealed that the 'special relationship' did not give Britain political omnipotence and in 1961 Prime Minister Harold Macmillan announced that his government would apply for EEC membership.

Although the USA welcomed the decision, Macmillan moved with characteristic languor. His vision was of economic union, with little place for the political dimension cemented into the foundations of the treaty. Moreover, there was opposition within the Community. French President General de Gaulle, suspicious that Britain would prove a Trojan horse for US influence, vetoed the application. He did the same with a second overture from the Labour government and only after his resignation in 1969 did the application receive a sympathetic hearing. Hence, in 1973, it was Edward Heath, clearer in his European intentions than his predecessors, who took the historic step. Yet British scepticism died hard. Labour had opposed the entry terms and, returning to office in 1974, held a promised referendum on continued membership with renegotiated terms. A 'Yes' vote duly came, with a 65 per cent turnout and a two-thirds majority, on 5 June 1975. However, the debate was by no means over. British statesmen had studiously avoided an explicit statement on the implied loss of national sovereignty (see Young 1998) and the gradual realization of this was to energize a body of **Eurosceptics** and prevent a whole-hearted commitment to the European project.

The Evolving Union

The career of the Community was to prove fitful, with periods of both stagnation (*immobilisme*) and dynamism. A steady process of enlargement had consequences for both structures and processes. The initial decade was dynamic, but was followed by four years of stagnation, beginning with de Gaulle's first UK veto. His retirement permitted further progress; the goal of advancing political union was affirmed at the 1969 Hague Summit and plans were made to coordinate foreign policy. In 1970 the Werner Plan argued for the harmonization of economic, fiscal and budgetary policy and 1979 saw the launch of the European Monetary System (EMS) and democratic elections for the European Parliament.

However, 1979 opened a further phase of tension when a new head of government, as nationalistic as de Gaulle, entered the stage and the UK was to establish its role as the 'awkward partner' (see George 1994). Britain declined to enter the EMS and, echoing her 'No such thing as society' sentiment on the domestic front, Margaret Thatcher was to declare:

> There is no such thing as a separate community interest; the community interest is compounded of the national interests of the ten member states. (Quoted in Urwin 1989: 369)

She began with a campaign to reduce the size of the UK contribution to the Community budget (see p. 187). The goal was not unreasonable; Labour also favoured negotiations. However, the tactics entailed denigrating the Common Agricultural Policy (CAP), regarded by the six original members as their greatest achievement, and Thatcher's style of diplomacy did little to enhance the UK's Euro-credentials.

The Single European Act

Preparations for the accession of Portugal and Spain reinvigorated the integrationist spirit. The Commission, under the presidency of avowed integrationist Jacques Delors, produced a white paper in June 1985, *Completing the Internal Market*. The following year saw the Single European Act, with its commitment to cooperation in foreign policy, strengthened social cohesion mechanisms and a programme for a genuine internal market by 1992, free of the non-tariff trade barriers which had persisted. The target year became a symbol of progress. Although signing the treaty, Thatcher was to pour a douche of cold water on the social dimension in a key speech at Bruges. Yet she did little to dampen the general enthusiasm for faster integration; an Intergovernmental Conference at Rome in December 1990 on Economic and Monetary and Political Union foreshadowed a major advance.

A centralized European government would be a nightmare. We have not rolled back the frontiers of the state at home only to see them re-imposed at a European level.
Margaret Thatcher, speech in Bruges (Sept. 1988)

The Maastricht Treaty: from Community to Union

The previously little-known Dutch town of Maastricht achieved celebrity in February 1992 as the site for the signing of the Treaty on European Union. Its

> **What's in a name?**
> Like the association itself the name has evolved. Initially the European Economic Community (often the 'Common Market'), the Single European Act re-baptized it the European Community, signifying concerns wider than trade. After the Maastricht Treaty the term 'European Union' gained wide currency and, although not strictly correct, was widely used to mean the EC. The Lisbon Treaty brought the three pillars under this title.

61,351 words went further than any other Community agreement in promoting integration. The event assumed additional significance because of its momentous historical conjuncture, including the end of the cold war, German reunification and the collapse of the Soviet empire. The term 'Union' signified that the EC became part of a wider framework of integration, to include foreign and security policy, and justice and home affairs. Yet it did not satisfy all. For true federalists the image would have been of a tree with three branches extending from a common trunk. What emerged was a temple built upon three pillars, combined but essentially separate.

In the common foreign and defence policy, the Western European Union (WEU), the existing joint defence association, was to become central. The justice and home affairs pillar was to see cooperation in various areas previously left within national competence. The pillar design meant that these were to remain outside the competence of the EC legislative and judicial institutions; reflecting cooperation rather than supragovernmentalism. This limitation was one of the proclaimed successes of the British government in the negotiations.

Amongst the treaty's most important features were the following.

- *EC citizenship*. Of both symbolic and practical significance, this allowed all nationals certain rights: to reside and move freely throughout the Community, and to vote and stand in municipal and European Parliament elections.
- *Policy competence*. This was extended to cover aspects of education, culture, public health, industry and consumer protection.
- *The institutions*. Decision-making procedures were made more supranational and the powers of the Parliament and the Court increased.
- *Subsidiarity*. This inelegant neologism established a principle of multi-level governance: EU institutions should act only where the objectives could not be better met at national level.
- *Social policy*. This became known as the Social Chapter protecting various workers' rights. It was opposed by the UK, which was allowed to opt out.
- *Economic integration*. The treaty placed renewed emphasis on the open market economy and monetary union, including the establishment of a single currency (the UK, along with the Danes, also negotiated an opt-out). Economic policy would be subject to qualified majority voting (QMV, see pp. 169–70).

Once signed, the treaty required ratifying by national assemblies and, in some cases, the courts. Stormy scenes in the House of Commons and the behaviour of his Eurosceptic MPs forced John Major to announce a confidence motion for 23 July 1993.

A minor advance also took place in the Netherlands. Sometimes billed as 'son of Maastricht', the 1997 Amsterdam Treaty proved a disappointingly puny child. Monetary union remained the main goal and reforms to voting procedures and the powers of the European Parliament were relatively modest.

The Nice Treaty: accommodating enlargement

The dramatic embrace of twelve further members from ex-communist Eastern Europe posed new problems and the Nice summit of December 2000 was called to approve a new treaty. Proving chaotic and fractious, this broke all records for length, extending the usual two-day schedule to five. In the early dawn of the final day, at 3.25, the weary leaders finally buried their differences over voting procedures and agreed changes to the EU decision-making process. Majority voting (see p. 169) was extended to over thirty new areas. The Blair government trumpeted as a success the retention of the veto in social security, taxation and immigration policy, yet these areas had never really been seriously threatened. The Nice Treaty was, like its Amsterdam predecessor, a compromise securing little more than the bare minimum, and the process was thrown into further disarray when the people of Ireland voted not to ratify it and a second referendum was required to secure their agreement. The entry of the twelve new members in 2004 called for more fundamental change, which was to prove hugely controversial.

The Lisbon Treaty: towards an EU constitution

In October 2004 a treaty was signed in Rome by EU national leaders. With a proclaimed purpose of establishing no less than a Constitution for Europe, it was to reveal popular misgivings when the question was put to citizens in referendums (see Hobolt 2009). Under the three-pillar structure of the EU only the EC had a legal persona, but the proposed constitution would merge the three, giving the EU treaty-making powers in its own name and placing foreign and security policy and justice and home affairs under the EU normal legislative system. Coupled with this would come an entirely new power structure, with a permanent EU president and an EU foreign minister. Supporters insisted that the proposals amounted to little more than a codification of previous treaties but, for critics, the dry text concealed an ambition to transform the EU into a different creature. To Eurosceptics it was a red rag of federalism.

There is not a single thing that we have yielded up that we said that we would not. The British veto is secured.
Tony Blair after the Amsterdam summit, quoted in *The Times* (18 June 1997)

While seventeen member states ratified the treaty, Britain, with scepticism in much of the media, the public and the political parties, prevaricated. It was to be spared embarrassment when the French government put the issue to its citizens who, in May 2005, said 'Non' by 55 to 45 per cent. This was echoed three days later by a decisive 'Nee' by 62 per cent of Dutch voters. The treaty could not be implemented and Britain could declare a referendum unnecessary. However, enthusiasts were not to be deterred. By January 2007, German Chancellor Angela Merkel was actively working to restart the negotiations.

While Germany wanted to salvage as much as possible, the French, under the right-wing Nicolas Sarkozy (who had defeated the socialist Ségolène Royale for the presidency), proposed a slimmed-down constitution and members began to bargain again. Tony Blair called for limits to further extensions of QMV. Germany wanted a change in the voting system which would disadvantage smaller nations (see p. 170). France called for a clear definition of EU borders and an end to entry negotiations with Turkey, Poland and the Czech Republic. The Netherlands wanted a veto over EU legislation for national parliaments. For those favouring the original constitution slimming down was betrayal, but for pragmatists it represented a more realistic model for an enlarged EU.

A fractious meeting at Brussels continued into the small hours, eventually agreeing a sixteen-page draft for a revised treaty. Attendance here was one of Tony Blair's last acts as prime minister. He opposed the replacement of the three-pillar model, arguing that this would put pressure on the government for a referendum, with a high possibility of a 'No' result. Hence the UK was allowed to opt out of cooperation in the areas of freedom, security and justice, and to 'opt in' to decisions on police and justice only where it wished. A national veto was also gained on foreign policy and defence and a protocol was agreed limiting the impact of the Fundamental Charter on Human Rights (see below). Britain also ensured that decisions on social security and tax laws remained subject to unanimous voting. Blair proclaimed a UK triumph but doubts remained over the validity of the foreign policy opt-out. With extensive diplomatic machinery, the EU would be fully capable of conducting collective negotiations regardless of British feelings.

The treaty was finalized following a conference in Lisbon, opening in July 2007. In order to avoid the appearance of a fully fledged constitution the treaty was presented in the form of amendments to the exiting treaties of Rome and Maastricht. The very term 'constitution' was expunged; it would be the Treaty on the Functioning of the Union (or the Reform Treaty). Reference to state-like symbols such as the EU flag and a 'national' anthem (although these exist) were absent. There was no stress on the primacy of EU legislation and a proposal to speak of EU 'laws' had gone into the

Brussels shredder; the traditional terminology of 'regulations', 'directives' and so on would be preserved. The draft also emphasized that the division of power was not set in stone so that, where appropriate, states could reclaim powers from the Union. Although reference was made to the Fundamental Charter on Human Rights, the text itself did not appear.

Yet extensive parts of the original constitution remained, including most of the institutional innovations. The EU would have a single legal persona and a permanent president would serve a two-to-five-year term. The idea of an EU foreign minister was transmogrified into the less provocative 'High Representative of the Union for Foreign Affairs and Security Policy', but it amounted to much the same thing. Although delayed until 2014, double majority voting would also be brought in.

The final stage in the tortuous process was ratification. The French and Dutch experiences left governments with little appetite for referendums and it was argued that, as mere amendments, this could be left to national parliaments. The only hitch was the Irish Republic, where the constitution demanded a referendum. Once again a sceptical public confounded the rest of Europe with a 'No', and further concessions were secured. In the UK, the Labour government was able to resist calls for a referendum on the grounds that its 'red lines' had not been not breached. Yet much of the press and a Eurosceptic Conservative Party remained opposed. For many, federalism had taken another step forward. Even Prime Minister Gordon Brown avoided any sign of excessive enthusiasm, arriving late to the summit and missing the main ceremony to leave an embarrassed Foreign Secretary representing him. The last country to ratify was the Czech Republic in November 2009 and the Treaty of Lisbon entered into force on 1 December that year.

Key Themes in EU Evolution

Within the broadly internationalist development of the EU are certain particular themes around which much controversy was to centre. At its heart lies one of the major political issues of the post-war decades: the question of membership itself. Only the Liberal Democrats express unalloyed enthusiasm and, in the UK Independence Party (UKIP), Britain has a party formed for the express purpose of exiting the Union. Four key aspects of EU evolution include the drive towards monetary union, the idea of a social dimension, the pattern of enlargement and the question of national sovereignty.

The road towards the euro

> **Plus ça change?**
> As long ago as the eighth century, Offa, the ambitious king of Mercia (i.e. England), attempted to take the country into the single European currency created by the emperor Charlemagne. This was the largest currency zone that had existed until the creation of the 'eurozone'.

In the days of empire sterling was a world currency and in the post-war years Britain remained enthusiastic about the Bretton Woods Agreement and preserving a sterling area. Yet paradoxically it had been decidedly cool towards European **economic and monetary union (EMU)**, dropping out of the system known as the Snake in the Tunnel in 1972 after only one year. As prime minister, Margaret Thatcher, against the advice of Chancellor Nigel Lawson, kept Britain out of the **Exchange Rate Mechanism** (ERM, based on fixed exchange rates). She was finally persuaded by John Major but the rate proved too high and the country fell out again on 'Black Wednesday' (16 Sept. 1992), following damaging currency speculation (see pp. 565–6).

> It was the European issue, far more than the poll tax, that brought [Margaret Thatcher] down. Her Commons speech opposing economic and monetary union of August 9, 1990 turned the Europhile wing of the party against her, and persuaded it to destroy her premiership.
>
> Andrew Roberts (historian), 'Margaret Thatcher: My tears for the iron lady' in
> *Daily Telegraph* (21 Nov. 2010)

The historic agreement at Maastricht was to take monetary union beyond the ERM with a **single currency** for all EU states. This would centre upon three institutions:

- a European System of Central Banks (ESCB) responsible for implementing domestic monetary and exchange rate policy and managing foreign reserves;
- a European Central Bank (ECB) under a council comprising the governors of the national central banks, with an exclusive right to issue bank notes;
- a European Investment Bank (EIB) to grant loans to underdeveloped regions.

John Major, heading a fractious and more Eurosceptic party, with many regretting the hasty dispatch of Thatcher, negotiated a derogation from these provisions.

After some initial doubts, what emerged was a multi-track development, with some states moving ahead of others. In May 1998, eleven countries formally adopted the single currency, the prosaically named euro. From January 1999 it was used for cheque and credit transactions, the new notes and coinage entering

Game, set and match for Britain. John Major's reading of his negotiating success at the Maastricht summit.

The financial heart of Europe: the euro sign outside the European Central Bank in Frankfurt

circulation in January 2002. By early 2007 the euro had surpassed the US dollar in terms of the combined value of cash in circulation. By the end of 2012, seventeen EU countries were in the eurozone. Of the remaining ten, Britain and Denmark had negotiated opt-outs, while Sweden and seven newer members from Eastern Europe had yet to meet the conditions for adopting the single currency.

Economic and monetary union: the debate

Monetary union is the linking of currencies to eliminate exchange-rate fluctuations. There are various arguments for a single currency. In the first place it is conducive to free trade, a key feature of the neoliberal agenda. It can also aid tourism, removing the cost of changing currencies and the uncertainty of unfamiliar notes and coins. Most importantly, it reduces opportunities for currency speculation. Arguments against monetary union centre on the loss of national control over financial policies including interest rates and inflation. With structural imbalances within the union, the weaker economies would impose strains upon the stronger. This became all too apparent in the global credit crunch, beginning in 2008.

After a second Labour victory at the polls in 2001 Tony Blair began to sound a more enthusiastic note; the expectation was that the question would be put to the people during that parliament. In opposition, Conservative leader William Hague had adopted Margaret Thatcher's position, fighting the 2001 general election on a platform of 'saving the pound'. He need have had no fear. Chancellor Gordon Brown maintained a cautious 'wait and see' approach, insisting that his enigmatic 'five economic tests' should be met before entry could be considered.

Within Britain feelings remained mixed. Some agreed with the Conservatives' most prominent Europhile, Kenneth Clarke, that within a generation no EU country would have its own currency. Fearing that Britain was once again sacrificing a 'seat at the top table' and risking being sidelined in the global economy, one senior mandarin was to lament: 'we'll be shut outside with our noses pressed to the glass' (*The Economist*, 1 May 1998). Yet despite the presence of the euro-friendly Liberal Democrats, the 2010 coalition government offered little hope to UK Europhiles. Indeed, the circumstances were moving sentiment even further from the single currency.

The global economic and financial crisis and ensuing 'credit crunch' triggered by the September 2008 collapse of US giant Lehman Brothers exposed structural imbalances within the eurozone. While Germany enjoyed a budget surplus, Greece, Italy, Ireland, Portugal and Spain suffered deficits and (Ireland excepted) poor productivity and low growth. Eurozone membership had given the weaker economies better access to low-cost borrowing, fuelling unaffordable levels of spending. Massive sovereign debts left them ill equipped to weather the crisis. Greece, and then Ireland, needed massive bailouts from the IMF and the EU. Strict austerity measures were required, creating suffering and social unrest. A pessimistic view was that the eurozone would break up if the patience of Germany, effectively shouldering the lion's share of the bailout burden, were to finally run out. Commentators began to think the unthinkable, predicting doomsday scenarios.

Yet the Union showed a determination to shore up its ailing economies. It was in many interests to do so. Certainly the indebted countries would not gain from leaving. Even contemplating such a move could see money haemorrhaging and economic disaster. Equally, the wealthier members would not want to push out the weaker for fear of encouraging contagion: a loss of confidence spreading throughout the eurozone in an irresistible domino effect. Moreover, despite everything, business and political elites could recognize that their economies benefited from the euro. Perhaps most significantly, the currency had totemic value and was buoyed up by the political will of EU leaders.

Yet the future remained uncertain, the structural imbalances likely to endure for years. One canvassed solution was the creation of a fiscal union, whereby states would sacrifice taxation, borrowing and spending decisions to the EU institutions and be bound together in complete economic integration. Cash transfers from rich to poor countries would be easy. However, citizens and politicians in the wealthy states could have little appetite for the transfer of sovereignty this would entail. For them the answer lay in economic reforms in the weaker states, with restructuring, productivity increases, improved competitiveness and a general belt-tightening.

The social dimension

The evolution towards a single currency is not the only EU issue bearing upon national economies. Another concerns social policy. The EU cannot have a social policy in the sense that a country does. Not responsible for schools, health care, social services and so on, it is limited to protecting workers within a largely capitalist system – a role with clearly economic implications. Article 118 of the Rome Treaty included provisions for the free movement of workers through equivalence in social security entitlement, educational exchange facilities, working conditions, labour law, vocational training, health and safety at work, rights of association and collective bargaining and equal pay for men and women. It also established a European Social Fund to promote worker mobility and created a framework for a Community vocational training policy.

We haven't worked all these years to free Britain from the paralysis of Socialism only to see it creep in through the back door of . . . Brussels.
Margaret Thatcher, speech to Conservative Party conference (Oct. 1988)

However, this aspect became more central as economies boomed and social costs, including pollution, health and safety-at-work problems and uneven economic development became apparent. World slump from the mid-1970s heightened awareness by not only precipitating unemployment but stimulating a resurgence of New Right thinking that threatened workers' security and conditions. Hence the 1980s saw renewed attempts to strengthen the social dimension with the Single European Act. A key figure was Jacques Delors. Formerly a socialist finance minister in France, his opening speech to the European Parliament as Commission President emphasized a European vision going beyond a gigantic market-place. His programme for the completion of the single market by 1992 included a range of social objectives to mitigate the disruption caused by economic restructuring.

After considerable debate, a Charter on the Fundamental Social Rights of Workers was adopted by the European Council in 1989. There was only one dissenting voice, that of Margaret Thatcher. The UK mood was to carry through to Maastricht, where Major negotiated a special opt-out of the Social Chapter. However, to the satisfaction of the unions, the New Labour government of 1997 signed up to the Charter at the Amsterdam summit, although government spin doctors stressed that there would be no urgency in its implementation. The rights in the Charter were further developed in the Lisbon Treaty. However, the UK government secured a written pledge that it could not be used by the European Court to alter its labour law, or other laws concerning social rights.

Let them have the Social Chapter, we'll have the jobs.
John Major, after the Maastricht summit

The British case against EU social rights legislation owes much to the neoliberal agenda, with its vision of a deregulated labour market with lower wages, making products more competitive and raising profits. There was also an argument based on the subsidiarity principle, social policies falling within that area of administration best left to national governments.

Enlargement

The Union has been subject to a continuous process of enlargement, raising a host of issues. From the original six in 1957, membership had reached twenty-eight by 2013, following eight enlargements. The largest occurred in May 2004, when the former communist states joined, to be followed by Bulgaria and Romania (figure 6.1).

Applicants are attracted by the prospect of access to EU markets, grant aid and a chance to participate in decision-making over trade issues. However, the process can produce losers as well as winners and negotiations can be tortuous (Schneider 2008). Not all countries want to join. Invited twice but, fearful of a Spanish invasion

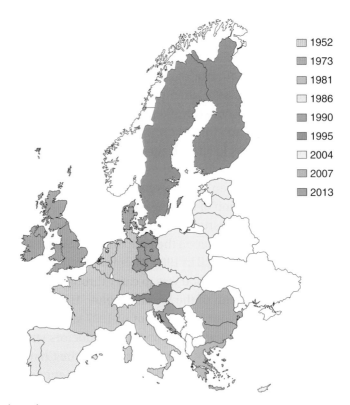

Figure 6.1 The enlarging Union

of their fishing waters, Norway voted 'No' in referendums. The Swiss have also seen their best interests lying outside the EU. Iceland, although a potential applicant, remained opposed to the Common Fisheries Policy.

In order to join, a state must fulfil certain economic and political conditions formalized at the June 1993 Copenhagen summit (the 'Copenhagen criteria'). These include democratic and secular government, the rule of law, an independent judiciary and a guarantee of rights and freedoms to citizens. The first step is to gain official candidate status. After this many issues need to be resolved, since any enlargement must be agreed to by all member states and by the European Parliament.

Despite the large expansion in 2004 there were still countries keen to enter. Croatia and the former Yugoslav Republic of Macedonia were recognized as official candidates. However, controversy over the use of the name Macedonia, and poor relations with Bulgaria, promoted opposition from Greece. Albania, Bosnia and Herzegovina, Montenegro and Serbia are also seen as potential candidates. Particularly controversial is the case of Turkey. Although recognized as an official candidate, major economic and social reforms are required. Some member states see its large Muslim population as a barrier to the secularism requirement. In September 2006 Pope Benedict XVI caused controversy over remarks about Islam and violence. As a cardinal he had spoken of a 'European identity' as something essentially Christian and historically opposed by the Ottoman empire. There is also a geographic factor, since only a small fraction of Turkish territory may be said to lie in Europe. Against this it may be argued that Cyprus (which *is* a member) is an island in the Middle East.

Implications of enlargement

> Europe in anything other than the geographical sense is a wholly artificial construct. It makes no sense at all to lump together Beethoven and Debussy, Voltaire and Burke, Vermeer and Picasso, Notre Dame and St Paul's, boiled beef and bouillabaisse.
>
> Margaret Thatcher, *Statecraft: Strategies for a Changing World* (2002: 328)

Enlargement enhances the political project of reducing the potential for war. In this respect the collapse of the Soviet empire created an historic opportunity. Yet with more members the process of deepening integration becomes more complex. The Lisbon summit sought to address the issues associated with enlargement but was one of the most fractious in EU history. The problems were many and complex. Greater diversity of cultures and economic situations make leadership more difficult. Voting procedures designed for a community of six, particularly the veto principle, become increasingly inappropriate. In an enlarged Union, the number of representatives in its institutions is increased, while the influence of each is reduced.

There is also the question of democracy. Enthusiasts and sceptics alike have agreed that the EU cannot progress without some enhancement of popular accountability and control. A democratic deficit has been apparent within most of the EU institutions (see chapter 7). Enlargement, with the principle of European citizenship, creates issues around immigration. Increased support for UKIP was believed by commentators to reflect popular fears on these issues rather than any desire to actually leave the EU. Finally, human rights issues arise as states with dubious reputations knock on the door. Further tensions relate to wealth redistribution, which poses heavy demands on the richer countries. Less developed countries also find themselves subject to a myriad of directives in areas such as food preparation and safety at work, which are expensive to implement without help.

There are grounds for anticipating that in an enlarged Union, with states at different stages of social and economic development, future integration will take place according to a principle of '**variable geometry**', permitting states to proceed at differing speeds. Indeed, this is built into the architecture of the Union. The Maastricht Treaty, in its schedule for achieving a single currency, established that no member would be forced along and no state could hold the others back. This enabled the UK and Denmark to stand outside. There is also the 1985 Schengen Agreement, absorbed into EU law by the Amsterdam Treaty, establishing a single international travel and immigration area free of border controls. This includes some non-EU states but, of the EU states, only the UK and Ireland remain outside. The Reform Treaty confirmed the right of states to reclaim powers from the Union and Britain negotiated a foreign policy opt-out. Critics worry that variable geometry could create a tiered association, with a dominant 'hard core' to the detriment of the others. Within the UK, Europhiles believe that a country such as the UK should be at the core where it can shape the agenda. However, the more extreme Eurosceptics, along with UKIP, see the UK striking out on its own in the global economy.

In international politics, no concept is less understood and more misused than that of sovereignty.

Josef Joffe, 'Rethinking the nation state: the many meanings of sovereignty', *Foreign Affairs* (Nov./Dec. 1999)

National sovereignty

The evolution of the EU, as a supranational association, has demanded some sacrifice of sovereignty by member states, a fact that may not have been made entirely clear to citizens during the UK entry debate. Little inflames feelings within the UK so much as the issue of national sovereignty. The concept can be seen as a defining feature of the national state, a symbol of freedom from oppression and a mark of dignity for citizens. It is treasured by rulers and protected in international law. However, those party to the debate do not always recognize that the concept of national sovereignty in the contemporary world is not as simple as much rhetoric implies. Despite its dominance in international discourse, the centralized nation-state is by no means the only way in which people can live or have lived. A relatively recent creation of modern Europe, it can be argued that, as traditionally understood, the state is becoming a practical and ethical anachronism.

The practical question

We saw in chapter 5 that the reality of national sovereignty today is questionable under a continuing process of globalization. Few domestic government policies are unaffected by exogenous forces, be they economic, social or cultural. Moreover, the proliferation of advanced weaponry decreases rather than increases sovereignty because confrontation to assert supremacy promises mutual destruction as well as giving power over nations to non-state actors, be they terrorists or freedom fighters.

It can be argued that international associations actually protect sovereignty rather than threatening it. One response to globalization comes in the growth of new political formations. Security alliances protect against invasion. Regional economic groupings combat transnational companies. The fight against terrorism and crime sees police and security forces amalgamating and systems of international law becoming increasingly important in the lives of citizens, organizations and states. Bodies such as the UN agencies unite governments and also work in partnership with international charities and business associations. The logic of European integration can be seen to lie within such developments. Some speak of pooled sovereignty as a protection of the state (Grahl and Teague 1990: 15).

The ethical question

Nationalism, which proclaims state sovereignty, can be a questionable virtue. Patriotism can sometimes deteriorate into racism and fascism, and it was to avert the latter that the movement for European integration arose. Today we witness an alarming paradox noted by Hobsbawm (1990) of increasing global interdependence coinciding with a revival of nationalism, often associated with religious fundamentalism, terrorism and ethnic conflict. A sovereign right of nations to do what they like within their own borders is increasingly questioned. Do governments have a right to violate human rights, persecute minorities or hold political prisoners? Religious persecution and atrocities in the Sudan, in Darfur, saw the Christian minority south oppressed by the Muslim north. In Zimbabwe, President Mugabe inflicted suffering on his own people. There are countless other examples. One of the justifications given for the invasion of the

The last refuge of a scoundrel.

Samuel Johnson (1709–84; British writer) on patriotism (meaning that it can be used to justify bad actions)

sovereign territory of Iraq was the cruelty of the rule of Saddam Hussein. There are other questions. Can one state claim a sovereign right to generate acid rain to fall on another? It can be argued that the maldistribution of world resources is in part perpetuated by nationalistic competition. During the career of the EU, despite horrors elsewhere, there has been no threat of armed conflict between its members.

Suspicion and Fitful Progress

The association has come a long way since 1951. Its major achievements include a complex institutional structure, a common body of law (the *acquis communautaire*), a wide range of policies and practices, and a spirit of cooperation that has replaced the hostility of the early twentieth century. However, progress has been fitful, with spurts of activity punctuated by periods of *immobilisme*. This is in large measure the result of a range of unresolved debates, many made more acute as a result of developments in Eastern Europe. There are fundamental questions about what the EU is and what it is to achieve. A central issue is **intergovernmentalism** versus **supranationalism**: is it to be merely an economic free-trade bloc or does it pursue the grander aim of political union? There is also the question of 'deepening' or 'widening': whether to concentrate upon further integration or to spread membership to more nations. Despite the EU's essentially supranational design, the diluted version of the ambitious constitution emerging from the Lisbon Treaty illustrates the reluctance of national governments to cede control to EU institutions. This reluctance has been most pronounced in security policy. Members failed to present a coherent front in the Gulf war, the war in former Yugoslavia and in the invasion of Iraq.

Debate often takes place within countries rather than between them and they resonate differently within each. It is likely that no country is as internally riven with mistrust and indecision as Britain, where interest groups and parties are split, sometimes to near destruction. With caution over its degree of commitment, a key question for Britain lies in the relative priority to be given to the competing alliance with the USA, where different social and economic models prevail (see Gamble 2003). The rise of UKIP, a party formally committed to withdrawal from the EU, and fuelled by a largely Eurosceptic press (Carey and Burton 2004), forces the mainstream parties to confront the issue. Although David Cameron promised a referendum on continued membership (assuming the Conservatives were still in power after the 2015 election), this did not prevent the dramatic surge in UKIP support in the 2013 local elections. Dismissed by some as a protest vote, reflecting popular anxiety about migration rather than a wish to sever links with Europe, it could not be ignored. Yet despite the unresolved debates, the EU has become a feature of the global landscape. In the next chapter we examine the institutional structure at the heart of this unique supranational project.

Key points

- Despite its imperialist history Britain remains an offshore island of Western Europe, sharing much of its history and culture.

- Of all Britain's relationships, none has generated more internal political heat than that with the EU.

- The association's origins lie in the attempt to repair the devastation wrought by the second world war and to prevent further war in Western Europe.

- The EU differs from all other international associations in that it creates a supranational authority.

- The career of the EU has itself been fitful, with periods of stagnation and dynamism.

- Edward Heath finally took Britain into the EC in 1973.

- The evolution of the association can be charted with reference to a number of landmark treaties.

- Central areas of debate include the single currency, social policy, enlargement and national sovereignty.

Review your understanding of the following terms and concepts

Amsterdam Treaty	eurozone	single currency
Brussels Treaty	exchange rate mechanism	Single European Act
Council of Europe	(ERM)	Social Chapter
economic and monetary	federalism	subsidiarity
union (EMU)	intergovernmental	supranational
EEC	Lisbon Treaty	Treaty on European
euro	Maastricht Treaty	Union
Eurosceptic	national sovereignty	

Questions for discussion and debate

Consider these propositions and be prepared to present the cases for and against. Try to produce debating propositions of your own.

1   Britain should have been at the centre of the European integration process.

2   Supranationalism is incompatible with the concept of the national state.

3   The promotion of peace within Western Europe is a more important goal than the creation of a free market.

4   The UK can aptly be termed 'the awkward partner' in the evolution of the EU.

5   An EU social policy is at variance with its free-market agenda.

6   UK reticence towards European integration is emotional rather than rational.

7   EU enlargement dilutes the integration project.

8   No euros please, we're British.

9   Governments should hold referendums on major EU treaties.

10   The 'Eurosceptics' are the Eurorealists.

Further reading

See also the reading for chapter 7.

Archer, C. (2008) *The European Union.*
Short but informative book with a pithy introduction to integration theories.

Bache, I. and George, S. (eds) (2006) *Politics in the European Union.*
A comprehensive and accessible blend of theory, history, institutions and politics of the EU.

Blair, A. (2005) *The European Union Since 1945.*
Concise and insightful account of the integration process. Contains abstracts from key documents.

George, S. (1994) *An Awkward Partner: Britain in the European Community.*
Examines and explains the tortuous nature of Britain's relations with Europe.

Lodge, J. (ed.) (1993) *The European Community and the Challenge of the Future.*
Collection of essays on various aspects by specialists.

Nugent, N. (2010) *The Government and Politics of the European Union.*
Detailed and informed account of the developing Union, with a useful companion
website.

Urwin, D. (1997) *A Political History of Western Europe since 1945.*
Addresses the major political and economic developments, including the
consequences of the end of the cold war and progress towards integration
post-Maastricht.

Young, H. (1998) *This Blessed Plot: Britain and Europe from Churchill to Blair.*
Excellent guide to the high and low politics of Britain's evolving position in
Western Europe.

For reading around the subject and some light relief

Jean Monnet, *Memoirs.*
Taste of the cocktail of passion and calculation in early integrationist moves.
Also insights on British emotional reservations.

Andrew Ian Dodge, *And Glory.*
Sci-fi set in a future where an EU superstate is sustained by nepotism,
violence and corruption.

Andrew Roberts, *The Aachen Memorandum.*
Intrigue, death, mystery and sex in the United States of Europe. Thriller,
satire, whodunit and futuristic fiction by Eurosceptic historian makes political
points while entertaining.

On the net

http://europa.eu/index_en.htm
Home page of the EU offers numerous links to the institutions and policy areas.

http://www.fedtrust.co.uk
Founded in 1945 by Sir William Beveridge, the Federal Trust is a research institute
studying European and global levels of government. A particular interest is
Britain's place in the EU.

http://www.epc.eu
Site of the European Policy Centre, a think-tank drawing members from all areas of politics, business and the professions, it is committed to making European integration work.

http://www.ukip.org
Visit the website of UKIP for a very negative view of the EU.

CHAPTER 7

THE EUROPEAN UNION: ANATOMY OF A SUPERSTATE?

Contents

Having examined the process of European integration and some of the associated debates, we turn to an analysis of the structure and role of the EU institutions. This chapter focuses on their composition, their internal workings, the relationships between them, and the legislative and budgetary processes. We also consider the debates surrounding their powers. Throughout we are concerned with the issue of democracy and the alleged democratic deficit. We see that the institutions and processes are evolving, but not without opposition and controversy.

The institutional architecture of the EU (figure 7.1) is more than a theme park of modernistic buildings and offices in Brussels, Strasbourg and Luxembourg; it is the physical embodiment of the values of supranationalism and testimony to the commitment of member states to unite. It is also a centre of power, a fact recognized by a host of interest groups who set up European offices for lobbying purposes.

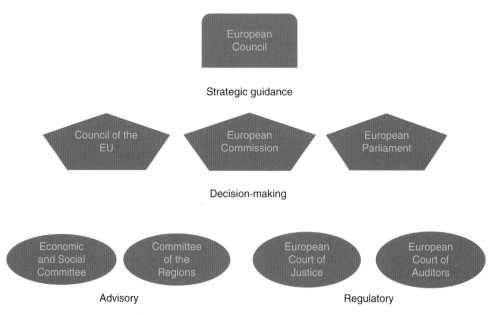

Figure 7.1 Institutions of the European Union

The Council of Ministers

Meeting in Brussels and consisting of national ministers, the Council of Ministers was created as the political head of the Union; from here come the decisions that increasingly shape the lives of people and organizations in member states. Not usually referred to as laws, decisions emerge as:

- *Regulations* – having immediate force of law;
- *Directives* – binding, but in practice leaving member states with leeway in implementation;
- *Recommendations and resolutions* – not compelling.

Its composition changes in order to bring together the ministers relevant to the policy area under discussion (trade, agriculture and so on). Of particular importance is the 'Ecofin' Council, comprising the economics and finance ministers. Meeting once a month, it considers a wide range of finance-related matters, including the budget. Leadership of the Council of Ministers rotates amongst the member states, each holding the presidency for a six-month period (semester). Most meetings are chaired by the relevant minister from the country holding the presidency. An exception is the Foreign Affairs Council, comprising foreign ministers and, following the Lisbon Treaty, chaired by the High Representative.

The Council is served by a bureaucracy of some 2000, headed by a secretary general. It is also aided by a Committee of Permanent Representatives (COREPER), comprising national ambassadors and their deputies. The system is held together by a dense web of official committees, subcommittees and working parties, some permanent and some ad hoc.

Voting procedures

Voting is an issue of fundamental importance to the Council, relating as it does to the sensitive question of national sovereignty. The Council tends to be a forum where ministers fight their corners in a nationalistic rather than a supranational way. Where voting is by unanimity or simple majority, those unhappy with a proposal can threaten to veto it. To mitigate this, the Rome Treaty made provision for a system of **qualified majority voting** (QMV) for certain policy areas. Disagreement over this resulted in the French boycotting the Community and, to resolve the deadlock, the 1966 'Luxembourg compromise' permitted a state to veto any proposal judged to threaten its vital national interest. Although not often used, it was a severe restriction.

The treaties specify which voting procedure applies in each policy area. These have progressively extended the scope of QMV, thereby restricting the opportunities

Table 7.1 QMV voting weights from 1 July 2013	
Country	**Votes**
Germany, France, UK, Italy	29
Spain, Poland	27
Romania	14
Netherlands	13
Greece, Portugal, Belgium, Czech R., Hungary	12
Sweden, Austria, Bulgaria	10
Slovakia, Denmark, Finland, Ireland, Lithuania, Croatia	7
Latvia, Slovenia, Estonia, Cyprus, Luxembourg	4
Malta	3
TOTAL	352

for obstructionism. Following the Lisbon Treaty, the inclusion of climate change, energy security and emergency aid saw most areas under QMV, but with unanimity remaining in the major areas of taxation, foreign policy, defence and social security. In practice unanimity is generally considered desirable on all issues. Under QMV each minister's vote is weighted to reflect population size but with some generosity to the smaller nations (Table 7.1). To pass a vote three conditions must be satisfied.

Those that did this must accept their responsibility before European history and Europeans. This is perhaps one of the worst crises Europe has ever seen.
Gerhard Schröder (German Chancellor), on Blair's blocking minority (June 2005)

1. The proposal must be supported by 260 votes from the total of 352 (about 74 per cent).
2. The proposal must be backed by a majority of members.
3. The states supporting the motion must represent at least 62 per cent of the total EU population.

A blocking minority may be put together by states aiming to reject a proposal. This requires 91 votes and the support of at least four members. Tony Blair led such a minority in June 2005 over a proposed deal on the seven-year budget, causing a political crisis.

Double majority voting

The Lisbon Treaty introduced a change with the requirement for double majority voting, under which a qualified majority requires the support of at least 55 per cent of ministers, who must also represent at least 65 per cent of EU citizens. This favours the larger nations, particularly Germany, with its population of 82 million. A redistribution of voting weights was to be phased in between 2014 and 2017.

A democratic deficit?

Much criticism of the Council centres on the idea of the **'democratic deficit'**. Although members have been elected to their own governments, they are not directly elected to the Council. The Council also tends towards nationalism rather than supranationalism. Voting is characterized by complex bargaining, compromising, log-rolling and arm-twisting (see Naurin and Wallace 2008). National interests are never far from ministers' minds; they aim to return to their own countries having 'brought home the bacon'. There has also been the issue of secrecy as the Council's deliberations were traditionally conducted behind closed doors. To address this, the Lisbon Treaty made provision for meetings to be public. In addition, an early-warning system was introduced to give national parliaments the right to comment on draft proposals and consider whether the principle of subsidiarity was upheld.

The European Council

In December 2000 French President Jacques Chirac arrived at the enormous Acropolis Centre at Nice with tears in his eyes. This was not due to federalist emotion, or even the promised confrontation with Britain's Prime Minister Tony Blair over the European rapid reaction force. The air outside was thick with tear gas thrown by his riot police at the massed ranks of protesters, including students, trade unionists and left-wing activists, protesting variously about the failure of governments to address social divisions within the EU, economic globalization and the EU record on human rights. In the following year a protester was shot at the Gothenburg meeting in Sweden.

Such violent events are prompted by meetings of the European Council and demonstrate a growing recognition of a key centre of EU power. Yet it was never planned to be so; the Rome Treaty did not create such a body. The European Council has been a product of an irresistible political evolution in which national leaders and foreign ministers have, from the early 1970s, come to play an increasingly dominant role through regular 'summit meetings'. Formalized at the Paris summit of December 1974 and recognized in both the Single European Act and the Maastricht Treaty, it is here that major community issues are thrashed out. The 1969 Hague summit gave the Community its 'own resources', the 1985 Milan summit will for ever be associated with the Single European Act, the 1989 Madrid summit with the Social Charter, the 1991 Maastricht summit with the Treaty on European Union and the Lisbon summit of 2007 with the revised EU 'constitution'.

These high-profile meetings originally took place two or three times a year under the chairmanship of the country holding the six-month presidency. As summits they were ornamented by lavish ceremonial and wining and dining for the political glitterati in the palaces and embassies of Europe's capitals, and this could offer national leaders a chance to impress. Tony Blair was fortunate in coming to it in his first year as prime minister but he also had the embarrassment of presiding over the launch of the single currency while his own country remained outside. Providing a major focus for media attention, the run-up to a summit usually sees protracted negotiations, febrile rumour-mongering and speculation. At the Nice summit of 2000 it was agreed that, in the light of the major enlargement, and for reasons of security, more summits would take place in Brussels.

A President of Europe?

The rotating presidency created a polycentric form of leadership, which was held to limit the scope for innovation (Hayward 2008: 2–3). The 'constitution' proposed at the 2004 Rome summit aimed to create a full-time position of President of the European Council. This survived as a particularly controversial aspect of the Lisbon Treaty. Seen by Eurosceptics as emblematic of a single federal European state, the position promised to change the face of the EU. The holder is sometimes dubbed 'President of Europe'.

The character of the office-holder has considerable bearing on the nature of the position. A charismatic and internationally recognizable figure could elevate the status of the presidency, possibly transforming Europe into a continental bloc rivalling the USA and China. The name of Tony Blair was touted from an early stage, with enthusiastic support from French President Nicolas Sarkozy. There was, however, considerable opposition, not least from British Conservatives, while the legacy of Iraq weighed heavily against him within the rest of Europe. The possibility of a strong president also evoked misgivings within the other EU institutions, fearing that it would elevate the Council at their expense. While the internet was alive with views and opinions, the actual choice was made by the European Council, operating with a mystery reminiscent of papal selection.

The final choice was of Herman Van Rompuy, once prime minister of Belgium. Appointed for a two-and-half-year term, renewable once, he was to serve from 1 December 2009. Gone was any expectation of charismatic leadership. Wags had long mocked the paucity of famous Belgians, and Van Rompuy was not calculated to increase their number. With modest ambitions and a hobby of writing Japanese-style *haiku* verses in Flemish, this president would be more a chairman than a 'traffic-stopping' celebrity. However, he had demonstrated skills as a consensus builder in Belgium's fractious politics, skills that were to be needed in the deepening eurozone crisis.

A democratic deficit?

Although they are national leaders, the members of the European Council are not elected as leaders of Europe. Moreover, their presence further testifies to the persistence of nationalism. As seen in chapter 6, the summit meetings can be extremely fractious. Thus it was at the Fontainebleau summit of 1984 that Margaret Thatcher fought successfully for a budget rebate, while Major claimed 'game, set and match' for Britain at Maastricht and Blair repeated the 'Britain first' mantra at Lisbon. He consulted Thatcher before his first EU summit and the priorities he outlined could have come straight from her handbag. David Cameron was to continue in similar vein, despite his coalition with the Euro-friendly Liberal Democrats, as European leaders wrestled with the crisis in the eurozone.

The European Commission

In the demonology of Eurosceptics, the Brussels-based Commission is redolent of a Kafkaesque superstate. Effectively the EU civil service, it is the institution most removed from democratic influence. The Commission is located mainly in Brussels in the Berlaymont building, and sometimes in Luxembourg and Strasbourg (when the Parliament is meeting there). A large bureaucracy of some 20,000 is divided into functional departments known as directorates-general. Each is headed by a director-general, rather like a Whitehall permanent secretary, responsible to a commissioner. In overall control is a secretary-general. Indeed, the Commission is more than a civil service. Not only does it implement policy, it has sole responsibility for initiating legislation by presenting proposals to the Council of Ministers and European Parliament. It also drafts the budget and conducts negotiations with non-member states. As the guardian of the treaties it can take nations, institutions and individuals before the European Court for any infringements.

The twenty-eight commissioners together form the College of Commissioners. The Nice Treaty envisaged reducing the number, which had risen due to EU enlargement, but this idea was dropped as a concession to the Irish Republic in 2008. (Before the 2004 enlargement the larger countries each sent two.) A commissioner is nominated by each member state, subject to European Parliament approval. They are required to swear an oath to espouse a supranational perspective, and sometimes can be accused of 'going native' in the heady Brussels atmosphere, putting them at odds with their own governments. Each is responsible for one or more policy portfolios and, like Whitehall ministers, face the danger of being dominated by their civil servants.

Britain's commissioners traditionally come from the two main parties and are

... neither seek nor take instruction from any government or any body.
Part of the solemn undertaking made by EU commissioners upon taking office

generally prominent ex-politicians; some might say failed politicians. Incumbents have included Neil Kinnock (who resigned the Labour leadership in 1992 after a second general election defeat), Chris Patten (a prominent Conservative MP before losing his seat in 1992), Leon Brittan (who resigned after the Westland scandal) and Peter Mandelson (forced to resign not once, but twice, from the Blair government). However, when Baroness Ashton was nominated by Gordon Brown, she was remarkable for being largely unknown.

The president

The Commission is led by its president, a high-profile figure in world politics. The position has been seen as the motor of integration and Jacques Delors, coming to office in January 1985 and reappointed four years later, was a particularly forceful advocate. Reviled by Eurosceptics, he was often pilloried in the British tabloids. Appointment must be with the common accord of member states and the Maastricht Treaty also made it subject to approval in the European Parliament. At the June 1994 Corfu summit, in a nationalistic move to appease his Eurosceptics, John Major vetoed the appointment of Jean-Luc Dehaene (a federalist and the preferred choice of France and Germany). The result was the appointment of Jacques Santer of Luxembourg, who was forced to resign in 1999 after becoming embroiled in a major corruption scandal.

His successor, the mild-mannered, bicycling, Bologna University Professor Romano Prodi, contrasted with his more charismatic predecessors. Described by political opponents as 'the Mortadella' (a rather bland sausage for which his city was famous), he was one of Italy's most successful post-war prime ministers. The particular talent he brought to the presidency was one much needed in the evolving EU: an ability to find consensus and compromise. He revealed himself to be a firm integrationist and was to criticize Britain's special relationship with the USA. He was succeeded by José Manuel Durão Barroso in 2004, previously prime minister of Portugal, who had to contend with the dramatic enlargement to twenty-seven and the vexatious 'constitution'.

An EU foreign minister?

It was considered important that the EU be represented to the outside world by a single commissioner. This led to the creation of the post of High Representative by the Treaty of Amsterdam. The position was expanded in the Lisbon Treaty to become effectively an EU foreign minister, combining the jobs of the foreign affairs and external affairs commissioners. The High Representative is Vice-President of the European Commission and chairs the Council of EU Foreign Ministers. The appointment is made by the European Council, subject to a vote of approval by the European Parliament.

However, like that of full-time president, the very idea of an EU foreign minister was controversial, as was the actual choice. Various candidates were considered and the choice of Britain's Baroness Ashton, put forward by Gordon Brown, was unexpected. She had no foreign affairs experience but was favoured by the centre-left leaders. Discontent continued during her stewardship. In the eyes of her critics, an unwillingness to travel, or to work abroad at weekends, made her peculiarly ill-suited to the role. She came under particular fire for being one of the few foreign ministers not to visit Haiti after the 2010 earthquake. In her defence it could be argued that the fault lay in the treaty itself. With the jobs of High Representative and Britain's European commissioner she was overloaded and faced with the time-honoured conundrum of 'being in two places at once'. However, those fearing a dominant and federalist interpretation of the role could take some comfort from the appointment.

> *Who do I call if I want to speak to Europe?*
> Attributed to Henry Kissinger

A democratic deficit?

Composed of bureaucrats and appointed commissioners, the Commission is the least democratic institution in the EU and its role occasions fierce argument in Britain. It is seen by Eurosceptics as driving the Euro-train at breakneck speed towards federalism, with no democratic accountability to the hundreds of millions whose lives are affected. Conscious of its vulnerability, the Commission has generally shown itself anxious to gain legitimacy by working in harmony with the European Parliament and welcoming consultation with interest groups at various levels. Some have called for the popular election of the College of Commissioners (see Smith 2005). However, the Commission is largely free from the constraints of national interest that bedevil the Council of Ministers and the European Council. It can aid the search for consensus and also take a broader and longer-term world perspective than transient politicians.

The European Parliament

Some citizens of continental Europe can expect to be disturbed at night by fleets of lorries trundling between imposing buildings in Brussels, Luxembourg and Strasbourg. Their cargo consists of many tons of documents, reproduced in all official EU languages on paper of various hues. The reason for this is nationalistic wrangling, which has prevented the establishment of a single seat for the EU's assembly. The single-chamber European Parliament holds plenary sessions one week every month in the splendid Palais de l'Europe at Strasbourg, while its administrative offices are in Luxembourg. In 2011 a cross-party group of MEPs set up the

The European Parliament building, part of the Leopold complex in Brussels

Photo: Ann Kingdom

Despite its three locations and multilingual operation, the annual running costs of the European Parliament are a very modest €0.3 for each EU citizen.

Single Seat campaign with the aim of avoiding this 'travelling circus' and saving an estimated €180 million. Although the Parliament's plenary sessions are the headline-catching occasions, detailed work is done in between, through a committee network working close to the heart of EU power at Brussels.

A president, elected by MEPs for two-and-a-half-year terms, presides over the Parliament. Much work is done through standing committees covering all important areas of EU policy, ranging from the budget and economic and monetary affairs to women's rights and gender equality. Servicing these operations is the work of the secretariat, located in yet a third venue, at Luxembourg.

Members of the European Parliament

The 766 Members of the European Parliament (**MEPs**) are elected for five-year terms by proportional representation within member states. Most use the d'Hondt method (see p. 284). The number from each country reflects population size but never exceeds 99 (table 7.2). Following the Lisbon modifications, the number of

Table 7.2 National representation at the European Parliament, June 2009	
Country	**MEPs**
Germany	99
France, Italy, United Kingdom	72
Spain, Poland	50
Romania	33
Netherlands	25
Belgium, Hungary, Greece, Czech Republic, Portugal	22
Sweden	18
Austria, Bulgaria	17
Denmark, Finland, Slovakia	13
Croatia, Ireland, Lithuania	12
Latvia	8
Slovenia	7
Cyprus, Estonia, Luxembourg	6
Malta	5
TOTAL	736

MEPs was increased from 736 to 751 and additional seats given to newer coun-tries. For European elections the UK is divided into twelve regions, each return-ing between three and twelve members (table 7.3). Within states, voting can often reflect domestic rather than Europe-wide issues. In the case of the UK, with UKIP standing on the paradoxical platform of leaving the Union, one issue can be EU membership itself.

Sitting in a semicircular chamber, MEPs do not confront each other like a govern-ment and opposition. However, rather than sit as national blocs, they form ideological groupings ranging from left to right (see figure 7.2). Members have conflicting loyal-ties: the parliamentary group, the EU itself, their national interest and their national party. The groups can have a degree of fluidity as parties merge and reform. The Euroscepticism of British Conservatives has often created major problems within the centre-right EPP group and, after the 2009 elections, to the dismay of moderate centre-right leaders such as Angela Merkel, David Cameron fulfilled a controversial pledge to leave the EPP and join a new anti-federalist group. This embraced right-wing MEPs from eight countries under the title 'European Conservatives and Reformists' (ECR). Cameron's twenty-six members constituted the largest national element, but they sat with some extremist bedfellows espousing anti-liberal sentiments, including opposi-tion to gay rights. Some Conservative MEPs were unhappy with the move.

Sometimes termed 'transnational parties' (Hanley 2007), these groupings are not

Table 7.3 Results for UK political parties in the 2009 European elections

Party	MEPs
Conservative	26
UK Independence Party	13
Labour	13
Liberal Democrats	11
Green Party	2
British National Party	2
Scottish National Party	2
Plaid Cymru	1
Sinn Féin	1
Democratic Unionist Party	1

Note: Another 25 parties or independents stood unsuccessfully, including Animals Count, the Fair Play Fair Trade Party and the Pensioners Party. With some 250,000 votes, the most successful was the Christian Party 'Proclaiming Christ's Lordship'.

Fingers on the buzzer: MEPs vote electronically in the European Parliament in Brussels, June 2011

Photo: European Parliament, © European Union

like parties in national politics. They do not have mass organizations or fight elections with clear manifestos and, with no executive to support, have little need for rigid party discipline. Indeed, a show of cross-group unity can actually be preferred, since this can strengthen the Parliament's hand in negotiating with Council and Commission.

Political complexion

Unlike most national parliaments, the European Parliament does not fall under the domination of a single party or coalition. However, it has shown an ideological complexion (figure 7.2). The first two elections produced a centre-right character based around the European People's Party (EPP). In 1989 the balance shifted to the centre-left, with increased Green representation which, although large enough to form a separate group, allied with the Socialists. The 1994 elections saw an almost Europe-wide swing back to the right except in the UK, where the first-past-the-post

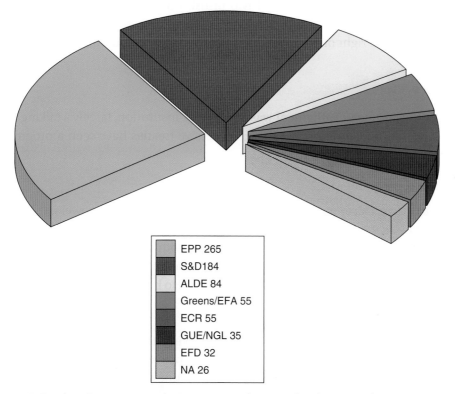

	EPP 265
	S&D 184
	ALDE 84
	Greens/EFA 55
	ECR 55
	GUE/NGL 35
	EFD 32
	NA 26

Figure 7.2 Political groupings in the European Parliament after the 2009 elections

Key: EPP = Group of the European People's Party (Christian Democrats); S&D = Group of the Progressive Alliance of Socialists and Democrats in the European Parliament; ALDE = Group of the Alliance of Liberals and Democrats for Europe; Greens/EFA = Group of the Greens/European Free Alliance; ECR = European Conservatives and Reformists Group; GUE/NGL = Confederal Group of the European United Left/ Nordic Green Left; EFD = Europe of Freedom and Democracy Group; NA = Non-attached voting system (except in Northern Ireland) greatly inflated Labour's representation. In 1999 the right consolidated its position (with the UK adopting PR).

Of particular interest were the 2004 elections, since enlargement had swelled the electorate to almost 344 million. Results showed a fall in support for governing parties and some gains for the more Eurosceptic parties. In Britain UKIP enjoyed a surge from three to twelve seats, to rival the Liberal Democrat presence. It was helped by media interest in some of its more exotic members, including TV personality Robert Kilroy-Silk (who later defected) and actress Joan Collins. However, enlargement did not markedly change the overall balance of power in the Parliament.

At the 2009 elections, with an electorate close to 400 million, the EPP secured 265 members, clearly outflanking the 184 of the Socialists. In the UK, domestic politics weighed against Labour. Losing six seats, the party dropped into a humiliating third place behind UKIP, which consolidated its presence with thirteen seats. A result that disturbed many was the election of two British National Party (BNP) candidates. The new presence of the European Conservatives and Reformists Group (ECR), positioned to the right of the EPP, added a conservative colouration.

Powers

Initially the European Parliament was a very weak institution, largely a talking shop. However, following continued debate, successive treaties have seen a progressive increase in its relative power.

General supervision

The Maastricht Treaty gave the Parliament general supervisory powers. It can take matters before the EU Court of Justice if, for example, it feels that the Commission or Council have failed to fulfil their obligations. With the power to investigate citizens' complaints against EU institutions and appoint an ombudsman to assist, it can also seek redress of grievance. Petitions can also be brought by EU citizens.

Scrutiny

National parliaments often have a role involving the scrutiny and control of executives. In the case of the EU, executive powers are shared between the Commission, the Council and the European Council, so the target is somewhat blurred. Nevertheless, a number of instruments are available.

- *Reports and enquiries.* The Commission regularly submits annual reports to Parliament, on issues such as the functioning of the Communities and the implementation of the budget. The Parliament can set up committees of inquiry to investigate possible violations of Community law by member states.

- *Question Time*. MEPs can table written and oral questions to the Council and Commission.
- *Approval of appointments*. Following the Lisbon Treaty, the range of appointments requiring parliamentary approval has extended to embrace the President of the Commission, the whole College of Commissioners, the President, Vice-President and the members of the Executive Board of the European Central Bank, the High Representative and the President of the European Council. Although the Parliament has never failed to approve a commissioner, its potential was seen when anticipated opposition to the Barroso Commission forced the proposal to be withdrawn without coming to a vote.
- *Censure of the Commission*. Formally the Parliament can dismiss the Commission *en bloc*. This has been seen as a draconian measure, a 'nuclear button' too dangerous to press. Even so, events reached fever pitch in January 1999 in a tense stand-off amidst parliamentary accusations of fraud, mismanagement and nepotism reaching to the highest level; the outcome was to become the greatest bloodbath in EU history. Outraged MEPs gave the commissioners an ultimatum: 'go with honour or be forced out without honour'. The ensuing mass resignations included that of the President himself, Jacques Santer.

A democratic deficit?

Although the Parliament is the Union's most democratic institution it had an unpromising start. Direct elections were not introduced until 1979 owing to the fear that the legitimacy conferred would erode national sovereignty. Today legitimacy is weakened by electoral turnout, which has progressively fallen. In 2009 it was only 43 per cent, with Britain well below average at 34. However, the Parliament can take a supranationalist perspective, which gives it something in common with the powerful Commission. The Commission has lent support, increasing its own legitimacy through association. It encouraged the gradual increase in the Parliament's power in legislation and the budget.

Other Institutions

The European Central Bank (ECB)

Located in Frankfurt, the European Central Bank was established on 1 June 1998 and formally recognized in the Lisbon Treaty. It works with the European System of Central Banks (comprising the central banks of EU states) and stands at the hub of the eurozone (seventeen countries in 2013; see p. 155). The Bank's role involves setting interest rates and controlling the money supply. It is run by a president and an executive board nominated by eurozone states. Overall policy is laid down by a governing council comprising the executive board and governors of eurozone central banks.

A democratic deficit?

The ECB operates independently of political intervention. This independence has been criticized by some leaders, notably French President Nicolas Sarkozy, who called for more action in politically sensitive areas such as growth, job creation and interest rates. It was thrust into the political limelight over the eurozone crisis in 2010. There is, however, some accountability to the Parliament and Council. The Council appoints the president, vice-president and members of the executive board and nominees must be approved by the Parliament. The president presents an annual report to a plenary sitting of the Parliament and also reports regularly to its monetary affairs committee.

The European Court of Justice (ECJ)

The existence of the Court testifies to the EU's uniqueness amongst international associations. Sitting at Luxembourg, it comprises a judge from each member state, serving six-year renewable terms. One judge is elected as president. As an international court, a court of appeal, a court of review and a court of referral, it aims to ensure that Community law is applied uniformly across member states. Actions may be brought variously by EU institutions, member states and natural or legal persons. The Commission is its best customer, having brought the greatest number of actions and been taken to the Court relatively frequently. Its procedures would be unrecognizable to anyone versed in the ways of UK courts. Advocates General present cases before judges and deliver reasoned opinions as to what the verdict might be. These are frequently followed. Decisions, which are made by majority, are binding upon member states.

A democratic deficit?

The role of the Court is deeply symbolic of the EU's supranational character. Some allege that it intrudes into the political arena. It has interpreted Council policy in various areas and can play a creative role, generally advancing a federalist vision through its interpretations and precedents (see Burley and Mattli 1993). It has ruled on the relative power of institutions and their relationship with member states. It also considers the constitutionality of laws passed by domestic legislatures. The 1990 *Factortame* case (see p. 98) brought home its ability to limit the legal sovereignty of the UK Parliament. Critics note that it works slowly, is expensive, and that many of its decisions have been seen as fudged compromises.

The Economic and Social Committee (ECOSOC)

The Brussels-based ECOSOC considers industrial policy. Members, comprising representatives of three interests – employers, workers and miscellaneous social and professional groups – are nominated by state governments for renewable four-year terms. As a consultative forum it lacks executive powers, although its existence represents a nod in the direction of corporatism (see pp. 596–7), a style of government more prevalent in continental Europe than in Britain.

The Committee of the Regions (COR)

Some see a vision of the future in terms of a Europe of regions rather than of nations. The Maastricht Treaty made provision for an advisory committee to articulate the regional voice and this held its inaugural meeting at Brussels in March 1995. Members are appointed by states, with most having clear party affiliations, and it shares a common organizational structure with ECOSOC. It is consulted when regional issues are considered and can also issue own-initiative reports. The Lisbon Treaty gave the committee the power to challenge new EU laws at the European Court of Justice over issues of subsidiarity.

The Court of Auditors

Comprising one member from each state and a bureaucracy of around 800 accountants and administrators, the Court audits the EU books. When satisfied that all is in order it issues a 'declaration of assurance' (see p. 188). It also issues various reports, including an annual one for the Parliament, and can bring actions before the ECJ. However, it is not without its critics.

The EU Legislative Process

It is through its laws and regulations that most people know the EU. The formal process of law-making begins with a proposal from the Commission to the Council of Ministers and Parliament. However, the Maastricht Treaty made provision for the Parliament to submit an 'own initiative' report to the Commission and request that it forms the basis of a proposal. In addition it examines and comments on the Commission's annual programme of proposed legislation. In considering a proposal the two bodies negotiate through rounds of readings. This entails much informal discussion, deal-making and lobbying, where interests extend beyond governments to a myriad of pressure groups operating in the Brussels hothouse (see

> **Scope of the EU legislative procedures**
>
> *Consultation*: taxation, industrial policy, agricultural policy
>
> *Co-decision*: the free movement of workers, the internal market, the whole of the budget, technological research and development, the environment, consumer protection, education, culture and health.
>
> *Consent*: citizenship, structural and cohesion funds, uniform electoral procedure, certain international agreements, accession of new member states and association agreements with other countries.

Coen and Richardson 2009). There are three procedures (consultation, co-decision and consent) and the treaties lay down which is appropriate in each policy area.

Consultation

From the outset a number of articles in the original EEC treaty required that draft legislation in certain sensitive areas be submitted to the Parliament for an opinion. The Commission decides whether to incorporate any amendments and submits it to the Council, which may accept, reject, or make further amendments. In the latter case the Council must vote unanimously.

Cooperation

Repealed by the Lisbon Treaty, this procedure is only of historical interest. Introduced in the 1986 Single European Act, it represented an important step along the road to greater power for the Parliament. In essence, it added a further stage to the consultation process, compelling the Council to consider Parliament's opinion and reach a 'common position'. Many policy areas were originally covered by this but were gradually transferred to the co-decision procedure.

Co-decision – the ordinary legislative procedure

This puts the Parliament on an equal legislative footing with the Council across a wide range of areas, including the budget. Some two-thirds of European laws are now made in this way. The procedure was introduced by the Maastricht Treaty to increase Parliament's power and simplified by the Amsterdam Treaty, which also enlarged its scope to include areas from the cooperation procedure, making the Parliament a 'big winner' (Duff 1997: 143). The Lisbon Treaty anointed it the 'ordinary legislative procedure' of the EU and extended it to the third pillar. In essence the process is a series of stages with some tortuous bargaining between the two institutions, always under the eye of the Commission (see figure 7.3). There

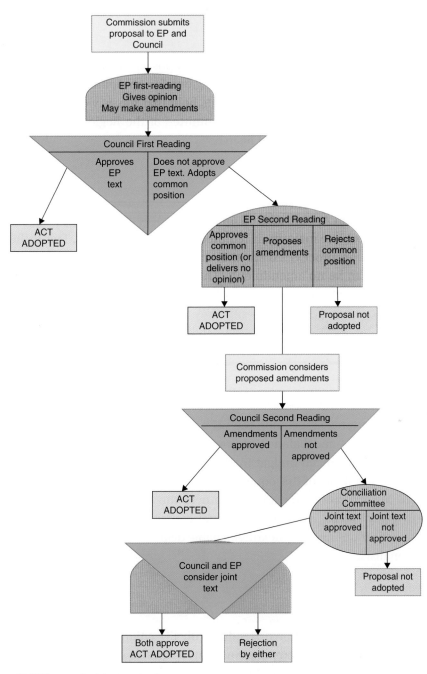

Figure 7.3 The co-decision procedure

is evidence that the co-decision procedure has made ministers more willing to compromise.

An early-warning system

Following the Lisbon Treaty, Commission proposals are also sent to national parliaments and the Committee of the Regions for an opinion on the principle of subsidiarity. If a majority of parliaments hold that this is violated, the Council or Parliament can vote it down. The Committee of the Regions can challenge a proposal in the European Court of Justice.

The consent procedure

The Single European Act introduced an assent procedure whereby parliamentary agreement, by absolute majority, is required for certain decisions. This is the same as the consultation process except that a proposal must be either accepted or rejected; there can be no amendments. The Maastricht Treaty extended its scope and the Lisbon Treaty renamed the procedure 'consent', classing it as a special legislative procedure.

The Budget

Like any international association the EU needs money and much can be learned about its dynamics and balance of power from a study of the budget. The EC Treaty calls for a balanced budget (Article 199); revenue must equal expenditure. However, the simplicity of this equation does not mean that the process is uncontroversial. Major political tensions arise over the redistribution of wealth from richer to poorer areas, the size of national contributions, the balance of power between institutions and the inextinguishable disputation between federalists and internationalists.

Scale

Although the budget has grown steadily with EU enlargement and the acquisition of new functions, it remains small by domestic standards, being capped at a specific percentage of total EU Gross National Income (GNI, 1.27 per cent in 2011). However, this can give a misleading impression; further expense is borne by member states, whose national bureaucracies share the task of policy implementation.

Revenue

Unlike national governments, which raise money by taxing citizens, international associations such as NATO and the UN are usually financed by members' contributions. They can never be entirely confident of funds; some states are too poor to pay, others may withhold payment in protest. For such reasons the ECSC founders instigated direct funding from levies imposed on production. However, when the EEC was created, inter-governmental wrangling resulted in a system of contributions related to national wealth. This source proved limited and, as crises threatened, the Community sought to raise its own resources. The consequent loss of national control would be offset by allowing the Parliament to share the budgetary role with the Council. The reform was introduced at the 1969 Hague summit. The 'own resources' were to come from customs duties, agricultural tariffs, sugar levies and, most importantly, a proportion of the VAT collected by member states.

> **The British Rebate**
> In 1984 Margaret Thatcher argued successfully for a UK rebate. It was claimed that, while the Common Agricultural Policy (CAP) consumed some 71 per cent of the EU budget, Britain, with fewer small farming enterprises, received little in farm aid. However, by 2011 the CAP accounted for only 40 per cent and some member states argued that the rebate should cease to apply.

Yet revenue remained inadequate and the 1988 Brussels summit agreed that, in addition, once annual Community expenditure was agreed, the total revenue from the existing resources would be calculated and the difference made up by a payment from each member state in proportion to its GNI. This became increasingly significant; starting at 10 per cent, it was to become the largest element of total revenue (figure 7.4).

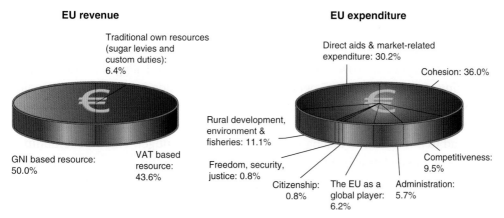

Figure 7.4 EU revenue and expenditure, 2011

Source: Data from *The EU budget in detail* http://ec.europa.eu/budget/budget_detail/current_year_en.htm

Expenditure

Generally the funds required by international associations are for running costs; they are not burdened with responsibility for substantive policies or redistributing income in the manner of states. However, with the Common Agricultural Policy, overseas aid and regional grants, the EU *does* pursue government-style objectives, making its budget not only far larger than those of other intergovernmental associations but different in character. Expenditure decisions usually create winners and losers, thereby producing high-octane fuel for political dispute. Rich countries tend to resist redistribution, poorer regions lobby for social and economic development grants, those with large agricultural constituencies favour price guarantees, and so on.

The budgetary cycle

The budget has provided a key site for trials of strength between the Council and the Parliament. More than an institutional power struggle, it encompasses the federalist/internationalist debate. In this the Parliament has shared the federal aspirations of the Commission, which promoted major budgetary reforms in 1988, increasing its influence. A budgetary cycle follows a number of stages in the EU financial year (1 January to 31 December). It opens with the proposal of annual spending plans by the Commission, which are negotiated between the Parliament and the Council of Ministers. Following the Lisbon Treaty this is through the usual legislative process, with the Parliament a co-legislator for the entire budget.

In addition there is the auditing of past expenditure by the Court of Auditors. The Parliament, with advice from the Council, decides on the basis of the Court's report whether to grant the Commission a 'discharge' with a 'declaration of assurance'. This is no mere technicality; fraud, alleged and uncovered, constitutes a major problem. In early 1998, misgivings over the 1996 budget led to discharge being deferred for a year. In November 1998 the Court considered alleged fraud and mis-spending of £3 billion, some 5 per cent of the total EU budget, precipitating a major crisis in the Parliament's relationship with the Commission (see p. 181). However, the problem has lain partly in the system, in which even minor accounting errors will lead to a refusal of a discharge for the whole EU budget. This can sometimes fuel exaggerated claims by Eurosceptics of a culture of fraud and mismanagement within the EU. Enlargement has seen membership of the Court swell to twenty-eight national representatives, making it cumbersome and less able to reach a consensus.

A Union United in Diversity

The institutional architecture of the European Union exists to serve the aspirations of peace, co-operation and economic growth. It can be called a success to the extent that there has been no third world war, the economies of member states have grown and many countries have joined, with others seeking to do so. However, as an actor on the world stage it has fallen short of the aspirations of federalists.

A unified Europe would influence the balance of power on the global stage, challenging US domination and speaking with a single voice. This requires strong, centralized democratic institutions and clear leadership. The Lisbon Treaty, although not the constitution envisaged at the Rome summit, aimed to move the institutions in this direction by injecting more democracy into the law-making process, taking more cognizance of the views of national parliaments, increasing the use of QMV in the Council, establishing a foreign minister in all but name and creating a permanent president of the European Council. Although the first two appointments to these positions did not promise dramatic changes in leadership style, the institutional structure contains much potential.

However, cultural differences make true unification difficult, more so with enlargement. European integration has been largely a product of elite initiatives with little reference to national electorates. Yet the ratification process of the Maastricht and Lisbon treaties revealed popular suspicion and discontent. Reform has been largely in terms of institutional structures, with less effort to forge a common culture and sense of European identity (Manent 2006: 67).

As the world's only supranational association, many problems of the Union must be unique. A likely scenario for the future will be slow progress towards integration, held back by the diversity of cultures and economic situations. Yet notwithstanding the critics, the federal drive is a genie that would not easily be returned to the bottle.

Key points

- Each EU institution has a distinctive role, and each is subject to debate, often centring on the notion of a democratic deficit.

- The Council of Ministers has a fluid composition and contains the leading politicians from member states. It was created as the main EU legislature.

- Voting methods within the Council of Ministers is an important area of debate, with a bearing on national sovereignty, which is reduced under QMV.

- The European Council comprises the heads of government and was not originally part of the EU institutional structure.

- The European Commission is the EU bureaucracy, responsible for proposing policies and overseeing their implementation.

- The European Parliament, consisting of elected MEPs, is the only democratic institution within the EU.

- The legislative process of the EU has continually evolved to increase the role of the Parliament.

- The nature of the EU budget provides it with its own resources, enhancing its supranational character.

- The future shape of the EU promises to be one of the most important factors influencing British politics in the twenty-first century.

Review your understanding of the following terms and concepts

co-decision procedure	democratic deficit	European Council
Committee of the Regions	double majority voting	European Court of Justice
consent procedure	Economic and Social	European Parliament
consultation procedure	Committee	European Union
cooperation procedure	European budget	MEP
Council of Ministers	European Central Bank	qualified majority voting
Court of Auditors	European Commission	

Questions for discussion and debate

Consider these propositions and be prepared to present the cases for and against. Try to produce debating propositions of your own.

1 QMV erodes national sovereignty.

2 The emergence of the European Council has held back the development of the EU.

3 Each EU institution suffers a democratic deficit.

4 The role of the European Parliament must be increased if the EU is to gain popular acceptance.

5   Without is 'own resources' the EU could never be truly supranational.

6   EU enlargement widens integration at the expense of depth.

7   The idea of European citizenship is a fantasy.

8   The European Commission is overmanned, overbearing and over there.

9   If the EU is to talk with a single voice there must be a 'President of Europe'.

10   Without the EU the UK would have little voice in world affairs.

Further reading

See also the reading for chapter 6

Bache, I. and Jordan, A (eds) (2008) *The Europeanization of British Politics.*
Illustrates how domestic politics cannot be understood without recognizing the influence of the EU.

Butler, M. (1986) *Europe: More than a Continent.*
An inside view by a UK permanent representative.

Coen, D. and Richardson, J. (2009) *Lobbying the European Union: Institutions, Actors, and Issues.*
Details the huge growth in EU lobbying over the past few decades.

McCann, D. (2010) *The Political Economy of the European Union.*
Argues that the core business of the European Union is the creation of an integrated European market and explains the complexities of the project.

Shore, C. (2000) *Building Europe: The Cultural Politics of European Integration.*
Argues that, while European integration has worked for technical, political and financial elites, it has failed to produce a common culture.

Watts, D. (2008) *The European Union.*
Sound introductory coverage of the EU institutions with useful concluding chapter on further development

For reading around the subject and some light relief

Edwina Currie, *The Ambassador*.
The EU a hundred years on is the most powerful state in the free world. Genetic engineering is widespread and the US Ambassador is sent over to investigate.

Julian Barnes, *England, England*.
Hilarious novel with satirical bite in which visionary tycoon Sir Jack Pitman recreates England as a theme park on the Isle of Wight, including replicas of Big Ben, Princess Diana's grave and Harrods.

Borgen
The popular Danish TV series (available on DVD) gives dramatic insight into one member state's political system and manages to make the choice of their European Commissioner as exciting as a car chase!

On the net

http://www.fco.gov.uk/europelindex.html
The Foreign and Commonwealth Office site includes UK policy on the EU.

http://europa.eu.intlindex.htm
The EU home page will lead you to a wealth of information on the EU, its policies and its institutions; available in any EU language at the touch of a button.

http://www.openeurope.org.uk/
Open Europe is a think-tank set up by leading UK business people. While sounding a sceptical note, it espouses the cause of radical reform rather than a British exit.

PART II
MOBILIZING THE DEMOS

The Greek *demos* means the people as a whole; when they control the government the polity can lay claim to the title democracy. Few polities today would not at least pay lip-service to the notion of democracy, but few fully realize its demanding ideals. In this section we examine the way in which the mass of the people are able to relate to government.

Chapter 8 considers people's attitudes towards government and politics and the structure of the society they inhabit. These attitudes form the bedrock of the system: the political culture that conditions what governments can and cannot do. Consciously or unconsciously they reflect the ideologies discussed in earlier chapters. These do not arise spontaneously; they are socially constructed by experience and conditioned through the process we consider in chapter 9 as 'mind politics'.

Chapter 10 turns to the most visible mechanism of participation, the electoral system, charting the grudging manner in which the powerful elite few extended the franchise to the mass, and did so in a way calculated to minimize damage to their own privileges. In chapter 11 we observe how modern elections operate, noting the behaviour of both voters and the politicians who seek their votes. Chapters 12 and 13 focus on the main products of the fully extended franchise, the modern political parties. These form the essential link between the people and their government. When these are understood we have some important keys for unlocking the mysteries of the British political system.

CHAPTER 8

THE SOCIAL CONTEXT: OUR DIVIDED SOCIETY

Contents

In this chapter we examine the social context in which British politics is enacted. A political system does not stand above society as an autonomous machine; it is as much part of society as our weather system is part of the planet's ecosphere. It has long been proclaimed that British society is benignly cohesive but we shall argue that this unity has been a veneer concealing the cracks beneath. The chapter includes four principal themes. The first examines a key feature of the political culture, the attitudes of people towards the political system. Do they trust figures in authority to act in the general interest? Are they willing to obey the law and respect the institutions of the state? The remaining sections expose great divides arising from class, gender and race.

Political Culture

Political culture is a rather vague concept referring essentially to the set of attitudes citizens hold towards society and the political system. It reflects myriad factors, including some already encountered in previous chapters: history, ideology, religion, geography, the constitution, and the institutions and range of informal practices associated with government. The study of political culture reminds us that maintaining a political regime depends upon thoughts as well as actions. For this reason much political activity at all levels is symbolic, aiming to make people happy with the system – to *legitimate* it.

A classic investigation of British political culture was carried out in the early 1960s by the American political scientists Almond and Verba (1963), who enthused that in Britain they had found a veritable jewel of a polity: nothing less than the ideal conditions for liberal democracy – a '**civic culture**' entailing respect for government and an unwillingness to resort to disruptive protest. There were three important ingredients in this civic mix: continuity, deference and consensus.

Continuity

We saw in chapter 4 that Britain has never made a dramatic revolutionary break with the past. The evolutionary pattern of change has preserved many ancient symbols and ceremonies. A brief republican period, seen as an aberration, was soon ended with the Restoration. However, critics see this conservative strain as holding back the process of social and political change. One symptom of this has been the preservation of deferential attitudes belonging to a distant monarchical past.

Deference

The best political culture for a capitalist state is a deferential one, where the masses willingly accept inequality and show little desire for change or to participate in government. Indeed, the essence of **deference** is that ordinary people believe that running the state should be left to those who 'know best'. It was noted by Walter Bagehot in 1867, when he argued that the masses were unable to understand the reality of government but were beguiled by a 'theatrical show' of monarchy and other *dignified* elements of the constitution.

Although the virtues of deference are questionable (for Aristotle, not to be involved in politics degraded one to the level of a beast), texts in the orthodox liberal-democratic tradition have generally admired it. This passivity was demonstrated in the depressions of the 1920s and 1930s (with the General Strike of 1926 failing to mobilize mass support). The feeling that things must be accepted has been seen as a very British characteristic, helping to explain why the Labour Party has been at its least electable whenever it has offered a radical programme.

A crisis of deference?

By the late 1960s orthodox writers began to fear that this 'civic society' was turning sour as a greater willingness to protest through unofficial strikes and demonstrations became apparent. When a miners' strike appeared to precipitate the downfall of Heath's government in 1974, the liberal-democratic apologists began a Cassandra-like lament that the country was becoming 'ungovernable'. To some extent Margaret Thatcher's call for a return to 'Victorian values' in the 1980s, and John Major's 'back to basics' campaign in the following decade, could be seen as nostalgic attempts to restore the age of deference.

By the opening of the twenty-first century British political culture was certainly different. Declining respect for the institutions of order such as the monarchy, priests, teachers and the police; 'laddish' behaviour, and a growing drug culture showed a society that had moved some way from the respect for hierarchy that had characterized the early post-war decades. Moreover, increasing voter apathy and a greater willingness to resort to various forms of direct action, sometimes leading to violence, suggested disenchantment with formal politics and its institutions.

However, the obituary for deference can be exaggerated. In 1980 Almond and Verba had 'revisited' the British political culture in a study that confirmed that, although there was cynicism, and even support for unlawful violence against the state, these attitudes were confined to a small, unpopular minority (see Kavanagh 1980). Labour leaders were actually condemning the actions of their non-deferential left-wing elements with as much ferocity as the Conservatives. From the early 1980s the rulers sought to persuade the masses that redundancies, cultural impoverishment and increasingly large differences in wealth were necessary for their own good. Thatcher denigrated the welfare state with reference to 'feather-bedding' and 'scrounging'. Her Employment Secretary, Norman Tebbit, coined a new catchphrase by suggesting that the unemployed should 'get on their bikes' in search of a job.

Like the General Strike, the recessions of the 1980s and 1990s were weathered with considerable patience and stoicism; in the acclaimed 1997 film, *The Full Monty*, the men cast aside by the economic system became not revolutionaries but strippers. In 1998, as French students took to the streets, their British counterparts were enduring reduced grants, student loans and tuition fees with largely token resistance. There was talk of Britain becoming a more **meritocratic** society in which the talented and thrusting would rise to the top. Yet curiously, such a society is not necessarily non-deferential. On the contrary, the 'success ideology' has been seen as a basis for quiescence by the working class and other disadvantaged groups in the face of social inequalities. Victims have only themselves to blame; revolution is unjustified.

Although newspapers increasingly report the behaviour of the high and mighty in non-deferential terms, the message remains broadly sympathetic to powerful capitalist interests. The Queen may have been mocked but it was a public-school-educated prime minister that media tycoon Rupert Murdoch helped to install in Downing Street in 1997. Despite the public's increased resort to direct action over issues such as animal rights and the environment from the 1990s, the Labour Party itself had swung massively to the right. When it finally regained office in 1997, it did so with the voices of its left-wing members muted, a tough law-and-order line and promises of 'no favours' for the unions. The crowds lining the route of the Queen Mother's funeral in April 2002 suggested that deference was by no means in its coffin. By 2010 Britain again had an Eton-educated prime minister with an aristocratic background. The following year saw the nation transfixed by a glittering royal wedding and one of the wettest June days in 2012 failed to dampen the spirits of the crowds lining the banks of the Thames to watch the royal barge sail past during the Queen's diamond jubilee celebrations.

Clearly the issue of deference is complex. Laddish behaviour, cheeky journalism and a refusal to vote do not suggest a politically assertive culture. Attitudes towards the constitution may offer a more fundamental guide and here the 1998 Human Rights Act may be instructive. This offers a chance to establish a rights culture in place of the subject culture preserved by the constitutional monarchy. It has conventionally been held that, unlike US or continental citizens, the great mass of the British have little interest in such matters. However, the Joseph Rowntree Reform Trust's large 'State of the Nation' survey of 2000 registered an increase in rights-based thinking, when compared with a 1995 survey, and it extended well beyond the drawing rooms of Hampstead (Dunleavy et al. 2001: 407–10). Ten years later, 52 per cent were 'strongly' agreeing with the statement that 'Britain needs a Bill of Rights to protect the liberty of the individual', with a further 28 per cent agreeing 'slightly'. Across a wide range of matters concerning their rights, the British were showing more demanding and assertive attitudes. The operation of the Act, a nod in the direction of a written constitution, may signal more fundamental changes to come.

Consensus

It can be argued that British political culture is highly consensual; the majority of the population are happy with the liberal-democratic system. The **consensus** can even extend to policy-making, the major parties having increasingly aimed for the centre ground. Yet the political culture is not as seamless and homogeneous as is sometimes thought. The UK was united partly by force, with lingering spatial tensions leading to new devolution settlements (examined in chapter 20). Beyond this, three other great fissures score the 'one-nation' landscape envisioned by liberal-democratic apologists: class, gender and race.

The history of all hitherto existing society is the history of class struggles.

Karl Marx, *The Communist Manifesto* (1848)

Classes Apart

Defining social class

Generally speaking, social classes categorize people on the basis of such characteristics as family background, occupation, income, manners, accent and privilege. **Class** is essentially about hierarchy and inequality, denoting social divisions similar to 'caste', 'rank', 'degree' and 'status'. Despite the claims of political leaders that Britain has evolved a 'classless society', it is of greater political significance in Britain than anywhere else in the English-speaking world. There are various bases for defining class, including the following.

Relationship to the means of production

More than any other thinker, Karl Marx made class central to his analysis (see p. 42). Under capitalism there is an essential dichotomy: a small upper class (or *bourgeoisie*) owning the capital needed for production, and a large working class (or **proletariat**) with only their labour to sell. The basic relationship between the two is exploitative.

Occupation

Another major figure in the study of class is German sociologist Max Weber (1864–1920). While accepting much of Marx's analysis, he argued that other factors were important, particularly the complex structure of the labour market. The capital-owning class contained *rentiers* and entrepreneurs, while the propertyless divided into those privileged with specialist skills and those without. Occupation is certainly a key variable, being generally correlated with a range of other factors – education, accent, social background, leisure activities, lifestyle, housing, and so on.

> *Misery and poverty are so absolutely degrading, and exercise such a paralysing effect that no class is ever really conscious of its own suffering. They have to be told of it by other people.*
> Oscar Wilde (1856–1900; Irish author and dramatist), *The Soul of Man under Socialism* (1891)

Socio-economic classification used by the Office for National Statistics (with examples of occupations in each class)

1 *Higher managerial and professional occupations*
   1.1 Large employers and higher managerial occupations: higher manager, company director, senior police officer, newspaper editor, top football manager
   1.2 Higher professional occupations: doctor, solicitor, engineer, teacher, airline pilot
2 *Lower managerial and professional occupations*: journalist, nurse/midwife, actor/musician, junior police officer, lower manager
3 *Intermediate occupations*: secretary, air stewardess, driving instructor, footballer
4 *Small employers and own account workers*: non-professional self-employed, publican, plumber, self-employed sportsperson, small farmer
5 *Lower supervisory and technical occupations*: craft worker, mechanic, train driver, foreman
6 *Semi-routine occupations*: traffic warden, caretaker, gardener, assembly-line worker
7 *Routine occupations*: cleaner, waitress, road-worker, docker
8 *Never worked and long-term unemployed*

Official surveys use an occupational classification that was revised in 1998 (for the 2001 census) to reflect the changing social structure: redundant workers setting up their own businesses, increased insecurity of employment, more women in work and the emergence of an 'underclass'. A widely used alternative occupational definition is that devised by the advertising industry, aiming to categorize people according to their consumption patterns.

> **Social class: advertising classification**
> In its efforts to persuade the right people to covet the right things, the advertising industry uses the following classification, which is widely used in social surveys.
>
> A   Higher managerial, administrative or professional
> B   Intermediate managerial, administrative or professional
> C1 Supervisory or clerical, and junior managerial, administrative or professional
> C2 Skilled manual
> D   Semi-skilled and unskilled manual
> E   State pensioners or widows (no other earnings), casual or lowest-grade workers and long-term unemployed

Income

It's not my burning ambition to make sure that David Beckham earns less money.

Tony Blair's comment during the 2001 general election campaign. (The ex-PM himself was reported to have earned £20 million in 2011)

Income generally shows wide variations between the few high earners and the many low earners. The early post-war period saw some reduction in income inequality, a trend enhanced by the tax system, but between the late 1970s and the end of the twentieth century an unprecedented increase occurred. In 1996, the gap between rich and poor was wider than at any time since 1886 (Goodman et al. 1997) and this trend continued under New Labour, with the richest fifth of the population increasing its share of national after-tax income to 45 per cent. By 2011 the OECD was reporting that the annual average income of the top 10 per cent of earners in the UK was just under £55,000, whilst the bottom 10 per cent averaged just £4,700 – with the gap between the richest and the poorest having widened between 1985 and 2010 (*Guardian*, 5 Dec. 2011).

Amongst those at the top end of the income range are the mega-earners. The Royal Commission on the Distribution of Income and Wealth (1976: 10) estimated that there were some 65,000 very highly paid employees in Britain in the 1970s. Globalization, financial deregulation, privatization and the tax revolution of the late 1980s were to swell this category into a new 'Super Class' (Adonis and Pollard 1997). Glimpses of this new breed were seen in high-profile examples such as 'Superwoman' Nicola Horlick, a working mother and City fund manager earning a reputed £1.15 million a year. The main driver in the rise of the super-earners was the financial services industry, with its US-dominated remuneration regime. The chief executives of the hundred largest UK companies were receiving on average £501,000 in 1995. There are also certain freakishly high, and usually short-lived, salaries earned by entertainers and sports personalities. In 2012, the Arsenal striker Robin van Persie was said to have turned down the offer of £300,000 a week from Manchester City, preferring instead to move to Manchester United for a weekly salary of 'just' £250,000 (*Independent*, 2 Nov. 2012). The popularity of such celebrities serves to legitimate the culture of inequality. Furthermore, tax breaks given to the 'fat cats' are justified by a theory that everyone else, even those in 'Cardboard City', benefits through the 'trickle-down effect'.

Wealth

Beyond earnings, there remains a basic dichotomy between a wealth-owning minority and the great mass. By 1997, the richest fifth of the British population were amongst the best-off in Europe (*Independent*, 15 June 1997). Even amongst the richest thousand, half the wealth at that time (almost £80 billion) was concentrated in the hands of the top 100. The proportion of wealth held by the richest, far from declining as it had in earlier decades, actually increased during the 1990s (table 8.1). As the new century opened, the millionaires' club was growing at a rate of 17 per cent a year.

Property is organized robbery.
George Bernard Shaw (1856–1950; Irish dramatist), Preface to *Major Barbara* (1907)

Table 8.1 Wealth ownership in the UK, 1923–1999 (percentages)

Year	Richest 1 per cent	Richest 5 per cent	Richest 10 per cent
1923[a]	61	82	89
1966[a]	31	56	69
1976	21	38	50
1986	18	36	50
1996	20	40	52
1999	23	43	54

[a] England and Wales only.

Source: Data from Atkinson and Harrison (1978: 159); *Social Trends* (2002: table 5.24).

Though wealth may take various forms – including stocks and shares, property and capital, which is handed down through the generations – the majority of those featured in the top thousand of the *Sunday Times* 'Rich List' now tend to be self-made millionaires. The list that had originally (in 1989) been dominated by inherited wealth and aristocracy, despite ten years of Thatcherism, now reflects wealth earned from commodities overseas, such as steel and oil. In 2013, Russian-born businessmen occupied three of the top five places and only one British-born citizen (the Duke of Westminster) had featured in the top ten in all twenty-five lists. The combined wealth of the thousand richest people in the UK had risen to £450 billion, with the number of billionaires (note, not millionaires) standing at eighty-eight (up from fifty-three in 2010).

> **Mind the wealth gap!**
> According to a study by the Office for National Statistics, total household wealth reached £10.3 trillion in 2008/10 (up from £9.1 trillion in 2006/8), but the gap between rich and poor was continuing to grow. The top 10 per cent of households, with a combined wealth of £4.5 trillion, were more than 500 times richer than the bottom 10 per cent (with only £8 billion between them).

Self-assigned class

There is also a subjective class structure, reflecting the way people perceive themselves (figure 8.1). The tendency in the post-war era has been for the working class to see themselves as going up rather than down in the world (though millionaire Sir Paul McCartney still termed himself working class). Despite politicians' claims that Britain was becoming a classless society, a BBC/ICM poll in September 1998 showed 55 per cent of people describing themselves as working class and 41 per cent as middle class, proportions that broadly accorded with an objective categorization. However, only 1 per cent claimed to be upper class, well below the objective assessment of 22 per cent. In 2011, the *Guardian*'s Polly Toynbee, commenting ahead of the launch of her BBC Radio series *The Class Ceiling*, reported the findings of a Britain Thinks poll that showed just 24 per cent regarded themselves as 'working class', 74 per cent 'middle class' and 4 per cent 'not sure'; no respondents categorized themselves as 'upper class'. Yet although self-assigned positions can be at variance with objective placings, they are important because they influence views on key issues, from the welfare state to trade unions, and thus voting behaviour.

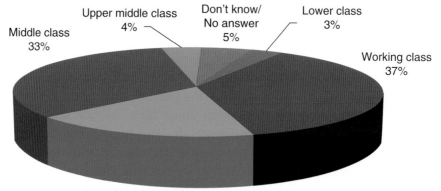

Figure 8.1 Self-assigned class: percentages identifying themselves as belonging to each class, 2009

Note: Less than 0.5 % identified themselves as upper class.

Source: Data from British Social Attitudes Survey, 2009.

An anatomy of the classes

When being described as rigidly class-divided, Britain is often contrasted with the USA, which is said to be classless. However, these are crude stereotypes; the USA is not without a social elite spanning the generations like an aristocracy, while mobility between classes is certainly possible in Britain. Goldthorpe (1987) found that 53 per cent of a sample of 10,000 British men surveyed in 1983 had changed classes. Yet Britain remains particularly class *conscious*. One indication of this is in attitudes towards the redistribution of income and resources: the rich resist it, and the poor favour it, more strongly than in comparable nations (Evans 1993: 133–4). Moreover, despite considerable social mobility in the mid-twentieth century, research shows that opportunities remain dominated by social origins and, unlike the USA, there is no evidence of a more open society (Devine 1997: 74).

Although the terms are used loosely, much discussion speaks of a broad threefold division into *upper class, middle class* and *working class.*

The upper class

The British upper class has evolved through a process of fusion and fission that amalgamated the landowning aristocracy, the lesser gentry, the financiers and the bourgeoisie who emerged with the industrial revolution (see Scott 1985: 29–35). In 1923, before the Labour Party and the welfare state had made any inroads into the pattern of distribution (see table 8.1), this powerful alliance constituted the richest fifth of the population, owning some 95 per cent of the nation's wealth. By 1972, with the welfare state at its peak, the richest fifth still claimed as much as 85 per cent, leaving 15 per cent to be shared amongst the rest (Urry 1985: 59–60). At the end of the twentieth century, 70 per cent of Britain's 60 million acres were still owned by less than 1 per cent of the population, while 77 per cent of the population lived on less than 6 per cent of the land. A decade later, in 2011, little had changed; with 0.6 per cent owning 69 per cent of the land.

> **Wealth, ancient and modern**
> Gerald Grosvenor, the Duke of Westminster, not only owns a sizeable chunk of London and large slices of Cheshire, North Wales, the Scottish Highlands, Ireland, Vancouver, Hawaii and Wagga Wagga, he had an income reported to be around £10,800 an hour in 1983 (*Sunday Times*, 20 Feb. 1983). With assets estimated around £4,700 million in 2002, he was back at the top of the *Sunday Times* 'Rich List' (7 April 2002), only to slip to eighth place (£7.8 bn) by 2013, behind foreign-born billionaires including the Hinduja brothers (10.6 bn), steel magnate Lakshmi Mittal (£10 bn) and Chelsea FC owner Roman Abramovich (£9.3 bn).

The holding of wealth is cumulative, since it generates considerable unearned income. For example, where the EU's Common Agricultural Policy once rewarded farmers for production, leading to the 'grain mountains' and 'wine lakes' of yore, it was, by 2011, apportioned instead on the basis of land 'farmed'. Whilst few would begrudge the National Trust the £8 million received as a result of this realignment in funding, critics question why the Duke of Westminster should receive £820,000 in EU subsidies, funded by taxpayers, simply by virtue of lands acquired in large part by an accident of birth (*Guardian*, 28 Nov. 2011).

> The stately homes of England,
> How beautiful they stand,
> To prove the upper classes
> Have still the upper hand.
>
> Noël Coward (1899–1973; British actor and playwright)

Members of this class share much in common in terms of background and values. Educated privately through the public-school system and disproportionately represented in the elite Oxbridge universities, their intense academic study has been

Classes apart. (a) A day at the races: picnicking at Royal Ascot;

complemented by a sense of training for leadership. Kinship (and old school) ties also ensure that family wealth is augmented rather than dispersed, while accountants and lawyers work assiduously to minimize the effects of inheritance and other taxes. Professional and social life further reinforce commonality. London clubs, golf clubs and freemasons preserve a sense of exclusiveness celebrated in ceremonies and great sporting events like the Lord's Test, Ascot, Wimbledon, Cowes, Henley Regatta, the Boat Race and the Grand National. At all these are hallowed places where ordinary folk may not enter: the Long Room at Lord's, the Royal Box and the Royal Enclosure.

The presence of the upper class is venerated with archaic symbols: a reigning monarch, a fully fledged aristocracy and a host of ancient sinecures such as Lord Lieutenant of the County and High Sheriff. The exclusion process is strengthened by a preoccupation with dress, manners and accent (mocked in Bernard Shaw's *Pygmalion*). These symbols of privilege serve to legitimate the inequality produced by modern capitalism. This explains why the British bourgeoisie sought not to overthrow the bastions of privilege but to ingratiate itself with the old elite through a process of social climbing. The class has shown a genius for survival, assimilating talented or successful members of the lower orders like a vampire sucking the life-blood of the young. This lack of rigid 'structuration' (Giddens 1979: ch. 6) helps to legitimate the system (anyone can become a millionaire, as the dot-com boom demonstrated).

> *We are forever being told that we have a rigid class structure. That's a load of codswallop.*
> Prince Edward, quoted in the *Observer* (21 Sept. 1997)

(b) A night in Tottenham High Road: sleeping rough

In terms of ideology the upper class exhibits a high degree of homogeneity, though there remains a broad division between the paternalism inherited from Tory traditions – a belief that privilege carries duties – and the hard-nosed whiggish tradition of individualism and competition resuscitated in the 1980s. In addition, much has been made of notions of racial superiority; members of the class saw themselves as shouldering the 'white man's burden' in the great days of empire and of being 'born to rule'. Ideologically their sympathies have generally been towards the right, which has usually meant supporting the Conservative Party, of which many have been members. However, they are equally willing to support Labour if it can deliver the enterprising low-tax regime they desire. Thus David Sainsbury, head of the supermarket dynasty, was an enthusiastic supporter of the New Labour government by which he was ennobled, and three of the top ten individual donations during the 2010 general election campaign were to the Labour Party (with the Conservatives netting seven).

The Establishment

> The Establishment talks with its own branded accents; eats different meals at different times; has its privileged system of education; its own religion, even, to a large extent, its own form of football.
>
> A. J. P. Taylor (1906–90; British historian), in *New Statesman* (8 Aug. 1953)

Linked with the notion of an upper class is that of the '**Establishment**', a vague but often-used term, popularized in the 1950s (Thomas 1959) and denoting a closed group comprising those in control of the leading institutions (public schools, church, monarchy and aristocracy, mass media, traditional professions, Parliament, armed forces, civil service, the City, and of course the owners and managers of industry). Many dislike the term, particularly those alleged to be part of it, and it is clearly related to the idea of the upper class, though some would use the term 'elite'. This is discussed further in chapter 19.

An Englishman's way of speaking absolutely classifies him. The moment he talks he makes some other Englishman despise him.
Professor Higgins, in Alan Jay Lerner's musical *My Fair Lady* (1956)

The middle class

Despite his essentially dichotomous view of class structure, Marx did recognize 'middle and intermediate strata'. However, he believed that the obligation to sell their labour, and hence their inability to accumulate capital, would mean that the middle class would ultimately become part of a massive proletariat. The fact that this has not happened in Britain has important implications for the legitimation process. The growth of a vast intermediate class can be seen as a process of ***embourgeoisement***.

Much analysis discusses politics and society in these terms, with the intermediate class commonly divided into three – upper, middle and lower – largely distinguished on the basis of occupation. The upper middle class broadly includes the intelligentsia, professional people and managers, termed the 'service class' or 'salariat' by John Goldthorpe (1982). The middle characteristically contains the petite bourgeoisie, a tenacious class of small business people who resist the drive to large-scale operation, while the lower middle comprises white- and blue-collar workers, who generally try to espouse middle-class values.

The Great British Class Survey

Conducted in association with the BBC in 2011, this suggested that traditional class divisions were outdated. After measuring economic capital (income, savings, house value), social capital (the number and status of people someone knows) and cultural capital (the extent and nature of cultural interests and activities), the researchers (Savage et al. 2013) proposed a more sophisticated seven-class model. It was claimed that this not only reflected the polarization in British society but also gave a much more nuanced picture of the fragmentation of its middle layers.

- *Elite*: the most privileged group, with the highest levels of all three capitals and distinguished from the other six classes through its wealth.
- *Established middle class*: a large and gregarious group, the second wealthiest, and scoring highly on all three capitals.
- *Technical middle class*: a small, distinctive, new and prosperous group but distinguished by its social isolation and cultural apathy.
- *New affluent workers*: a young socially and culturally active group, with middling levels of economic capital.
- *Traditional working class*: although scoring low on all three capitals, not completely deprived, and having reasonably high house values (due to having the oldest average age at 66).
- *Emergent service workers*: a new, young, urban group, relatively poor but with high social and cultural capital.
- *Precariat (precarious proletariat)*: the poorest, most deprived class, scoring low for social and cultural capital.

A classless society?

Many saw the Thatcher era as the final seal on the creation of this middle-class-dominated society, which enthusiasts, including John Major and Tony Blair, preferred to call a *classless* society. There is clearly much in the *embourgeoisement* thesis; capitalism changed dramatically during the twentieth century. However, it can be argued that the idea of the classless society contains an element of mythology, obscuring the continued holding and control of great wealth by the few. Indeed, during a decade of Thatcherism 'old money' prospered as never before in the

The charm of Britain has always been the ease with which one can move into the middle class.

Margaret Thatcher, in the *Observer* (27 Oct. 1974)

post-war era. Adonis and Pollard (1997) argued that class barriers actually *increased* during the 1990s. Middle-class vulnerability was demonstrated throughout the 1980s and 1990s as professions such as university lecturers, civil servants and doctors saw their jobs threatened by governments intent upon reducing the tax burden placed upon the rich. The public-sector cuts imposed by the 2010 Conservative–Liberal Democrat coalition also fell on these same middle-class professional groups, which Labour leader Ed Miliband designated the 'squeezed middle'.

The working class

Today the term 'working class' is not employed in the Marxist sense. 'Work' can range from investment banking to road-sweeping but few would place them together in their class location. Again, although condemned to idleness, the unemployed are generally placed within the working-class category. The essential feature of this class is that its members lack wealth and power. Yet this great majority of the British people can only be designated as a class in the very loosest of senses and it lacks the homogeneity Marx ascribed to it. There are multifarious distinctions within it in terms of race, colour, spatial distribution, income, gender, occupation and, most importantly, in perceptions of the capitalist system.

A shrinking class?

The decline of mining and heavy industry, new (post-Fordist) industrial practices and the globalization of the production process have eliminated many jobs and decimated traditional communities. Lockwood (1966) saw the working class splitting into three: traditional proletarians such as miners and shipworkers, who showed great class solidarity; traditional deferential workers, with a sense of hierarchy and respect for their 'betters'; and privatized workers, with an individualistic view of life and work and upwardly mobile aspirations. These were to become electorally significant from the late 1970s.

Our human stock is threatened . . . single parents from classes 4 and 5 are now producing a third of all births. If we do nothing, the nation moves towards degeneration.
Sir Keith Joseph (1918–94; Conservative politician), speech to Birmingham Conservatives (Oct. 1974)

Is the working class shrinking? Goldthorpe's (1987) class schema identified a shrunken working class as the upgrading of employment in a range of occupations created a new enlarged middle class. In contrast, neo-Marxist Erik Olin Wright (1985) argued that the essential class structure remained unchanged for most of the twentieth century: a large proletariat at the bottom comprising a range of new non-manual but unskilled occupations that stood in the same vulnerable position vis-à-vis capital as the old working class, a small bourgeoisie at the top and an even smaller middle class sandwiched between. The insecurity of employment for many blue-collar and routine clerical workers leaves them little different from manual workers.

Mind the gap: an underclass?

Marx also saw a class below the working class – the *lumpenproletariat*. During the 1980s and 1990s J. K. Galbraith (1993) postulated a widening gap between a prosperous majority living securely in a 'culture of contentment' and a depressed minority of the socially vulnerable – the unemployed, low paid, homeless, elderly, handicapped, chronically sick, disabled, ethnic minorities, single-parent families, those with low educational attainments and those dropping out of the 'rat race' of competitive society. They have been characterized by American sociologist Charles Murray (1990) as an **underclass**, a term criticized by Adonis and Pollard (1997) as an elitist argument concealing the true extent of poverty by implying it to be confined to a small minority. Indeed, economic journalist Will Hutton (1996: 105–10) argued that government policy from the 1990s, deliberately fostering widespread inequality, had resulted in what he termed a 30/30/40 society.

The 30/30/40 society

- *Top 40% privileged*: Tenured, secure, full-time jobs or self-employed, a category shrinking by 1 per cent a year.
- *Middle 30% structurally insecure*: Part-time work, little protection.
- *Bottom 30% disadvantaged*: Unemployed, economically inactive, marginalized.

The Joseph Rowntree Foundation's 2011 report, *Monitoring Poverty and Social Exclusion*, found that more than 2.5 million individuals were living in households experiencing 'deep poverty' – defined as having a household income of less than 40 per cent of the median (Aldridge et al. 2011). Social geographer Danny Dorling (2011) drew a picture of stark inequality using a variety of indicators, replacing the Beveridge goals of freedom from ignorance, want, idleness, squalor and disease with elitism, exclusion, prejudice, greed and despair.

Class and politics

What has class to do with politics? Class is essentially about who has what in society and its political effects are felt in voting behaviour, the media, the realm of ideas and attitudes, education and health. Domination within a wide range of social relationships is often based upon class. Does domination go further than this: can one class collectively dominate the whole of society? In other words, does Britain have a ruling class? This important question is explored throughout this book and particularly in chapter 19.

The Monstrous Regiment: Sexism in British Society

The First Blast of the Trumpet Against the Monstrous Regiment of Women.
Title of pamphlet by John Knox (1505–72; charismatic Scottish preacher)

In turning to the question of gender we are by no means leaving the issue of class because women have been predominant in the lower echelons of the class structure. Moreover, in all classes men tend to dominate women. This remains true despite the fact that from 1979 to 1990 Britain had a woman prime minister.

British patriarchy

British culture is **sexist** and patriarchal: a woman's social position has been largely fixed by the men in her life, mainly her father and husband. Working-class culture has been particularly male-dominated, with the trade union bastions of **patriarchy**. The domination is betrayed in our very language, with the repetitious use of the male pronoun: not only have committees largely been headed by chairmen, even God is a man. In the human race we are all *Homo sapiens*; where is the *Femina sapiens?*

The modern pattern of domination by gender did not originate with the capitalism that shapes life today. In many African cultures women spend the day in hard physical labour while the men remain largely idle, Asian civilizations retain rigid sexist traditions and under Islamic Sharia law the treatment of women is seen as repressive. As long ago as 300 BC, in an idyll by Theocritus, Praxinoa, a fine lady, rushes away from a show at the royal palace telling her friend: 'I must be getting back. It's Diocleidas' dinner time, and that man's all pepper; I wouldn't advise anyone to come near him when he's kept waiting for his food' (Seltman 1956: 134). However, male domination and the concept of the family unit have proved functional for capitalism by providing a means for the reproduction and maintenance of labour.

Women and work

The oldest profession?
Even when women have full rights, they still remain factually down-trodden because all house work is left to them. In most cases house work is the most unproductive, the most barbarous and the most arduous work a woman can do.

V. I. Lenin (1870–1924; Russian communist leader),
Collected Works (vol. XXX: 43)

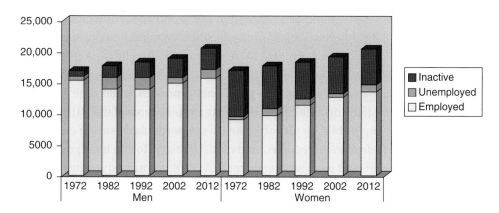

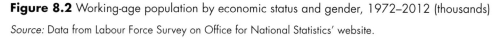

Figure 8.2 Working-age population by economic status and gender, 1972–2012 (thousands)
Source: Data from Labour Force Survey on Office for National Statistics' website.

The multi-faceted subjugation of women is nowhere better illustrated than in paid employment. The growth of capitalism made possible a sharp distinction between two forms of work: the *commodity production* of industry and *domestic production* at home. However, the latter is not usually considered real work at all and housewives socialized by the commodity production ethos tend to say: 'I don't have a job'. Figure 8.2 illustrates the extent to which women continue to be classified as 'economically inactive' (a category including housekeeping).

For many women, paid employment must be fitted around the full-time domestic production role, yet this has not significantly altered the basic organization of work practices. The effect is to exclude women from many sections of the labour market. An additional problem is that of the single-parent family – largely a euphemism for families without a man, marital break-up or unintended pregnancy usually leaving the children with the mother. The position can be particularly degrading as the need for an income, coupled with an inability to give a full-time commitment, often oblige women to accept menial, low-prestige occupations. Immigrant women, sometimes from particularly sexist societies, are even more vulnerable, often accepting sweatshop conditions and denied unionization. Even professional women can expect to be dominated by their male colleagues, denied promotion by a 'glass ceiling', while those returning to work after child-rearing tend to occupy positions far lower than their qualifications warrant.

The propensity to gravitate towards menial jobs means that, unlike men, women tend to work in a more limited number of occupations. Over half are in three service sectors – distributive trades, secretarial and miscellaneous unskilled (e.g. catering, cleaning). They are also found predominantly in caring work such as nursing, primary education and social services, thereby reinforcing the cultural definition of their identity as servers rather than creators. Although changes in employment patterns

Mother is the dead heart of the family, spending father's earnings on consumer goods to enhance the environment in which he eats, sleeps and watches the television.

Germaine Greer (Australian-born feminist), *The Female Eunuch* (1970)

from the early 1980s saw a rapid acceleration in the recruitment of women into the workforce (figure 8.2), this was largely in the flexible, vulnerable, poorly unionized and low-paid service industries. By 2012 there were nearly 8 million people working part time, almost 80 per cent of whom were women. The increasing casualization of the labour force saw women taking low-paid, part-time jobs while their husbands suffered redundancy (Hutton 1996: 106). The austerity measures of the 2010 coalition government, involving public sector job losses, were particularly severe on women. In March 2012 the *Independent* reported that of 210,000 jobs lost in local government since 2010, over 68 per cent were among women. A GMB union study found thirty-six councils in England and Wales where all job losses were among women.

Political implications of sexism

Women have served all these centuries as looking-glasses possessing the magic and delicious power of reflecting the figure of man at twice its natural size.

Virginia Woolf (1882–1941; English writer), *A Room of One's Own* (1929)

As was amply demonstrated in the suffragettes' battle for the franchise (see chapter 10), a male culture has not welcomed women in politics. Women's issues have tended to remain off the political agenda and women themselves have rarely become political activists; far less unionized than men, they may even withhold support from their husbands when on strike. Women have been poorly represented on the TUC and, although attitudes have become more sympathetic, there remains much deep-seated sexism within trade unions. Despite the influx of women MPs since 1997, Parliament remains an overwhelmingly male club (see chapter 14), seen at its most bizarre when pontificating on abortion, at times appearing to view the foetus as male property placed in the womb for safe keeping.

During the 1970s, legislation on sex discrimination and equal pay marked the inauguration of a sex equality strategy. However, the legalistic removal of barriers by governments committed to a minimalist state role did little to change behaviour. Indeed, policies from the 1980s were particularly bad for women, with much rhetoric on the theme of family breakdown. Women could be blamed for failings such as low educational standards, drug abuse among the young and juvenile delinquency. Social policies shifted the care of the old, chronically ill and handicapped from the state to the family under a policy termed 'Care in the Community'. The freezing of child benefit payments also specifically targeted women. Labour in power initially appeared no less harsh in the eyes of many of its critics, with its policy of getting single mothers off state benefits and into work (a policy supported by most of its record new intake of women MPs).

Deeply sexist attitudes vein state institutions. It will be apparent throughout this book that the world we are examining is one of male dominance. The vast majority of cabinet ministers, judges, higher civil servants, MPs, councillors, soldiers and police are still male. Despite becoming Britain's first woman prime minister, Margaret Thatcher was to appoint no other members of her own sex to her Cabinet.

A study of the north-east, published in 2000, which was not considered atypical, revealed men comprising 87 per cent of the region's MPs, 77 per cent of its elected councillors, 74 per cent of its housing association members and 66 per cent of the regional arts council (Durham University 2000). Hence, over eighty years after granting women the vote, the political system still served 'to institutionalize and reproduce inequalities between the sexes' (Lovenduski 1996).

Women on top?

However, as seen in chapter 3, feminism is now a recognized ideology and the women's movement is part of politics. A number of concessions have been gained in the areas of equal opportunities and pay, and women have been appointed to some high-profile positions: there has been a woman speaker in the Commons and the first two Lords speakers were women, Stella Rimington became head of MI5 and Elizabeth Filkin replaced Sir Gordon Downey as Parliamentary Commissioner for Standards. However, in 2001 the latter two were to depart under clouds, falling foul of whispering campaigns within the male establishment club. A similar fate befell Mo Mowlam, despite the great advances she had made as Northern Ireland secretary. Women have also been involved in some major *causes célèbres*, not least the Greenham Common encampment against Cruise missiles. By the end of the twentieth century, girls were outperforming boys in school and women were finding it easier to pursue professional careers.

A record number of women entered Parliament in 1997 and a record number had positions in Blair's first Cabinet, rising to seven after his 2001 election victory. Although the most senior positions, such as chancellor, home secretary and foreign secretary, have generally remained in male hands, there have been notable exceptions to the rule. Labour's Jacqui Smith (2007) and the Conservatives' Theresa May (2010) both served as home secretary and Labour's Margaret Beckett became the first female foreign secretary in 2006. Yet in 2010 Cameron appointed only four women to his Cabinet (less than 20 per cent). This compared unfavourably with other western democracies at the time. According to the Centre for Women and Democracy, women made up 53 per cent of the Cabinet in Spain, 50 per cent in Sweden, 38 per cent in Germany, 33 per cent in France and 31 per cent in the USA.

Race and Politics

Over the course of the 1990s, Britain became an increasingly multiracial society (table 8.2), the ethnic minority population having grown from some 3.2 million in 1992–4 to 3.7 million in 1997–9, a rise of 15.6 per cent (*Population Trends*, 2001). The fastest-growing groups were the Muslim Bangladeshi and Black African populations

Table 8.2 Ethnic composition of the British population, 1996/7 and 2000/1 (millions)

Year	White	Black	Indian	Pakistani/ Bangladeshi	Chinese	Other/ mixed
1996/7	52.9	0.9	0.9	0.8	0.1	0.6
2000/1	53.0	1.3	1.0	0.9	0.1	0.7

Source: Data from *Social Trends* (2002: table 1.4).

(30 and 37 per cent, respectively). Over the same period the white population had increased by only 1 per cent, reaching 53 million. The process was further accelerated by an increase in asylum applications and the economic migration that accompanied each stage of EU enlargement, and by differential birth rates between those different ethnic groups resident within the UK (table 8.3). Yet there is a deep-seated, indelible **racism** within the political culture. Although many white people may doubt this, few with a West Indian or Asian background could agree with them: race and racism lie at the very heart of their social and economic experience.

Table 8.3 Population and population growth by ethnic group, England and Wales, 2001–2009 (thousands)

Ethnic group	Mid-2001 population	Mid-2009 population	Percentage of total population	Average annual percentage growth*
White	47,745.2	48,188.9	87.9	0.1
Non-'White British'	6,641.2	9,127.1	16.7	4.7
Mixed	672.0	986.6	1.8	5.8
Asian	2,316.6	3,219.5	5.9	4.9
Black	1,165.4	1,540.1	2.8	4.0
Other	460.9	874.1	1.6	11.2
All groups	52,360.0	54,809.1	–	0.6

* Natural change plus net migration.

Source: Data from Office for National Statistics, *Population Estimates by Ethnic Group 2002–2009* (2011: table 1).

What is racism?

The human species may be said to consist of several races distinguished by superficial physical characteristics (size, colour of hair and skin, etc.). These are only broad distinctions: many individuals do not fit the physical type suggested by their racial origins and intermarriage further blurs the picture. Recognition of these differences is not racism. Racism is the practice of discriminating against people on the grounds of race. Some regimes (the European fascists in the 1930s and South Africa in the days of apartheid) have been openly based on the belief that racial differences justify inequality, the implication being that some races are morally or intellectually superior. Apart from being ethically objectionable, this is quite impossible to sustain because of differences in cultural environments. It is about as logically defensible as the distinction Gulliver encountered in Lilliput based upon the method of eating a boiled egg, which resulted in bloody war for 'six and thirty moons' between the 'Big-Endians' and 'Little-Endians'!

All those who are not racially pure are mere chaff.
Adolf Hitler (1889–1945), *Mein Kampf* (1925–6)

Manifestations of racism

Although racism in Britain today does not take the open and violent forms seen in Nazi Germany, the American deep south, or apartheid South Africa, it has permeated every nook and cranny of life, from the membership of clubs and societies to sport, housing, newspapers, employment, education and everyday language. The most openly racist white people have a rich lexicon of derogatory terms, ranging from 'our coloured cousins', 'nigger' and 'wog', to the more obscene. Such attitudes are also found in state institutions, with the police and army subject to particular criticism (see chapter 23).

Source: Mary Evans Picture Library

In Great Britain racism is smouldering like the funeral pyres in the areas of foot and mouth.
Stern (German magazine, May 2001)

When Hitler and Mussolini were taking power in the 1930s, Britain had its own fascist movement, led by Sir Oswald Mosley. Although making minimal impact, fascist and far right parties have continued to exist, including the National Socialist Movement, the National Front, the British Movement and the British National Party (BNP). The BNP enjoyed a string of electoral successes at local level (see chapter 13), but failed to win a single seat in the 2010 general election, despite fielding some 300 candidates. Although its leader, Nick Griffin, publicly abandoned the goal of an 'all-white Britain' in 2009, the party's rank and file are still widely seen as espousing racist sentiments. The rise of the UK Independence Party (UKIP) can be seen partly as a response to a fear of immigration rather than any particular animosity towards the EU.

As racist patterns continue, the threat of further resistance, including violence, increases. One result has been for ethnic minorities to turn inwards, living a self-contained existence in decaying inner-city ghettos and abandoning the ambition to participate on equal terms in society. In December 2001, the Cantle Report on serious race riots earlier that year in Oldham, Bradford and Burnley revealed ethnic and white communities living separate existences and lacking a sense of common civic identity. It is the young with no experience of a home other than Britain who feel the greatest sense of alienation and despair and who are likely to vent their frustration in rioting. By the late 1990s, most major cities had experienced clashes between young blacks and the police. The case against white youths accused of murdering black youth Stephen Lawrence in 1993 was initially dismissed for lack of evidence, though the Macpherson Report into the affair suggested an underlying racist culture amongst the police. Public sensitivity to the issue of racism and policing was shown in the serious rioting in London and other cities after the police shooting of Mark Duggan in August 2011.

The roots of racism

The British have long attributed their supremacy to God, who is frequently enjoined to 'make us mightier yet'. Hence it is not surprising that Jews in particular have been vilified. The late-Victorian journalist W. N. Ewer mocked: 'How odd of God, to choose, the Jews', and from Shakespeare's *Merchant of Venice* to Dickens's Fagin they have been depicted as miserly and grasping. Similarly, the Irish (notwithstanding Wilde, Shaw, Joyce, Behan, Heaney et al.) have long been considered inferior. The great age of discovery revealed to West European eyes a vast world of 'savages': inferior beings to be tamed, trained and deprived of their land, culture and property. The seventeenth-century slave trade made the English curiously interested in race. Part of the justification for this abomination was a belief that Africans were so inferior in character and brain that to be enslaved by the white man was actually an improvement! Rudyard Kipling's 'The white man's burden' appears to justify colonization and imperialism as being beneficial for the subjugated peoples:

Take up the White Man's burden –
And reap his old reward:
The blame of those ye better,
The hate of those ye guard.

British thought and British society has never been cleansed of the Augean filth of imperialism.
Salman Rushdie (b. 1947; British Indian novelist), in *New Society* (9 Dec. 1982)

The development of the empire as an integral part of British capitalism had a particular significance for today's racist attitudes. The British defeated European rivals in the pillage of the New World, where they subjugated the indigenous populations. By the closing decades of the eighteenth century, once the Indian subcontinent had been retrieved from the French, the empire was the largest the world had ever experienced. Truly they were a master race. Victorian scientists pictured mankind in terms of a great hierarchy, with the white Englishman invariably at the top and the negro just above the ape at the bottom. The claimed superiority was largely attributed to the dominant class, not to the lower orders labouring in conditions scarcely better than those of slaves. However, the extension of the franchise obliged establishment forces to seek their support, a seemingly impossible enterprise accomplished through the Disraelian concept of 'one nation'. In this great legitimating myth the empire was invoked as a unifying symbol, serving to bestow splendour on even the most lowly; they were part of the race that ruled the world. This sentiment was to bequeath a lasting sense of **xenophobia**.

Recognition of this legacy came from Home Secretary Jack Straw in July 2000, when he attributed the hooliganism of English football fans abroad to a distorted sense of patriotism that was part of the 'baggage of empire'. The feelings are not confined to those of a different colour. The general unease with the EU is testimony to a problem many British people have with those from any other country. A 2001 British Council poll of young people in seventeen countries showed these sons of Britannia to be widely regarded not as 'cool' but as arrogant, often drunk and 'xenophobic' (Burke 2001).

The pattern of immigration

Contrary to the Victorian theory, the British 'race' is in no sense pure; it is a mongrel breed including Celts, Romans, Anglo-Saxons, Normans and Danes that would struggle to be accorded class status at a *Homo sapiens* Crufts Show. After 1066 the country was host to further waves of immigration: the medieval period saw large numbers of Jewish settlers, at the end of the seventeenth century came the Huguenots escaping persecution in France, and the eighteenth-century Irish famine brought a further major influx. It was never in the British nature to welcome the newcomers. In 1601 Elizabeth I issued a proclamation to remove the country's few black people and a 1605 Act restricted the rights of aliens. However, time

We shall have to start progressively removing their rights. If bloodshed and racial strife are the result, then all I can say is that that is an acceptable price to pay for clearing out the immigrants.

Anthony Reed-Herbert of the National Front, quoted in *The Times* (24 June 1976)

generally soothed irate feelings and the immigrants were well integrated, some to become very successful (amongst the most successful were William of Orange, the Hanoverians and the Saxe-Coburgs). Intermarriage frequently meant that the only sign of foreign origins was an unusual name, and sometimes even these were changed. (Conscious of its German connotations, the Saxe-Coburgs prudently changed their name to Windsor during the first world war.)

A new wave of immigration began in the post-imperial era. The 1948 British Nationality Act gave common British citizenship to all Commonwealth citizens, providing a labour source to compensate for shortages at home. Workers from India, Pakistan and the West Indies were encouraged through recruitment drives by public bodies such as the NHS and London Transport. Their willingness to undertake uncongenial, low-paid work enabled some traditional industries, such as textiles, to survive in an increasingly competitive world economy. Governments aimed to manipulate public opinion to accept the new influx (Paul 1997: 65). Although the first of the immigrants (mainly men) met with resistance, they were buoyed up by the expectation that, as in the past, they would become integrated. However, such optimism proved illusory. Despite the efforts of bodies such as the Runnymede Trust, fighting for racial equality and social justice, a second British-born generation remained as black as its parents, excluded from better jobs, confined to poor housing in inner-city areas, with inferior education and health care and subject to racially inspired violence. Problems intensified as the long boom of western capitalism ran out of steam. The black population, particularly vulnerable to the automation of manufacturing and textile industries, suffered disproportionately as unemployment began to rise (figure 8.3). Adding insult to injury, they were seen as one of the *causes* of unemployment.

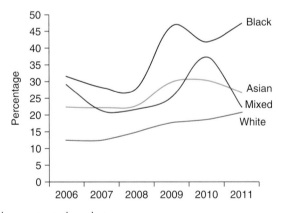

Figure 8.3 Unemployment rate by ethnic group

Note: Unemployment rate is calculated as a proportion of the economically active population.

Source: Data from Office for National Statistics, *Statistical Bulletin* (June 2012).

The break-up of the Soviet Union prompted a new wave of immigration as people fled from the horrors of ethnic cleansing, tribal war and economic collapse. The accession of many former Eastern Bloc states to the EU, most notably that of the so-called A8 states in 2004, only served to accelerate the process. According to EU estimates there were 265,000 A8 nationals living in the UK by May 2004 (Barrell et al. 2007: table 1), with the figure trebling over the course of the next five years. Whether called asylum-seekers, bogus asylum-seekers, economic migrants or illegal immigrants, the incomers inflamed the passions of the tabloid press and prompted a reaction from politicians in the form of stricter laws, tighter appeals procedures, voucher systems and detention centres. Despite tabloid alarm, however, the great majority of non-EU applications to remain are turned down.

Institutional racism

Racism can be enstructured into the very institutions of society through laws and habitual practices. It can be found in the legal system, the civil service and educational institutions. The 1999 Macpherson Report highlighted the problem within the police service. David Wilmot, Chief Constable of Greater Manchester, caused considerable shock when he admitted to **institutional racism** within his own ranks. Critics can claim that racism has been institutionalized through legislation (passed by both major parties) designed to restrict the immigration of certain ethnic groups. The 1958 Notting Hill race riots marked a grim watershed, leading to the first post-war Immigration Act in 1962. This restricted entry from the black Commonwealth to those able to show they were coming to a specific job, or able to offer a particular skill. Women were subject to strict physical examinations, including a degrading internal virginity test.

The grim reality of the Smethwick election result in 1964 (when an openly racist Conservative using the slogan 'If you want a nigger for a neighbour, vote Labour' won a stunning victory) and increasing anti-black hysteria led Labour to introduce even tougher restrictions in 1965, allowing deportation by the Home Secretary (without a court hearing) of any illegal immigrant of less than five years' standing. A new style of rhetoric, speaking of the 'small crowded island', transformed what had been far-right views into respectable orthodoxy. Home Secretary Roy Jenkins, hitherto a notable advocate of the humane society, stressed the 'social factor' limiting the number that could be absorbed. In 1968 the Commonwealth Immigrants Act (to stem immigration from turbulent Kenya) was rushed through Parliament in only two days. The Conservatives consolidated the position in 1971 with an Act restricting entry to patrials (those with parents or grandparents born in the UK), while the 1981 British Nationality Act effectively closed the door to non-whites, though keeping another open for 6 million patrials and the 200 million in the EC.

Racism and politics

> Members of Parliament who represent ethnic minorities – unlike their colleagues who sit for prosperous suburban seats – are always criticised for advancing the claims of their constituents. It is part of the racism which afflicts our society.
>
> Roy Hattersley, *Who Goes Home?* (1996: 284)

The politics of Britain logically gives ethnic minorities and working-class whites more reason to unite than divide, yet racism has appeared at its strongest among unskilled workers. Even within the active left there has been a strong vein of racism, particularly evident in the trade unions. Immigrants have been seen as depressing wage levels and taking employment from indigenous workers. The TUC has pressed enthusiastically for action against illegal immigrants and there is a lengthy catalogue of disputes involving racist behaviour by members and officials. Hence, although Labour has received more solid support from ethnic minorities than from working-class whites, its trade-union roots have inhibited its response. The Scarman Report on the 1981 Brixton riots criticized 'the low level of black representation in our elective political institutions' (Scarman 1981: 16). Yet Labour remained strongly opposed to black sections, thereby denying black people the distinct political voice afforded to women. It was not until May 2002 that Labour's Paul Boateng made history by becoming the first black member of the Cabinet. In 2010 Baroness Warsi was appointed as a Conservative minister without portfolio, the first Muslim woman to serve in a Cabinet.

As I look ahead, I am filled with foreboding. Like the Roman, I seem to see 'the River Tiber foaming with much blood'.
Enoch Powell (1912–98; Conservative MP), speech expressing his fears over immigration (20 April 1968)

The reality of British political culture means that 'there are votes for the picking in fanning the flames of racial resentment' (Crewe 1983: 263), though it has been argued that racism is a weapon of last resort for conservative parties, particularly in the post-cold-war period (Thranhardt 1995: 337). The racist vote was most effectively garnered for the Conservatives by Enoch Powell, whose lurid speeches lamented the submergence of a halcyon English age under the great alien tidal wave. A Gallup poll exposed the stark truth that 75 per cent of the population were broadly sympathetic to his sentiments (Marwick 1982). Fascism had given racism a bad name but Powell made it 'respectable amongst those who saw the Tory party as the epitome of conformist respectability' (Bhavnani and Bhavnani 1985: 150). By

> The party must learn that holding three or four receptions for Asian millionaires every year does not amount to a race relations policy. Whenever I go to central office the only other black face is the security guard at the door.
>
> John Taylor (defeated Conservative candidate at Cheltenham in 1992 general election, 12 Oct. 1993)

the late 1970s, therefore, the National Front had seen its popular support eroded by the Conservatives who, with their hard-line immigration stance, had stolen its central political message.

Powell was known to be greatly admired by Margaret Thatcher, who herself warned of the danger that 'this country might be swamped by people with a different culture' (Sivanandan 1981: 145). Upon becoming Conservative leader she was seen by some as 'a poor man's Enoch Powell' (Johnson 1985: 114). While the neoliberalism of the New Right was not itself racist, its authoritarian strand took a hard line on social issues. From here came a 'new racism', its message shrouded in a language of social responsibility. Stressing Englishness, national identity and common cultural history, it attacked multiculturalism (Gordon and Klug 1986), while MP Norman Tebbit regarded support for visiting cricket teams as a 'test'. In the 2001 election campaign, Conservative leader William Hague spoke of a Britain that was soon to become a 'foreign land', sparking off new accusations that the party was sending out a covert racist message. A year later, Labour Home Secretary David Blunkett caused public controversy by suggesting that asylum-seekers were 'swamping' some British schools.

Hence the claim that there is a gentleman's agreement among politicians not to use race for political advantage may be bogus; racism helps sustain class domination. From the 'one-nation' appeal of Disraeli, Conservatives have vaunted patriotism as more honourable than class loyalty. Yet in the words of Dr Johnson, patriotism was 'the last refuge of a scoundrel'. Unlike that of gender, the racial division has not cut across class. Despite a growing number of upwardly mobile Asians (Saggar 1992: 207), black people belong largely to the working class, so racism weakens working-class solidarity, particularly during economic recession. The depression of the early 1990s saw a tide of racial assaults accompanied by burgeoning support for the BNP in London's East End, as well as in some cities in the northwest. Such results cause alarm by revealing that, in the privacy of the polling booth, many voters are willing to give their support to the openly racist party. Similarly, the growing success of UKIP in the twenty-first century was also often attributed to its opposition to immigration rather than simply popular disenchantment with the EU.

Brothers in law: race relations legislation

Governments have shown themselves to be aware of the problems. Attempts to curb racism were seen in the 1965, 1968 and 1976 Acts designed to outlaw discrimination, and the establishment of the Commission for Racial Equality (CRE) to enforce their provisions. The Macpherson Report led to the first new piece of race relations legislation for twenty-five years. The Race Relations (Amendments) Act (2000) (which came into operation in April 2001) extended existing provisions against racial discrimination to previously excluded public bodies, including hospitals, the prisons service and the police. The Equality Acts of 2006 and 2010 brought further changes, transferring the responsibilities of the CRE, the Equal Opportunities Commission and the Disability Rights Commission to a new Equality and Human Rights Commission (EHRC), and consolidating existing legislation that outlawed discrimination on the grounds of race, gender and disability. However, it is debatable just how far legislation can change deep-seated prejudices. The CRE was seen by many as a toothless watchdog, its critics routinely pouring scorn on what they dubbed the 'race relations industry' (Banton 1985: vii). It remained to be seen whether those who saw the CRE's role as being to legitimate oppressive legislation, as opposed to improving the life experiences of black and minority ethnic Britons, would be any more convinced by the body that replaced it.

Covering the Cracks

Britain's deferential, united civic culture is rather more complex and tense than that venerated by liberal apologists. The working of the polity cannot be explained in terms of a large natural consensus. Class, gender and racial cracks in the social fascia are plastered over with political spin and concealed beneath unwritten constitutional wallpaper. It is in exploring how this is accomplished that one gains the key to the true spirit and genius of the system. This long exploration begins in the following chapter.

Key points

- Political culture is an imprecise term encompassing history, institutions and attitudes within a nation towards the political system.

- Characteristics ascribed to British political culture include continuity, homogeneity, deference and consensus.

- There is a case for arguing that the post-war era has seen a decline in deference.

- Class has been seen as a particularly salient feature of British political culture.

- Class can be defined in terms of various factors, such as occupation, income and wealth.

- A basic class division in much discussion identifies an upper, middle and working class.

- Politicians have argued that Britain is now a classless society.

- Beneath the apparent tranquillity of consensus fester gender and racial tensions.

- Britain has a patriarchal political system in which women have not been encouraged to participate.

- Racism is found in various forms in Britain and is particularly persistent where skin colour prevents long-term assimilation.

Review your understanding of the following terms and concepts

bourgeoisie	institutional racism	sexism
civic culture	meritocracy	underclass
class	middle class	upper class
consensus	patriarchy	working class
deference	political culture	xenophobia
embourgeoisement	proletariat	
Establishment	racism	

Questions for discussion and debate

Consider these propositions and be prepared to present the cases for and against. Try to produce debating propositions of your own.

1 A nation's political system reflects its political culture.

2 Deference is no longer a feature of British political culture.

3 The British working class is shrinking.

4 The Marxist distinction between the owners of capital and the workers remains valid.

5 A post-cold-war wave of economic migrants and asylum-seekers has rekindled racism in Britain.

6 A cohesive society can be multiracial but not multicultural.

7 Racism does not have any significant effect on British politics.

8 You can change your class, but not your colour or gender.

9 Britain's political culture is changing.

10 Women have no place in politics.

Further reading

Adonis, A. and Pollard, S. (1997) *A Class Act: The Myth of Britain's Classless Society*.
Argues that, far from diminishing, class barriers are intensifying.

Almond, G. A. and Verba, S. (1963) *The Civic Culture* (reprinted 1989).
Remains a classic text, despite subsequent developments.

Almond, G. A. and Verba, S. (eds) (1980) *The Civic Culture Revisited*.
Readings re-evaluate the civic culture in the light of events.

Atkinson, W., Roberts, S. and Savage, M. (eds) (2012) *Class Inequality in Austerity Britain*.
Critical interrogation of the interests behind the austerity programme pursued by the 2010 coalition, identifying damaging effects on class inequality.

Bruce, S. (2012) *Politics and Religion in the United Kingdom*.
Analyses links between Protestantism and modern democracy and the impact of religion, including ethnic minority values, on political alignment.

Childs, S. (2009) *Women and British Party Politics: Descriptive, Substantive and Symbolic Representation*.
Examines women's participation at the mass and elite level in contemporary British politics in the post-1997 period.

Dorling, D. (2011) *Injustice: Why Social Inequality Persists*.
Draws a picture of stark inequality in which the Beveridge goals of freedom from ignorance, want, idleness, squalor and disease are being replaced with elitism, exclusion, prejudice, greed and despair.

Dunleavy, P. et al. (2005) *Voices of the People: Popular Attitudes to Democratic Renewal in Britain.*
A revised version of the 2001 original, reports a ten-year series of opinion polls on constitutional and democratic issues commissioned by the Joseph Rowntree Reform Trust. Finds more support than is commonly supposed for a variety of reforms.

Fryer, P. (1988) *Black People in the British Empire.*
Explores the exploitation of the colonies and presents an alternative view of the place of black people in British history.

Giddens, A. and Sutton, P. W. (2010) *Sociology: Introductory Readings.*
Lively readings from a wide variety of sources.

Giddens, A. and Sutton, P. W. (2013) *Sociology*, 7th edn.
Illustrates how the discipline of sociology addresses many of the questions important to the study of politics.

Lovenduski, J. and Norris, P. (eds) (1996) *Women in Politics.*
Focusing on Britain, provides an overview of women's attitudes, behaviour and representation in policy areas affecting them.

Solomos, J. (2003) *Race and Racism in Britain*, 3rd edn.
Detailed analysis of race relations and forms of racism in British society.

Whiteley, P. (2011) *Political Participation in Britain: The Decline and Revival of Civic Culture.*
Well-researched analysis of political attitudes, behaviour and forms of participation in contemporary Britain.

For reading around the subject and some light relief

A huge body of English literature deals with the factors that divide societies; a small selection is included here.

Martin Amis, *London Fields.*
Surreal vision of London life: four people bound together in a modern urban torment of class, wealth and squalor, destroying themselves within a decaying world.

Billy Bragg, *England, Half-English.*
This album from the most politically engaged of Britain's song-writers addresses the vexed questions of 'Englishness' and nationalism.

Jilly Cooper, *Class.*
Light essay by a proud daughter of the upper middle class.

Edwina Currie, A *Woman's Place.*
According to John Julius Norwich, this 'does for Parliament what D. H. Lawrence did for gamekeeping'.

Danny Dorling, *The 32 Stops: Lives on London's Central Line.*
A novel approach to the social geography of London.

Eric Hobsbawm, *Fractured Times.*
Collection of essays and articles by eminent historian charting changes in culture (from architecture to shopping) throughout the twentieth century.

Kazuo Ishiguro, *The Remains of the Day.*
Moving class novel with powerful political overtones. (Also a film.)

Jeremy Paxman, *The English: A Portrait of a People.*
Entertaining inquiry into Englishness.

George Bernard Shaw, *Pygmalion.*
Witty but subversive comedy on upper-class manners and gender relationships by the Irish genius. (Alternatively, see the less subversive musical/film, My *Fair Lady.)*

Alan Sillitoe, *Saturday Night and Sunday Morning.*
Portrait of working-class life in 1950s Britain. A hard-drinking, hard-fighting, young working-class rebel comes up against social barriers and conventions. (Also a film.)

On the net

http://www.ons.gov.uk
The Office for National Statistics is the official source for up-to-date socioeconomic information.

http://www.jrf.org.uk/
The Joseph Rowntree Foundation is concerned with reducing poverty and social exclusion. Its website includes reports into a wide variety of social and economic issues.

http://www.migrationwatchuk.co.uk/
A think-tank concerned with the often-controversial issues of immigration
and asylum, Migration Watch describes itself as independent and non-political.

http://www.runnymedetrust.org/
The UK's leading independent racial equality think-tank publishes research and
policy advice, much of which is freely available from its website.

MIND POLITICS: WHAT WE THINK

Contents

In this chapter we turn to the processes shaping people's views and attitudes – the politics of the mind. Mind politics arises from the need for social stability. There are various ways of maintaining this, from the brutal use of force and fear, through attempts by the state to ease the effects of inequality (welfare policies), to more subtle psychological processes that discourage the disadvantaged from rebelling. Here our focus is on those institutions particularly concerned with what we think. We begin by examining informal political influences encountered through the family, the peer group, religion, school, the arts and the advertising that is so central to our capitalist society. Next we consider two profoundly important sources of mass communication – the press and broadcasting. We conclude by examining the impact of a development that is reshaping the contemporary world: the revolution in information and communications technology.

Political Socialization

While the British state has been willing to employ force against citizens at certain points in history, it is preferable that people live with some degree of contentment. The distribution of power and material goods in society, and the form of government, have generally led people to feel that their political and economic systems are fair and just, and that their political ambitions could be achieved without violence or rebellion. Inequality has largely been justified in terms of promoting the common good and has not prompted the violent revolutions seen in many polities.

Defining political socialization

How Nature always does contrive
That every boy and every gal,
That's born into the world alive,
Is either a little Liberal,
Or else a little Conservative!

W. S. Gilbert, *Iolanthe* (Act II)

The process whereby people acquire their attitudes towards politics is termed **political socialization**. A major flaw in typical studies of political socialization is a preoccupation with voting behaviour, but there is much more to the socialization process than explaining the mysteries whereby boys and girls grow up to be Conservatives, Liberal Democrats, Labourites, or even supporters of the BNP. It is upon the socialization process that the stability of the whole system depends; it determines whether successive generations will vote at all, whether they will be apathetic abstainers, cynics, activists, or perhaps revolutionaries.

A central legitimating feature of a political culture is the notion of the neutral state: one that does not favour one section of society over another. This may be promoted by venerating basic constitutional principles such as the rule of law and the impartiality of state institutions (civil service, police force, judiciary). We shall see in later chapters that the institutions themselves play a part in the socialization process in many subtle ways. However, in addition to the state's direct role in reproducing supportive attitudes we find a range of non-state institutions extending into civil society. In addition, there are institutions specially created to talk to (not with) the masses: the communications media.

The family

As Philip Larkin put it in the often-quoted lines from 'This Be the Verse':

> They fuck you up, your mum and dad.
> They may not mean to, but they do.
> They fill you with the faults they had
> And add some extra, just for you.

The family is the first source of attitude formation we encounter. Despite the role played by mothers, it has been an essentially patriarchal organization tending to reproduce sexist attitudes towards gender roles. Xenophobia and racism, as well as love and tolerance, may also be learnt in this private world. The family is also a power structure in which parents exercise authority, although characteristically on the basis of love. Hence we grow up understanding that authority is generally in our own interests. This can help explain why the political right lays great stress on the family; it helps to reinforce a social organization where a dominant class is accepted in the interest of the whole nation. However, the family can also socialize people into non-capitalist, altruistic values such as mutual care and equality, which is why it cannot in itself provide a sufficient basis for mind-shaping in a capitalist society.

British family life is changing as a result of the growth of non-white communities, feminism and a greater plurality in social norms. Families from the Indian sub-continent traditionally honour family loyalty and conformity, including arranged marriages. These values clash with the liberal competitive environment outside, placing conflicting pressures on children. In families of West Indian origin, although fewer mothers aged 20–45 live with a husband than among the comparable white population, these single mothers can gain support from their extended kinship networks (Giddens 2001: 190). Through the influence of feminism, patriarchy is less strong among many younger couples and more domestic chores are shared. Greater plurality in lifestyles produces far more unmarried couples living together and rearing children. There is also more tolerance of gay and lesbian 'marriages', as institutionalized under the 2004 Civil Partnerships Act, with the 2013 Marriage (Same Sex Couples) Act offering the prospect of full gay marriage. In spite of such developments, however, governments of all political creeds have often sought to reaffirm the more traditional family values.

The peer group

The importance of relationships based on school, work and leisure has been stressed by psychologists such as Mead and Piaget. There are strong social pressures to conform to **peer group** norms in many respects, such as dress, musical taste and attitude towards sex. Since peer relationships are usually based on consent, pressures to conform can be more acceptable than those imposed by parents or teachers. Because of their exclusive as well as inclusive nature, peer groups can engender racist and sexist attitudes. They may also encourage crime, particularly amongst disaffected young men, and reinforce drug culture and gang membership. Peer-group influence is intensified by the burgeoning growth of social networking. Falling electoral turnouts amongst the young may also be partly explained by peer-group influence.

Religion

Despite the Enlightenment view that religion and politics should not be mixed, in reality they are rarely far apart. For much of the medieval and early modern period, most educated people were formally church officials. Leading office-holders in the church such as Thomas Becket, Cardinal Wolsey and Archbishop Cranmer were also key political and administrative figures. The English Reformation saw the church formally wedded to the state as the Church of England, headed by the monarch. During the industrial revolution capitalism drew its inspiration from the puritan

Religion is the sigh of the oppressed creature, the heart of a heartless world, just as it is the spirit of an unspiritual situation. It is the opium of the people.
Karl Marx,
Introduction to
Critique of Hegel's Philosophy of Right
(1844)

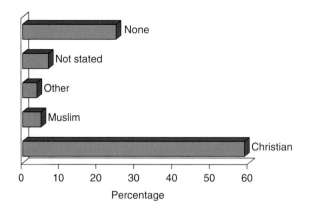

Figure 9.1 A secular society? Declared religious affiliation in England and Wales, 2011 (percentages)

Note: Other includes Hindu (1.5%), Sikh (0.8%), Jewish (0.5%) and Buddhist (0.4%).

Source: Data from 2011 census.

doctrines of nonconformity. Stressing frugality and saving, these justified the great accumulation of wealth necessary to consolidate the capitalists' position. However, they saw the Church of England as the religion of the upper middle class.

From the eighteenth century, with the emergence of the great urban masses, social services were pioneered by the churches, including early ventures into mass education in which nonconformist and Anglican organizations competed for the minds of the population. However, capitalism is about selling dear and buying cheap; it could not operate if people did unto their neighbours as they would have them do unto them. Hence British Christianity has been concerned to explain the divine ordination of inequality in this world ('The rich man in his castle, the poor man at his gate') with the promise of more egalitarian conditions confined to the next, making a particular virtue of the passive acceptance of one's lot. Marx saw this as a vital cog in the machinery of subjugation and exploitation. Not only has religion socialized people into accepting inequality, it has purveyed patriarchal values.

Today Britain is regarded as a secular society with less place for religion (figure 9.1); it is said that faith in science has replaced faith in a God, with Sunday shopping replacing churchgoing and non-believers increasing from 15 per cent of the population in 2001 to 25 per cent in 2011, according to census data. Although many people claim to believe in a God, 59 per cent identifying themselves as Christians (down from 72 per cent in 2001)and some 40 per cent professing membership of the Church of England, only around 1 million attend a service each week (according to the Church's own figures). Indeed, whilst 79 per cent of Muslims, 74 per cent of Sikhs and 70 per cent of Hindus claim to practise their religion, just one in three British Christians do so (Department of Communities and Local Government 2011: 18).

> The Church of England and the Church Universal have a proper interest in
> the ethics of the financial world and in the question of whether our financial
> practices serve those who need to be served – or have simply become idols that
> themselves demand uncritical service.
>
> Rowan Williams (Archbishop of Canterbury, 2003–12), in the *Financial Times* (1
> Nov. 2011)

However, tensions in Northern Ireland, the presence of Britain's ethnic minorities, the rise of new religious movements and church leaders' increased willingness to enter the political domain (see p. 73) mean that religion has by no means disappeared from politics. Indeed, most politicians would be as loath to declare themselves atheists as they would be to profess a lack of interest in football! Often speaking in what critics saw as messianic terms, Tony Blair ascribed his political thinking to Christianity.

Britain's non-Christian religions

The presence of significant numbers of Sikhs, Hindus and Muslims, as well as smaller sects such as Mormons and Rastafarians, has presented new issues for the British polity as religious, racial and political issues have become enmeshed. Although not essentially a new problem (Britain's Jewish population has long existed within the predominantly Christian culture), the more fervent (sometimes fundamentalist) views can promote clashes. The *fatwa* passed by the Ayatollah Khomeini on author Salman Rushdie over his *Satanic Verses* followed demonstrations and symbolic burnings of the book by some British Muslims. There are also implications for feminism, with some Muslims calling for, and establishing, separate schools for their daughters as a means of limiting their ambitions (Cahanum 1997: 244–7).

The December 2001 Cantle Report on race riots earlier that year (the worst for many years) revealed a strong religious factor uniting Muslims. Paradoxically, the government was pressing ahead with a policy of increasing the number of state-funded faith schools. The events of 9/11 also revealed the potential for religion to affect political attitudes, as television screens featured alarming scenes of some British Muslims apparently celebrating in the wake of the terrorist act and advocating *jihad* (holy war). CCTV footage of three British-born Muslims, along with a fourth who had lived in the country since the age of five, preparing to bring chaos to the streets of London in the suicide attacks of 7 July 2005 only served to underline the point. However, following the brutal murder of Drummer Lee Rigby in 2013, hacked down before startled onlookers in broad daylight, the Muslim community was at pains to distance itself from the Muslim converts alleged to have committed the atrocity.

The postmodernist scepticism towards Enlightenment thinking and materialism opens the door to the pursuit of eastern religions, forms of meditation, informal variants of Christianity, paganism, and even mystical practices such as astrology. The rejection of established religion can be seen to parallel a rejection of established political institutions and be reflected in new forms of direct action. Indeed, certain strands of feminism and environmentalism also embrace spiritual values.

There are those who fear the effect of religion on the political culture. Biologist Richard Dawkins has spearheaded a movement of unbelievers (atheists) who are particularly opposed to introducing children to religious ideas before their minds have reached maturity.

Education

Education is simply the soul of society as it passes from one generation to another.

G. K. Chesterton (1874–1936; British writer), in the *Observer* (6 July 1924)

The British school system is sharply dichotomized, with the private sector preparing the future controllers of the state machine and the state system aiming to manufacture the smaller cogs in the wheel. The state sector, for the most part, is shaped by civil servants, many of whom have never themselves darkened the doors of its institutions. In this process of cultural reproduction children learn more than is outlined in the official syllabus; there is also a 'hidden curriculum', by which they learn their place in society. Like the family, the school is hierarchical in structure, and ideally the staff exercise their authority in the interests of pupils, further legitimating the idea of elite dominance.

> A very large part of English middle-class education is devoted to the training of servants . . . In so far as it is, by definition, the training of upper servants, it includes, of course, the instilling of that kind of confidence which will enable the upper servants to supervise and direct the lower servants.
>
> Raymond Williams (1921–88; left-wing writer), *Culture and Society* (1958)

Generations of British children have come to understand their culture through what is alleged to be their country's history. In reality it has largely been the history of the elite: the kings and their conquests. The heroes of school texts are figures like Richard the Lionheart and Henry VIII; of John Wilkes and Thomas Paine children have remained largely ignorant. Although Karl Marx worked in England, and lies buried in Highgate Cemetery, a British child can negotiate the scholastic assault course with little more than a superficial knowledge of perhaps the most influential social thinker of the age. Ethnic minorities have challenged the relevance of British history as a basis for understanding their own cultural backgrounds and this has led to some modifications. Yet was obliterating the history of those from the black Commonwealth really any stranger than excluding working-class history?

A level playing field? Cricket at one of Britain's leading public schools

The idea of the state providing education as a *consumption good* to be enjoyed as a gift of citizenship can be at variance with capitalist values, which regard it as more of an *investment good* providing training for work. New Labour, with its 'Education, Education, Education' mantra, made much of the link with jobs, renaming the Department of Education and Science the Department for Education and Employment (DfEE) in 1997, and rebranding it the Department for Education and Skills (DfES) in 2001. This kind of philosophy is consistent with an inegalitarian society. A substantial body of research confirms that British education has served to reinforce inequality rather than reduce it (Giddens 2001: 510–15). Of course, many teachers are unhappy with the utilitarian ethos. This accounts for an often tense relationship with government; belittled by some politicians and feeling poorly paid, teachers have been placed under increasing pressures with competitive league tables and performance management.

The arts

Ever since Johannes Gutenberg set up his printing press in Mainz in 1440, the power of literature has been both cherished and feared by the mighty. Although offering a means of legitimating their position by directly shaping mass attitudes, it carries a dangerous potential for exposing the privilege of the few to the eyes of the many. Even the idea of a Bible that everyone could read was once seen as dangerous, and radical news sheets circulating during the industrial revolution appeared as an insidious virus in the body politic. The words of geniuses such as Shakespeare, Tolstoy, Dostoevsky, Dickens, Milton and Shelley can be elevating, but a workforce with a soaring spirit had little place in the logic of unbridled capitalism.

It was not until towards the end of the nineteenth century, when it was realized that industry could no longer function without an educated workforce, that mass literacy became state policy. Yet the results were to disappoint. Critics perceived only the rise of a demeaning mass culture usurping the real world of art and (possibly subversive) ideas, offering only a 'candy floss world' and 'sex in shiny packets' (Hoggart 1958). The Frankfurt School of neo-Marxist thinkers argued that undemanding homogenized forms of culture removed from the masses the power to look at the world critically. German philosopher Jürgen Habermas saw this as stifling democracy, replacing the 'public space', in which opinion forms through open discussion, with manipulation and thought control.

Advertising

The morality of free-market capitalism is based upon the belief that if everyone buys and sells wisely, according to self-interest, all will be well. The consumer is said to be sovereign. This is questionable in practice because people are generally denied enough information or wisdom to know what is in their own interest. It can be argued that modern capitalism is not at all happy to let people decide for themselves what they want; it is concerned with making them want what is most profitable to produce. Companies devote huge proportions of their budgets not to making products or rendering services but to altering our thoughts. Advertising is a mega-industry concerned expressly with getting into our heads and shaping our desires. Although promoting a particular product, it generally subscribes to the ethos of free-market capitalism and usually favours the political right. However, the political place of advertising in mind politics goes even deeper. We shall see in later chapters that it plays a direct part in politics, with parties investing enormous funds to sell themselves to voters.

The Print Media

The British have traditionally been great readers (or at least great buyers) of newspapers, circulation figures being the highest in the western world. In January 2011, the Audit Bureau of Circulation (ABC) reported that national daily newspapers had a combined circulation of around 10 million copies, with the circulation of Sunday nationals totalling around 9.5 million (*Guardian*, 11 Feb. 2011). There is less enthusiasm for serious weeklies, where more detailed analysis may be found. The mass readership preference is for lightweight material, with magazines devoted to celebrities the clear favourites. Rapid advances in communications technology have extended the reach of the press, with various online versions available at the click of a mouse. Indeed, these may be expected to supersede ink-based journalism within a few decades.

In addition, there is a recognized division between the quality press (or **broadsheets**) and the **tabloids** (or 'red tops'). However, although the broadsheets are said to influence the opinions of the intelligentsia, including journalists themselves, the tabloids outstrip them in terms of both circulation and readership (figure 9.2). It is also worth noting that, according to the National Readership Survey (NRS), actual

> *In the tabloids, virtually every Tory has the stature of Winston Churchill, every Labourite is a lying Leninite.*
> Glenn Frankel (*Washington Post* journalist), quoted in the *Independent* (15 April 1992)

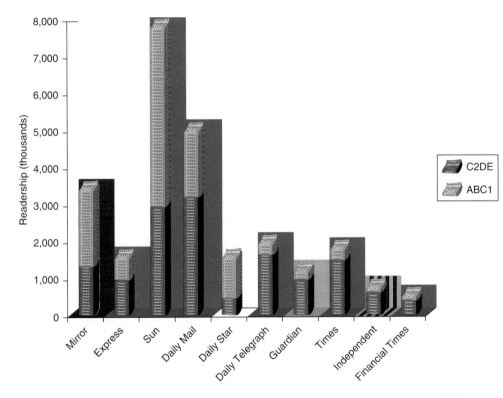

Figure 9.2 Readership of daily national newspapers by social class ahead of the 2010 general election

Note: Colours indicate the electoral outcome favoured by each paper

Source: Data from Kavanagh and Cowley (2010: table 14.1).

readership exceeds sales by an average ratio of around 3:1. In January 2010, for example, the *Sun* had 2.7 readers per copy, whereas 4.4 individuals claimed to read the *Guardian* for every copy in circulation.

Broadsheet readers tend to be the best informed about politics, are more interested and feel more confident that they can influence things. Tabloid readers have similar views to non-readers, suggesting that tabloids do not contribute much to political knowledge. However, even among the better educated, they are more popular than the broadsheets (Newton 1998: 155). Because the country is small, the major newspapers are national, producing considerable uniformity of view and centring on London. Provincial morning and evening dailies are in decline, being confronted with 'free-sheets' containing advertising and human-interest stories, force-fed through the letterboxes of urban households or shoved into the hands of weary commuters struggling to navigate a path through the rush-hour traffic.

Partisanship

Part of the process of legitimation is an exhortation of the rights of the **free press**. These values were fought for in the eighteenth century against a secretive ruling class, when it was even necessary to smuggle reports of proceedings out of Parliament. Until the mid-nineteenth century government sought to exert influence over the press through censorship, legal constraints and financial measures (Kuhn 2007: 31). A free press is held to be one of the defining characteristics of the liberal state: a democracy must have freedom of speech for its journalists and free access to information for citizens. However, this freedom must logically allow the press organs to support particular ideologies and political parties, which gives them a major opportunity to influence popular attitudes. Hence it is a source of political power.

Britain has a particularly **partisan** press. Although sometimes critical, newspapers have traditionally spread a generally right-wing message, favouring the Conservative Party and the Labour right. Hence, *The Times* attributed the Conservative 1987 election success to 'the good sense of the majority of voters'. There is an extremely close association between newspaper readership and voting, dwarfing many of the other electoral variables. However, not all readers are aware of the bias: the calculatedly down-market appeal of the *Sun* actually led one-third of its readers to believe it to be a Labour paper (Newton 1986: 324) even before it became one!

As governments become increasingly obsessed with 'spin', so the influence of the press worries them more. Yet the extent to which newspaper bias affects voting

Freedom of the press in Britain is freedom to print such of the proprietor's prejudices as the advertisers don't object to.

Attributed to Hannen Swaffer (1879–1962; British journalist)

> **What the papers said during the 1992 election campaign**
>
> MAJOR DEFIES LABOUR MOBS, *Daily Mail*, 21 March
>
> THREAT OF RETURN TO PICKET TERROR, *Sun*, 24 March
>
> LABOUR TO RATION MORTGAGES, *Daily Mail*, 23 March
>
> THE KICKBACK: THE SECRET TAX THAT WILL ALLOW LABOUR TO REWARD ITS UNION PAYMASTERS, *Daily Mail*, 1 April
>
> NAZI RIOTS IN BRITAIN: PR AIDS FASCISTS CLAIMS BAKER, *Sun*, 7 April
>
> BAKER'S MIGRANT FLOOD WARNINGS: LABOUR SET TO OPEN DOORS, *Daily Express*, 7 April
>
> IF KINNOCK WINS TODAY WILL THE LAST PERSON TO LEAVE BRITAIN PLEASE TURN OUT THE LIGHTS, *Sun*, Election morning
>
> IT'S THE SUN WOT WON IT, *Sun*, The morning after

should not be seen as the central issue. Between elections they exert an insidious influence on attitudes, influencing the political culture. The message they emit will be partly influenced by capitalist interests through their purchase of advertising space (see Kuhn 2007: 39–40).

> **The power of advertising**
> According to Ofcom, £3.23 billion was spent on newspaper advertisements in 2010 out of a total advertising 'spend' of £15.68 billion. Though the advertising spend in newspapers has now been overtaken both by television advertising and online advertising, it remains a significant revenue stream for newspaper proprietors, at a time when newspaper sales are in decline.

Content: 'All the news that's fit to print' (motto of the *New York Times*)

Selling newspapers is business, and profit maximization means maximizing circulation. This results in a quest for the lowest common denominator, with the tabloids favouring sensationalism, trivialization and titillation. There has also been a deep-seated racism in the sentiments and language, which can break out into hysterical **jingoism** whenever foreign relations become in any way turbulent. At times of crisis the state has overtly demanded that the press becomes its instrument. During two

Something someone, somewhere, wants to suppress; everything else is just advertising.
Lord Northcliffe's definition of news

world wars dishonest reporting was deemed necessary to stiffen people's resolve and the newspaper barons were flatteringly brought into government to ensure their cooperation. During the Falklands war, in an orgy of bellicose press chauvinism, the Argentineans became the 'Argies' and the infamous *Sun* headline 'Gotcha!' gloried in the agonizing deaths of foreigners as they abandoned the stricken cruiser *ARA General Belgrano* for the icy waters of the South Atlantic. Sport evokes similar sentiments: the German teams become 'krauts', while the *Daily Star* headline in March 1998 concerning the French allocation of World Cup tickets read 'FROGS NEED A GOOD KICKING'.

> Forget all this crap about politicians – who's interested, eh? You only write this bollocks so that you can look good with all your fucking mates in Westminster. The readers don't give a fuck about politics.
>
> Kelvin MacKenzie as *Sun* editor, to his political editor, Walter Terry. Quoted in Peter Chippindale and Chris Horrie, *Stick it up Your Punter!* (1990)

Much tabloid reporting is preoccupied with the doings of a glitterati of soap stars, super-models, sports personalities and royalty, with those not falling into any of these categories increasingly drawn from the ranks of reality-TV stars, whose requisite fifteen minutes of fame is routinely spun out for months, sometimes years. Where stories of substance do appear, reporting invariably concentrates on the immediate, to the exclusion of background analysis. Sectarian attacks in Belfast, for example, were reported with little mention of the historical context of Ulster politics.

The press barons

The proud boast that the British press is not owned or controlled by the state must be countered with the observation that it lies broadly in the hands of a neo-liberal Establishment. Never widely dispersed, ownership narrowed even further during the post-war era. The celebrated *Times*, founded in 1785, was not intended for the masses. Inescapably an organ of the Establishment (a 'parish magazine' for the upper classes, recording their births, marriages and obituaries), it claimed for much of its life to be a newspaper of national record (offering an objective, definitive account of events). The rise of the 'popular' papers followed the extension of adult literacy at the end of the nineteenth century with the creation of the *Daily Mail* (1896), *Daily Express* (1900), *Daily Mirror* (1903) and *Daily Sketch* (1908). These were the first mass-circulation papers and were to generate vast revenues from advertising, thereby keeping down their prices.

I run the Daily Express *purely for propaganda and for no other purpose.*
Lord Beaverbrook, to the Royal Commission on the Press (1948)

Papers were owned by private individuals who became formidable '**press barons**'. The awe in which they were held by politicians meant that they often became real barons, with elevation to the peerage: Alfred Harmsworth (*Mirror, Mail* and *The Times*), regarded as the father of modern journalism, became Lord Northcliffe; his younger brother Harold (*Mail*) became Lord Rothermere, and the Canadian Max Aitken (*Express*) became Lord Beaverbrook. A second generation included Cecil Harmsworth King, nephew of Lord Northcliffe, who hugely expanded the family empire into the world of magazines and television. A rival empire was headed by Lord Thomson of Fleet (*The Times* and *Sunday Times*), a Canadian who had expanded his interests from Canada to Scotland, where he had become a millionaire through commercial television. Subsequently the Australian Rupert Murdoch was to build up the mammoth News International empire, owning, amongst others, *The Times*, the *Sunday Times*, the *Sun* and the *News of the World*, as well as a number of US papers, including the *New York Post* and the *Wall Street Journal*.

> What the proprietorship of these papers is aiming at is power, and power without responsibility – the prerogative of the harlot throughout the ages.
>
> Stanley Baldwin (1867–1947; Conservative leader), attacking Lords Rothermere and Beaverbrook in an election speech (18 March 1931)

Despite protestations to the contrary, owners are regularly criticized for exercising editorial control. Upon buying the *Mirror* Robert Maxwell declared: 'I have invested £90 million. There can only be one boss, and that is me' (Bower 1988). This is not illegal but it does give an individual awesome power. Murdoch conducted a continuing crusade in favour of free-enterprise culture, doing much to enhance the neoliberal project of the right. This power is recognized by politicians. Tony Blair courted Murdoch assiduously, even to the extent of becoming godfather to one of Murdoch's daughters. Doors swung open as he gained his place in the *Sun*, and indeed the *News of the World*, with articles, usually ghosted by ex-journalists turned **spin doctors** (Scammell 2000: 182), appearing regularly under his name. On BBC TV's *Newsnight* (17 March 1997), Labour's campaign director Peter Mandelson declared: 'We have earned the *Sun's* support'. As the 1997 general election approached, the *Sun's* eve-of-poll headline read: 'WHO BLAIRS WINS'. By the time of the 2001 election virtually all the papers were supporting New Labour's brand of modified neoliberalism, with some openly scornful of Conservative leader William Hague.

Upon assuming the Conservative leadership David Cameron followed Blair's courtship style (to an extent not fully appreciated until the revelations of the

Sunset for Labour and Gordon Brown in 2009

Leveson inquiry in 2012; see below). As a result, a douche of cold water was poured over Gordon Brown's 'fight to win' speech at Labour's 2009 annual conference when, on the same day, the *Sun* announced its switch to the Conservatives.

Self-control: avoiding lying in the *Sun*

News does not come in labelled packages; it must be selected from a great writhing mass of reality. What we read as 'news' is what others decide to print, and this crucial exercise of journalistic discretion does not treat all sections of society equally. This results in continuing debate around the issue of regulation.

The essential feature of a free press is that it is not state regulated. In a free society one should have the right to 'publish and be damned'. Those who feel they have a grievance have recourse to the courts and the libel laws. It is argued that, rather than **official censorship**, the only acceptable form of regulation is self-regulation. This has come through a Press Complaints Commission (PCC), a body of laypeople and editorial and managerial representatives from within the industry, set up on a voluntary basis to protect their freedom, hear complaints, chastise for misreporting and administer a code of conduct drawn up in 1991. However, critics regard it as a toothless watchdog and it was made something of a mockery by the tabloids. Following the Calcutt enquiry, a statutory framework for the press was proposed in 1993 but a largely united profession was hotly opposed to it.

The royal family were to become particular targets, with transcripts of the 'Squidgygate' and 'Camillagate' tapes (conversations between Princess Diana and Prince Charles and their respective lovers) appearing in the tabloids. Watched and photographed incessantly, sometimes secretly, Princess Diana was literally pursued to her death by the *paparazzi*. Instant hypocrisy reigned as they mourned the 'People's Princess', although one US tabloid, *The National Enquirer*, was too late to withdraw its current edition, carrying the front-page headline 'Di Goes Sex Mad'. This tragic incident led to some toughening up of the code and in 2010 the PCC received over 7,000 written complaints, more than three times as many as ten years earlier.

However, events were to lead to entirely new levels of concern. In August 2006 the police had arrested *News of the World* royal editor Clive Goodman and private investigator Glenn Mulcaire over allegations that they had illegally accessed messages (hacked) recorded on the mobile phones of members of the royal household. Both were found guilty and received prison sentences, while the paper's editor, Andy Coulson, resigned. (Within a month he was appointed by David Cameron as the Conservatives' Director of Communications, going on to head the coalition government's communications operations.) A can of worms had been opened with revelations that the paper's reporters had, from 2003 to 2007 (under Coulson's editorship), hacked into the mobile phones of a range of celebrities and politicians. Some £1 million had been paid out to settle cases that threatened to reveal damaging evidence. A major scandal erupted as a stream of prominent people, including actor Hugh Grant and author J. K. Rowling, alleged that they had been victims. Most shocking to the public was the hacking of the phone of murdered schoolgirl Milly Dowler. Murdoch was driven to close this best-selling Sunday newspaper in 2011 and further arrests and resignations followed.

Concern was expressed by the Commons Culture, Media and Sport Committee and in July 2011 Lord Justice Leveson was appointed to head an investigation into 'the culture, practices, and ethics of the press', including 'contacts and the relationships between national newspapers and politicians' and 'the press and the police'. The Inquiry began taking oral evidence from a stream of A-list celebrities and politicians and was to uncover the astonishing depth of the relationships between politicians and the Murdoch empire. TV broadcasts of the proceedings became compulsive daytime viewing as the public were to learn of Cameron horse-riding with *News of the World* editor Rebekah Brooks, attending parties at her home – where meetings with the Murdochs were possible – and signing-off his emails to her with the tag LOL.

Shaping events by just 'having a word' in private is still the habit of the Establishment. Fortunately we now have a more disrespectful press to publicise these contortions.
Sir Peter Hall (theatre director), *Making an Exhibition of Myself* (1993: 197)

> I am so rooting for you tomorrow not just as a proud friend but because professionally we're definitely in this together! Speech of your life? Yes he Cam.
>
> Text from *Sun* editor Rebekah Brooks to David Cameron (7 Oct. 2009), on eve of Conservative conference, reported in the *Guardian* (14 June 2012)

Reporting in November 2012, Leveson concluded that the relationship between politicians and press had been too close and that press behaviour, at times, had been 'outrageous'. Its recommendation included the creation of a new self-regulating body, independent of current journalists, serving editors, government and business interests, to be active in promoting high standards. With power to investigate serious breaches and apply sanctions, it should be backed by legislation. The editors of the main newspapers broadly accepted most of the proposals, though with strong reservations about statutory backing, reservations that were shared by Shami Chakrabarti, Director of Liberty (and an adviser to Lord Leveson's inquiry). David Cameron shared these concerns, seeing this as a Rubicon that 'should never be crossed', by challenging the principle of a free press. However, in March 2013, under pressure from Labour and the Liberal Democrats, he was forced to make concessions. A new body backed by a Royal Charter was to be created with the power to levy fines up to £1m and insist upon front-page apologies where required. Although voluntary, those refusing to sign up would run the risk of incurring draconian 'exemplary' damages if subsequently sued for some aspect of their reporting.

(W)hen it comes to regulation, I just beg for some care – because this is a very complex situation . . . We want democracy not autocracy.
Rupert Murdoch in evidence to the Leveson enquiry (April 2012)

Freedom of the press poses conundrums for democracy. Greater protection for ordinary people against harassment and embarrassment may also allow the high and mighty to evade democratic scrutiny. Again, while official censorship spells totalitarianism, press freedom in a class-based society can allow the wealthy to manipulate the ideas and attitudes of the masses, providing a leverage on the polity regardless of which party reigns. This is political power; it is not difficult to see why Thomas Carlyle called the press the 'Fourth Estate'.

The Broadcast Media

For many years broadcasting was largely the preserve of the BBC, seen as a particularly venerable organization (affectionately known within establishment circles as 'Auntie'). Established in 1927 as the successor to a private pioneer, the British Broadcasting Company, it has a Royal Charter to broadcast and is financed independently of the Treasury through viewers' licence fees. In its early years, under its legendary Director General Sir John (later Lord) Reith, it built up a reputation for elitism, pomposity and sycophancy towards the institutions of the state, particularly the monarchy. It was so much an arm of the Establishment that wireless news readers, though invisible to their audience, wore evening dress, the uniform of the upper class. The development of television has lessened such attitudes, though vestiges remain, as in the reverent tones of commentators at great state or sporting occasions (particularly if attended by royalty) – royal weddings and funerals, the Lord Mayor's parade, Royal Ascot and the Oxbridge Boat Race.

The BBC began television broadcasting from Alexandra Palace in 1936 and by 1966 was transmitting to virtually the whole country. It enjoyed a comfortable monopoly until a traumatic challenge came in the form of commercial TV. If the BBC stood for the high Tory element within the Establishment, commercial TV represented its thrusting, free-marketeering spirit. In 1954, after prolonged political infighting among various factions within the Establishment, the IBA (later to become the ITC) was created by the Conservative government to grant licences and (renewable) franchises to regional private broadcasting companies financed by advertising. Its patronage was regal and the franchise to operate commercial TV was described by Lord Thomson (who became a millionaire) as a 'licence to print money'. Although the regional structure implied plurality, the biggest companies belong to massive leisure and media conglomerates, most major programmes are intended for national transmission through a networking system and the main news programmes come from London.

Today, television is a significant factor in British politics, completely transforming the nature of elections, orchestrating political debate, creating a cult of personality politics, helping to elevate the executive, reducing the role of Parliament and projecting the monarchy into a new era of political theatre. Although radio is by no means dead, television has long since become the organ of a truly mass culture, the principal means of informing perceptions of the political world. Avid watchers tend to form a category similar to tabloid readers – older, on lower incomes and with fewer educational qualifications, but in all classes the habit is increasing. The 1997 British Social Attitudes Survey revealed that while 10 per cent of the population were watching for less than an hour a day, an equal proportion were keeping vigil for seven hours. By 2012, according to the 2013 Telescope report (TV Licensing 2013), viewers were devoting on average around four hours a day to their screens (including an hour of news programmes), up from around three and a half hours in in 2006.

The power of TV over minds is potentially Orwellian, a fact testified to in advertisers' willingness to contribute currently some £4 billion a year to the coffers of the commercial TV (and radio) companies (Ofcom 2010). Purveying anything from soap powder to soap opera, it is recognized by politicians as a searing spotlight which can heighten their fretful hour on the political stage or consume them like moths near a candle flame. Margaret Thatcher made mastery of the medium her first priority and Tony Blair's easy TV manner was seen as an essential asset to his party. In news reporting, the projection of visual images suggests a reality greater than that of the printed word, defying scepticism and compelling belief. A Labour Party rally held in the huge Sheffield Arena on the eve of the 1992 general election greatly inspired many of those present. However, in the hands of the TV producers it was to enter folklore as a grotesque miscalculation by leader Neil Kinnock. Action replays of his repeated exultation 'Are we all right!' left the toes of middle England curling with embarrassment.

Multi-media moguls

Modern concentrated ownership, made possible by deregulation from the 1980s, follows the classic advanced capitalist model, with complex transnational conglomerates combining diverse interests in electronic communications, broadcasting, cable TV and the leisure industry. Replacing the press barons, the new-style **multi-media moguls** own TV companies, film studios, publishing houses, film libraries and software companies, as well as newspapers. They are typified by Rupert Murdoch. His empire expanded into satellite and cable through his BSkyB TV company and controlled Hong-Kong-based Star TV, covering the gigantic markets of India and China. He also acquired a half-stake in Twentieth Century Fox (later taking full control of the company), as well as several US TV stations and the US publishers HarperCollins. Another conglomerate was created in 1996 when the *Express* titles were bought by the Labour-supporting Lord Hollick (ennobled by Neil Kinnock), whose group controlled Meridian and Anglia TV. Although having more independence, the *Guardian* (alongside its Sunday sister paper, the *Observer*) and *Independent* are still caught up in this web of multi-media ownership. The concentration is even found in the so-called local press, once a basis for radical agitation, about half of which has been progressively bought up by a few large companies.

Following further franchise consolidation in 2000, two companies, Granada Media and Carlton Communications, controlled 91 per cent of the ITV network in England and Wales. In the ratings war both adopted avowedly populist strategies unlikely to increase political reporting or raise BBC standards (Stanyer 2001: 357). The scope for concentrated cross-media ownership was further advanced with the passage of the 2003 Communications Act, which allowed Granada and Carlton to merge, forming ITV plc. The new company controlled the licences to broadcast the third terrestrial channel (re-branded ITV1) across England, Wales and much of Scotland. It also cleared the way for Murdoch to bid for Channel Five, although his wider ambitions were curbed by preserving the rule preventing newspaper tycoons owning more than 20 per cent of an ITV licence. The channel was ultimately purchased by Richard Desmond, whose company, Northern and Shell, also owned the *Daily Express* and the *Star*, as well as a number of magazines and subscription-only television channels. Crucially, the Communications Act also created a new super-regulator, Ofcom, replacing nine existing bodies with one.

In this new competitive environment the domestic companies, already losing major sporting events to the wealthy cable and satellite empires with no public service mandate, face an uncertain future. The political potential residing in this multi-media power was demonstrated by Italian mogul Silvio Berlusconi, who used his empire to promote his own political career, becoming prime minister at the head of his own right-wing Forza Italia party. Anxieties were roused when Rupert Murdoch announced the intention of extending his media reach by taking over full control of the satellite broadcaster BSkyB. Although culture secretary Jeremy Hunt was revealed in the Leveson inquiry to be in favour of the bid, it was withdrawn owing to the phone-hacking scandal.

Regulation and impartiality

Regulation of the broadcast media is more stringent than that of the press, requirements including a remit for public service broadcasting and impartiality. The broadcasters come under two main regulatory bodies: the BBC Trust (BBC), established under Royal Charter in 2007 to replace the Board of Governors; and Ofcom, which replaced the Independent Television Commission (ITC) in 2003, as the body regulating commercial television and radio. Regulation becomes more complex with the digital convergence of all forms of news media and the growth of multi-channel output. In this digital market-place the requirement for public service broadcasting places broadcasters under strain when they are also subject to evaluation in terms of ratings arising from the need to attract advertising or justify the licence fee. Soaps, lifestyle programmes, talent contests and general entertainment displace arts, classical music, drama and serious news analysis (Bergg 2004: 12).

Impartiality is a continually controversial issue, with governments and all main parties regularly monitoring news coverage and crossing swords with the BBC over allegations of bias. Moreover, political impartiality means impartiality between political parties and interest groups, not between social classes. Critics have consistently alleged an anti-working-class bias in news programmes (Glasgow University Media Group 1976, 1980, 1982; Eldridge 1993), although their findings have been questioned (Harrison 1985). Military conflict is often contentious and during the Iraq invasion the Labour government frequently alleged BBC bias against its policy. However, the key point remains that the idea that TV reporting can be impartial and objective involves subjective judgement and is fraught with difficulty. Some argue that unbiased reporting is not possible. The prevailing culture may influence how journalists present news in ways of which they are not conscious.

Journalists

While owners have much power it is journalists who stand before the cameras and microphones or wield pen and mouse. Some prominent journalists come from lower-middle-class backgrounds; the BBC's John Humphrys, unrelenting scourge of evasive politicians, was born in a working-class area of Cardiff and did not attend a university. However, most of those writing for the broadsheets or fronting the news and current affairs programmes come from middle- and upper-middle-class backgrounds. A career in journalism, with an inside track to the top, ranks high amongst the glittering prizes the Establishment offers bright young Oxbridge graduates. During their careers they get to know leading figures in the arts, business and politics, and are unlikely to bite the hands that can offer them enticing titbits of useful information. Editors in particular live very close to the heart of the Establishment.

The succession of **sleaze** cases from the 1990s saw journalists in more challenging mode. The *Guardian* pursued minister Neil Hamilton, alleging acceptance of payments for tabling parliamentary questions on behalf of Harrods owner Mohamed Al-Fayed. In its sleaze hunt it also indicted Jonathan Aitken, who eventually found himself in prison. In 1998 New Labour staffers-turned-lobbyists, Derek Draper and Roger Liddle, were trapped in a 'cash for access' scandal. In 2011 Defence Secretary Liam Fox was hounded from office for events surrounding his relationship with his close friend Adam Werritty. In 2012 Conservative Party co-treasurer Peter Cruddas was caught by undercover reporters appearing to offer exclusive access to David Cameron in return for party donations of £250,000. Yet while uncovering personal misbehaviour, these developments do not challenge the Establishment at a radical level. Only in the case of the involvement of the *Daily Telegraph* and other papers in the exposé of MPs' expenses (see p. 418) can the press be seen to have taken on the Westminster Establishment in a more concerted way, with some conspiracy theorists regarding the Leveson Inquiry as a backlash orchestrated by the political elite.

In the Westminster village many journalists can become friends with officials and politicians, who can of course furnish them with valuable copy. Although causing some ministerial heads to roll, the interest is often in the peccadilloes (often sexual) of those in high office. If journalists have radical leanings, the structure of the news industry will largely neuter them. Stories can be edited, career advancement can be blocked by management and, in the final analysis, recalcitrants can be sacked. The promotional progress for those of humbler origins in the provincial press will serve to socialize them into the ways of the Establishment or filter them out before they reach the holy grail of Fleet Street or Wapping. Little distinction can be made at the elite level between broadcast and print journalists, who move easily between the two platforms. The tendency towards upper-middle-class domination is strengthened by the high kudos associated with a TV career. Interestingly, in spite of the increasing frequency of regional accents in broadcast television and radio, TV journalists from ethnic minority backgrounds often speak with impeccable middle-class accents.

The close proximity between journalists and politicians can also be seen in the way the latter (particularly ex-ministers) can, as a sideline, pick up the pen themselves. While articles are often ghosted, some, such as Winston Churchill and Roy Hattersley, have distinguished themselves in print. In the USA and continental Europe journalists entering politics must give up their day jobs, but in Britain they may do both. The distinction between the two professions is further blurred when the journalists put their skills at the disposal of the politicians. At the retirement of a leading Fleet Street editor, Mrs Thatcher was able to offer public thanks for a key speech he had written for her (Preston 1997). Use of the media was to reach new heights under New Labour, the Prime Minister and his colleagues producing a stream of regular self-justifying articles in both tabloids and broadsheets, a trend continued by David Cameron and coalition cabinet ministers. Ex-journalists were also to become prized as government directors of communications, as seen in the cases of Bernard Ingham, Alastair Campbell and Andy Coulson.

He wields far more power than many of the elected politicians at the high table of government.
Andrew Rawnsley on Alastair Campbell, Blair's press secretary, in the *Observer* (1 Nov. 1998)

Ruling the Waves: Political Interference

The structure of broadcasting is intended to prevent politicians from meddling. Some evidence of independence was seen in 1998 in a joint BBC–ITC proposal to scrap party political broadcasts and restrict electioneering broadcasts, on the grounds that they bored the audience. However, whenever it appears that the Establishment cannot count on the kind of *reportage* it desires, an underlying feeling that broadcasters should be subservient to the state is forced out into the open. Lord Reith laid down the ground rules during the 1926 General Strike, recording in his diary that the government 'know that they can trust us not to be really impartial' (Stuart 1975: 96).

Patronage

The BBC Trust and ITC commissioners are appointed by government from the ranks of the great and the good. Requiring no particular expertise or knowledge of broadcasting, they have reflected the British tradition of amateurism where, in the old cliché, who you know is rather more important than what you know. The 2003 Communications Act and other changes that came in its wake went some way towards placating public concern. The BBC Trust, though similar in size and composition to the Board of Governors it replaced, is on a tighter rein, although the appointment in 2011 as chairman of Chris Patten, life peer, ex-Conservative MP, ex-European Commissioner, ex-Governor of British Hong Kong and Chancellor of the University of Oxford since 2003, confirmed a preference for establishment figures.

Each authority delegates day-to-day operations to a director general, whom they appoint. Cautious selection generally reduces the need for sacking, but should an incumbent decide, like Beckett or Sir Thomas More, to turn from his patron and serve a higher god, their martyrdom can always be speedily effected. The 1980s saw the Thatcher government roused to fury, culminating in January 1987 with the sacking of Director General Alasdair Milne, a move foreshadowed in the appointment as chairman of the Board of Governors of Thatcherite Marmaduke Hussey, who delivered the *coup de grâce* (Milne 1988). He subsequently made the controversial appointment of John Birt, who was to criticize his own journalists for being too robust with politicians. The fact that Birt's successor in 2000 was Greg Dyke, known to have contributed £50,000 to Blair's leadership campaign and general election campaigns (Scammell 2000: 177), did nothing to quell fears over patronage. It was not without irony, therefore, that Dyke's departure, effectively forced out by the BBC governors, came in the wake of the 2004 Hutton Report into the death of weapons inspector David Kelly which, to much surprise, exonerated the government and criticized the corporation's handling of the story. However, the shortest-serving director general was to be George Entwistle, forced to resign in 2012 after only fifty-four days in the post, following a BBC *Newsnight* report falsely implicating Lord McAlpine in a child abuse scandal.

Intimidation

Although some broadcasting journalists aim for a robust style, they can come under attack. In 1986 Norman Tebbit weighed in heavily against the BBC and Kate Adie for her reporting of the launching of the US attack on Libya from Britain in non-jingoistic terms. John Humphrys of Radio 4's *Today* programme and other well-known figures, such as Jeremy Paxman, Andrew Marr and Anna Ford, have all come under fire. In December 2001, Labour Party chairman Charles Clarke accused Humphrys of 'propagating the view that politicians are cynical and basically are not to be trusted' (Humphrys 2001). In his Radio 4 programme *Battle for the Airwaves* in March 2013, journalist Nick Robinson revealed that Lord (Peter) Mandelson had once tried to get him fired for his political reporting.

Direct pressure

There are certain formal means whereby governments may influence the media, including Defence Advisory (DA) Notices and the Official Secrets legislation (see p. 527). However, of greater importance are the informal workings within the body of the Establishment. Lord Reith suppressed news that the government did not want broadcast, establishing the principle that 'the vaunted independence of the BBC was secure so long as it was not exercised' (Taylor 1965: 246).

Unwillingness to displease was demonstrated in 1962 when *That Was The Week That Was* introduced a level of popular satire hitherto unseen. Its style was little more than that of an Oxbridge undergraduate revue, part of the middle-class movement that generated *Beyond the Fringe* and the magazine *Private Eye*. However, gamekeepers made effective poachers and the programme startled deferential working-class viewers reared on the unctuous tones of BBC reportage. Amongst other things it stirred up the Profumo scandal, destabilized the Macmillan government and generally disturbed the Establishment. BBC Director General Hugh Carlton Greene appeared to lose his nerve and the programme was taken off the air in 1963 on the pretext of an impending general election (which did not actually materialize until 1964).

> What changed between January and March 1987 was not the facts or the quality of the programme but the scale to which the [BBC] governors' political and personal views intruded into the corporation's whole management.
>
> Duncan Campbell, on the banning of his controversial programme *Cabinet*, quoted in the *Independent* (30 April 1988)

Pressure became much more intense in the 1980s with the Thatcher government's diagnosis of too many with liberal leanings in the establishment kitchen. During the Falklands war, mindful of the effect of Vietnam war reporting on the American public, broadcast coverage of the task force was restricted and the government prevented the rapid transmission of TV pictures to British audiences (House of Commons Select Committee on Defence 1982: xiv).

Evidence of BBC compliance came under New Labour when, in November 1998, it banned discussion of the sexuality of Peter Mandelson in its *Any Questions* radio programme. There was anger amongst journalists and one of the panellists,

Please will all programmes note that under no circumstances whatsoever should the allegation about the private life of Peter Mandelson be repeated or referred to on any broadcast.

Edict issued to BBC staff, reported in the *Observer* (1 Nov. 1998)

Northern Ireland Secretary Mo Mowlam, described the act as 'a serious error on the part of the BBC' and 'insulting'.

News management

We are dealing with a press that basically wants to do us in.
Alastair Campbell, as Labour Party media chief, *Guardian* interview (17 Feb. 1997)

Establishment practices have long allowed the government to propagate the official line through the media. A tidal wave of official information is washed up on the beaches of Fleet Street and Broadcasting House each day; many journalists live by the source, faithfully trotting out the platitudes from the press releases. So house-trained were the Westminster journalists that officials organized them into a formal club, the **Lobby**, complete with rules and regulations and assembling in the Members' Lobby, where ministers and spin doctors would throw them unattributable titbits of information. Blair's press secretary agreed in March 2000 to end the practice of non-attribution so that 'sources close to the prime minister' became 'Alastair Campbell'. In April 2002 it was agreed that the Lobby would be opened up to other journalists, but members of this exclusive club argued that this would make it easier for the news managers to evade their forensic skills.

From the early 1980s the parties began to take control of the media into new waters. Thatcher's and Blair's press secretaries became readily recognizable figures in the political firmament, bullying and cajoling journalists, and furnishing their political charges with carefully crafted 'soundbites'. The Labour Party in opposition had focused heavily on **news management** from its media centre in Millbank Tower. Alastair Campbell began to lean on the BBC, complaining, in September 1995 for example, that Tony Blair's conference speech had not been the lead item in the news broadcasts. Deep levels of cynicism were exposed when Jo Moore, a special adviser to the then Transport Secretary Stephen Byers, circulated an email directly after the 9/11 shock, suggesting that it was 'now a very good day to get out anything we want to bury. Councillors' expenses?'. David Cameron showed himself no less interested in the dark art of news management when he hired Andy Coulson from the *News of the World* as his own press secretary.

However, it cannot be assumed that there are no people in broadcasting for whom the goal of genuine neutrality is real (Glasgow University Media Group 1976: xii). The very fact that governments complain and interfere is evidence of this. The establishment of the second commercial channel, Channel Four, initially a wholly owned subsidiary of the Independent Broadcasting Authority and now controlled by the publicly owned Channel Four Television Corporation, has shown courage in permitting the airing of non-orthodox points of view, including on the Iraq invasion. Courageous reporting does exist, but it can never be taken for granted.

New Media, New Messages

From the time that our ancestors inscribed hieroglyphics on cave walls, technology has shaped communications culture. Marshall McLuhan coined a memorable phrase when he proclaimed that 'the medium is the message'; the way information is conveyed affects what it says. While it has evolved steadily over the centuries, recent advances in information and communications technology (ICT) have generated a breathtaking acceleration, making the internet one of the central drivers of the globalization process that defines the contemporary world. Bill Gates, founder of the Microsoft empire, was once said to be 'the richest man in the world'. With a monopoly hold over cyberspace, he and his like promised to become the greatest media moguls of all.

The controllers of the 'old media' have been quick to recognize the challenge posed by the new, in which they made huge investments. Newspapers established online versions (initially free-to-air, with some later becoming subscription services) and broadcasters began to provide internet news reports and interactive sites in which subjects of broadcasts could be further explored. The BBC website soon became one of the largest in Europe, with well in excess of two million pages, its News Online receiving millions of hits on a newsworthy day. In September 1997, the Press Complaints Commission extended its remit into online material. The symbiosis with the capitalist economy was demonstrated as broadcasters diversified into e-commerce, with even the BBC's beeb.com offering goods and services linked to programmes on specialist subjects such as gardening and cooking.

The government itself joined the party with its *Knowledge Network*, providing departmental facts and figures. Even the government websites carried advertising, with well-known large companies making significant contributions. There was also the launch of the Number Ten website, providing coverage of Prime Minister's Questions in Parliament, lobby briefings, chat rooms and 'good news' stories to win public acclaim. The latter was the result of government suspicion of press reporting, most of which Alastair Campbell placed in two categories: 'crap and total crap'.

In September 2000 the government went further with UKonline, to present news to the British public in the way it wanted it presented. The idea of government controlling the news agenda had previously been tried during the 1926 General Strike, when an official newspaper evoked considerable cynicism. Critics, including civil servants themselves, dubbed the new website Pravda.com (Carr-Brown 2001), but the government was not to be steered away from its chosen path. As the websites of many government departments – and even Number Ten's own site – grew apace, citizens were given access to a wealth of information on public services through the new DirectGov portal, which had replaced UKonline in 2004, and was later re-branded as Gov.UK, professing to be 'simpler, clearer, faster'. With advances in technology came the possibility (tantalizing to some, alarming to others) of greater interactivity (dubbed Web 2.0). The idea that the online relationship between those in office and the broader public could become a genuinely two-way experience was demonstrated as the government made provision for searchable online petitions that could be signed with a single click.

Who's watching whom: new public space or Orwellian nightmare?

The US government (which had initially seen the internet as a defence instrument) spoke of an 'information superhighway', implying some kind of ordered development. The British government responded enthusiastically, seeking to promote wide access with a policy to get computers into all schools and schemes to help the poor get online. However, for some the more appropriate image was of a playground, uncoordinated and anarchic, where individuals inhabit a world of cyberspace – the world wide web – expanding like forest fire at a rate of 200 per cent each year. Not condemning people to passivity, it offers the opportunity to reclaim the public space that sociologists such as Habermas believed to have been eroded. Social media such as Facebook and Twitter connect millions of users and span continents. Amateur journalists can pre-empt the professionals with blogs, videos and opinion. Mass demonstrations and disturbances can be planned from activists' studies and bedrooms, as demonstrated by anti-globalization protests, the totemic 'Arab Spring', the English riots of 2011 and the worldwide Occupy movement in 2012.

   Such developments pose a serious threat to those who wish to control minds and ideas. While the Bible could be banned with relative ease, cyberspace is more difficult to patrol. Will technology be harnessed to create the 'Big Brother' society dreaded by Orwell? The spectres of paedophilia and terrorism are invoked to help justify attempts at official scrutiny and regulation. By the early twenty-first century no one in Britain could send an email or access a website in privacy. In July 2000, the Regulation of Investigatory Powers Act, allowing state interception of all emails, became law. In the interests of national security, service providers were required to hand over details of people's internet activities. A number of high-profile police swoops demonstrated the penetration of the official eye. Such developments caused concern to the civil liberties lobby but the 9/11 attack provided all the justification governments required.

   In April 2012 government plans to allow intelligence agencies to monitor the internet use and digital communications of every person in the land even drew criticism from Sir Tim Berners-Lee, whom they had appointed as an adviser. Although Nick Clegg declared that the so-called 'snooper's charter' would not happen while the Liberal Democrats were in government, Home Secretary Theresa May appeared to be harbouring thoughts of resurrecting just such a bill.

A destruction of human rights.
Sir Tim Berners-Lee (inventor of the world wide web) on government plans to monitor internet use; reported in the *Guardian* (17 April 2012)

Mind Politics

In shaping our attitudes the agencies of socialization form a rich informational cocktail. Family, education, peer group, class background and so on will influence the way we attend to the messages received from advertisers and the media; what we hear may influence our careers, ethics, lifestyles and friendship patterns. This mix forms the ideological bedrock of the political system and its importance cannot be overestimated.

Back in November 1998 the *Observer* published a list of what it claimed were the 300 most powerful people in Britain, as chosen by a panel of eight worthies (Hutton 1998). Prime Minister Tony Blair headed the list but second and third came two who did not even live in the country, Rupert Murdoch and Bill Gates! Moreover, in fourth place came Peter Mandelson who, prior to his ignominious downfall at the end of the year, had honed the ability to control the media probably more than any British politician before him. Never before had a government entered office with so firm a conviction of the need to monitor and shape public opinion. More than ever the new 'sultans of spin' make modern politics a psychological game – **mind politics**.

It is through mind politics that the powerful can make patterns of privilege seem beautiful in the mind of the mass. Although all inegalitarian polities must achieve this if they are to survive, few have done so as smoothly as Britain. On the other hand, Thompson (1995: 42–3) reminds us that passivity can be overstated; the hold of the media does not eliminate the chance for people to form and refine their ideas in the public spaces, be they pubs, clubs or the new spaces created on the internet. The arena of mind politics contains tensions that determine who thinks what, when and how. Our exploration of this psychological dimension of the polity must continue throughout the book.

Key points

- There is a mental as well as a behavioural dimension to politics. This mental climate shapes the political culture.

- In order for a polity to function, people must share some broad consensus on its desirability; it must enjoy legitimacy.

- Attitudes towards politics are developed through a process of political socialization.

- Important agents of political socialization include the family, the school, the peer group, religion, the arts and advertising.

- The mass media stand in a key position to shape popular attitudes.
- It is in the interests of those with wealth and power to induce others to share their own views on what is legitimate.
- The political battle can thus be seen in ideological terms.
- This hegemony is not absolute; ideologies contrary to the one favoured by establishment interests may circulate; the world-wide web and the growth of social networking increase the potential for this.
- Politics can thus be seen as a fight for the minds of people, as well as a struggle for power, material goods or control of the means of production.

Review your understanding of the following terms and concepts

broadcasting impartiality	new media	Press Complaints
broadsheet	News International	Commission
free press	news management	regulation
jingoism	Ofcom	sleaze
Leveson Inquiry/Leveson	official censorship	social networking
Report	peer group	soundbite
lobby	political socialization	spin doctor
media mogul	press baron	tabloid
mind politics	press partisanship	Web 2.0

Questions for discussion and debate

Consider these propositions and be prepared to present the cases for and against. Try to produce debating propositions of your own.

1 The peer group is the most potent agent of political socialization.

2 Political socialization is a process that continues throughout life.

3 A political culture is more clearly manifest in people's behaviour than in what they say in response to questionnaires.

4 The freedom to own newspapers is not the same as a free press.

5 Advertising is the kiss of death to crusading journalism.

6　The independence of the BBC is secure so long as it is not exercised.

7　The British press cannot regulate itself.

8　Governments have a right to expect loyalty from the mass media.

9　The internet and social networking must alter the way people form political attitudes.

10　Newspapers should report politics neutrally.

Further reading

Barnett, S. and Gaber, I. (2001) *Westminster Tales: The Twentieth-Century Crisis in Political Journalism.*
Argues that independent critical political reporting is undermined by factors such as multi-media ownership, competition and a changing culture of journalism in the interests of the powerful.

Bartle, J. and Griffiths, D. (eds) (2001) *Political Communications Transformed: From Morrison to Mandelson.*
Employs empirical studies to trace changes in the culture of politics and the media since 1945.

Cockerell, M., Hennessy, P. and Walker, P. (1984) *Sources Close to the Prime Minister: Inside the Hidden World of the News Manipulators.*
Written from an insider perspective, the title says it all.

Curran, J. and Seaton, J. (2009) *Power Without Responsibility: The Press, Broadcasting and the Internet in Britain*, 7th edn.
Introduction to the history, sociology and politics of the media in Britain.

Easton, D. and Dennis, J. (1969) *Children and the Political System: Origins of Political Legitimacy.*
Classic study of the vital early years of political socialization.

Gibson, R., Nixon, G. and Ward, S. (2003) *Political Parties and the Internet.*
Considers the powers of the internet to re-engage the public in politics.

Hollingsworth, M. (1986) *The Press and Discontent: A Question of Censorship.*
Details right-wing bias in the press.

Ingham, B. (1991) *Kill the Messenger.*

Memoir by Thatcher's press secretary lamenting the unhealthy state of current affairs broadcasting in Britain.

Kuhn, D. (2007) *Politics and the Media in Britain*.
A detailed account of the complex relationship between the media and politics, including key policy issues such as ownership and regulation.

McNair, B. (2000) *Journalism and Democracy*.
Argues that political communication in Britain is becoming more democratized.

Pilger, J. (1998) *Hidden Agendas*.
Crusading journalist reports the voices that consensual news-definers filter out. Also trenchant critique of media ownership and management.

Thompson, J. B. (1995) *The Media and Modernity: A Social Theory of the Media*.
Analyses the way in which modern societies affect and are affected by the media.

Watts, D. (1997) *Political Communication Today*.
Theoretical perspectives on the role of media in politics as well as interesting anecdotes. Notes the rise of a 'tyranny of the soundbite'.

Wayne, M. (1998) *Dissident Voices: The Politics of Television and Cultural Change*.
Analyses TV portrayal of events in the last decades of the twentieth century, examining its role as a subversive medium.

For reading around the subject and some light relief

Ray Bradbury, *Fahrenheit 451*.
Nightmare future vision where government firemen burn all books. (Also a film.)

Robin Oakley, *Inside Track*.
Senior BBC journalist recounts anecdotes of his close encounters with the powerful.

Peter Chippindale and Chris Horrie, *Stick it Up Your Punter!*
Frank story of the *Sun*. Contains nudity and strong language!

Barry Hines, *Kes*.
Goes into the mind of a working-class boy and the narrow world it is permitted to perceive. (Also a film.)

Richard Hoggart, *The Uses of Literacy*.
Argues compellingly that mass literacy has not been used to edify the masses.

Henrik Ibsen, *An Enemy of the People*.
Play in which mass opinion is mobilized against a man trying to advance the public good against capitalist interests.

S. Milgram, *Obedience to Authority: An Experimental View*.
Classic but controversial study showing that people can go to dangerous extremes in their willingness to obey those in power.

John Sergeant, *Give Me Ten Seconds*.
Thoughtful and witty account of major political events and the job of reporting them by ITN political editor.

Michael Shea, *Spin Doctor*.
Fiction close to modern reality. Chilling Machiavellian landscape beyond the eyes and ears of democracy. Author should know; he was the Queen's press secretary.

Orson Welles, *Citizen Kane*.
Classic film exploring personality and motives of newspaper baron.

On the net

The availability of all the broadsheet newspapers (both current and retrospective) on the internet enables their treatment of particular political events to be easily studied. The web addresses are all in a similar form (http://www.telegraph.co.uk) and easily obtainable.

The Press Complaints Commission (www.pcc.org.uk) was a useful site for information on the operation of the press but the Leveson Inquiry marked its demise. However, despite controversy, its successor will emerge and will be easily traceable.

http://www.ofcom.org.uk/
Ofcom regulates TV and radio sectors as well as other forms of communication. Its site includes annual reports, news releases and statistics.

CHAPTER 10

THE MACHINERY OF DEMOCRACY: THE ELECTORAL SYSTEM

Contents

In this chapter we scrutinize the machinery supposed to make Britain a democracy, the means whereby ordinary citizens formally participate in politics. This is the electoral system, or rather, the various electoral systems operating in the United Kingdom of Great Britain and Northern Ireland. We begin by considering the origins and nature of representation within democratic systems. In so doing we introduce the concepts of direct democracy and representative democracy, both in general terms and in the UK context, whilst at the same time identifying some other models of representation. This discussion naturally leads us on to outline the way in which elections to the Westminster Parliament currently operate, before charting that crucial chapter in British political history, the evolution of the electoral system. We conclude with an evaluation of the Westminster electoral system itself and consider alternatives, some of which are also in use in the UK. This leads to the key issue of electoral reform.

Democracy and Representation

The origins of democracy

Over 300 years before the birth of Christ, Ancient Greece consisted of many small self-governing city-states. Adopting a variety of methods and institutional frameworks for conducting public affairs, they presented a unique laboratory for the empirical study of government. As we saw in chapter 1, many of the Greek philosophers, particularly the Athenians, saw democracy as the most desirable form of government, a belief they bequeathed to modern civilization.

Direct democracy

In order to be entirely democratic a system of government should permit all citizens to take part in making public policy. There have been examples of such **direct democracy**: the Greek city-states made some provision for it and early parish government in Britain saw the community meeting in the church precincts to make decisions about such issues as roads, bridges and law and order. The government of the small communities formed by the New England settlers in America (referred to as 'town hall' democracy in its modern incarnation) was also widely participative in character, as are the Swiss cantons today. Although direct democracy in the modern nation-state has generally been seen as impractical, in an age of advanced technology the use of electronic means of consultation makes it more feasible (see p. 265).

The Greek city-states were very small and intimate, covering an area no larger than around thirty square miles. With a considerable number of slaves, citizenship was restricted to fewer than 20,000; abortion, infanticide and a liberal attitude towards homosexual relationships kept populations under control. Yet even these polities were too large to govern themselves directly. A mass forum cannot conduct the kind of deliberation necessary for decision-making; this must be entrusted to a smaller group and, if the democratic ideal is to be protected, the selection of this group, and its **accountability** to the people as a whole, are key. The Greek city-states made provision for popular voting and office-holding by rotation, with various penalties for unsatisfactory officials. In Athens, candidates were elected to a large panel from which office-holders were selected by drawing lots. They believed that those, like Macbeth, who thrust themselves forward with 'high-vaulting ambition', would be the most unsuitable for high office.

Representative democracy

In these devices we see the origins of **representative government**. Although a state may be run by a small group of rulers, not unlike a monarchy or an aristocracy, they are not there by virtue of any personal qualities (birth, wealth, religious status, physical strength or even intelligence) but as *representatives* of everyone else. They act in the name of the people and the people retain the right to control and even remove them.

Democracy in Britain

Although Britain formally has a system of representative democracy based on elections, it falls far short of the Athenian ideal. Indeed, for long it was believed by the ruling Establishment that only a relatively small proportion of the population should vote. Ordinary people were said to enjoy a form of paternalistic 'virtual representation' – the aristocracy could be assumed to take the views of all classes into consideration when making decisions. However, the **franchise** (eligibility to vote) was gradually extended as a result of radical leaders fighting for their rights (see pp. 269–75). Those who regarded themselves as the ruling class became fearful of mass rule, seeking new ways to limit democracy. This they did by keeping MPs unpaid, charging electoral deposits, developing party machines to dominate elections, refusing to adopt working-class candidates and inhibiting the rise of a working-class party.

The Tamworth Manifesto
A set of electoral promises was first made by the Conservative leader Peel on an historic occasion in 1834 to the 586 electors of his Tamworth constituency. The 'Tamworth Manifesto' marked a new style of campaigning based on the mandate.

In addition, they developed a highly elitist theory of representation in which MPs were supposed to act according to their own discretion, with no particular regard for their constituents' opinions. The view received its most authoritative enunciation by Edmund Burke (1729–97) in a famous address to his constituents in Bristol, when he stressed that what they were to expect from him was not servitude but the exercise of 'judgement and conscience'. This representative view of democracy (or 'trustee model') remains deeply ingrained in British political culture, part of the all-important machinery of deference in which the masses forgo their right to influence the high and mighty. An alternative view of representation is presented by the **mandate** model, whereby election is seen to empower and perhaps oblige the party elected to government to fulfil those promises made in its **manifesto**. In the reality of modern political life we hear both models championed, with politicians choosing the one that best suits their argument at any given point in time.

Direct democracy in Britain

Referendums

> A device so alien to all our traditions … which has only too often been the instrument of Nazism and Fascism.
>
> Clement Attlee's 1945 opinion of referendums (widely shared in the immediate post-war period

Fear of the mass has also been seen in a disinclination to put questions directly to the people through **referendums**, although continued membership of the EC was decided in this way in 1975, and in 1979 referendums were held on Scottish and Welsh devolution. However, the constitution and political culture are beginning to show signs of change. In 1995 Tony Blair noted that 'in the case of major constitutional change, there is clearly a case for that decision to be taken by the British people'. Referendums were subsequently held on Scottish and Welsh devolution in 1997, and on the London Assembly and mayor and the Northern Ireland peace agreement the following year. In his 2001 party conference speech, Blair expressed a strong preference for a referendum on entry into the single European currency during that parliament. Further referendums followed: on the creation of an elected regional assembly for the North East (rejected in 2004), on greater powers for the Welsh Assembly (approved in March 2011) and on the introduction of the Alternative Vote (AV) system in elections to the Westminster Parliament (rejected in May 2011). Referendums were also making their appearance in local government.

As the idea of direct democracy has entered the veins of the body politic, opposition parties, pressure groups and citizens have felt more able to demand referendums. However, critics argue that, by asking only 'yes' or 'no', referendums may oversimplify issues, be unduly influenced by those controlling information and undermine representative government and parliamentary democracy. In most recent referendums the party (or largest single party) in government has obtained the outcome it desired. Some efforts have been made to level the playing field. Following the recommendations of Lord Neill's Committee on Standards in Public Life, for example, the 2000 Political Parties, Elections and Referendums Act introduced state funding of £1.2 million, to be shared equally between the rival campaigns. The government is now also required to remain neutral, no longer using the machinery of the state to promote its preferred outcome.

E-democracy

The term 'e-democracy' is commonly applied to the use of the internet and other communication technologies as a means of enhancing political communication and decision-making. Top-down initiatives, often seen as being motivated more by a desire to cut costs through paper-free operations than by a wish to enhance democracy, have given way to greater interactivity (dubbed Web 2.0) and action initiated by grassroots activists. Crucially, campaigners have also begun to use such technologies as a means of communicating with one another as well as for lobbying public officials. Jackson and Lilleker (2009) explore the implications of MPs' engagement with the internet, particularly the extent to which e-democracy is facilitating representation, beyond simply enhancing the traditional relationships between MPs and their constituents. Thus groups that would previously have struggled to organize and articulate their views effectively for want of material resources have found their voice. The internet-based campaigning group '38 Degrees', for example, regarded as a powerful political force, played a key role in the coalition government's U-turn on its proposal to sell off Britain's publicly owned forests. The UK government, for its part, has also come to embrace e-democracy as a way of eliciting the views of citizens. The e-petitions initiative, once regarded as somewhat tokenistic, gained greater credence in 2011 as a result of the coalition's announcement that any online petition exceeding 100,000 signatures would be passed to the Commons Backbench Business Committee, with a view to scheduling a debate on the issue (see p. 447).

Anyone who can claim to understand this issue in simple black and white terms is either a charlatan or a simpleton!
Harold Wilson on EC membership, quoted in Anthony Sampson, *The Essential Anatomy of Britain* (1992: 15)

Democratic avalanche
With a claimed (virtual) membership of over 1 million in 2012, 38 Degrees takes its name from the angle at which an avalanche occurs. Mobilizing supporters via the internet, its declared aims are to 'deepen democracy' by enabling people to act together to create an 'avalanche for change', but legislative proposals on election spending could curb its operations.

Citizens' juries and assemblies

Although New Labour was often criticized for its centralizing tendencies, Gordon Brown expressed support for a number of initiatives during his time at Number Ten, most notably the use of **citizens' juries** and **citizens' assemblies**. Both devices are used widely elsewhere. A citizens' jury consists of a small panel assembled to take evidence and, ultimately, deliver its verdict on a government proposal. Whilst the final decision remains with elected politicians, guided by the panel of experts who review the jury's verdict, the use of such juries in many US states and in Germany is seen to enhance the democratic process. Citizens' assemblies tend to involve a broader and more representative cross-section of the population. Whereas a citizens' jury may only involve handfuls of participants, assemblies can engage hundreds or even thousands of citizens. In this way citizens might be able to enjoy the kind of 'public conversation' widely advocated by those favouring a codified constitution for the UK. Crucially they could be given the power to make binding decisions, as opposed to simply advising politicians. The principle could also be adapted to provide an online reading stage for public bills, an initiative considered by the 2010 coalition government.

Recalls

The **recall** is a device that gives voters the opportunity to petition for a public ballot that can remove an elected official from office before the end of their term. Used widely outside the UK, most notably in many US states, the recall is controversial because it appears to strike at the heart of representative democracy. Recalls are particularly problematic when motivated by political animosity, as opposed to issues of competency or alleged impropriety. In the wake of the 2010 MPs' expenses scandal, all three of the main UK parties pledged to bring forward proposals that would allow the public to unseat MPs found guilty of financial irregularities.

The electoral process today

The British are frequently invited to the polls. In addition to five-yearly general elections, local elections take place somewhere every year, elections for the Scottish Parliament and for the Welsh and Northern Ireland assemblies occur every four years, and European Parliament elections are held at five-yearly intervals. A variety of electoral systems are employed in these, as outlined below. However, electing members to the House of Commons remains the high point in the political calendar and here the system used is known as **simple plurality** or first-past-the-post. General elections take place around a framework of voters, constituencies and candidates.

Voters

Today Britain has a universal franchise. With certain exceptions (those guilty of electoral malpractice, aliens, imprisoned criminals and members of the House of Lords), all citizens over the age of eighteen are eligible to vote in Westminster elections. A lively debate arose in the wake of a 2005 ruling by the European Court of Human Rights that imprisoned criminals should be allowed to vote. (There are fewer restrictions in the cases of elections to local government, the devolved legislatures and the European Parliament.)

Constituencies

The basis for representation is spatial; MPs represent areal **constituencies** (650 in 2010, including 18 in Northern Ireland) and a general election is in effect a number of simultaneous contests, each returning a single member. Constituency populations tend towards equality (at around 69,000). However, there have been significant variations. At the 2010 general election, for example, the Isle of Wight constituency comprised 110,924 eligible voters, whereas the MP elected to represent Na h-Eileanan an Iar (formerly the Western Isles) had only to appeal to 21,837 souls. Borisyuk et al. (2010) give a detailed analysis of some of the problems associated with unequal constituency populations, particularly disproportionality and electoral bias.

Population movements are monitored by Boundary Commissions, independent bodies chaired by the Speaker of the House of Commons, which normally recommend changes every ten to fifteen years, following lengthy consultation. These can have important consequences. Post-war readjustments to reflect declining inner-city populations tended to favour the Conservatives, although the 1994–5 review may have contributed to their 1997 defeat (Johnston et al. 1998) as a number of safe constituencies disappeared or became more marginal. This periodic redrawing of constituency boundaries inevitably forces those MPs representing doomed constituencies, or those becoming highly marginal, into a 'chicken run' towards what are seen as safer seats. The proposal to drastically redraw the map to reduce the number of constituencies from 650 to 600 in time for the 2015 general election, ostensibly to achieve further equality and a more efficient House of Commons, appeared to critics to be being rushed through with unseemly haste, with token consultation and little consideration for social geography. Many MPs, particularly Labour, contemplated their future nervously (with the party apparently set to lose around twenty seats). However, these plans were put on hold until at least 2018 in the wake of a Commons defeat for the government in January 2013 (344:292), a reversal precipitated by the Liberal Democrats' decision to withdraw support in a tit-for-tat reaction to the part played by many Conservative backbenchers in the forced abandonment of the coalition's blueprint for Lords reform six months earlier.

Candidates

Although almost any resident British citizen over the age of eighteen may stand, most of those elected are over thirty. The youngest MP returned to the Commons at the 2010 general election was Labour's twenty-five-year-old Pamela Nash, representing Airdrie and Shotts. The police and armed forces, certain civil servants, judges, Anglican and Roman Catholic clergymen, and those ineligible to vote are all excluded. There are few independents, virtually all clothing themselves in party garb. Notable exceptions to this rule have included white-suited journalist Martin Bell, who in 1997 spectacularly defeated Conservative Neil Hamilton on an anti-sleaze ticket in Tatton, and Dr Richard Taylor, elected to represent Wyre Forest in both 2001 and 2005 – although he registered himself as belonging to the Independent Kidderminster Hospital and Health Concern Party (with lively website and newsletter). Independents normally have little chance unless one or more major parties steps down in their favour, as occurred in both these cases.

Each candidate must formally appoint an agent, who ensures compliance with electoral law and will probably also be the campaign manager (organizing canvassing, press conferences and so on). Most agents are well versed in the arts of political intrigue and some are highly professionalized.

The Electoral Commission

This statutory body was established in November 2000 under the Political Parties, Elections and Referendums Act (PPERA). Independent of the government, it is charged with the task of monitoring elections and reports directly to Parliament, via a committee chaired by the Speaker.

General elections

A general election follows a number of stages.

1. *Naming the day.* The date was not traditionally fixed by law, with the government's term of office merely being subject to a five-year maximum. Under this system, the process was initiated when the prime minister asked the Queen to dissolve Parliament, giving the government something of an advantage. However, the 2011 Fixed Term Parliaments Act established a system of fixed-term, five-year Parliaments, with the first election under the new calendar due to take place on 7 May 2015.
2. *Mobilizing the electorate.* The 1983 Representation of the People Act set a minimum of seventeen days between calling the election and the day itself, a requirement retained in the Fixed Term Parliaments Act. There is no upper limit, but by convention a campaigning period is normally four to six weeks. During this time, candidates and parties conduct what have become increasingly sophisticated stratagems designed to woo voters.

3. *Determining the result.* Voting has been the essence of simplicity, an 'X' being placed alongside the name of a single candidate. In this simple plurality system, the candidate with the most votes – the 'first past the post' (FPTP) – is the winner.

> **Sore loser?**
> In 1997 the voters of Winchester gave Liberal Democrat Mark Oaten victory by only two votes. Unwilling to accept defeat gracefully, his Conservative opponent challenged the validity of the result and a by-election was held. However, perhaps sensing a lack of sportsmanship, the voters endorsed Oaten with a resounding 21,556 majority.

4. *Forming the government.* A general election results in the emergence of a government, usually formed from the party with an **absolute majority** in the House of Commons. In a two-party system a simple majority will necessarily be absolute, but with more parties complications set in; *hung Parliaments* may emerge and politicians have to retire to rooms (smoke-filled in less health-conscious times) to consider **coalitions** or party agreements. In 1974 Edward Heath, leader of the narrowly defeated Conservative Party (297 seats), conducted a tentative flirtation with the Liberals (14 seats) before conceding defeat to Labour (301 seats). By the time he called the 1997 election, John Major headed a minority government dependent on Ulster Unionist support. In the wake of the 2010 general election, a week of febrile negotiation ultimately resulted in the drafting of a formal coalition agreement between the Conservatives and the Liberal Democrats.

> **By-elections**
> By-elections are called in particular constituencies following an MP's death or retirement. These provide a measure of government popularity and allow minority parties to shine. The Conservatives suffered a series of defeats throughout the 1979–97 period, frequently with swings against them in the 20–30 per cent range. Yet although stimulating political debate and media hype, these contests provide a poor guide to long-term trends. The party in power is often victim of a 'protest vote' from those wishing to administer a 'kick in the pants' without dislodging it, and the successful minority parties are usually banished to the wilderness at the next general election.

Economizing with Democracy: Evolution of the Electoral System

The history of Britain's electoral system is no account of legalistic reform, nor a psephological nightmare of figures, swings and majorities, but a story of violence and political struggle in which the prize was control over the state. Reforms were not born of rational thought or an enlightened desire for democracy on the part of the powerful; they came after a slow and painful political labour. The belief (perhaps misguided) of those calling for reform since the seventeenth century was that entry into the House of Commons would advance their political ambitions. This conviction averted revolutionary challengers from rocking the constitutional boat, making British history more tranquil than it might otherwise have been.

A democratic travesty

At the beginning of the nineteenth century the system was a democratic travesty. Of a total population of 16 million, a mere 400,000 were eligible to vote in parliamentary elections. Of the two chambers, the House of Lords was reserved for those of noble birth while the Commons was largely peopled on the basis of patronage and corruption. MPs came from two types of constituency. *Counties* showed no consistency in size or population and the franchise was tied to landownership; each returned two MPs. *Boroughs* were towns that had at some time been granted royal charters. Here franchise rights varied widely and, although some allowed almost universal male suffrage, the scope for malpractice was considerable. In the

Show of Hands for a Liberal Candidate.

Source: Mary Evans Picture Library.

so-called 'rotten boroughs', the population had shrunk since their days of medieval splendour, leaving a mere handful of citizens (Dunwich had fallen into the sea and Old Sarum had a population of zero). In 'pocket boroughs', rich landowners controlled elections through threats and bribery, while the new thriving and populous industrial towns, many with highly efficient local government institutions, remained starved of representation at Westminster. Voting was not secret and, since MPs were obliged to be entirely self-financing, candidature was restricted to the wealthy. Parliament was thus held securely in the grip of a landed Establishment.

Forces for change

In common with most other institutions, the electoral system was transformed to serve the ends of the new industrial bourgeoisie. For the emergent class, archaic practices of law, administration and government were not the cherished legacies praised by Burke but barriers to enterprise, trade and social advancement. The clash was typified in the 1815 Corn Law which, by denying free trade, blatantly favoured landed interests over commerce. The bourgeoisie realized that the parliamentary compost required some more earthy additives for the bloom of private enterprise.

Justifying claims for a stronger voice in Parliament through the utilitarian arguments of the philosophical radicals, they called for representative government through rational and fair elections. Although self-interested the bourgeoisie required allies, whom they found in the bottom half of the curious social sandwich in which they were squeezed. Here was a working class that they themselves had, in Marx's view, 'called into existence', whose potential for insurrection was made more ominous by the chilling excesses of the French Revolution. It offered a force that, if harnessed, could drive the piston of reform as effectively as steam power drove their industry.

Wellington's victory at Waterloo in 1815 did little to relieve the misfortunes that war had heaped upon the poor. Economic slump, the return of soldiers and Irish immigration produced unemployment, destitution and rising costs. The workers were willing to accept the leadership of middle-class radicals working for a reform promising them a voice in Parliament. Agitation operated on a number of fronts, with Hampden Clubs (named after a great seventeenth-century parliamentarian), radical city newspapers, strikes, marches, mass meetings and political discussion classes to prepare ordinary people for rule.

The 1832 Reform Act

Although working-class agitation was easily suppressed by state violence (as in the 1819 Peterloo Massacre), voters felt that the Whigs (later to morph into the Liberal

Party) were better able to reduce the tension in the long term. In 1830 they were returned to government after almost fifty years of continuous Tory rule. The scene appeared set for a democratic revolution, but once in office they revealed no less a respect for property than the Tories. The difference lay only in their view that factories, machines, raw materials and even the urban labour force could represent property as well as rolling acres in the countryside. In the 1832 Reform Act many small boroughs lost their MPs as seats were redistributed to the more populous counties and new urban kingdoms where the bourgeoisie reigned.

The working class gained nothing. The franchise was parsimoniously extended (from around 500,000 to just over 700,000) to middle-class male property-owners (valued at £10 or more a year). MPs remained unpaid, potential candidates faced a prohibitive property qualification, electoral corruption was not eliminated and wealthy individuals could still exert undue control. Of course, the Whigs had never wanted popular democracy; they had dreamed only of a prudent middle-class control over Parliament from which they could command their empire of trade at home and around the world.

Chartism

The radicals' disappointment led to bitterness, violence and renewed calls for electoral reform. In 1836 William Lovett formed the London Working Men's Association, which drew up a *Charter* incorporating the following demands:
1. universal manhood suffrage;
2. annual election of parliaments (to render bribery prohibitively expensive and increase accountability);
3. abolition of the property qualification for candidates;
4. payment for MPs (to enable the poor to serve);
5. equal-sized constituencies (to make all votes of equal weight);
6. secret ballot (to end intimidation).

Working-men's clubs emerged under the mantle of **Chartism** but Parliament rejected their demands and those favouring violence rather than argument took the initiative. The government's reaction revealed it to be as willing as its Tory predecessors to use draconian methods involving imprisonment, vigilantes (special constables and spies) and the army. By the late 1840s Chartism was a spent force, battered by the power of the very state in whose government it wished to participate.

The Representation of the People Act 1867

In the 1860s, partly as a result of unease over the American civil war, popular attention again focused upon electoral reform as a means of containing unrest. In 1866 a Liberal reform bill was defeated by a combination of government rebels and Conservatives. The government resigned, to be replaced by a Conservative minority government led by Disraeli who, to the surprise of many, promptly introduced the 1867 reform bill. Dropping the restrictive property qualifications, this enfranchised all male urban householders. In 1868, with around two and a quarter million eligible voters, it was now possible to speak of a *mass electorate*. This had far-reaching consequences: to attract mass support and keep out working-class parties, politicians were forced to take serious interest in social conditions, education and trade union rights.

The 1867 Act further underscored the supremacy of the Commons over the Lords, marking the end of the ascendancy of Parliament over the executive. The so-called 'Golden Age', which began in 1832, was closed by the rise of disciplined parliamentary party cadres (see p. 457), affording ministers a grip over the legislature that the Tudors would have envied. From this time the voters, not the Commons, would choose governments.

The full impact of the reforms could not take effect without certain other measures. The 1872 Ballot Act made voting secret; workers no longer had to risk their livelihoods by opposing their employers' interests. The Corrupt and Illegal Practices Act (1883) reduced bribery and the following year the electorate was almost doubled by the Franchise Act, which introduced virtual universal male suffrage by extending the 1867 provisions to rural constituencies. The Redistribution of Seats Act (1885) had the profound effect of making the working class a majority of the electorate. However, the franchise was still withheld from certain categories of men, and all women were excluded. MPs were still not paid as such and voters were obliged to select from two competing factions of the elite rather than choose genuine working-class representatives.

The politician who once had to learn how to flatter kings has now to learn how to fascinate, amuse, coax, humbug, frighten or otherwise strike the fancy of the electorate.
George Bernard Shaw, in Preface to *Man and Superman* (1905)

Votes for women

Throughout the reform era, the phrase 'one man, one vote' meant exactly that; women continued to be regarded by middle and working class alike as political ciphers. Hence, their struggle for political equality was even harder. The potential increase in the electorate would be considerably larger than any before, a fact contemplated with consternation by the male Establishment and intensifying its resistance.

The achievement of near-universal male franchise was a potent catalyst. The idea of a middle-class male monopoly might have irked some of their wives, but extending the right to all men, regardless of social status, was even more intolerable. Various associations formed, such as the Nottingham Female Political Union (1838), the Sheffield Association for Female Suffrage (1851) and a Woman's

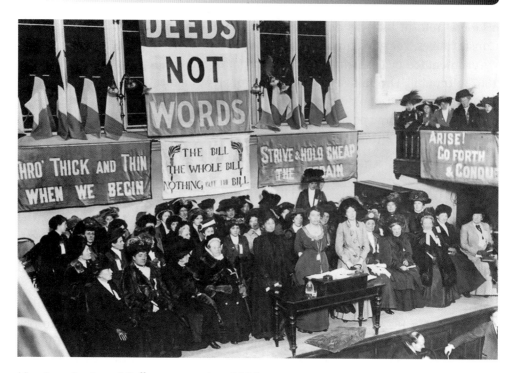

Monstrous Regiment? Suffragette meeting, 1908

Franchise League (1889). In 1897 Millicent Fawcett sought to unite the movement in the National Union of Women's Suffrage Societies, but the approach was too timid for some and in 1903 Emmeline Pankhurst and her two daughters established the Women's Social and Political Union, which became the most famous instrument of the **suffragettes**.

The movement began with education and propaganda but the pipe-smoking, leather-armchaired Establishment and Asquith's Liberal government were uncompromising and prepared to employ the same state force that had resisted the Chartists. Suffragettes were subject to ridicule, physical attack, forcible ejection from meetings, imprisonment and hard labour. Victorian judicial attitudes were conditioned by the mysteries of child-bearing; menstruation was a common explanation for female deviancy and suffragettes were said to be suffering with their ovaries or from spinsterhood (Kennedy 1992). Hunger-strikers were sadistically force-fed through the nose, an ordeal leaving some permanently injured. To avoid creating martyrs, the government passed the notorious 'Cat and Mouse' Act in 1913, enabling it to release weakened hunger-strikers only to re-imprison them upon recovery. Yet they could not prevent Emily Wilding Davison's dramatic martyrdom when, in the same year, she fell under the galloping hooves of the King's horse in the Derby.

The most important thing women have to do is to stir up the zeal of women themselves.
J. S. Mill, letter to Alexander Bain (14 July 1869)

War and the franchise

Where Asquith would not help the women the Kaiser could. The arrival of an enemy at the gate produced domestic truce and the Pankhursts rallied their supporters behind the flag. On 15 July 1914 they staged their final demonstration, marching down Whitehall to demand not the vote but the 'right to serve'. Their reward was the 1918 Representation of the People Act, which A. J. P. Taylor (1965: 94) described, with apparently unintended irony, as the victory 'of the radical principle of "one man, one vote"'. This gave women the vote and completed the male franchise but it still stopped short of full equality: men could vote at twenty-one but fear that young women might prove radical, engendered by socialist revolutions in Europe, limited their participation to the mature over-thirties. (The 1928 Equal Franchise Act brought women into equality with men, and was followed by the 1929 Labour victory, perhaps justifying establishment fears.) The 1918 Act added more new voters than all previous franchise acts together. It also gave women the right to stand for Parliament and later that year seventeen did so. Although Lady Astor, amidst some ceremony, made history as the first woman MP, the occasion did not mark the opening of any floodgates. The advance of women in Parliament continued to be held back by constituency organizations' unwillingness to adopt them as candidates. Not until the Labour Party introduced all-women shortlists prior to the 1997 general election did the real breakthrough come, with the entry of 121 women MPs, 101 of them – later dubbed 'Blair's babes' – representing Labour (see p. 338).

Women had always fought for men and for their children. Now they were ready to fight for their own human rights.
Emmeline Pankhurst (1858–1928), *My Own Story* (1914)

Votes for youth

War had led some to muse on the anomaly that, while young people of eighteen could be required to fight and die for the country, they were not entitled to vote for those who sent them into battle. But it was not until the 1960s, with improvements in education at all levels, many more adolescents going to university and a prevailing cult of youth that Harold Wilson, in tune with the *zeitgeist* (to establishment shock the Beatles received MBEs), lowered the voting age to eighteen in the 1969 Reform Act. His reward was rebuff in the next general election, though perhaps by a smaller majority than would otherwise have been the case, and in 1974 the young vote helped him back to power (Butler 1995: 69). Today debate centres on the possibility of a further lowering of the age to sixteen.

The extension of the franchise had been gradual and grudging. The effect of the 1832 Act was to give the vote to a mere 20 per cent of the men in England and Wales. After 1867 this became 33 per cent, reaching 67 per cent in 1884. Full adult franchise was withheld until 1928. No major concession was secured without the threat of violence. How have these enfranchised voters been represented through the ballot box? To answer this question we must study the mechanics of the electoral system.

The British Parliamentary Electoral System: Disproportional Representation?

The first-past-the-post (FPTP) system is said by its supporters to be quintessentially British, uniquely fitted to the political culture. It is conducive to bipartisan politics, offering electors a clear choice and producing stable majorities, moderate policies and an ethos of strong government. Extremist or frivolous parties are excluded; despite its 30,000 membership in the 1930s, the British Fascist Party did not gain a single seat in Parliament. Stable, single-party governments – which remain the norm – can generally count on a full term, enabling them to enforce their electoral mandate without the kinds of compromises often forced by the need for coalition-building or fear of a coup. The system also produces a coherent opposition – a 'government in waiting' – and allows a regular alternation of governments. The relatively small single-member constituencies permit close links between MPs and people and ensure that the interests of far-flung regions are not forgotten at Westminster. Moreover, its simplicity makes it easily understood, voters are used to it and a fairly high turnout is said to demonstrate their satisfaction. However, these virtues are open to question.

Problems with first-past-the-post

The kind of economy that we are faced with is going to be a market economy, and we have got to make it work better than the Tories make it work.

Neil Kinnock, Labour Party conference speech (1988)

Critics of FPTP question the virtues detailed above.
- *Clear choice.* This idea is belied by the tendency of the two main parties to converge on the centre ground (the much-heralded 'end of ideology'), minimizing the policy differences between them. The post-war consensus was broken only by Thatcher, and it was not long before Labour was moving rightwards across a wide policy range. Sometimes, on certain crucial issues, such as Europe, the fissures run largely *within* the parties rather than between them.
- *Strong and stable single-party government.* Throughout the twentieth century Britain experienced some twenty-one years of government by a combination of parties – either a coalition or a national government. There have also been periods when a single party in office has lacked an absolute majority, sustained only by a third-party agreement. Major was brought to his knees by his Eurosceptics and obliged to rely on Irish MPs, while the inconclusive 2010 general election results led to the formation of a coalition. Curtice (2010) considered why FPTP failed to deliver single-party majority government in 2010 and what this could mean for electoral reform.
- *Moderate government.* Thatcher demonstrated, to both admirers and critics, that the system did not necessarily prevent a degree of extremism.

- *Mandated government.* A victorious party cannot always be expected to execute all its promises as, for example, when the Conservatives jettisoned their 1992 pledge not to increase VAT, or when Labour introduced university top-up fees in spite of making an explicit pledge not to do so in their 2001 manifesto. Similarly, the Conservative manifesto in 2010 promised no top-down reorganization of the NHS but the coalition of which it was the main partner embarked on it with alacrity.

- *Single-party opposition.* For much of the early twentieth century the Liberals coexisted with Labour in opposition. In 1983, the system was kind to Labour, masking the strength of the centre-party vote, yet with 46 seats in 1997, 52 in 2001 and 62 in 2005, the Liberal Democrats could lay some claim to be part of Her Majesty's Loyal Opposition.

- *Regular alternation in office.* Even in the post-war era, when this thesis appeared most plausible, by 1997 the Conservatives had reigned for thirty-five years (figure 10.1) and, once in office, the New Labour government enjoyed power from 1997 to 2010.

- *Close MP–constituency link.* The dominance of the party machines means that constituencies increasingly find that candidates with few local connections are 'parachuted' from London to be foisted on them. Prospective candidates will tote themselves around the country in the search for a seat, sometimes maintaining

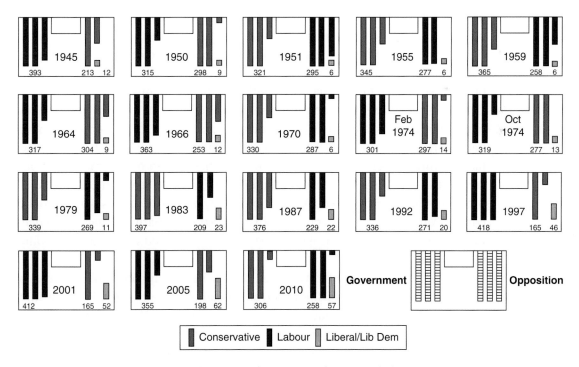

Figure 10.1 Party dispositions in the House of Commons after general elections, 1945–2010

only a token constituency address. Citizens of South Yorkshire found themselves represented by Londoners Nick Clegg and Ed Miliband.

- *Simplicity*. The choice of **proportional representation** (PR) for elections to the European Parliament, a hybrid Additional Member System for the devolved assemblies and the Greater London Assembly, as well as increasingly sophisticated approaches to tactical voting, give the lie to the claim that Britons need simplicity.
- *Popularity*. The record low turnout at the 2001 general election (59.4 per cent) and disappointing turnouts in 2005 (61.4 per cent) and 2010 (65.1 per cent) have done little to substantiate claims that the system is popular. Indeed, apathy is seen as a major issue in British politics. Despite Labour's 247-seat majority over the Conservatives in 2001, only one in four of the eligible electorate had actually placed a cross beside a Labour candidate. Research has shown turnout in proportional systems to be some 9 per cent higher than in the non-proportional (Lijphart 1994).

Beyond questioning the virtues claimed for the system, there are other criticisms.

- *Disenfranchisement*. A single-member constituency, in which only one set of opinions can ever be represented, leaves many votes 'wasted'. Even votes cast for successful candidates are superfluous where majorities are large, as in many northern Labour seats (so-called 'wasted surpluses'). Such constituencies remain impervious to national swings and thousands of voters have no influence. Local party oligarchs become the effective electorate (or 'selectorate') through their right to select candidates. Experiments with **primary elections** – as used in Totnes by the Conservative Party in 2010 – offer a partial solution to this problem, but the use of such devices has been both limited and inconsistent.
- *The third-party blues*. Despite gaining widespread national support, third parties may not be in a position to win many constituencies. The Liberal Democrats have been particularly vulnerable. Between 1997 and 2010, thanks to targeting and tactical voting, their support became more concentrated but, attracting 23 per cent of the votes, just 6 per cent behind Labour, their 57 seats (in 2010) fell disproportionately below Labour's 258. Conversely, minority parties with spatially concentrated support can achieve a disproportionate parliamentary presence. In 2010, Scottish and Welsh nationalists together secured nine seats with only 656,780 votes.
- *Over-amplification of opinion change*. It has been estimated that a shift in support from one party to the other of only about 1 per cent will result in a change in Parliament of about thirteen seats: in 1997, a 10.3 per cent swing to Labour gave a 147-seat gain; in 2010, a 4.9 per cent swing nationally from Labour to Conservative saw Labour lose 90 seats and the Conservatives gain 96.
- *Legitimacy crisis*. Once there are more than two horses in the race, in any

constituency, 'winners' may take their seats at Westminster with well over half their constituents having voted against them. In this simple plurality system the absolute number of votes is immaterial; MPs can quite easily be elected with 30 per cent of the votes.

- *Disproportionate majorities*. Anomalies at constituency level are transposed to Westminster; since 1935 no governing party has polled over half the votes cast although almost all have enjoyed substantial majorities. With 42.3 per cent of the votes in 1987, the Conservatives were able to push through the poll tax, buoyed by 57.8 per cent of the seats in Parliament. Blair's lead over the Conservatives in terms of votes in 2005 (2.8 per cent) was 4.2 points lower than Cameron's lead over Brown in 2010. Yet, whereas Labour was returned with a 64-seat majority, the Conservatives were obliged to form a coalition with the Liberal Democrats, having fallen 21 seats short of an overall majority. It is even possible for the majority party in Parliament to poll fewer votes than the opposition, as in 1951 and February 1974.

- *Policy discontinuity*. The fact that government change entails a clean sweep of an entire government threatens policy continuity. Critics cite 'stop–go', 'see-saw' policies as a cause of Britain's economic performance in comparison with Western Europe, where continuity is often secured through coalitions in which centre parties remain in power.

- *Issue submergence*. The pressure towards bipartism means that voters are offered only two very broad policy *tables d'hôtes*. They cannot choose, say, Labour's education policy and the Conservatives' policy on law and order. This justified the dubious claim by Nick Clegg's Liberal Democrats that no referendum was required on House of Lords reform because all parties had included this in their manifestos and therefore all voters must want the reform.

The Alternatives to First-Past-The-Post

Continuing debate surrounds the FPTP system, with various alternatives canvassed. These may be broadly categorized as majoritarian, proportional or hybrid (i.e. some mixture of the two).

Majoritarian systems

Alternative vote (AV)

This well-known system is used for the Australian House of Representatives. It cannot produce genuine proportional representation (PR) because it operates on the basis of single-member constituencies, but it does ensure that members have

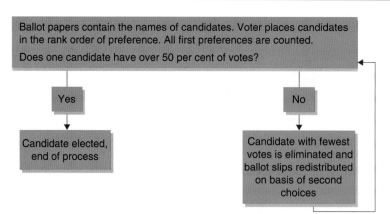

Figure 10.2 The alternative vote system

an absolute majority by considering their alternative preferences (**preferential voting**) of those voting for minority candidates (figure 10.2). The possibility of this system coming into use for the House of Commons arose with a referendum put to the British people (but rejected) in May 2011 (see p. 284).

Supplementary vote

This variation on the AV system avoids overvaluing third and subsequent preferences (which may not carry the same levels of conviction) in the redistribution process. It came into prominence by being recommended by Labour's 1993 Plant Report. The ballot paper is the same as in FPTP but voters choose a single second preference. If no candidate wins over 50 per cent of the vote, all but the first two are eliminated and their votes redistributed. This system is used for the election of local mayors (including the Mayor of London).

Second ballot

Instead of voters expressing a second preference, if no candidate secures an absolute majority a second election is held. During the interim period, weak parties may withdraw and others indulge in horse-trading over policies, while voters can think again and abstainers may decide to turn out. The system is used in France, where in the 2002 presidential election the Front National's Jean Marie le Pen fared well on the first ballot but was swept aside on the second.

Proportional systems

Many polities use a system of PR, seeking an assembly that broadly mirrors the pattern of support in the country. Thus the Conservatives' 33 per cent of the vote in 2001 would have translated into 217 seats under pure proportionality, rather than the 166 they gained under FPTP. There are various forms of PR, of which the following are the principal basic models.

Party list

Widely used in Western Europe, including Denmark, Finland and Belgium, this system is based upon **multi-member constituencies**. Parties prepare lists of candidates, and candidates are returned in the list order. The percentage vote obtained by each party in each region is calculated and seats are awarded on a pro rata basis. Some systems allow voters to split the ticket between parties. The **party lists** may be 'open' (voters can indicate their favoured candidates) or 'closed' (voters merely indicate the party of their choice). The closed party list system has been used for the British European Parliament elections since 1999, except in Northern Ireland, where STV is used. The closed list increases the power of the party machine and is thus less democratic, a point emphasized by the House of Lords in opposing its use for the European Parliament elections.

The multi-member constituency
This is fundamental to the PR principle. If in a given constituency party X polls 60 per cent of the votes, party Y 30 and party Z 10, a minimum of ten candidates must be returned if strict proportionality is to be observed. This implies that constituencies cannot be small; indeed, a 'constituency' may be a large region or, as in the case of the Netherlands, a whole country.

Single transferable vote (STV)

STV is probably the best-known PR system. A version was used in Britain between 1918 and 1948, when multi-member university seats existed. It was also recommended by the Kilbrandon Commission on the Constitution for the separate assemblies it advocated for Wales and Scotland. Today it is used in Northern Ireland for the European Parliament, the Northern Ireland Assembly and local government. It is also used in Scottish local government elections. Although requiring multi-member constituencies, these may be relatively small (usually three to five MPs). Parties may put up as many candidates as there are seats, and voters are thus given considerable choice. The procedure has three main stages.

1. Voters record on the ballot paper their order of preference for candidates.
2. An **electoral quota** (EQ) is calculated using the droop formula:

$$EQ = \left[\frac{\textit{Valid votes cast}}{\textit{Seats} + 1} \right] + 1$$

3. First preferences are counted and those obtaining the EQ are elected. If seats remain vacant, surplus votes for successful candidates are redistributed on the basis of second choices, so that further candidates reach the EQ and no votes are wasted. If all seats cannot be filled in this way, the last-placed candidate's ballot papers are redistributed on the basis of second choices.

STV ballot papers
Although STV is complicated for those doing the counting, it should be simple for voters, who merely number the candidates in order of preference. However, research by Democratic Audit (Dunleavy et al. 1997) found that ballot papers were difficult to understand. The system was rejected by the Jenkins Commission as being too great a change from FPTP and outside its remit of maintaining the constituency link.

Mixed or 'hybrid' systems

Additional member system (AMS)

This system combines single-member constituencies with proportionality. The voter has one vote for a constituency MP under FPTP and an additional one for a party list. The balance between the two can vary; the more 'additional' or top-up members, the greater the proportionality. Various versions are employed in Germany, Italy and Mexico and it is now used in New Zealand as the 'mixed member proportional' system. In the UK it has been adopted for elections to the Scottish Parliament, the Welsh Assembly and the London Assembly.

AV-plus

A very British reform
Charter88 believes that the strength of AV-plus is that it has been specifically designed to fit in with Britain's political culture . . . [it would] foster a more productive and efficient style of politics.
Extract from Charter88 press release (Nov. 1998)

Voting takes place as in AMS, but constituency members are chosen by AV rather than FPTP. It was recommended for Westminster elections by the 1998 Jenkins Commission, which proposed 80–85 per cent of MPs elected for constituencies (reducing the number of constituencies to 530–560), with the remaining 15–20 per cent selected from regional lists.

Movement for change

First-past-the-post has many critics yet it has shown a dogged persistence. The problem for reformers has been that it serves the dominant party well. A 1970s reform campaign orchestrated by academics and politicians gained considerable momentum but came to nothing, partly through lack of strong public feeling (see Finer 1975). The two major parties had long resisted reform, but a third consecutive defeat in 1987 concentrated the collective Labour mind. Within the party a vigor-

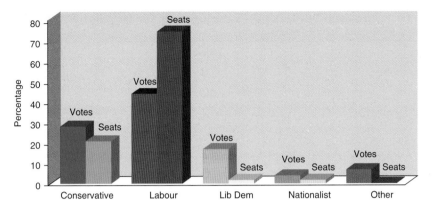

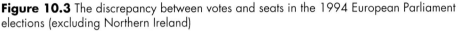

Figure 10.3 The discrepancy between votes and seats in the 1994 European Parliament elections (excluding Northern Ireland)

Source: Data from Butler and Butler (1994: 221).

ous Campaign for Electoral Reform emerged, with over sixty MPs and presided over by Professor (later Lord) Raymond Plant, who had chaired a Labour-sponsored working party on electoral reform. Reporting in April 1993, shortly after a fourth consecutive general election defeat, it recommended a regional list system for the European Parliament and a supplementary vote system for the House of Commons. Once in office Tony Blair established an independent commission to consider reform, chaired by Liberal Democrat Lord Jenkins of Hillhead, one of the 'Gang of Four' who had once dreamed of breaking the mould of British politics. The report, published in October 1998, recommended AV-plus.

Although broadly welcomed by those campaigning for reform, there was no action before the 2001 election and Labour's second huge majority gave it little incentive to move. However, events moved on. Britain's adherence to FPTP proved particularly anomalous in the case of the European Parliament, where the purpose is not to form a government (a key argument for FPTP). The UK was the only member state not to be using PR and the 1994 elections produced angry complaints from frustrated centre-right European leaders. While the continent generally swung to the right, the Socialist group (PES) boosted its representation from 198 to 221 (a 4 per cent rise in the vote giving them seventeen more seats, owing to the distortion from the British result, whereas PR would have produced only around six seats: figure 10.3). In response, Britain introduced PR for the 1999 European elections. The result was a trouncing for Labour and a demonstration that small parties can gain a foothold under PR (table 10.1), the Liberal Democrats being particular beneficiaries.

Devolution introduced further proportionality into the UK. Members of both the Scottish Parliament and Welsh Senedd are elected for four-year terms by

AV or not AV
At present, the UK uses the 'first past the post' system to elect MPs to the House of Commons. Should the 'alternative vote' system be used instead?

The question put to the British people in the 2011 referendum

Table 10.1 European Parliament election results for England, Scotland and Wales, 1994 and 1999 (seats won)

Party	1994	1999
Conservative	18	36
Labour	62	29
Liberal Democrat	2	10
UKIP	–	3
SNP	2	2
Plaid Cymru	0	2
Green	0	2

Note: Northern Ireland continued to elect its three MEPs by STV.

AMS. They began with 73 constituency members and 56 from party lists in Scotland, while in Wales the numbers were 40 and 20. The d'Hondt system is used, which gives smaller parties a chance in the list ballot through a divisor that effectively reduces the vote of parties with members already elected. Thus, as shown in figure 10.4, although Labour secured twice as many votes in the list ballot as its nearest rival in the Glasgow region in 1999, it gained no list seats at all because it already had ten constituency seats. The system even delivered a Socialist member to the Parliament. The Northern Ireland Assembly uses STV to elect its 108 members in order to ensure that, in an unusually fractious polity, all voices are heard.

In a changing climate the Liberal Democrats seized upon the chance of reform in the construction of the coalition agreement in 2010, the outcome being a national referendum held on 5 May 2011. The system put to the British electorate was AV, a modest change that would preserve the majoritarian principle. However, many Conservatives did not share the enthusiasm of their coalition partners and lent their support to the 'No' campaign. Unfortunately for the cross-party 'Yes' campaign, the proposal was closely associated with the Liberal Democrats and came at a time when their popularity was at a low point. The electorate also showed little appetite for reform, the result being a resounding 'No' from 68 per cent of those who bothered to vote. On a turnout of 42 per cent, it can only be assumed that the majority of the population had little interest in the change offered.

Effects of PR in Britain

Despite the many criticisms of FPTP, the result of the 2011 referendum meant that the topic of electoral reform for Westminster was kicked well into the long grass of politics. Nevertheless, the introduction of PR for Westminster elections remains of

1. Constituency results

Constituency	Party	Constituency	Party
Glasgow Anniesland	Labour	Glasgow Maryhill	Labour
Glasgow Ballieston	Labour	Glasgow Pollock	Labour
Glasgow Cathcart	Labour	Glasgow Rutherglen	Labour
Glasgow Govan	Labour	Glasgow Shetleston	Labour
Glasgow Kelvin	Labour	Glasgow Springburn	Labour

2. Working out the allocation of regional seats

$$\text{Regional figure} \quad = \quad \frac{\text{total number of regional votes for the party in the region}}{\text{number of seats won so far} + 1}$$

	CON	LAB	LIB DEM	SNP	SSP	Elected
Total votes	20,239	112,588	18,475	65,360	18,581	
Seats won so far	0	10	0	0	0	
1st divisor	0 + 1 = 1	10 + 1 = 11	0 + 1 = 1	0 + 1 = 1	0 + 1 = 1	
1st regional figure	20,239	10,235	18,475	**65,360**	18,581	SNP
2nd divisor	1	11	1	2	1	
2nd figure	20,239	10,235	18,475	**32,680**	18,581	SNP
3rd divisor	1	11	1	3	1	
3rd figure	20,239	10,235	18,475	**21,786**	18,581	SNP
4th divisor	1	11	1	4	1	
4th figure	**20,239**	10,235	18,475	16,340	18,581	CON
5th divisor	2	11	1	4	1	
5th figure	10,120	10,235	18,475	16,340	**18,581**	SSP
6th divisor	2	11	1	4	2	
6th figure	10,120	10,235	**18,475**	16,340	9,290	LIB DEM
7th divisor	2	11	2	4	2	
7th figure	10,120	10,235	9,328	**16,340**	9,290	SNP

3. Filling the allocated seats with candidates on the party lists

SNP	LIB DEM	CON	SSP
Nicola Sturgeon	**Robert Brown**	**William Aitken**	**Tommy Sheridan**
Dorothy-Grace Elder	Moira Craig	Tasmina Ahmed Sheikh	Frances Curran
Kenny Gibson	Mohammed Khan	Michael Fry	Rosie Kane
Sandra White	Mary Paris	Mary Leishman	Jim Friel
Maire Whitehead	Iain Brown	Assad Rasul	Ann Lynch
John Brady	Judith Fryer	Rory O'Brien	Robert Rae
Bill Wilson	Matthew Dunnigan	Colin Bain	David McKay
Kaukab Stewart	Clare Hamblen	Murray Roxburgh	Heather Ritchie
Bashir Ahmad	Callan Dick	Iain Stuart	Caroline Moore
Tom Chalmers	Laurence Clark		
Gavin Roberts	James King		
Jim Byrne			

Figure 10.4 PR in action: Glasgow Region, Scottish Parliament election, 1999 using the d'Hondt additional member system

Note: Candidates elected are in bold type.

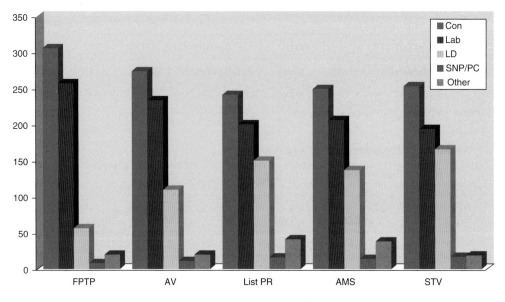

Figure 10.5 The 2010 general election under several different electoral systems

Note: List PR by region; STV with small multi-member constituencies (3–5).

Source: Data from Electoral Reform Society (2010: 63).

great interest to political scientists. It would in all probability revolutionize British politics, although different systems would yield differing results. Various sophisticated simulations have attempted to predict their impact for different general elections (see, for example, Sanders et al. 2011, for what the 2010 outcome might have been under AV). The Electoral Reform Society's simulated results for several different systems are shown in figure 10.5.

The possible effects of PR could be wide-ranging, including the following.

• Campaigning styles would probably become even more centralized. In New Zealand, the reform saw the parties fundamentally changing their strategies, moving from constituency targeting as they sought to maximize votes everywhere (Denemark 1996).

• Parliamentary representation of minority parties would increase at the expense of the old duopoly. It could also include the rise of disruptive parties such as the BNP.

• Entirely new parties might emerge onto the national scene, though even in the 2010 election, 135 registered parties fielded candidates (Electoral Commission 2010: 32).

• Depending on the system chosen, hung Parliaments and coalition government could become more common. Both Scotland and Wales have experienced extended periods under coalition executives.

- Centre parties, despite minority status, would gain authority and could expect to remain part of successive coalitions. After the first New Zealand election under the new system, the seventeen MPs of the Maori-based New Zealand First party found themselves in a pivotal position.
- In the longer term, smaller parties might lose their minority status, becoming more attractive once people felt that votes would no longer be 'wasted'.
- Alternatively, electors might decide that they preferred a two-party system and reduce their support for minority forces.
- The 'broad churches' of the major parties might fragment into their different factions – Old and New Labour, Eurosceptic and Europhile Conservatives.
- Turnouts might rise if voters felt their votes would not be 'wasted'.

A Crisis of Legitimacy?

At the beginning of the twenty-first century Britain found itself with a problematic electoral system. By 1997, the eighteen-year Conservative reign had been the longest since the Great Reform Act of 1832. The thirteen years of Labour rule that followed hardly served to redress the balance. If some people come (as did the Northern Ireland Catholics) to feel the system gives them no constitutional means of influence, a crisis of legitimacy looms. The new millennium opened with the record low turnout of 59 per cent in 2001. Despite improvements by 2010, critics continued to believe that it was 'Time for a change'. The decisive 'no' vote in the 2011 AV referendum, however, would suggest that a compelling case for abandoning FPTP is yet to be made, at least in the eyes of most voters.

What the Tories need, did they but know it, is electoral reform. They could then divide into the two parties – European Social Democrat and English Nationalist – that they are.
Andrew Rawnsley (journalist), in the *Observer* (6 July 1997)

Key points

- British democracy is based on the principle of representative government, where the few govern on behalf of the many.

- Representative government can have various, and contrasting, interpretations.

- The evolution of the British electoral system has been slow, with extensions to the franchise conceded grudgingly.

- Today a number of different electoral systems operate in the UK, but for Westminster the FPTP system remains.

- The FPTP principle is not proportional but can produce strong, single-party government.

- FPTP has favoured the continued dominance of two parties, which helps explain its persistence.

- The alternative to FPTP is PR, under which the number of seats awarded reflects the proportion of votes received by a party.

- The offer of AV in elections to the Westminster Parliament was comprehensively rejected in a referendum held in May 2011.

Review your understanding of the following terms and concepts

additional member system (AMS)

alternative vote (AV)

Chartism

citizens' assembly

citizens' jury

coalition

constituency (single-member/multi-member)

d'Hondt system

direct democracy

electoral quota (droop quota)

first-past-the-post (FPTP)

franchise

simple plurality (FPTP)

hybrid (or 'mixed') system

majoritarian system

mandate

manifesto

party list (national/regional; open/closed)

preferential voting

primary election

proportional representation

referendum

recall

representative government

single transferable vote (STV)

threshold

Questions for discussion and debate

Consider these propositions and be prepared to present the cases for and against. Try to produce debating propositions of your own.

1 The grudging extension of the franchise reveals establishment fear of democracy.

2 The electoral mandate in British politics means very little in practice.

3   For all its defects, the British electoral system ensures strong government.

4   The need to secure a broadly proportional outcome should outweigh all other considerations when choosing an electoral system.

5   The use of hybrid or 'mixed' electoral systems in some UK elections has done more harm than good.

6   PR is appropriate for the European Parliament but not for Westminster.

7   A system of PR would destroy the role of the constituency MP.

8   The introduction of primary elections into British politics would have dangerous consequences.

9   A system of recall of those elected to public office would enhance democracy.

10 The introduction of PR for elections to Westminster would revitalize British politics.

Further reading

Butler, D. (1995) *British General Elections Since 1945*.
Concise and accessible historical account of elections and electioneering.

Cracknell, R., McGuiness, F. and Rhodes, C. (2011) *General Election 2010*.
A House of Commons Library research paper providing accessible and clearly presented analysis of the 2010 general election.

Electoral Commission (2010) *Report on the Administration of the 2010 UK General Election*.
The official review of the work of the Commission in respect of the 2010 general election. Contains a wealth of material on electoral administration and party registration, as well as pointers for the future.

Electoral Reform Society (2010) *The UK General Election 2010 in Depth*.
A helpful overview of the 2010 UK general election which provides some interesting insights into how the election might have panned out under alternative electoral systems.

Farrell, D. (2011) *Electoral Systems: A Comparative Introduction*.
Outlines the mechanics and histories of various electoral systems operating around the world, capturing the flavour of what it is like to vote under each.

Fraser, A. (2013) *Perilous Question: the Drama of the Great Reform Bill 1832*.
Something of a political thriller as Tories and Whig reformers battle it out.

Journal of Elections, Public Opinion and Parties (2005–); formerly *British Elections and Parties Review* (1997–2004) and *British Elections and Parties Yearbook* (1991–6).
A more-or-less annual publication including authoritative essays on elections, electoral reform, referendums, etc., and a variety of useful data.

Kavanagh, D. and Cowley, P. (2010) *The British General Election of 2010*.
Latest in line of studies dating from 1945. Lively, accessible and conscious of the politics behind the numbers.

Johnston, R., Pattie, C. J., Dorling, D. and Rossiter, D. (2010) *From Votes to Seats: The Operation of the British Electoral System Since 1945*.
Examines how, under FPTP, geographical factors influence results.

Norris, P. (1996) *Electoral Change since 1945*.
Accessible overview looking at change and the causes of change.

For reading around the subject and some light relief

Anthony Trollope, *Phineas Finn*.
Parliamentary politics of the 1860s, including voting reform (secret ballot and eliminating rotten boroughs) as well as political skulduggery.

H. G. Wells, *Ann Veronica*.
Controversial when first published. Relationships between men and women against suffragette background.

P. G. Wodehouse, *Much Obliged, Jeeves*.
An old school chum of Bertie's is standing for the House of Commons, and Aunt Dahlia has offered the use of Brinkley Court as a general HQ for the campaign. Life then becomes complicated.

Virginia Woolf, *Night and Day*.
Novel dealing with suffragette issues.

On the net

http://www.electoral-reform.org.uk
Campaigning organizations, such as the Electoral Reform Society, provide plenty of material on the working of the electoral system, electoral reform and other electoral systems.

http://www.parliament.uk/about/how/
The 'How Parliament works' site includes a useful section on the various electoral systems used in Britain.

THE *VOX POPULI*: HOW PEOPLE VOTE

Contents

In this chapter we consider electoral behaviour, asking why and how people vote, and noting the impact and relative importance of race, gender, age and class. This leads us on to consider the behaviour of the politicians and their spin doctors in one of the most visible events in modern politics: the election campaign. We conclude by questioning the extent to which modern campaigning methods have genuinely changed the dynamics of voter choice.

The philosophical radicals argued that if everyone voted, governments would be forced to rule for the good of all. Yet universal franchise has not resulted in anything resembling popular rule. Traditional elites have maintained their ascendancy and capitalism has continued its dominance. This conundrum partly reflects the Burkean notion of representation. It may also be explained by the way people have used the vote, the study of which is known as **psephology**.

Pebbleology?
The ancient Greeks voted by placing pebbles in jars. The Greek word for pebble is psephos. *Hence we have 'psephology'.*

Why Do People Vote?

> The returns from voting are usually so low that even small costs [time, energy, etc.] may cause voters to abstain.
>
> A. Downs, *An Economic Theory of Democracy* (1957: 274)

Since any single vote, even in a marginal constituency, has a negligible impact, it can be argued that a rational being might be better occupied tending pigeons or reading Shakespeare than entering the polling booth. Game theory (Kanazawa 1998) would predict that electoral turnout should be zero! Some countries (such as Australia) attempt to combat the disinclination to vote by making it compulsory. Others view the right to **abstain**, to say 'a plague on both your houses', as a democratic freedom in itself. However, according to Johnston and Pattie (1997), 'voluntary' abstainers often belong to the more deprived sections of society, who see politics as largely irrelevant, while 'involuntary' abstainers will only overcome difficulties (e.g. illness) if the local situation promises a close contest.

The decision to cast a ballot may reflect various sentiments: class solidarity, a herd instinct, a sense of civic duty, or (particularly among women) a tribute to those who fought for the franchise. Voters questioned in a MORI poll for the Electoral Commission (2001) cited habit and civic duty as their main motives (36 and 20 per

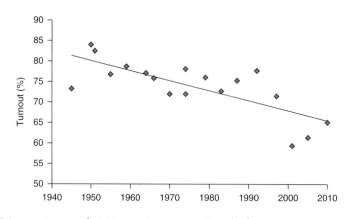

Figure 11.1 Increasing apathy? Turnout in post-war British elections

Bad officials are elected by good citizens who do not vote.

attributed to George Jean Nathan (1882–1958; American drama critic)

cent, respectively). Voting is an endorsement of the political system itself; mass abstention would constitute a legitimacy crisis.

However, the proportion of the population staying at home on election day has been rising steadily (figure 11.1). Indeed, at 59 per cent, turnout in 2001 was the lowest since the achievement of universal suffrage in 1928, despite postal voting being more readily available. Most commentators ascribed the unexpectedly steep fall in turnout to Labour's victory being seen as a foregone conclusion (Electoral Commission 2001: 16), but turnout did not improve significantly in 2005 (61.4 per cent) or 2010 (65.1 per cent). Compared with most of their European neighbours (table 11.1), the British appear to be decidedly unenthusiastic voters. Whether innovative voting methods will make a significant difference remains to be seen.

Table 11.1 National variations in turnout (%) in European Parliament elections, 2009

Country	Turnout	Country	Turnout	Country	Turnout
Luxembourg	91	Spain	44	Portugal	37
Belgium	86	Sweden	44	Hungary	36
Malta	79	Estonia	43	UK	35
Italy	66	Germany	43	Czech Republic	28
Denmark	60	Austria	42	Slovenia	28
Cyprus	59	Finland	40	Poland	27
Irish Republic	55	France	40	Romania	27
Latvia	53	Bulgaria	37	Lithuania	21
Greece	52	Netherlands	37	Slovakia	20

Note: Voting is compulsory in Belgium, Luxembourg, Cyprus and Malta

Source: Data from Mellows-Facer et al. (2009: 23)

What do people vote for?

Conflicting interpretations of what exactly one is supporting when placing an 'X' on the ballot paper reflect different views on the function of elections. Ostensibly voters are supporting a *candidate*, but even charismatic figures attract a limited personal vote. Most voters feel they actually vote for *parties*, a view reinforced by the theory of the mandate. For some, however, the general election is a presidential-type contest in which they are choosing a prime minister (see p. 304).

Party Identification and Voting

Studies have shown that most people are stable voters, always supporting the same party (Butler and Stokes 1969), while a more volatile minority are described as '**floating voters**'. Since the 1970s, however, an increase in net volatility has resulted in greater support for centrist and nationalist parties (figure 11.2). The explanations for **electoral volatility** and stability are key elements in the study of electoral behaviour and are considered below.

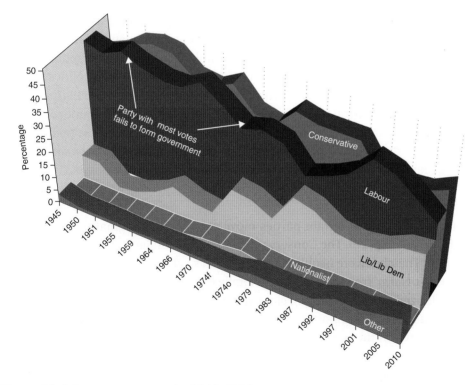

Figure 11.2 Post-war voting trends, 1945–2001

Source: Data from Kavanagh and Cowley (2010: table A1.1).

> **Volatility in the electorate**
> Gross volatility refers to the total amount of vote-switching, as revealed by large-scale national sample surveys, while net volatility represents the final effect.
> If 10 per cent of Labour voters switch to the Conservatives, while 10 per cent of Conservative supporters move in the opposite direction, the gross volatility would be 20 per cent but the net figure would be zero. Such hidden volatility is commonly referred to as 'churn'.

Stable party identification

There are various hypotheses as to why people repeatedly support the same party.

Loyalty

Loyalty is fundamental to human existence, producing the cohesion needed to withstand hostile environments. It was not only Dumas's legendary trio who recognized this; unity lies at the very heart of politics, facilitating the formation of associations – basic units of political action. Loyalty towards a political party inspires the **party identification voting model**. Around 80 per cent of voters have identified with a party in much the same way as they take sides in other great contests – the Cup Final, the Grand National or the Boat Race. This model does not postulate that voters act with self-interested calculation; they vote unthinkingly, habitually, responding only to vague mental images of the parties. In the 1950s and 1960s, when politics reached 'the end of ideology', with little partisan differentiation, there were high turnouts (over 80 per cent) with 90 per cent of voters sticking to their party. Butler (1995: 66) argued that 'most citizens vote as they always voted – and usually as their parents voted before them'. Although loyalty has been supplanted by other factors (see below), many voters still retain a tribal attachment to a party.

Ideology

Within the ideological terrain parties move as much by pragmatism as principle (see figure 2.1 on p. 26). The Conservatives under Macmillan were social democrats but under Thatcher were neoliberals, while Blair's Labour Party effectively dropped the word 'socialist' from its lexicon. Generally the middle classes are more ideologically polarized than the working class and all three main parties tend to be closer to their middle-class supporters (Crewe 1993: 104). Thatcher's revival of ideological distance between the parties may have accounted for some partisan dealignment (see p. 301) and there were sightings of Essex Man pursuing a rugged individualist lifestyle in the terrain of the south-east. However, despite Thatcher's crusade, voters' ideological positions changed very little and tended towards the left rather than the right (Crewe 1988).

Gender

Despite male establishment fears of radicalism, working-class women have tradition-ally shown a greater propensity than their husbands to vote Conservative. Various explanations have been offered for this. In the first place, they were less exposed to the forces heightening class consciousness associated with employment in large indus-trial undertakings – camaraderie, unionization and clubs, pubs and sport. An alterna-tive explanation was that greater longevity gave them more chance to lose the radical fervour of youth (see Hills 1981). Hence Norris (1993) argues that rather than a gender gap one should consider a gender–generation gap. Both explanations suggest no causal link between voting and gender as such. Indeed, there are so many differences between the social experiences of men and women that any suggestion that they vote differently for some biological reason must be highly suspect. Moreover, the distinc-tion between male and female voting behaviour has diminished. The 1979 general election was the first in which more men voted Conservative than Labour. Margaret Thatcher may have actually antagonized some women. Following her departure, the 1992 general election saw the gender gap re-open, but in both 1997 and 2001 exit polls showed virtually no difference between the sexes, and the 2010 general election saw the traditional pattern reversed: 38 per cent of men and 36 per cent of women voted Conservative; 31 per cent of women and 28 per cent of men voted Labour.

Age

The universal franchise was at first limited to those over twenty-one, in the belief that the young are more likely to question established values and favour radical policies. Surveys tend to confirm this view (figure 11.3), though the differentials give no cause for establishment alarm and do little to substantiate Shakespeare's claim.

Crabbed age and youth cannot live together: Youth is full of pleasure, age is full of care.
William Shakespeare, *The Passionate Pilgrim*, xii

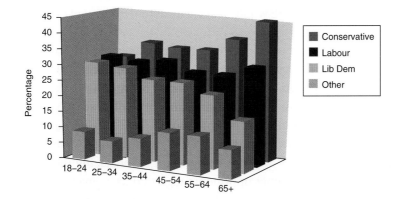

Figure 11.3 Voting by age, 2010

Note: Percentage in each age group voting for each party.

Source: Data from Cracknell et al. (2011: 36).

Although the youngest cohort was more Conservative than Labour in 1992, suggesting the effect of a generation socialized by unbroken Conservative rule, the greatest rise in the Labour vote in 1997 was amongst the young. However, disappointment may have set in, since an estimated six out of every ten 18–24-year-olds stayed away from the polling booths in 2001, making them the most apathetic or uninterested age group (Electoral Commission 2001: 15). By contrast, in 2010 TV viewers were alarmed by scenes of frustrated first-time voters (inspired by the leaders' debates and Nick Clegg's student-tuition-fee 'pledge') being denied their right to vote by the long queues preventing them from reaching the door of the polling station by 10 p.m.

The increasing potential of older people's votes is shown as Age Concern (now Age UK) mounts roadshows and produces glossy brochures to mobilize the 'grey vote'. At the time of the 2010 general election, researchers at Leicester's De Montfort University estimated that more than 40 per cent of votes nationally would be cast by the over-55s (Davidson 2009: 8), while Cracknell et al. (2011: 36) showed that turnout was highest among the over-65s (at 76 per cent).

Race

Black and minority ethnics (BME) have generally been less inclined to register to vote than whites. However, those of Asian descent are more likely to vote than their white neighbours, while Afro-Caribbeans are less so. At the 2005 general election only 83 per cent of eligible BME respondents claimed to be registered to vote, compared to a figure of 95 per cent amongst white respondents (Electoral Commission 2005: 16). Turnout amongst BME groups was also lower, with a 'claimed turnout' of just 59 per cent compared to 72 per cent amongst non-BME groups. With the actual turnout (61.4 per cent in 2005) generally falling some way short of 'claimed turnout', the 59 per cent figure for BME would suggest an actual turnout of nearer 50 per cent amongst these groups.

Amongst those members of the BME community who do cast a ballot, the strong preference has been for Labour. In 2005, some 58 per cent of BME voters supported Labour (Ipsos-Mori 2006: 4). There have been grounds for thinking that non-manually employed Asians, a growing category, will gradually defect (Studlar 1983), but such predictions may be premature. The parties have increasingly courted the ethnic minority vote, though without explicitly focusing on race relations or immigration issues. In 2001, however, in emphasizing the asylum-seeker issue, William Hague took what opponents regarded as a covertly racist position, re-igniting long-standing divisions within his party and exposing a deep structural fault-line (Saggar 2001: 759). In a similar vein, the Conservative's 2005 campaign, orchestrated by the Australian consultant Lynton Crosby, focused heavily on the issue of immigration.

What the papers say

Unlike broadcasters, newspapers can adopt a partisan stance during an election. It is debatable whether readers choose papers that reflect their views or are influenced by what they read, but the correlation between voting and newspaper choice is strong. The *Sun*, with its least politically interested but most volatile readership (Miller 1991: 192), has been much feared by politicians. Its 1992 post-election boast, 'IT'S THE SUN WOT WON IT', was not merely self-aggrandizement (Harrop and Scammell 1992); in 1997, 2001 and 2005 it switched to Labour, again backing the winning party. Switching again in 2010 it achieved the more modest success of a Conservative-dominated coalition.

We saw in chapter 9 how the press has tended to favour the political right, with tabloid support for the Conservatives reaching fever pitch in the 1980s. However, in a surprising turnabout, which could be dated to Black Wednesday (September 1992), the British press became more agents of dealignment than stability as they lined up behind New Labour. The pattern remained much the same in 2001 and 2005. On the morning of 7 June 2001 the *Sun* greeted its readers with the prediction that Blair was poised to win an historic second term, 'and he will do so with *The Sun's* support'. In fact this view was shared by most other papers, with only the *Daily Mail* and *Daily Telegraph* dissenting. Of course it is a moot point as to whether the press had moved to New Labour or New Labour had moved towards the position preferred by the media barons. Blair's courtship of Rupert Murdoch was one of the most compelling symbols of New Labourism. If the party were to disappoint, its new friendships could soon sour – as they ultimately did. By Christmas 2010, it was David Cameron who was partying in the home of Rebekah Brooks, then chief executive of News International, with James Murdoch, son of Rupert.

Social class

The most durable explanation for party identification has been class. In four successive general elections in the 1960s and 1970s some 80 per cent of the middle class consistently voted Conservative, while about 70 per cent of the working class supported Labour (Gallup 1976). Yet **cross-class voting** – the presence of working-class Conservatives and middle-class Labour voters (so-called deviant voters) – which became more evident from the 1980s, shows that class identification has never provided a complete explanation.

The phenomenon of the working-class Conservative is crucial to the pattern of hegemony in British society; it has enabled an upper-middle-class elite to maintain its supremacy. Fears of the mass working-class vote haunted the nineteenth-century Establishment as the franchise was extended, they need not have lost any sleep. Around one-third of working-class voters were consistently to support a party

Class is the basis of British politics: all else is embellishment and detail.
Peter G. J. Pulzer, *Political Representation and Elections in Britain* (1967: 98)

with its origins in the aristocracy and largely dedicated to preserving traditional privileges and inequalities. This apparent puzzle has excited various hypotheses.

- *Political deference.* A deferential political culture (see p. 196) sees the working class voting for their 'betters', whom they believe to be 'born to rule'. Norton and Aughey (1981: 175) perceive working-class Conservatives as individuals who 'prefer, despite not having . . . privileges, what is known and predictable in the system and who believe that this is how things should be'.

- *Social aspiration.* For many members of the working class the desire for self-betterment is seen in ruggedly individualist terms rather than collectivism. D. H. Lawrence (1950: 119) speaks of his own working-class community in which 'it was a mother's business to see that her sons "got on"'. The individualism in Conservatism can appeal to this sense of aspiration and to 'be Conservative' in a working-class community can, in a snobbish way, represent social improvement in itself.

- *Neighbourhood.* Working-class voters in predominantly middle-class areas show a greater propensity than others to be Conservative. It may be, of course, that people choose to live among those holding similar values to their own.

- *False consciousness.* Marxists, notably Gramsci (1971), have argued that the working class are led to the mistaken belief that their lowly role in life is in their self-interest, perhaps divinely ordained. This **false consciousness** is fostered through ruling-class hegemony which has forestalled revolution.

However, underlying this debate should be a realization that the British working class has not been driven by strongly left-wing attitudes or egalitarian instincts. There is considerable genuine support for many right-wing positions, ranging from attitudes to race and immigration and the monarchy to council house sales, law and order, trade union reform and social security 'scroungers'. The popularity of Enoch Powell between the 1960s and 1980s testifies to many of these sentiments, while the TV character Alf Garnett, a grotesque caricature of the working-class Conservative, evoked ready recognition to become a loved national symbol. New Labour showed a keen awareness of these attitudes across a wide policy range.

In contrast, a not insignificant proportion of the middle class (social classes AB) have supported Labour – traditionally around 20 per cent but rising to 30 per cent in 2001 (28 per cent in 2005 and 26 per cent in 2010). Possible explanations for this include the following.

- *Intellectual socialism.* The intelligentsia are, by definition, likely to take a more reasoned rather than an entirely self-interested view of politics. Much Labour support and leadership has been drawn from this group, with the elitist Fabian movement a significant force from the outset. The Conservatives have fared markedly worse in those Conservative city constituencies (including Oxford and Cambridge) with high concentrations of professional middle classes, university dons and students.

- *Residual class loyalty.* Not all upwardly mobiles pull up the ladder; some remain faithful to the values of their parents.
- *Public-sector employment.* Public-sector employees are predominantly middle class and, by the 1970s, comprised around 30 per cent of the workforce. They have a career interest in welfare-orientated policies and a natural antipathy to the right-wing preference for a small state. (An exception is the police force.)
- *Mistrust of the New Right.* Some 'one-nation' Conservatives were uncomfortable with the neoliberal policies of the post-1979 Conservatives. By branding them 'wets', Thatcher showed little inclination to keep their support, though her successors, particularly David Cameron, tried to win them back.

Volatile voting patterns

Non-stable voters are particularly important because, although they may constitute only a small proportion of the electorate, they precipitate the **electoral swings** that can sweep governments from office. A movement of only 3.6 per cent in 1964, for example, served to erase a seemingly impregnable Conservative majority. Increased volatility became a striking feature of the 1980s and 1990s, so that it could be said that 'the majority of British voters no longer readily identify with a political party' (Johnston and Pattie 1996: 299). Similarly, the 1997 and 2001 Labour landslides suggested that many lifelong Conservative voters had changed allegiance. Today, explanations of voting behaviour are more complex than in the days of stability.

Partisan dealignment

From 1945 the overall level of class-based voting for both major parties began to fall until over half the electorate was rejecting the class imperative (Crewe 1986: 620). **Partisan dealignment** (figure 11.4) was confirmed using a sophisticated multi-dimensional definition of class as well as one based simply on occupation (Rose and McAllister 1986). The collapse was particularly injurious to Labour. Between 1945 and 1970 its share of the vote had stood, like that of the Conservatives, at around 45 per cent; by the 1980s it had plummeted to around 30 per cent. Its dramatic recovery in 1997 clearly demonstrated the features of dealignment (Denver 1998: 210), a swing of 10.3 per cent (almost double that of the previous record swing in 1979) indicating high volatility. Of those who had voted in 1992, almost a quarter had changed allegiance. Class-based voting reached an historic low, with non-manual workers dividing evenly between Labour and Conservative.

The third force

The bipartisan model was threatened as a rejuvenated Liberal Party offered electors a third choice. Its share of the vote rose dramatically from 7 to 19 per cent between

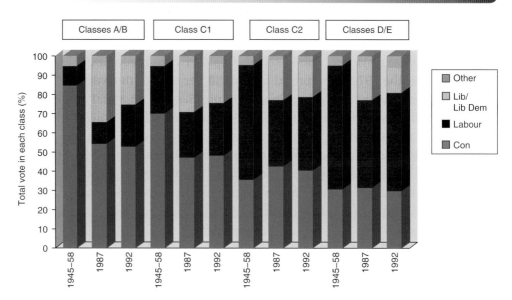

Figure 11.4 Partisan dealignment: class voting from 1945–58 to 1992

Source: Data from Abrahams (1958), ITN/Harris poll in the *Independent* (13 June 1987) and Curtice (1997: table 3).

1970 and 1974 (see figure 11.2). The SDP further muddied the partisan water when it entered the fray in March 1981. Support for the Liberal–SDP Alliance remained buoyant (25 per cent in 1983 and 23 per cent in 1987), and as the Liberal Democrats they claimed 18 per cent of the vote in 1992, rising to 23 per cent by 2010.

Tactical voting

The entry of a third horse in the electoral race opened the door to **tactical voting**: supporting a party, or candidate, that is not the first choice to *prevent* the least-liked being elected. There was some evidence of this during the 1980s; opposition parties that had finished in second place in the previous election generally improved more than those finishing lower (Curtice and Steed 1987, 1992). Newspapers began to launch campaigns to encourage tactical voting, advising voters how to get this or that candidate out, and in 1997 a 'Get Rid Of the Tories' (GROT) campaign was orchestrated by Democratic Left. With forty-six seats, the Liberal Democrats were the principal beneficiaries. By 2001 the electorate were showing even greater sophistication. Some, including pop singer Billy Bragg, used the internet to organize 'pairing' arrangements between constituencies whereby voters would effectively 'trade' their votes. An eve-of-election *Observer*/ICM poll (*Observer*, 3 June 2001) revealed hundreds of thousands prepared to vote tactically to keep out Conservatives where the Liberal Democrats were in second place. In the 2010 contest, with prospects of a hung parliament in mind, tactical voting became a prominent issue. The *Daily Mirror* produced a tactical voting guide: 'How you can save Britain from a Tory nightmare', listing seventy-one key marginal seats. Labour politicians themselves came under fire for covert messages to vote 'to keep the Tories out'.

A shrinking working class

Although working-class loyalty to Labour may have remained solid, movement away from the party during the 1980s may also be explained by the class itself shrinking (Heath et al. 1987). Since the early 1970s the percentage of manual workers in Britain has declined from around 47 to around 30, while the proportion of people belonging to the salaried managerial class has risen from around 18 per cent to well over 30 per cent. Indeed, figures published by the Office for National Statistics in 2011 showed that 45 per cent of workers were categorized in the top three employment groups (managers and senior managers, professional occupations, and associate professionals and technical), with just 18 per cent working in the bottom two groups (process plant and machine operatives, and elementary occupations).

A new working class

The working-class tendency to acquire middle-class values and lifestyles (*embourgeoisement*) was accelerated by the Conservative ethos of aggressive individualism. Ivor Crewe identified a 'new working class' – owner-occupiers, especially in southern England, in private-sector employment and non-unionized – which could be contrasted with the 'old' or 'traditional working class', swelling the ranks of the working-class Conservatives (*Guardian*, 15 June 1987). Among the new working class Labour's share of the vote fell from 45 per cent in 1979 to around 34 per cent in 1987. By 1997, however, New Labour, with some support from the *Sun*, had managed to shape its appeal to these key voters.

Geographical cleavage

From the 1970s, with a major new shift in the sands of electoral geography, psephologists could no longer speak of a uniform national swing sweeping the whole country. A deep fissure was opening between the predominantly Labour-voting north and the more Conservative south (with a lesser Labour–Conservative divide between the west and the east). This **north–south divide** had been present in the 1930s but had largely been erased in the 1945 Labour landslide (Johnston et al. 1988: 9). Intimations of the renewed division came as nationalist movements in Scotland and Wales gained momentum. Regional differentiation continued during the 1980s, reinforced in 1992 by the geography of recession (Pattie et al. 1993). Although the electoral map of May 1997 left no trace of blue in Scotland, Wales or large areas of the north and south-west, New Labour had begun to shade the south-east red, making the divide less marked. The 2010 general election saw the divide beginning to reappear, with the Conservatives winning 126 seats to Labour's 6 in the Eastern and South East regions and Labour securing 67 seats to the Conservatives' 9 in Scotland and Wales.

Sectoral cleavage

The growing role of the state since 1945 has created a fundamental dichotomy or **sectoral cleavage** between those whose lives are predominantly locked into the public sector, who tend to support Labour, and those operating largely within the private sector, who are more likely to vote Conservative (Dunleavy and Husbands 1985). Conservatives generally oppose big government and their policies (council house sales, privatization, welfare cuts) do little to gain support from either public-sector providers or clients. The cuts implemented by the coalition government from 2010 starkly exposed this divide.

Personality voting

A process of 'presidentialization', encouraged by the media, has tended to reduce elections to contests between party leaders. In 1983 Michael Foot cut a poor figure and in 1987 and 1992 there was some evidence of a Kinnock factor blighting Labour. By contrast, for much of her reign Margaret Thatcher excited personal admiration, and within three months of taking over as Labour leader John Smith's popularity rating had overtaken Major's. From July 1994 Blair consistently dominated, with an average rating of 39 per cent to Major's 19 and Ashdown's 14. His personal ascendancy continued when Hague took the Conservative helm. A poll on the eve of the 2001 general election revealed that, in response to the question 'Who do you think would make the better prime minister?', an overwhelming 67 per cent favoured Blair (*Observer*, 3 June 2001). After the election, a BBC/ICM recall poll found 30 per cent of former Conservative voters giving Hague as their reason for deserting the party. Some critics evoked a phrase then current in a popular TV quiz programme: 'William Hague, you are the weakest link'. Robin Cook, a highly talented Labour politician, ruled himself out of any leadership contest on the grounds of appearance, having been likened to a 'garden gnome'. Gordon Brown, described as a 'disgruntled dour Scot' in a book by former Labour First Minister of Scotland Henry McLeish, was widely seen as an electoral liability for Labour in 2010. The so-called 'Bigotgate' episode was symptomatic of a lack of grace. Brown's performance in the first-ever televised election debates between the main party leaders, where the Lib Dem leader Nick Clegg excelled and David Cameron acquitted himself adequately, only served to add credence to the view that he was ill-equipped to compete in a modern election campaign.

Shoparound voting

The **consumer voting model** sees voters as shoppers in a political market place (Downs 1957; Himmelweit et al. 1985: 70; Rose and McAllister 1986), choosing policies as they choose a powder that 'washes whiter' or a lager to reach inaccessible parts. Saunders (1995: 136), for example, found that Labour's promise to renationalize the water and electricity industries frightened off 'a substantial proportion' of its potential supporters who had bought shares. Generally Labour has fared better in areas such as health, employment and education, the Conservatives traditionally inspiring more confidence in law and order, defence, taxation and the economy. Furthermore, the Conservatives' failure to dent Labour's majority in 2001 was partly attributed to its fixation on asylum-seekers and the euro (Hague's 'seven days to save the pound') to the exclusion of issues that mattered to people, such as health and education. In 2010 the Liberal Democrat pledge on student fees was very enticing but shoppers were to find that the final product was not what it said on the tin.

Slings and arrows

Outrageous fortune between elections can send short-term shock waves through the electorate. Examples include the Profumo affair, the winter of discontent and the Falklands War (curiously Suez did not precipitate a Conservative fall). England's world cup victory was said to have helped Labour in 1966. Conversely, the eruption of scandals, such as cash-for-questions under Major and cash-for-honours under Blair, also coloured voters' perceptions, while the MPs' expenses scandal did little to encourage them to make the effort to vote. The global banking crisis also cast a fatally dark shadow over Brown's premiership.

The economy, stupid!

There is a long-standing belief that voters support the ruling party if the economy is doing well and shift to the opposition if it is doing badly. In 1979 the Conservatives came to power after Labour's economic 'winter of discontent' and enjoyed continuing success until 'Black Wednesday' in September 1992 finally sank their reputation for economic competence. In fact, given the Conservative record on the economy, the electorate's faith was, to some, one of the puzzles of British politics (Newton 1993), and by 1997 it had been eroded (Denver 1998: 212). The importance of the economy appeared to have been borne out in 2001, when falling unemployment, income tax pegged and Gordon Brown's burgeoning reputation for economic prudence all helped Labour to secure a second term, followed by an historic third term in 2005. However, by 2010, in the midst of the world economic crisis, the Conservatives were able to discredit Labour's economic record.

It's the economy, stupid.

Aide memoire in the Clinton office during the 1992 US presidential election

Feeling good

The objective state of the economy, although a key reading on the political barometer, may not accord with voters' perceptions. The notion of the 'feelgood factor' entered journalistic parlance as a measure of the latter. Despite improvements in certain economic indicators, it remained elusive in 1997, confirming Will Hutton's thesis of the 30/30/40 society (1996: 105–10); under rampant capitalism even those in employment may feel insecure. Thus John Major had the curious distinction of winning in a recession (1992) and losing in an upturn (1997).

* * *

Finally, it must be remembered that, despite the considerable body of academic and commercial research since the 1950s, the reasons why people vote as they do remain obscure. Human motives and emotions are not easily unlocked by the researcher with the clipboard. People may be self-interested consumers of policies but are not entirely so; 'some form of conditional altruism may be at work' (Gavin 1996: 322). Moreover, views can be manipulated through processes intended to affect thoughts and attitudes: mind politics. At election times, this layer of politics comes to the fore in the campaigns the parties wage.

Influencing Voters: Politicians and the Election Campaign

Packaging the parties

Despite its limitations, the consumer voting model is important in a way its proponents may not intend; while it may not entirely account for voters' behaviour, it does explain that of the politicians, pundits, parties and the parasitic psephological media, all of whom operate as if it were true. Politicians like to think that the country is enraptured by their comings and goings and make punishing efforts to inform, analyse and persuade in the **election campaign**, one of the most compelling symbols of modern politics. Prior to the passage of the Fixed Term Parliaments Act, the real campaign was preceded by a 'phoney war' during which the prime minister teased the pundits and opposition over the election date. In both 1992 and 1997 campaigning effectively began well before the starting pistol was formally fired. Upon taking over the premiership from Tony Blair in 2007, Gordon Brown tantalized the nation for a few indecisive weeks before settling on a tenuous period of office.

Traditionally campaigns involved an unveiling of manifestos, followed by hustings and public meetings, door-to-door canvassing, flattering constituents and

"Oh no — canvassers — pretend we're not in..."

kissing sticky babies, with candidates fighting individual constituency battles. Local campaigning and the role of party activists on the nation's doorsteps can still be crucial (Seyd and Whiteley 1992: ch. 8; Whiteley et al. 1994: 213–18). The Liberal Democrats' successes between 1997 and 2010 were achieved by targeting key seats, often moving reinforcements in from neighbouring constituencies. In 2001, Labour sent its biggest guns to 'battleground' target seats so that, while there was a national swing of nearly 2 per cent to the Conservatives, there was no swing from Labour in its key marginals. Conservative advances were either in seats they already held, or in those where Labour had no chance.

However, more than ever campaigns are conducted by the central party machines, with a sophistication undreamed of a few decades ago. It is a battle of media spin doctors and large-scale advertising, with enormous sums being spent. From 1979 the Conservatives, backed by mighty capitalist enterprises, called the tune. However, learning much from Clinton in the USA, Labour had raised the art to new levels by 1997, operating from its high-tech media centre at Millbank. Indeed, its offensive can be said to have begun the moment Blair took over as leader, with technology, discipline, focus groups, grooming of leaders and news management honed to a fine degree (Kavanagh 1997). The new style of campaigning led to increasing concern over the level of national campaign expenditure by the two main parties and attempts to control this came in the 2000 Political Parties, Elections and Referendums Act (see p. 343).

Today politicians have become products to be packaged and sold. Their actions (speeches, interviews and photo opportunities) are planned in detail by public relations gurus. What they say, how they dress, their hairstyles, where they go, whom they meet, which politicians or party they attack, which section of the electorate they target, by whom they will be interviewed on television – all is decided for them after careful analysis. Even the manifestos are written by media men. In 2010 the Conservative manifesto, introduced by David Cameron in Battersea power station, took the form of a glossy hardback – *Invitation to Join the Government of Britain*. The spin doctors have emerged from the shadows, becoming as familiar to *aficionados* as the politicians themselves. Criticized as 'control freaks', they can stifle any real debate, emphasizing personalities rather than policies (see Scammell 1995).

Campaigns are physically and psychologically gruelling. Politicians rise early, travel daily to and from London, attend frequent strategy meetings, make and remake speeches, give daily press conferences, sweat before television cameras and snatch only a few hours' sleep in each 24-hour cycle. Increasingly they must cope with an effervescent social media. All takes place under the scrutinizing eyes of the journalists, eager for a gaffe or an encounter with a banana skin. Yet politicians need the media and provide 'battle buses' to ferry journalists around with them. This can be a two-edged sword. Eager photographers were on hand in May 2001 to record both the Welsh egg hurled at Labour's John Prescott and the quick counter-punch delivered to the assailant, and following his 'Bigotgate' gaffe in 2010, a hapless Gordon Brown was obliged to make a televised return to the home of the offended Mrs Duffy to seek forgiveness.

Campaigning has taken an increasingly aggressive and negative direction; rather than promoting their own policies, parties attack their opponents. In 1997, Conservative posters featured Blair with 'demon eyes', while in 2001 Labour portrayed a grotesque vision of Hague with Thatcher's coiffure. Broadcasters aid and abet by reporting the campaigns themselves rather than fundamental issues. They also concentrate on party leaders. In the 2010 campaign, Brown accounted for 74 per cent of the Labour Party citations in those news programmes analysed, with Cameron taking 71 per cent of Conservative citations and Clegg 72 per cent for the Lib Dems (Kavanagh and Cowley 2010: 273).

Television has become ever more dominant. Although political commercials are not allowed in Britain, slick party election broadcasts use skills developed in advertising. A highly acclaimed production presenting Neil Kinnock, written by Colin Welland and directed by Hugh Hudson (director of *Chariots of Fire*), was said to have lifted the Labour leader's rating by 16 percentage points in 1987 (Harrison

1987: 154). However, such campaigns create tensions at party headquarters as the advertising consultants and party officials vie for control (Hollingsworth 1997). When let down by the traditionally Conservative press in 1997, John Major turned to television for salvation, accepting a challenge to a US-style head-to-head debate with Tony Blair (who promptly refused to pick up the gauntlet). In office, Blair again refused such encounters in 2001 and 2005, but in 2010 Brown rose to the challenge, agreeing to share the ring with both David Cameron and Nick Clegg. The three set-piece debates were heavily controlled and carefully orchestrated, but they were widely seen as having had a significant impact on public perceptions.

Throughout all, the public are reduced to passivity. People cannot confront and heckle as they could at the traditional hustings; a foot projected through the screen will do nothing to register opposition to the relentless talking head, and questioning can only take place vicariously through the medium of the professional interviewer. 'Phone-ins', permitting the public to address politicians directly while others listen, do little to capture the robust spirit of true debate. Questions can be carefully monitored beforehand and an awkward or abusive caller reduced to mute impotence at the press of a button. The spin doctors seek to manipulate and bully the media, so that what appears on the screen or across the airwaves is 'politics on the politicians' terms', with little real information dispensed by the 18-second 'soundbite' (Harrison 1992: 170).

In the 2001 campaign interest waned. Sales of several newspapers fell during the month: the *Express* group by 2.8 per cent, the *Sun* by 1.3, the *Mirror* by 1.1 and *The Times* by 0.7. People also voted with their remote controls; while the soap operas maintained their viewing figures, audiences for BBC's 6 p.m. news and ITN's *News at Ten* both fell during the campaign (Deacon et al. 2001: 666–7). However, a new factor also came into play: the internet (see Coleman 2001). While the parties tried e-marketing their policies and the established media provided more detail through their websites, members of the public were also able to take a less passive role by exchanging information and arranging vote-swapping and pairing. Such trends continued in 2005 and 2010.

Monitoring the campaign

The analogy with selling is strengthened by the ever-increasing use of market survey organizations commissioned by the media and the parties to conduct **opinion polls** on voting intentions and related matters (figure 11.5). There were fifty-seven published nationwide polls in 1992, but the polling errors identified in that year resulted in some cooling off; with forty-four in 1997 and just thirty-one in 2001. With confidence restored, the number of polls topped forty at the 2005 general election and reached a new high in 2010, with eleven different polling

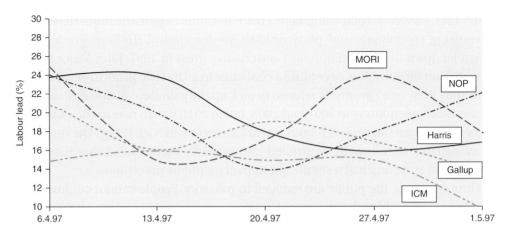

Figure 11.5 An exact science? Labour's lead over the Conservatives according to the last published poll during each week of the 1997 election campaign

Source: Data from Butler and Kavanagh (1997: table 7.2).

companies involved in the campaign (Kavanagh and Cowley 2010: 246) and the nine largest companies alone accounting for ninety-two separate polls (Cracknell et al. 2011: 68).

There are grave dangers in such saturation and some countries ban polling during election campaigns. Sometimes the polls themselves displace real news. Believing with Oscar Wilde's Lady Bracknell that statistics 'are laid down for our guidance', the 'bandwagon effect' may lead people to be swept along like sheep to be on the winning side. Alternatively, supporters may stay away if they see their party is well ahead, while lukewarm voters may be galvanized to assist one falling behind, in a kind of boomerang effect.

Moreover, pollsters may get their predictions wrong. They emerged with much egg on their clipboards as the Conservatives secured their 1992 victory against all expectations (Butler and Kavanagh 1992: 146). Interviewees may have been expressing their disapproval of government policies while still intending to support it in the secrecy of the ballot box. In addition, a late swing to the Conservatives, differential abstention rates, a higher propensity to vote among Conservative supporters and sample bias may all have contributed to the errors. The pollsters revised their methods and 1997 was seen as a critical test (figure 11.5). When Labour romped home, they claimed to have redeemed themselves. Yet with such a landslide how could they have failed? Ivor Crewe (1997) pointed out the need for some modesty. Had the result been narrower (as they usually are), and allowing for the margin of error, some polls would almost certainly have been wrong. However, despite such reservations, it is true that polls taken in the 2001, 2005 and 2010 campaigns were largely accurate in their predictions.

'Sound and fury, signifying nothing'?

Whether the new campaigning trends are desirable or effective is debatable. Familiarity with modern advertising tactics may induce voter scepticism. Short, easy-to-remember messages exorcize all subtlety from discussion and the sheer quantity of coverage may induce torpor and apathy; in 1997 and 2001, increased campaigning coincided with falling turnouts. Finally, the great expense and energy may well be wasted. Although the Conservatives' 1987 campaign was often in disarray they found themselves drinking the champagne with a handsome parliamentary majority and, in 1992, John Major stepped back from the spin doctors' wizardry to take a soap-box into the shopping precincts and gained the last laugh. Although Labour spent over £7 million on press and poster advertising in 1997, many commentators regard this election as one the Conservatives lost by their own disarray. Indeed, in the view of some psephologists, elections are won and lost before the campaigns ever begin (Clifford and Heath 1994: 21). The 2001 result certainly bore this out, with the Labour lead virtually unchanging throughout both its term of office and the campaign itself. The Electoral Commission (2001: 17) concluded that the campaign 'did little to persuade people that their vote mattered'. The 2010 election saw new Conservative leader David Cameron inspiring his party with an assertive and confident style, pitted against a distinctly lacklustre performance by Gordon Brown. In the TV debates Nick Clegg appeared to excite the nation with vows to break free from traditional politics. Yet in the event his party lost five seats and no party gained a parliamentary majority and, to the surprise of many, the Labour vote largely withstood the onslaught.

'I agree with Nick': one of the televised debates prior to the 2010 general election

Participation Beyond the Ballot Box

Declining levels of turnout at UK elections have inevitably given rise to talk of a nascent participation crisis. It would be a mistake, however, to measure political participation simply in terms of the proportion of eligible voters passing through the polling booth or marking a cross on a ballot paper in the comfort of their own kitchens. Whilst participation in formal politics, most notably in voting and individual membership of mainstream political parties (see Table 12.1), has declined in Britain since the 1950s, other forms of political participation have experienced an upsurge.

As Noreena Hertz noted in the *Observer* (10 June 2001): 'It's not about apathy . . . while voting is waning, alternative forms of political expression . . . are all on the rise'. Burgeoning pressure group activity and the rise of less formally structured social movements, spontaneous demonstrations and direct action can be seen to offset the decline in electoral turnout. Indeed, these more 'gladiatorial' forms of participation might even be said to be qualitatively more worthy than 'spectator' activities such as simply voting, or signing a direct debit mandate in favour of one's preferred party. The rise of a 24-hour news media and the growth of internet-based communication through social networking sites and the blogosphere have also provided novel opportunities for political engagement, just as other modes of participation have fallen out of favour. The willingness of the government to engage with e-democracy, and more direct forms of involvement such as citizens assemblies and citizens juries (see p. 266), might also be seen as evidence of the evolution of a new participatory democracy in Britain, rather than presaging a looming crisis. Even the innovation of televised debates between the leaders of the three main parties at the time of the 2010 general election can be said to have stimulated political engagement and discourse. The three set-piece debates attracted massive audiences, the first pulling in an average of 12.4 million viewers (Kavanagh and Cowley 2010: 266) – just shy of the 12.6 million votes Labour polled back in 2005.

The falling turnouts that so concern politicians may signal a lack of interest in the politicians themselves, or in the conventional politics that they practise, but this is by no means an indication of an absence of concern over the nature of society and the quality of people's lives. Hence the study of politics does not end with the statistical charts of the psephologists. Political activity continues between elections, and is often more dramatic and engrossing as parties in government appear to forget their manifesto promises, opposition parties criticize and make new promises, and people voice their opinions and demands. We turn to these themes in future chapters.

Key points

- A fully extended franchise is seen as the hallmark of a modern democracy.

- However, many people exercise a right not to vote.

- Abstaining at election time is often described as lack of interest and is seen as a crisis for democracy.

- It is possible to regard abstention as a rational act, given the minimal effect of any single vote.

- Of those that regularly vote, most are stable supporters of a particular party.

- However, the latter decades of the twentieth century saw a process of partisan dealignment as other short-term factors began to exert influence.

- Politicians and parties regard elections as extremely important, going to great lengths to win support, particularly during the election campaign.

- The modern national election campaign is far removed from the constituency-based face-to-face hustings of old.

- Unlike broadcasters, newspapers can adopt a partisan stance during an election and have a major presence in campaigns.

- The actual impact of the electoral campaigns remains in some doubt as, for many voters, other factors have already made up their minds.

Review your understanding of the following terms and concepts

abstention
churn
class alignment and
   dealignment
consumer voting model
cross-class voting
deviant voter
electoral stability and
   volatility

electoral swing
embourgeoisement
floating voter
manifesto
opinion poll
partisan alignment and
   dealignment
party identification
political participation

psephology
referendum
sectoral cleavage
spin doctor
swing
tactical voting
turnout

Questions for discussion and debate

Consider these propositions and be prepared to present the cases for and against. Try to produce debating propositions of your own.

1 There are many reasons why some working-class voters support the Conservative Party.
2 Opinion polls do as much to shape public opinion as to quantify it.
3 Ethnicity, age and gender should play an increasing part in explaining voting behaviour in Britain today.
4 Social class remains the main determinant of voting behaviour.
5 Voting is a duty of citizenship.
6 Rational people do not vote.
7 The 24-hour mass media and the rise of the internet have transformed British election campaigns.
8 Voting behaviour in Britain is habitual rather than rational.
9 Falling turnouts do not mean political apathy.
10 It does not matter what the papers say.

Further reading

Butler, D. (1995) *British General Elections Since 1945*.
Concise and accessible account of elections and electioneering in the second half of the twentieth century.

Butler, D. and Kavanagh, D. (2002) *The British General Election of 2001*.
Kavanagh, D. and Butler, D. (2005) *The British General Election of 2005*.
Kavanagh, D. and Cowley, P. (2010) *The British General Election of 2010*.
The last three titles in a long line of Nuffield election studies dating from 1945. Lively, accessible and conscious of the politics behind the numbers.

Denver, D., Carman, C. and Johns, R. (2012) *Elections and Voters in Britain*.
A lively and detailed introduction to the vagaries of voting behaviour in the UK, with analysis of the 2010 general election.

Fisher, J. and Wlezien, C. (eds) (2011) *The UK General Election of 2010: Explaining the Outcome.*
Data-rich examination of the election, looking for enhanced understanding of the outcome.

Himmelweit, H., Humphreys, P. and Jaeger, M. (1985) *How Voters Decide.*
Explains the consumer voting model and tries to show that attitudinal variables are more relevant than class in explaining voting.

Kavanagh, D. (1995) *Election Campaigning: The New Marketing of Politics.*
Thorough analysis of post-war campaigning strategies, tracing the link with media developments and a process of Americanization.

Mugham, A. (2002) *Media and the Presidentialisation of Parliamentary Elections.*
Analysis of press and TV reporting of election campaigns, noting the increasing importance of party leaders.

Norris, P. (ed.) (2001) *Britain Votes 2001.*
Norris, P. and Wlezien, C. (2005) *Britain Votes 2005.*
Geddes, A. and Tonge, J. (2010) *Britain Votes 2010.*
Informative accounts by various academics. Examine issues such as falling turnout.

For reading around the subject and some light relief

Melvyn Bragg, *Autumn Manoeuvres.*
Cumbrians work out their personal and public salvation with passion and deceit during 1970s election campaign.

Douglas Hurd, *Truth Game.*
A stylish novel by a once-leading politician.

H. G. Nicholas (ed.), *To the Hustings.*
Entertaining election stories.

Simon Walters, *Second Term.*
A Labour prime minister longs for a second term in office. He is helped by a flame-haired beauty, spin doctor Charlie Redpath. As the general election approaches, the tension mounts.

On the net

The websites of the leading newspapers and the BBC usually contain detailed reports of electoral results, often with details of each constituency.

http://www.electoralcommission.org.uk/
Beyond the operation of the system, the Electoral Commission site is particularly informative, including reports on a range of related matters such as election expenditure and cases of electoral fraud.

CHAPTER 12

THE POLITICAL PARTIES: MASSES, LEADERS AND POWERS BEHIND THRONES

Contents

Although unknown to the constitution, political parties dominate the real world of politics; they are defining symbols of the modern age. The chapter falls into three parts. The first focuses on the anatomy of the mass party organization. The second examines internal party dynamics: cohesion, power relationships, control mechanisms and the basic relationship between mass membership and leaders. The final sections analyse the location of the parties within the structure of power in society at large, addressing the sensitive issue of funding: who pays the piper and do they call the tune?

Political Parties

Defining parties

Any political movement can describe itself as a party, but in a democracy **political parties** are essentially associations with a common set of beliefs and goals, aiming to take office by constitutional means. Some commentators see the quest for office overriding all else, portraying parties as vote-maximizing machines (analogous to profit-maximizing firms) prepared to pursue any policy that commands support (Downs 1957: ch. 7). This is particularly true where the system is dominated by two parties. However, parties usually reflect ideologies to some extent, though over time they may pick and choose from the ideological cafeteria in the quest for support. The goal of taking control of government means that the major parties offer policies across a wide range of issues. However, there may also be small parties with a more narrow concern, such as the environment. Yet even these single-issue parties sometimes try to widen their appeal in the quest for votes.

The modern mass party

The major British parties are large associations essentially comprising three elements: a parliamentary cadre of elected MPs, a bureaucracy and a large extra-parliamentary membership in constituency associations (figure 12.1). We shall see in the next chapter that these **mass parties** evolved as a direct result of extensions to the franchise.

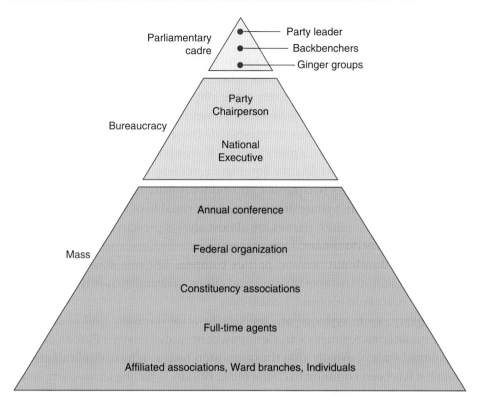

Figure 12.1 The organization of a mass party

Functions of parties

Beyond providing a government (or opposition), parties play multifarious roles in political life. Elections are their great celebrations: they energize campaigns, feed the media and mobilize voters. In addition, they organize the life of Parliament; without them the Palace of Westminster would be an empty shell. They also shape popular opinion, set the political agenda, stimulate public debate and, in doing so, help to provide political education. Recruiting people into politics and training them in the Machiavellian arts is another party function; historically Labour has been important in enabling working-class participation. Mass parties also bring together diverse demands in a process termed '**interest aggregation**', constructing the compromises that help maintain social stability. When out of government they continue to play a crucial role, providing political opposition, without which democracy is in peril. In the 1983 election campaign Conservative minister Francis Pym expressed fear of too weak a Labour opposition; similar concerns were expressed by some commentators after Labour's post-1997 triumphs, when the Conservatives seemed in disarray.

No Government can be long secure without a formidable opposition.
Benjamin Disraeli, *Coningsby* (1844: book 11, ch. 1)

The party system

Parties in a democracy do not exist in isolation. The British parties have been inextricably entwined, cross-fertilizing each other with philosophy, policy, strategy and organizational form. They have even made physical contact, to fight or to hold together in the warm embrace of coalition, sometimes even exchanging vital fluids as factions have surged from one to impregnate the other. Each party can therefore only be understood as part of a **party system**. It is usual to classify these in terms of number of parties and their relative dominance, thereby distinguishing four types.

- **Multi-party**: more than two parties; governments usually coalitions.
- **Two-party**: two parties share dominance, each capable of forming an entire government. In reality, minor parties are almost always present and a more realistic term is 'two-party dominant'.
- **Single-party-dominant**: several parties compete but one stands like Gulliver among the Lilliputians, able to command either an overall majority or remain the dominant partner in successive coalitions.
- **Single-party**: such 'systems' are unlikely to arise naturally and occur mainly under totalitarian regimes (Nazi Germany, communist Eastern Europe or certain ex-colonial states), usually after the opposition has been forcibly eliminated.

Fruitcakes, loonies and closet racists.
David Cameron on the UK Independence Party during a phone-in on the London radio station LBC (2006) (perhaps regretted)

Although it has been common to characterize Britain as having a two-party system, this must now be subject to qualification. There is an important third-party presence in the form of the Liberal Democrats, which was thrust into the front line as part of the 2010 coalition government. In addition there are usually around fifty fringe parties representing minority and sometimes bizarre interests, including, for example, the British National Party (BNP), Animals Count and the Pirate Party of the United Kingdom.

Anatomy of the Mass Party

The constituency associations

> I find most of them boring, petty, malign, clumsily conspiratorial and parochial to a degree that cannot be surpassed in any part of the United Kingdom.
>
> Alan Clark (1928–99; Conservative MP), on his local constituency organization, *Diaries* (26 Nov. 1985)

Consisting of the thousands of ordinary members who never expect to stand for office or even make a speech, these locally based organizations are crucial in fighting elections. A wise MP will keep on very good terms with the constituency organization, requiring from the more active members many long hours of unpaid work: stuffing envelopes, organizing campaigns, distributing propaganda, holding meetings, liaising with the local media and canvassing from door to door. In addition, they raise funds and recruit new members. Each has an organizational structure with a chairperson and executive committee of some kind, and many employ full-time agents. New Labour took particular care to strengthen the professional core of its Constituency Labour Parties (CLPs). Probably the most politically significant act undertaken by local associations is the selection (and sometimes deselection) of parliamentary candidates, although this is increasingly influenced by the central machines (see pp. 337–9).

Ward associations

The grassroots structure may be further fragmented into ward committees, reflecting the community substructure and based on local government electoral boundaries. These are active in local politics, providing councillors and fighting local elections. They promote the 'community politics' approach favoured by the Liberal Democrats and increasingly spoken of by the main two parties.

Individual membership

In principle anyone can join a political party. Workers are volunteers devoting their spare time to political activity; for some it is a hobby, for others an obsession. Indeed, it is at this level that some of the fiercest zealotry is encountered, from the 'wild-eyed' hard left to the 'goose-stepping tendency'. Controversy was aroused in 2013 when one of David Cameron's close friends was alleged to have described grassroots activists as 'mad, swivel-eyed loons'. Of course, by no means all local activists are extremists, though most feel more strongly on issues than the general public (Seyd and Whiteley 1992: 216–17). Membership is also a social activity, involving parties, fundraising dinners and auctions, concerts and so on; the Young Conservatives were traditionally admired as a dating agency and marriage bureau. At one time Conservative associations were controlled by local aristocrats, but they are now largely in the hands of local businessmen and professionals. In the case of Labour the trade unions have been prominent.

Parties partly judge their strength by membership size but records are often haphazard and it is difficult to assess this as it waxes and wanes with the political climate. Throughout the 1970s and 1980s falling numbers tended to leave the zealots in command and in the 1990s party leaders worked to widen membership. Labour was particularly successful (Table 12.1), its army of foot soldiers peaking at some 400,000 by 1997, the key year when the pattern of government power changed.

There are a fair number of constituency parties in the commuter belt which are run by people who, frankly, might quite properly be labelled neo-fascists.
Unnamed Conservative MP quoted in S. Ingle, *The British Party System* (1987: 83)

Table 12.1 Estimates of the membership of the three main parties for selected years, 1951–2011 (thousands)

Year	Conservative[a]	Labour	Liberal/Liberal Democrat
1951	2,900	876	
1965	2,250	817	279[b]
1975	1,220	675	190[b]
1987	1,000	289	138[c]
1992	500	280	101
1997	400	405	87
2001	311	272	73
2005	258	198	73
2010	177	193	65
2011	c. 130–170	193	49

[a] Conservative membership figures are particularly difficult to estimate. The party itself estimated 750,000 in 1996, but Pinto-Duschinsky's survey (1997) suggested only 350,000–400,000.
[b] Data for previous year.
[c] Includes SDP.

Source: Data from McGuinness (2012: table 1)

Apathy rules?
Political party membership is dwarfed by that of the larger charities, such as the National Trust, with almost three million members.

Despite success at the polls, Conservative party membership had plummeted from a high point of three million in the mid-1950s to only a few hundred thousand. The decline was particularly rapid during the eventide of the Major government, membership falling by 40 per cent between 1994 and 1997 (Pinto-Duschinsky 1997). Unlike that of Labour, its membership base was not being renewed; one estimate suggested that over 95 per cent of members were thirty-five or older (Whiteley et al. 1994: 42), the youth membership (Young Conservatives plus students) having fallen from around 34,000 in 1979 to only 10,000 in 1997 (Conservative and Unionist Party 1997: 2). Indeed, by the late 1990s the membership was quite literally dying; sacks of voting slips sent out in September 1997 to endorse William Hague's leadership being returned marked 'Deceased'. After the initial euphoria of its 1997 victory, Labour membership began to haemorrhage steadily, as those who had joined to oust the Conservatives gradually became disillusioned. Cameron's election as Conservative leader in 2005 produced a short-term boost but then, with some prominent defections to UKIP, sank to a lower level than before he was elected (Helm and Jones 2006). The unpopularity of the Liberal Democrats after joining the Conservatives in a coalition in 2010 also served to deplete their forces, numbers falling to around 49,000 in 2011.

Other associations

- *Affiliated associations.* In addition to individual membership, the Labour Party has offered a form of indirect membership whereby associations such as socialist societies and trade unions affiliate, producing an inflated paper membership. The result was often union domination and part of New Labour's recruitment strategy was to curb this.
- *Intermediate-level associations.* Neighbouring associations may combine for purposes of coordination at area, regional or provincial levels. European elections, with their larger constituencies, also bring adjacent organizations together.
- *Federal organizations.* The constituencies are united through federal organizations; the Conservatives form their National Union (see p. 357) while the CLPs form the Labour Party as such.

Red flag and blue rinse: the annual conference

The parties hold various conferences, the most significant of which is the annual autumn conference which, in an age of mass communications, is an important shop window. Although bringing all sections together, the **party conference** is really a jamboree in which all who have laboured in the fields on behalf of their leaders may draw near to pay homage. The events are rituals which could interest anthropologists as much as political scientists (see Faucher-King 2005). They last for several days, often in the pleasant environs of the seaside at the end of the season but before the weather is too cold to enjoy a publicity-seeking dip. All takes place before the assembled press corps and unblinking eye of the television camera, supplemented with a ball-by-ball commentary by the pundits and blog postings and tweets from participants and observers.

The order of play entails a succession of debates on resolutions submitted by members, with speakers drawn from sections of the party. Formally the Labour and Liberal Democrat conferences have a policy-making role (see below). Voting in the Labour conference has involved a particularly controversial feature – the **block vote**, whereby trade union delegates enjoyed overwhelming influence by casting votes weighted to reflect the size of their memberships. An acute embarrassment to the party's modernizers, this became a key target after the 1992 election defeat.

The appropriate parliamentary leader (minister or shadow minister) will usually conclude a debate, individual popularity being gauged by the length and intensity of the applause. The audiences have their favourites. It was at conferences that Neil Kinnock made his rousing attack on Labour's far left that changed the party's fortunes and where Thatcher made her memorable 'The lady's not for turning'

Source: Cartoon by Paul Thomas, published in the *Daily Express* (5 Oct. 1998), reproduced by permission of the British Cartoon Archive, University of Kent: www.cartoons.ac.uk

declaration. During the New Labour years Blair delighted audiences. It is often the more extreme views that gain the plaudits. A Conservative home secretary often has the most difficult time since, however tough the rhetoric, it may not satisfy the demands of the hanging-and-flogging school of penal reform. Likewise, Labour conferences have often exposed a sharp duality between the parliamentary leaders preaching moderation and trying on capitalist clothes, and the fundamentalist prophets who see sackcloth and ashes as the only garb suitable for those who have repeatedly betrayed the faith.

The significance of a conference can be heightened by political circumstances. In 1963, when Conservative leader Harold Macmillan lay in hospital, a dramatic letter from him was read out saying that the time had come to choose a new leader. This can be contrasted with the 2005 Conservative conference, when again a leadership contest dominated. Here David Davis, long regarded as the heir apparent, turned in a lacklustre performance, no match for David Cameron. Thatcher gained much from the Falklands victory, and in 2001 Blair was able to ride out unpopularity over privatization when the 9/11 attack enabled him to make a 'statesmanlike' appeal for national unity.

Planning party conferences has become a complex operation. Conference

No member of the conference wants to let down the party in front of the national [TV] audience. Everybody is on his best behaviour, naturally a great aid to the leadership.

Ian Gilmour
(Conservative MP),
The Body Politic
(1969: 80–1)

managers make strenuous efforts to ensure that the boat is not rocked. Conservative leaders for long demonstrated a clear superiority in the art of stage management, employing public relations experts to orchestrate their entrances and exits, though under Major they began to lose their sense of decorum. In the Labour Party, speakers often emerged believing that, like justice, the washing of disgusting linen should be seen to be done, preferably using the launderette of television. However, the party learned its lesson and by the 1990s had acquired consummate public relations skills. Party managers were able to keep the Iraq invasion off the agenda in 2005 and one aging delegate, Walter Wolfgang, was manhandled out of the hall for daring to shout 'Rubbish' during a speech by Labour Foreign Secretary Jack Straw.

Conferences tend to spill out, both socially and politically, into the surrounding environs. The foyers of conference halls are festooned like bazaars with stands set up by sympathetic pressure groups and stalls selling trinkets and memoirs of party grandees or even scandalmongers. Parties of the non-political kind proliferate and there is a brisk business in fringe meetings, where figures 'managed' out of the main event, such as John Redwood (after his challenge to Major), Ken Livingstone, Tony Benn or George Galloway, can expound their views in an atmosphere often more lively and stimulating than in the official forum. Increasingly the media direct attention here; Michael Heseltine claimed that his fringe appearance in 1988 received 'more serious coverage than for any speech I ever made at a Conservative conference' (Pienaar 1988).

All conferences aim to end on an uplifting note, often with singing (traditionally 'The Red Flag' for Labour, while Conservatives have been known to appropriate Elgar's 'Land of Hope and Glory'), and a rousing speech from the leader – a key test of political virility. Yet although some are much publicized, most are soon forgotten when the Westminster routine resumes (Kavanagh 1996).

The central machinery

The executive

As large organizations parties need executives to direct their business. Most prominent is Labour's National Executive Committee (NEC); its membership is determined by elections from various sections of the party (figure 12.2) and it elects its own chair and vice-chair. Although constitutionally the servant of the mass party, the NEC's practical role has been leadership. Meeting regularly, it had a key position in policy formation, various subcommittees submitting conference resolutions. However, it could embarrass the leadership; the trade unions were for long able to control a majority and the method of election meant that it could be captured by the left. Hence, a key part of the modernizers' strategy was to reduce NEC power (Lent and Sowemimo 1996: 126–7).

Ex Officio Party Leader Deputy Leader General Secretary EPLP leader							
Unions	Socialist Societies	Constituency Parties	Local Parties	PLP/ EPLP	Front bench	Treasurer	Youth rep.
Elected at Annual Conference. At least six must be women	Elected at Annual Conference. (Unopposed)	Elected by all members. Cannot be MPs. At least three must be women	Elected at Association of Labour Councillors. At least one must be a woman	Elected at Annual Conference. At least one must be a woman	Nominated by Cabinet	Elected at Annual Conference. (Unopposed)	Elected at Youth Conference.

Figure 12.2 Composition of the Labour NEC, 2009

Source: Data from Labour Party website.

The Conservative Party comes under the control of its Central Office, established in 1870 largely as a personal machine to serve the leader. Significant developments took place between 1906 and 1911 during opposition, when the key position of party chairman (responsible for running the Central Office) was created, to be held by a cabinet-ranking MP. The Liberal Democrat Federal Executive, with representatives from all sections of the party under the leadership of the party president, is responsible for directing, coordinating and implementing party activities.

The bureaucracy

Employing paid officials rather like civil servants, these are the professional backbone of the parties. Situated within a stone's throw of Westminster (Labour in Brewer's Green, the Conservatives in Millbank Tower and the Liberal Democrats in Great George Street), they have relocated from time to time in response to party finances. Working under the party leaders, the bureaucracies have a wide range of management and control functions over the voluntary arms, coordinating local activities, providing a link with the leader and giving advice and information. They conduct public relations (liaising with the media, advertising and producing party literature), manage the annual conference, organize research and service back-bench committees. They also oversee candidate selection policy and maintain the central list of favourites and hopefuls seeking constituencies. Most crucially, they administer party finances and fundraising. Increasingly, service in the administrative arms of the parties is seen as the first step in a parliamentary career.

The parliamentary cadres

At the apex of the party structure sits the parliamentary cadre of MPs, including the leader, the front bench and the backbench organizations (see p. 433). The political mainsprings of Parliament, the extent of their independence from the rest of the party is a key question in political analysis.

Conscience and brain: satellite groups and policy wonks

Within and around the main parties is an expansive and ever-changing constellation of smaller organizations or ginger groups comprising varying combinations of MPs and members. These are of huge, and sometimes unrecognized, influence in party politics. Sometimes forming in response to particular events or policies, they can give a party much of its character, claiming variously to be its soul, its conscience, or its ideas bank, though often seen by leaders as unwanted carbuncles or diabolical incarnations requiring surgery or exorcism. Work in a think-tank can often be a springboard to a political career, either as a ministerial adviser or even an MP. Ed Balls, for example, worked as a research fellow for the Smith Institute before entering Parliament in 2005. The links between these bodies, their funders and the parties can sometimes be the sources of controversy and even scandal. One, involving Atlantic Bridge, and its links with US neo-cons and big business, led in 2011 to the resignation of Cameron's Defence Secretary, Liam Fox.

Conservative

In 1883, the Primrose League was formed in an attempt to keep alive the 'one-nation' spirit of Disraeli (being a reference to his favourite flower), a cause later taken up by the Tory Reform Group (established in 1975 to resist the neoliberalism of Thatcher). Together with several pro-European groups, the latter became part of an umbrella organization attempting to develop policies to appeal to the broad mass of the electorate – Conservative Mainstream. The Bow Group, a political research group founded by Conservative intellectuals in 1951 as a counterpoise to Labour's Fabian Society, also professed moderation, disseminating its message through its journal, *Crossbow*.

On the far right of the party, the Monday Club was formed in 1960 to oppose Macmillan on South Africa. The spirit of Thatcherism has been preserved by a number of associations, including specifically Eurosceptic groups, such as Conservatives Against a Federal Europe and the Bruges Group, which plagued John Major. Other well-known right-wing think-tanks include the Centre for Policy Studies and the Adam Smith Institute. Under Cameron, Policy Exchange, with an annual budget around £2 million, was hugely influential; it had played a part in his assuming the party leadership. Also important was the Centre for Social Justice, set up in 2004 by ex-party leader Iain Duncan Smith. However, by early 2013 Cameron was under enormous pressure from Fresh Start (see below).

Labour

The Fabian Society, instrumental in the birth of the Labour Party, has been central to its thinking since the party's inception. Although appearing moribund during the 1980s, in the 1990s it was rejuvenated, becoming closely aligned with the Institute for Public Policy Research, set up to pioneer the party's intellectual fightback. There has been no shortage of other ginger groups, the best known being Tribune (propagating its views through the journal of that name). Founded in 1964, it has often been troublesome, but also highly respected and influential, and has included some prominent figures. Militant Tendency believed in a mission to oppose the Fabian tradition of moderation, using the Trotskyite tactic of entryism into the party. Michael Foot expelled the five-member editorial board of its journal, *Militant*. During the cold war, CND also penetrated deeply into the Labour ranks. On Labour's right was the Manifesto Group, established in 1974, though its first two chairpersons went on to help form the SDP. Demos was launched in 1993 by Martin Jacques, formerly editor of *Marxism Today*. The Institute for Public Policy Research, established 1988, was seen as a training ground for many Labour special advisers. Compass was formed in 2003 to promote the 'progressive' left in the party and held conferences attended by Labour cabinet ministers. The Smith Institute was particularly close to Gordon Brown. The groups are not always welcomed; in 1998 Tony Blair accused the Grass Roots Alliance of posing as 'critical supporters' while really being 'outright opponents' (*Independent*, 26 Sept. 1998).

Beyond the Westminster hothouse are youth movements, such as London Young Labour, women's sections and faith sections such as the Christian Socialist Movement combining religious and political beliefs.

Non-party think-tanks

Some think-tanks do not profess party affiliation. The Foreign Policy Centre comments on the impact of globalization on foreign and domestic policy and Chatham House enjoys fame for its research on international affairs. However, such bodies often have an ideological orientation. Charter88 (now Unlock Democracy), contributed much to the New Labour mood.

Inside the Parties: Tweedledum and Tweedledee?

Historically, the internal processes and power structures of each party reveal significant differences. Yet at the same time the pressures of modern politics produce a contagion effect, with parties coming to resemble each other in the competition for power.

Internal cohesion

In a multi-party system each party stands for a narrow interest or ideology, thereby promising internal solidarity. However, one of the *raisons d'être* of parties in a two-party system is interest aggregation – they cast their policy nets wide as 'catch-all' parties (Kirchheimer 1966). This can generate tension between ideology and political expediency within a party, which constitutes a key focus for analysis.

Factions and tendencies

For long, history showed the Conservatives as the most successful, Labour continually searching for an antidote to the virulent factionalism coursing through its veins. This has been explained through a distinction between the concepts of faction and tendency (Rose 1964). A **faction** is a group united across a wide front. Labour has been said to contain two factions broadly differentiated in left–right terms, confronting each other on a wide range of issues and producing a fundamental fault line. In contrast, Conservative disagreements tended not to precipitate the same formations every time. *A* and *B* might oppose *C* on one issue, but on another *A* and *C* might unite against *B*, these fluid **tendencies** never destroying overall cohesion.

> *What a genius the Labour Party has for cutting itself in half and letting the two parts writhe in public.*
>
> Cassandra (William Neil Connor; 1910–67; Irish journalist) in the *Daily Mirror*

However, this can be debated. The Conservatives have had an historic problem with foreign relations, reflecting a divide between the old Tory strain emphasizing nationhood and the whiggish element of thrusting commerce. This produced divisions over the Corn Laws in the 1840s, imperial protection in the early twentieth century, Indian government in 1935, South Africa under Macmillan and Rhodesia in 1965 (Norton 1978). This re-appeared under Thatcher, who dichotomized the party with disagreements over Europe. Major suffered from her legacy and Hague, while talking of reuniting the party, was to fight the 2001 election opposing the euro, thereby forcing his Europhiles into confrontational mode. David Cameron sought to reunite his party but after an initial honeymoon period was again faced with a Euro divide, this time exacerbated by the coalition with the pro-Europe Liberal Democrats. Calling itself Fresh Start, a group of his MPs formed in 2011 with a membership twice the size of that of Liberal Democrats in the coalition, to demand that Britain seize back control of employment and social laws from the EU. His problem became more acute with the rise of UKIP, signalled by its electoral success in the 2013 local elections. Backbenchers and even some front-bench colleagues became more strident in their Euroscepticism, some even calling for a leadership challenge.

While the Conservatives fought amongst themselves, New Labour was able to grow new skin over its old scars and, under Ed Miliband, lay claim to the 'one-nation' mantle of Disraeli. Socialistic elements became muted; the goal was gaining and holding power.

Social composition

Although the Conservatives have been able to command a wide range of electoral support, their traditional membership came from a narrow and homogeneous social base within the upper middle class and petite bourgeoisie. However, the Thatcher era added a new meritocratic breed to the mix and Cameron pursued a diversity agenda. Yet the Conservative Party remains predominantly a middle-class in character. By contrast, the PLP has been more a microcosm of society, wider class tensions being reproduced within its own ranks. The New Labour intake introduced increased homogeneity around a meritocratic norm, with 75 per cent university educated, a trend that was to continue into 2010 (Sutton Trust 2010: 2).

Experience of office

A party forming a government is constitutionally and politically pushed towards coherence. The doctrine of collective responsibility, official secrecy, the need for Commons' support and the duty to represent the whole community all conspire to unite. A long history of office gave the Conservatives considerable exposure to these forces. After its 1997 victory, Labour's spin doctors worked strenuously to keep backbenchers 'on message' and were rewarded with impressive majorities in 2001 and 2005. This was ended by the narrow defeat of 2010.

Hegemonic consciousness

The belief in one's right to rule can give party members a sense of mission that binds. For long the Conservatives regarded themselves (and were regarded by others) as the 'natural' party of government. Even in opposition they tended to remain united, believing office was never far away. By contrast, some Labour members saw the party's role primarily in terms of protest. This was very evident during the early 1980s and the essential project of Kinnock, Smith and Blair was that of convincing the party it could govern, a task resumed by Miliband after 2010.

Ideology

Ideology might be expected to unite, but it can have the opposite effect. Labour traditionally espoused socialism but this can have a variety of meanings, imply-ing contrasting strategies. Successive leaderships regularly sought to reduce the 'red in tooth and Clause Four' commitment to socialism, Gaitskell's attempts to disembarrass the party of this talisman proving particularly disruptive. In contrast, the Conservatives' traditional goal has been office, with pragmatism taking precedence over ideological purity. Even Thatcher was more pragmatic than is sometimes acknowledged. Labour under Blair jettisoned much ideological baggage, including the old Clause Four; even the term 'socialist' was largely abandoned. Upon taking the Conservative helm in 2005 David Cameron's early moves were also pragmatic, to the extent of welcoming a coalition with the Liberal Democrats in 2010. However, by 2013 ideological differences were threatening to destabilize the party.

Personalities

The leading members of the parliamentary parties, often termed the 'big beasts' of the Westminster jungle, can be fierce rivals, tending to gather followers who will rally to their support. Figures such as Lloyd George, Churchill and Aneurin Bevan all exercised a disruptive influence. When in government there can be tension, particularly between prime minister and Chancellor of the Exchequer. In one of the most bitter rivalries in modern politics, the New Labour split between Blairites and Brownites (see chapter 13) and the departure of Blair re-opened the old schism in the form of 'old' versus 'new' Labour. A battle for the succession in 2006 also revealed splits within the Liberal Democrat ranks. Within the Conservative Party figures such as Michael Heseltine, Kenneth Clarke and Michael Portillo have all attracted followings.

Not while I'm alive he ain't.
Ernest Bevin's reply when an MP remarked to him that Labour colleague Herbert Morrison was 'his own worst enemy'

Choosing (and removing) the leader

The selection of leaders and their security of tenure are two factors with important implications for a party's well-being and culture.

Conservative

The process whereby Conservative leaders emerged was for long shrouded in a mystique that would even have puzzled England cricket selectors. The party elders, including the outgoing leader, would take soundings within the upper echelons of the party and a new heir would emerge. This was not necessarily corrupt or even irrational; it permitted sensitivity to candidates' qualities and reflected intensity of feeling in a way that a simple vote could not. However, in choosing Sir Alec Douglas-Home the party found itself with a leader who seemed out of touch with the times and in 1965 election by MPs was introduced. Soundings were still to be taken amongst peers and MEPs, and MPs were required to consult their constituency associations. First Heath and then Thatcher were so appointed. By 1997, with only a rump of 164 MPs remaining to choose Major's successor, there was considerable unease in the constituencies and (unsuccessful) calls for a one-member-one-vote system.

Table 12.2 Conservative leadership elections, 1965–2005 (number of votes)

Candidate	1st ballot[a]	2nd ballot	3rd ballot	Membership vote[b]
1965				
Edward Heath	150	–	–	
Reginald Maudling	133	–	–	
Enoch Powell	15	–	–	
1975				
Hugh Fraser	16	–	–	
Edward Heath	119	–	–	
Geoffrey Howe	–	19	–	
John Peyton	–	11	–	
James Prior	–	19	–	
Margaret Thatcher	130	110	–	
William Whitelaw	–	79	–	
1989				
Anthony Meyer	33	–	–	
Margaret Thatcher	314	–	–	
1990				
Michael Heseltine	152	131	–	
Douglas Hurd	–	56	–	
John Major	–	185	–	
Margaret Thatcher	204	–	–	
1995				
John Major	219	–	–	
John Redwood	89	–	–	
Spoiled papers/ abstentions	22	–	–	

Finally, a special constitutional conference in March 1998 decided upon an **electoral college** for leadership contests, to include all party members, choosing from a shortlist of two determined by a series of ballots of backbench MPs (the 1922 Committee), working on an elimination principle (table 12.2). This ensured that the winning candidate would have 1922 Committee support. However, it opened the door to tactical voting and could lead to the candidate with the greatest appeal to ordinary members being rejected. Coming into operation sooner than Hague would have wished, the system soon revealed its flaws with openly vicious leadership contests (see p. 375). After short-lived tenures for Iain Duncan Smith

Table 12.2 (continued)

Candidate	1st ballot[a]	2nd ballot	3rd ballot	Membership vote[b]
1997				
Kenneth Clarke	49	64	70	
William Hague	41	62	92	
Michael Howard	23	–	–	
Peter Lilley	24	–	–	
John Redwood	27	38	–	
2001				
Michael Ancram	21	17	–	
Kenneth Clarke	36	39	59	100,864 (39%)
David Davis	21	18	–	
Iain Duncan Smith	39	42	54	155,933 (61%)
Michael Portillo	49	50	53	
2003				
Michael Howard	No Contest			
2005				
David Davis	62	57		64,398 (32.4%)
David Cameron	56	90		134,446 (67.6%)
Liam Fox	42	51		
Kenneth Clarke	38			

[a] Prior to 2001, to win at this stage, a candidate required an overall majority plus a 15% lead over nearest rival.

[b] Turnout 79% in 2001.

and Michael Howard, the party reverted to its toff image with the election of Eton-educated David Cameron.

The security of tenure of Conservative leaders can be uncertain. There is a tradition of staunch loyalty to a leader when in office but it is coupled with a reputation for eliminating old warriors that would be envied by the Mafia (Bruce-Gardyne 1984: 22). With the exception of Bonar Law, every incumbent appointed during the twentieth century was either forcibly removed or placed under heavy pressure to go. Like the manager of a league football team, leaders appear safe as long as they deliver victory. Thus, all suffered some Achilles heel. For Chamberlain it was Munich, for Churchill, by the late 1940s, it was age and drink, for Eden Suez, for Macmillan his stance towards Africa and Europe and the Profumo scandal, and for Douglas-Home an unfashionable aristocratic style.

Born to rule? David Cameron and Boris Johnson in the Bullingdon Club, Oxford

Election made removal even easier, opening up the possibility of annual challenges. Heath, whose mistake was an economic 'U-turn', added to the distinction of being the first elected leader that of being the first to be 'unelected'. Thatcher's dispatch in 1990 came not because she had lost an election but because some thought she was likely to; the poll tax was her pons asinorum (see p. 670). Major was called a ditherer and his undoing was Europe and sleaze within the party. Hague's reign was short and without distinction, his humiliation in the 2001 general election a damning indictment of his 'save the euro' campaign slogan. Duncan Smith was driven out by his colleagues and for Howard the scale of losses in 2005 was a sufficient sign to go quietly.

> 'I must congratulate you on the combination of loyalty and restraint that you have shown in going on television to announce your intention to vote against the prime minister in the Leadership Election.'
>
> 'Alan, I'm perfectly prepared to argue this through with you if you'll listen.'
>
> 'Piss off.'
>
> Alan Clark on his encounter with Edwina Currie behind the Speaker's chair during the tense moments surrounding the fall of Thatcher, in *Diaries* (21 Nov. 1990)

Labour

From the outset, the Labour leadership was elective, with voting initially the exclusive right of the PLP. In theory, leaders were subject to annual re-election but, although Wilson unsuccessfully threw down the gauntlet before Gaitskell in 1960 and Tony Benn challenged Kinnock in 1988, this has largely been avoided. After criticism from the left it was agreed that the electoral college choosing the leader and deputy should be widened to embrace the trade unions (40 per cent), the constituency associations and the PLP (30 per cent each). Paradoxically, the reform actually increased the leader's security in three ways: it gave authority over all sections of the party; the PLP lost any moral right to a vote of no-confidence; and the cumbersome procedure could inhibit challenges.

In 1993 union influence was reduced by making the proportions in the electoral college equal thirds, and both unions and constituency parties were obliged to adopt the principle of 'one member, one vote' (OMOV), producing an electoral college of millions. Votes from each section are expressed in percentage terms so that the vote of an MP (or MEP) counts for much more than that of an ordinary member. An AV system of voting takes place, with the lowest-ranked candidates being eliminated (Table 12.3).

With no one opposing, there was no need for an election in the case of Gordon Brown, but the election of Ed Miliband in 2010 saw the process in full swing and illustrated its idiosyncrasies. Brother David, the favoured choice of the MPs/MEPs and CLPs, led in the first three rounds only to falter at the final hurdle. It was section three of the electoral college (affiliated members) that swung the vote in favour of the younger sibling and left him leading a somewhat startled party.

Evidence shows Labour leaders to be more secure than their Conservative counterparts: Attlee was able to cling to office far longer than his younger colleagues wished; Gaitskell, although his reign was turbulent, died with his leadership boots firmly laced; and Harold Wilson was sufficiently secure after fourteen years that his resignation surprised both colleagues and pundits. Even James Callaghan, after stormy battles with the left, was able to depart with dignity, as was Neil Kinnock

Table 12.3 Labour leadership election, 2010 (percentages)

Candidate	Round 1	Round 2	Round 3	Round 4
Diane Abbott	7.42	–	–	–
Ed Balls	11.79	13.23	16.02	–
Andy Burnham	8.68	10.41	–	–
David Miliband	37.78	38.89	42.72	49.35
Ed Miliband	34.33	37.47	41.26	50.65

after the election defeat of 1992. The departure of Michael Foot came closer to a Conservative-style hounding from office. He had proved an electoral liability, nicknamed Worzel Gummidge (a scruffy but well-meaning scarecrow featuring in a current TV series) by *Private Eye*. Blair had become unpopular but his resignation was announced after an election success rather than a failure, and without a clear date. Unlike most Labour leaders, Brown's departure was marked by considerable dissatisfaction with his performance.

Liberal Democrats

Until 1976 the Liberals had followed their traditional practice of allowing the parliamentary cohort to choose the leader. However, following Jeremy Thorpe's resignation over the Norman Scott scandal, party-wide election was instigated. Merger between the Liberals and the SDP in 1988 resulted in a new constitution for the Liberal Democrats in which the leader would be elected by all party members. The 2007 contest, with all but two possible contenders standing aside, gave victory to Nick Clegg over Chris Huhne by the astonishingly close margin of 1.2 per cent (Table 12.4).

Table 12.4 Liberal Democrat leadership election, 2007

Candidate	Votes (all party members)	Percentage
Nick Clegg	20,988	50.6
Chris Huhne	20,477	49.4

Generally, post-war Liberal leaders appeared secure in office: in 1967 Jo Grimond left with dignity, continuing as a respected party elder; and although Thorpe's position became untenable, he survived for an astonishingly long time. David Steel, though subject to some rough treatment, remained secure until he voluntarily stood down in 1988 for the SDP merger. Paddy Ashdown's resignation, after eleven years of unchallenged supremacy, was both voluntary and surprising. However, with Charles Kennedy, things changed. His performance evoked widespread expressions of no confidence, leading to a bitter resignation. The ensuing election in March 2006 gave an overwhelming majority to Sir Menzies 'Ming' Campbell, but his enforced resignation came after only seventeen months, clearing the way for Nick Clegg.

A hollow crown?

Although Labour has offered its leaders a relatively secure tenure, this does not necessarily mean they are the more powerful. It may be in the interests of party members to preserve a weak leader in order to enjoy greater freedom to rule from behind the throne. Caesar was slain not because he was weak but because he was powerful. The uncertainty of the tenure makes the party leadership a lonely position, many incumbents becoming brooding and paranoid, and fearing amongst their retinue those who, like the lean and hungry Cassius in Shakespeare's *Julius Caesar*, lie awake at night and 'be never at heart's ease whiles they behold a greater than themselves'. Tony Blair had more reason than most to heed this message. Although not lean, Brown was hungry for power. More than any other party member the leader has to remember that, while the opposition may be ranged on the opposite benches, one's enemies sit behind.

Paranoid and deluded.
Reported description of Tony Blair by supporters of Gordon Brown (April 2006)

Candidate selection

To be a genuinely national force a party must field over 600 candidates. Their selection represents a widely based patronage exercise, theoretically giving the mass membership a key 'gatekeeper' role and offering considerable power to shape the Westminster presence. Local oligarchs with entrenched loyalties and fiefdoms can use the selection process as a means of consolidating their own power. Hence, tension can arise as the central organizations, with their own lists of approved candidates, seek influence, either to make their parties mirror the demographic face of Britain or to 'parachute' in favourites with no affinity with the constituency. While there are strong arguments for more women candidates (see Childs 2009: ch. 4), local associations often have strong male traditions and this was to become a source of tension between national party leaders and the local members.

Conservative

In theory anyone can apply to be a Conservative candidate; selection committees may be faced with the mammoth task of reducing a list of a hundred or so to a short-list of around six. These are subjected to scrutiny: interviewed, invited to deliver an address and their profession and lifestyle noted. Those with spouses have been preferred and these may be vetted for acceptability on platform and in drawing-room. Throughout the process Central Office presence is felt but local associations have traditionally resisted pressure. De-selection can be used as a weapon. Many local associations resented the manner of Thatcher's departure and Major was obliged to appeal to activists not to act against MPs who had supported Heseltine's challenge. Big names are not necessarily favoured: as ex-Chancellor, Norman Lamont was spurned by eight associations without even an interview before securing Harrogate and Knaresborough for the 1997 election.

Until the post-war Maxwell-Fyfe reforms it was possible for wealthy aspirants effectively to purchase nomination by agreeing to contribute to party funds. A preference for breeding and education produced a predilection for company directors and executives and lawyers. However, from the 1980s, a new kind of professional politician began emerging, the policy 'wonks' and lobby consultants discussed above (p. 327), with little experience beyond Westminster. On becoming party leader David Cameron sought to alter the image by opening the central list and encouraging a diversity of people to apply. With particular attention to the position of women see (Childs and Webb 2011), he challenged the party's opposition to all-women shortlists. Under his initiative US-style 'open primary' selection meetings were held in some constituencies where local oligarchs were obliged to allow local people of any party to attend and vote. Warrington South was secured by Small Businesswoman of the Year 2003, Fiona Bruce. Particular media interest was aroused by an open primary in Totnes, involving a postal ballot of every registered voter. The winner, from a shortlist of three women, was political outsider Sarah Wollaston, who went on to enter Parliament. In the 2010 general election 151 (24 per cent) Conservative candidates were women. Cameron's initiative also produced forty-four ethnic minority candidates. However, his moves sparked off a backlash from local parties and the typical Conservative candidate has remained middle class, middle aged, white, married and male.

Labour

Here the selection process has been somewhat different. The original lists are considerably shorter because applications are restricted to those nominated by affiliated associations. At one time candidates were differentiated between sponsored and non-sponsored. **Sponsorship** meant that nominating associations met a substantial proportion of election expenses and made a contribution to funds. As a result selection was often controlled by union-dominated general management committees which chose the safer seats, leaving younger and more radical candidates favoured by the NEC with unwinnable ones. It also betrayed a male bias (see Lovenduski and Norris 1994).

The system was modified in 1996, with contributions going to the CLPs in general rather than to particular candidates, opening up the possibility of directing resources away from safe seats, where they were not needed, to the marginals. To increase the representation of women, the centre introduced women-only shortlists in 1989, but perhaps the most controversial innovation was the agreement in 1993 to establish such lists for 50 per cent of all winnable seats. Hotly resented by many CLPs, the policy was declared illegal in 1996 under the 1975 Sex Discrimination Act but was legalized by the Labour government in 2002. In 2005, national leaders suffered a spectacular embarrassment at the hands of former Labour Welsh Assembly member Peter Law. Standing as an independent in protest against an imposed all-women shortlist, he overturned a 19,000 majority in Blaenau Gwent, Labour's safest Welsh seat, to defeat Maggie Jones. In 2010, Labour fielded 190 women but many were in marginal seats, a disadvantage given the prevailing political climate.

Although ethnic minority candidates stand for Labour, they have frequently fought unwinnable seats. Prior to the 1997 election disputes arose in inner cities with sizeable BME populations where incumbent white MPs were loath to step aside. Sometimes mass signings of new Asian CLP members influenced candidate selection. In certain cases NEC inquiries revealed irregularities, with some names either not on the electoral register or even fictitious. A number of court cases ensued and candidates were imposed through NEC intervention.

Liberal Democrats

Local associations are responsible for selecting Liberal Democrat candidates drawn from a national approved list, but an emphasis on community politics has permitted considerable local autonomy. For the 1999 European elections the party adopted 'zipped lists' – alternating men and women. Subsequently the rule was changed to require that shortlists of two to four should include at least one member of each sex, and those of five should contain at least two of each sex. In the 2010 general election 134 of the party's candidates were women. Although the rules require selection processes to pay due regard to ethnicity, in 2011 the party had no ethnic minority MPs, MEPs, MSPs or AMs.

Who selects?

The choice of candidates is a clear area where the mass memberships of the parties can exert influence. Initially Labour's central machine generally sought a greater influence than Central Office over selection. Many of the party's leading figures were 'parachuted' in, including party leader Ed Miliband, descending into the South Yorkshire constituency of Doncaster North in time for the 2005 general election. However, David Cameron saw changing the Conservatives' image ('de-toxifying' it in the view some commentators) as central to his project to regain power. The Liberal Democrats have been less centrally driven, although leader Nick Clegg did himself arrive in the safe Sheffield Hallam seat by the same route as the Labour leader in time for the 2005 general election.

Power within parties: mass rule or iron law of oligarchy?

> Lenin's method leads to this: the party organisation at first substitutes itself for the party as a whole. Then the central committee substitutes itself for the party organisation, and finally a single dictator substitutes himself for the central committee.
>
> Leon Trotsky (1879–1940; Russian revolutionary), quoted in N. McInnes, *The Communist Parties of Western Europe* (1975: ch. 3)

Choosing leaders and candidates is linked to the power relationships within the parties. Does power lie with the masses, the vital life blood of the parties, or with the small number who form the leadership? This is a major area of debate in the study of modern politics. There are two extreme models: top-down, in which the mass obediently plays follow-my-leader; and bottom-up, where the party practises internal democracy and MPs are seen essentially as delegates. The emergence of the local associations in the nineteenth century created fears of mass control. Ostrogorski's famous 1902 study sounded a dire warning that the parliamentary parties had created monsters that would soon undermine representative democracy. Others feared the reverse – that the mass membership would be denied influence. In the early twentieth century the German/Italian sociologist Robert Michels enunciated his well-known **iron law of oligarchy**, postulating that within any mass party ineluctable sociological, organizational and psychological processes would result in domination by a small elite (Michels 1962).

Genesis

Because the Conservative and Liberal parties originated as parliamentary group-ings, the extra-parliamentary organizations were from the first seen as their handmaidens. There was never any reason to address the question of control; it remained within the provenance of the elite. Attempts by Joseph Chamberlain and Randolph Churchill to establish some degree of democratic control within their respective parties came to nothing. However, the conception, birth and growth of the Labour Party (see chapter 13) implied a quite different relationship. As the offspring of the trade union mammoth, the Labour Representation Committee was essentially subservient. Even the title 'leader' was denied in favour of 'chairman', who was co-equal with the NEC chair. However, the process of evolution was to see party leaders distancing themselves from the unions.

The party constitution

Like the country over which it has so long presided, the Conservative Party had no formal constitution but party literature has generally paid homage to the leader's supremacy. Hague secured the endorsement of a formal constitution at a special March 1998 conference but this did little to limit the leader's power. The Labour constitution imposed an ostensibly democratic pattern of authority, with three centres of policy formation: the PLP, the NEC and the annual conference. Policy was to be determined by the annual conference on the basis of a two-thirds major-ity. In 1945, NEC chairman Harold Laski argued that if Attlee, as prime minister, attended the three-power peace conference at Potsdam his position should be approved by the NEC. However, Attlee rejected this interpretation (McKenzie 1967:

330). The dominance of the party conference declined from the 1950s (see Minkin 1980) and constitutional reforms under Blair (over Clause Four revision and NEC composition) further strengthened the leadership. With elitist origins formed in the days before the mass electorate, the Liberal constitution was decentralized in 1983, giving a predominantly 'bottom-up' character. This was preserved by the Liberal Democrats, making the federal conference sovereign. A conference rejection of coalition NHS policy in 2011, for example, led the leadership to reconsider their position. Most conference resolutions are drawn up by the party's central Policy Committee.

Patronage

The ability to make appointments to various positions within a party can work to strengthen a leader's position. When in government this power is enhanced through the range of honours and positions dispensed in the name of the monarch. Candidate selection can also be a formidable patronage instrument of the party leaders, which the major parties increasingly use.

The position of prime minister

When a party assumes office its leader inherits the supreme powers of the Crown, and when ejected these clouds of glory may be trailed into opposition. This has given an advantage to Conservative leaders. Whenever Labour leaders experienced power they too wore a halo of authority, though until 1997 such periods were tantalizingly short-lived, punctuated by lengthy spells in the wilderness, when the steel discipline of office softened in the heat of internal friction. However, once he became prime minister, Tony Blair was to develop an iron grip over the party to match that of any Conservative leader. The formation of the 2010 coalition subjected the Liberal Democrats to entirely new pressures, with the leadership having to make compromises to support government policies at variance with the wishes of many grass-roots members.

Attitudes towards office

The hegemonic consciousness of the Conservatives has not only enhanced their cohesion, it has recognized the importance of the party elite in securing power. Hence, when displaced, the mass loyally followed the leadership in any policy revision designed to regain office. In contrast, the idea of some on the left, that it is better to lose than compromise, often curbed Labour leaders' ability to shape policy. However, by 1997 the party hungered more for office than for pure socialism, becoming voter responsive rather than activist orientated. At the same time the Conservatives seemed to lose the appetite, with divisions over Europe debilitating a succession of leaders.

Winning is the sine qua non and a lot of leeway must be allowed to a leader who is successful.
Ben Pimlott (1945–2004; historian and former Fabian chairman), quoted in the *Observer* (12 Jan. 1997)

Modern campaigning

Contemporary electoral politics is about highly disciplined parties fighting centrally controlled campaigns (see chapter 11). Manifestos are focused on the leaders, members are expected to be 'on message' and annual conferences are stage-managed. General elections have become presidential in character and the media depict them in terms of gladiatorial battles between leaders.

The charisma factor

As discussed above, personalities matter in real-world politics. Members of organizations look for leadership and charismatic figures will tend to rise. Figures such as Gladstone, Disraeli, Lloyd George and Churchill dominated their parties. While Attlee was not a man to thrill an audience, he could inspire confidence. Labour's disarray in the 1950s and early 1960s in part reflected the combative character of Gaitskell, while the relative calm under Wilson can be largely attributed to his ability to pour liberal quantities of oil on the party's sea of troubles. Macmillan charmed while Thatcher inspired. In contrast, Major appeared dithering and weak. Kinnock did not charm or enthuse the electorate but Blair achieved unparalleled popularity ratings. In contrast, the gods appeared less generous to a succession of his Conservative opponents. When Brown succeeded Blair he began to lose control of his party, while with his PR skills and rousing conference speeches Cameron re-established the authority of the Conservative leadership.

Mr Blair's New Labour has become the natural party of deference in which power flows from the top.
The Times (21 Sept. 1997)

Policy-making

Ultimately the issue of power is related to policy determination. It can be argued that, in a democratic party, policy should be made by the membership. However, the views of activists can often be at variance with those of 'the mass of those who actually provide the vote' (Butler 1960: 3). McKenzie (1967: 635) argued that such fears were unnecessary, the imperatives of political life (electioneering and governing) providing a procrustean bed forcing any party to become oligarchic. Labour's left-inspired reforms in the early 1980s reflected the views of its leftist membership but were electorally disastrous. The modernization process diluted the mass voice, transforming the party in line with the Michels thesis. Similarly, Cameron sought to pull his party towards the centre ground. The imperative of a universal franchise in British politics is that leaders must bypass their own mass membership to appeal to the wider electorate.

Who Pays the Piper?

As Electoral Commission reports reveal, maintaining a complex organization and fighting elections in the modern age are expensive undertakings. The way the parties feed their gargantuan financial appetites produces another key area for debate in party politics today.

Expenditure

Some of the expenditure might seem bizarre. In the 2005 campaign the Conservatives paid £5,000 for the rights to Andrew Lloyd Webber's song 'Take that look off your face'. Michael Howard's make-up cost £1,000, but the Liberal Democrats needed £2,000 for Charles Kennedy's, and spent a further £5,000 on his wardrobe. Cherie Blair's hair was considered enough of an asset to warrant the addition of £7,700 to Labour's expenses. Labour even invested £299 on *Star Trek* suits in targeting Conservative John Redwood, nicknamed the Vulcan in Parliament. There were also considerable sums paid to various gurus and advisers such as Labour's Philip Gould, who pocketed £143,000 for his services. However, this was dwarfed by the £441,000 the Conservatives paid to Australian advertising wizard Lynton Crosby – a costly way to raise the party's share of the vote by just 0.5 per cent.

Although parties are legally required to stick to constituency spending limits, the focus is on the national campaigns, where there have been no limits. More was spent fighting the 1997 election than ever before, the Conservatives and Labour together accounting for £47 million. Expenditure levels were reduced after 2001, following the 2000 Political Parties, Elections and Referendums Act (PPERA). For the 2005 campaign, total spending reached £36 million, falling to around £25 million in 2010, although this was largely a result of the decline in Labour funds.

Income

Unlike private corporations, the parties are not profit-making enterprises. They must rely on donations from others. Do the donors expect something for their money? The issue raises compelling questions about power and democracy. The classic distinction between parties and interests becomes blurred; the two are bound together by chains of gold.

Conservatives

> We need funds and I look to the City of London to give a lead in providing that support which as businessmen they should be prepared to give, in view of our efforts to make their business safe.
>
> Appeal by Conservative leader Stanley Baldwin in the *Daily Telegraph* (2 Feb. 1926)

The CBI's character, and perhaps its main raison d'être, is geared to a dialogue with government . . . But it must be emphasised that the CBI is politically neutral.
John Davies (CBI Director General), quoted in Ian Gilmour, *The Body Politic* (1969: 351)

The funding of the Conservative Party was one of the mysteries of British politics. Until 1968 no accounts were published at all, and when they did appear they were economical with ink. Although becoming more detailed in 1993, they continued to conceal the size of private donations. Although much constituency energy is directed towards fundraising, at critical points like general elections the broadly capitalist interests of Britain have regularly reached for their wallets to achieve what was generally regarded as a key requirement of successful capitalism – a Conservative government. The party chair and treasurer had the task of rattling the begging bowl before industry, but this was for long as difficult as fishing in a trout farm.

A prolonged period of opposition from 1997 saw harder times, with both constituency funding and corporate donations declining (see Pattie and Johnston 1996; Whiteley et al. 1994). The party became heavily reliant on donations from party chairman Lord Ashcroft. The May 2005 electoral battle was a landmark in that, for the first time, the party was outspent by Labour with a total of £17.9 million. However, the usual position was restored in 2010, when the Conservatives mustered £16.6 million, only marginally less than their 2005 outlay and very close to the limit imposed on total party spending by the PPERA.

Labour

Until 1997, the Conservatives were able to bombard the public with posters, newspaper advertisements and polished election broadcasts on a scale that could demoralize Labour. Traditionally, Labour's funds came from the poorest section of society: under the 1913 Trade Union Act, the unions were entitled to collect a political levy from individual members to form a political fund. New Labour sought to widen its support base with a recruitment drive and a search for new friends in the unfamiliar territory of the corporate boardrooms and the world of celebrity. Little could better symbolize the New Labour style. By late 1996 the new sources were accounting for some 25 per cent of income and by 2002 were contributing around two-thirds. However, the tide was to change. For the 2010 campaign Labour's expenditure, at £8 million, was only half that of the Conservatives.

Liberal Democrats

The financial appetites of the two major parties threaten to leave a centre party with little potential sustenance. Liberal Democrats rely heavily on members' donations and fundraising activities and of necessity must fight lean campaigns (spending only £2.3 million in 1997 and £2.5 million in 2001). However, for the 2010 campaign, the party was able to find some £4.7 million, thanks in large part to the controversial £2.4 million from Michael Brown (see below).

Regulating the donors

The reliance on private donations raises fears that public policy will favour a rich few rather than society at large. Although the Commons Home Affairs Committee had recommended regulating donations, Prime Minister John Major refused Lord Nolan's request to inquire into the area. However, under Labour, reform began with the 1998 report from Lord Neill's Committee on Standards in Public Life. This recommended a raft of restriction and controls, with an independent electoral commission to police the system. The recommendations were broadly accepted and included in PPERA. The 2001 general election was the first to be fought under the new rules. Subsequent modifications to reporting and permissibility thresholds for donations and loans were made by the Political Parties and Elections Act 2009 (PPEA). By the time of the 2010 general election the cap on national party spending was placed at £19.5 million, and the level over which gifts had to be declared was £7,500 for a central party and £1,500 for a constituency association. However, although regulation can set rules, it can come up against the ingenuity of the party financiers, which raises various concerns and sometimes promotes scandals.

Come dine with me

Businessmen, socialites and other wealthy individuals like to rub shoulders with those in power. When in government both Labour and Conservative fundraisers have contrived social meetings with ministers. Membership fees for dining clubs, with names such as Millennium and Premier, need not be classed as donations. David Cameron came to office promising to clear up party funding, but in 2012 found himself embroiled in a 'cash-for-access' scandal after party treasurer Peter Cruddas was caught in a sting operation by journalists posing as businessmen. Sounding like a street trader, he was filmed apparently offering meetings with the Prime Minister for large sums of money. Although this was not illegal, Cameron was quick to distance himself from his colleague (who resigned) but declined to name the millionaire donors whom he had recently wined and dined in Number Ten and at his country retreat of Chequers.

'Neither a borrower nor a lender be'

The wise advice on borrowing from Shakespeare's Polonius to his son Laertes was not heeded by the parties. In March 2006 it emerged that Lord Levy, Labour's chief fundraiser, had secured around £14 million in some secrecy. This came in the form of loans rather than donations and therefore evaded the rules of disclosure. The taking of a loan is not illegal but the question asked by critics was, were they borrowed on normal commercial terms which would be repaid, or would they later be written off, making them in effect gifts? Indeed, one of the lenders, Dr Chai Patel, a health entrepreneur, revealed that he had been asked to loan the money rather than make a gift because of the transparency rule.

Labour, having revealed the sources of its loans, placed pressure on the Conservatives, who had also been indulging in the practice, amassing debts of around £24 million (*The Times*, 25 March 2006). Initially the party claimed that lenders had been promised secrecy but finally revealed a list of socialites, business tycoons, philanthropists, wealthy individuals and city investors who had funded its debt (*Guardian*, 1 April 2006). It was following these developments that the Electoral Administration Act 2006 extended the declaration requirements to loans and credit facilities.

Feathers and favours

Personal vanity can drive politics as much as the quest for power. From a life peerage to a position on a quango, there are numerous ways in which a government can stroke the feathers and otherwise adorn the deserving. The practice of selling honours is not new. In 1616 Sir John Roper bought a title from James I for £10,000. In 1920, Liberal prime minister Lloyd George was embroiled in a scandal which led to the 1925 Honours (Prevention of Abuse) Act, making the sale of honours a criminal offence. There were also allegations against Harold Wilson and Margaret Thatcher. Lord Shackleton, a former member of the Privy Council's Political Honours Scrutiny Committee, declared in the House of Lords that he believed honours were effectively being bought.

From 1979, around 6 per cent of companies were making donations to the Conservative Party and they received about half of all knighthoods and peerages – a statistical correlation unlikely to be accidental (Bogdanor 1997a). In March 2006 the Conservative Party, under pressure, revealed to the Electoral Commission that in 2004 party leader Iain Duncan Smith had proposed four men for peerages, three of whom had made substantial donations to the party (Lawson 2006).

But it was Labour that was to find itself embroiled in a major scandal. By 2006, of twenty-two people who had 'loaned' £100,000 or more to the party coffers, seventeen had received honours. Of those giving £1 million or more, all but one had received a knighthood or a peerage. In May 2000 an independent Lords Appointments Commission had been created to vet nominations for life peerages and in March 2006 it blocked awards of peerages for four big Labour donors (each £1 million plus) nominated by Blair. The media smelled blood and a 'cash for peerages' scandal unfolded. There were accusations that Labour had breached the 1925 Act and police inquiries followed. Tony Blair was subject to questioning three times and Labour's fundraiser Lord Levy was arrested. When released on bail he declared that he would not be Tony Blair's 'fall guy'. Finally the Crown Prosecution Service declared in July 2007 that it would not bring any charges owing to a lack of direct evidence that honours for loans had been agreed in advance. Yet the investigation had severely undermined the party.

Nobody gives money to a political party for nothing. They all want their feathers stroked from time to time . . . some . . . more often and more lovingly than others.
Senior Conservative, quoted in the *Observer* (20 June 1993)

Friends abroad

A particularly sensitive issue for the Conservatives has been the extent to which they sought and received overseas donations. Lord McAlpine (1997) was to report in his memoirs how, a year after retiring as party treasurer, he was asked by John Major to solicit funds from a wealthy benefactor identified as Greek shipping tycoon John Latsis (*The Times*, 3 March 1997). Contributions also came from Hong Kong and there were even donations from individuals involved in the Yugoslavian civil war, including an associate of human rights violator Radovan Karadzic (Fisher 1997). In response the 2000 PPERA laid down that parties could accept money from overseas sources only if they could prove they were carrying on business in the UK. However, this left loopholes, allowing foreigners to channel cash through UK-based companies. Many of these were tax exiles, individuals domiciled abroad for tax purposes and labelled 'nondoms'. Amidst much controversy, Michael Ashcroft, Conservative Party treasurer, donated £3 million from the tax haven of Belize (and was subsequently nominated by William Hague for a life peerage). Media suspicion arose as to the reasons why, in March 2006, at least ten of those lending to the Conservative Party had asked for their money back rather than have their identities revealed (*Guardian*, 1 March 2006).

While Conservative donors were the most controversial figures, with donors such as Lakshmi Mittal and the packaged food tycoon Sir Gulam Noon, New Labour was also benefiting from such aid. The Liberal Democrats also received help from nondoms. An Electoral Commission inquiry was launched over Majorca-based trader Michael Brown, who gave £2.4 million through his London-based investment arm. Embarrassment increased when he was convicted of fraud in November 2008 but the Electoral Commission ruled that the donation had been received in good faith and need not be repaid.

Measures to close the loophole came in Section 10 of the 2009 PPEA, prohibiting parties from accepting donations of more than £7,500 from individuals not ordinarily resident and domiciled in the United Kingdom. However, faced with mounting expenditure, the Labour government fought shy of asking the Electoral Commission to enforce the new rule in time for the 2010 general election.

A policy bazaar?

> It is a far cleaner method of filling the party chest than the methods used in the United States. Here a man gives £40,000 to the party and gets a baronetcy. If he comes to the leader of the party and says 'I subscribe heavily to party funds, you must do this or that', we can tell him to go to Hell.
>
> Lloyd George, quoted by Dominic Lawson in the *Independent* (18 April 2006)

I don't believe these people would have given a bean unless there were enough nods and winks that Tony was, of course, very grateful.

Henry Drucker (political fundraiser) on contributions to Labour, quoted in the *Independent* (30 April 1998)

It is said that money talks and the concern arises that it may talk in terms of government policy. While the buying of honours may appear unsavoury, in a democracy this is the more serious issue. When wealthy individuals and corporations contribute money to help parties win elections, will they expect to influence policy? Traditionally the suspicions were that the unions influenced Labour while the Conservatives served the capitalist interests. As New Labour turned to business, the issue became more complex.

Prior to the 1997 general election, northern millionaire Paul Sykes promised Conservative candidates up to £3,000 towards election expenses if they were prepared to repudiate their leader's 'wait and see' policy over the single European currency; 237 took the wealthy man's shilling (*Guardian*, 30 April 1997). A defining moment occurred in November 1997 when the New Labour government reneged on a key pre-election promise to ban tobacco advertising in sport. Motor racing mogul Bernie Ecclestone, who had donated £1 million to the party just prior to the election, had an urgent meeting with Britain's new Prime Minister and the decision was made to exempt Formula One motor racing from the ban. The result was media outcry and an embarrassed Blair 'apologized' on Sunday television.

In January 2002 a new embarrassment arose over the collapse of US energy giant Enron and the accountancy firm Arthur Andersen, under investigation by the US Congress over allegations of false accounting on a massive scale. Critics claimed that a £36,000 reception sponsored by Enron had cleared the way for a takeover of Wessex Water and the ending of a moratorium on building gas-fired power stations. However, Conservative moral outrage looked less convincing when Enron's former European chairman revealed that the company had contributed to both parties. Conversely, funds may be withheld by those unhappy with government policy; BA openly threatened to cut donations to the Conservatives for this reason. In February 1998 Labour's largest benefactors (UNISON, the Transport and General and the GMB general union) threatened cuts of £400,000 in donations because of government policy (*Independent*, 23 Feb. 1998).

Party funding remains a somewhat murky area of political life, with economy of the truth, suspicions, accusations, claims and counter-claims leaving no clear picture of how it is accomplished. It is obvious that the reforms introduced by legislation cannot completely eliminate the problems that arise when finance and politics meet. Parties need funds, donors will always be sought and rules can be bent or evaded. For many reformers, such as Unlock Democracy (and the 1976 Houghton Committee), only state funding (as in continental European democracies and Canada) can end questionable practices and reduce the climate of suspicion. However, this is also not without problems.

State funding

Advocates of state funding argue that it would break the link between private wealth and public power. Indeed, there is already some public funding, including free delivery of one election leaflet per candidate and free party political broadcasts. In addition there is Short Money, named after Edward Short, Leader of the House of Commons in 1974 when it was introduced ('Cranborne Money' in the Lords). This is paid to the opposition parties in Parliament. There is also indirect state aid through postage and research costs. The 1998 Neill Committee did in fact rule out large-scale public funding but recommended an increase in Short Money. In March 2006, former civil servant Sir Hayden Phillips headed an inquiry into party funding, which recommended a limited increase in state funding and a capping of private donations.

Yet large-scale state funding might not be a universal panacea and itself raises new questions. Parties vary in size, and what would be the formula for determining the level of funding for each? Would it favour existing parties and inhibit the formation of new ones? Would frivolous parties be eligible? Should the state finance dark forces wishing to undermine democracy or persecute minorities? Should taxpayers have to pay for parties they oppose? With no need to raise funds, would parties abandon local associations and lose touch with their grass roots? Would state funding come with a degree of state control? Moreover, such a system would be difficult to monitor. There is also a fundamental question of the freedom of citizens to use their money according to personal choice.

However, there is one restraint in a democracy, which is the ability of critics and the media to scrutinize and publicize. Neill recommended transparency in all financial activity. As we have seen, scandals associated with fundraising are not infrequent: cash for questions, cash for access, cash for honours and cash for policies have all led to embarrassment, resignations and even police investigations when exposed to the sunlight of public debate. The parties must heed these signs.

* * *

This chapter has examined the structure and internal organization of the political parties. However, it does not explain their centrality to the political system as a whole. In the next chapter we chart the development of party politics in Britain.

Key points

- A political party is an association formed for the purpose of entering government (usually by constitutional means).

- Although parties often claim to reflect ideologies, the quest for electoral support weakens this link.

- The main British political parties consist of three elements: a parliamentary cadre, a bureaucracy and a mass membership.

- The question of where the power lies within each party is an important subject for analysis.

- This can be examined with respect to organization, internal democracy, leadership appointment, patronage, candidate selection and policy-making.

- The central goal of maximizing votes leads parties to resemble each other in many respects.

- The need for funds makes the British parties dependent on private donations and raises profound questions about the public interest and democracy.

Review your understanding of the following terms and concepts

1922 Committee	interest aggregation	party conference
all-women shortlist	iron law of oligarchy	party executive
candidate selection	mass party	single-issue party
catch-all party	multi-party system	single-party system
constituency association	Parliamentary Labour	think-tank
faction	Party	two-party system
fringe party	party bureaucracy	ward association

Questions for discussion and debate

Consider these propositions and be prepared to present the cases for and against. Try to produce debating propositions of your own.

1   Political parties bring ideology into politics.
2   Democracy within a political party is not a necessary condition of a democratic state.
3   The longevity of the Conservative Party is the result of its lack of ideology.
4   Labour leaders are more secure than their Conservative counterparts.
5   The 'iron law of oligarchy' remains irrefutable.
6   Tweedledum and Tweedledee best characterizes the differences between Britain's main parties.
7   The financing of British parties undermines the democratic process.
8   All-women shortlists in candidate selection cannot be justified.
9   Party conferences are little more than PR exercises.
10   Parties are indispensable in modern government and politics.

Further reading

Most general books on British politics will have much to say on political parties. More focused titles can be found, such as the following. (See also reading for chapter 13.)

Bochel, H. (ed.) (2011) *The Conservative Party and Social Policy.*
Examines the development, sources and content of Conservative social policy and their influence within the coalition.

Clark, A. (2012) *Political Parties in the UK.*
Up-to-date account of the main UK parties, including those active in the devolved systems.

Driver, S. (2011) *Understanding British Party Politics.*
A comprehensive overview of British party politics with attention to the effects of devolution.

Garner, R. and Kelly, R. (1998) *British Political Parties Today.*
Considers the party system following the advent of the Blair government.

Griffiths, S. and Hickson, K. (eds) (2009) *British Party Politics and Ideology after New Labour.*
Much-needed debate from academics and politicians on the intellectual roots of the main British parties. Considers whether there was a decisive ideological shift away from Thatcherism under New Labour and highlights ideological controversies within parties.

McKenzie, R. (1967) *British Political Parties.*
Presents the thesis that political constraints force parties to resemble each other.

Michels, R. (first published 1911) *Political Parties.*
Classic statement of 'iron law of oligarchy'.

Muller, W. D. (1977) *The Kept Men.*
Illustrates the early trade-union sponsorship of Labour candidates.

Peele, G. (1991) *British Party Politics: Competing for Power in the 1990s.*
Focuses on the problems of party management and leadership, techniques for marketing parties and party organization.

Quinn, T. (2012) *Electing and Ejecting Party Leaders in Britain.*
An interesting study that finds that increased democratization of the process does not significantly change the type of leaders chosen.

Riddell, P. (1996) *Honest Opportunism: The Rise of the Career Politician.*
Charts the changing character of the parliamentary parties with the rise of the career politician.

Seyd, P. and Whiteley, P. (1992) *Labour's Grass Roots.*
Whiteley, R., Richardson, J. and Seyd, P. (1994) *True Blues: The Politics of Conservative Party Membership.*
Illuminating empirical analyses of mass memberships.

Willetts, D. (1996) *Blair's Gurus.*
Lively right-wing challenge to a battery of New Labour thinkers (Hutton, Marquand, Kay, et al.).

For reading around the subject and some light relief

Jeffrey Archer, *First Among Equals.*
Ambitious politician attempts to climb the greasy party pole. By ambitious politician who slipped down.

Wilfred Fienburgh, *No Love for Johnnie.*
Love, romance and committee meetings in the Labour Party. (Also a film.)

Chris Mullin, *A Very British Coup.*
Labour MP explores (old) Labour's problems in dealing with the Establishment.

Simon Walters, *Tory Wars: Conservatives in Crisis.*
A light-hearted account, packed with inside information exposing the internal machinations, dirty tricks and bitter enmities within a party.

Jim Wilson, *The Labour Man.*
Comic novel. Labour has a majority of one, and all depends on a newly elected MP who, tortured by his socialist ideals and the contradiction between power and honour, disappears.

On the net

http://www.labour.org.uk
http://www.conservatives.com
http://www.libdems.org.uk
http://www.greenparty.org.uk/

The websites of the major (and minor) political parties usually outline their organizational structures, procedures and policies, as well as providing information on their key personalities.

CHAPTER 13

PARTY POLITICS: FROM ELITES TO MASS PARTICIPATION

Contents

This chapter, by charting some key moments in the development of Britain's political parties, is also a story of British politics. It is inextricably linked with the development of democracy, as the extensions of the franchise and changing social conditions forced the parties to respond to the demands of a mass electorate. It makes it clear that parties in a democracy should not be seen in isolation; it is in their essential nature to be linked through competition, contagion and sometimes cooperation. The chapter is divided into what may loosely be termed eras, such as that of the new liberals, Thatcher or New Labour. We end with an intriguing question for British politics: the possible opening of a new era, one of coalition politics.

Genesis

The British party system is best understood through its evolution, which is also the evolution of the country's democracy. From the settling dust of seventeenth-century constitutional struggles emerged two parliamentary groupings – the Tories, a land-owning cadre avowing fidelity to the King, and the Whigs, devoted to trade and the parliamentary cause – which dominated into the nineteenth century. As **cadre parties** they existed only in Parliament and had little ideology save the protection of self-interest. These primitive organisms were forced under the radical sun, to crawl from the mud of eighteenth- and early-nineteenth-century court and parliamentary intrigue onto the hard ground of democracy. The nineteenth-century extensions of the franchise opened the age of the modern mass party.

The Conservatives: the era of Peel and Disraeli

By the 1820s, under the leadership of the Duke of Wellington, the Tories appeared to be collapsing before the radical pressures unleashed by the industrial revolution, fatally vulnerable before any extension of the franchise. However, following the 1832 Reform Act, they experienced an unexpected revival under resourceful leader Sir Robert Peel (1788–1850), who gave them a *raison d'être* beyond self-interest by identifying with a view of conservatism expressed not by a Conservative but by the Whig, Edmund Burke (see p. 38). Asserting tradition over radicalism, it was exceedingly attractive to those whose interests lay in the status quo – the landed gentry. Thus did the Conservative Party rise, phoenix-like, from the ashes

The right honourable gentleman [Sir Robert Peel] caught the Whigs bathing and walked away with their clothes.

Benjamin Disraeli, Commons speech (28 Feb. 1845)

of the old Tory Party. However, another crisis occurred in 1846, the party splitting over the repeal of the Corn Laws, which ended tariff protection of agriculture, favouring commerce and industry at the expense of land. Two groups emerged: the more radical one (containing many who had entered Parliament as a result of the 1832 Reform Act), favouring free trade, moved towards the Whigs, with whom they finally merged (forming the Liberal Party). The future of the landed interests again seemed vulnerable but the party was to find a second visionary to lead it from the wilderness. Benjamin Disraeli (1804–81) not only parted the difficult waters of further franchise extensions, he also created an image to carry the party into the era of mass politics.

Disraeli's inspiration was to perceive how the interests of privilege could be allied to those of the ordinary folk whose votes were needed. With a rallying cry of 'one nation', he stressed the Conservative claim to be the natural guardians of *all* sections of society, evoking the empire as a symbol to unite them as members of a dominant race. The life-saving bond entailed a paternalistic commitment to social reform through legislation regulating the sale of food and drugs, public health, artisans' dwellings, river pollution, factory conditions and trade unions. So effective was the strategy that it was a Conservative government that felt confident enough to extend the franchise further in 1867. In gaining working-class support Disraeli had laid the foundations for the modern Conservative Party.

However, after his death the future looked bleak as the traditionalists reasserted their influence. They were saved by the tormented obsession of Liberal leader Gladstone with the Irish question. Splitting the Liberals in 1886, this propelled a group of unionist defectors, led by a radical Joseph Chamberlain, into the Conservative ranks. Subsequently the party acknowledged its commitment to Ireland's link with the mainland by adopting the title 'Conservative and Unionist Party'. The influx returned to the party some Whiggish blood, enabling it to accommodate the rising bourgeoisie, who were increasingly dominating the social order. The Tory and Whig strands offered a formidable electoral potential, which was to become fundamental to the party's remarkable width of appeal.

The Liberals: the era of Gladstone

You cannot fight against the future. Time is on our side.
W. E. Gladstone, speech on the Reform Bill (1866)

The Liberal Party was a major force for only around half a century. In its heyday it experienced some great periods of office, its social and constitutional reforms standing as its monument. Yet like a figure in classical tragedy, the party (and its leaders) seemed to contain from the first the seeds of self-destruction. The modern party was established in 1859 through the fusion of the old Whigs with the new radicals and the free-trade faction haemorrhaging from the Tories. This latter infusion provided one of its greatest figures, William Ewart Gladstone (1809–98), whose austere presence, the very antithesis of the polished Disraeli, dominated in the nineteenth century. Drawing on Enlightenment ideals, the rationale of liberalism lay in the idea of freedom from the state; impatient with traditional institutions it supported business and commerce through *laissez-faire* and free trade. Beyond the economy there was Irish home rule, nonconformity, parliamentarianism and social reform.

The emergence of mass parties

The two great Reform Acts (see pp. 271–3) hardened the fluid parliamentary alliances with a new sense of discipline, greatly enhancing the leaders' authority. It was no longer possible to gain election through corruption and the parties fostered organizations in the constituencies (registration societies) to ensure that all sympathizers would vote. The local associations also gained the crucial responsibility of choosing candidates.

To oversee the local activists two London clubs – the Carlton for the Conservatives and the Reform for the Liberals – became party headquarters and federations of local organizations were established to forge a sense of national unity. The Liberal Registration Association, founded in 1861, was followed in 1867 by the National Union of Conservative and Unionist Associations. The mass membership suggested problems of control: the Conservative Union seemed content to serve the leaders but the Liberal Federation claimed rights over party policy, which Gladstone resisted. Both associations also held annual conferences in which the toilers in the constituency fields could voice their opinions. By the end of the century the mould for the modern system had been cast: parties were ideologically based mass organizations, led by elites, seeking office by courting the electorate.

Challenge to the Established Order: the Rise of Labour

One of the remarkable aspects of franchise reform was the failure of a working-class party to capitalize on the potential in the mass vote – a manifestation of the power of the dominant classes to keep participation as a choice between two elites. They did this by showing some concern for the working class. Conservatives set out their 'one-nation' stall while the Liberals embraced the new liberalism and promoted major social reforms in the early twentieth century (national insurance, pensions, unemployment benefits and employment exchanges). However, a revolutionary ideology was taking shape; Marx's trenchant critique of liberalism meant that things could not remain as they were. Socialist movements were forming and some working-class activists sought to enter the parliamentary stage themselves.

Labour pre-history

The Labour Party was born of a long and painful confinement. Although opposed by establishment forces, the Chartists had argued from the 1830s for a working-class parliamentary voice. In 1869 the trade unions created a Labour Representation League but, although two of its thirteen candidates were returned in 1874, it showed little promise. Some working-class candidates also managed to enter Parliament under the Liberal banner; by 1885 there were eleven Trade Union Liberal MPs. However, the Liberals remained reluctant to cooperate with them. Keir Hardie, Ramsay MacDonald and Arthur Henderson, who rose to be giants of the Labour movement, were all spurned as candidates – had things been different, there might never have been a Labour Party.

During the 1880s and 1890s a socialist dynamic came from three associations. At the extreme left was the London-based Marxist group, the Social Democratic Federation (SDF), led by H. M. Hyndman. Of different character was the Fabian Society, founded in 1884 by George Bernard Shaw and the indefatigable social researchers Sidney and Beatrice Webb. It took its name from Quintus Fabius Maximus ('the Delayer'), a Roman general who achieved success by small, cautious moves and delaying tactics rather than reckless bravado – such was the avowed strategy of **Fabianism**. Most important was the Independent Labour Party (ILP), founded in 1893 to pursue moderate socialism and numbering amongst its members Philip Snowden, Ramsay MacDonald and Keir Hardie. Yet in the 1880s there were only some 2,000 active socialists in the entire country. Despite meagre social improvements, the working class remained content to vote for the elite duopoly and the ILP gained little support. However, a more aggressively socialist New Unionism introduced a fresh dynamic. In the late 1890s, damaging defeats in large strikes made the case for direct parliamentary representation more compelling.

MacDonald owes his pre-eminence largely to the fact that he is the only artist, the only aristocrat by temperament and talent in a party of plebeians and plain men.
Beatrice Webb (1858–1943; Fabian Society founder member), *Diary* (May 1905)

Emerging from the womb

In 1900, the Trades Union Congress (TUC) made the momentous decision to seek a parliamentary presence. The might of sixty-five trade unions, with their hundreds of thousands of members, combined with the intellectual vigour of the three small organizations to establish the Labour Representation Committee (LRC). Significantly, its strategy was to be in the Fabian tradition: revisionist ('Labourism') rather than revolutionary socialism. At a very early stage the SDF disengaged from the inhibiting embrace.

The Conservative government reacted with intense hostility, portraying the movement as a threat to the constitution and requiring harsh treatment. A series of judicial decisions, culminating in the infamous Taff Vale judgment of 1901 (holding that unions could be cripplingly sued by employers for loss of profits resulting from strike action), convinced more unions of the need to combine under the new banner, and MacDonald, as LRC secretary, worked to develop a national mass organization.

Labour and the Liberals

Although a fundamental principle of the new party was to oppose established elites, an early pragmatic advantage was gained by a secret agreement with the Liberals. Each party would withhold candidates from selected constituencies to unify the anti-Conservative vote. Through this stratagem the new party signalled its entrance onto the parliamentary stage as the Liberals scored a landslide victory in the 1906 general election. Twenty-nine Labour MPs together took the title Parliamentary Labour Party (PLP). The election also saw the return of twenty-four Lib-Labs, union candidates standing under the Liberal banner. For the first time there was a formidable working-class phalanx in Parliament. An early success was the 1906 Trades Disputes Act, reversing the Taff Vale judgment. However, their prime object was to ingratiate themselves with the Establishment by demonstrating *responsible* behaviour (Miliband 1961: 28). The Liberals felt no threat and formed a highly distinguished government, laying the foundations of the British welfare state, with Winston Churchill and David Lloyd George forming a formidable duo.

Yet these were turbulent times. The Liberal programme led to a dramatic confrontation with the House of Lords, spearheaded by the radical Chancellor of the Exchequer, Lloyd George, resulting in the 1911 Parliament Act (see chapter 14) and near civil war over Ireland (see p. 629). Labour became more closely wedded to the Liberals, a development derided by its left wing, which argued for a distinct identity. The first world war provided an opportunity for this.

War and the Inter-war Era

The year 1914 marks the beginning of the Liberals' decline. It was the party's misfortune to be in office at the outbreak of war. As prime minister, Herbert Asquith became the leader of a coalition in 1915 but soon proved unequal to the task. 'His initiative, if he ever had any, was sapped by years of good living in high society' (Taylor 1965: 14) and, following a series of military defeats, he was ousted in 1916 by Lloyd George, who headed a new coalition with a Conservative majority.

For Labour, war provided a taste of office and a chance to demonstrate patriotic qualities. It shed its pacifist garb and MacDonald (supported by the pacifist ILP) resigned the leadership to be replaced by Arthur Henderson, who gained influence and was even included in the war cabinet. However, dealings with international socialism led to his ejection in 1917, leaving him free to prepare for the greater role that Liberal disarray seemed to promise. With MacDonald and intellectuals such as Sidney Webb, Henderson drew up a new socialist constitution, including the famous *Clause Four*, with its commitment to public ownership of the means of production, distribution and exchange. It also recognized the importance of widening party membership, making provision for individuals to join constituency associations in their own right rather than as trade unionists. The 1918 conference formally approved a wide programme, *Labour and the New Social Order*, which was to be the mainspring for policy for the next thirty years.

The immediate aftermath of war proved disastrous for the Liberals. Lloyd George rushed into an opportunistic general election in 1918, offering further coalition government. Coalition candidates were endorsed with a letter signed jointly by Lloyd George and Conservative leader Bonar Law, dubbed the 'coupon' by Asquith, leader of the independent Liberals, in sarcastic evocation of wartime rationing. Asquith lost his seat and only twenty-eight of his supporters were returned, but Lloyd George had played into the hands of the Conservatives, delivering his own party into a political netherworld.

Though faring badly against what was an anti-socialist alliance, Labour demonstrated its muscle by fielding 361 candidates, a considerable increase on its previous best of 78 in 1910, and the freak circumstances gave little indication of real trends. The coalition proved unpopular and, after a string of by-election failures (mainly gains for Labour), Bonar Law agreed, at a momentous meeting of Conservative MPs at the Carlton Club in 1922, that it was time to bid farewell to Lloyd George before he destroyed the Conservatives as he had the Liberals. As a by-product, a new institution had been created: the Conservative 1922 Committee. The Liberals were left in disarray, candidates fighting the ensuing general election as either 'Lloyd George' or 'Asquith' Liberals.

Labour: a viable government

Labour's parliamentary strength rose to 142 in 1922, giving it second-party status. The number of ILP-sponsored candidates reached 32, with an influx of intellectuals giving a wider appeal and more rhetorical virtuosity. It began to attract ambitious young Liberals despairing of the schism within their own party. With increased parliamentary strength, the heady possibility of taking over the reins of government could be contemplated. Ambitions were realized in late 1923 when Conservative prime minister Stanley Baldwin dissolved Parliament over tariff reform. Although the Liberals revived with 158 seats, Labour increased its presence to 191 (39 ILP). The single-issue nature of the election meant that, despite its 258 seats, the government had been rejected. The Liberals felt justified in supporting Labour, which momentously ruled for ten months as a **minority government**. Not surprisingly, so tenuous a period of office produced little reform and was attacked by socialist purists. This was a harsh judgement on the leaders, who had been faced with a task hitherto the preserve of those with wealth, position and a solid tradition of parliamentary organization. Labour providing a government was, like the proverbial dog walking on its hind legs, remarkable for being done at all.

Labour versus the Establishment

The experience offered a stark illustration of establishment power. The government was undermined with alarmist propaganda and deceit, Anglo-Soviet relations being a particularly sensitive area. The final straw came in the Campbell case. The Attorney General's decision to drop sedition proceedings in a minor case against the editor of a small communist journal was fanned up as evidence of corruption. The Liberals grew nervous, withdrawing their support and forcing MacDonald to dissolve Parliament. The 1924 election campaign saw one of the shabbiest scandals of British politics – the Zinoviev letter (see p. 748). Chilling press warnings that a vote for Labour was a vote for a Soviet system saw the Establishment regain its hold on the tiller.

Yet the value of Parliament to working-class aspirations was underlined in the abysmal failure of the 1926 General Strike, which renewed commitment to the Labour Party. With 288 seats it emerged from the 1929 election as the largest single party; it was a turning point in British politics. The Liberals had crossed the electoral Rubicon, the bias of the electoral system beginning to weigh against them. Their future seemed to lie only in some form of union with Labour and a second minority government was formed, though for the Liberals the embrace was to be that of the praying mantis.

MacDonald's disgrace

However, Labour was also to encounter troubled waters. From the outset the government was severely hamstrung by the Liberals in the Commons and the Conservatives in the Lords. Problems were exacerbated by economic depression, the Cabinet split over expenditure cuts (particularly unemployment benefit) as a condition of international loans and, on 23 August 1931, MacDonald resigned as prime minister. However, the following day he stunned colleagues by accepting the King's invitation to form a Conservative-dominated *National Government*. Together with some followers he was disowned by his party and in the coalition became a prisoner of his Cabinet. He was obliged to fight the next election (1931) in the grip of the coalition; 'National candidates' sought a 'doctor's mandate' to heal the country's maladies. Labour fared disastrously with only 46 seats and Conservatives dominated the new coalition. For Labour, these events marked the end of an era,

Sit down, man, you're a bloody tragedy.
Cry by MP James Maxton, during Ramsay MacDonald's last speech in Parliament

fortunes remaining at a low ebb until the 1935 election. Ex-barrister Clement Attlee became leader, the first to lack genuine working-class credentials, and although not recovering its 1929 position, the party revived with 154 seats, while the Liberals drifted further into the wilderness.

The Liberals: decline and fall

The collapse of the Liberal Party remains one of the cautionary tales of British politics. Despite a landslide victory in 1906 and a period of great reform, a decade after the outbreak of the war it had a parliamentary presence of only forty-two. There is no simple explanation. One historian likened the demise to that of a frail old gent, troubled by a variety of serious ailments (Labour, suffragettes, Ireland), with misfortunes compounded by a meeting with a rampaging bus (the war); his state of health is easy to diagnose but not the actual cause of death (Wilson 1966: 20–1). In this political whodunit a number of suspects may be assembled along with the butler in the drawing room:

- a congenital tendency to fragment;
- strong personalities whose ambitions overrode party interest;
- the prolonged fight with the suffragettes;
- the misfortune to be in office at the outbreak of the war;
- an inability to adapt to a harsher twentieth-century climate (see Dangerfield 1936);
- the loss of radical reformers like Chamberlain, Dilke, Churchill and Lloyd George;
- a healing of the old social cleavage between landowners and capitalists, who began to unite as Conservatives (Taylor 1965: 172);
- the failure to embrace leading Labour figures;
- a willingness to allow Labour to gather strength through electoral pacts (Wilson 1966: 19);
- defections to Labour in the inter-war years;
- the British electoral system.

War and the end of an era

Once again war intervened, leading to Labour's further entrenchment. Agreeing to join a coalition, provided it would not be led by Neville Chamberlain (discredited for his appeasement policy), it could claim to have brought Winston Churchill (by now a Conservative) to power. It did well in the apportionment of offices, with Attlee and Greenwood both in Churchill's first war cabinet of five. Attlee became generally recognized as deputy prime minister.

During the inter-war years a number of small parties emerged. The Communist Party was founded in 1920, though its attempts to affiliate to Labour were rebuffed. Welsh nationalism was reflected in the establishment of Plaid Cymru in 1925.

Nationalism was stronger in Scotland, coalescing into a party in 1928. In 1932, Oswald Mosley left the Conservatives to found the British Union of Fascists, which grew to over 30,000 members.

The Era of Consensus: the End of Ideology?

After the war Churchill agreed to an early general election. The 1945 result gave every indication of a revolution in British politics, a Labour landslide producing its first overall majority. The swing in the marginal seats introduced a new kind of Labour MP, drawn from the professions and giving the PLP a broader character. Despite a regime of severe post-war austerity, the government embarked upon an agenda intended to shake the foundations of economic and social life with a range of welfare reforms envisaged in the 1942 Beveridge Report. The aura of office increased the leader's authority, further buttressed by trade union loyalty, but Attlee remained anxious for establishment respect, reining in socialistic expectations and even expelling extreme left-wingers.

The popular verdict prompted alarmist talk in middle-class drawing rooms and concentrated Conservative minds, enabling them again to demonstrate the protean qualities that preserved them throughout the era of modern politics. The architect of recovery was R. A. Butler, whose strategy was to challenge Labour at its own game by embracing the new agenda.

By the end of its first hectic term the government was showing fatigue strains; many stalwarts were past their prime, some stricken with illness and some dead. Furthermore, people were weary of austerity. In 1950 Labour narrowly clung to office but, lacking confidence, Attlee returned to the country the following year. This time, although Labour polled more votes than had ever previously been cast for a British party, the electoral system produced a Conservative parliamentary majority. Butler had fashioned a bipartisan consensus that began a peace spoken of by the Archbishop of York in Shakespeare's *Henry IV*, when 'both parties nobly are subdued, and neither party loser'. Termed 'Butskellism', by combining the names of two significant party figures, it characterized a period when both parties accepted the principal tenets of the welfare state and Keynesian economics.

Yet the tranquil consensus interpretation can be misleading; a minority within Labour, led by Aneurin Bevan, was never comfortable pitching the manifesto tent in the middle of the ideological field and this prompted enervating infighting. After tenacious resistance, Attlee finally departed in 1955. His replacement, the sternly moderate Hugh Gaitskell, inherited worsening disciplinary problems. Moreover, the supportive trade union old guard was passing on and the largest union, the TGWU, had fallen under the leadership of left-winger Frank Cousins.

The masters now
We are the masters at the moment – and not only for the moment but for a very long time to come.
Sir Hartley (later Lord) Shawcross (1902–2003; member of 1945 Labour government), Commons speech (2 April 1946)

Some Conservatives were also unhappy with consensus. When Churchill finally stepped down, party and government had seemed healthy and the succession passed to the smoothly aristocratic Anthony Eden. Yet despite an early election success in 1955, domestic problems mounted, his popularity rating nose-dived and he was certainly in no state to handle the Suez Crisis in 1956 (see p. 138), which traumatized the Establishment and split the party. Retiring in humiliation, Eden left a party in morbid contemplation of loss of office and possibly two decades in the wilderness.

Winds of change: the Macmillan era

> By far the most radical man I've known in politics wasn't on the Labour side at all – Harold Macmillan. If it hadn't been for the war he'd have joined the Labour Party. . . Macmillan would have been Labour Prime Minister, and not me.
>
> Clement Attlee, quoted in James Margach, *The Abuse of Power* (1981)

The wind of change is blowing through the continent. Whether we like it or not, this growth of national consciousness is a political fact.
Harold Macmillan, speech in South African Parliament (3 Feb. 1960)

Eden's departure exposed the arcane process whereby the Conservatives chose their leader. Party elders conducted soundings and Harold Macmillan was preferred over the diligent Butler. Yet the succession was to prove inspired. With an Edwardian dilettantism concealing shrewd recognition of the consensus era, he was able not only to rebuild the party substructure but modernize its facade. He also restored self-confidence at home and repaired the damage to Anglo-American relations, earning the cartoonists' moniker 'Super Mac'. Yet despite his success the right mistrusted him. In 1960 the hostile Monday Club formed to lament 'Black Monday', when he made a celebrated speech on reform in racist South Africa.

Labour in the wilderness

The Suez crisis proved no help to Labour. Although shocking the intelligentsia, a popular jingoism was shared by many Labour supporters. In 1959 the Conservative majority reached 100, a third successive defeat leaving Labour reeling. The post-war inheritance seemed to have been squandered and younger members began to talk of policy revision. In *The Future of Socialism* (1956), Anthony Crosland

> Do you think that we can become overnight the pacifists, unilateralists and fellow travellers that other people are? . . . some of us . . . will fight, fight and fight again to save the party we love.
>
> Hugh Gaitskell, speech to Labour Party Conference (5 Oct. 1960)

argued that in an age of affluence public ownership was an anachronism. Gaitskell agreed, confronting the left in a momentous 1960 party conference, where he suffered an heroic failure to remove Clause Four from the party constitution. He was more successful in rejecting unilateral nuclear disarmament as party policy the following year.

The Night of the Long Knives

The government had its own troubles. On 13 July 1962, beset by economic problems and falling popularity, a desperate Macmillan reversed the action of *Julius Caesar*, removing one-third of his Cabinet in the greatest bloodbath in the party's history: 'The Night of the Long Knives'. However, it was the exotic Profumo affair that brought the leader's failing touch to a wider, tabloid-devouring public. The party's image was also not helped by the early 1960s penchant for cynicism and satire. Oxbridge undergraduates began poking fun at the Establishment in the theatre (*Beyond the Fringe*), in the press (*Private Eye*) and on television (*That Was The Week That Was*).

> **Scandal**
> The **Profumo scandal** arose from an intriguing *ménage à trois* involving a defence minister, John Profumo, who resigned in 1963, a high-society prostitute (Christine Keeler), a Russian naval attaché and a host of exotic bit players including Mandy Rice Davies (a prostitute), Stephen Ward (an alleged procurer of ladies for the gentry) and a mysterious man (believed to be a respected pillar of the Establishment) featured in photographs wearing a black mask (and little else). It is doubtful if the public were concerned with the security aspects of the affair. The massive newspaper coverage showed the main interest to lie in the intoxicating contemplation of hanky-panky in high places.

Constitutional change in the Conservative Party

Macmillan's retirement through ill-health in 1963 led to controversy. The patient Butler was again the natural heir, but the aristocratic Sir Alec Douglas-Home was raised from entombment in the House of Lords by renouncing his title. He continued the party's Tory rather than its Whig strain but seemed out of touch with the *Zeitgeist*. In the 1964 election campaign, Harold Wilson, Labour's adroit new leader, mocked Home's aristocratic antecedents. Labour won a narrow majority of four; with a different leader the Conservatives might have secured a fourth term. It was agreed that a ballot of the parliamentary party should become the basis for leadership selection and Home resigned.

He is used to dealing with estate workers. I cannot see how anyone can say he is out of touch.
Lady Caroline Douglas-Home, speaking of her father's suitability as prime minister, quoted in the *Daily Herald* (21 Oct. 1963)

The white heat of technology: the Wilson era

> The Labour Party is like a stage coach. If you rattle along at great speed everybody inside is too exhilarated or too seasick to cause any trouble. But if you stop everybody gets out and argues about where to go next.
>
> Harold Wilson, quoted in Leslie Smith, *Harold Wilson: The Authentic Portrait* (1964)

Having acceded to the Labour leadership in 1963 as a result of Gaitskell's unexpected death, Wilson brought a more conciliatory tone, his style said to have been modelled on the charismatic and youthful President Kennedy. Confident enough to ask for a stronger mandate in 1966, he increased Labour's overall majority to ninety-six, the influx of middle-class professionals reinforcing his 'white heat of technology' rhetoric. Although the left were dissatisfied, the party began to look more like a 'natural' party of government during this optimistic decade – the 'swinging sixties'. There was some surprise when the government was ejected in 1970 and the glittering decade closed.

On the fringe

During the consensus era the Liberal Party had been no more than a bit player, to some a buffoon, to others a figure of tragedy. In the bipartisan scenario it had no place, being neither regionally based nor radical. In Northern Ireland Sinn Féin reappeared as a political force in 1955, contesting all twelve seats (although their three successful candidates were disqualified as felons). In 1970 the Social Democratic Labour Party (SDLP) was founded as the moderate vehicle of the Roman Catholic minority. At the same time, cracks began to appear in the Ulster Unionist Party, which had dominated Northern Ireland's Westminster representation: Ian Paisley, standing as a Protestant Unionist, captured the North Antrim seat (see chapter 20).

Heath: towards neoliberalism

Conscious of Wilson's appeal, the Conservatives had applied Newton's Law of Motion to politics by attempting to counter with an equal and opposite force. Edward Heath, the first leader to be elected, was also the first hailing from the party's *petit bourgeois* strain and he worked to manufacture a technocratic image. Pulling off an unexpected coup and surprising his own party as much as his opponents, he gained an overall majority of thirty seats in 1970.

A long-standing Europhile, he led the nation into the EEC in 1973 and moved towards a neoliberal economic agenda at home. However, inflation and rising unemployment led to policy reversals, branded 'U-turns' and taken as evidence of weakness. In the face of unrelenting union hostility he called an ill-timed general election in February 1974, asking 'Who governs?' Although a majority supported him, the electoral system again thwarted voters. Yet Labour lacked an absolute majority and Heath flirted with the Liberals over a possible pact before conceding defeat. The indeterminate situation forced Wilson to return to the country in October, but an overall majority of only three did little to clarify the confusion. The efficacy of two-party politics was beginning to look doubtful.

In April 1976 Wilson shocked his party with his unexpected retirement, bequeathing to James Callaghan bad union relations, economic crisis, IMF-imposed monetarism (see p. 564) and public-sector strikes. By-election defeats rendered the government increasingly fragile, until it could be sustained only with the life-support machine of the 1977/8 Lib–Lab pact. All was to culminate in some cold and gloomy months of 1978/9 – the 'winter of discontent' – with the media and some academics proclaiming a crisis of governability. The government finally lost a no-confidence vote in March 1979 and the Conservatives returned rejuvenated. Again they had used their time in the reformatory of opposition gainfully, emerging ready to take British politics into a new era.

'No such thing as society': the coming of Thatcherism

Heath's humiliation in 1974 had led to further ordeal by election and in February 1975 he lost the leadership of his party to Margaret Thatcher. As a grocer's daughter she was clearly in the same *petit bourgeois* line and was to seize radical initiatives on all fronts. The objective was no less than a frontal assault on post-war social democratic orthodoxy. She was advised by think-tanks where, outside the formal party machinery, the alchemy of neoliberalism was brewing that was to alter the course of British politics. The 1979 general election was critical. The new leader avowed that, as a woman, she would be permitted just one chance, and the spoils of victory promised riches in the form of a gushing supply of North Sea oil, available for generous tax cuts or increased welfare spending, according to political fancy. Thatcher also recognized the increasing importance of the mass media, engaging Saatchi and Saatchi to harness the skills of Madison Avenue. The result was a sixty-seat majority over Labour, and Britain's first woman prime minister.

Any woman who understands the problems of running a home will be nearer to understanding the problems of running a country.
Margaret Thatcher, quoted in the *Observer* (8 May 1979)

The Thatcher Era: Fractured Consensus or New Centre?

Initially the new programme faltered; the Cabinet contained a large contingent of 'wets' inherited from Heath, who impeded progress. Unemployment rose and Thatcher's popularity sank to an all-time low for a prime minister. However, a lifeline came from the South Atlantic, the Falklands crisis giving her the boost she needed; in an upsurge of popular chauvinism her ascendancy became virtually absolute. The years between 1983 and 1987 saw an ideological flowering of the New Right, though people spoke not of conservatism but of 'Thatcherism'. The 1987 general election gave the Conservatives a third term with a majority over Labour of 147. However, the pattern of support was becoming increasingly concentrated in the prosperous south-east. In asserting 'there is no such thing as society' Thatcher had renounced the party's 'one-nation' appeal.

As if on a see-saw, the fortunes of Labour sank as Conservative stock rose. Michael Foot, once a doyen of the left, replaced Callaghan as leader in 1980 but deep fissures remained within the party over Europe, the unions and the economy (see Meredith 2008). For some the left-wing pressures became too great: choosing flight rather than fight, in March 1981 they founded the Social Democratic Party (SDP) with a mission to reclaim the centre ground. Labour's 1983 manifesto was described from the right as 'the longest suicide note in history'. In the final stages of the campaign the party's support began to wilt before the new centrist force and only the quirks of the electoral system ensured its survival (figure 13.1). Foot resigned and Neil Kinnock, who had moved to the centre, was elected leader. Though fighting a much better campaign in 1987, the result was again failure.

On the fringe, the Ecology Party re-launched itself in 1985 as the Green Party, achieving some success in local elections. National Front support fell away, partly won over by Thatcher's brand of Conservatism, and internal splits saw it re-emerge in 1983 as the British National Party (BNP).

The rise of the third force

Growing from a rib plucked from Labour's breast, the SDP appeared as one of the most dramatic post-war party developments. Dubbed 'the Gang of Four', its leading figures were seasoned parliamentarians and their rhetoric spoke of 'breaking the mould' of **adversarial politics** and re-introducing consensus through European-style coalitions (supported by electoral reform). By late 1981 its mass membership had mushroomed to some 70,000 and the party scored some notable by-election victories, including the return of Gang members Shirley Williams and Roy Jenkins.

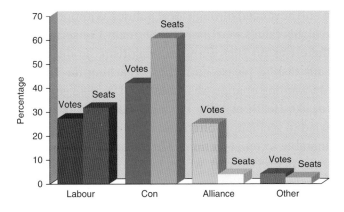

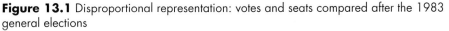

Figure 13.1 Disproportional representation: votes and seats compared after the 1983 general elections

Developments gave new heart to the Liberals and in 1983 and 1987 the two parties fought under a common Alliance banner. However, the electoral system denied them a parliamentary representation proportionate to their vote (figure 13.1). Liberal leader David Steel opened discussions on complete merger, which took place in March 1988, Paddy Ashdown was elected leader, and an all-member ballot adopted the name Social and Liberal Democrats.

The end of an era

Events in late 1990 were to rock the Conservatives. Dramatic resignations by Chancellor Nigel Lawson and Geoffrey Howe (deputy prime minister) intimated that all was not well in Cabinet, the main source of dissatisfaction being Thatcher's lukewarm European vision and her domineering style. Fierce hostility towards the poll tax had seen her popularity plummet below 30 per cent. A leadership challenge by Michael Heseltine forced a humiliating second ballot and, after consulting her cabinet colleagues individually, Thatcher made the decision to resign. John Major emerged from the shadows as the new leader, rewarding Heseltine with a cabinet seat. Thus, the longest premiership since 1827, marked by three electoral triumphs and dramatic policy advances, was terminated not by the electorate nor the party rank and file, but by the Conservative establishment in perhaps the most brutal political knifing in modern political history. The wound was to fester into the next era.

The Major years: things fall apart

Major's succession continued the trend away from the party's aristocratic roots. In contrast to his two main rivals, he had left school at sixteen, experienced

But there was one more duty I had to perform, and that was to ensure that John Major was my successor. I wanted – perhaps I needed – to believe that he was the man to secure and safeguard my legacy.
Margaret Thatcher,
The Downing Street Years (1993: 860)

unemployment and advanced through local politics. Without Thatcher's confrontational style or zeal, his values were more traditionally Conservative. When Thatcher asserted that there was no such thing as 'Majorism' he did not dissent (Norton 1993a: 60). Yet his task to please both those yearning for Thatcherism by other means and those wanting change was daunting. His 1992 general election victory was unexpected; like Heath in 1970, he could take considerable personal credit. Yet pragmatism led to vacillation, often described as dithering, and a flimsy majority left him vulnerable to rebel factions. The most troublesome of these were the Eurosceptics (some in his Cabinet), whom he described, in an unguarded moment at a BBC studio, as 'bastards'.

Major's enemies were emboldened with a sense of mission and the fires were fanned by newspaper editors who did little to conceal personal dislike of the Prime Minister. Ratification of the Maastricht Treaty was a tense process and did not end his problems. The humiliation of 'Black Wednesday' (see pp. 565–6) was seen as a defining moment of a blighted premiership. Tensions reached a crescendo in June 1995 when, in an astonishing resignation of the party leadership, Major threw down the gauntlet, demanding that his critics 'put up or shut up'. His endorsement was only lukewarm.

New Labour, New Consensus

> The Great Parliamentary Sausage Machine which sucked in public opinion at one end and spewed out popular politics at the other.
>
> Roy Hattersley, retrospectively, on the 'Labour Listens' initiative, in *Who Goes Home?* (1996: 284)

It had been apparent to Labour leaders that the party was no longer tuned to the march of history. The New Right agenda was recognized throughout Europe by socialist parties in or out of government. Even the USSR had fallen under the *perestroika* of Mikhail Gorbachev, who had established a surprising rapport with Thatcher. The hard left saw any attempt to don Thatcher's clothes as a perverse form of transvestism, but a policy of expulsion removed some 200 of them. By 1989 opinion polls were consistently placing Labour in the lead, but an unexpected fourth successive defeat in 1992 left many to ponder whether Britain had become a one-party state. Some declared Kinnock's triumphalist behaviour to have snatched defeat from the jaws of victory.

Kinnock's successor, John Smith, slid into place to continue the modernization project of widening the appeal of the party and two fresh-faced MPs joined the

National Executive Committee: Tony Blair and Gordon Brown. Smith's untimely death in 1994 was to foreshadow an era of Labour power that few would have imagined possible. In determining the succession the most important move, reportedly made in the Islington restaurant Granita, was the agreement of Shadow Chancellor Gordon Brown to stand aside in favour of Tony Blair to avoid splitting the modernizing vote. The result came as no surprise, Blair being supported by all sections of the party's electoral college.

Trust me, I'm a spin doctor

Unlike Kinnock, or even Major, Blair sported no working-class credentials. Educated at Fettes College, Edinburgh, one of Scotland's foremost private schools, he had progressed via St John's College, Oxford, to become a barrister, entering Parliament as MP for Sedgefield in 1983. Like all his generation he was starved of office but had shadowed some key areas. Just forty, and with a barrister's verbosity, a careerist wife, Cherie, two sons and a daughter, he was a spin doctor's dream. If Blair had a model it was that of Labour's nemesis, Margaret Thatcher. Master of the soundbite, he spoke of 'fairness not favours' for the unions, no more 'tax and spend' on the economy and, on Labour's other Achilles' heel, he would be 'tough on crime and tough on the causes of crime'. In industrial disputes he studiously withheld support from strikers while seeking the confidence of business leaders, even wooing media baron Rupert Murdoch. The mission was to reassure 'middle England'. He took a tough line with dissidents and, in perhaps the most symbolic act, succeeded where Gaitskell had failed. On 29 April 1995, at a special conference at Methodist Central Hall, Westminster, where seventy-five years earlier the original Clause Four of the party constitution had been adopted, the party voted for its reform.

Within a short time, party membership had risen substantially (table 13.1) and Blair's own popularity dwarfed that of Major and Ashdown (Dorey 1995: 258). For critics, 'New Labour' showed more froth than substance. The spin doctors dispensed with ideology to follow the beacon of the opinion polls. At their head was Peter Mandelson (grandson of earlier Labour moderate Herbert (later Lord)

To create . . . a community in which power, wealth and opportunity to be in the hands of the many not the few.
Part of the reformed version of Clause Four of Labour's constitution

Table 13.1 Increase in Labour Party support, 1992–1996		
Category	**1992**	**1996**
Members	279,000	400,000
Donors	3,500	71,000
Sponsors	30,000	60,000
Source: Data from Labour Party NEC reports.		

Morrison) and Blair's press guru, Alastair Campbell. There was a particular emphasis on the control of information (see Kettell 2006).

The acid test arrived with the general election of May 1997. Although suggested by the polls, the sheer size of the majority came as a shock, with 418 seats to the Conservatives' 165. Modernizers saw it as an overwhelming endorsement of their strategy. If symbols were needed they were aplenty. At the 1998 Labour conference, avowedly the last at Blackpool, with its old Labour odour of fish and chips, delegates wore name badges sponsored by a supermarket chain (though some refused), while journalists from the radical magazine *Red Pepper* were banned.

Conservative meltdown

Entirely banished from the Celtic fringes, the Conservatives suffered their worst defeat since 1832. It meant the end for Major and within hours hats were in the ring, from which the young William Hague emerged (see pp. 332–3) to lead the party through what some commentators saw as the Conservatives' 'most futile period of opposition in the last one hundred years' (Collings and Seldon 2001: 624).

The Liberal Democrats had enjoyed a string of by-election successes and, during the 1992 campaign, Ashdown had consistently outscored the other leaders. With twenty MPs, a rising membership and a more secure financial position, the party was poised for progress. In addition, with two seats in the 1994 Euro-elections, there was a breakthrough onto the EU stage. (The Greens, with the same percentage vote, gained none.) The 1997 general election result produced the biggest third-party breakthrough of post-war history, their forty-six seats promising to become significant should Labour cohesion melt in the heat of internal friction.

On the fringe

The 1992 general election saw nationalist support remaining stable. With four seats Plaid Cymru was one up on 1987 and the Scottish Nationalists (SNP) maintained their three. As Major's majority shrank the parliamentary significance of the Ulster Unionists had increased until, just before the 1997 election, they held the balance of power. In 1997, Plaid Cymru retained their four seats and the SNP gained another three. However, devolution was to mean a changed climate for the nationalists (see chapter 20).

Eurosceptic feeling led to the formation of two single-issue parties committed to withdrawal from the EU. The UK Independence Party (UKIP), set up in 1993, was initially overshadowed by the Referendum Party of wealthy Eurosceptic businessman Sir James Goldsmith. After his death UKIP increased its membership to almost 10,000. It gained three MEPs in 1999, but in the 2001 general election all but six of its

428 candidates were to lose their deposits. The Greens mainly made their presence felt more as a pressure group, greening the agendas of the main parties. As with UKIP, it was PR that gave them real opportunities – two MEPs, one MSP and three Greater London councillors were to carry the green flag.

Life was bleak on the far left. Britain's Communist Party had declined since the 1950s, relaunching itself in 1991 as the Democratic Left with some 6,000 members – more a pressure group than a party. Militant Tendency and the Socialist Workers' Party also found little resonance with the times. On the far right, the BNP caused ripples by winning a council seat in east London in 1993, and in 2001 it was to gain over 16 per cent of the vote in Oldham.

These are my principles, and if you don't like them I've got others.
Attributed to Groucho Marx (1890–1977; comedian)

From Butskellism to Blatcherism?

Finally back in power, Labour hit the ground running. The 1997 Queen's Speech detailed twenty-two bills covering a wide range of areas. However, the government had chosen a procrustean bed in its promise to preserve Conservative spending limits. It would be difficult to find a better indication of a return to consensus politics. For critics this was Thatcherism by other means. The economy would be led by the market, shaped and refined by the state rather than regulated. The policies were justified variously by reference to Christian values, communitarianism, stakeholding and a so-called 'third way' (see p. 45). Blair could argue that New Labour had come to terms with the modern world; in a globalizing economy, debates about the state versus the market were no longer appropriate platforms for economic thinking (Kenny and Smith 1997: 227–8). On the eve of the 2001 general election an *Observer*/ICM poll gave Blair an 18 per cent lead over Hague on the question 'Who would get the best deal for Britain in Europe?', the area the Conservative leader had tried to make his own.

Prior to the 1997 general election, the Liberal Democrats had been engaged in 'constructive opposition' and Paddy Ashdown had been having secret talks with Blair, in the hope of a possible coalition. The size of the Labour majority ruled this out and in January 1999 Ashdown stunned his party by announcing his retirement. Charles Kennedy assumed the leadership and there was a further cooling in the party's relationship with Labour.

With Blair having so successfully plundered the centre-right wardrobe, the Conservatives could find little to wear. It had been a party of empire but this was gone. It had been a party of the Union but had no MPs in either Wales or Scotland, and devolution was now a bitter pill that could only be swallowed. It had been a party of high moral values but was now mired in sleaze. It had been a party of constitutional stability but Labour was instigating change on many fronts. Europe was divisive and there were fears that the party could split as it had over the Corn Laws in 1846, which had been followed by twenty-seven wilderness years.

An historic second term: from Ramsay MacDonald to Ronald McDonald

The 2001 general election proved a particularly significant triumph for Labour, yielding 413 seats with (only) 42 per cent of the vote. The party appeared to have established itself as one that business could trust. The transformation was symbolized at the September 2001 conference, with the logo of the sponsoring fast-food chain prominently displayed inside the hall. However, this was not the Labour Party of old, and the cost of victory was disenchantment in the old working-class heartlands, where support had fallen by 4 percentage points (Curtice 2001). Relations with the trade unions were becoming less harmonious and Blair's parliamentary troops were becoming increasingly rebellious (see Cowley 2005). It was an appalling election night for the Conservatives, who managed to gain only one extra seat, raising their Commons force to 166. In defeat Hague took the immediate decision to fall upon his sword, securing for himself an unenviable place in history as the first Conservative leader for eighty years not to have been prime minister.

Who's for the poisoned chalice? The Tory leadership after Major

Hague's departure plunged the Conservatives into a leadership contest using an untried method of election (see p. 332). The most likely heir apparent, Michael Portillo, launched his bid with a reception in a glitzy London restaurant. With charisma to spare and, despite relative youth, considerable government experience, he exuded an aura of success and seemed the man most likely to heal the party's wounds. However, knives were sharpened as high ambition met low intrigue in the Westminster hothouse. The final 1922 Committee ballot delivered the knockout blow: the two contenders to go before the wider party membership would be Kenneth Clarke and Iain Duncan Smith. Again, the MPs had rejected the candidate most feared by their opponents. Final victory went to Duncan Smith, who had been one of the Eurosceptic 'bastards' damaging the party's chances in 1997. However, the change did little to revive the party's standing in the opinion polls. The new leader's lack of charisma led him to take refuge in an image of the 'quiet man', silent but inwardly strong like John Wayne in a film of that name. The decibel level remained low and his tenure was to be short-lived.

Towards Coalition Government

Labour and Iraq

The euphoria of Labour's second-term achievement was soon to evaporate as the government became embroiled in a complex web of intrigue, half-truths and ministerial resignations surrounding the highly controversial decision to support US President George W. Bush in invading Iraq in 2003. It was the beginning of the end of the Blair era. Events moved ominously towards war, with the USA loath to seek a solution through the UN. Ignoring the opinion of European leaders, and the largest street demonstrations seen in modern times, Blair stood shoulder to shoulder with Bush while former Foreign Secretary Robin Cook and Development Secretary Clare Short resigned from the Cabinet and 139 Labour MPs rebelled in a critical Commons vote. However, the Conservatives supported Blair and the invasion went ahead. In a remarkably short time the conflict was said to be over and in December 2003 Saddam Hussein was captured and gruesomely executed.

Careful post-war inspection failed to find the alleged weapons of mass destruction (WMD) and critics proclaimed a foreign relations disaster greater than Suez. Indeed, in terms of deaths and suffering it was of a quite different magnitude. At the 2003 party conference Blair echoed Thatcher's 'the lady's not for turning' boast with the assertion that he had 'no reverse gear'. However, the claim became embarrassing as, with Sunni insurgents and Shia death squads kidnapping, bombing and

If this is not a civil war, then God knows what a civil war is.
Iyad Allawi, Iraq's former interim PM, speaking on BBC TV (19 March 2006)

torturing, the Iraq road looked increasingly like a cul-de-sac. Labour approached the 2005 general election under a cloud but, with 356 seats from 36 per cent of the vote, again benefited from the electoral system. Given the circumstances, it remained a remarkable testimony to the political skills of the leader as well as the fact that the Conservatives had, unlike the Liberal Democrats, also supported the invasion.

A 'dodgy dossier', a suicide and two resignations

In September 2002, in an effort to strengthen public support, the government released a dossier which it claimed would detail the threat posed by Iraq. This chillingly asserted that the country possessed weapons of mass destruction ready to be deployed against the people of Britain (or any other country) within 45 minutes. This was contrary to the reports of UN weapons inspectors working in Iraq. BBC journalist Andrew Gilligan reported an assertion of a high-ranking government official that the dossier had been 'sexed up' by government spin doctors. The source of the leak was discovered and his name allowed to enter the public domain. Subsequent events saw David Kelly, an experienced member of the Iraq weapons inspectorate, brought before the Commons defence committee for a public grilling. Pressure apparently led to his suicide. Further dramatic events followed the report of Lord Hutton, appointed by the government to investigate. To the surprise of many, this largely exonerated the government while castigating the BBC, leading to the resignations of both Director General and Chairman of the board of governors.

Conservatives: finding the Blair antidote

From being one of those forcing Major into his 'back me or sack me' challenge, Duncan Smith too was forced, in October 2003, to throw down the gauntlet before detractors. Unlike Major in 1995, his position was precarious. The twenty-five names required to force a no-confidence vote came forward, some delivered with a flourish to the 1922 Committee office and others dispatched furtively in plain envelopes. The vote was to prove fatal, heralding the fourth leadership change in eight years. Former home secretary and Shadow Chancellor Michael Howard praised Duncan Smith's 'courage and dignity' but there was little surprise when he emerged as the favourite and his enthronement was uncontested.

Yet Howard failed to make any serious dent in the Prime Minister's armour and the 2005 general election defeat was his signal to go. It was almost with relish that he announced his intention to make way for a younger leader, while making a significant shadow cabinet reshuffle and bringing in the relatively unknown

Conservative Party leaders since 1900	
1900 Marquis of Salisbury	1957 Harold Macmillan
1902 Arthur Balfour	1963 Alec Douglas-Home
1911 Andrew Bonar Law	1965 Edward Heath
1921 Austen Chamberlain	1975 Margaret Thatcher
1922 Andrew Bonar Law	1990 John Major
1923 Stanley Baldwin	1997 William Hague
1937 Neville Chamberlain	2001 Iain Duncan Smith
1940 Winston Churchill	2003 Michael Howard
1955 Anthony Eden	2005 David Cameron

The centre ground has always been a morass.
Norman Tebbit (former Conservative Party Chairman) on David Cameron's attempt to reposition the party, in the *Independent* (31 Jan. 2006)

David Cameron. The favourite candidate was Shadow Home Secretary David Davis, but at the party conference in Blackpool Cameron seized the initiative with a barnstorming speech. The result, in December 2005, was humiliation for Davis.

Born in 1966, Cameron could be seen as the party's antidote to Blair. Eton- and Oxbridge-educated, young, media friendly and entering Parliament in 2001 as MP for Witney in Oxfordshire, his rise had been rapid. Deputy Chairman of the party by 2003, he had become a front-bench spokesman the following year. Like Blair his rhetoric suggested a readiness to ditch party shibboleths, aiming to shift the party towards the centre ground. His supporters rejoiced that for the first time since 1992 the party had a leader untainted by Black Wednesday. Yet those with better memories could recall that he had been an economic adviser to Chancellor Norman Lamont at that very time.

Liberal Democrats: youth to the helm

The Liberal Democrat parliamentary cadre had risen to fifty-two in 2001. With both major parties now tarnished by Iraq, in disarray over their leaderships and with festering policy divisions, the party approached the 2005 general election with hopes of supplanting the Conservatives as the main opposition. Their key strategy was to target constituencies with large Muslim populations. The result was 22 per cent of the vote, delivering sixty-two seats, the highest number for a party bearing the name Liberal since 1923. Despite this success it was felt that Charles Kennedy had not made the most of a unique electoral opportunity. A deeper problem was his revelation in January 2006 that he was dealing with a continuing alcohol problem. Treasury spokesman Vince Cable promised to deliver a letter signed by ten frontbenchers calling for his resignation. The dispatch appeared brutal. His remaining supporters alleged him to be victim of a vicious *coup* by allies of heir apparent

Liberal/Liberal Democrat leaders since 1900	
1900 Henry Campbell-Bannerman	1967 Jeremy Thorpe
1908 Herbert Asquith	1976 David Steel
1926 David Lloyd George	1988 Paddy Ashdown
1931 Herbert Samuel	1999 Charles Kennedy
1935 Archibald Sinclair	2005 Menzies Campbell
1945 Clement Davies	2007 Nick Clegg
1956 Jo Grimond	

and deputy leader Sir Menzies Campbell, whom they dubbed 'Ming the Merciless'. Instrumental in the outcome had been Nick Clegg's decision not to stand against Campbell.

Yet the matter was not settled. Apart from his age (64), Campbell's very manner, that of the pin-striped Scottish lawyer, made him appear almost a figure from a bygone age. The gravitas he had exuded as foreign affairs spokesman seemed to elude him and in October 2007 he announced his resignation after a tenure of only nineteen months. The man who took over as interim leader declined to stand on the grounds that, in his mid-sixties, he could hardly expect to succeed one moving aside on the grounds of age. Yet, with parliamentary wit and perceptive economic understanding, Vince Cable was to shine and some colleagues (and perhaps the man himself) regretted his decision. The announcement of Clegg's victory over Chris Huhne in December 2007 fulfilled most media predictions.

> The House has noticed the remarkable transformation in the last few weeks from Stalin to Mr Bean, creating chaos out of order rather than order out of chaos.
>
> Question Time comment (28 Nov. 2007) by Vince Cable on Gordon Brown (previously dubbed 'Stalin') over his handling of a party funding scandal. Widely regarded as the best parliamentary put-down of the year

As former Manchester United manager Tommy Docherty said, 'We got beat four-nil and were lucky to get the nil'.
Colin Fox (SNP leader), on his party's 2005 result, quoted in *Red Pepper* (6 I May 2005)

At the fringe

Minority parties fared variously in the 2005 election. In Northern Ireland there was a move against the moderates but, in a surprising development, the polar extremes were to find it possible to work together as the peace process moved forward (p. 637). In Scotland the nationalists suffered an 18 per cent fall in votes but their tally of six seats exceeded predictions, while the Scottish Socialists saw their vote fall from 3 to 1 per cent. In Wales election night was bleak for Plaid Cymru, which failed to take a target seat and lost another, leaving them with three MPs.

There were mixed fortunes for English parties. In Bethnal Green and Bow, George Galloway (expelled from Labour for his opposition to the Iraq invasion), standing for his newly formed Respect Party, defeated Blairite loyalist Oona King. Although winning no seat, the Greens raised their vote. Despite fighting its biggest campaign, UKIP failed to make a breakthrough. On the far right the BNP made a modest surge to record its highest ever vote share in a parliamentary election. Its leader, Cambridge-educated Nick Griffin, had worked to de-toxify the party's 'tattooed skinhead' image.

Labour: Downing Street wars

It became apparent that the Granita deal carried a condition: at some point Blair would stand aside for Brown. However, in March 2006 he conceded on Australian radio that his promise not to fight another general election could have been a mistake. Bitter feuding continued between the two camps as Blair teased Brown by refusing to announce a departure date. The Blairites alleged that the Chancellor, with tentacles extending into every corner of Whitehall, was using the Treasury to derail his leader's policy designs. It was even suspected that he had stoked up the fires leading to a damaging loans-for-honours scandal. The two protagonists denied any animus, but their smiling joint public appearances failed to convince. Finally, in May 2007, Blair announced his retirement, ending an era that, in the view of many commentators, fell short of the promise of its opening years (see Seldon and Kavanagh 2005).

Blairites believed the Prime Minister had been pushed and wanted a fight for the leadership. From amongst the young Turks David Miliband was canvassed, but he held back. Eventually the desire for unity saw opposition fall away, producing a coronation rather than a contest. In June 2007, to a standing ovation from Labour MPs, Gordon Brown fulfilled a burning ambition to take control of the ship of state. More of an ideologue that Blair, Brown had grown up as a 'son of the manse' in Scotland. With an impressive academic background, he had entered Parliament in 1983 as MP for Dunfermline East and had established a formidable reputation. In terms of ministerial experience he appeared supremely well qualified, having served as a high-profile chancellor for the entire period of Labour government.

Alleging that Brown lacked a mandate, David Cameron called for an immediate general election and the party machines set themselves on stand-by. But with

I have come back here, to Sedgefield, to my constituency. Where my political journey began and where it is fitting it should end.

Opening of Tony Blair's retirement announcement in his constituency, widely quoted in the media (10 May 2007)

his popularity short-lived, Brown stepped back from the brink. In the Commons he began to look uncomfortable in the face of taunts by Cameron, while his first anniversary as prime minister coincided with the Henley by-election, when Labour suffered the ignominy of finishing fifth, trailing the Greens and the BNP and losing its deposit. The media detected a 'stench of death' around the government that was reminiscent of John Major's last days in office.

With some irony, the great global 'credit crunch', beginning in the autumn of 2008, presented Brown with a lifeline. This was an area where he appeared in command, acting promptly to inject equity into British banks and provide guarantees on bank debt in a bid to stimulate inter-bank lending. With global influence his actions were much praised by respected American economist and Nobel Prize winner Paul Krugman:

> Mr Brown and Alistair Darling . . . have defined the character of the worldwide rescue effort, with other wealthy nations playing catch-up. (*New York Times*, Oct. 2008)

However, the domestic test would be the general election in May 2010. Here his lack of campaigning savvy was palpable and the era of New Labour drew to a close.

Five days in May

Own Goal

That was a disaster – they should never have put me with that woman. Whose idea was that? Ridiculous. . . she was just a bigoted woman.

Gordon Brown's unfortunate electioneering gaffe after a pre-arranged meeting with a voter in April 2010

The 2010 general election was to produce the most dramatic constitutional development of the post-war era. From the start the opinion polls were issuing strong warnings of a hung parliament, a possibility strengthened by a major innovation in British campaigning. A series of US-style 'presidential' televised debates allowed the leaders of the three main parties to share a platform. As they debated and argued, Liberal Democrat leader Nick Clegg made a surge in the polls.

Coalition negotiations

In the event, with 57 seats (a loss of five), the Liberal Democrats did not fare as well as might have been expected (or deserved, with almost one-quarter of the popular vote). However, the Conservatives also failed to capitalize on Labour's travails and, with 306 MPs, fell short of the 326 required to dominate the Commons. Labour's tally of 258 was better than many expected and the hung parliament forecasts proved correct. Five days of feverish negotiation and speculation followed (Kavanagh and Cowley 2010: ch. 10). Labour argued that a coalition with the Liberal Democrats would be possible with the support of fringe parties and, aware of Clegg's antipathy towards him, Brown offered to resign his party's leadership. However, the arithmetic was always against this, and a coalition agreement (replacing their respective manifestos) was forged between the Liberal Democrats and Conservatives. A key feature of this was a commitment, dear to Liberal Democrat hearts, to a referendum on the electoral system.

Fraternity under test

Within the Labour Party Gordon Brown had little alternative but to resign and the party was thrown into a leadership contest. The claim to fraternity was tested quite literally when the two main contenders emerged as the brothers Miliband. Using its complex AV system the party elected Ed, although David had been the choice of the MPs and party members (see p. 335). It was the affiliated associations that finally swung the result on the fourth round, David retiring to the backbenches bitterly to rue previous occasions when he could have moved to seize the crown. In April 2013 his dislocation from British politics was completed with the announcement of his resignation from Parliament and the abandonment of the South Shields constituents he had vowed to serve. Arguing that his continued presence would be a 'distraction' to his brother's leadership, he accepted the appointment by the Chancellor of the Exchequer as Crown Steward and Bailiff of the Manor of Northstead (see p. 416).

Labour Party leaders		
1906 Keir Hardie	1922 Ramsay MacDonald	1980 Michael Foot
1908 Arthur Henderson	1931 Arthur Henderson	1983 Neil Kinnock
1910 George Barnes	1932 George Lansbury	1992 John Smith
1911 Ramsay MacDonald	1935 Clement Attlee	1994 Tony Blair
1914 Arthur Henderson	1955 Hugh Gaitskell	2007 Gordon Brown
1917 W. Adamson	1963 Harold Wilson	2010 Ed Miliband
1921 J. R. Clynes	1976 James Callaghan	

At the fringe

The 2010 general election saw two parties gaining their first-ever seats: party leader Caroline Lucas in Brighton Pavilion for the Greens and Naomi Long unseating the DUP's Peter Robinson in Belfast East for the Alliance Party of Northern Ireland. George Galloway also won Bradford West for his Respect Party.

Life in coalition

The coalition began in an atmosphere of harmony, with commentators remarking upon the similarity and personal chemistry of the two public-school-educated party leaders. Cameron's offer of five cabinet posts was certainly too good to refuse and Clegg was rewarded with the title Deputy Prime Minister. However,

'Best friends?' David Cameron and Nick Clegg in the Number Ten rose garden, May 2010

posing for the smiling photographs in the rose garden of Number Ten was the easy bit. The coalition promised substantial cuts in public expenditure, which were justified by ascribing the budget deficit largely to Labour mismanagement rather than the economic crisis rocking the world. Many of those who had voted Liberal Democrat had not anticipated the enthusiasm with which the party appeared to embrace the austerity agenda. Amidst various sources of discontent, one was toxic. The party had committed itself to phasing out university tuition fees and many MPs, including Clegg, had signed a National Union of Students pledge to this effect. However, with mass demonstrations in London and elsewhere against the policy of allowing universities to raise the cap from £3290 to £9000, Clegg experienced the fickle nature of popularity and some hard truths about coalition government.

The first nationwide barometer reading for the coalition came in the local elections of May 2011 – also the occasion for the promised referendum on the introduction of the AV electoral system. Campaigning turned nasty and some suspected fault lines in the coalition, with Clegg accusing the Conservative-dominated 'No' camp of peddling 'lies, misinformation and deceit'. Cameron appeared to renege on an agreement that the coalition leaders would not play central roles in the campaign. When votes were counted it was a nightmare for the Liberal Democrats.

The party lost nine of the English councils it controlled, including Sheffield, the city harbouring Clegg's own constituency. Even more demoralizing was a massive rejection of electoral reform, with only 32 per cent in favour of change. As the austerity agenda unfolded, the government became increasingly unpopular, despite some major U-turns. A second disappointment was to come for Clegg and his party in 2012, when another of their pet projects foundered – a bill for House of Lords reform being derailed by Conservative backbench opposition (see p. 408). His embittered party claimed that the Conservatives had broken the coalition agreement and in January 2013 the Liberal Democrats withheld support for the boundary changes bill, which would have benefited the Conservative Party. Two months later, the Liberal Democrats went so far as to ally themselves with Labour over plans to regulate the press following the Leveson report (see p. 244). The coalition was to experience a further shock in August 2013 in the rejection of the government's emergency motion over military intervention in Syria (see p. 458). Both coalition partners found backbencher support wavering. As events moved towards the 2015 general election, tension continued to mount, as their respective backbenchers voiced growing resentment against the compromises that life in coalition demanded. At the same time, Labour was not ruling out the possibility of a future coalition with the pivotal third party.

Britain's Party System

Under the influence of the first-past-the-post electoral system, a broadly **bipartisan** political pattern has evolved in Britain. This is held by apologists to have features peculiarly favourable to democracy and contrasted with West European multipartism. Much writing has extolled virtues such as strong single-party government and a regular alternation of governments in office. Yet these virtuous features can be subject to sceptical review.

The parties in Parliament

Strong single-party government has not invariably been the case. Although the May 2010 general election produced the first coalition since the second world war, the twentieth century saw some twenty-one years of rule by a combination of parties (see Driver 2011). Those formed under wartime conditions were marked by strength, not weakness. There have also been periods when a governing party, weakened by a lack of an absolute majority, has been sustained only by an agreement with another party. As recently as 1997, the Major government needed Ulster Unionist support. The notion that a bipartisan system produces frequent alternation in office is also unconvincing. In the early decades of the post–war era the Conservatives sustained the claim to be the natural party of government, with the lion's share of office (see figure 10.1). After 1997 the Labour Party had its own era of extended office, only to be ended by a coalition.

The parties in the country

Looking beyond Westminster, there is even less evidence of a two-party culture. Not until the immediate post-war decades did Labour and the Conservatives begin to carve up the popular vote, and the period was brought to an end with a groundswell of support for the nationalists and centre parties. Since the 1960s there has been an accelerating process of fragmentation. In 1983 and 1987 the Alliance polled around a quarter of the total votes, slightly less than Labour (28 and 30 per cent, respectively) and over half the number polled by the victorious Conservatives. In the 2010 general election, the national vote was shared fairly evenly between the three main parties (36 per cent for the Conservatives, 29 for Labour, and 23 for the Liberal Democrats). Another measure of party support is local government, where from the 1980s the Liberal Democrats could not be seen as a 'third party' in many areas.

The fragmentation has extended beyond the main three to a range of significant minor players. The BNP made progress in local government, achieved two MEPs in 2009, and fielded 338 Westminster candidates in 2010. The Green Party put up 335 candidates in 2010 and actually won a seat. George Galloway's Respect Party managed to survive into 2010 with eleven candidates and secured one seat. In 2010 the SNP and Plaid Cymru won nine seats between them and Northern Ireland parties gained a total of eighteen seats between them (Kavanagh and Cowley 2010: 350–2). Perhaps most significantly, UKIP broadened its appeal, gaining seats in the European Parliament, fielding as many as 558 Westminster candidates in 2010 and making dramatic advances in 2013 in by-elections and local elections.

The bipartisan nature of Parliament may be something of a distortion produced by the electoral system. If a system of proportional representation were ever to be introduced it could bring Britain to an historical watershed. Parties waiting in the wings would hear their cue, soliloquies and dialogues perhaps giving way to turbulent crowd scenes and a rather more colourful *dramatis personae*. However, following the result of the 2011 AV referendum, constitutional reformers would be advised not to hold their breath.

Key points

- The early British parties were loosely organized parliamentary cadres, becoming mass parties as a result of franchise extensions.

- From the first the Labour Party was a mass party.

- Labour made its early advances by working with the Liberals, whom it finally eclipsed as the main rival to the Conservatives.

- The early post-war years saw an era of party consensus around a welfare state and Keynesian economy.

- This lasted until the Thatcher premiership, which was sufficiently stamped with her personality to be designated an era.

- Labour moved leftward and some members cast adrift to form the Social Democratic Party.

- This was to merge with the Liberals to form the Liberal Democrats.

- Labour began moving back towards the centre, rebranded as 'New Labour'.

- In 1997 the party regained power and experienced its longest term of office. Tony Blair stamped his personality on the period.

- Amidst acrimony Blair passed the leadership to Gordon Brown, who was to preside over defeat in the 2010 general election.

- This produced a hung parliament and the formation of a peacetime coalition, which could, or could not, herald a new form of British politics.

Review your understanding of the following terms and concepts

adversary politics
bipartisan politics
Butskellism
cadre party
Clause Four
coalition
Eurosceptic

Fabianism
Gang of Four
Militant Tendency
minority government
modernizer
Night of the Long Knives
Profumo scandal

registration society
single-issue party
sleaze
Thatcherism
Tory
Whig

Questions for discussion and debate

Consider these propositions and be prepared to present the cases for and against. Try to produce debating propositions of your own.

1. The widening of the franchise was the key factor in the emergence of the modern political party.
2. Parties evolve largely by 'stealing each other's clothes'.
3. The Liberal Party was assailed by numerous forces.
4. The post-war era of party consensus could never have lasted.
5. Blair's modernization of the Labour Party was a master-class in modern statecraft.
6. A two-party system cannot adequately reflect a pluralist society.
7. The Liberal Democrats can never supplant either of the two main parties.
8. A charismatic leader is the key to a party's success.
9. There is more dissent within the main parties than between them.
10. There can be no long-term place for coalition government in British politics.

Further reading

Any historical account of developments in British politics will say much on the parties. In addition, biographies and diaries of leading figures can contain much on the friendships and rivalries. There are also studies of particular parties by both scholars and practising politicians. Some examples are given below but there are numerous other sources to discover. (See also reading for chapter 12.)

Bogdanor, V. (2011) *The Coalition and the Constitution.*
Short accessible book examining the significance of coalition government for Britain.

Childs, S. and Webb, P. (2011) *Sex, Gender and the Conservative Party: From Iron Lady to Kitten Heels.*
David Cameron's attempts to feminize his party.

Driver, S. (2011) *Understanding British Party Politics*.
Shows how multi-party politics had already established itself as a feature
of contemporary British political life well before the formation of the 2010 coalition.

Heppell, T. and Seawright, D. (eds) (2012) *Cameron and the Conservatives: The Transition to Coalition Government*.
Conservative perspective on the formation and early working of the 2010 coalition.

Jenkins, S. (2006) *Thatcher and Sons*.
Argues that Blair and Brown set out to consolidate and develop the Thatcher legacy.

Ludlam, S. and Smith, M. (eds) (2000) *New Labour in Government*.
Ludlam, S. and Smith, M. (eds) (2003) *Governing as New Labour*.
Examine this key era in British party politics.

Norton, P. (ed.) (1996) *The Conservative Party*.
Essays by academics and a Conservative MP. Editor's opening chapter probes deeper philosophical grounding.

Pelling, H. and Reid, A. J. (2005) *A Short History of the Labour Party*, 12th edn.
Clearly narrated and economical account of the rise of the party.

Shepherd, J. and Laybourn, K. (2013) *Britain's First Labour Government*.
Reassesses Ramsay MacDonald's tense reign as the first British Labour prime minister.

Toynbee, P. and Walker, D. (2001) *Did Things Get Better?*
An audit of New Labour's successes and failures. Title asks the question. Answer is sometimes 'yes', sometimes 'no'.

Wilson, I. (1966) *The Downfall of the Liberal Party 1914–1935*.
Probes a key event in modern political history.

For reading around the subject and some light relief

David Boothroyd, *The History of British Political Parties*.
History and background of every British party that has featured in British politics since 1832. Also looks at some of the more memorable participants in the party battles.

Jonathan Coe, *What a Carve Up!*
Satirical novel detailing the rising fortunes of the wealthy Winshaw family during the neoliberal revolution.

Benjamin Disraeli, *Sybil, or: the Two Nations.*
A romance by the great Conservative prime minister, celebrating his own vision of Toryism.

David Hare, *The Absence of War.*
Play showing the trials and frustrations of a Labour leader in a class-conscious society. Said to be based on Kinnock experience.

Alan Hollinghurst, *The Line of Beauty.*
Booker-Prize-winning novel centring around the life of a coke-snorting, gay, sex-addicted Oxford graduate living in London (who gets to meet Mrs Thatcher). Deals with hypocrisy and the acceptance of homosexuality within the 1980s Conservative Party.

David Nicholls, *One Day.*
A modern romance, starting in 1988, and stretching over some eighteen years against a background of significant political events.

Andrew Rawnsley, *Servants of the People.*
Spin doctors, intrigue, ambition and feuds. The inside story of New Labour and more.

Scandal.
Film/DVD of the Profumo affair which shook the Conservative establishment.

Jack Straw, *Last Man Standing.*
Former Labour minister's memoirs, crafted with literary elegance, cover the party's rise and fall from the mid-1960s to its 2010 defeat.

On the net

http://www.labour.org.uk/
http://www.conservatives.com/
http://www.libdems.org.uk/home.aspx
http://www.greenparty.org.uk/

The websites of the major (and minor) political parties offer some details of their recent developments, in addition to their organization and policies.

PART III

GOVERNMENT AT THE CENTRE

Significantly we do not arrive at the formal centre of British government until the middle of the book. This underlines the fact that politics is by no means confined to the Palace of Westminster and those who inhabit it. In chapters 14 to 18 we address the most central and exhilarating concepts in politics – official power: who holds it, who uses it, and who is able to influence its exercise. Our search takes us through the most ornate institutions of government (the monarchy and Parliament) to the heart of the Westminster/Whitehall complex, the Cabinet, the prime minister and the higher civil service. Finally, in chapter 19, we delve even deeper into the mysteries of power by seeking sources of influence lying below the surface of ministerial pomp in a world of pressure group politics and in even more shadowy recesses of political life. We shall find that, although all may not be as it seems, nothing is without significance; every cam and cog in the machinery of state has a function and our task is to try to discover what that is.

CHAPTER 14

POMP AND CIRCUMSTANCE: MONARCHY, LORDS AND COMMONERS

Contents

In this chapter we meet the more ornate parts of the constitution, the parts foreign tourists come to see and which are shown on the postcards they send home. These include the monarchy with its robes, jewels and golden coaches; the Palace of Westminster housing the two chambers of the legislature, and the people who occupy them. Here we see much flummery lovingly preserved from bygone ages, a celebration of the much-vaunted continuity of the British constitution. However, although as lifeless as the waxworks at Madame Tussaud's, like the mystic ritual of high church and courts, the ceremonial is by no means without significance. It induces respect and reverence for authority; it is the living dead of the constitution.

Parliament

Britain's constitutional triptych

Parliament formally comprises the monarchy, the House of Lords and the House of Commons. The two houses have a very tangible presence as the picturesque Palace of Westminster, one of London's major landmarks. Situated grandly on the bank of the Thames at the end of Whitehall, it is a popular tourist destination, around a million visitors a year queuing to be conducted on guided tours and purchase trinkets marked with the prestigious portcullis logo (also found on its official notepaper).

The beautiful architecture is not merely ornamental, it is deeply symbolic. Following severe fire damage in 1834, it was restored in the Gothic style to reflect the belief that Britain's civil liberties stemmed from medieval achievements. The chambers have a cathedral-like aura, intimidating all but the initiated. Around them a labyrinth of corridors, quadrangles and staircases leads to offices, committee rooms, smoking-rooms, tea rooms, and of course bars. MPs and peers can be seen variously talking in intimate clusters, meeting groups of eager constituents, playing host to interest-group representatives or lobbyists, or perhaps lying low in places of refreshment trying to avoid such encounters.

The chambers are surprisingly small and could not seat all members if they were to descend simultaneously. This is quite deliberate; another opportunity to rebuild was presented by the German Luftwaffe in 1941 but the decision was taken to retain the sense of intimacy conducive to debate. Unlike most chambers, the benches are

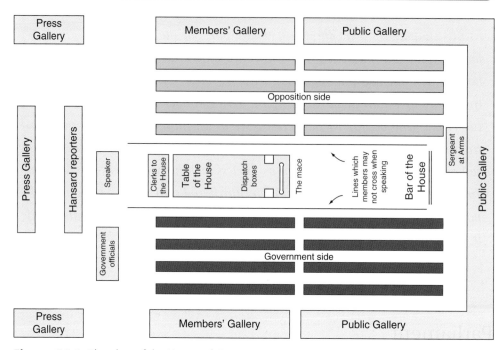

Figure 14.1 Chamber of the House of Commons

arrayed in a confrontational manner (figure 14.1) and, in the Commons, the front ranks are two swords-lengths apart, commemorating an age when the thrust and parry of debate could be more than figurative.

Within walking distance, standing at the end of the Mall, is perhaps the greatest tourist attraction of all. As the third pane of this constitutional triptych, Buckingham Palace is the London home of the British monarch. With a history dating from well before the dawn of democracy, the monarchy remains a significant feature in political life.

The evolution of Parliament

The three elements of Parliament represent the great estates of the realm which have fought over the centuries for control of the state: the Crown, the aristocracy and the common people. Its origins lie in the assembly of Anglo-Saxon kings which met as the Witenagemot. In Norman times kings governed assisted only by their officials, although the country was divided into territorial units ruled by barons whom the kings would summon as the *Magnum Concilium* for discussion, advice and to raise money. The barons gradually demanded more control, securing this through the Magna Carta signed at Runnymede in 1215. Herein lies the origin of the House of Lords.

The House of Commons was conceived in the kingly practice, from the thirteenth century, of calling additional meetings of the less-important local representatives, the commoners (knights from the shires and burgesses from the incorporated towns), as a further source of revenue. They would assemble humbly before the monarch, who would tell them how much was required and dispatch them to find it, leaving the aristocracy to discuss important matters of state. However, the Commons, recognizing its potential power, began making demands. When expensive wars forced Edward III (1327–77) to summon frequent parliaments, they took the opportunity to attach a list of desired reforms when accepting the tax demands. At the beginning of the fifteenth century Henry IV agreed that grants of funds would only be initiated in the Commons, recognizing the lower house as part of Parliament.

This hold over the purse-strings saw the gradual erosion of the monarch's position. Coming soon after the profligate Henry VIII (1509–47), Elizabeth I (1558–1603) recognized this reality and was careful to court Parliament. However, the Stuarts lacked the Tudors' realism and Charles I sought to govern without parliamentary consent, raising taxes directly from towns ('ship money'). By this time the Commons had become powerful enough to oppose him and events led to the Civil War (1642–6) between the Royalists (Cavaliers) and the parliamentarians (Roundheads). It resulted in Charles losing not just the Crown but a head upon which to rest it. Britain entered upon a brief period as a **republic** (1649–60) with the Puritan Oliver Cromwell supreme as 'Lord Protector'.

The Restoration in 1660 saw Charles II return from exile in glory, but things were to be different. He was a *constitutional monarch*, constrained by Parliament. The anniversary of his father's execution was marked by a grizzly ceremony in which Cromwell's disinterred corpse was hung on the infamous gallows at Tyburn. Yet James II could not accept the limitations and further skirmishes culminated in the Glorious Revolution of 1688, which placed William (of Orange) and Mary (daughter of James II) on the English throne, their powers clearly restricted in the 1689 Bill of Rights. It was not until the 1701 Act of Settlement that the subordinate position of the monarchy was satisfactorily established, made easier by the fact that the Hanoverian line (starting with George I in 1714) had little interest in British affairs.

The upper house had also been abolished during the republic and was reinstated at the Restoration. Under the 1689 settlement the Commons would concern itself with commerce while the Lords attended to affairs of state, including foreign policy, subject to the convention that money supply was in the sole gift of the Commons. However, the Commons remained under the control of aristocratic and royal factions, both exercising an often-corrupt influence on elections and nominations. It was not until the great nineteenth-century Reform Acts that the *coup de grâce* was delivered on the old order, through the moral authority acquired by the Commons through the popular vote (chapter 10).

I would rather hew wood than be a king under the condition of the king of England.
Charles X of France (1757–1836)

Yet the message was not immediately clear to their lordships. In 1883 they rejected the second Irish Home Rule Bill and the reforming Liberal government of 1905 found eighteen of its bills rejected. Matters came to a head when Chancellor Lloyd George, needing £16 million in extra revenue to finance the planned social programme, as well as to build *Dreadnought* battleships, determined that the money should come principally from taxing the landed interests, against whom he had been conducting a campaign. His 1909 'People's Budget' was rejected by the Lords, precipitating a constitutional crisis in which a reluctant monarch, weakened by 'four gargantuan meals a day together with endless wine, brandy, whisky and cigars' (Cross 1963: 106), was told he might be forced to create sufficient new government-supporting peers to swamp the opposition. The result was major reforms in the powers of the upper house.

The nature and functions of all three of the institutions comprising Parliament are subject to continuing debate.

The Monarchy

Britain today has a **constitutional monarchy**, which means that although the Queen may be said to *reign*, she does not *rule*. Perhaps the monarchy's last dying gasps were heard under Victoria. Initially influenced by her consort Albert (who took his authority seriously) and later encouraged by the flattering Disraeli, she made several efforts to exert the royal prerogative (a set of powers available only to the monarch). It was the lot of the austere Gladstone to school the Queen in her role and cut the modern pattern of British democratic kingship (Magnus 1963: 42–7).

Today the monarch formally continues to hold hundreds of prerogative powers, the extent and scope of which are largely determined by convention. They range widely, but are generally exercised only on advice (usually prime ministerial) and conflict has been rare since the beginning of the twentieth century.

The formal role of the monarchy

The Queen holds a number of official positions, including the following.
- *Head of state.* Whether or not a monarchy, each nation has at its head a figure who embodies the state in the eyes of its own people and of the world. In many cases this is an elected president but in Britain it is the Queen rather than any elected politician.
- *Head of the executive, legislature and judiciary.* Formally, the prime minister is the Queen's first minister, she prorogues and summons Parliament, the civil servants are the servants of the Crown, the nation's finances are managed by

Her Majesty's Treasury and judges are the Queen's judges, appointed by Her Majesty.

- *Commander-in-Chief of the armed forces.* Members of the royal family frequently hold ceremonial military ranks and the armed forces and police are constitutionally servants of the Crown, supposedly symbolizing their independence from party politics.
- *Fidei defensor.* The Reformation established the Anglican Church with the monarch at its head as 'defender of the faith'. Many royal ceremonies have a religious nature, including the coronation itself. However, with increasing multiculturalism, Prince Charles has spoken of being the defender of the *faiths* and in June 2002 the shoeless and garlanded Queen paid her first visit to a Hindu temple during her silver jubilee tour. Moreover, in 2011 the rule banning the spouse of a Roman Catholic from taking the throne was repealed.
- *Head of the Commonwealth.* This is an area where the Queen's authority is not subject to prime ministerial guidance. Some Commonwealth countries even accept the monarch as head of state but others do not.

With these positions comes a range of ceremonial duties, including appointments to state positions, from the prime minister down; the proroguing and summoning of Parliament (the 2011 Fixed Term Parliaments Act removed the prime minister's power to request a dissolution, except in the case of a no-confidence vote); delivering the Queen's Speech to Parliament; governing the Anglican Church; chairing meetings of the Privy Council; signing treaties; awarding honours; making official visits to other nations and entertaining foreign leaders in Buckingham Palace. When newly elected US President Barack Obama made his first official visit to Britain in 2009, a meeting with the Queen was high on the ceremonial agenda. However, these official positions and functions are all constrained within a straightjacket of constitutional monarchy. In her official duties the Queen acts largely on the advice of her ministers.

Why study the monarchy?

The absence of real governmental power leads some commentaries on politics and sociology to omit the monarchy. This may be intended to betoken a jettisoning of meaningless symbolism in order to focus on the world of reality but it is a mistake, betraying a short-sighted and superficial vision. The monarchy affects modern politics by being a significant element in political culture.

Funding

The monarchy does not come cheap. In 1761 George III agreed to surrender the income from the Crown Estate (worth some £200 million a year by 2007) in

The use of the Queen, in a dignified capacity, is incalculable. Without her in England, the present English government would fail and pass away.
Walter Bagehot, The English Constitution (1867: ch. 2)

exchange for a regular grant from Parliament – the Civil List – to cover expenditure relating to the monarch's official duties. Although remaining constant for a considerable time, it was revised under Elizabeth II to keep pace with inflation. Other expenses include the upkeep of five palaces and the travel costs of up to 2,500 official engagements annually, which are met by Grants-in-Aid from government departments. In addition there is the Privy Purse (income generated from the sole surviving Crown Estate in the monarch's hands – the Duchy of Lancaster), primarily used to cover official expenditure not met from the Civil List.

The Queen's private expenditure is met from her own considerable personal fortune, its precise size subject to much speculation. Estimated at £350 million in 2008, this may have been overstated. Although her property includes two royal residences, Sandringham and Balmoral, certain 'inalienable' items are held not as private property but on behalf of the nation (though most of the nation will never see them). These include the internationally renowned art collection, heirlooms in the Queen's jewellery collection and the Crown Jewels.

For long the Queen's income was exempt from tax and death duties, giving her a touch similar to that of King Midas and enabling her to outdistance all aristocratic rivals (some of whom, even after the second world war, were actually richer than the King). While they were collecting the tickets for the exhibitions and zoos on their estates, the wealth in the royal coffers continued to grow. When part of Windsor Castle (which was not insured) was destroyed by fire in November 1992, the Conservative government's immediate response was to shoulder the £50-million repair burden. However, this uncharacteristic generosity with taxpayers' money provoked controversy, and from 1993 the Queen joined her subjects as a client of her tax inspectors. The money for the restoration was raised by opening Buckingham Palace to a fee-paying public. In addition, the Civil List was cut to the bone, leaving only the Queen herself, the Duke of Edinburgh and the Queen Mother. A city accountant became guardian of the royal finances. The parliamentary annuities paid to the remaining members of the royal family to enable them to carry out official duties are now repaid to the Treasury by the Queen. However, further controversy followed the Queen Mother's death in 2002, when the contents of the will were not revealed and no death duties paid.

The monarchy today

Buckingham Palace, the main royal residence, stands in London at the end of the Mall in some 40 acres of gardens. Together with Horse Guards' Parade, Westminster Abbey and the Palace of Westminster, all within a cannon's shot of each other, it is part of a baroque Disneyland of the past, gradually becoming overgrown by a towering office-block jungle. Inside the palace, courtiers and flunkeys, with titles and sometimes costumes of a bygone age, perform the tasks of running the monarchy industry. Many are themselves nobly born and treasure their families' links with the sovereign, passing the positions down through the generations. Today's monarchy is distinguished by certain characteristics.

Hereditary

No one votes for the British Head of State. Although faltering from time to time, the succession is based on inheritance, Elizabeth II being the fortieth monarch since the Norman Conquest. Traditionally the rule of primogeniture has applied, meaning that any male child took precedence in the order of succession over his sisters. Had Elizabeth II had a younger brother she would not have become monarch. However, at the Commonwealth Heads of Government meeting in October 2011, attended by the Queen, it was agreed unanimously that the rule would no longer apply. This was subsequently ratified in the 2013 Succession to the Crown Act. Had Prince William sired a daughter in July 2013, she would have taken precedence over any subsequent brothers.

Pomp and ceremony

While Britain is not alone as a constitutional monarchy (Luxembourg, the Netherlands, Belgium, Spain, Sweden, Denmark and Norway are the same), it is unique in the degree to which the pomp and **ceremonial** have been preserved. (The Scandinavian royals have been slightingly dubbed 'bicycling monarchies', having reduced ostentation.) The British monarchy can on great occasions in the royal life-cycle (births, weddings and funerals) reach a scale only matched in Hollywood epics.

Political neutrality

Although informed on a weekly basis by the prime minister, the Queen remains above the political fray. She does not vote; neither is she expected to express partisan opinions.

Familial

Like the Mitchells of the East End or the Archers of Ambridge, the Windsors of Belgravia present to the public an extended family supported by a galaxy of bit-players. Royal weddings, new offspring and dramatic marital disasters provide gripping storylines. The wedding of Prince William to the commoner Catherine Middleton brought another glamorous player into this everyday story of royal folk.

Loyal subjects: crowds line the streets for the marriage of Prince William to Kate Middleton, April 2011

Popularity

Before the second world war, shaken by the abdication crisis, the future of the monarchy was uncertain, but the war itself and the post-war era, including the coronation, saw it recover. Although the period following the dramatic death of Princess Diana in 1997 led to a view that the Queen's popularity was plummeting, 200,000 people were to file past her mother's coffin as it lay in state in Westminster Hall in April 2002, while around a million lined the streets for the funeral procession. The response to the marriage of Prince William to Catherine (Kate) Middleton in 2011 showed little sign of any diminution of popular interest, while the diamond jubilee celebrations of 2012 saw thousands at the concert at Buckingham Palace. Neither did unseasonable weather dampen the spirits of the crowds turning out to watch the royal flotilla along the Thames and millions turned out as the Queen proceeded around the country on her jubilee tour, confounding predictions that the event would prove an embarrassing flop.

A throne behind the power

Beyond the largely ceremonial and cultural functions is the possibility that monarchs can exert real influence. Unlike prime ministers they are not troubled by popular opinion, elections, party infighting and power rivalries. Enjoying office for as long as they remain alive, their experience can be a source of wisdom. Although believing a republic had insinuated itself beneath the folds of a monarchy, Bagehot enunciated a famous trio of royal rights: to be consulted, to encourage and to warn. In 1884 even Gladstone formally thanked Queen Victoria for her 'wise, gracious and steady exercise of influence' (Magnus 1963). When David Cameron became prime minister the Queen had worked with eleven of his predecessors, giving her more experience of public life than any political figure. This influence is likely to be greatest over non-ideological issues (Bogdanor 1996a), particularly the Commonwealth, a point borne out by former prime minister James Callaghan (1987: 382):

> The Queen's initiative on Rhodesia [openly disapproving of Ian Smith's declaration of UDI] was a perfect illustration of how and when the Monarch could effectively intervene to advise and encourage her Ministers . . . with complete constitutional propriety.

Moreover, in conditions of constitutional crisis powers may go beyond Bagehot's modest assessment. Few would deny that the monarch would be justified in intervening if events 'subverted the democratic basis of the Constitution' (Jennings 1959: 412). Even in less dramatic circumstances the powers to dissolve Parliament and appoint the prime minister could become real. Although no dissolution request has been refused since before the 1832 Reform Act, this could happen if, in the words of Sir Alan Lascelles (former private secretary to both George VI and Elizabeth II), 'the existing Parliament was still vital, viable and capable of doing its job' or if the monarch 'could rely on finding another prime minister who could [govern] . . . with a working majority' (Hennessy 1994).

The possibility of such powers being used has loomed on at least six occasions: in the spring of 1950 when the general election cut Attlee's majority from 146 to 6; in July 1953 when Churchill and Eden were seriously ill; in January 1957 following Eden's post-Suez resignation; in October 1963 following Macmillan's resignation; in March 1974 when the narrowly defeated Heath attempted to do a deal with the Liberals, and finally with the prospect of a hung parliament after the 2010 general election. Constitutional expert Robert Hazell, warning of the effect that uncertainty might have on the financial markets, lamented that 'the rules are not clear and hard to find' (Woolf 2010). Senior civil servants, royal courtiers and Cabinet Secretary Sir Gus O'Donnell went into overdrive as they sought to clarify the role the Queen might be required to play. Guidance was sought in memos, written by Robert Armstrong, the prime minister's principal private secretary, at the time of the 1974 crisis. Once Brown resigned as prime minister many outcomes in the choice of successor were possible. Crisis was averted by the emergence of a tenuous coalition.

On the whole it is wise in human affairs and in the government of men to separate pomp from power.
Winston Churchill, speech in Ottawa (1952)

A hollow crown?

While supporters of monarchy extol its virtues and agnostics dismiss it as a harmless sideshow, those of a more republican disposition paint a different picture.

Out of touch

The life experience of the Queen, despite her known enthusiasm for *Coronation Street*, can hardly be said to have brought her into contact with the feelings of ordinary people. Her personal circle has remained largely within the aristocracy. According to a BBC report (25 Feb. 1998), Prince Charles apparently managed to complete a nine-day trip round Central Asia in 1996 without once saying hello to the small press party with him. At the death of Princess Diana many were offended by protocol that forbade the flying of the flag at half-mast while the Queen remained at Balmoral with her grandsons and there were fears (which proved unfounded) that she would be booed at the funeral.

Vulgarization

If Bagehot were to return he would have cause to rue the day he praised the elevating virtues of royal ceremonial. Today the masses gape through the vulgarizing lens of the tabloid press. The 'Royals' have been elevated to the status of showbiz celebrities and hounded round the world by the *paparazzi*, aptly named the 'rat-pack'. The intense scrutiny led the Queen to label 1992 her *annus horribilis*. Princes William and Harry were to feature as part of Britain's celebrity culture, their socializing and girlfriends reported in glossy magazines and tabloids, along with showbiz stars and reality TV personalities. The labour of the Duchess of Cambridge and Prince George's subsequent entrance onto the stage were followed in minute detail.

Falling popularity

The popularity of the monarchy is a varying barometer. According to one opinion poll in 1997, less than half the population supported the monarchy; the proportion thinking the country would be worse off without the royals falling from 70 per cent in 1994 to 48 per cent (*Guardian*, 12 Aug. 1997). While Royal scandals do little to help, weddings, funerals and jubilees can promote revivals. Clearly the adoration of the public cannot be taken as a stable factor.

An uplifting moral force?

Although in the 1950s Princess Margaret had denied herself marriage to Group Captain Peter Townsend on account of his divorce, by 1996 she herself, and three of the Queen's children, were divorced. Some spoke of a dysfunctional family when the romance of Prince Charles and Lady Diana Spencer, which had enchanted millions, disintegrated in a moral morass in 1992, when first the 'Camillagate' and then the 'Squidgygate' tapes allowed the world to hear of the fairytale couple's infidelities. Those who had cheered along the wedding route were to discover that, sitting sedately in row three during the glittering ceremony in Westminster Abbey, was Charles's mistress, Camilla Parker-Bowles (see Holden 1997).

Democracy as deception: panem et circenses

The expectations of modern British constitutional kingcraft were virtually defined by Walter Bagehot in 1867. He argued that 'the masses of Englishmen are not fit for an elective government; if they knew how near they were to it, they would be surprised and almost tremble' (1963: 97). The monarchy was the keystone in the dignified facade concealing the real processes of government from the uncomprehending masses (particularly women). Bagehot's views reflected an elite fear of the extending franchise but, where J. S. Mill argued for more political education, he preferred constitutional sleight of hand. Like the emperors of imperial Rome, the powerful would provide bread and circuses to divert popular attention from affairs of state. However, a political culture that values deception is one that can tolerate secrecy and even lies.

Legitimation of inequality

Unlike other constitutional monarchies, Britain's does not stand alone; it is the tip of an aristocratic iceberg of inherited wealth and titles, the survival of which, to critics, is one of the political wonders of the world. This legitimates elitism and maldistribution of wealth, helping to keep the social soil fertile for capitalism. Chapter 8 noted the high levels of inequality in Britain and the continuation of class stratification.

A neutrality myth?

Finally, the convention of political neutrality is open to question. Although the sovereign is not allowed discretion in the choice of prime minister, political implications can be seen in the very concept of royalty. Disraeli's 'one-nation' Conservatism made the Crown one of its symbols. Patriotism could be expressed by voting Conservative. Indeed, the Queen is head of the Anglican Church, long mocked as the Conservative Party at prayer.

Critics even find suggestions of political leanings at times. The failure to invite Labour ex-prime ministers Tony Blair and Gordon Brown to the royal wedding in 2011 was seen by some as a political statement. Labour MPs sat stony-faced as the Commons wished Prince William and Kate Middleton well. On another occasion, former Australian prime minister Bob Hawke disclosed that the Queen had argued with Thatcher on policy and Ben Pimlott's 1996 biography prompted tabloid headlines: 'The Queen's a Lefty'.

Peter Mandelson: You're a secret Blairite. Prince Charles: I gather Mr Blair is a secret me.
Sunday Times (15 June 1997)

Particular controversy has concerned the Prince of Wales, who, although the future monarch, has sought to champion a wide range of causes, including the environment, organic food and architecture. Legend has it that, as a student, he had asked the Master of Trinity if he could join the university Labour club, and in 1988 he criticized Conservative social policy. In July 2011 the *Independent* reported that he had summoned ministers to meet him eleven times since the formation of the coalition in May 2010.

How long to reign over us?

Death of a princess

She was always trying to get across to people like us.

East London girl, on Princess Diana, quoted by Simon Jenkins in *The Times* (3 Sept. 1997)

The monarchy debate was thrust to the front pages with the death of Princess Diana in 1997. She had spoken of being the 'Queen of people's hearts' and her funeral became her tragic coronation, provoking an unprecedented mass outpouring of grief. Yet this was no demonstration of love of royalty. Rejected and effectively banished on her divorce, and stripped of her royal rank, she could be seen 'a totem of protest against that ring-fenced elite that has quietly run Britain from gentlemen's clubs and secret societies' (Holden 1997). Whether the monarchy should be abolished or reformed, few could imagine it remaining unchanged.

> **Attitudes to the monarchy following the death of Princess Diana**
> Which of these options for the monarchy would you prefer?
>
> - Continue in its present form: 12%
> - Continue but be modernized: 74%
> - Be replaced with a republic when Queen dies: 5%
> - Be replaced with a republic immediately: 7%
>
> *Observer*/ICM poll in the *Guardian* (17 Sept. 1997)

Alternative images of the monarchy

- *Abolition.* While abolition, and even execution, has been a principal basis for much constitutional evolution (until the first world war monarchy was prevalent throughout Europe), Britain's relatively smooth transition to democracy has never produced a sustained republican call. The Cromwellian interlude soon gave way to a restoration. Despite the 1997 Labour government's wide-ranging constitutional reform programme, the death of Princess Diana saw Labour spin doctors working to protect the image of the monarchy.
- *A bicycling monarchy.* A scaling down to Dutch or Scandinavian proportions would entail less ostentation and less attention to 'minor Royals'. Jack Straw, as

Labour's home affairs spokesman, had affirmed such a vision. Yet for many this would destroy the magic.

- *A hands-on monarchy.* Diana's style was to pay more attention to meeting ordinary people while retaining the glitter. The Queen's eve-of-funeral broadcast declared that 'lessons would be learned'. However, such a transformation might prove difficult for a family schooled in the art of the stiff upper lip rather than the gentle touch.

- *A fresh-start monarchy.* Some have argued that his divorce and remarriage rendered Prince Charles an unacceptable monarch, with 53 per cent of those polled in September 1997 expressing approval for Prince William to take the institution into the new century (*Guardian*, 17 Sept. 1997). Yet the popular weather vane swung again and by 2011 a YouGov survey conducted for *Prospect* magazine showed a preference for Charles as next king by a 45 to 37 per cent margin. In 2012, the 86-year-old Queen announced that she was indeed long to reign over us; there would be no early retirement. Although her fitness and stamina were evident during the 2012 jubilee celebrations, in 2013 Prince Charles began to take her place at some key events, including the Commonwealth Heads of Government Meeting in Sri Lanka, and Camilla Parker-Bowles, as the Duchess of Cornwall, was assuming an increasingly public role.

> *Among my contemporaries I am reckoned to have weathered rather well.*
> Queen Elizabeth II, quoted in Ben Pimlott, *The Queen* (1996)

In defence of monarchy

It can be argued that there is a place for constitutional monarchy in the modern world. In a democracy, it is generally good for politicians to be kept down to size. They are supposed to represent the interests of others and should be restrained from self-aggrandizement. Thatcher's style in the late 1980s was criticized by some as inappropriately imperious and her funeral in 2013 did indeed represent that of a head of state. For most abolitionists the solution lies in some form of elected presidency. However, this could mean disruptive battles over the succession. Thomas Hobbes argued for the hereditary principle to avoid this.

The monarchy's uncertain future is tied in with a host of other political and constitutional variables, including the demise of press deference, demands for a written constitution, reform of Parliament, the future of the Commonwealth and Britain's place in Europe. However, the institution has shown considerable flexibility and durability. Perhaps it is uniquely fitted to British political culture. There is perhaps more to the debate than constitutional logic. As Bogdanor (1996a: 421) states:

> If the conjunction of monarchy and democracy may seem a contradiction, it would be well to bear in mind Freud's aphorism that it is only in logic that contradictions can not exist.

> **Regal longings**
> *We have become a grandmother.*
> Margaret Thatcher as prime minister

The House of Lords

> If, like me, you are over 90, frail, on two sticks, half deaf and half blind, you stick out like a sore thumb in most places, but not in the House of Lords.
>
> Ex-prime minister Harold Macmillan (Lord Stockton), quoted in the *Observer* (19 May 1985)

Beneath the monarchical tip of the iceberg has long floated an edifice of ancient privilege – a fully fledged aristocratic class of titled lords and ladies, sighted on special occasions and in special places such as the royal enclosure at Ascot, Cowes and, most visibly of all, in the House of Lords. It has remained one of the most curious of the anomalies in British public life, defying any rule book of democratic and secular politics. The general atmosphere of the upper house has been seen as somnambulant, likened to a mausoleum or adduced as evidence of life after death. However, by the opening of the twenty-first century it was possible to say that some remarkable institutional changes had given the House a new complexion and a significant role in politics (Dorey and Kelso 2011: 217).

The membership of the House has been a highly contentious issue. Originally composed largely of members of an unelected aristocracy, by 2011 it contained 789 members, only 90 of them **hereditary peers**, and 26 of them, known as the Lords Spiritual, there by virtue of being senior bishops of the Church of England, and the remainder being **life peers** appointed by the monarch on the advice of the prime minister or of a newly created House of Lords Appointments Commission. This composition was a product of New Labour's reform programme. Before the 2005 Constitutional Reform Act there was another category, the Law Lords (see below). However, the question of composition was by no means settled and remains a major source of constitutional debate, to be examined below.

This is a rotten argument, but it should be good enough for their lordships on a hot summer afternoon.
Civil servant's note on a ministerial brief, read out by mistake in Lords debate; quoted in Lord Home, *The Way the Wind Blows* (1976)

Another place

Although cryptically referred to in the Commons as 'another place', the Lords is linked to the lower house by a short corridor. Constitutionally the upper house, the layout of the chamber broadly resembles that of the Commons, with government and opposition facing each other. Here the upholstery is red rather than green and there are some benches facing the throne to accommodate a substantial body of **cross-benchers** (members not committed to a party). Debates are rarely acrimonious. The party machines have been less dominant than in the Commons, around a third of members being cross-benchers, often having renounced former allegiances.

Despite the leisurely atmosphere, the House has come to work harder in recent years. Sittings take place from Mondays to Thursdays for about thirty weeks a year, usually between 2.30 and 7.00 p.m. Only towards the end of the session do they meet on Fridays. The central throne is reserved for the monarch for great ceremonial occasions and, until 2006, debate was chaired by the Lord Chancellor, sitting in front of the throne on the traditional 'Woolsack', symbolizing national prosperity through trade. In November 1998 there was agreement on some minor reductions to the pomp surrounding the office, allowing the Lord Chancellor to dispense with breeches and tights in favour of trousers at certain less ceremonial times, though traditionalists feared the office was losing its dignity. A more dramatic reform in the 2005 Constitutional Reform Act saw the chairing role passing to a new creation, a Lords Speaker, elected for five-year terms from amongst the peers by fellow members. The mood of change was heightened by the fact that the first two new occupants of the Woolsack happened to be women. In 2006 Baroness Hayman became the first holder of the £100,000-a-year office, to be replaced in 2011 by Baroness D'Souza.

The functions of the House of Lords

> The House of Peers, throughout the war,
> Did nothing in particular,
> And did it very well.
>
> The Peers in W. S. Gilbert and Arthur Sullivan, *Iolanthe* (Act 2)

Generally speaking, second chambers can represent various interests, provide parliamentarians who are more independent of the executive, and share the burden of parliamentary duties (Russell 2001). The British House of Lords shares a number of functions with the House of Commons, including legislation, debate and scrutiny of the executive (see chapter 15). For long the House also fulfilled a function not common to upper chambers. Contravening the principle of the separation of powers it was the nation's final court of appeal, acting though the Law Lords led by the Lord Chancellor, head of the judiciary. This exercised critics and the 2005 Constitutional Reform Act transferred the appellate function to a newly created UK Supreme Court housed in the historic Middlesex Guildhall on London's Parliament Square, but a stone's throw from its previous location.

At the opening of the twenty-first century it could be argued that the House was performing its functions more effectively than it had throughout the previous century. With many independent-minded and highly qualified life peers it brought much-needed wisdom and expertise to Parliament. Yet, not without some irony, its vulnerability in the face of reformers increased under the 2010 coalition government and the reforming zeal of Deputy Prime Minister Nick Clegg.

The end of the peer show: a very British reform

One of the main controversies surrounding the Lords has been its composition. Traditionally, membership was based on hereditary right; certain people were 'born to rule', a distinction acquired by emerging from a particular womb following an aristocratic impregnation. The system could have been purpose-built to produce maximum controversy yet it proved remarkably resistant to change.

At the opening of the twentieth century Lloyd George, who regarded the Lords with contempt, had intended the 1911 Parliament Act, limiting the powers of the House, to be a stop-gap, a prelude to more radical reforms. However, despite much huffing and puffing, for long no wolf emerged with the constitutional lung power to blow the House down.

Some reform came in the 1958 Life Peerages Act, through which 'life' peers (whose titles could not continue beyond their own lives) could be appointed, thus reviving the House with a transfusion of fresh (though not always young) blood. Of the regular attenders, Conservatives did not have an overwhelming majority but, if all their hereditary members had descended, they could swamp the House. These were the 400 or so 'backwoodsmen' and, if the trumpet sounded, they could forsake their estates to answer the call, as they did in 1968 to vote against a trade ban on Rhodesia and in 1998 to defeat New Labour's proposed closed-list system for EU elections. Peers who had never voted before, and who did not even know their own leaders, were to be found wandering in bewilderment around the precincts of Westminster.

Although people looked to Labour for action, they did so in vain for many years, the party barking in opposition but unwilling to bite in office. A 1968 white paper announced some half-hearted reforms but these were defeated, dashed on the rocks of a somewhat unholy alliance between those on the right (favouring the status quo) and on the left (favouring the constitutional bulldozers). New Labour's 1997 manifesto again promised reform and, in office, Tony Blair sought to redress the Lords' inbuilt Tory domination, his first honours list containing thirty-one 'working' Labour peers. The Liberal Democrats gained eleven new working peers and the Conservatives five.

In October 1998 a two-stage timetable for fundamental reform was announced. The first was intended to sweep all hereditary peers from the chamber. However, unbeknown to the public, and indeed to his own party leader, the leader of the Conservative peers, Lord Cranborne, hatched a deal with Blair whereby, rather than total expulsion, ninety-two hereditary peers would remain for an interim period. Conservative leader William Hague showed his view of Cranborne's efforts by sacking him but the deal stood. Under the provisions of the House of Lords Act 1999, the ninety-two were elected by their fellow members, and a further ten were

Table 14.1 Party strength in the House of Lords, 1 April 2009

Party	Life peers	Hereditary peers	Bishops	Total
Conservative	149	48	0	197
Labour	211	4	0	215
Liberal Democrat	67	5	0	72
Cross-bench	171	33	0	204
Bishops	0	0	26	26
Other	14	2	0	16
TOTAL	612	92	26	730

Note: Excludes 11 peers on leave of absence.

Source: Data from: http://www.parliament.uk/directories/house_of_lords_information_office/analysis_by_composition.cfm 8 April 2009.

reprieved with life peerages. The effect on the composition of the House is shown in table 14.1. The second stage was to be considered by a Royal Commission under Conservative peer Lord Wakeham.

The Wakeham Report

Reporting in January 2000, Wakeham saw the role of the upper house as a 'revising and deliberative assembly – not seeking to usurp the role of the Commons'. With no hereditary peers, it would comprise 550 members, some elected and some nominated. Direct election would be used for only a 'significant minority' to represent the regions, with most members appointed by an independent commission, selecting from all sectors of society without reference to party, gender or race.

Despite some government revision the proposals evoked a barrage of criticism from opposition parties, the Commons Public Administration Committee and many of the government's own supporters. Lord Wakeham lamented that his 'hard-fought consensus' had been abandoned (Tempest 2002). The result was a government climbdown and yet another review. A joint committee of MPs and peers would produce further proposals, to be put to a free vote in both Houses, offering seven options ranging between the two extremes of 100 per cent elected and 100 per cent appointed. The free vote came on 4 February 2003. The first result was from the Lords, where peers voted by a decisive 335 to 110 for an all-appointed chamber. In contrast, the Commons rejected every one of the options.

The coalition under stress

It was the Liberal Democrats who became the next champions of Lords reform. The 2010 coalition government offered them their big chance. Bruised by heavy local election losses in 2011, and the referendum rejection of the AV electoral

All experience, for the last 100 years, shows that incremental reform is the way to do it. The big bang theory won't work.

Jack Cunningham (Labour MP, chairman of the joint committee on reform), in the *Guardian* (27 Feb. 2003)

system, party leader (and Deputy Prime Minister) Nick Clegg seized the initiative on this front. The party favoured a fully elected chamber but, after some compromises within the coalition, a bill was introduced in June 2012 for a House comprising 360 elected, 90 appointed, up to 12 bishops, and up to 8 additional 'ministerial members'. Those elected would serve fifteen-year, non-renewable terms, and would be elected by thirds. Not all those favouring reform approved of the particular model.

Labour declined to assist. But it was opposition from Clegg's coalition partners that finally derailed his efforts. A 'programme motion' that would have set a timetable for the bill had been withdrawn to allow Cameron more time to persuade the Conservative recalcitrants to change their minds. This he was unable to do, and the bill was consigned to the growing scrapheap of failed Lords' reforms.

The debate

The Lords reform debate has never been conducted in a political vacuum; from the time of Lloyd George party interest has never been absent. New Labour enhanced its reformist credentials by ejecting most of the hereditary peers, but also eliminating a key source of Conservative opposition. The Conservatives have traditionally opposed reform of a chamber that served them well. The Liberal Democrat call for an STV-elected house could also be seen as self-serving, reflecting their quest for more proportional representation. Yet the debate goes beyond party interest. The principal alternatives – direct election, patronage, appointment by independent commission and the hereditary principle – each have strengths and weaknesses.

The people's choice: direct election

Election is the basis for populating most upper houses. This is based on democracy, the right of people to choose and remove those involved in their government. It bestows legitimacy, an essential condition of stable government. Yet valid objections have been made to an elected Lords.

Why we think that, unlike France, India, Germany... God knows where, we can't have an elected upper house that works I don't understand.
Lib Dem Baroness Shirley Williams, speaking on BBC TVs *Newsnight* (9 Jan. 2002)

- *'Gridlock'*. Two houses of comparable legitimacy would be prone to the stalemate sometimes seen in the USA. Wakeham expressed the view that a largely elected house would be a recipe for 'damaging conflict' (Lord Chancellor's Department 2001a: para. 11.6). Moreover, with different electoral cycles the possibility of clashing mandates increases.
- *Constituency confusion*. Elected members representing constituencies would compete with MPs as the people's trouble-shooters and confuse constituents
- *Party domination*. An elected chamber might mean the end of the cross-bencher, with candidates lining up behind party leaders. The Lord Chancellor argued

before the Commons Public Administration Committee: 'If you convert it to an elected house the whips will take over'.

- *Professionalization.* Election might also bring in a further wave of professional politicians with little experience of the wider world.
- *Lower quality.* Some have suggested that an elected house would become a refuge for those who had failed in Commons elections.
- *Loss of experience and wisdom.* A cull of the life peers would sacrifice an enormous wealth of experience and expertise. Eminent people would not have the time or inclination to enter the murky world of street politics.
- *Unnecessary.* If the house were to become little more than a talking shop, it might not require the legitimacy of election.
- *Not-accountable.* The fifteen-year non-renewable terms proposed in 2012 would remove a key feature of representative democracy: the ability to 'throw the rascals out'.

Royal favourites: political patronage

As stated above, a strong argument for an appointed house comes from the inclusion of those with widespread knowledge and experience drawn from areas such as the arts, sport, law, medicine, business, academia and science. It also enables those who have held high government office to continue to contribute. In June 1992, Margaret Thatcher entered the chamber, along with many of her former Cabinet. (Michael Foot, true to his principles, became the first Labour leader since 1935 to spurn the honour.) Moreover, the practice does not mean a politically neutered House; Blair's 'interim' reform, injecting additional Labour peers, did not reduce obstructionism (see pp. 441–2). The voting record after the first year revealed only three-quarters of these to be regular supporters.

However, **patronage** is generally regarded as a dangerous practice and has many critics.

- *Undemocratic.* Figures can ascend the greasy poll to key positions in government without confronting the electorate. Blair brought in long-time friend Lord Falconer as Solicitor General and Gordon Brown recalled Peter Mandelson from his duties as European Commissioner to be Business Secretary. Upon becoming prime minister in 2010 David Cameron created more peers in a single year than any of his predecessors.
- *Lack of independence.* Appointment can favour political supporters who will toe the line rather than constrain the executive. Some cite the case of Canada, where an appointed second chamber has been seen as a government poodle. On the *Breakfast with Frost* programme in November 2001, Lord Wakeham lamented: 'I wanted an end of Tony's cronies'.
- *Thwarting the electoral verdict.* Patronage enables MPs to overcome rejec-

tion by the electorate, as when Lynda Chalker, transmogrified into Baroness Chalker, remained at Overseas Development despite the adverse judgement of her constituents in 1992.

- *Corruption.* Lloyd George was notoriously guilty of dispensing honours in exchange for donations, and legislation banning this was made in 1925. However, allegations of corruption arose in 2006 over a number of large secret loans finding their way into Labour Party coffers before the 2005 general election; some of the lenders had been nominated for peerages (see p. 346).
- *Prime ministerial power.* Patronage powers give immense leverage to any leader. A monarchical hangover, this allows prime ministers to act like kings.

Appointment by commission

Like patronage, appointment by independent commission could bring in expertise and experience. It could also produce a large number of independents and remove the opportunities for corruption associated with patronage. Such a commission was set up in May 2006 as part of the first stage of Lords' reform. (It was the commission which uncovered the 'cash for honours' scandal.) As a non-partisan independent body it was given three roles:

- to take over from the prime minister the role of making non-partisan recommendations for life peerages to the Queen;
- to vet all nominations for life peerages, including those from political parties;
- to scrutinize candidates added to the honours lists, such as those nominated for political services.

However, critics question the true independence of an appointments commission.

- *Appointment.* It would be necessary to appoint the commission members. Could this role be entrusted to politicians?
- *Politicization.* A commission might be subject to lobbying. Would the role become politicized?
- *Rule by the great and the good.* A commission might tend towards 'safe choices'. The chamber could become populated with the 'usual suspects' from the Establishment as commissioners appointed in their own likeness.
- *A social microcosm.* If the commission leant more towards ordinary folk ('people's peers'), these might lack the political antennae to survive in the febrile atmosphere of Westminster.

Born to rule: the hereditary principle

Can anything be said in the modern age for a system based on the idea of inheritance? There is no doubt that many hereditary peers have, over the ages, taken their responsibilities very seriously and contributed much to public life. It is not entirely irrational to argue that a belief that one is born to rule can promote leadership skills. Plato advocated training the guardians from birth, while Hobbes supported hereditary monarchy to avoid a disruptive battle for power. Compared with the life peers, their hereditary colleagues have less reason for sycophantic manoeuvring and their road to Westminster did not involve the compromises and backroom skulduggery required of party apparatchiks. Whether those willing and able to fight for office are best fitted for it is indeed debatable. The presence of dictators the world over testifies to this. The Ancient Greeks believed that those longing for power were, by definition, the least suited to it. In some cases they drew lots for office; today we choose juries on a similar principle. Those with wealth and position do not fear sacking for criticizing the executive and are free from the temptations that might corrupt. Indeed, in January 2009 a scandal arose when four Labour life peers were accused of taking money to table amendments to bills.

There are, of course, arguments against the hereditary principle.

- We would not, for example, appoint someone as a brain surgeon merely because her father was one. Empirically it would be hard to find overwhelming evidence for aristocratic supremacy in the fields where talent and intelligence matter.
- Seen as a relic of a bygone age, the hereditary principle was rejected by the Royal Commission, the white paper, the Liberal Democrats, the reformist lobby and even the leader of the Conservative Party. Perhaps the most remarkable thing is that it was able to persist into the twenty-first century.

The chains of history

Why has the preservation order remained so long on this ancient edifice? Perhaps establishment interests found symbolic value in one of the remaining bastions that only the select (or the selected) might enter. A key element in British political culture, Britain's upper house symbolized hierarchy and exclusion, reminding the mass where they belonged – on the outside. However, another argument is that it has been reformed by the subtle evolutionary process that has characterized the British polity. What now exists bears little resemblance to the House that resisted Lloyd George's taxation policies. Britain may be evolving a unique chamber which, through its life peerage system, contains an array of talented people – leading figures in the worlds of the arts, science, industry, some of them Nobel prize-winners – who can contribute to the legislative debate on the basis of knowledge and reason rather than party allegiance.

The House of Commons

The third element in the parliamentary triptych is the only one that may be called democratic. Housing 650 Members of Parliament (MPs) chosen by popular election from a population of some 60 million, the House of Commons is also the chamber of the prime minister and the majority of government ministers. In the chamber they occupy the front benches sitting to the right of the Speaker. Across the chamber the leading members of the opposition confront them. Other MPs sit in rows behind their leaders; they are the backbenchers. However, although the cockpit where Britain's political Titans confront each other on a daily basis, it is by no means free of flummery and ceremony.

Parliamentary mumbo-jumbo

The Commons embraces Westminster ritual from the very beginning with the annual opening of Parliament. Black Rod, the officer responsible for maintaining order in the House of Lords, carrying an ebony cane for the purpose, summons the Commoners to hear the Queen's Speech. Much is conducted in Norman French. When he approaches the lower house the doors are slammed in his face (because in 1642, the last time the Commons allowed the monarch in, he arrested five members). Undeterred, he gives three solemn knocks, the doors are opened and the MPs, led by the prime minister and opposition leader, advance in pairs like a *corps de ballet* towards the 'other place'. The flummery of the ceremony engages 'ladies of the bedchamber' in long evening dresses and officials with Ruritanian titles such as 'silver stick in waiting'.

MPs are required to swear an Oath of Allegiance to the Crown. This is a problem for those with republican principles and some Labour MPs have done so with tongue in cheek. Two Sinn Féin MPs, elected in 1997, were denied office space at Westminster for their refusal. The longest-serving member enjoys the title 'Father of the House' and, with no compulsory retirement age, there is competition for the honour.

In understanding Commons discourse there are various arcane terms requiring translation. The 'usual channels' means consultation between party whips; in the chamber MPs should refer to each other as 'honourable friends' or 'honourable members' for this or that constituency. Until 1998 members raising a point of order in a division did so wearing an opera hat while remaining seated. Privy Councillors (cabinet and ex-cabinet members and leading members of the opposition parties) enjoy certain privileges: 'right honourable', rather than 'honourable', they receive precedence in debate. New Labour came to power in 1997 promising to end such flummery, but the chamber has seen many Young Turks seduced by the ritual and comforts of the Westminster club and little changed.

State Opening of Parliament: Black Rod escorts the Speaker and MPs back from the House of Lords after the 2011 Queen's Speech

Photo: Catherine Bebbington/Parliamentary copyright

The Speaker

> I have neither eye to see, nor tongue to speak here, but as the House is pleased to direct me.
>
> William Lenthall, in the House of Commons on 4 January 1642, in reply to Charles I asking if he had seen five MPs whom he wished to arrest. A classic statement of the Speaker's role

At the centre of Commons life is the Speaker, who chairs debate. Yet there is more to the role than this: sometimes adorned with wig and black robes, the Speaker also presides over a variety of solemn ceremonies often held in his or her official baroque residence within the Palace of Westminster. Although now considered an honour, the position was once unenviable, entailing facing the monarch on behalf of MPs; a newly elected Speaker thus makes a show of resistance before being forced into the chair by colleagues.

Piss-up in a brewery? This lot couldn't organise an orgy in a massage parlour or a sit-in at the Parker Knoll factory.
Simon Hoggart (journalist) on the election of Speaker Martin, in the *Guardian* (24 Oct. 2000)

The Speaker is elected by MPs. The choice was usually for well-respected uncontroversial figures, although this was to become less common, with the election of Betty Boothroyd, as the first woman Speaker, seen as a landmark. The 300-year-old election procedure was traditionally no less archaic than the office and its dress. A nominee was put forward and then, if there was a rival, an amendment was proposed, and a debate and a vote would follow. If there were further rivals the process would be repeated for each. In the October 2000 contest the list became unusually long, making the process tortuous, if not ludicrous. As a result the Commons agreed that future Speakers would be elected by secret ballot. This system was first used in in 2009, following the resignation of Speaker Martin after a troubled reign (the first Speaker to so depart since 1695). He was replaced by Conservative John Bercow, scarcely a less controversial choice.

The Speaker is attended by the Sergeant at Arms, equipped with sword and mace. Responsible for maintaining order, he will eject the unruly, including MPs banned by the Speaker, and could imprison enemies in the clock tower (renamed the Elizabeth Tower in 2012 to honour the Queen's diamond jubilee) of Big Ben. In January 2008 Jill Pay became the first woman to hold the position of Sergeant at Arms and this was also the first non-military appointment. Each day the Speaker leads a dignified procession into the House following the Sergeant, and during debate the mace rests on the table at the centre of the chamber. Michael Heseltine etched his name in parliamentary folklore by brandishing it in the face of the Labour enemy; only by prostrating himself before the House the following day did he gain forgiveness.

In debate, the Speaker must shed political affiliation and call members fairly, and with due weight to their expertise, interest and status. However, MPs can sometimes feel unfairly treated. Conservatives questioned the impartiality of Speaker Martin and his successor Speaker Bercow, claiming in January 2011 that there were 'very worrying' questions about his impartiality.

The Speaker gives rulings on points of procedure, emergency debates, money bills and **parliamentary privilege**. The latter are rights and immunities from court action granted to MPs to ensure free debate. Discipline within the House is another of the Speaker's responsibilities. Although there are often raucous scenes, turbulence is nothing new. Conservative opposition to Lloyd George's 1909 'People's Budget' produced uproar, giving many modern altercations the air of the proverbial vicarage tea party. Where MPs persist in bad behaviour the Speaker will 'name' them, whereupon they are banned for a prescribed period. Thus in July 1992 Dennis Skinner was ordered from the House for refusing to withdraw the unparliamentary term 'wart' as a description of Agricultural Secretary John Gummer. However, in 2010 Labour's Tom Watson, in deference to the Speaker, withdrew his declaration that Education Secretary Michael Gove was a 'miserable pipsqueak of a man'.

It is expected that members will accord the Speaker great respect but tensions can emerge. In December 1995 Speaker Boothroyd summoned the Conservative Chief Whip for a serious dressing down after a whispering campaign against her by his colleagues. There were claims that the strong Glaswegian accent of Speaker Martin was difficult to understand, but defenders alleged this to be snobbery. Some thought it inverse snobbery when, in November 2001, he sacked an experienced secretary for being 'too posh'. Speaker Bercow came under attack when detractors claimed that the dignity of the office suffered when his wife Sally posed semi-naked for a magazine, and appeared on the TV show *Celebrity Big Brother*.

The timetable

The life of a *parliament* is the period between two general elections. Following the 2011 Fixed-term Parliaments Act this was set at five years. Prior to this, it would not normally exceed five years, but could be concluded at any time within this period by a prime minister seeking a dissolution. A parliament can, however, be terminated at any time following a vote of no confidence or if the House itself resolves to call an early general election.

The parliament is divided into annual *sessions* commencing each autumn, punctuated by *recesses* over Christmas, Easter, Whitsun and summer. A session ends with a prorogation. A Daily Agenda (formerly the Order Paper) outlining each day's events is the responsibility of the Leader of the House liaising with the Opposition (available on the internet). Although a cabinet member, the Leader is expected to protect the debating opportunities of backbenchers. From January 2003 the normal working day has ended at 6 or 7 p.m. At one time debates regularly continued into the small hours as *all-night sittings*, but modernization efforts in the 1990s reduced their frequency in a quest for a more 'family-friendly' house. However, helpful only to those MPs with homes near Westminster, the reform remained controversial. On Fridays, sittings usually adjourn by mid-afternoon, enabling MPs to return to their constituencies.

'The best club in London'

The House has for long retained the characteristics of a Victorian establishment club, with bars, smoking-rooms and leather armchairs. A useful quality is to be 'clubbable', to be able to mix easily and enjoy a good joke. While ideologies may separate them, MPs can form cross-party friendships, with clubs for activities ranging from skiing and football to chess and jazz. However, the club ethos was challenged in May 1997 with the entry of a veritable regiment of women. Many changes were demanded, such as an earlier end to the working day and the establishment of a

I think that it is the best club in London.
Mr Tremlow on the House of Commons, in Charles Dickens, *Our Mutual Friend* (1864–5)

> **The times they are a-changin'**
> New, younger MPs of both sexes have, probably, brought more sex into
> Parliament.
>
> Lib Dem MP Dr Evan Harris, leading calls for condom machines in the Commons,
> quoted in the *Guardian* (13 March 1998)

crèche, though calls for breastfeeding in the chamber and the closure of a rifle range went unheeded.

There is no job description for an MP, each making of it what they will. Some do much, some little. Those yearning to ascend the 'greasy pole' must define their role in conformity with a culture of obedience (see chapter 15). There is little glamour in this. If they seek the limelight with a controversial article or a challenging speech they run the risk of incurring displeasure. Some may experience a sense of *ennui* and spend time in the many tea rooms and bars, sometimes appearing 'tired and emotional' (MPs are never drunk) and sometimes even falling into casual adultery. Some will continue with their professional careers, but the 'full-time' MPs have two stages upon which to act, one in Westminster and one in their constituencies.

> **Chains of office**
> A 1624 resolution passed by the Commons demands that MPs fulfil their full
> term. Only death or disqualification will permit them to shed their responsibilities.
> However, puzzled citizens may note that certain MPs, including Tony Blair and
> David Miliband, have been able to forsake their constituents when it suited them.
> They do so on the principle that no one holding a paid office of the Crown
> may be an MP. The Chancellor of the Exchequer therefore appoints them to one
> of two sinecure positions: either the Crown Steward and Bailiff of the Chiltern
> Hundreds or Crown Steward and Bailiff of the Manor of Northstead.

Parliamentary matters

Wednesdays excepted, MPs spend their mornings dealing with correspondence, sitting on committees, meeting constituents and receiving lobby groups. They work in premises round about, including Portcullis House, where many have offices, and in the corridors, tea rooms and bars of Westminster. In the afternoons and evenings they may attend debates in the main chamber, meet fellow MPs, feed information to the press, gossip and plot; Parliament is a hot-house of rumour, character assassinations, secret agreements and broken confidences.

Dishonourable members: private interests and public confidence

Part-time representatives

Some MPs have not seen the work as a full-time job. Conservatives have characteristically held company directorships, worked in the professions (often law), or been large-scale landowners. Labour members also supplement their incomes, often through journalism. It is argued that outside employment keeps MPs in touch with the real world, although critics may question how many ordinary people inhabit the boardrooms of industry, the Inns of Court, or even the inns of Fleet Street and Wapping.

Concern led to the establishment of a Register of Members' Interests in 1975 requiring them to declare all outside employment. This revealed a variety of directorships, associations with financial institutions and multinational corporations. Indeed Kenneth Clarke, when out of office, not only supplemented his MP's salary with directorships, he also found time to present highly entertaining jazz programmes on radio. The issue re-emerged with a series of scandals involving cash for questions and lobbying by MPs (discussed in chapter 19) which led, in October 1994, to the establishment of a Committee on Standards in Public Life, a non-departmental public body chaired first by Lord Justice Nolan. No longer could Parliament be trusted to regulate its own conduct.

Reporting in May 1995, Nolan concluded that the Register was inadequate. To combat the deadly sins available to MPs he set out seven 'Principles of Public Life' and a draft code of conduct. An independent Parliamentary Commissioner should police the system, though with final judgements remaining with Parliament. In November 1995, with votes split 322 to 271, MPs grudgingly agreed to disclose income related to their work in Parliament. While outside interests were to be permitted, all remuneration was to be declared and paid parliamentary work for lobbyists should cease. Sir Gordon Downey (ex-Comptroller and Auditor General) became the first to hold the position of Parliamentary Commissioner for Standards, and a Select Committee on Standards and Privileges was established.

However, the commissioner had fewer powers than the Ombudsman or Comptroller and Auditor General. The power to send for persons and papers, take oral evidence, publish findings and impose sanctions lay with the select committee. Hence, the commissioner was confined within the framework of the 'Westminster club' (Woodhouse 1998). The system's frailties were starkly exposed when Elizabeth Filkin took over from Downey. Frustrated at every turn, she felt herself the victim of 'unchecked whispering campaigns and hostile press briefings'. Speaker Martin criticized her publicly (Cracknell 2001). The final insult came when her three-year term expired; the Commons commission chaired by the Speaker decided that rather than renew her contract she should reapply – effectively a sacking. In 2009 commissioner

Frank Field was forced to pull out of the 2009 contest for Speaker because his strong sense of morality offended his fellow MPs.
Daily Mail (19 June 2009)

Nolan's seven Principles of Public Life
Selflessness
Integrity
Objectivity
Accountability
Openness
Honesty
Leadership

John Lyon (unkindly described as an 'establishment stooge' by *Private Eye*) found himself faced with a new scandal, one that was to shake Westminster to its roots and enter the roll of parliamentary dishonour as the MPs expenses scandal.

Extravagant claims

A process set in motion by a Freedom of Information Act request concerning MPs' expenses led to the leak of a CD containing detailed information. The information was drip-fed to an astonished public by the *Daily Telegraph* over the summer of 2009 and revealed a litany of financial misbehaviour by the people's representatives. As a so-called 'John Lewis list' and dubious claims made for second-home allowances ('flipping'), a floating duck-house and the upkeep of a moat hit the headlines, few MPs appeared as honourable as their formal titles proclaimed. There was additional outrage that they had long tried to block the release of the information.

The party leaders competed with each other in condemnation (although none were exempt from criticism). An attempt to draw a line under the affair came by commissioning an enquiry by civil servant Sir Thomas Legg. Published in February 2010, his critical review found the system 'deeply flawed' and demanded that £1.3 million be returned by 392 former and current MPs. However, the outcome was demoralization and disgrace for MPs, many of whom chose not to fight the next election. Some even found themselves imprisoned. Most dramatic was the resignation of Speaker Martin in May 2009. However, a number of members of the House of Lords were also found guilty of expenses fraud, some even spending time in one of her majesty's other institutions. It was argued that, for MPs, the problem lay in salaries (Table 14.2), which had been held down for political reasons. A culture had emerged in which they would routinely supplement their incomes with inflated claims.

Table 14.2 Parliamentary salaries, April 2010

Position	Salary (£)
Backbench MP	65,000
Select committee chair	80,319
Cabinet minister	134,565
Speaker	134,565
Prime minister	142,500

Amateurs or professionals

This issue goes to the heart of democracy, being concerned with what kind of people become MPs. Before 1911 they were expected to give their services freely, unsullied by pecuniary motivation. Reflecting an historic establishment fondness for amateurism this meant that, as on the county cricket and rugby union fields, only the wealthy were welcome. Until as recently as 1964 MPs received only the equivalent of part-time salaries, working- and lower-middle-class members often being unable to eat in the Westminster dining rooms. In July 2001, when MPs voted themselves rises beyond an independent review board's recommendations, there was much criticism. Yet it can be argued that effective representation requires the participation of all classes. Low salaries tend to make Parliament a rich man's club and threaten democracy.

Representing the People

A system of representative democracy is one in which chosen individuals run the state on behalf of the masses. Before the extensions of the franchise, the peers in the House of Lords were said to protect the interests of the masses through a system of 'virtual representation'. Today it is the MPs who are the representatives of the people. However, MPs could well suffer confusion in coming to grips with their role since there are various interpretations placed on the concept of representation.

Opinion leaders

It can be argued that the responsibility of MPs is not to reflect the wishes of others but to exercise wisdom and follow conscience, doing what they believe to be right. In the eighteenth century Edmund Burke (see p. 264) made a celebrated statement of this view, which sees Parliament not as a gathering of delegates but a deliberative assembly, leading public opinion rather than following it. While politicians are frequently called upon to take a lead over an issue, few would advocate such an openly elitist view of representative government today, as politicians follow the lodestone of public opinion.

Your representative owes you, not his industry only, but his judgement; and he betrays, instead of serving you, if he sacrifices it to your opinion.
Edmund Burke, addressing his Bristol constituents (1774)

Social workers

> Being a backbencher is really a very good job; . . . and if they've got intelligence and guts and a good relationship with their constituents then it's a better job than in most parliaments of the western world.
>
> Michael Foot (1913–2010; former Labour leader), interviewed by Bill Jones in *Talking Politics* (vol. 9, no. 3)

MPs can find much employment in dealing with constituents' concerns. This is an area largely free from the straitjacket of party discipline and it has increased significantly with the growth of the welfare state, MPs' role in the ombudsman system (see p. 706), increased volatility amongst voters and the need to secure re-adoption by local parties. An influx of women might also be expected to give a higher priority to constituency work (Norris 1996c). MPs themselves have encouraged developments, advertising regular surgeries, holding public meetings, developing websites, tweeting and entering the 'blogosphere'. The careerist MP may find in the constituency dimension a means to attract attention and gain fuel for parliamentary questions and adjournment motions. Yet there are costs. MP Austin Mitchell suggested that 'to be a good constituency MP is . . . downgraded by the ambitious' (Mitchell 1994: 703). Moreover, MPs are not trained counsellors, social workers or civil rights lawyers, but their deflection from the Westminster role may be welcomed by an executive eager to swell its power.

Delegates

MPs can also be said to represent their constituencies as a whole, going to Westminster with a remit to fight for the area. This is sometimes termed 'pork-barrel politics' as they aim to 'bring home the bacon' by, say, resisting proposals to close a hospital or gaining funding for a new ring road. Sometime MPs will seek the views of constituents on how to vote. This can lead to issues of conscience for an MP when party policy conflicts with the local interest. This tension became more acute as the 2010 coalition government sought cuts in public expenditure.

Advocates

Interest groups are keen to have their case represented in Parliament and can develop a range of formal and informal links with MPs. Sometimes members hold honorary positions in charities and other associations. So overt are the relationships that the Speaker will often choose MPs to speak not on the basis of constituencies but because of the interests they are known to represent. The knowledge MPs can gain from these relationships can enhance debate and improve legislation. However, there are dangers. Constituents can be neglected and it has been noted (Norris 1996b) that multiple interests have appeared to be associated with safe seats, where members need to spend less time courting their constituents.

From the late 1970s developments took an alarming turn when MPs appeared to be acting as lobbyists and seeking personal reward. Concerns led to the reforms discussed above and continue to surface. In 2010, a Channel 4 sting operation by the *Dispatches* programme filmed leading MPs talking to an undercover reporter posing as an interviewer seeking well-connected lobbyists. Television viewers were to watch Labour ex-minister Geoff Hoon declaring that he wanted to do something that 'frankly makes money'. He was suspended from the PLP.

A social mirror: microcosmic representation

> A Parliament elected by the universal suffrage of voters grouped according to geographical areas is about as truly representative as a bottle of Bovril is a true representative of an ox.
>
> Eleanor Rathbone (1872–1946; independent MP and women's rights campaigner),
> in the *Observer* (29 March 1931)

Another understanding of representation is that the social make-up of the Commons should resemble that of the population as a whole, that it should be a microcosm of society. This is justified on the grounds that issues associated with various social categories cannot be properly considered without their members present. How like their fellow citizens are these occupants of the green benches of the Commons? The 2010 intake, coming in the wake of the expenses scandal, produced some 35 per cent new MPs, almost double the usual number, and offering a greater possibility of change. Yet when placing them under the microscope we find a make-up which differs from that of the general population in significant ways.

Age

Despite something of a cult of youth amongst party leaders, the Commons tends to mirror the more mature population, with the majority in the 40–60 age group. In 2010 Sir Peter Tapsell became the Father of the House, a title made particularly appropriate in that, at 81, he was also the oldest MP. Labour has tended to be the older party. In 2010, 60 per cent of its MPs were over 60, while 60 per cent of Conservatives were under 60 (Criddle 2010: 321). With an average age of 49, the class of '97 lowered the age profile but the infusion of youth was not to last. By 2005 the average had risen to 51, and in 2010 it stood at 50, with Labour's 26-year-old Pamela Nash the baby of the House. Clearly the young have some right to claim they are under-represented. However, it can be argued that maturity is a desirable quality in rulers. The wisdom of age was valued by the Ancient Greeks, hence the term 'Senate'. Perhaps a more negative consequence is a death rate, in modern times, of some four MPs per year.

Education

Increasingly MPs tend to be among the more highly educated; Labour's graduate count more than doubled between 1945 and 2001, from 32 to 67 per cent. Of the

2010 intake, 73 per cent of Labour and 80 per cent of Conservative and Liberal Democrat MPs had been to university. For much of the post-war period the majority of graduates were from Oxbridge and, despite an increase in those from other institutions, this proportion remained high. Percentages for the 2010 intake were largely the same as in 2005 for Labour (17), but Cameron's drive to recruit non-Establishment figures also saw a drop in the Conservative percentage (43 to 34), while that of the Liberal Democrats also fell (32 to 28).

Social class

The type of school attended gives some indication of social background. Traditionally private schools provided the pre-university education for the majority of Conservatives (mainly Eton, but also Harrow and Winchester). During the 1980s this began to change, with more from the state grammar school assault course. However, by the end of that decade the party had reverted to its tradition of social exclusivity (see Baker and Fountain 1996). Fee-paying schoolboys have not been absent from Labour's ranks. Of the 2010 intake, 14 per cent of Labour MPs, 54 per cent of Conservatives, and 40 per cent of Liberal Democrats had been to private schools. With twenty of its alumni in the House (nineteen Conservatives and one Liberal Democrat), Eton appeared as the most successful avenue to political success (Criddle 2010: 326).

Occupation

Occupational backgrounds also tend to distance MPs from their constituents. They stretch Conservative and Labour MPs further apart, with the Liberal Democrats standing closer to the former (Table 14.3). Since 1945 all parties have included a high proportion classed as professional, although in the case of Labour these have mainly been teachers and academics. Despite its business-friendly image, less than 10 per cent of the New Labour intake entered Parliament with such backgrounds. There was little change in 2010, with 8 per cent of Labour MPs, 40 per cent of Conservatives, and 20 per cent of Liberal Democrats claiming business

Table 14.3 Occupation of MPs elected at the 2010 general election

Occupation	Conservative	Labour	Liberal Democrat
Professional	107	89	22
Business	125	20	11
Miscellaneous	72	127	23
Manual	2	22	1

Source: Data extracted from Criddle (2010: 327).

backgrounds. Indeed, Conservatives are not merely businessmen, they are big businessmen. Of the 273 company directors elected to Parliament in the first three decades following the second world war, no fewer than 245 were Conservatives. In 2010, a hundred Conservative MPs described themselves as company directors or executives, compared with eight for Labour and seven Liberal Democrats (Criddle 2010: 327).

Manual workers are virtually unrepresented on the Conservative and Liberal Democrat benches and their number has declined sharply in Labour's ranks, from over 40 per cent in 1945. However, unlike their Conservative and Liberal Democrat colleagues, Labour MPs are often first-generation middle class, having working-class parents (Cowley 2001: 826).

Political experience

One significant trend, continuing in 2010, was a growth in those whose occupations have been entirely in politics as 'staffers': political advisers and those working for parties as organizers, researchers or consultants. The 2001 Parliament contained 44 Labour staffers, 18 Conservatives and 4 Liberal Democrats, rising in 2010 to 52 Labour, 31 Conservatives and 7 Liberal Democrats. Although providing experience in the dark arts, such a grounding moves MPs further away from those they represent. They include many of the parties' luminaries; indeed, Ed Miliband, David Cameron and Nick Clegg had all worked in such a capacity.

A background in political activity is not entirely new. For long MPs have cut their political teeth in local government; of the 1997 intake, 70 per cent of Liberal Democrats, 64 per cent of Labour and 25 per cent of Conservatives had been councillors. In addition, Labour has always relied on a considerable body of MPs with a trade union grounding and has become a home for several student union ex-presidents. Within the Conservative Party an ethos of being born to rule has produced political dynasties where the young have been reared and educated with statesmanship in mind.

Sexual orientation

If the House is representative of the wider population in this respect, then a number of gays and lesbians must choose life in the parliamentary closet. After the 2001 general election, the *Guardian* recorded eight openly gay or lesbian MPs, including Labour's Ben Bradshaw and Chris Smith. Generally, such admission does little to enhance a political career. Michael Portillo's mention of early homosexual experience may have cost him the Conservative leadership in 2001. The tabloid newspapers can take a threatening line. Labour's Nick Brown came out under threat of exposure by the *Sun*, which also ran the headline 'TELL US THE TRUTH TONY – ARE WE BEING RUN BY A GAY MAFIA?'

Oh, Mr Bryant, it's after dark – shouldn't you be on Clapham Common?
Tabloid editor Rebekah Brooks to gay MP Chris Bryant at a Labour conference; reported variously and featured on BBC's *Panorama* (18 Jul 2011)

> They are behaving like Smithfield meat-porters – love the Queen Mum and bash the queers.
>
> Conservative MP David Ashby upon being deselected by his constituency after losing his libel case against the *Sunday Times* over allegations of homosexuality. Quoted in Criddle (1997: 197)

Even openly gay MPs tend not to place themselves as representatives of the gay community. Gay rights campaigner Peter Tatchell has inveighed against their failures to support anti-discrimination legislation against lesbians and gay men and there have been threats of a systematic 'outing' campaign. However, a *Guardian* poll (10 Nov. 1998) revealed public attitudes becoming more relaxed and the 'outing' of Peter Mandelson on television by gay journalist Matthew Parris did little to harm him.

Gender

The House of Commons is not so much a gentleman's club as a boy's boarding school.
Lib Dem MP Shirley Williams, on Granada TV (30 July 1985)

In the debate over the resemblance of the Commons to society at large, nothing generates as much heat as the issue of gender. Only a small proportion of MPs have been women (figure 14.2). Not becoming eligible for election until 1918, the first three all represented seats formerly held by their husbands. A poor record leaves Britain out of step with many other western democracies. In Sweden, for example, around 40 per cent of MPs are women. In 1928, when franchise equality was gained, suffragette Millicent Garrett Fawcett declared: 'Our cause is a long way from full success'; today the Fawcett Society continues her mission. Although women actually join political parties in similar numbers to men, they have not tended to seek nomination, neither have they been favoured by selection

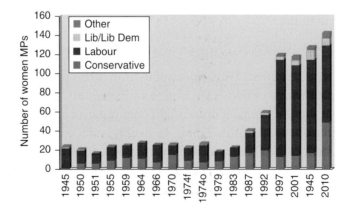

Figure 14.2 Women MPs 1945–2010

> ### Inappropriate questions
> * So what will your husband do for sex if you get the job?
> * How is your husband going to get his evening meal if you're at Westminster?
> * You should be wearing red. Are you wearing red knickers?
>
> Questions asked of women at local candidate selection committees, reported in P. Watson and M. Kite, 'Most unwanted', *The Times* (1 Aug. 2000)

committees. Of 4133 candidates in the 2010 general election, only 862 were women (Criddle 2010: 328).

The 1997 breakthrough, with 120 women elected, doubled their previous number. However, plaudits belonged largely to Labour, the Conservatives returning only 13, and the Liberal Democrats 3. This reflected Labour's policy of all-women shortlists (see p. 338). In Parliament, New Labour women began forming networks to work together (Lovenduski 1997: 719). However, although immaculately turned out, they promised little that was radical and the media were soon mocking 'Blair's Babes' and the 'Stepford Wives'. The prediction that they would produce more humane policies took something of a knock in the debate on the invasion of Iraq, when Blair's women were largely in support.

Monstrous regiment or Blair's Babes? Tony Blair with some of the Labour women MPs, May 1997

The 2010 general election produced a total of 143 women MPs, a modest increase of only 15 compared with 2005. As Conservative leader, David Cameron had initially pledged himself to a target of 50 per cent women candidates. While rejecting all-women shortlists, he established a central priority list (A-list) of candidates who already had successful careers outside politics. Although the Fawcett Society found him falling short of his ideals, the 2010 result saw a significant increase in the proportion of women on the Conservative benches, doubling from 8 to 16 per cent. However, the 2012 resignation of Louise Mensch, one of the most glamorous of the intake (a successful 'chick-lit' author), cast some doubt on the efficacy of recruiting 'celebrities'. Despite its losses, Labour could still claim the most success in terms of gender equality, with 81 women MPs (31 per cent, up from 28 per cent in 2005), while the Liberal Democrats trailed with only 7 (down from 16 to 8 per cent).

Ethnicity

Fear of racist voting has been a factor holding back the representation of ethnic minorities, with parties fighting shy of black candidates. Progress has been slow but in 2010 27 non-white MPs were returned: 15 Labour and 11 Conservative. A key factor is the contesting of winnable seats. Despite the Liberal Democrats fielding 46 non-white candidates, more than either of the two main rivals, none gained a seat. The Conservatives made the greatest advance by deliberately placing candidates in winnable seats. However, Labour maintained its lead in diversity by producing the first three Muslim woman MPs, though all-women shortlists were avoided in predominantly Muslim areas for fear of Asian resistance (Criddle 2010: 321).

Representing diversity

Increasingly parties make efforts to ensure that their parliamentary profiles reflect the society they serve. This broadly means moving away from the image of the white, middle-class, heterosexual male. David Cameron used PR skill to re-brand the Conservative Party. Indeed, a shortlist centrally imposed on Surrey East did not include a single white male (Criddle 2010: 316). However, beyond the categories considered above are numerous others, including adherents to various religions, atheists, the disabled, the illiterate, and so on. Moreover, microcosmic representation conflicts with the Burkean view of representation as leadership. It can be argued that the function of representation means more than resembling those represented. An accused burglar would not expect to be represented in court by another burglar. In practice, MPs move between the varying interpretations of their role. We shall see in the following chapter that in fulfilling its functions Parliament requires a variety of talents.

* * *

This chapter has introduced what may be termed the three main estates of the realm. However, their composition and structure do not explain their role in the governance of the country. To understand this we must look beyond structure to the functions Parliament performs. These are the focus of the next chapter.

Key points

- All polities contain ceremonial elements, though Britain is particularly rich in this respect.

- Bagehot took an exceedingly elitist view of such ceremony, its purpose being to keep the masses in the dark about the process of government.

- Britain has a constitutional monarchy.

- The idea that the monarchy is above politics is open to question.

- The future of the monarchy is an ever-present feature of contemporary debate.

- The House of Lords, with its composition still reflecting breeding and prime ministerial favour, may appear a relic of an undemocratic age.

- Yet it has evolved within British politics to offer some unique benefits.

- In the House of Commons Parliament comes closest to making Britain a representative democracy.

- Any idea that the Commons is (or should be) a microcosm of society is questionable.

Review your understanding of the following terms and concepts

'another place'	cross-bencher	Standards and
appointments commission	hereditary peer	Privileges
backbencher	Leader of the House	parliamentary privilege
bicameral	life peer	patronage
Black Rod	Lord Chancellor	Privy Councillor
Civil List	Lords' Speaker	Register of Members'
Committee on Standards	Order Paper	Interests
in Public Life	Parliamentary	Speaker
constitutional monarchy	Commissioner for	'usual channels'

Questions for discussion and debate

Consider these propositions and be prepared to present the cases for and against. Try to produce debating propositions of your own.

1 Ceremony and display are a necessary part of the process of government.
2 The life peerage system offers Britain a unique constitutional asset.
3 Without the mass media the British monarchy would die.
4 The abolition of the monarchy would have dangerous consequences.
5 An influx of women MPs can do little to change British politics.
6 Parliament cannot be described as representative unless it is a microcosm of society.
7 Outside jobs make better MPs.
8 Parliament can never protect itself against sleaze.
9 The value of the hereditary peers is underestimated.
10 The only solution to the problem of the House of Lords is abolition.

Further reading

See also reading for chapter 15.

Bagehot, W. (first published 1867) *The English Constitution*.
Elitist and somewhat disdainful of the masses, but contains enduring truths about the relationship between the rulers and the ruled, and the place of symbolism in politics.

Bogdanor, V. (1997) *The Monarchy and the Constitution*.
Accessible academic analysis of the monarchy in politics. Ultimately a defence of the institution.

Cannadine, D. (1999) *The Decline and Fall of the British Aristocracy*.
Historical chronicle explains the eroding wealth, power and prestige of the British nobility.

Dorey, P. and Kelso, A. (2011) *House of Lords Reform Since 1911: Must the Lords Go?*
Explains why House of Lords reform has proved so problematic since 1911.

Kavanagh, D. and Cowley, P. (eds) (2010), *The British General Election of 2010*.
Includes a very comprehensive analysis of the composition of the Commons by Criddle.

Norris, P. and Lovenduski, J. (1994) *Political Recruitment: Gender, Race and Class in the British Parliament*.
Examines the relative dearth of women, black and working-class MPs and discusses whether the social bias in the political elite matters.

Rogers, R. and Walters, R. (2006) *How Parliament Works*, 6th edn.
Perceptive (and sometime amusing) insights into the workings, daily life and character of Parliament.

For reading around the subject and some light relief

Julian Critchley, *Palace of Varieties*.
An entertaining insight into an MP's role by one of its mavericks.

Edwina Currie, *A Parliamentary Affair*.
Obsessive ambition, eroticism and political intrigue.

Paul Flynn, *How to be an MP*.
The most borrowed book from the Commons library.

Frances Edmonds, *Members Only*.
A sharp and witty analysis of the Commons from a feminist perspective.

Anthony Holden, *The Tarnished Crown*.
Express columnist and keen monarchy watcher with republican sympathies.

Sara Keays, *The Black Book*.
Novel by former amour of minister Cecil Parkinson about the 'black book' in which whips record the sins of their fellow MPs.

Kitty Kelley, *The Royals*.
Fearless American iconoclast turns her attention on the House of Windsor.

Peter Morgan, *The Audience*.
Play imagining the Queen's weekly meetings with her prime ministers, described as 'the dirty dozen' by Helen Mirren's Queen Elizabeth II.

Andrew Morton, *Diana: Her True Story.*
Book which put the cat among the corgis on the break-up of the fairytale marriage.

The Queen.
Stephen Frears' film covering the events surrounding the death of Princess Diana, with Helen Mirren as the Queen.

Sue Townsend, *The Queen and I.*
Life for the royal family on a council estate.

On the net

http://www.royal.gov.uk
The monarchy's website will welcome you with official information on its history and changing role. Numerous links will take you to the lesser members of the royal family and even provide pictures.

http://www.parliament.uk
Parliament's home page offers links to the Commons and Lords and an enormous amount of information on parliamentary history, customs and procedure.

https://www.gov.uk
This government website will open a door to sites of various other parliamentary appendages, such as the Committee on Standards in Public Life.

CHAPTER 15

PARLIAMENT AT WORK: NOT TO REASON WHY

Contents

In this chapter we turn from the overtly ceremonial and structural aspects of Parliament to its governmental role. We begin by noting the overwhelming dominance of political parties, before turning to the central functions of sustaining a government, making legislation, debating, and scrutinizing the executive. Beyond this we consider how the proceedings of Parliament are brought to the attention of the population in whose name it operates. We conclude by trying to look behind the formal trappings to evaluate Parliament's essential role today.

Parliament's procedures are scrupulously regulated by its Standing Orders. However, these make no mention of the most pervasive source of influence within the chambers, committee rooms and even the bars and terraces – the political parties. Journalist Martin Bell, entering as an independent on an anti-sleaze ticket in 1997 was, in his white suit, a lone figure. This rather dimly glowing torch of independence was carried on after June 2001 by Dr Richard Taylor, representing Wyre Forest until losing to the Conservatives in 2010. In the same year Caroline Lucas won an historic victory in Brighton, but was the sole representative of the Green Party rather than an independent.

The idea that Parliament has its own distinct identity is really part of the dignified constitution; such life it has is breathed into it by the parties through their front-bench teams, forming the government and shadow government respectively, and their massed backbench ranks. What is the *raison d'être* for such dominance? For the majority party it is nothing less than producing and sustaining a government; for the others, the less heroic role of opposing and waiting.

The Parliamentary Parties: Sustaining the Executive

In Britain we believe we have a democratic government, yet no one voted for it as such; citizens choose only MPs. The government emerges as the creation of the House of Commons. Does this mean that the Commons is master of the government? The doctrine of parliamentary sovereignty (see p. 97) would seem to imply this, but the reality is rather different. The government is formed from the party, or coalition, that can count on majority support within the Commons; its survival depends on its MPs. Their loyalty becomes, quite literally, a matter of political life or death. This fact dominates Westminster, with profound implications for the way Parliament performs each of its functions.

Today party leaders are invariably from the Commons; in earlier times they came from the Lords, but Lord Salisbury, who retired in 1902, was the last of this breed. In 1906, after a landslide victory, the leading Liberals in the Commons – Asquith, Grey and Haldane – plotted (unsuccessfully) to dispatch their leader, Henry Campbell-Bannerman, to the Lords, knowing that this would neuter him and allow Asquith in the Commons to become *de facto* prime minister (Cross 1963: 14–15). Conversely, in 1963, Alec Douglas-Home had to renounce his peerage and enter the Commons before he could become prime minister.

Backbench organizations

Backbench organizations meet regularly once or twice a week. The Conservatives form the 1922 Committee (see p. 360), whose chairman, elected annually by the backbenchers, retains direct access to the leader and is always a commanding party figure. Proceedings are conducted informally with few rules, day-to-day affairs being organized by an executive committee of around fifteen, also elected annually. When in government the party leader and ministers are not members but the leader may attend and address the Committee, the event usually being something of an occasion. The Committee plays a key role in the election of the party leader (see p. 332).

The Labour Party formed its near-equivalent in 1923 as the Parliamentary Labour Party (PLP). This is not exclusively a backbencher group; the leaders are also members, as are its members in the House of Lords. At one time the party leader chaired the PLP but in 1970 the two positions were divided, with members electing the chair annually. It is usual for the sitting member to be returned unopposed but in 2006 Ann Clywd was ousted by Tony Lloyd, who challenged her on the grounds that she was too close to party leader Tony Blair. In opposition the front-bench team was elected annually as the 'shadow cabinet' but, on becoming leader, Ed Miliband ended this practice, thereby increasing his power of patronage. Since 1980 the PLP has formed one element in a party-wide electoral college (see p. 335). When in office, a liaison committee, with one-half government representatives and one-half elected by the PLP, acts as a channel of communication between leader and backbenchers.

The vicissitudes of the electoral system leave third parties at their weakest on the parliamentary stage and their organization is more informal. At one time it was unkindly said that the Liberals could hold their meetings in a bus shelter, but with a breakthrough to sixty-two members after the 2005 election the Liberal Democrats could laugh at the joke. In opposition the leading members of the parliamentary party termed themselves a shadow ministerial team, but with increasing numbers became sufficiently emboldened to adopt the term 'shadow cabinet' – a title contested by their Conservative rivals.

In the upper house things are more relaxed but all three parties have a leader and chief whip (see below). The near-equivalent of the 1922 Committee is the Association of Conservative Peers. Labour peers may attend PLP meetings but also meet separately.

There remains an element of mystery about the workings of the backbench organizations. Although the PLP agreed to press reporting of its meetings in the 1970s, there is no constitutional requirement that they conduct their affairs before the public gaze. Sometimes meetings can be fractious and the party whips will take note of disquiet within the ranks. The 1922 Committee practises its rites behind closed doors and sinister stories have circulated, some of the earlier ones started, not surprisingly, by Lloyd George. On balance, the evidence is that, although having less formal authority, it receives a more studious ear from party leaders than does the PLP. Loss of confidence can see ministerial heads roll; this may have been the case in the resignations of several of Major's ministers in the 1990s, and the dispatch of Thatcher in 1990 demonstrated just how brutal the Committee can be. Charles Kennedy and Menzies Campbell received similar treatment from their Liberal Democrat colleagues.

Policy influence

The parliamentary parties establish committees specializing in particular policy areas, regions of the country and items of legislation. Front-benchers will often consult with these when aspects of their portfolios are under consideration. In opposition, there is some feeling in the PLP that votes should be binding on the front bench, a conflict avoided by the Conservatives since shadow ministers can chair the committees. Influence tends to be weaker when a party is in government as the leaders become more remote. Not wishing to antagonize their troops, however, they generally take soundings on the general mood through the whips. Edward Heath's reputation for aloofness contributed to his downfall. The all-male club atmosphere of the House placed Mrs Thatcher at a disadvantage, though she encouraged cabinet colleagues to act as her eyes and ears in the bars, tea rooms and corridors. Although work on the party committees enables MPs to gain experience and specialized knowledge, they also make demands on their time (see Norton 1994).

The culture of obedience

> ### Obedience or impotence
> The principle of Parliament is obedience to leaders. Change your leader if you will, take another if you will, but obey No. 1 while you serve No. 1, and obey No. 2 when you serve No. 2. The penalty of not doing so, is the penalty of impotence.
>
> Walter Bagehot, *The English Constitution* (1867)

Although rebellions can happen, the role of backbench MPs today is largely one of humility, their lot to follow rather than lead, as satirized by Sir Joseph Porter in Gilbert and Sullivan's *HMS Pinafore*:

> I always voted at my party's call,
> And never thought of thinking for myself at all.
> I thought so little they rewarded me,
> By making me the leader of the Queen's navy.

While loyalty to the cause will be a factor, a prime motive for such obedience is ambition; careers are advanced through the patronage of those above. Discipline becomes stronger for government members. Indeed, even in free votes prime ministers may expect loyalty from this 'payroll vote', as John Major did over the abolition of corporal punishment in state schools in November 1996. Those entering the House later in life and with little further ambition may lack the incentives to grovel, yet such members rarely exhibit radical tendencies.

The mavericks

> ### The price of milk and dissent
> Unfortunately I think that not only are they two posh boys who don't know the price of milk but two arrogant posh boys who show no remorse, no contrition and no passion.
>
> Conservative MP Nadine Dorries on her party leader and his chancellor, on the BBC's *Daily Politics* (April 2012)

A small category of MPs, scorning the party leaders and placemen, will speak their minds and can be more influential than docile colleagues. Enoch Powell, for example, caused both major parties to harden their lines on immigration, while the Eurosceptics influence attitudes towards European integration. Sometimes these mavericks spend their earlier years as orthodox careerists. Powell was Minister of

Health in 1962, and Michael Heseltine, who was poised at the crossroads between orthodoxy and Mavericksville in the late 1980s, was to return as a pillar of the Major government. Fiery Welsh radical Aneurin Bevan succumbed to the warm embrace of orthodoxy for a time as the siren of office beckoned, while Tony Benn strayed progressively leftwards throughout a long career. Those who have enjoyed front-bench status but have been dispatched to the backbenches following a reshuffle can also prove awkward. When Labour Home Secretary Charles Clarke made this unwelcome journey in 2006 he became a vociferous critic of the government, as did the Conservative Liam Fox after being forced to resign in 2011. Mavericks are not always without ambition; a rebellious stand on a populist issue may prove advantageous (see Pattie et al. 1994). Harold Wilson resigned from the government in 1951 over NHS charges but by 1964 was prime minister, and Iain Duncan Smith, a Euro-rebel under Major, became party leader in 2001. However, MPs really falling foul of the leadership can be expelled from the party (see below).

Uncritical mass

> I am unique among MPs in that I can say when I don't know. I can say I've changed my mind and I can say I've made a mistake. That's what being independent is about. The mistakes I make are my own mistakes and they are not forced on me by a party whip.
>
> Martin Bell, 'On being an independent MP', *Talking Politics* (13(1), Summer 2000)

Newer MPs are more likely to toe the line than the old-stagers. With only 62 rebellions in 941 votes in its first three years, Labour's 1997 contingent, replete with newcomers, was the most loyal of the post-war era. Of the pre-1997 vintage, 32 per cent rebelled at least once, compared with only 25 per cent of the freshers. The new women proved the most loyal of all, with a 14 per cent rebellion rate (White, M. 2001). It can be argued that this level of obedience was a product of widespread agreement amongst Labour MPs and a belief that they could exert influence behind the scenes (Cowley 2001: 827). As a government's term progresses, and the number passed over or returning to the ranks grows, discipline weakens. Major found this when he followed Thatcher into Number Ten, and towards the end of the Blair premiership the rate of revolts and threats of revolts had reached destabilizing levels (see Cowley 2005). By 2013, pressure from the Eurosceptics on David Cameron was beginning to reach the level endured by John Major.

While we were in opposition Humphrey Atkins had been a most objectionable Chief Whip, and had marked my card. ... he gave me a spastic 'dressing down' for smashing one of the House telephones.
Conservative MP Alan Clark, *Diaries* (1 Jan. 1990)

The mechanics of discipline

A key figure in **party discipline** is the chief **whip**, aided by assistant whips. In the Conservative Party the leader makes the appointments but Labour's whips are elected by fellow MPs. In both cases their loyalty is to the leadership, ensuring that members will generally remain 'on message' and be in the House to vote as required. The title comes appropriately enough from the world of the hunt, where the 'whipper in' is charged with keeping the hounds in order. The whips circulate weekly memorandums outlining the pattern of business and showing the relative importance of the votes by underscoring the request to attend with one, two or three lines. A 'three-line whip' indicates top priority, with grave consequences for backsliding, ranging from a dressing-down to a 'withdrawal of the whip' (a form of excommunication, to be restored only when the offender has purged his political soul).

Labour has proved far more likely to use stern measures, even resorting to expulsion. In 1954 the whip was withdrawn from fiery radical Aneurin Bevan and seven of his supporters. Under New Labour several MPs suffered this fate, including Ken Livingstone, expelled in April 2000 for running as an independent in the London mayoral election. George Galloway went in October 2003 for his outspoken criticism of the attack on Iraq. Yet stern measures do not always work. In November 1994, eight Conservatives abstained over the European Communities (Finance) Bill, which the Major government was treating as a vote of confidence. The government scraped home and the whip was withdrawn from the rebels. However, far from becoming pariahs, as 'the whipless wonders' they were to enjoy a collective notoriety, gaining much media attention. The whip was restored the following April with little sign of atonement. Again, Ken Livingstone, after his expulsion, went on to win the London mayoral election and George Galloway returned to Parliament in 2005 as head of his newly formed Respect Party.

> **Pairing**
> An unofficial practice allows that, if an MP cannot be present to vote in a particular division, an arrangement can be made with an MP of an opposing party that he/she will also not attend. Pairing arrangements can exist between two MPs on a long-term basis. Whips will usually be satisfied if an absent member has arranged a pair. However, the practice is not allowed on matters of great importance.

The constituency associations can also be part of the machinery of obedience. Of the seven left-wing rebels voting against Eden over Suez, four failed to secure re-adoption as parliamentary candidates. In the 1960s, Wilson employed canine imagery to warn Labour rebels that although every dog might be permitted one bite, he should not forget that his constituency 'licence' would need renewing. Among the Conservatives, Sir Anthony Meyer, who had the temerity to challenge Thatcher for the party leadership in 1989, suffered de-selection soon afterwards, and in 1997 the Reigate association deselected sitting MP Sir George Gardiner, a Eurosceptic who had described Major as a ventriloquist's dummy.

Discipline has been more relaxed in the upper house and cross-voting can be acceptable. Despite dignified titles (Captain of the Gentlemen at Arms and his deputy, the Captain of the Yeomen of the Guard), the whips have few sticks with which to fright the souls of old warriors and, in the case of hereditary peers, few carrots to dangle before the eyes of those who already own much of the country.

We'll swing together

Yet in the final analysis backbenchers and leaders are in the same boat; discipline is in everyone's interest. The fratricide under Major contributed to the Conservatives' disastrous result in 1997, many finding themselves blackballed by the electorate from the 'best club in London'.

A ministerial training ground

The reason that ambition can be an important factor in ensuring discipline lies in Britain's unusual fusion of powers. Convention requires that ministers and other government members have seats in Parliament, usually in the Commons. A denial of the separation of powers, this convention arose from the monarchs' desire to have their ministers in a position to manage Parliament. The 1701 Act of Settlement attempted to sever this link but its value to the executive led to its persistence into the modern age.

Once in Parliament, the ambitious must aim to impress their party leaders through speeches, parliamentary questions, committee work, mastery of legislative detail, ability to be 'clubbable' and of course their loyalty. The first rung on the ladder is often appointment as a parliamentary private secretary to a minister. This unpaid position, as a general assistant, is loaded with opportunity. Through this process ministers (and shadow ministers) can emerge who have proved themselves equal to the heat of the parliamentary fray and ready for the dispatch box. However, there are dangers; ambitious MPs may put courtship of their leaders above loyalty to the House.

Three-line whips are very rare, and if I get 150 peers in to vote, using a really strong two-line whip, I am doing jolly well.
Lord ('Bertie') Denham (Conservative chief whip in the Lords), in the *Independent* (27 April 1988)

Making Laws

Parliamentary sovereignty lies at the heart of the British constitution. Parliament is the legislature, free to make any law it chooses, not bound by previous laws, and subject to no legal restraint from any other constitutional body. Although constrained by EU membership, it is always free to secede from this association. However, we shall find that in practice parliamentary supremacy is not all it seems.

The legislative process

All Acts of Parliament begin life as **bills** which, broadly speaking, are of two kinds.

- *Private bills* are introduced by some body (a local authority or public corporation) wanting some special power in the form of a *by-law*. These were common in the nineteenth century as the local bourgeoisie (as councils or ad hoc authorities) sought new powers to develop the industrial cities.
- *Public bills* constitute the lion's share of all legislation, becoming the normal laws of the land. Although most are government bills, some are introduced by private members.

Some bills may contain both public and private elements, in which case they are known as hybrid bills. The legislation concerning the Channel Tunnel involved hybrid bills.

All bills travel a lengthy **legislative process** (figure 15.1). For public bills this was to be completed within a single session, otherwise they were 'lost' and had to start from the beginning in the following session. However, following the Modernization Committee's 1998 report, certain bills may be 'rolled' over, a practice that increased from 2003. The first to be so treated was the Financial Services and Markets Bill, carried over into the 1999–2000 session. If necessary, the legislative process can be accelerated (the 1911 Official Secrets Act was rushed through the Commons in a single day, as were the 1998 Landmines Bill and the 2000 Northern Ireland Bill re-imposing direct rule).

Bills pass through both Houses, usually originating in the Commons but sometimes in the Lords. With its packed programme, the 1997 Labour government introduced several major pieces of legislation (including the Crime and Disorder Bill, the Higher Education Bill and the Human Rights Bill) in the upper house.

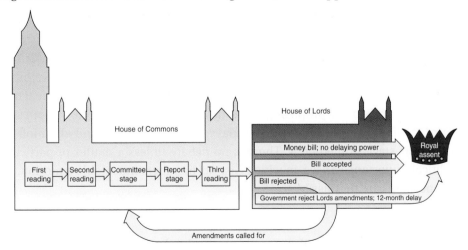

Figure 15.1 The legislative process

The progress of a bill introduced in the Commons involves the following stages.

- *Pre-legislative scrutiny.* Consultation documents and white papers often precede major legislation to permit widespread discussion. Increasingly, governments release draft bills for pre-legislative scrutiny by select committees and in May 2002 it was agreed to make specialist staff available to assist MPs in this.
- *First reading.* This is a formality when the bill is introduced by its sponsor who, in the case of government bills, is a minister. The House orders the bill to be printed and sets a date for the second reading. The bill is prepared by parliamentary draughtsmen with the exactitude of lawyers. Although a second reading is rarely denied, this can happen, and was the fate of the Shops Bill (on Sunday trading) in April 1996.
- *Second reading.* The broad principle of the proposed legislation is debated, but modifications are not permitted. Although voting takes place, rebels rarely use this stage to mount a protest, a notable exception being the ninety-one Conservatives voting against the House of Lords Reform Bill in July 2012, which was subsequently withdrawn.
- *Committee stage.* The bill is considered clause by clause, sometimes leading to proposed amendments. Meetings take place 'upstairs' in a **Public Bill Committee** (formerly a standing committee). Membership of somewhere between sixteen and fifty reflects party balance in the House, giving the government the advantage. Following a 2006 report of the Modernization Committee, the committees are able to take evidence from experts and interest groups. For matters of major constitutional importance, as with the devolution legislation, this stage can take place before a Committee of the Whole House.
- *Report stage.* The committee reports back to the House, which debates the clauses and proposed amendments in detail. In the case of major bills this may take several days. Amendments may be agreed, but many are introduced by the government as a tidying-up function. Voting usually follows party lines but, if the government's own supporters stand up, the boat may begin to rock. Thus, in April 1988 the Conservative majority was slashed to a humiliating twenty-five in the report stage of the 'poll tax' bill. Blair suffered his first parliamentary defeat over the 2005 Terrorism Bill, proposing ninety days' detention of suspects without trial.
- *Third reading.* This final stage is nowadays largely a formality and often follows the report stage immediately. There is no debate unless a matter of particular political importance arises, in which case six members must table a motion. No amendments are permissible.

House of Lords

From the Commons the bill proceeds to the Lords, to follow a similar route. Generally no serious challenge is expected; if amendments are proposed, the bill returns to the Commons, but if these are rejected the Lords are then expected to comply gracefully. Moreover, in the case of manifesto commitments, the Salisbury Convention requires that the Lords will never frustrate the will of the elected House. Only if a government was clearly acting unconstitutionally (say, attempting to extend its life beyond five years) would continuing opposition be regarded as justified. Thus, for example, despite receiving an eloquent and informed mauling by Lord Lestor QC and the Law Lords, the Commons reversed all amendments to the 1993 Criminal Justice and Public Order Bill.

Yet their Lordships have not proved powerless. Under the 1949 Parliament Act, they have the right to delay non-money bills for twelve months. Again, the very process of returning a bill with amendments takes time and, before the provision for bills to 'roll over', delay could amount to government defeat, particularly towards the end of a session when a legislative backlog has built up. Moreover, defeats in the Lords can be embarrassing to governments, generating adverse publicity. The 1980s and 1990s saw greater assertiveness, with over a hundred defeats.

New Labour fared no better, with some thirty defeats in each session up to its 1999 interim reform. In July 1998 the Higher Education Bill was so batted back and forth that it was termed 'ping pong in ermine'. The European Parliamentary

Another Place? Debate in the House of Lords

Photo: Parliamentary copyright

Elections Bill, at the very end of the 1997/8 session, suffered five defeats. Here the introduction of closed lists could be seen as a constitutional matter, but many argued that such draconian action was unwarranted. Finally the 1949 Parliament Act was invoked, enabling the Commons to override the Lords. Significantly, the 1999 'interim' reform did little to stem the tide, with thirty-six defeats in the first session, some on flagship measures. Contrary to expectations, ejecting the battalions of hereditary peers appeared to have lessened the self-restraint. In 2004 the peers even broke the Salisbury Convention in opposing the anti-foxhunting bill and causing the Parliament Act to be invoked again – only the fourth time since 1949. Another bout of 'ping pong', over plans to outlaw the 'glorification' of terrorism, saw the ball returned six times before peers finally complied in March 2006.

Royal Assent

La Royne le veult. Norman French formula for the Royal Assent

In the final stage of the legislative process the Queen formally approves the bill, whereupon it becomes an **Act of Parliament**. This stage has been entirely ceremonial since Britain became a constitutional monarchy; the Royal Assent was last withheld in 1707, by Queen Anne. The Royal Assent is also the final stage of the Scottish legislative process.

Restrictions on legislative influence

The greatest constraint on the legislative influence of Parliament as a body is the fact that the government will get its own way most of the time owing to its majority, which is also reflected in the composition of the Public Bill Committees. There are also other ways in which governments can limit Parliament's influence. Standing orders introduced in 1902 enable the government to decide what subjects could be raised and for how long they would be discussed (dubbed 'Balfour's railway timetable'). Both front benches accept this curtailment, the opposition recognizing that they too may enjoy the advantages when in office, and negotiations between them are conducted by the whips through 'the usual channels'. Devices curtailing debate include the following.

- *Closure motions.* These permit the House to agree to a member's request that 'the question be now put' without further discussion.
- *The guillotine.* While tedious speakers are not decapitated, the debate itself is put under the blade at a government-determined time. This usually leads to opposition accusations of steamrollering, as in the case of the Devolution Referendums Bill in June 1997. In 2010 David Cameron aroused anger over threats to use a guillotine to curtail House of Lords debate on the Parliamentary Voting System and Constituencies Bill.
- *Programme motions.* Like the guillotine, these are allocation-of-time motions.

Introduced following recommendations of the Modernization Committee, they set a limited number of sittings for the passage of a bill.

- *The kangaroo.* Only a limited number of the proposed amendments are discussed, 'hopping' over the others like the antipodean marsupial. This is mainly used in committee and is applied at the discretion of the Speaker.

There are other ways in which legislative debate is limited. The committee stage necessarily excludes the majority of MPs from detailed discussion. Lack of time sometimes infuriates members. Shadow Home Secretary Ann Widdecombe and three colleagues vented their anger with a sit-in at the committee stage of the Criminal Justice and Police Bill in March 2001. Once a bill has been passed the committee disbands, allowing no opportunity for MPs to build up specialist expertise.

In addition, much power is passed to civil servants to frame detailed clauses through statutory orders and regulations. Although freeing Parliament from 'technical details', as long ago as 1929 Lord Chief Justice Lord Hewart (1929: v) feared the dangerous 'pretensions and encroachments of Bureaucracy', in which he discerned a 'new despotism'. Most Acts conferring such powers contain provisions for Parliament to consider **delegated legislation** and pass affirmative or negative resolutions.

Private members' legislation

It is here that Parliament comes nearest to a policy-initiating role. **Private members' bills** are introduced by individual MPs rather than the government. They can also be introduced in the Lords although, if they get as far as the Commons, they do not have priority. Despite various restrictions, some MPs use the opportunity to demonstrate parliamentary flair and make their mark, as did Roy Jenkins (obscene publications), David Steel (abortion law reform) and Margaret Thatcher (admission to public meetings).

Three means are available for private members' legislation.

- *The ballot.* In each session a ballot (drawing lots) is held for those wishing to present a bill. Many MPs have definite legislative ambition, but some, lucky in the ballot but without clear plans, will be besieged by pressure groups with ideas of their own.
- *The ten-minute rule.* At the opening of business on most Tuesdays and Wednesdays a ten-minute period is allowed for a backbencher to introduce a bill. If approved it will then run the normal course of a private members' bill. An MP wishing to do this must be first to the door of the Public Bill Office on the Tuesday or Wednesday morning three weeks before the day on which they wish to present the bill. Some members have resorted to sleeping overnight outside the office in order to be first there.

- *Presentation*. Here members may introduce the title of the bill but not speak in support of it. They must give notice of their intention. Although publicity may be gained, such bills rarely become law.

The hurdles

Nothing better betokens the humility of MPs than the provision made for them to introduce bills of their own. The reefs upon which they can founder are various.

- *Luck of the draw*. Demand outstrips the niggardly supply of opportunity and a ballot selects the first twenty of those applying. Of these lucky ones, fewer than half will ever see their bills discussed, let alone complete the obstacle course to become an Act.
- *Procedural problems*. A mere thirteen Fridays are reserved for balloted bills, during which time they must attempt to negotiate all the legislative hurdles. Friday is the day when many return to their constituencies and there is a danger that the House will not be quorate. Malevolent opponents may 'talk' the bill out, preventing debate from closing, as happened to Labour backbencher Mike Foster's attempt to ban foxhunting in March 1998, despite a 250 majority in favour on first reading. Between 1967, when David Steel steered his abortion bill through, and 1988, when David Ashton introduced another on the same subject, no fewer than fifteen private members' bills on abortion law fell foul of procedural devices.
- *Government attitude*. If a government wishes, it can put various spanners in the legislative works. It may mobilize its majority to strangle a bill at birth. Alternatively, if it welcomes the measure, a government can make time available. This is a convenient means of passing legislation with which, for reasons of discretion or cowardice, a government may not wish to be associated, as happened in the cases of homosexual law reform and abortion. Sometimes a government will make known a number of topics upon which it would welcome private members' bills. A government may induce a member to drop a bill in order to bring in a similar one of its own, as in the case of the 1965 Health Services Complaints Act. This tactic may be used to water down a proposal, as with the 1988 reform of the Official Secrets Act.

Even if a bill meets an ignominious end, however, MPs have had an opportunity to publicize their views and stimulate debate. Michael Foster's failed foxhunting bill, for example, later re-emerged as a government bill.

Legislation from Europe

EU membership produces an alternative source of law affecting British people. Critics see this as an assault on parliamentary sovereignty and MPs have sought some element of control. In May 1974 a sixteen-member European Scrutiny Committee was established to examine draft European Commission proposals. However, unable to question the legislators, it can only recommend further consideration by an appropriate committee or the House. Even here no amendments can be made; the House debates the proposal as a 'take note' motion in the hope that ministers will reflect its views in Brussels. In Denmark the Folketing enjoys far greater powers to influence its government's position in Brussels. Matters are additionally complicated because the Westminster and Brussels timetables are not synchronized and proposals may surface during a recess. The Lords also has a European scrutiny committee, working through seven specialist subcommittees. The Lisbon Treaty (see p. 186) reflected concern over the role of national parliaments and laid down an early-warning system giving them the right to receive and comment on draft proposals in the light of the principle of subsidiarity.

The value of the legislative process today

The legislative process bestows an official seal of approval. Ordinary people can rest in their beds secure in the knowledge that the laws affecting their lives have satisfied their elected representatives, rather in the way that a car might pass its MOT test. Or can they? Although outwardly the process remains essentially that of the nineteenth-century 'Golden Age', it has become in some measure part of the dignified constitution. Like all such ceremonial, much of its value lies in its ability to beguile and deceive. Yet, although the legislative process may have little *policy* influence, it remains of considerable *political* significance as a means of legitimation. Moreover, it would be mistaken to conclude that all stages of the process are as empty as the Royal Assent. Revolts in both Commons and Lords can sometimes change government bills. And beyond this, legislative debate fulfils two important roles: *publicity* and *criticism*. Although imperfect, these cannot be dismissed as contributions to democracy.

Debates in Parliament

Another major parliamentary function is debating issues of the day ('parliament' derives from the French *parler*). On occasions debate can be heated and may continue into the small hours although, since 1994, the government has used its 'best endeavours' to avoid such late-night sittings. Practice has varied over the years, with various experiments and attempts at modernization. Opportunities for debate include the following.

- *The **Queen's Speech**. Delivered in the House of Lords with much pomp and ceremony at the beginning of each session, this catalogue of proposed legislation (written by the prime minister) is debated over the following five days.

- *General government debates.* The government will normally devote around fifteen days each session for debate on topics of its choice. It will choose subjects in which it can appear in a favourable light but can also float ideas and hear views on green or white papers, and outline its position.

- *Opposition Days.* Originally called Supply Days, these are twenty occasions when the topic is chosen by the opposition parties (in proportion to numerical strength). Here the aim is usually to attack the government. The Liberal Democrats scored a notable triumph when, in April 2009, the Labour government was defeated on a motion on Gurkha settlement in Britain, its first defeat on an opposition-day motion since coming to power in 1997.

- *Estimates Days.* Since 1981, three days have been set aside each session for debating the Estimates (of government expenditure), with topics chosen by the Liaison Committee (comprising the chairs of other committees).

- *Adjournment debates.* On four days a week, a half-hour debate at the end of the sitting traditionally allows the House to consider an issue without having to vote. The Speaker chooses Thursday's subject; on other days, MPs are selected by ballot and the topics raised often concern constituency matters. A minister will reply. The final adjournment debate before a recess is a larger affair, the motion selected by party leaders. A further series of debates takes place on Tuesdays and Wednesdays in the ancient banqueting chamber, Westminster Hall. Usually on non-controversial issues, these are chaired by special deputy speakers who, unlike the Commons Speaker, do not relinquish their political identities.

- *Emergency adjournment debates.* A government may propose 'That this House do now adjourn' at the beginning of the day to debate an emergency, such as happened over the Gulf war of 1991.

Subjects proposed to be raised on the Motion for the Adjournment of the House in Westminster Hall on Wednesday 20 May 2009

Start time	End time	Member	Subject
09:30	11:00	Miss Anne McIntosh	Primary care trust criteria for allocating beds to elderly patients
11:00	11:30	Anne Main	Allocation of school places
14:30	16:00	Jeremy Corbyn	London Metropolitan University
16:00	16:30	Siobhain McDonagh	Progress of Better Healthcare Closer to Home strategy
16:30	17:00	Mark Hunter	Future of the Nimrod project

- *Emergency debates under Standing Order No. 24.* Here an MP can ask for an adjournment to debate a 'specific and important matter that should have urgent consideration'. The agreement of the Speaker must be sought and such debates are infrequent. One was held on 6 July 2011 when Speaker Bercow acceded to a request by Labour MP Chris Bryant concerning phone hacking by journalists.
- *Private members' motions.* In each session a number of Fridays are reserved for motions put by private members. Although constituency matters may be raised, debates often centre on government policy.
- *E-petition debates.* In 2006 the government set up an e-petition site which began to produce some embarrassing demands. It soon attracted 1.6 million signatures from those opposed to plans to introduce road pricing and there were even demands for Prime Minister Gordon Brown to quit. It was suspended ahead of the general election to be re-launched in June 2010 with the promise that any campaign backed by 100,000 signatures would trigger consideration for debate in Parliament (see p. 265).
- *Backbench business time debates.* The 2010 coalition government established a system whereby backbenchers could bring forward debates of their choice. The equivalent of thirty-five days in the House were allocated for these. An eight-member Backbench Business Committee considers MPs' proposals, including those raised in e-petitions or national campaigns. Topics can cover almost any subject; in 2011 they ranged from the future of the nation's pubs to onshore wind energy. MPs responded enthusiastically but were soon critical of the restriction on time and of crowding out by e-petitions.

Early Day Motions

Citizens may read that their MP has put down, or signed, an **Early Day Motion** (EDM), though may never see any record of the debate. This puzzle arises because an EDM is today a colloquial term for a notice of a debate with no expectation that it will ever take place. A number of such motions are tabled each day. MPs will sign them rather like a petition to register their feelings on a subject. One signed by sixty-nine of his backbenchers in June 1992 gave John Major a forbidding warning of his Eurotroubles to come. Sometimes much can be achieved, as when an EDM in November 1994 forced minister Michael Heseltine to abandon plans to privatize the Post Office.

Empty debate

Despite the opportunities, commentators have criticized the way Parliament uses its debating powers.

- *Blind loyalty.* Debate is rather a misnomer. Often there appears to be little real cut and thrust as members tend to recite prepared briefs, rarely responding to previous points and not even remaining in the chamber to hear how others respond. Final votes reflect not the qualities of wit or wisdom but party loyalty.

- *Backbench frustration.* In calling members the Speaker is supposed to look to those with particular expertise or interest, but frequently MPs are left seething at not having been called. The inexperienced spend fruitless hours preparing speeches never delivered. Speakers can be attacked for being over-conscious of the rights of Privy Councillors.

- *Superficiality.* Debate can emphasize meretricious rhetorical skills. Members performing stylishly may triumph over less articulate colleagues. As deputy prime minister, John Prescott's use of the English language led to mockery from the opposition.

- *Ya-boo politics.* The televising of Parliament brought into shocked viewers' homes scenes of booing, fist-waving and shouting down, often likened to a bear garden. Indeed, the Speaker's plaintive cry of 'Order, Order' became the 'signature tune' of the broadcasts.

- *Insubstantial.* Commons debates can be of low quality. Ministers rely blindly on a crutch of bureaucracy (providing statistics, arguments and information), while the opposition struggles to build its case on the basis of outside advice, intuition and invective. In the Lords the hereditary peers represented a narrow interest but the presence of life peers, appointed because of some particular expertise (from the professions, the arts, industry or academia), can often sustain a higher level of debate. The presence of scientists is of particular significance, given their almost complete absence from the Commons.

- *The empty chamber.* Backbenchers do not always support each other well; once opening speeches have been made they can drift from the chamber, re-emerging only to cast their all-important votes. Absenteeism was made even easier by a 'deferred vote' system introduced in December 2000, allowing MPs to submit a sheet showing their voting intentions for the following week without even entering the chamber. To critics this was a sop to the new influx of women MPs, some of whom were unhappy about long hours (see Black 2000).

A Select Committee on Modernization of the House of Commons reviews the practices and procedures of the House. It has made various recommendations, such as keeping questions and answers brief and calling upon members to respond to comments of previous speakers and, having spoken, to remain in the chamber. It has also suggested that the Speaker cease to give Privy Councillors precedence. Its reports led to the additional debates on Tuesdays and Wednesdays in Westminster Hall.

Debates in Parliament take the form of a party clash rather than a dialogue between executive and legislature. There is value in this in that issues of the day can be articulated and publicized; an informed opposition is a crucial element of democracy. However, in the effort to hold the executive more effectively to account, Parliament has sought other means. It is to these that we now turn.

Scrutiny of the Executive

It is said that the price of freedom is eternal vigilance; the idea that Parliament should scrutinize the executive remains a key aspect of its rationale. MPs probe through **parliamentary questions** and through an updated version of an ancient instrument – the select committee.

Questions in the House: a fretful hour

One of the few opportunities MPs have to shine is during **Question Time**: every day (except Fridays) government members face an hour of questions on their portfolios. A relatively modern innovation, it began in the nineteenth century as a reaction to an enlarging executive. The occasion can prove testing to ministers. Although answers are prepared by civil servants (work in the upper echelons of a department can come to a virtual standstill while this is done), the hour receives keen media attention and those who falter may be earmarked as political liabilities; for junior ministers it can be make-or-break time.

Oral and written answers

Questions may, at the choice of the member, receive an oral answer in the chamber or a written one (indicated by an asterisk on the order paper). With almost 50,000 questions tabled each session, about three-quarters receive written answers. The distinction has considerable importance. Written answers can be prepared by civil servants and arouse little media attention. With oral answers, ministers are forced to become personally involved, which gains publicity.

Supplementary questions

Ministers cannot get away with merely reciting a civil servant's brief; they must also be prepared to deal with follow-up questions. Skilful MPs will lure the minister to the dispatch box with an innocuous question, only to unsheathe a rhetorical stiletto. Supplementaries have steadily increased, reducing the number of questions answered each day from around sixty in the 1920s to around twenty. This leaves some forty questions unanswered in the House, although they will be printed (together with written answers) in the following day's *Hansard* (the report of parliamentary proceedings). Successive Speakers have urged members to cut supplementaries, but this reduces their power and is resisted.

Ask me another
In July 2002 it was revealed that John Bercow (as an MP) had tabled an average of 121 written questions a week (annual cost £565,278), the longest running to 10,195 words.

Prime Minister's Questions (PMQs)

The highlight occurs on Wednesdays at midday, when for half an hour the prime minister stands at the dispatch box. Parliamentary broadcasts frequently place this at the top of the bill. There are more oral questions for the prime minister than any colleague, ranging widely over issues of the day. Sometimes these can be deflected to the responsible minister but, to prevent this, members adopt the strategy of enquiring into the prime minister's immediate plans and engagements, and following this up with their real concern, for which the prime minister may not be prepared. Nowadays most MPs merely table their questions as 'engagements'. Subsequent 'engagement' questions are not even answered once a reply has been given to the first and the MPs go straight to their supplementaries. Opposition leaders have special opportunities to question the prime minister. Although Wilson, Thatcher and Blair all appeared to revel in the opportunity to enthuse supporters and ridicule opponents, the occasion can be fraught with danger. Gordon Brown lacked the assurance of his predecessor and faced a formidable opponent in David Cameron.

Question Time in question

The present system owes much to Balfour's reforms at the beginning of the twentieth century, which were intended to restrict rather than encourage debate. Amongst other things, he instigated the *written answer* and limited the time for oral questions. By replacing two fifteen-minute sessions for PMQs with one of thirty, Tony Blair was seen to be further weakening the system. Various other problems remain.

- *The rota.* Particular ministers come to the dispatch box on certain days only; issues can become stale and a backlog develops.
- *Written answers.* Although providing much detailed information, these cannot be subject to spontaneous debate.
- *Time.* Despite various suggestions for improvement (an extended question hour, Friday sessions), Question Time remains a rather inadequate fifty-five minutes.
- *Evasion.* Ministers have an increasing capacity to evade by claiming that a matter lies outside their control (local government, civil service agencies and the NHS, for example). They may also refuse on grounds of security or 'public interest'.
- *Party domination.* Despite MPs' alleged freedom at Question Time, the parties spread their tentacles. Governments can 'plant' questions, detailing tame backbenchers to ask what they want asked, or crowd out opposition questions. This reached a new low under Blair, forcing Speaker Boothroyd to complain of 'sycophantic questions'; the 'new women' were said to have been particularly 'helpful' to the Prime Minister in this respect (White, M. 2001).

Promises, Promises!

Andrew MacKinlay: Does the Prime Minister recall that, when we were in opposition, we used to groan at the fawning, obsequious, softball, well-rehearsed and planted questions asked by Conservative members of the right honourable Member for Huntingdon [Mr Major]? Will my right honourable friend distinguish his period in office by discouraging such practices – which diminish Prime Minister's Question Time – during this Parliament?

The Prime Minister: I fully respect my honourable friend's independence of mind, and shall do my very best to ensure that he retains it.

Exchange between Labour backbencher and Tony Blair during Prime Minister's Questions (*Hansard*, 3 June 1998)

Scrutiny by committee

Much of the work of Parliament is done by committees. Many are **select committees** drawn from all parties to fulfil some function on behalf of the House. Thus the Procedure Committee regulates its internal working, the Committee on Standards guards ethical standards and oversees the work of the Parliamentary Commissioner for Standards (see p. 417), and the Modernization Committee considers reform. Select committees are also involved in policy issues (in the nineteenth century they functioned rather like royal commissions) or are used to gather information. In addition, they are increasingly being used to consider draft bills prior to the first reading.

One of the most successful has been the Public Accounts Committee (PAC), created in 1861 to examine the departmental accounts. This provided a model for a pattern of reform that began in the 1960s. However, the major advance came under the 1979 Conservative administration, which created twelve committees covering the major spending departments. Superior to anything seen before, they can choose the topic for investigation, call for persons and papers and are served by a staff. They can also appoint advisers to prevent witnesses pulling the wool over MPs' eyes. In July 2011 the Culture, Media and Sport Select Committee succeeded in getting media mogul Rupert Murdoch to appear before it (despite his being a US citizen) to face questions on phone hacking by journalists working for his newspapers. Public hearings can often be seen on TV, with the MPs sitting at horseshoe-shaped tables grilling witnesses. Some have produced stinging reports; the Treasury and Civil Service Committee has been particularly scathing of economic policy.

Committee membership reflects party strength in the House and is kept small (around eleven), with the chairing role shared between parties and the system overseen by the Liaison Committee. Established for the complete duration of a parliament, they cannot be disbanded by government. A Committee of Selection decides the membership at the beginning of a parliament, but makes its decisions from names suggested by the party whips. Since June 2010 members have been able to decide which of them should hold the chair.

House of Commons Select Committees, 2012–13

Departmental	**Non-departmental**
Business, Innovation and Skills	Administration
Communities and Local Government	Armed Forces Bill
Culture, Media and Sport	Backbench Business
Defence	Environmental Audit
Education	European Scrutiny
Energy and Climate Change	Finance and Services
Environment, Food and Rural Affairs	Liaison
Foreign Affairs	Members' Expenses
Health	Political and Constitutional Reform
Home Affairs	Privileges
International Development	Procedure
Justice	Public Accounts
Northern Ireland Affairs	Public Administration
Scottish Affairs	Regulatory Reform
Transport	Science and Technology
Treasury	Standards
Welsh Affairs	Statutory Instruments
Work and Pensions	

The House of Lords also operates a successful select committee system but, rather than shadow departments, these concentrate on four main areas: Europe, science, economics and the constitution.

A mandarin's charter

However, if the executive conceded with one hand it took with the other. A hitherto unknown assistant secretary in the Civil Service Department secured modest immortality in May 1980 by codifying some earlier guidelines as the Osmotherly Rules: a hitchhiker's guide to the committee galaxy designed to keep officials out of trouble. The black holes of questioning into which civil servants should not allow themselves to be lured included:

- advice to ministers;
- interdepartmental policy exchanges;
- matters of political controversy;
- confidential information supplied by firms or individuals;
- delicate information concerning foreign powers.

Furthermore, in no circumstances were MPs to receive extracts from cabinet papers or to be told anything about cabinet discussions. Decision-making details were also to be clasped to the bureaucratic bosom. These guidelines could be seen as a mandarin's charter and gave an indication of the official view of Parliament's place in government.

Problems with select committees

The Westland affair (see below) foreshadowed a number of areas of difficulty for the committee system, including the following.

- *Interference with composition.* John Major's administration infuriated its own backbenchers by removing a raft of independently minded (i.e. awkward) members from committees by 'inventing' a rule that no MP could serve for over twelve years. After its June 2001 election triumph the Blair government sought to remove Gwyneth Dunwoody and Donald Anderson from their positions as chairs of the Transport and Foreign Affairs committees respectively. However, MPs (including the Leader of the House) were so incensed that they resisted and the two were reinstated. The Liaison Committee has called for appointments to be placed in the hands of an independent panel of MPs.
- *Prime ministerial reticence.* Prime ministers have been reluctant to appear before select committees. Following the Pergau Dam scandal in 1994 (concerning government aid for a Malaysian dam being tied to arms contracts) Margaret Thatcher refused to face the Foreign Affairs Committee. The Liaison Committee suggested that it might question Tony Blair but he declined on the grounds that a convention existed that prime ministers did not appear. However, his argument was hotly contested by the Public Administration Committee and he eventually relented, appearing for the first time on 16 July 2002, thereby establishing a new convention to be honoured by both Brown and Cameron.
- *Intimidation.* Some committee members, conscious of their careers, are easily frightened. Government whips can accuse them of disloyalty. This happened to Labour's Diane Abbott as a member of the Foreign Affairs Committee (*Sunday Times*, 24 May 1998). In July 2011 it was reported that members of the Culture, Media and Sport Committee were warned off pursuing phone hacking, with threats that media giant News International would 'investigate' their own private lives.
- *Leaking.* Some appear to agree that loyalty to party bosses comes before loyalty to Parliament. The Foreign Affairs Committee report on the arms-to-Sierra-Leone affair was leaked to the Foreign Secretary before publication and Labour's Ernie Ross was forced to resign from the committee as a result. Further investigations revealed Labour MPs on other committees guilty of similar practices.
- *Government pressure.* Under the Major government, whip David Willetts was

Everyone thought it was very harsh on David Willetts. All he was doing was his job.
Former Conservative whip, in the *Independent* (14 July 1997)

accused in 1997 of attempting to influence the Members' Interests Committee in its investigation into the cash-for-questions scandal of the 1990s. Called before the Committee on Standards and Privileges, his answers were seen as 'dissembling', and he was forced to resign in December 1996. Evidence later emerged that attempts to influence select committees were widespread (*Independent*, 14 July 1997).

- *Non-cooperation.* In the Westland affair a leak came from the Department of Trade of a letter relating to the Westland helicopter company. The Defence Committee launched an investigation. However, in January 1986 the government prevented key civil servants from testifying. Thus Parliament was never to know the extent of Downing Street's involvement in what the Cabinet Secretary admitted to be the 'discourtesy, impropriety, and unwisdom' of the leak (Evans 1986b). In January 2002 Lord Birt, Blair's special adviser responsible for 'blue skies' thinking, refused to appear before the Transport Committee, claiming that officials were better qualified to answer questions.

Scrutiny and the constitution

Given their paucity of resources (staff, advisers, expenses for witnesses, time and formal powers), the committees can be said to have achieved much. They have produced hundreds of reports, publicized some important issues and sometimes influenced government policy. However, they work under a major constitutional handicap. Across the Atlantic congressional committees exert considerable sway, their chairpersons nationally recognized figures able, as British television viewers witnessed in the Watergate, 'Irangate' and Monica Lewinsky hearings, to put the US executive on the spot. However, British committees could never operate with the same authority. Congress is set within a constitutional separation of powers (see p. 94); in Britain all the formidable powers the government has to control Parliament can be used to limit its committees. Moreover, some have argued that the whole development is misguided. Parliamentary debate is traditionally wide-ranging, concerned with points of broad principle. For such critics the micro-level scrutiny of the committees may lose sight of the ideological wood for the trees.

Today in Parliament: the Fourth Estate

> Burke said that there were Three Estates in Parliament; but, in the Reporter's Gallery yonder, there sat a Fourth Estate more important far than they all.
>
> Thomas Carlyle (1795–1881; Scottish essayist and historian), *On Heroes and Hero Worship* (1841)

Whatever its limitations, Parliament remains the nation's central democratic forum with a key role in voicing the demands of citizens (Norton 2005: 12) Even though debate rarely leads to direct policy change, it can have a longer-term effect by influencing public opinion. Hence the mechanisms for reporting Parliament's proceedings to those it represents become crucially important. Although all debate and discussion is faithfully reproduced in *Hansard*, the vast majority of people wishing to follow the proceedings of Parliament do so through the mass media. The occupants of the press gallery and those operating the cameras and microphones are part of a functioning democracy.

Press reporting of Parliament did not come easily; it was secured after a tortuous history, with many rights gained through struggles in the eighteenth century. Broadcasting developed more recently but also met with resistance. Not until March 1976 did the Commons agree to sound broadcasting and the television cameras did not begin operating until November 1989 with the debate on the Queen's Speech. By the time this 'experiment' began, Australia, Austria, Belgium, Canada, France, Greece, Holland, Italy, Japan, West Germany and the USA had all accepted the principle. Perhaps official reticence was hardly surprising in the most closed and secretive political culture in the western world, where democracy, unlike justice, has been deemed better for not actually being seen.

Bad news

However, media coverage is open to criticism on various fronts.

- *Selectivity and sensationalism.* It is impossible to cover everything said in this palace of a million words. Journalists must be selective, seeking the essence of a speech or debate, and the bias of the press will influence what they select. This has generally favoured Conservative or centrist Labour politicians, with 'rowdyism' on the left being reported in lurid detail. Selection can also highlight the 'worst' aspects of debate, encouraging members to play to the gallery. As with sports coverage, editing concentrates on 'highlights'.
- *Simplification and trivialization.* In the tabloids single-syllable words are *de rigueur*, while the broadsheets have a tradition of amusing 'Parliamentary Sketch' columns, often highlighting the antics of the more bizarre and exotic parliamentary creatures. Broadcasters are concerned with ratings. In 1998, *Yesterday in Parliament* was removed from Radio 4's FM frequency for fear of losing listeners.
- *News management.* Much reporting merely relays information disseminated by ministers, press secretaries and spin doctors through press releases and the exclusive club of Westminster journalists known as the Lobby (see p. 252).
- *Extra-parliamentary reporting.* The media can reduce the status of Parliament by

encouraging statements outside its precincts. Although the ministerial code of conduct lays down that policy statements should first be made to the Commons, not the media, this is not always followed. Important announcements frequently first appear in the press and on Radio 4's *Today* programme.

> **'Twas ever thus**
> *The Times* has made many ministries. When, as of late, there has been a long continuance of divided Parliaments, of governments which were without 'brute voting power', and which depended upon intellectual strength, the most influential organ of English opinion has been of critical moment.
>
> Walter Bagehot, *The English Constitution* (1867: ch. 1)

The case for the fourth estate

Doughnutting
MPs may cluster around an MP speaking while the cameras are on. This will make the chamber appear less bare, give support to the colleague and perhaps catch the eye of constituents.

Towards the end of the first decade of the twenty-first century an issue arose in which the judiciary began issuing 'super-injunctions' to prevent press reporting of the activities of certain firms and individuals and this even extended to the reporting of questions asked in Parliament. Yet the case for shining the public spotlight on Parliament is that, having been courted for their votes, people should be allowed to witness the results of their choices. In a televisual age, if the cameras did not enter the House, coverage would be confined to studio confrontations between academics, journalists and a chosen few media politicians or ex-politicians: not public debates but private debates upon public matters. In Westminster, the official public gallery is small and usually full of sightseeing tourists. However, the electronic public gallery contains some 60 million at home as well as a worldwide audience. But with jeering MPs and an expanse of empty green leather benches, people do not always like what they see.

From Golden Age to Golden Sunset?

An incessant theme of post-war debate has been the reform of Parliament, the underlying critique centring on its inability to bridle, or even effectively scrutinize, the executive.

A 'Golden Age'?

It is sometimes contended that, from its origins, Parliament has never been strong vis-à-vis the executive, and that it is not in the nature of the British constitution that it should be. However, there was a '**Golden Age**', between the 1832 and 1867 Reform Acts, when MPs really mattered. This was before the parties began to dominate, when governments were genuinely vulnerable to being turned out of office without a general election (as in 1852, 1855, 1858 and 1866), and ministers could be individually censured and forced to resign. MPs controlled the organization of the House and could shape policy through debates. Information could be demanded from government, and select committees would conduct authoritative investigations and even draft legislation. During this period the legislative process began with a formal request for leave to introduce the bill, justification being required before a first reading. Second and third readings, and the committee stage, were genuinely critical scrutinies in which MPs set their own time and secured amendments. Gladstone's financial reforms subjected public expenditure to real control.

However, this period was ended with the rise of tighter party discipline. MPs were to become members of their parties first and of the House second. Despite some attempts at modernization, including the creation of the Backbencher's Business Committee, some probing work by select committees and a Speaker (Bercow) committed to advancing the case of the House against the executive, the unity of Parliament remains like that of a gigantic pantomime horse in which two ill-matched thespians wrestle with each other about who should be the head. The result is executive domination, which runs like a fault line throughout the system (Grant 2009: 56).

Friendly fire: will the real opposition stand up!

If parties have consolidated the executive hold over Parliament they can also imperil it. It is within the parties that the real executive/legislature tension can be seen (Brand 1992). A government's own backbenchers can become an effective opposition. This important facet in appreciating the role of Parliament has been a key theme in a continuing analysis by Philip Norton. From the 1970s the governing party's MPs were becoming less disciplined, resulting in a greater incidence of government defeats. Heath (1970–4) experienced six such setbacks, three on three-line whips. The 1974 Labour government suffered no fewer than fifty-nine defeats, although there were special circumstances, including fragile majorities, minority government and the uneasy Lib–Lab pact.

The Conservatives' success in broadening their social base brought in young meritocrats displaying less instinctive loyalty, which helped to make Major's government increasingly vulnerable. Following his resignation, Norman Lamont spoke in June 1993 of a government 'in office but not in power'. As his majority dwindled, Major's hands became tied over his Northern Ireland initiative and individual MPs could even take advantage with threats to withhold support unless constituency demands were met.

A new MP entering the chamber with Winston Churchill remarked that it was time to face the enemy. 'No', came the reply; the facing benches contained the 'opposition', the 'enemy' sat behind!

Neither does a secure majority always guarantee peace since backbenchers may feel free to air their consciences without real damage. In 1964, when Labour had the barest of majorities, Wilson could enjoy loyal support, but after his 1966 victory the left began to make demands, particularly on defence issues. Similarly, the seemingly impregnable Thatcher governments experienced many challenges and some backbench victories were gained with the 1982 amendment to the immigration rules, and defeats on the 1986 Shops Bill and 1990 National Health Service and Community Care Bill. Revolts in April 1988 over the poll tax and housing benefits also forced government concessions.

After Major's troubled reign, Blair's government was to reassert the position of the executive through unprecedented attention to party discipline. MPs were allegedly being kept 'on message' by spin doctors; in March 1998 Tony Benn reported in *Tribune* that they regularly received faxed personalized press releases ready to be sent unchanged to their local newspapers. However, things were to change with time and the number of disgruntled and rebellious backbenchers grew (see Cowley 1999). The government was to suffer four Commons defeats within a ten-month period, beginning in November 2005 when a controversial amendment to the Terrorism Bill, to allow suspects to be held without charge for ninety days, was defeated (by 322 to 291). With forty-nine Labour MPs rebelling, opposition leaders claimed that Blair had lost his authority and should resign. This was followed in January 2006 with the loss of two motions to reject Lords amendments to the Racial and Religious Hatred Bill, which Shadow Attorney General Dominic Grieve described as 'a victory for Parliament'. The Brown government suffered three defeats in its relatively short reign. One, in April 2009, glamorously supported by actress Joanna Lumley, opposing restrictions on the right of Gurkhas to settle in the UK, was carried by 276 to 246. The 2010 coalition government could be seen as particularly vulnerable, with many disgruntled MPs from both partners hating the process of compromise with their erstwhile opponents.

The power of government backbenchers was spectacularly demonstrated in August 2013 over the government's emergency motion on military action against the Assad regime in Syria, following alleged use of chemical weapons in contravention of international law. First obliged to water down the motion, Prime Minister David Cameron was to be embarrassed as thirty of his own backbenchers, together with nine Liberal Democrats, voted against it, leading to an unexpected government defeat by thirteen votes (272 to 285).

Hence, the power to check the executive, while real, is contingent, limited by factors such as a government's majority, the time during which it has been in office, the extent to which it moves away from its core support and the effectiveness of internal party discipline. However, this is not the constitutional check of a genuine separation of powers. In the USA, by contrast, Congressional leaders cannot also be members of the executive, neither do they depend on executive patronage for advancement. President Clinton, for example, was subjected to unremitting hostility and lost some of his most cherished legislative ambitions. In July 2011, Barack Obama, in the midst of economic crisis, was compelled to compromise over the US debt ceiling. Significantly, it is sometimes the House of Lords, more free from the straitjacket of party discipline, that provides the greater resistance in Britain.

Denouement: a deeper function exposed

If Parliament is limited with respect to its key roles, what then is its function in modern politics? Perhaps the answer lies in Bagehot's analysis of the value of monarchy and the dignified parts of the constitution: outward display serving to beguile the masses, leaving the real process of government in the hands of a political elite.

It is crucially necessary for the economically and politically powerful that the House of Commons should have this apparent centrality in British political life, because it stands alone in the constitution as the embodiment of democracy. Without it there would be little to justify the exercise of state power. Politicians of all hues, representatives of powerful interests, the media and civil servants, all pay unctuous tribute to the idea of parliamentary sovereignty. More than any other institution, it can foster a popular belief that ordinary folk control their rulers. In other words, it is one of the most powerful legitimating devices in the political system. In the following chapter we shall look deeper into the modern executive that so dominates the political landscape.

Key points

- Parliament is the constitutional seat of sovereignty in Britain.
- It is largely energized by political parties, with little real identity of its own as the collective voice of the people.
- The House of Commons effectively sustains the executive.
- Party discipline, absolute majorities and the absence of a separation of powers mean that parliamentary sovereignty is effectively hijacked by the executive.
- The principal functions of Parliament include legislation, debate and scrutiny of the executive. In all these the executive holds the whip hand.
- EU membership limits parliamentary sovereignty.
- Because Parliament is the forum for popular debate, media reporting is constitutionally significant.

■ There are latent powers lying with Parliament that backbenchers may use.

■ To an extent Parliament serves to conceal the reality of power in Britain.

Review your understanding of the following terms and concepts

Act of Parliament	Liaison Committee	Queen's Speech
adjournment debate	Opposition Day	Question Time
backbench organization	parliamentary question	select committee
Early Day Motion	party discipline	supplementary question
emergency debate	private and public bill	whip
Hansard	private member's bill	written answer
legislative process	Public Bill Committee	

Questions for discussion and debate

Consider these propositions and be prepared to present the cases for and against. Try to produce debating propositions of your own.

1   The party backbench organizations perform essential roles in Parliament.

2   Party discipline reduces MPs to lobby fodder.

3   The legislative process is nothing more than an anachronism.

4   EU law-making seriously erodes parliamentary sovereignty.

5   The parliamentary question is a two-edged sword.

6   Opportunities for private members' legislation should be increased.

7   Parliament's most significant power lies in debate.

8   Select committees provide MPs with a potent weapon.

9   The broadcasting of Parliament does little to enhance democracy.

10   The House of Commons is part of the dignified constitution.

Further reading

The workings of Parliament are of course much written about, creating hundreds of sources, both printed and electronic. (See also reading for chapter 14.)

Baldwin, N. (2005) *Parliament in the 21st Century*.
Essays from thirty politicians and academics on many aspects of parliamentary reform in the light of recent developments.

Brand, J. (1992) *British Parliamentary Parties: Policy and Power*.
Illustrates how intra-party tension can constitute the real executive–legislative tension.

Grant, M. (2009) *The UK Parliament*.
Introduction to the history, structure and functions of Parliament, with a topical evaluation of its role.

Norton, P. (1993) *Does Parliament Matter?*
'Yes', says one of Britain's leading authorities.

Norton, P. (2005) *Parliament in British Politics*.
Searching, authoritative and comprehensive analysis of both Houses of Parliament by an academic with an insider's view.

Richards, P. G. (1970) *Parliament and Conscience*.
Illustrates the backbencher's role in legislating on sensitive issues of morality.

Riddell, P. (2000) *Parliament under Blair*.
Finds the Blair government unwilling to admit to the diminishing power of Parliament.

Rush, M. (2001) *The Role of the Member of Parliament since 1868*.
Analysis of the socioeconomic transformation of the Commons from the mid-nineteenth century.

Rush, M (2005) *Parliament Today*.
Parliamentary government in theory and practice illustrated with historical, recent and contemporary examples.

For reading around the subject and some light relief

Tony Banks, *Out of Order.*
Parliamentary anecdotes from a colourful MP.

Hilaire Belloc, *Mr Clutterbuck's Election.*
Satire on early-century political life.

Sir Henry Channon, *Chips.*

Famously indiscreet diary of 'Chips' Channon, who moved in the world of gossip, malice, glamour and power in the period between the abdication of Edward VIII and the coronation of Elizabeth II. Was the inspiration for Alan Clark.

Alan Clark, *Diaries.*
Celebrated irreverent account of Westminster life and much else. See also Peter Bradshaw's entertaining parody, *Not Alan Clark's Diaries*, based on his *Evening Standard* feature.

Michael Dobbs, *House of Cards.*
Follows the progress of evil chief whip, Francis Urquhart, who will stop at nothing for power. Fictional of course. Also on DVD.

Greg Knight, *Right Honourable Insults.*
Tory MP of Tony Blair: 'He's so vain he'd take his own hand in marriage', and so on. Hundreds of wicked insults from the experts.

Matthew Parris, *Great Parliamentary Scandals.*
Entertaining mapping of the moral swampland of British politics over four centuries.

Matthew Parris, *Chance Witness: An Outsider's Life in Politics.*
Candid and entertaining autobiography by the *Times* parliamentary sketch writer and former Conservative backbencher.

Howard Spring, *Fame is the Spur.*
Labour politician's rise to power and subsequent disillusionment.

On the net

http://www.parliament.uk/business/publications/hansard/
Today's Parliament reflects the power of the internet and provides a wealth of material. Access verbatim daily reports of proceedings in both the Commons and Lords on the *Hansard* website. You can also read past Commons debates from November 1988 and Lords debates from1995/96.

http://www.parliament.uk/business/publications/committees/recent-reports/
Read the reports of select committees here.

Most members now also have websites of their own and many write blogs, giving a more personal viewpoint than the official reports in *Hansard* and select committee reports.

CHAPTER 16

THE HEART OF GOVERNMENT: OF CABINETS AND KINGS

Contents

In this chapter attention turns from the elected assembly to the relatively small group of MPs who head the executive arm of government, and to the environment in which they work. The complex territory around the cabinet system constitutes Britain's core executive. The chapter comprises two broad sections. The first begins by examining the nature of cabinet government and its evolution in Britain. Next we map the anatomy of the core executive, identifying a range of associated political debates. In the second section we turn to one of the most compelling questions of modern government: the role of the prime minister. Is it becoming more presidential in character? Or is the modern core executive so complex that the question is simplistic? This chapter tells us much about the living constitution, revealing a dense network of relationships and dependencies in which power is diffuse and appears in many guises.

The Core Executive

The executive arm of government dwarfs the other two arms of legislature and judiciary. However, when we speak of executive power we are concerned with the centre of political authority: the head of the executive. Decisions made here determine how we live, how we are educated, our health, our employment and perhaps, where war is concerned, how we may die. Formally the head of the British system of government comprises the prime minister and around twenty other senior ministers, most heading ministries. This is the **Cabinet**, which works through weekly meetings in the Cabinet Room at the prime minister's residence, 10 Downing Street, a familiar backdrop for the comings and goings of the important and self-important.

The Cabinet and the government

Journalists often write as if the terms 'Cabinet' and 'government' are synonymous. In the eighteenth century this was largely true. Today the Cabinet is but a small part of a complex governmental web comprising around one hundred politicians, forming a hierarchy ranging from secretaries of state to junior parliamentary private secretaries assisting ministers (figures 16.1 and 16.3). This web of power

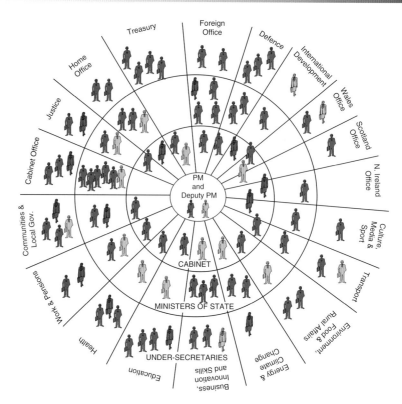

Figure 16.1 The Cabinet stands at the centre of a web of government

Note: This example shows the Conservative–Liberal Democrat coalition government in 2013. The Leader of the House of Lords is also a member of the Cabinet.

extends even further to embrace the senior public servants at the heads of the departments of state and executive agencies to form the '**core executive**' (see Dunleavy and Rhodes 1990).

Government by Cabinet

In the multitude of counsellors there is safety.
Proverbs (xi: 14)

The Ancient Greek philosopher Plato believed that rule by a benign 'philosopher king' would be the most perfect form of government. However, this could only exist in an ideal world; in reality it would deteriorate into the *worst* form – tyranny. Regimes that have terrorized populations have characteristically been dominated by single rulers – tyrants, dictators and demagogues, their very names synonyms for oppression. Constitutions are designed to prevent tyranny; this is what the English sought to do in 1215 and 1689 and the Americans in 1787. After Stalin the Russians vowed they would never again permit one person so much power. Yet the British executive, inheriting the powers of the monarch and able to dominate Parliament, knows no constitutional constraints. Hence, faith in **cabinet government** is crucial.

Cabinet government entails the sharing of authority, with decision-making based upon discussion and compromise. However, this self-moderating form of government is only protected by conventions and these are among the most fragile in the constitution. If there is a document to be consulted, it is the *Ministerial Code* (formerly *Questions of Procedure for Ministers*), finally released in 1992 after some fifty years of official secrecy. However, the dry passages of dos and don'ts of this ministerial highway code say little about the politics of power. For this reason, one of the most crucial questions in modern British politics is whether cabinet government is real or just one more myth in our slippery and elusive constitution.

> *This is not a collective government. We have to accept that the old model of Cabinet government is as dead as a doornail.*
> Whitehall insider to Peter Hennessy (1998:12)

Evolution

The history of the Cabinet cannot be traced as a continuous line linking a distant past indissolubly to the present. The modern Cabinet owes much to political forces generated by the rise of capitalism and is linked with the nineteenth-century constitutional reforms. It is certainly true, however, that monarchs have always surrounded themselves with small bands of loyal advisers and confidants and this helps explain the structure of the modern executive and the culture of power within it.

The Privy Council

By the sixteenth century the practice of monarchical consultation had become institutionalized in the Privy Council, a body that had itself evolved from a council of royal advisers in Norman times (the *Curia Regis*). The following century saw the Civil War and the republican period, with government through *executive committees*. This proved unworkable, but after the Restoration, when Charles II sought to re-establish what he believed to be his divine right to rule alone, he found the Privy Council difficult and resorted to a smaller group, a committee of the council. This was labelled the 'cabinet' as a term of abuse, a synonym for 'cabal' – a devious, inner group. The modern Cabinet remains constitutionally a committee of the Privy Council, members retaining the title 'right honourable' for life. Consigned to the dignified part of the constitution, the full Council nowadays meets only rarely, to mark great state occasions such as the sovereign's marriage or death.

The Glorious Revolution

In 1681 Charles II dissolved Parliament, establishing an alternative 'Oxford Parliament'. The ensuing struggle led to the 'Glorious Revolution' of 1688, resulting in the flight of James II (who had acceded in 1685), and his ultimate replacement by William (of Orange) and Mary. Matters of state were transacted in the full Privy Council and, to prevent royal influence over the legislature, ministers were excluded from Parliament. However, this principle was soon abandoned because

Parliament wanted ministers in its midst for questioning. Had it been retained, Britain might have developed a separation of powers and a significantly different constitution. As it was, membership of Parliament, rather than being forbidden, became an essential requirement of office, thereby clearing the way for a fusion of powers – Bagehot's 'efficient secret' of the constitution.

The Act of Settlement

Later anxiety about the succession, resulting from the death of Queen Anne's son, was allayed in the Act of Settlement (1701) establishing the Hanoverian succession. George I and George II are said to have shown little interest in British politics between 1714 and 1760, thereby allowing the Cabinet to become increasingly dominant, but there were also more fundamental forces at work. Ministers had in fact met in the absence of the monarch during Anne's reign (1702–14), and when George III attempted to reassert a degree of royal authority in 1784 he was castigated as unconstitutional; the roots of the modern Cabinet had taken hold. Hence, five years before the French revolution, George III made the last appearance of a monarch in the Cabinet (until the Queen attended a cabinet meeting in 2012). The monarch reigned but the Cabinet had effectively hijacked the royal prerogative. It did not, however, possess all the essentials of its modern counterpart.

More women in Cabinet? The Queen attends a cabinet meeting in her diamond jubilee year

- Responsibility was to the Crown rather than to Parliament, so that it was possible to govern without a majority.
- Parliamentary groupings (Whigs and Tories) were only loose coalitions, making it possible for a Cabinet to contain representatives of both and enjoy cross-party support in the House.
- Cabinet members were responsible only for their own ministries and quite prepared to attack each other's policies.
- The resignation of the First Lord of the Treasury (the prime minister) did not mean that other ministers should also depart.
- A significant number of MPs owed allegiance to neither 'party' and could be courted through patronage and bribery.

The industrial revolution

The rise of the industrial bourgeoisie in the nineteenth century challenged the *ancien régime*; the new men entered Parliament through the extended franchise and dominated it through party discipline. This added a second dimension to the power of the Cabinet.

- Cabinets became more tightly knit, with members drawn from one party only.
- Members accepted collective responsibility for policy.
- So long as their backbenchers remained loyal, governments enjoyed a degree of supremacy unknown since the Tudors.

Here was the modern Cabinet: relatively autonomous and drawing authority from various constitutional and political sources, including its lineage to the Privy Council, its inheritance of the prerogative powers of the Crown, and its domination of the constitutionally sovereign Parliament.

An Anatomy of the Cabinet

Collective responsibility

> Now, is it to lower the price of corn, or isn't it? It is not much matter what we say, but mind, we must all say the same.
>
> Attributed to Lord Melbourne (1779–1848; Whig prime minister), quoted in Walter Bagehot, *The English Constitution* (1867: ch. 1)

The constitutional basis of cabinet government is sometimes said to lie in the doctrine of **collective responsibility**, which implies a form of collective decision-making.

Interpreted variously by participants and commentators, it generally implies the following features.

- All (or several) members play a part in formulating policy.
- All members support each other in public (even if privately disagreeing).
- Any member unable to lend support should resign. This can happen regularly and usually represents a major political upheaval, as in the cases of Michael Heseltine and Robin Cook.
- Cabinet proceedings are regarded as confidential (though resignees earn the right to a resignation speech revealing their reasons).

The convention probably originated in the eighteenth century when ministers sought to strengthen their hand vis-à-vis the monarch by sticking together. Today its prescriptive force lies in the ideal of collective decision-making as an alternative to rule by one individual, be they president or monarch. However, submerging differences can be stressful. Once in opposition, former Home Office minister Ann Widdecombe, in a passionate Commons speech, revealed the tension between her and Home Secretary Michael Howard over the dismissal of prison service chief Derek Lewis. Howard was never to shake off her declaration that he was a man with 'something of the night' about him. Again, Geoffrey Howe's momentous resignation speech, marking the beginning of the end for Thatcher, revealed anguish submerged beneath a famously ovine exterior when he lamented the futility of

> trying to stretch the meaning of words beyond what was credible, of trying to pretend there was a common policy. . . (House of Commons speech, 13 Nov. 1990)

In practice, cabinet leaks enable journalists to reveal much cabinet disagreement. Throughout history there have been 'agreements to differ' over divisive issues. One such occurred in the run-up to the 1975 referendum on continued EU membership. In the 1990s a number of Major's ministers remained in the Cabinet while known to be at variance over the EU. In 2003 Tony Blair effectively broke the convention by allowing Clare Short to remain in his Cabinet while voicing opposition to his policy towards Iraq.

The formation of the 2010 coalition government placed new stresses on the convention. From the outset the differing manifestos of the two parties had to be merged as the Coalition Agreement, but the agreement was not always entirely agreeable. At an early stage the Liberal Democrat pledge on student tuition fees had to be effectively sacrificed, at considerable cost to the party and its leader. Further disagreement emerged over the AV referendum, reform of the House of Lords and the Leveson Inquiry. This erupted into open hostility in February 2013 when the Liberal Democrats voted with Labour to thwart Conservative legislation to revise the constituency boundaries.

Collective responsibility or collective expediency?

An important reason for the doctrine's persistence is political expediency (which is why we even find it applied to the shadow cabinet). A united front has proved a valuable asset, whereas a divided government can be more easily attacked by its opponents. Moreover, the collective cloak can be thrown over all members of the government, usually encompassing around one-third of the parliamentary party. The doctrine can thus be a basis for party discipline, giving the government a reliable 'payroll vote'.

Cabinet structure

Within the cabinet hierarchy, the seniormost members hold titles such as Home Secretary, Foreign Secretary, or Secretary of State for this or that. Generally ministers are not expected to have specialist knowledge. Indeed, regular reshuffles positively discourage this; they are generalists rather than specialists. The status of a position can vary with circumstances and personalities. Attlee held the position of deputy prime minister during the war but when Howe was given the role it was seen as an insult. When Heseltine took the position under Major, some even saw him as the *de facto* prime minister. The position gained a particular significance in 2010 when it was given to Nick Clegg in the coalition government. Greatest status goes with the post of Chancellor of the Exchequer, often seen as the rival to the prime minister. A Cabinet can also contain ministers without portfolio, their responsibilities reflecting a prime minister's priorities. This appointment was used for a time by Tony Blair to include trusted aide Peter Mandelson, and David Cameron appointed Sayeeda Warsi, indicating his BME sensitivities (but dispatched her in his first reshuffle).

Social complexion

Cabinets were traditionally drawn largely from the social elite, many having aristocratic backgrounds, but in both major parties there has been a steady increase in the *petit bourgeois* element (figure 16.2). In terms of education, ministers have been by no means typical of those they govern, a high proportion having attended public school (particularly Eton) and Oxbridge. However, Blair's first Cabinet contained only four Oxbridge alumni (including the Prime Minister himself). Apart from Gordon Brown, every prime minister since 1937 who attended university has been to Oxford. The 2010 coalition government saw some reversion to tradition, with 62 per cent educated privately and 69 per cent from Oxbridge universities. It was also a very wealthy Cabinet. The *Daily Mail* (23 May 2010) reported that twenty-three of the twenty-nine ministers entitled to attend cabinet meetings were millionaires.

Like Parliament, the Cabinet has been largely a male preserve, women often

We still thought in terms of appointing a statutory woman. 'Who should she be?' asked Ted [Heath]. 'Margaret Thatcher', was my immediate reply.
James Prior (Conservative cabinet member), A Balance of Power (1986)

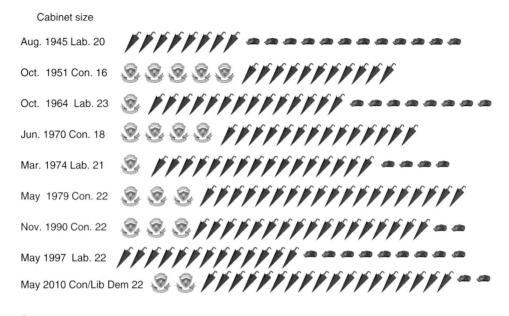

Cabinet size

Aug. 1945 Lab. 20

Oct. 1951 Con. 16

Oct. 1964 Lab. 23

Jun. 1970 Con. 18

Mar. 1974 Lab. 21

May 1979 Con. 22

Nov. 1990 Con. 22

May 1997 Lab. 22

May 2010 Con/Lib Dem 22

 Aristocrats (with hereditary titles amongst grandparents)

 Middle class

Working class (fathers with manual occupations)

Figure 16.2 Social complexion of incoming Cabinets, 1945–2010

Source: Data from Butler and Butler (1994: 66), *Dod's Parliamentary Companion* (1998), Waller and Criddle (1997) and estimates from various on-line information sources.

having had only a token presence. Ironically, Thatcher showed no desire for female company and Major's first Cabinet contained no women. Blair began with five women, rising after his 2001 victory to a magnificent seven. There was also a new attitude. While the older women, like 58-year-old Margaret Beckett, were content to do the job on men's terms, the younger representatives, such as Patricia Hewitt and Tessa Jowell, sought to change the rules, integrating motherhood into their working lives. David Cameron's first Cabinet contained five women but this was reduced to three in the 2012 reshuffle.

Experience

A minister reaching cabinet rank will normally be experienced in government. However, Blair's first team began at a considerable disadvantage as a result of a prolonged period in the wilderness of opposition and Cameron's was similarly inexperienced. Indeed, its Liberal Democratic members had not only never experienced office, they had possibly not even contemplated the prospect.

Size

The size of the Cabinet is no mere technicality; it has implications for the way it works. Eighteenth-century cabinets contained around five to nine members, which grew to twelve to fifteen in the following century, and by Asquith's time had reached twenty-three, whereupon the figure remained fairly constant (figure 16.3). Although other ministers may attend at certain times, the law allows for twenty-two salaried members. This is large by international standards; the US president, for example, surrounds himself with only around ten cabinet colleagues. Critics generally believe British cabinets to be too large for effective collective decision-taking but various pressures tend to increase size.

- *Growth in the public domain.* Since the nineteenth century, government has taken on many more areas of responsibility. Wilson defended his Cabinet of twenty-three on the grounds that it was 'inconceivable that important sectors of our national life should be excluded' (Walker 1972: 35).
- *Bureaucratic pressure.* Representation in Cabinet remains politically important to departments as they compete for resources.
- *Outside pressure.* Outside Westminster, groups see in cabinet composition indications of a government's priorities.
- *Parliamentary pressure.* Leading party figures usually have bands of supporters in the House pressing for their inclusion. When the coalition government was formed in 2010, Liberal Democrat MPs looked to cabinet membership for confirmation of their significance.
- *Factionalism.* A prime minister will try to appease factions of party opinion; hence Major's inclusion of his troublesome Eurosceptics. In the 2010 coalition Cameron was obliged to give generous recognition to the Liberal Democrats.

It's probably better to have him inside the tent pissing out, than outside the tent pissing in.
President Lyndon Johnson on FBI Director J. Edgar Hoover, quoted in the *New York Times* (31 Oct. 1971)

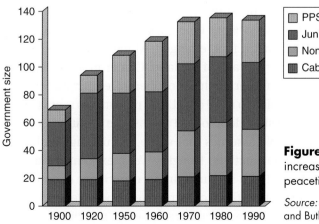

Figure 16.3 The increasing size of peacetime governments

Source: Data from Butler and Butler (1994: 66).

Critics allege that large cabinets can be slow and cumbersome; vulnerable to factional-ism ('wets' and 'drys' for Thatcher, Blairites and Brownites for Blair); liable to leak – 'The more you have,' said Harold Wilson, 'the more people can be got at' (Hennessy 1986: 149); and lacking a strategic vision as ministers develop departmental tunnel vision. Reformers have advocated some form of slimming down in ways such as the following.

- *A policy cabinet*. One of the most discussed models is the **policy cabinet** advo-cated by Leo Amery (1947), who served under Bonar Law and Baldwin. He argued for around six members, each free of departmental ties, to take an overarching strategic perspective. Ex-chancellor Nigel Lawson put forward a similar proposal in 1993. The nearest version of the model was Churchill's 1951 experiment: in a Cabinet of sixteen he appointed three non-departmental 'Overlords'.

- *War cabinets*. The exigencies of war have produced some enforced experiments. In 1916, Lloyd George's war cabinet contained five members, as did Churchill's in the second world war. Even the skirmish with Argentina in the 1980s saw the fleeting emergence of a war cabinet. In the tense period following 9/11, Tony Blair operated unilaterally until, bowing to pressure, he created a war cabinet of eight.

Blair's war cabinet, 8 October 2001

John Prescott, Deputy Prime Minister	Gordon Brown, Chancellor
Jack Straw, Foreign Secretary	David Blunkett, Home Secretary
Geoff Hoon, Defence Secretary	Robin Cook, Leader of the Commons
Clare Short, International Development Secretary	Admiral Sir Michael Boyce, Chief of the Defence Staff

- *Inner cabinets*. While outward forms remain, informal evolution takes place beneath the surface. One such has been the rise of what has been termed the **inner cabinet** – a small group of ministers closest to the prime minister, meeting independently and informally. Major's inner group varied with the matter under consideration. Under Blair, a 'big four' emerged, which took the decision to cede power over interest rates to the Bank of England. Cameron worked through 'The Quad' (himself and George Osborne plus the Liberal Democrats Nick Clegg and Danny Alexander), but the plan to rebel over Lords reform was reportedly hatched by a 'secret seven', with the shed door locked against the coalition partners.

Yet the policy-cabinet principle assumes that strategic thinking can be separated from day-to-day departmental matters. Douglas Wass, ex-joint head of the civil service, questioned this in his Reith Lectures: 'In my experience of administration I have found it almost impossible to think constructively about general policy issues if I have not been involved in particular practical cases' (1984: 29).

Cabinet committees

> **Informing the people**
> He agreed that no Prime Minister has ever explained why the numbers and membership of Cabinet Committees were kept secret. Why were they? I asked. There was a long pause. 'Erm,' said the former Secretary to the Cabinet. 'Well. Erm. Are we on the record or off the record?'
>
> 'On the record.'
>
> 'Then I think I'd rather not go into that.'
>
> Lord Hunt (ex-Cabinet Secretary), interviewed by Michael Davie in the *Observer* (11 Oct. 1987)

Modern governance in Britain is enmeshed in a dense network of committees and sub-committees (table 16.1), the growth of which is one of the most significant post-war constitutional developments. Yet it long remained cloaked in secrecy, with accounts pieced together from memoirs, leaks, press guesswork, and occasional parliamentary statements. In 1972 Patrick Gordon Walker gave some clear

Table 16.1 Cabinet committees for the 2010 coalition

Name	Chair	Deputy Chair
Coalition Committee	David Cameron (C)	William Hague(C)
	Nick Clegg (LD)	Chris Huhne (LD)
National Security Council	David Cameron (C)	Nick Clegg (LD)
European Affairs	William Hague (C)	Chris Huhne (LD)
Social Justice	Iain Duncan Smith (C)	Danny Alexander (LD)
Home Affairs	Nick Clegg (LD)	Kenneth Clarke (C)
Public Health (sub-committee)	Andrew Lansley (C)	Danny Alexander (LD)
Olympics (sub-committee)	Francis Maude (C)	Danny Alexander (LD)
Economic Affairs Committee	George Osborne (C)	Vince Cable (LD)
Reducing Regulation (sub-committee)	Vince Cable (LD)	Philip Hammond (C)
Banking Reform	George Osborne(C)	Vince Cable (LD)
Parliamentary Business and Legislation	Sir George Young (C)	David Heath (C)
Public Expenditure	George Osborne (C)	Danny Alexander (LD)

C = Conservative; LD = Liberal Democrat.
Source: Cabinet Office website, September 2010.

indications in his book *The Cabinet*, Mrs Thatcher acknowledged them in the House in 1983 and the following year *The Times* published a detailed list. Finally, in 1992, the Whitehall ribcage, if not the flesh, was detailed in X-ray, with the official release of full details, including terms of reference and membership. These are now readily available on the internet.

In principle, committees are created to assist the Cabinet, which remains the 'parent' body. There are two broad categories – ad hoc and standing committees.

Ad hoc committees

Created for specific problems, these have only ephemeral lives. The first was established in 1855 to handle the Crimean war, to be followed by others concerned with aspects of foreign policy. Towards the end of the nineteenth century, with a massive tide of legislation, more committees emerged to formulate policy and draft bills. Although the number has since fallen, they remain very important. Thatcher controlled strategy towards the 1985–6 miners' strike in this way, and the coalition government created an ad hoc committee for the 2012 Olympic Games.

Standing committees

Dating from a later period, the first of these was the highly successful Committee of Imperial Defence (CID), with its network of sub-committees. Its creation in 1903 marked a watershed in cabinet government. Concerned with particular areas of policy (education, defence, the economy, and so on), standing committees have a more durable existence.

Composition and functions

The committees characteristically include a core of cabinet ministers, some junior ministers, and civil servants attending as the secretariat or in their own right. Sometimes outsiders are included. Tony Blair caused some consternation in July 1997 by announcing a new cabinet committee chaired by himself and including five Liberal Democrat MPs, amongst them leader Paddy Ashdown, to focus on issues of mutual interest, including the constitution. Veteran MP Tony Benn prophesied 'the beginning of the end' of party government. The coalition committees created in 2010 may have justified his fears (see table 16.1).

Government by committee?

In 1967 Wilson formally enhanced the status of the committees, decreeing that matters should only be reconsidered by the full Cabinet with the agreement of the chairs. Some committees have exceedingly high status, often chaired by the prime minister or another senior minister. A Coalition Committee of 2010 was jointly chaired by the two party leaders. The great 1944 Education Act was largely

Most of my work when I was Minister of Education was done outside the Cabinet, and hardly referred to the Cabinet at all.

Lord Butler, interviewed by Norman Hunt (later Lord Crowther–Hunt) in the *Listener* (16 Sept. 1965)

the product of a committee led by R. A. Butler. Mrs Thatcher herself chaired committees on the economy and other key areas and Blair's reforming constitutional committees were chaired by Lord Chancellor Derry Irvine. Although their role is recognized in the *Ministerial Code*, there remains an underlying fear that they reduce the Cabinet to a rubber stamp, leaving no room for ministers to discuss each other's policies or take an overall strategic perspective. The cabinet committee system is paralleled by one of official committees that prepare the ground. There is a danger here that decisions may really be made before the politicians actually meet, with ministers being given briefs that foreclose their options.

From substance to shadow

Even less known to the constitution than the Cabinet is its shadow on the opposing front bench at Westminster. Often ignored in studies of government, the **shadow cabinet** constitutes a ready-made governmental cast waiting in the wings; its members are shadow ministers with shadow portfolios and the leader is the shadow prime minister. It is a particular feature of a two-party system, where a foetal government will lie curled in the womb before the general election with a clear manifesto. This means that voters can have some idea of what an alternative government will look like and what it will do. However, this advantage disappeared with the formation of the coalition in 2010, when two shadows were merged, not under a manifesto but a coalition agreement.

In the eighteenth century parliamentary factions would organize into groups to oppose those in office. If a government seemed likely to fall, lists of possible ministerial teams would begin to circulate. The relatively frequent fall of governments meant that there were always ex-ministers in Parliament; thus the 'ex-Cabinet' was the forebear of the shadow cabinet. Once a general election meant the removal of a government *en bloc*, it followed that a new one must be ready to emerge overnight.

Although the difference between shadow and substance is that the former has no executive responsibility, in many respects they function in a similar manner: holding meetings, appointing specialist committees and practising secrecy (and suffering leaks). They also practise collective responsibility and members can resign, as did Labour's Tom Watson in 2013 in order to be able to speak more freely.

Shadow cabinets are valuable to democracy. Americans see little of any alternative president until the campaign period and do not see the Cabinet until well after. In Britain, Her Majesty's Loyal Opposition is an alternative government displayed on the shelves of the Westminster supermarket. The role is officially recognized with salaries for the opposition leader and chief whip. Yet its value is reduced by lack of information; ex-mandarin Sir Douglas Wass (1984) argued that it should be power-assisted with an official department.

The Cabinet Office

The core executive territory is by no means the exclusive preserve of politicians. Standing at the epicentre of power is an extremely powerful section of the civil service – the Cabinet Office. Employing some 2,000 officials, it is organized into sections and units responsible for various aspects of government business, such as the machinery of government, senior public appointments and top management. Its role has increased since the 1980s as various new specialist units have been added, enlarging it by some 300 per cent. It contains both the prime minister's office and the **Cabinet Secretariat**.

The Cabinet Secretariat

With the exception of its head, the **Cabinet Secretary**, the 200 or so civil servants comprising the secretariat are seconded from other departments to these prestigious positions within the super-elite of the service. Its ostensible functions are similar to those of any other secretariat: circulating information to the Cabinet and its committees, preparing and distributing papers and agendas, advising on procedure and taking minutes (known as conclusions). It also conveys decisions to departments and monitors their implementation. These functions give it great political significance. Its role in establishing compromise solutions that enable ministers to present a unified front, both domestically and to the EU Council of Ministers, affords considerable influence (figure 16.4). Beyond these functions, it also deals on an ad hoc basis with difficult constitutional and political issues. In

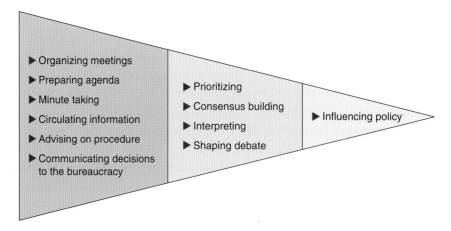

Figure 16.4 Administrative functions have political implications

2010 Cabinet Secretary Sir Gus O'Donnell played a major role in setting up the coalition.

Evolution

Until the early twentieth century it was traditional for the Cabinet to work informally with no agendas or minutes and no officials present. The only records were notes and personal letters from prime minister to monarch or diary entries (Gladstone's diaries are a particularly rich source of information). Sometimes ministers were unclear about outcomes, their civil servants being obliged to deduce what might have been decided. This seeming madness had some method: meetings were regarded as highly secret and the involvement of non-elected outsiders as unconstitutional. However, the first world war was to undermine such niceties. When Lloyd George took over he commandeered the much admired secretariat of the CID, including its head, Maurice Hankey, for the war cabinet. Housed in huts in the garden of 10 Downing Street, it became known as the 'garden suburb'. After the war the innovation was reappraised; opponents associated it with Lloyd George's overbearing style and the Treasury saw it as a rival in Whitehall. However, the 1918 Haldane Report on the machinery of government recommended its retention.

> Now that the Cabinet's gone to its dinner,
> The Secretary stays and gets thinner and thinner,
> Racking his brains to record and report,
> What he thinks what they think they ought to have thought.
>
> Anon., quoted in S. S. Wilson, *The Cabinet Office to 1945* (1975)

As the main architect of the secretariat Hankey deserves an honoured place in the bureaucratic hall of fame. Remaining to serve five very different prime ministers (Lloyd George, Bonar Law, Baldwin, Ramsay MacDonald and Chamberlain) in a variety of circumstances (war, reconstruction, coalition and both Labour and Conservative administrations), he demonstrated the value of the new machinery. Today the cabinet secretary is frequently described as the most powerful civil servant. In 1983 he was also designated head of the civil service. In 2012, the two roles were again separated, with the appointment of Sir Jeremy Heywood as cabinet secretary and Sir Bob Kerslake as head of the civil service. In addition to Herculean formal responsibilities, cabinet secretaries can find themselves in politically sensitive trouble-shooting roles, as was Sir Robert Armstrong over the 'Spycatcher' and Westland affairs and Sir Robin Butler over the Scott inquiry and alleged breaches of the rules on MPs' outside interests. They will also consider cases where a minister may appear in breach of the *Ministerial Code.*

The minutes: how they run

Initially Hankey kept near-verbatim accounts, attributing opinions and attitudes to individuals (as in the Cabinet Secretary's notebook shown in figure 16.5). Criticized

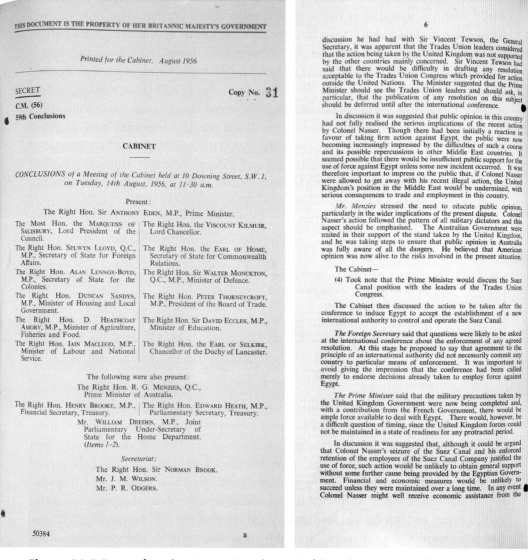

Figure 16.5 Extracts from the Minutes ('Conclusions') of the cabinet meeting of 14 August 1956, which discussed the looming Suez crisis, together with a page from the Cabinet Secretary's notebook (opposite) corresponding to part of the same discussion

Note: In the notebook, individual speakers are identified by their initials but the typed minutes do not attribute particular views to particular ministers and are couched in more moderate language.

Source: National Archives (document reference CAB/128/30 and CAB/195/15).

P.M. Mil. Preparations. Necessary : we must be ready. Labour Party accept that. But N. may act further – employees : Br. community : stopping ships. Tho' we can't hold our troops in readiness indefinitely.

W.M. In planning, seeking greatest flexibility possibility. By reducg. num of troops & considering how long oper'd. cd. be held poised.

P.M. We have completed plan. Have enough force to deal with situation. F.O. cont's makes it more than enough. But occasion is not it!

I.M. Attitude of T.U.C. Tewson is v. feeble. Thinks u.K. more isolated over this than we are. Re. wing motions on f. affairs can't pass T.U.C. w'out risk with u.S. T.&G.W. unions, now under Cousins, cd. be decisive. All we can do is ensure resol'n & debate is as little embarrassing as poss. – eg. defer publ'n until after conference. F.O. might also brief T.U.C. leaders.

P.M. Better for me to do that. I.M. V. well. – with me.

P.M. Consequences. If we lose M/E, we are finished. Shd. that be brought home more clearly to public?

L.P. That is best ground on which to stand.

S.Ll. cf. Nasser's own book. u.S. at last understand this.

L.P. Combine 2 arguments by saying : either internat'l control or leave it to dictator – & we know what dictators are. Plug the second part of argument. For we must bring N. down.

P.M. Doubt if we shall bring him down, w'out force.

M. u.S. attitude to force. u.S. will be heavily on our side.[i] They understand effect, not only on Canal, but on M/E. gen.

[i] They don't want u.N. – intolerable delays. They will stand to a good position resol'n. iii) They are beginning to think of econ. sanctions. If u.S. will apply them hard, it tends to bring them on to use - force. They don't want that now, a/c Election s) if they stand out of it, R. might stand aside too. But, if strong resol'n, followed by sharp econ. pressure (eg. dues) – other measures may come in, for N's popularity may wane : if large line-up against (incldg. u.S.) & no revenue to Canal. Dictator's stock, when it begins to fall, falls fast.

Favoured start is W'ton : import'c of getting u.S. thoroughly involved.

S.Ll. Agree. That's why I hope B. will move resol'n in conference.

K. No weakening on internat'l management.

A.B. Impose sol'n by force – p. opinion will back it.

W.M. w'out some provocative act by N., doubt if opinion will back use of force. Must watch this.

I.M. Agree with A.B. – believe we may have more support than appears.

as unconstitutional, this was modified to include only a general view of the debate, making it possible to use the 'conclusions' as the directions for civil service action. This practice places the secretariat in a pivotal position, with disturbing possibilities. In a break during a meeting, Richard Crossman examined the notes of Cabinet Secretary Sir Burke Trend and was shocked to see that the report of the Prime Minister's position was 'not the substance of what he had said, and if it had been the substance he would have divided the Cabinet' (Crossman 1975: 103–4). Under Blair the quality of the minutes changed, with much important business transacted elsewhere and a more informal flow of discussion. The secretariat were left to write things up as best they could so that some non-cabinet ministers (and no doubt future historians) found them among 'the least important part of their weekly reading' (Hennessy 1998: 11).

The Prime Minister: Elective Dictatorship?

When I was a minister I always looked forward to the Cabinet meeting because it was, apart from the summer holidays, the only period of real rest which I got.
Nigel Lawson, quoted by Michael White in the *Guardian* (29 Sept. 2001)

Cabinet government: dead or sleeping?

Any idea that Britain is governed by a tightly knit team is grossly simplistic; it is hard to discern where any particular decision is actually taken. The modern Cabinet is but one body in a labyrinthine network at the heart of the state machinery. It can be argued that it is little more than a fiction, a device whereby senior ministers share responsibility for tricky decisions. Meetings are mere formalities during which senior ministers may even sit working through their own papers. It is now time to replace the wide-angle lens with a microscope and peer more deeply into the heart of state power. In particular, we must address a crucial debate of the modern era: the position of the prime minister.

Who is the prime minister?

On 17 April 2013 a visitor from another planet would have believed itself to be at the funeral of a very special person, nothing less than a head of state. Yet this was not so. The British head of state was herself sitting quietly in one of the pews of St Paul's Cathedral. This was the funeral of Margaret Thatcher, a mere elected politician and not a president but a prime minister. Or was it? For some it was a state funeral in all but name, adorned not only with pomp, but with the military hardware normally associated with royal ceremonial (see p. 485). This circumstance draws our attention to one of the most salient debates in British politics.

The prime minister is not elected as such but is invited by the monarch to form a government on the basis of being able to command a majority in the Commons. Normally this means the leader of a single majority party, yet this has been less common than is usually realized (see p. 383). Under a coalition or party pact the prime minister is most likely to be the leader of the largest party, although both Lloyd George (Liberal) and Ramsay MacDonald (Labour) headed Conservative-dominated coalitions. Again, the minority partners might influence the choice. Thus Labour refused to serve under Chamberlain in 1940 and in 1987 David Steel of the Alliance declared that serving in a Thatcher-led coalition would be 'inconceivable'. Similarly, in the run-up to the 2010 general election Liberal Democrat leader Nick Clegg let it be known that he had no appetite for a coalition under Gordon Brown.

The circumstances of political life often mean that prime ministers will be of mature years, with substantial political experience (table 16.2). In 1964, however, Labour's thirteen years in the wilderness meant that Wilson had only been Secretary for Overseas Trade and President of the Board of Trade and in

Table 16.2 Age and experience of prime ministers since 1902			
Name (and party)	**Date of first coming to office**	**Age**	**Years in Commons before becoming PM**
Balfour (Conservative)	1902	53	28
Campbell-Bannerman (Liberal)	1905	69	37
Asquith (Liberal)	1908	55	22
Lloyd George (coalition)	1916	53	26
Bonar Law (Conservative)	1922	63	22
Baldwin (Conservative)	1923	56	15
MacDonald (Labour)	1924	58	14
Chamberlain (Conservative)	1937	68	19
Churchill (coalition)	1940	65	38
Attlee (Labour)	1945	62	23
Eden (Conservative)	1955	57	32
Macmillan (Conservative)	1957	62	29
Home (Conservative)	1963	60	15 (+ 13 in Lords)
Wilson (Labour)	1964	48	19
Heath (Conservative)	1970	53	20
Callaghan (Labour)	1976	64	31
Thatcher (Conservative)	1979	54	20
Major (Conservative)	1990	47	11
Blair (Labour)	1997	43	14
Brown (Labour)	2007	56	24
Cameron (Conservative)	2010	43	6

1979 Mrs Thatcher's experience amounted to four years as Secretary of State for Education and Science. Tony Blair and David Cameron came to the office, like MacDonald in 1929, with no ministerial experience whatsoever. Lack of experience can be compensated for by youthful vigour; Mrs Thatcher took the reins at the relatively young age of 54 but, at 43, both Blair and Cameron were veritable infant prodigies. On the other hand, when 64-year-old James Callaghan moved from 11 to 10 Downing Street in 1976, Wilson was able to claim that he was 'making way for an older man'. But coming to office in 1783 at the age of 24, William Pitt well deserved his epithet 'the Younger'!

Evolution of the office

It was the Hanoverians, through lack of kingly interest in things British, who allowed Sir Robert Walpole (1676–1745), the First Lord of the Treasury, to fill the power vacuum. He is usually cited as the first prime minister, though the term was used abusively, to deplore his pre-eminence over his colleagues. After his fall in 1742, his immediate successors were denied the same authority. However, by the time of Pitt the Younger, the position had become firmly established by constitutional convention. Even so, to be the cabinet leader was not to be supreme. The purpose of the historic constitutional struggles had been to curb monarchy, not replace one with another. Early prime ministers were regarded as only *primus inter pares* (first among equals). Indeed, when highlighting the significance of the nineteenth-century Cabinet, Bagehot placed little stress on the role of the prime minister. Subsequent developments saw a shift in the balance of power so that, by 1963, Labour minister Richard Crossman was to argue in the introduction to a reprint of Bagehot's great work that

> . . . the post–war epoch has seen the final transformation of Cabinet Government into Prime Ministerial Government. (Crossman 1963: 51)

The prime minister as president?

This question is central to an understanding of modern British government. Real-world **presidential government** takes various forms; some presidents share power with a prime minister, as in France, while others, as in Germany, are mainly symbolic figures, rather like the British monarch. However, exponents of the presidential prime-ministerial thesis think in terms of a powerful figure such as that of the USA, where incumbents stand in a particular relationship with the other political structures.

- *Head of state.* This position gives presidents special powers not available to others.
- *The people.* Presidents are in effect directly elected in a country-wide constituency, enjoying supreme legitimacy.

- *The Cabinet.* Members are not elected but appointed by the president on the basis of personal choice and, being unelected, have no independent source of legitimacy.
- *The bureaucracy.* The upper echelons of the bureaucracy are appointed by the president on the basis of political sympathy.
- *A personal department.* Presidents are served by a formidable White House staff and the Executive Office of the President, providing powerful intellectual and political support.
- *The legislature.* Presidents are not members of Congress and their position is independent of its support.

Yet despite their personal ascendancy, presidents face certain *restrictions*. The separation of powers allows the judiciary to examine the constitutionality of executive actions and Congress can block presidential legislation and veto certain appointments.

The constitutional position of British prime ministers appears to bear little resemblance to that of US presidents: they are not heads of state and not directly elected; their cabinet choice is restricted to members of Parliament; they are not independent of the legislature; the bureaucracy is permanent rather than politically appointed; and there is no prime-ministerial department like the Executive Office of the President. However, our examination cannot end with the formal constitutional position; on the contrary, this is where it begins.

[Tony Blair] has torn up the constitution and become far more presidential than any other Western leader. We don't even have the checks and balances they have in the US.

A 'senior Liberal Democrat', quoted in MacAskill and White (2001)

A state funeral in all but name: the Iron Lady is laid to rest

Head of state

Although this position is formally held by the monarch, in many respects the prime minister functions as a head of state. The important prerogative powers of the Crown, such as appointing ministers, agreeing treaties and even declaring war are only exercised on prime-ministerial advice. Moreover, foreign trips and meetings with other heads of state cast a presidential gloss, Thatcher characterizing her encounters with President Reagan as meetings of 'two heads of state'. Regular European Council summits enhance this impression. Early in his premiership Blair came to the presidency of the European Council and journalists began to speak of 'President Blair' with some irony. A hagiography on *Blair's 100 Days* by a Labour staffer even employed the term as a chapter title (Draper 1997). At the death of Princess Diana it was Tony Blair, rather than the Queen, who expressed the nation's sorrow.

The prime minister and the people

Although prime ministers are elected only as constituency MPs, political practice provides an increasingly **populist** link with the whole nation (figure 16.6).

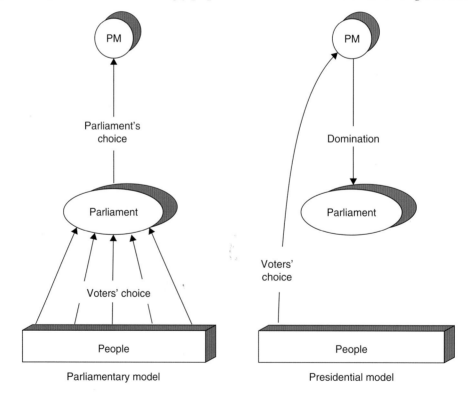

Figure 16.6 Choosing the prime minister

General elections

It can be argued that modern general elections are effectively contests between party leaders. The result is that prime ministers can claim a personal mandate. Before the 1987 election Mrs Thatcher proclaimed: 'I can handle a big majority'. In the 2010 campaign the three main party leaders took part in US-style televised 'presidential debates' (see p. 311).

The media

Journalists look to Number Ten for the main story and prime ministers' press offices have become increasingly dominant in politics, feeding journalists with a 'carefully filtered version' after cabinet meetings (Hennessy 1986: 5). As the term 'spin doctor' has gained currency, government has increasingly become the art of communication, with prime ministers' press secretaries rising to become key figures. On 15 June 2000, Blair began a new style of regular televised press briefings, very much in the manner of presidential briefings from the White House.

Opinion polls

The increasing application of market research techniques tends towards personalization, dwelling on the ratings of party leaders and thereby enhancing their pre-eminence. General election campaigns and day-to-day politics are regularly reported in terms of the poll ratings of the party leaders.

Image politics

> Quite suddenly, he who had been looked upon as something of a bore became both a formidable debater and a funny speaker. . . he set out deliberately to make himself amusing, writing out his jokes in longhand, late at night.
>
> Alan Watkins (journalist) on Harold Wilson, in the *Observer* (19 Oct. 1986)

Party leaders themselves play the game, paying attention to their images. Wilson modelled himself on the youthful President Kennedy but Thatcher carried image-making further; following the advice of PR gurus she altered her hairstyle, expression, clothes and even the pitch of her voice. The failures of Kinnock, Hague and Brown has been attributed at least in part to image. Blair appeared to mirror much of the style of President Clinton. Lifestyle factors, such as holidays with pop idol Cliff Richard, added to the 'cool' image. David Cameron dazzled his party conferences and his friendship with TV personality Jeremy Clarkson added some glamour.

Weak and hopeless. Norman Lamont (former chancellor) on John Major, quoted in *The Times* (29 Jan. 1994). He claimed to have been misquoted but was absent from Major's honours list in July 1997

Political culture

Finally, it can be argued that the British actually prefer strong figures at the helm. 'Churchillian' is a term of approbation and Thatcher and Blair were applauded, while Major's willingness to consult with colleagues was often seen as 'dithering'. British history is replete with examples of great individuals – from kings and generals to explorers and social reformers; there are few 'great' committees or working parties to stir the imagination. The admired leaders of the Knights of the Round Table and the Merry Men of Sherwood Forest were by no means *primus inter pares*.

The prime minister and the Cabinet

This relationship lies at the heart of the debate and contains various facets.

Creating the Cabinet

Like the procreation of eels, it is slippery and mysterious.
Claud Schuster (Permanent Secretary to the Lord Chancellor's Office, 1915–44) on the relationship between PM and Cabinet

The appointment of the Cabinet from amongst parliamentary colleagues is a powerful source of patronage, giving an iron grip over all those wishing to attain, or keep, high office. Moreover, the life peerage system allows non-MPs to be brought in. Thus Baroness Warsi entered Cameron's Cabinet in 2010. With the right to hire comes the even more devastating power to fire. Her Majesty's ministers hold office at her first minister's pleasure and those incurring displeasure can have their careers abruptly terminated.

Cabinet meetings

The conduct of meetings remains securely under the prime-ministerial thumb. With control of the agenda Wilson was able to prevent debate on devaluation and Thatcher avoided economic strategy and the Trident missile system. Blair prevented full-scale debate on the euro, economic policy and missile defence. Indeed, he was reported as dispensing altogether with formal agendas 'in the sense of an item by item discussion', preferring to choose the order of topics during the meeting (Hennessy 1998: 11). Furthermore, as chair the prime minister decides who shall speak, when, and at what length; dissident voices can be limited or studiously ignored. Even seating can be manipulated: Heath placed the *ingénue* Margaret Thatcher at an inconvenient position, from which she found it difficult to interject, and Lord Home (1976: 192) tells how Macmillan avoided having the 'steely and accusing eye' of Enoch Powell facing him across the table. The prime minister can also decide the frequency and length of meetings; under Blair they were reported to be cursory affairs, taking place once a week on Thursdays, often for little more than forty minutes. Finally, prime ministers can define precisely what was decided through their prerogative to sum up and shape the content of the all-important cabinet 'conclusions'.

Collective responsibility

When ministers feel they are inadequately consulted they have constitutional grounds for complaint. Yet today the doctrine decrees little more than that all support the prime minister or resign. Blair's first Cabinet was tightly bound and some ministers were rapped over the knuckles by Alastair Campbell, his press secretary, for stepping out of line. Critics described Thatcher's Cabinet as an echo chamber for her voice.

Cabinet committees

Cabinet committees might seem to offer ministers opportunities for influence. However, it is the prime minister who manages the network – appointing members, designating chairs and chairing those critical to major initiatives. In 1979 Thatcher took control of the 'E' committee on the economy, packing it with sympathizers.

Sofa government

Prime ministers can engineer meetings with close colleagues (sometimes inner cabinets, sometimes 'bilaterals') in order to avoid critical members and officials. Blair went further to appear detached from his colleagues (Norton 2003: 547–52). The 2004 report by ex-Cabinet Secretary Robin Butler on the use of intelligence before the Iraq invasion characterized his style as 'sofa government'. Even non-cabinet members can be involved in major decisions. Under Blair, Jonathan Powell (chief of staff), Alastair Campbell (director of communications) and Peter Mandelson were in many important groups, while Chancellor Gordon Brown, Foreign Secretary Jack Straw and Defence Secretary Geoff Hoon found themselves sidelined (Perkins 2001).

It is possible for prime ministers to take momentous decisions virtually alone. Attlee's move to develop a nuclear capability did not come before the Cabinet. Similarly, in 2002, amidst tension within the country and his own party, Tony Blair effectively agreed to support the bellicose stance of US President George W. Bush towards Iraq.

The Cabinet now – and I don't think there is any secret about this – doesn't make decisions.
Robin Butler (Cabinet Secretary) on the Blair Cabinet; quoted by Boris Johnson in *The Spectator* (2004)

Policy initiative

With no specific portfolios prime ministers can range freely over policy, choosing involvement in successful or 'sexy' areas. It is in foreign affairs that they can find the greatest scope; Thatcher will for ever be associated with the Falklands war, while Blair intervened over Kosovo, Sierra Leone and missile defence. Northern Ireland was another area where he upstaged his minister: despite her earlier work, Mo Mowlam became a bystander as Blair (with Mandelson and Powell) took over. Blair's most dramatic opportunity came with the 9/11 attack and the 'war on terrorism'. The once august Foreign Office appeared in decline as he effectively installed an alternative foreign policy directorate in Number Ten. Cameron appeared content to leave his ministers free but was quick to move in with U-turns when policies appeared unpopular.

The prime minister and the bureaucracy

When US presidents take office they sweep like new brooms through every nook and cranny of the White House. While their wives have traditionally changed curtains and wallpaper, they have changed the people, some three or four thousand of them. This is the **spoils system**, giving awesome power to reward, bribe and command. In contrast, incoming prime ministers are faced with a marble face of public bureaucracy, constitutionally beyond their power of appointment and as permanent as the Sphinx. Or are they? The idea that the public service is beyond the reach of political manoeuvring is but one more myth of British public life.

'One of us'

Though less dramatic and sudden than the presidential shake-out, prime ministers are able to control key positions and distribute considerable prestige and power throughout the state. Effectively inherited from the monarch, since Walpole's day these powers have been used to enhance prime-ministerial standing (figure 16.7). Positions within the prime minister's gift include:

- honours (peerages and knighthoods), subject since 2000 to the involvement of the House of Lords Appointments Commission;
- state offices (armed forces, church);
- government posts (from senior ministers to parliamentary private secretaries);
- ministerial advisory posts;
- top jobs beyond Whitehall in the huge diversity of quangos;
- Whitehall (although conventionally immune from the web of patronage, Margaret Thatcher began to influence senior appointments – see p. 537).

Moreover, with no parliamentary or judicial vetoes, the prime minister is not accountable for appointments in the way that a president is.

In the 2010 coalition, Cabinet Office minister Francis Maude sought reform to allow ministers to be formally involved in the appointment of senior civil servants and in 2012 Cameron vetoed the appointment of an official to the top position in the Department of Energy. In addition to exercising patronage, the prime minister can shape the very architecture of government, thereby determining what it is capable, or not capable, of doing. The administrative skyline can be transformed overnight with the creation, amalgamation and dismantling of departments (see p. 513). The number of agencies, quangos, ministerial advisers, cabinet committees and interdepartmental taskforces can all be modified in response to a prime minister's favoured policy initiatives.

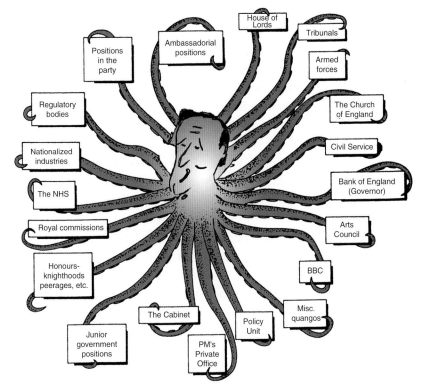

Figure 16.7 In an age of patronage to make Walpole blush, the tentacles of prime-ministerial patronage reach deeply into the state machinery

A personal department?

Without departments of their own, prime ministers must stand alone against cabinet colleagues powered by high-octane information and advice from their bureaucratic forces. Yet this is a misleading picture; today's prime ministers are not without support.

Personal offices

Personal offices contain staffs of around 100, comprising the following:
- *Private Office*. Housekeeping functions, managing day-to-day affairs.
- *Political Office*. Responsibility for party and constituency matters.

Press Office

Recent decades have brought into prominence a new and dominant political presence, the prime minister's press secretary or 'Director of Communications'. The function is frequently labelled 'news management'. Thatcher's Bernard Ingham became better known than many politicians and his belligerent style was replicated by Blair's Alastair Campbell. Appointees come well versed in the ways of Fleet Street (dubbed 'The street of shame' by *Private Eye*) and present the prime minister in the most favourable light. They can even brief against their rivals (Geoffrey Howe being described as a 'semi-detached member' and Gordon Brown as 'psychologically flawed'). In July 1997 Blair insisted that all ministerial speeches, press releases, interviews and media appearances be cleared with his press office.

Policy units

Policy experts drawn from various walks of life can assist a prime minister with ideas on policy. Wilson introduced a policy unit in 1974 and Thatcher brought in a succession of eminent figures. It was a policy unit that produced Major's 'big idea' – the Citizen's Charter. Under Blair this instrument was made even stronger with the intention of giving the government a 'steel centre' (Mandelson and Liddle 1996). Senior civil servants were obliged to see their advice overturned by 'policy wonks' only a few years out of Oxbridge. In December 1999, an answer to a House of Lords question revealed that the staff in Number Ten had grown by 50 per cent (Sherman 2002).

The Cabinet Office

The Cabinet Office is increasingly seen as a bureaucratic shell within which a further battery of units can be housed. These units have played an increasingly important role in policy, undermining both the Cabinet and its committees. Thatcher's Efficiency Unit, under businessman Sir Derek Rayner, was of enormous significance. From this acorn grew such initiatives as the Ibbs Next Steps programme (see p. 514). Under New Labour, policy units proliferated, with one for most new initiatives, and a Minister for the Cabinet Office was created. The position remained, to be occupied by Francis Maude in the 2010 coalition government, along with a ministerial team sharing a range of specialized responsibilities, from political and constitutional reform to volunteering and the 'big society'.

The Cabinet Secretary

At the head of the Cabinet Office is a figure often described as the most powerful in government. The cabinet secretary works closely with the prime minister and can be a tower of strength. From the beginning Lloyd George relied heavily on Maurice Hankey. Sir Burke Trend, who served from 1963 to 1973, denied that he was 'the Prime Minister's exclusive servant' (Hennessy 1985) but worked closely with Wilson, accompanying him, for example, to Washington as an equal and opposite force to Nixon's Henry Kissinger (Wilson 1974: 947). Thatcher established an exceptional rapport with Sir Robert Armstrong – her 'oracle' (Hennessy 1986). Under Blair, Sir Richard Wilson was adjudged by a leading journalist to have become 'immersed

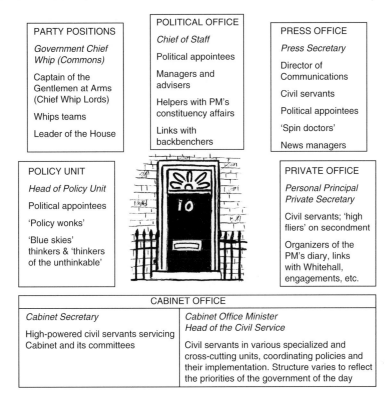

Figure 16.8 A Prime Minister's department?

in New Labour's presentationally driven culture' (Rawnsley 2001). In 2012 David Cameron entrusted Sir Jeremy Heywood with the sensitive job of investigating the 'plebgate' scandal which led to the resignation of his bicycling chief whip over a fracas with the Downing Street police.

External think-tanks and advisers

Prime ministers can also look outside for advice and support. Thatcher maintained contact with a number of right-wing intellectual groups, including the Centre for Policy Studies, the Institute of Economic Affairs and the Adam Smith Institute. Blair turned to bodies such as the Fabian Society, the Policy Studies Institute and Demos, often placing New Labour wrapping around Thatcherite policies (Pilger 1998: 83). Cameron favoured the right-wing Policy Exchange. The use of **think-tanks** and advisers is by no means a recent phenomenon, as Lord George Brown (1972) bemoaned:

> I resigned on a matter of fundamental principle, because it seemed to me that the Prime Minister [Wilson] was not only introducing a 'presidential' system into the running of the government . . . far too often outsiders in his entourage seemed to be almost the only effective 'Cabinet'.

What's in a name?

If British prime ministers were to have their own department, resembling the US president's Executive Office, it would, perhaps more than any other development, 'symbolise the shift from cabinet to prime ministerial government' (Jones 1983: 84). Today the resources available to prime ministers are formidable (figure 16.8). This may explain why, despite repeated speculation, the temptation to establish a formal department is resisted. In evidence to a House of Lords select committee inquiry into the Cabinet Office in 2009, Professor Peter Hennessy declared that Britain has 'a prime minister's department in all but name'.

The prime minister and the legislature

Finally there is a relationship in which the prime minister is constitutionally stronger than the US president, who is severely constrained by the separation of powers. In the case of Britain, a culture of party discipline (see chapter 15) gives the executive an astonishing degree of control over the legislature; the prime minister, as head of the executive, gains hugely from this.

Sharks and banana skins

There are no true friends in politics. We are all sharks circling and waiting for traces of blood to appear in the water.
Alan Clark (Conservative ex-minister) after the fall of Thatcher, *Diaries* (30 Nov. 1990)

There can be no doubt that Britain's ancient, ambiguous and elusive constitution leaves a formidable armoury in the hands of the prime minister. However, in the real world of politics, where personalities and interests clash, prime ministers can find their weapons double-edged. Any idea that they are *de facto* presidents must be hedged with reservations.

Head of state

However grandly the premier may strut the stage, Britain remains a constitutional monarchy, reminding elected leaders that they, and their powers, are mortal, the ability to use the royal prerogative being constrained by political factors. In the case of the government defeat in 2013 on its motion on military intervention in Syria, Miliband compelled Cameron to renounce its use, the Prime Minister ruefully declaring his respect for the will of the Commons in three short words: 'I get it'.

The people

Although general elections can be fought on the basis of a leader's popularity, public opinion can be fickle. A poor showing in the polls can damage, as Thatcher discovered in November 1990. Despite his dominance, Tony Blair ended his reign with a considerably dented reputation and Gordon Brown, crippled by a serious lack of popularity at the time of the 2010 general election, appeared weak.

The Cabinet

The Cabinet is not always compliant. Unlike presidential appointees, its members are career politicians who, like Macbeth, entertain vaulting ambitions of their own. Within the Cabinet sits the likely heir apparent and plots and rumours of plots are regular features of political reportage. Even the seemingly impregnable Blair had reason to lie awake at night as ambition continued to gnaw at his chancellor's heart. Indeed, he had to accept something of a dual administration, with considerable power lying in Brown's hands. The relationship bore comparison with the mid-nineteenth-century partnership between Lord Palmerston, whose interests lay overseas, and his chancellor Gladstone. Prime ministers need to keep friends in the Cabinet. Cameron resisted widespread calls for the head of Jeremy Hunt over News Corporation's BSkyB bid in 2012.

Cabinet selection is subject to political constraints and there will be a core of senior MPs with strong followings who cannot be omitted. Moderate Labour leaders have been obliged to endure some unwelcome company from the left. The fear of prime ministerial displeasure does not afflict all. Thatcher's wealthy foreign secretary, Lord Carrington, could afford an outspoken line.

The ability to butcher can also be questioned. Certain figures can be unsack-able; Major feared sacking troublesome enemies in his 1992 victory reshuffle and Blair could never remove Brown. Even ex-cabinet members can exert a troubling presence on the backbenches. Macmillan, for example, was weaker after his 'Night of the Long Knives'. Some ministers are willing to resign and, when they do, they earn the right to a resignation speech, which can have serious, if not fatal, consequences. Geoffrey Howe produced one of the most bitter denuncia-tions in modern history, helping to precipitate Thatcher's downfall, while Blair was undermined by Clare Short's and Robin Cook's speeches. Neither is collective responsibility always the gag it might seem. Most prime ministers feel plagued by leaks; Thatcher was to lament in her memoirs the lack of some 'good men and true'.

The bureaucracy

Despite some degree of politicization, the civil service remains largely perma-nent and civil servants are able to moderate the actions of prime ministers. It was reported that Gordon Brown received a stern warning from Cabinet Secretary Gus O'Donnell about alleged bullying of his staff. In 2011, an inquiry by O'Donnell confirmed that Defence Minister Liam Fox had broken the *Ministerial Code*. The structuring of the bureaucratic environment is often done to satisfy colleagues rather than increase prime-ministerial power and patronage appointments can be questioned. Early beneficiaries of the Blair regime were quickly dubbed 'Tony's cronies'. There are limits to the extent to which press officers can be recruited from

Prime Minister, you will not bother yourself about the New Hebrides.
Reported reply from Thatcher's Foreign Secretary Lord Carrington, when asked for details, quoted in the *Guardian* (1 March 1989)

the 'street of shame'. Cameron's choice, Andy Coulson, was forced to resign in 2011 following the *News of the World* phone-hacking scandal and later found himself under police investigation and arrest. The use of think-tanks and advisers can also backfire. Thatcher's reliance on the advice of Sir Alan Walters led to the embarrassing resignation in 1989 of Chancellor Nigel Lawson. Regarded as David Cameron's favourite think-tank, Policy Exchange attracted some derision as a 'neo-con attack dog'.

The legislature

While Parliament, with its captive audience, affords a stage for the adroit performer, it can prove a political graveyard for the less endowed. For Major and Brown Prime Minister's Questions could prove embarrassing to their supporters. Indeed, even the strong performers have testified in memoirs to attacks of stage fright before appearing. Despite his oratorical talents, Tony Blair fought shy of the chamber, with an attendance record worse than that of any modern prime minister (Rose 2001: 134–5). As chapter 15 shows, there are other caveats. Select committees can be penetrating and MPs can sometimes cast off their party loyalty. Moreover, as a prime minister's term lengthens, the number of the demoted or never-promoted rises, increasing the threat of backbench revolts.

The Achilles' heel

Finally, the prime minister has a weakness entirely unknown to a president. Having been elected by the people a president's security of tenure is absolute. Only upon some gross misdemeanour (such as Watergate) should the process of impeachment roll into action. In contrast, prime ministers occupy their positions only as long as the party is prepared to back them. Without this they lose all legitimacy to rule. Thatcher was once praised by colleague John Biffen as 'a tigress surrounded by hamsters', but on 21 November 1990 the hamsters were to bite. Perhaps as a consequence, Major lived a tenuous existence amidst constant rumblings of discontent and rumours of challenge. Even the once-dominant Blair was finally forced out in an atmosphere of party disaffection and declining PLP support. Increasingly David Cameron appeared weak in the face of the same Eurosceptic threat that had plagued Major.

Politicians are sustained through the setbacks which are their inevitable lot by conviction, self-belief and good luck. Lloyd George was fortune's favourite.

Roy Hattersley, David Lloyd George: the Great Outsider (2010)

Destiny and disposition

Hence, the prime minister's powers are potential, their reality depending largely upon two factors: *prevailing contingencies* and the *personality* or character of the incumbent.

The contingency factor

There is always an underlying tension between politics and fate, with economic movements, scandals and the forces of globalization setting the framework in which politicians act (see Gamble 2000). Like sports stars and businessmen, they need a helping hand from Lady Luck; the circumstances surrounding a prime minister's reign are, in no small part, a matter of fortune. Attlee was obliged to reign during the years of post-war austerity while Macmillan inherited the years of plenty. Health can also be a factor (see Owen 2008); Macmillan handed over to Home on such grounds and Gaitskell's untimely death gave Wilson his big chance, as did John Smith's to Blair. British victory in the 1966 football world cup and the popularity of the Beatles may have helped Wilson, contributing to the feel-good factor. Heath was forced into humiliating U-turns amidst world economic crisis and Callaghan was squeezed by the IMF and undermined by those upon whom he most relied – the trade unions. Major reaped the bitter harvest of a fractious party and an overheated economy, but for 'Black Wednesday' he could not entirely blame his stars; as chancellor it was he who had persuaded Thatcher to enter the ERM at a fatally high rate. Tony Blair surfed on the crest of a wave of fortune. He led a party united by weariness of opposition and faced a flagging Conservative opposition. Upon victory in May 1997 he inherited a relatively healthy economy and a popular mood for a change, while crisis in the world economy left Gordon Brown with little reason to thank the gods of political fortune.

Circumstances will call for different styles; an individual can seem right for one situation but wrong for another. Wars have been of particular significance. Asquith and Chamberlain appeared unequal to the challenge while Lloyd George and Churchill thrived, though in the aftermath were less sure-footed. Suez proved to be Eden's downfall. In contrast, the Falklands war saved the unpopular Thatcher, an inflexible style re-branded as 'resolution'. Globalization is another contingency which confronts all modern prime ministers (see Rose 2001), exposing them to external factors such as the European Council, where the prime minister is but one amongst equals, or the 'special relationship', where Blair's alignment with George W. Bush was to cast a shadow over his tenure.

Another card in the hand of fate is the parliamentary arithmetic. While Thatcher and Blair sailed on buoyant majorities, Major's twenty-one-seat margin in 1992 soon haemorrhaged, leaving little scope for manoeuvre, and in 2010 Cameron faced the difficult position of leading a coalition.

The personality factor

Weber noted charisma as a significant source of power and Asquith etched his name in the textbooks by declaring that the office of prime minister is 'what its

Changing times
*Events dear boy,
events.*
Attributed to Harold
Macmillan

Shit happens.
David Cameron,
speech at *Spectator*
annual parliamentary
awards 2010

holder chooses and is able to make of it'. All prime ministers share a fondness for power and, having risen up the greasy pole, are likely to possess political skill. However, each is unique, and the informal nature of the office permits infinite scope for interpretation. This helps to explain why the debate remains unresolved and of unquenchable interest.

Although Churchill emerged from the war as a giant, in the early post-war years incumbents interpreted their role cautiously, content to preserve the constitutional status quo. Charisma is not a term associated with Labour's Clement Attlee, although his modest efficiency has led many to dub him Britain's greatest twentieth-century prime minister. Macmillan exuded charm and is credited with having been surprisingly radical, but Labour leaders were repeatedly accused of wilting in the face of the Establishment. However, things were to change under Thatcher. Even before coming to office, the effect might have been anticipated. Interviewed in the *Observer* (25 Feb. 1979), she appeared to reject the very principle of cabinet government: 'As prime minister I could not waste time having any internal arguments'. In this era, personalized politics in Britain came of age. A child reared during these years would be unable to understand why William Pitt (the Elder) was compelled to resign in 1761 because the majority of his Cabinet refused to support his policy towards Spain. Major brought a quite different personality, accused of having 'all the charisma of a provincial bank clerk' (Charmley 1998: 124). Without Thatcher's confrontational style or zeal, he was to be plagued by accusations of weakness, and many believed his deputy Michael Heseltine (sitting on fourteen cabinet committees) to be something of an *eminence grise*.

In opposition the youthful Tony Blair had certainly not looked *primus inter pares* as he stamped his modernizing imprint on his party, even rewriting the totemic Clause Four. Columnist Andrew Grice (1997) was not alone amongst Westminster-watchers in prophesying that 'the overwhelming influence on Blair in power will be Labour's arch-enemy, Margaret Thatcher', whose style he professed to admire. In a similar fashion David Cameron, with confidence and panache, was able to snatch the leadership from the grasp of colleague David Davis.

A Monarchical Culture?

The last twenty years of the second millennium saw a testing of the ambiguities, myths and conventions that had long misted any clear vision of the British constitution. Britain's ancient monarchical lineage is no mere curio; it has deep implications for contemporary politics. Executive powers are derived from the royal prerogative, a power supposed to come from God. Together with a hijacking of the supremacy of Parliament, this bestows an authority surpassing that of monarchs of old. Constitutional authority Anthony King (2001: 1–21) draws a distinction between 'power-sharing' and 'power-hoarding' regimes. The Netherlands is an example of the former; Dutch ministers serve *with* not *under* their prime minister, cabinet members come from various parties, and meetings last a long time and really make policy.

The tercentenary of the Glorious Revolution was celebrated in 1988 in a most muted manner (privatization of the steel industry receiving far more publicity). In marked contrast to the French celebration of 1789 the following year, the British appeared to see little to applaud in the notion of freedom from tyranny. With the monarchical character of the British constitution laid bare, Charter88 declared:

> No country can be considered free in which the government is above the law. No democracy can be considered safe whose freedoms are not encoded in a basic constitution.

However, although rich in the resources of constitutional and political power, prime ministers operate under the constraints of the wider environment. The core executive, a complex web of interrelating structures and processes, extends to encompass the departments of state and even the security and intelligence services (Dunleavy and Rhodes 1990). Beyond the executive terrain journalists, media moguls, business magnates and trade union leaders also penetrate the shell of the core executive. Dispersed throughout this network, power becomes elusive and fluid and the answer to the question 'where does it lie?' can never settle simply upon either Cabinet or prime minister. Hence, issues concerning the working of the cabinet system do not tell us all we need to know about policy and power. The next chapter takes us further into this labyrinthine world.

Elective dictatorship. Lord Hailsham's description of the British constitution in his 1976 BBC Dimbleby lecture

Unlimited power is apt to corrupt the minds of those who possess it. William Pitt the Elder (1708–78), House of Lords speech (9 Jan. 1770)

Key points

- Formally, Britain has cabinet (as opposed to monarchical or presidential) government. This implies government based on discussion, compromise and moderation.

- This system is recognized constitutionally in the convention of collective responsibility.

- The modern Cabinet does much work through a system of committees.

- The Cabinet Office lies at the bureaucratic heart of the executive.

- Executive power in Britain cannot be appraised without considering the office of the prime minister.

- The term *primus inter pares* suggests that the prime minister shares powers with his cabinet equals.

- With no separation of powers or written constitution, a prime minister is potentially more powerful than a typical president.

- In addition, a large range of political factors serve to enhance a prime minister's authority.

- However, there are still constraints and incumbents vary in their capacity to exploit the position.

Review your understanding of the following terms and concepts

cabinet committee	elective dictatorship	Privy Council
cabinet government	inner cabinet	royal prerogative
Cabinet Office	news management	Shadow Cabinet
Cabinet Secretariat	patronage	spin doctor
Cabinet Secretary	policy unit	war cabinet
collective responsibility	presidential government	
core executive	press secretary	

Questions for discussion and debate

Consider these propositions and be prepared to present the cases for and against. Try to produce debating propositions of your own.

1 Cabinet government is a protection against tyranny.

2 The Cabinet Secretariat has excessive power in British government.

3 The Shadow Cabinet is a vital part of British democracy.

4 The personality of a prime minister largely determines the nature of the role.

5 The 'presidentialization' of British government is a product of the media.

6 'News management' is not a legitimate role for a government press secretary.

7 Collective responsibility is a dead convention.

8 Cabinet members have considerable power to curb the power of the prime minister.

9 The British Cabinet is no more than a rubber stamp.

10 The British love a strong leader.

Further reading

Blick, A. and Jones, G. (2010) *Premiership: The Development, Nature and Power of the Office of the British Prime Minister.*
Presents theories of the development, nature and power of the premiership.

Bogdanor, V. (ed.) (2010) *From New Jerusalem to New Labour: British Prime Ministers from Attlee to Blair.*
The history of post-war Britain in terms of its prime ministers. Essays by historians with some insider knowledge.

Burch, M. and Holliday, I. (1996) *The British Cabinet System.*
Well-crafted case studies showing the increasing centralization of power in the context of the core executive.

Foley, M. (2000) *The British Presidency.*
Title leaves no doubt where the author stands on the key debate; the Blair premiership is seen as the 'clinching proof'.

Gerrard, J. (2011) *The Clegg Coup: Britain's First Coalition Government Since Lloyd George.*
Early analysis of the operation of Britain's first peacetime coalition government by a journalist and Liberal Democrat insider.

Hennessy, P. (1986) *Cabinet.*
Lively account by academic and master journalist with an intimate knowledge of the geography of the corridors of power.

Hennessy, P. (2000) *The Prime Minister: The Office and its Holders Since 1945.*
Charts the gradual move towards presidentialism with a vividly empirical account of premierships in an unfailingly engaging and accessible style.

Kavanagh, D. and Seldon, A. (2000) *The Powers Behind the Prime Minister: The Hidden Influence of Number Ten.*

With unprecedented access to contacts inside 10 Downing Street, the authors reveal how successive prime ministers consolidated their power

Lee, S. and Beech, M. (eds) (2011) *The Cameron–Clegg Government: Coalition Politics in an Age of Austerity.*
Sixteen academic specialists appraise the formation of the 2010 coalition and its programme.

Rhodes, R. A. W. and Dunleavy, P. (1995) *Prime Minister, Cabinet and Core Executive.*
Examines the centre of the web of power in Britain.

Rose, R. (2001) *The Prime Minister in a Shrinking World.*
Charts the changing nature of the office since 1945. Examines the paradox that, while power at Westminster increases, power on the world stage diminishes.

Smith, M. (1999) *The Core Executive in Britain.*
Emphasizes the fluid network of relationships around Britain's cabinet system.

Young, H. (1989) *One of Us.*
Excellent account of Thatcher in government. Clever punning title sets the tone.

For reading around the subject and some light relief

Bad as political fiction can be, there is always a politician prepared to make it look artistic by comparison.
Christopher Hitchens (1949–2011; journalist and social commentator)

Biographies and autobiographies of the actors in the Number Ten sphere abound and are too numerous to mention. Many should be read with caution.

Michael Dobbs, *To Play the King* and *The Final Cut.*
Sequels to *House of Cards*. Evil chief whip Francis Urquhart becomes prime minister and his eventful career reaches a dramatic conclusion. You may like this, I couldn't possibly comment. (Available on DVD.)

Robert Harris, *The Ghost.*
Outlandish *roman à clef* about a prime minister whose foreign policy is made in the interests of the US. Resemblance to any living person purely coincidental.

Robert Harris, *Good and Faithful Servant.*
The inside story of the Thatcher regime told through an account of the developing role of her controversial and dominant press secretary Bernard Ingham.

Douglas Hurd, *Vote to Kill*.
A troubled Tory PM is betrayed by someone inside Number Ten and is soon fighting for his own life as well as that of his government. Former foreign secretary Douglas Hurd has seen much of it.

Nicholas Jones, *The Control Freaks: How New Labour Gets its Own Way*.
BBC political correspondent gives a no-holds-barred critique of New Labour media manipulation.

David Owen, *In Sickness and in Power*.
Ex-foreign secretary, Gang-of-Four member and qualified doctor examines how their state of health affects leaders and their decisions.

Christopher Meyer, *DC Confidential*.
Fascinating and alarming exposé of the human side of power by Britain's one-time ambassador to Washington. Blair emerges as shallow and vainglorious, star-struck by American razzmatazz.

Charles Moore, *Margaret Thatcher: the Authorized Biography*.
A sympathetic account, but with a sense of the absurd, by the former editor of the *Daily Telegraph*, who had unprecedented access to Thatcher's private papers.

Ben Pimlott, *Harold Wilson*.
Rehabilitation without hagiography of a key post–war prime minister.

Sue Townsend, *Number Ten*.
A satirical tale of prime minister Edward Clare, from author better known for Adrian Mole diaries.

On the net

https://www.gov.uk/government/organisations/prime-ministers-office-10-downing-street
Website at the heart of government, with information about past prime ministers as well as current activities.

http://www.cabinet–office.gov.uk
In addition to reports on Cabinet Office responsibilities, hear former cabinet secretaries talk about their time in office.

https://www.gov.uk/government/history/10-downing-street
Historical story of Number Ten, includes a virtual tour along the corridors of power and even a profile of Larry, Chief Mouser to the Cabinet Office!

Although purporting to explain how government works, all these websites should be viewed with due scepticism.

CHAPTER 17

THE VILLAGE OF WHITEHALL: OF MINISTERS AND MANDARINS

Contents

In this chapter we move to the engine room of the modern state – the central government bureaucracy, constitutionally part of the executive arm of government. We first detail the anatomy of the modern civil service and its evolution. We also note a large area of state administration which takes place beyond the civil service and at an arm's length from the government. Next we examine the bureaucrats who rub pin-striped shoulders with ministers in the process of government. What kind of people are they? Do their life experiences resemble those of the people they serve? From this we turn to a contentious issue that has characterized this world of power: official secrecy. This leads to the key debate on the influence of the bureaucrats: are they really the 'obedient servants' they claim at the end of their polite letters?

An Anatomy of a Bureaucracy

The British **civil service** is the central government **bureaucracy**, its function in the great liberal-democratic scheme of things to serve faithfully the people's elected representatives. Writers in the apologist tradition have had no difficulty in believing this to be the case, depicting the bureaucrats in the way seventeenth-century painters portrayed the nobility, in romantically idealized poses without warts or wrinkles. Thus E. N. Gladden (1967: 199) notes: 'On its record of public service it stands unchallenged, setting an example that the lesser breeds of official strive, almost hopelessly, to emulate'. This tradition of approval is partly explained by the fact that many writers (like Gladden) are themselves ex-members. Sir John Hoskyns (1984: 4), an outsider brought in by Margaret Thatcher to shake up this comfortable world, observed:

> No one is qualified to criticise . . . unless he has first hand experience of working in it. But if he has worked in it, then there is a convention that he should never speak about it thereafter except in terms of respectful admiration.

Empires fall, ministries pass away but bureaux remain.
Duc d'Audiffret-Pasquier (1823–1905; French statesman)

The constitutional position of the civil service has been said to entail three related characteristics.

- *Permanence*. Political storms may rage and politicians be swept in and out of office but the bureaucrats cling like pin-striped limpets to the solid grey rocks of Whitehall. They are career civil servants, not political appointees. This means

Picture 17.1 The stone face of bureaucracy

that, while acting in a position subservient to a minister, they may freely offer advice, warnings and criticism.

- *Neutrality.* Taking no sides and favouring no class, in their work civil servants remain above the sordid world of politics, the very embodiment of the liberal-democratic ideal of the *neutral state*. Without this they could not be permanent.
- *Anonymity.* Ministers alone are *responsible* to the outside world (through Parliament) for departmental actions. Civil servants remain in the shadows, neither named nor blamed when issues are debated. The person answerable is the minister, who is subject to democratic constraint.

However, the myths and ambiguities clouding the British constitution are nowhere more evident than in the role of the civil service. In this chapter, we must try to substitute a microscope for rose-tinted lenses, first setting the scene by identifying our specimens and the environment in which they civilly serve.

The civil servants

Not all state employees are civil servants. They may broadly be defined as servants of the Crown working in a civil (non-military) capacity and not holding political or judicial office. Said unkindly in caricature to be rarely civil and never servile, they are popularly thought of as grey, passionless beings who sometimes exercise discretionary power over our lives. However, despite evident efforts by some writers to avoid over-exciting their readers, the role of the civil service in our lives is certainly not a boring subject; it is about nothing less than running the state we live in. When examining the balance of power in society, its role must be central.

Civil servants may be broadly dichotomized as industrial and non-industrial. Thus, although the figure of popular imagination wears a suit and carries a rolled umbrella, many are obliged to roll up their shirt sleeves, others have stripped to the waist in government dockyards, and the exotic Quentin Crisp entitled his autobiography *The Naked Civil Servant* because, when posing for students in state art colleges, he wore nothing at all. Today the industrial civil service (primarily employed by the Ministry of Defence) has shrunk to minute proportions. The non-industrial service has broadly comprised three main elements: *administrators* – those concerned with running the state machinery and shaping government policy; a category of *specialist groups* containing experts such as scientists, doctors and lawyers; and a set of departmental classes implementing policy in areas such as taxation, benefits and social services.

From the mass of workers at its base to its tiny elite pinnacle (figure 17.1), the service has been something of a social microcosm. However, our principal focus is on the 1 per cent at the top, those whose daily lives bring them into intimate contact with government ministers. Many are located in the dignified corridor surveyed by Nelson from his vantage point in Trafalgar Square and leading to the Palace of Westminster. This is Whitehall, by which metonym this bureaucracy is popularly known. Often termed the **mandarin** class, the term recalls the high officials in imperial China. At the top is the Senior Civil Service, comprising some 4,000 members from grade 5 upwards. Traditionally known as deputy secretary, under

From mander, to command, 'mandarin' is not a Chinese word; it was used to describe the officials (Khiouping) by the Portuguese colonists at Macau. Mandarins were appointed on the basis of imperial birth, long service, illustrious deeds, knowledge, ability, zeal and nobility.

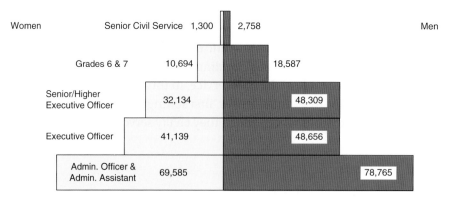

Figure 17.1 The civil service hierarchy: full-time staff in post by grade, March 2012

Source: Data from *Civil Service Statistics* (2012).

secretary and assistant secretary, in more managerial times they take the titles of director general, director and assistant director. At the apex in each department, and retaining their traditional titles, sit the permanent secretaries. The most senior mandarins meet formally as the 'Top 200', to coordinate the work across departments. The 2012 coalition government promised to simplify the grading structure, Cabinet Office minister Francis Maude aiming to follow the model of Tesco, with only ten grades between a shelf stacker and chief executive.

The genesis of the modern civil service

Like many institutions, the structure and ethos of the civil service owes much to its evolution. Orthodox accounts stress the nineteenth-century reforms, which are said to have replaced the corruption of an old aristocratic order with rational administrative principles. Less readily acknowledged is the fact that these reforms made this powerful state institution the property of the bourgeoisie.

Its ancestral roots lie in the courts of Anglo-Saxon kings who required clerks to accompany them around the realm. As officers of the royal household, their functions persisted through episodes of constitutional turbulence, with some offices, such as the Chamber and the Wardrobe, gradually giving way to newer ones. However, there was no single service and many positions were little more than sinecures, with appointments made through nepotism and bribery. Civil servants were often the sons of the aristocracy too dull to survive in any other walk of life such as church, law or army. The autobiography of the novelist Anthony Trollope (1883) recounts his own selection process.

> I was asked to copy some lines from *The Times* newspaper with an old quill pen, and at once made a series of blots and false spellings. 'That won't do, you know' said Henry Freeling to his brother Clayton. Clayton, who was my friend, urged that I was nervous and asked that I might be allowed to do a bit of writing at home and bring it as a sample on the next day. . . With a faltering heart I took this on the next day to the office . . . But when I got to 'The Grand', as we used to call our office in those days, from its site, St Martin's le Grand, I was seated at a desk without any further reference to my competency. No one condescended even to look at my beautiful penmanship.

Salaries were supplemented by bribes and gifts, a practice well documented by diarist Samuel Pepys (entry for 1 April 1663), who served in the Admiralty in the mid-seventeenth century.

> Going out of Whitehall, I met Capt. Grove who did give me a letter directed to myself from himself. I discerned money to be in it and took it, knowing, as I found it to be, the proceed of the place I have got him . . . But I did not open it till I came home to my office; and there broke it open, not looking into it till all the money

was out, that I may say I saw no money in the paper if ever I should be Questioned about it. There was a piece of gold and 4/– in silver. So home to dinner with my father and wife.

The rise of the industrial bourgeoisie

Eighteenth-century radicals lamented the failings of the service and a campaign for reform emerged under Burke and Fox. However, it was the new industrial bourgeoisie that fashioned the modern service. A critical element was the experience of empire, where the model for reform was found: the Indian Civil Service (ICS), which had evolved from the East India Company to become a complex instrument of British colonial rule. It was manned by the brightest sons of the bourgeoisie, who would take the passage to India, reigning there as the epitome of the over-dressed, over-confident Englishman (depicted by writers such as E. M. Forster). The fading sepia photographs suggest that the adventure was luxuriantly pleasurable and exceedingly good for the ego.

The young bureaucratic conquistadors prepared themselves to rule a race about which they knew little, in a climate for which they were singularly ill-suited, by means of the newly revived public school system with its umbilical link to the universities of Oxford and Cambridge. Under the stimulus of men like Thomas Arnold of Rugby, these schools became forcing houses for transforming the sons of rough-talking businessmen into scholars and (more importantly) gentlemen. They sought to place a stamp of superiority on their alumni through the study of the classics, team games and a hierarchical prefect system which, while appearing sado-masochistic, simultaneously stressed a natural right to rule and passive obedience. The ICS used examinations in selecting candidates, and the classics, the intellectual diet of the universities, were seen as the best indication of excellence. As **generalists**, with no practical skills, successful candidates confidently sailed away to command a vast subcontinent. The ICS seemed to the bourgeoisie to offer the very best model upon which to reform the home administration.

The Northcote–Trevelyan Report (1854)

What we must look for here is, first, religious and moral principles; secondly, gentlemanly conduct; thirdly, intellectual ability.

Dr Thomas Arnold (1795–1842; headmaster), address to his scholars at Rugby School

This report, the result of an enquiry established by William Gladstone, then Chancellor of the Exchequer, drew a blueprint for radical reform. Its driving spirit was Sir Charles Trevelyan, a zealous member of the ICS. The report recommended that the separate departments be amalgamated to form a single *home civil service*. The work was characterized hierarchically, from clerical routine, through a range of executive functions, to the intellectualism of policy-making. Recruitment was to reflect these distinctions in appropriately Platonic terms: men of iron would labour at the lower levels, while the upper echelons were reserved for the men of gold forged on the public school/Oxbridge anvil.

Merit would replace patronage and nepotism. Yet in this praiseworthy ideal lay the key to a bourgeois capture of the service. The examinations would be geared to the Oxbridge syllabus and neither the aristocrats nor the working classes could match the sons of the bourgeoisie on such territory. The report was warmly welcomed by Gladstone; the class he represented would have 'command over all the higher part of the civil service, which up to this time they have never enjoyed' (Morley 1903: 649). The old guard were not blind to the writing appearing on their decaying walls, Queen Victoria worrying where 'the application of the principle of public competition is to stop' (Magnus 1963: 118).

The twentieth century

The fact that the civil service took this shape is by no means remarkable: it was fashioned to serve a new political order. What is remarkable is that, as society changed during the twentieth century, the model persisted. Even an era of reform instigated by Thatcher, including the Next Steps initiative, which undermined the Northcote–Trevelyan principle of a single service (see p. 514), could not penetrate the bastions of the mandarinate.

The modern structure

Following nineteenth-century reforms, the civil service grew steadily. In 1900 membership stood at around 50,000 but growth was promoted by two world wars and the emergence of a complex welfare state, reaching a peak of 763,000 in 1976. With a changing political climate the number fell, standing at around 470,000 in 2011.

Outside London is a national diaspora of civil servants (figure 17.2), many working in semi-autonomous **executive agencies**, leaving a central core around Whitehall of some 50,000 (the size of the whole service in 1900). Although the sands regularly shift in the political winds, there are usually about nineteen ministerial departments, a similar number of non-ministerial departments and around sixty-five executive agencies. In addition there is a large and diverse range of non-departmental public bodies (NDPB) often termed quangos (see pp. 514–18).

The EU impact

Membership of the EU makes increasing demands on Whitehall. Although there is no special department of European affairs, those departments closely involved (Treasury; Environment, Food and Rural Affairs; Education; Business, Innovation and Skills) have established dedicated EU sections. While the Treasury and Cabinet Office are the traditional leaders, in an internal power struggle the Foreign and Commonwealth Office (FCO) found a lifeline to arrest its declining importance. Some members serve on the UK Permanent Representation at Brussels; once

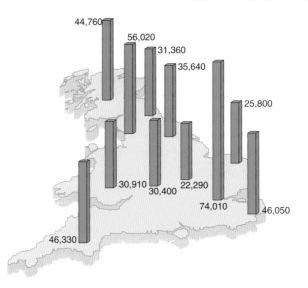

Figure 17.2 The national distribution of permanent civil servants, 2012

Source: Data from *Civil Service Statistics* (2012).

breathing its heady air they can be accused of 'going native', becoming forgetful of the Whitehall world as they act on the larger stage of European summitry (Sampson 1992: 40–1).

Political factors

Structure is no technical matter lying outside politics. The beauty of the unwritten constitution is that it can be forever reinvented at prime ministerial whim, often for some political purpose. Indeed, the very creation of the modern civil service was itself a political project. During the 1960s and 1970s a fashion for departmental fusion created new giant departments such as Health and Social Security (figure 17.3). These provided empires for prominent politicians and enabled governments to remove controversies from the public eye by resolving them within departments. By the mid-1970s the climate began to change and the giants were dismantled, but within days of Labour taking office in 1997, John Prescott's Department of Environment, Transport and the Regions (DETR) was born – an empire created to satisfy the political ambition of the Deputy Prime Minister. Further reforms in 2002 saw Local Government and the Regions come under the grandiosely named Office of the Deputy Prime Minister. In 2005 came the fusion of the Inland Revenue and HM Customs and Excise which, in the words of the minister, would 'pool information on those cheating the tax system' (Burnham and Pyper 2008: 143).

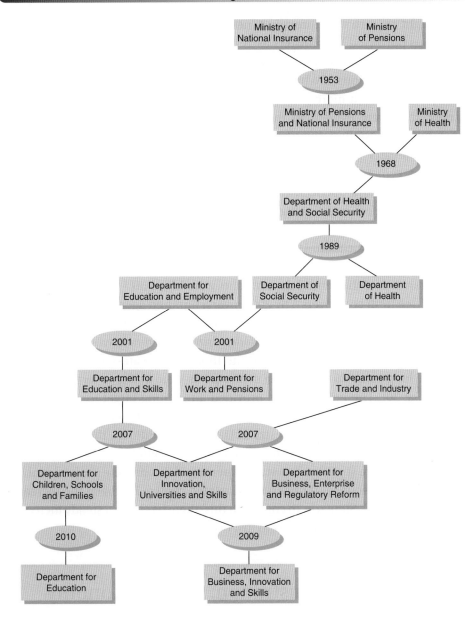

Figure 17.3 Departmental fission and fusion

Reinventing government: executive agencies

The greatest structural change to the service was agencifcation and it was by no means outside politics. A body of rightish thought (**public choice theory**) depicts bureaucrats as profligate users of public money, intent on enlarging their empires and 'over-supplying' their services (see Niskanen 1973). Governments from the

1980s sought to curb this through a 'new public management' movement. The process was portrayed by ministers as 'reinventing government', following the title of a book by US authors Osborne and Gaebler (1992). Reform proposals began to strike at the foundations of Whitehall like Exocet missiles.

The quest was for a more private-sector style of management. Such aims were not new; they were evident in the 1961 Plowden Report and the 1968 Fulton Report, but all these initiatives had been skilfully neutralized by the mandarins. However, Margaret Thatcher moved with greater reforming zeal than any predecessor. Management consultants were brought in at various levels and Sir Derek Rayner, of Marks and Spencer, was made head of an Efficiency Unit in 1979. A system of 'scrutinies', questioning established practices, achieved more than any previous initiative.

Next came agencification. Under Robin Ibbs the Efficiency Unit produced the 1988 'Next Steps' report, which presaged the large-scale fragmentation of the service. Branches of the central departments were **hived off** – a reform that was by no means free from controversy. By 2001, over a hundred agencies were employing around three-quarters of all permanent civil servants. The New Labour government proposed to go further, publishing its *Modernising Government* white paper in 1999 (Cabinet Office 1999b). This continued the theme of private-sector management and before long some 25 per cent of senior posts were being advertised (Cabinet Office 1999a: 30). The new agencies provided a tempting target for **privatization** (Burnham and Pyper 2008: 135) and the Blair government set about the process with a particular focus on the Ministry of Defence. In addition, the programme of public–private partnerships and the private finance initiative (PFI) continued to leave the civil service structure in a state of perpetual flux and the professional lives of civil servants insecure and uncertain. A related change has been the increasing casualization of staff. Similarly, to cope with this, there has been a steady increase in part-timers, from one in ten in 1999 to just over one in four by 2011.

Arm's-length Administration: Quasi-autonomy, Quasi-democracy

The architecture of the state goes beyond the civil service. An extensive world of public administration comprises a diverse category of what are termed Non-Departmental Public Bodies (NDPB). Journalists and politicians regularly refer to them as **quangos** (Quasi-Autonomous Non-Government Organizations). The acronym is employed rather loosely and often pejoratively; some might prefer the *Daily Telegraph's* 'Quite Unacceptable And Nasty Government Offshoots'. An alternative term is QGAs (Quasi-Governmental Agencies), while a report by Democratic Audit (Weir and Hall 1994) catalogued the vast menagerie of what it termed EGOs (extra-governmental organizations). Although set up by government, often on a statutory basis, these are bodies operating at an 'arm's length' from democratic control and accountability. Usually funded from the national exchequer, they are run by boards appointed by ministers. There are a number of reasons for **'arm's-length' administration**.

- *Historical.* Many important state functions (e.g. education, housing and medical services) grew up under local boards rather than at the centre.
- *Commercialism.* When the state becomes involved in commercial activities the traditional institutions and rules are seen as inappropriate.
- *Expertise.* Many areas of policy require knowledge and experience beyond the scope of politicians and bureaucrats (e.g. drug safety, the environment, the school curriculum).
- *Artistic and technical judgement.* It has been felt that bureaucrats and popularity-seeking politicians are ill equipped to make judgements about distributing funds to the arts and sciences.
- *Moral issues.* Certain areas of life have been felt to be beyond political judgement (e.g. race relations or film censorship).
- *Protection of civic freedom.* A fundamental plank of a free society is that certain state functions must be free from political control (e.g. broadcasting, police).
- *Judicial matters.* The constitutional principle of the separation of powers requires that institutions responsible for the administration of justice must be beyond government control.
- *National security.* Certain matters lie with the security services and are kept beyond the eyes and ears not only of Parliament but even of ministers.
- *Efficiency.* It is often more rational to provide services through locally based bodies able to respond to local conditions.

The quangos providing these services are known variously as tribunals and inquiries, advisory bodies, consultative councils, Crown bodies, public corporations, regulatory bodies, self-financing regulatory agencies (SEFRAS) and executive councils.

Quangos in politics

The principle of arm's-length administration is to insulate certain state responsibilities from the hurly-burly of politics. Yet any idea that this can be done is open to question. Quangos often operate in acutely sensitive areas: unemployment, race relations, nuclear energy, inner-city riots, police violence, local government reform, education, the NHS, university grants, the arts, railways, water supply, broadcasting, and so on. Even judicial decisions can be subject to political controversy. Their existence itself remains controversial, criticized from both left and right. The left view with misgivings the reduction in accountability while the right fear the insidious extension of state tentacles. The wide disparity of bodies in this category makes generalization difficult, but key areas of debate include the following.

Scale

The unending debate over what is or is not a quango arises in part from government attempts to minimize the apparent number and critics' desire to maximize it, the latter frequently evoking the term 'explosion'. Incoming governments regularly announce plans for a bonfire of the quangos. The 2010 coalition proved no exception. Claiming that, under its Labour predecessors, the number had soared to some 1,162 at a total cost of £64 billion, and with sixty-eight quango chiefs enjoying salaries of up to £624,000, George Osborne, in one of his first acts as chancellor, announced a £500-million cull.

Representation

> Is he really suggesting that one should engage in a series of silly questions to all the people on quangos as to what their political affiliation might be? Are you or have you ever been a Conservative – is that the sort of society the Hon. Gentleman wants?
>
> John Major responding to Nolan's recommendation that quangos should be more representative, quoted in the *Guardian* (12 May 1995)

Generally, members of quangos are chosen from the great and the good – those white, middle-class, middle-aged males carrying the 'safe pair of hands' kitemark. This bias obviously discriminates against the lower social classes and ethnic minorities. There is also under-representation of women. Cabinet Office figures released in 2009 revealed them to make up just 33 per cent of appointees.

Accountability

Not elected and not subject to the Access to Meetings Acts, most quangos can assemble behind closed doors, need not expose their documents to the withering sunlight of scrutiny and cannot be called to explain themselves; nor are they called upon to resign in the manner of ministers. For example, when the Lottery Commission turned down Virgin's bid in favour of Camelot in December 2000, although Camelot had been rejected earlier, Commission chairman Sir Terry Burns could not be called to account. Without accountability any system of government is open to corruption, or charges of corruption, and allegations of sleaze and venality are frequently made.

Patronage: of placemen and toadies

Appointments to quangos are made largely on the basis of patronage, a practice as old as the constitution itself. Monarchs have regularly placed favourites in positions of power and prestige and Britain's constitutional monarchy bequeaths to a prime minister much patronage power. According to the *Independent on Sunday* (23 March 1999), Lady Denton, a junior trade and industry minister with responsibility for 804 public appointments, confessed to never knowingly appointing a Labour supporter.

Concern about patronage led the Commons Public Accounts Committee to place the matter within the remit of the Nolan Committee in 1994 and its recommendations for appointments to executive non-departmental public bodies included the following:

- all appointments to be made after advice from an independent panel;
- at least one-third of membership to be independent;
- regulation by an independent Commissioner for Public Appointments;
- the Public Appointments Unit to be removed from the Cabinet Office and placed under the Commissioner;
- secretaries of state to make annual reports on appointments;
- candidates to report any political activity undertaken during the previous five years (Nolan 1995).

The government's response was to produce a code of practice and create a Commissioner for Public Appointments. For critics such as Hall and Weir (1996) this did little to address the problems. Despite Nolan, New Labour was soon accused of cronyism as its supporters, often 'celebrities', began to populate its boards and task forces. The second Commissioner for Public Appointments, Dame Rennie Fritchie, concluded that NHS bodies were being systematically packed with Labour councillors, whom opposition leader William Hague called 'placemen and toadies'. Beyond the issue of appointing ideological supporters is the suspicion of rewards, including those for donations to party coffers. Of the 450 directors on the boards of the companies in the FTSE 100 Index making donations to the Conservative Party in the 1990s, 150 were appointed to quangos. Only 50 appointments came from the remaining 480 directors of companies *not* making donations (Fisher 1997). New Labour did not escape criticism. An early example was Greg Dyke, appointed as BBC Director General, who had donated some £50,000.

Who's afraid of the quango?

Governments regularly come to office promising to save taxpayers' money and to do this they promise to cut the public sector. At this point it is the quangos that appear most vulnerable and the fighting talk is of a 'bonfire of the quangos'.

None did this so zealously as the 2010 coalition government. A swathe would be cut through the sector, with functions either transferred to civil service departments or local government or abolished altogether. Writing on PublicService.co.uk (24 Feb. 2012), scholars Chris Skelcher and Matthew Flinders feared that such a cull would seriously reduce the involvement of citizens in the business of government and lose the services of distinguished experts. In January 2012 a National Audit Office report, *Reorganising Central Government Bodies*, cast doubt on the government's grasp of the costs of the functions being transferred or of the transitional costs involved.

However, despite regular criticism, quangos are unlikely to become an endangered species. Not only do they perform some crucial (indeed indispensable) functions, they offer governments some extremely useful political tools, enabling them to wash their hands of embarrassing matters, disclaim responsibility for unpopular policies, evade parliamentary scrutiny and keep areas off the political agenda. Patronage power also provides a large bag of goodies with which to encourage and to repay favours. We find that the great and the good move in and out of quangos from the other peaks of social, academic and economic life. Virtually all can be counted upon to favour an establishment line; if they develop a maverick streak they can be removed as easily as they were appointed. This was demonstrated in the case of Professor David Nutt, chairman of the Advisory Council on the Misuse of Drugs. After repeatedly clashing with the government over drugs classification, and with scientific evidence to back his position on policy, he was sacked in 2009 by Labour Home Secretary Alan Johnson. Hence there remains in British public life today more than a little whiff of early-nineteenth-century venality and nepotism.

The Culture of Whitehall

Following the nineteenth-century reforms the civil service evolved its own particular culture, which preserved its elitist character. It has been likened to an Oxbridge college, with much attention to status, ritual displays of courtesy, esoteric speech codes involving Latin phrases and much cricketing jargon, and a general air of superiority.

Social make-up: unrepresentative bureaucracy?

Post-war mandarins have been asked to run a complex welfare state. How far has the service reflected the society it serves in terms of gender, race and social class? Has the selection process aimed for a representative bureaucracy?

Gender

The Victorian era was marked by male hegemony, shown in all-male London clubs, limited education for girls and a male House of Commons supported by a male electorate. The civil service reflected this culture. Although the diaries of Richard Crossman conferred a modest fame upon Dame Evelyn Sharp, the first woman permanent secretary, she remained a rare bird. While their opportunities in the service have improved (no longer forced to retire if they marry), women have remained under-represented at the upper levels (see figure 17.1). Their value has been seen to lie in performing routine tasks as administrative assistants and casual employees.

> **Diary of Jim Hacker: Oct. 27th**
> 'How many Permanent Secretaries', I asked Sir Humphrey, 'are there at the moment?' 'Forty-one I believe.' A precise answer. 'Forty-one,' I agreed pleasantly. 'And how many are women?' Suddenly Sir Humphrey's memory seemed to fail him. 'Well broadly speaking, not having the exact figures to hand, I'm not exactly sure.' 'Well, approximately?' I encouraged him to reply. 'Well,' he said cautiously, 'approximately none.'
>
> J. Lynn and A. Jay, *The Complete Yes Minister* (based on TV series) (1981: 355)

In opposition Labour had published in 1986 plans for a Ministry for Women. However, in government this was scaled down to a Women's Unit with responsibility for 'gender mainstreaming' throughout Whitehall, calling upon departments to consider women's needs in policy-making. Yet this did not guarantee influence and the results disappointed. The government appeared to place greater emphasis on its Social Exclusion Unit, with which the Women's Unit was later merged to form a Women and Equality Unit (Squires and Wickham-Jones 2002).

In line with wider cultural changes, the employment level of women has increased. In 2010 over half of all civil servants were women. However, many were still performing the more routine tasks and, of the part-time staff, some 95 per cent were women. Moreover, there has been a tendency for more men than women to be paid above the advertised rate, while more women than men received less than the rate. At the most senior levels women accounted for around 28 per cent, a figure which compared favourably with that of women in top positions in FTSE 100 companies. At the very highest level, however, of forty-two permanent secretaries in January 2011, only eight were women. Although Cabinet Secretary and Head of the Civil Service Gus O'Donnell had promoted a diversity agenda, when the post was split between Jeremy Heywood and Bob Kerslake in 2012, the position of women appeared to be reverting to former times, with the first four permanent secretary appointments going to men.

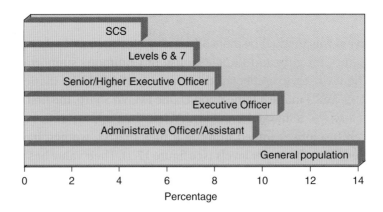

Figure 17.4 Ethnic minorities in the civil service and the general population, March 2012

Source: Data from *Civil Service Statistics* (2012).

Race

Not only male, the civil service has also been seen as pale. The issue of employing those from ethnic minorities was hardly one to engage the nineteenth-century reformers. Even in more recent times it has not been a major area of concern and, despite the target of 3.2 per cent at senior level by 2005 (proposed in the 1999 Wilson Report), prospects in the upper echelons have been limited (figure 17.4). In October 1997 Labour MP Keith Vaz, in a report based on replies to parliamentary questions tabled between May and July 1997, described the failure to recruit Asians as a 'national shame'. The Foreign Office and the Ministry of Defence were singled out for particularly poor records. By 2010 the percentage of ethnic minority civil servants had, however, increased to 9.2 per cent (*Civil Service Statistics*, 2010).

Social class

> If we're going to provide a public service, we can provide it better if we can understand and represent who we are serving. I want the civil service to look like the Number 36 bus.
>
> Treasury solicitor Paul Jenkins at 2009 Civil Service Live conference

Nowhere has the Northcote–Trevelyan legacy been more evident than in the class make-up of the mandarinate. Moulded from the same establishment clay as the heads of industry, commerce, the City, the army, the church and the ancient professions, its members attended the same schools and universities (see Kellner and Crowther Hunt 1980: 193; Theakston and Fry 1989: 132), joined the same London clubs (the Athenaeum and the Oxford and Cambridge being particular favourites) and met at the same house parties. Class bias has been reinforced by working-class graduates' disinclination to apply, reflecting low expectations of success. However, the appointment of Sir Andrew Turnbull as cabinet secretary in 2002 represented some degree of change. Unlike his three predecessors (who had spent their school-days at Harrow, Eton and Radley College, respectively), he was a product of the state system and under clubs in his *Who's Who* entry he listed Tottenham Hotspur! His successor, Sir Gus O'Donnell, followed the new mould, with a degree from the University of Warwick before Oxford. He had been an economics lecturer prior to joining the Treasury. However, Sir Jeremy Heywood, who took up the post of cabinet secretary in 2012, had been educated at an independent Quaker school, thence going to Oxford, the LSE and Harvard Business School.

Socialization

Although there has been some increase in the number of state-school entrants, in coming from the diligent middle classes they may be pursuing personal ambition rather than social reform. Moreover, despite meritocratic procedures, career advancement requires informal patronage from above and the ambitious will need to catch the eye of their superiors (Richards 1996: 665). Consciously or unconsciously, like the chameleon, they will assume the colours of their environment, joining the right clubs, attending the right parties and adopting the right speech codes.

Skimming the milk: selecting mandarins

The selection process is the key to understanding mandarin culture. Northcote–Trevelyan established that potential mandarins would enter directly into a closed upper elite – the Administrative Class. From the start entrants inhale the oxygen of power, meeting and even advising ministers. This at once removed the requirement to work through the ranks, while also preventing aspirants rising from the lower strata. Subsequent reforms maintained this principle of a 'Fast Stream', providing a gilded staircase to the top. After a filter of written tests a small number have proceeded to a 'house party', modelled on the selection system for army officers, involving several days of subjective assessment searching for ill-defined 'right qualities'. This policy of meritocratic recruitment was to lead to a form of elite cloning through which the service could reproduce in its own image.

Between 1965 and 1986, Oxbridge entry swelled to 75 per cent (Theakston and Fry 1989: 132). An *Economist* analysis (19 March 1994) of the 'true mandarinate' found that, of twenty permanent secretaries, sixteen had been to private schools and fourteen were from Oxbridge. These proportions had remained remarkably stable throughout the twentieth century. In June 1996 the government revealed that of Leeds University's 349 applicants in 1995, just 2 per cent entered the Fast

The British tradition of public administration is aristocratic, the French is republican.
Robert Skidelsky, 'The British Tradition of Administration', lecture delivered to a Moscow conference (17 Oct. 2007)

Stream – compared to 10.6 per cent of Oxford applicants. Universities with strong science backgrounds (such as Aston and Brunel) had no successful candidates at all (*Financial Times*, 13 June 1996). Beyond entry is the issue of career progression. Advancement, while subject to various 'objective' meritocratic processes, has been controlled through more secretive, club-like practices at the highest level. According to Richards (1996), formal procedures can be but a facade to legitimate decisions.

'Yes Permanent Secretary'

There are those who are always on the side of authority and quite exceptionally adept at formulating the answer that will be most acceptable to those at the top. It is no secret that they get on better than those who are outspoken and speak their minds.

E. N. Gladden (retired civil servant), *Civil Services of the United Kingdom* (1967: 199)

Although there had been some modest change in the characteristics of top officials during the post-war decades, the twenty-first century opened with the Whitehall village still largely inhabited by the white, middle-class, middle-aged male (Rhodes and Weller 2001). That the issue remained central was seen in the 2009 Civil Service Live conference (a networking of civil servants designed to share best practice), when senior civil servants recognized their recruitment bias towards the traditional elite of privately educated Oxbridge graduates. Permanent secretary at the Ministry of Defence Bill Jeffrey (2009) argued that the old school tie still 'probably matters far more than it should, but less than it did'.

The expertise of the mandarins: gentlemen versus players?

Social bias in the upper echelons can be defended with the argument that the criterion is brains, the apparent class domination arising because the best and brightest issue from the loins of intelligent and successful parents. Yet severe doubts have been expressed about the mandarins' expertise. While doctors attend medical schools and lawyers study law, Britain's mandarins, in sharp contrast to the practice in many other countries, have remained largely untouched by the disciplines relevant to their work (sociology, economics, civil engineering, and even social and public administration).

It is argued that high-level work requires *generalist* rather than *specialist* abilities, a preference redolent of the nineteenth-century reforms. Yet in truth the reformers had little choice; it was classics that the public schools and universities taught, so it had to be classics for the examinations. Had practical subjects been examined, the 'barbarians' from the urban technical colleges might have entered the establishment gates. This approach could work during the nineteenth century, with the state's minimalist 'night-watchman' role, but the post-war era brought government into new areas of economic and social life. Britain slipped behind its main competitors as civil servants wrestled with problems they did not understand, their cultivated air of superiority concealing shallow dilettantism (see Balogh 1968). The retention of the generalists' hegemony was justified variously. Only they knew their way around the Whitehall system, only they could understand the (equally generalist) minister's mind; that is, the best people to lead the blind would be the blind. Legitimation came in a doctrine which declared that experts must be 'on tap, not on top'.

The arrival of a Labour government in 1964 promised an attack on both social exclusiveness and amateurism and a committee was established under Lord Fulton. Its 1968 report castigated the 'cult of the amateur' yet, of over a hundred recommendations, one was politely declined – that entrants should possess *relevant* degrees. In the eyes of critics this seemingly small reservation effectively sabotaged the enterprise. By the 1990s, the generalists' promotion prospects were still considerably brighter than those of the specialist (Richards 1996). The importance of the issue was illustrated in the economic crisis faced by the 2010 coalition, a 2011 report from the think-tank Demos casting doubt on the ability of Treasury mandarins to cope (Ussher and Walford 2011). While claiming there had been improvements, Cabinet Office minister Francis Maude conceded at a Civil Service Live conference that specialists still 'don't always get afforded the same status and authority that they need'.

Mandarins in the hereafter: life beyond Whitehall

Mandarins have not feared retirement; indeed, some greet their professional demise with the relish of Christians in Foxe's *Book of Martyrs*, so certain are they of paradise to come. The close of a career brings rather more than a pocket watch; titles have been dispensed twice a year in the honours lists. These awards reflect status reached rather than any particular contribution; senior figures expect peerages. Although the practice was curbed under Major and Blair, the rewards do not end with ennoblement. Though gone, the mandarins are not forgotten, their names are entered upon the list of the great and the good from which are chosen the heads of university colleges, quangos and government commissions. Thus was Sir Thomas Legg (a long-serving 'Sir Humphrey' and Garrick Club member) brought in to investigate the arms-to-Sierra-Leone affair in May 1998. In 2004, Lord Butler, ex-cabinet secretary and by then Master of University College, Oxford, was enlisted to conduct an inquiry into the intelligence relating to Iraq's weapons of mass destruction (which he found flawed).

There is also a tendency, once the winter of retirement threatens, for some to migrate like starlings to the warm climes of the private sector in merchant banks and industry (Balogh 1968: 21). In the 1980s, public service could increasingly be seen as a prelude to private gain (see Doig 1984) and senior mandarins could feel considerable anguish if they had not ensured that when the Whitehall door closed another was ready to open. It is not difficult to see why an unrivalled knowledge of the workings of Whitehall should be prized by private interests, including multinational companies. In 1994, amidst controversy, Sir Duncan Nichol, NHS chief executive, joined the board of BUPA, Britain's largest private health care organization. Similarly, in 2007 Sir Kevin Tebbit, former permanent secretary at the Ministry of Defence, became UK chairman of Finmeccanica, the global aerospace, defence and security company. Critics have feared that civil servants in key positions, but with an eye on the future, might be 'inclined to take a general view of things not awkward to large private interests' (Balogh 1968: 23).

Restrictions have been introduced but remain light. For two years after leaving the service appointments are subject to an independent vetting body, the Advisory Committee on Business Appointments. With its membership drawn from the great and good, it seldom, if ever, turns down a request, and its declarations are only advisory.

Secrets of Success

The issue of state secrecy has long coloured debate on the civil service. This can be seen as a monarchical inheritance. State information belongs to the Crown not the people; the thirteenth-century oath sworn by Privy Councillors (the term means *secret council*) and lovingly preserved made secrecy a constitutional article of faith, institutionalized as the convention of collective responsibility.

Whitehall may be characterized as an incestuous 'village'. The inhabitants of Whitehall-on-Thames have their own private world of shared experiences 'united by coherent patterns of praxis' (Heclo and Wildavsky 1974: 2). This image has been particularly apposite with respect to sharing information with outsiders: locals like to keep themselves very much to themselves. Yet the mandarins are supposed to serve the world outside and if they are miserly with information they threaten democracy. In a detailed analysis of Britain's civil service, Burnham and Pyper (2008: 190) concluded that it 'is at its least modernised . . . when it comes to access to information'.

Information and power

Endemic throughout British government, **official secrecy** is perhaps the real *vice anglais*. It is a necessary instrument of a dominant elite; ignorance among the masses helps maintain deference. Official information has long been seen as the property of the high and mighty, who have been as likely to distribute it as they have their land, money and capital. The civil service, as keeper of the keys to the informational vaults, was to make British government one of the most closed in the world. Not only is secrecy bad for democracy, it can be bad for the health. People have been denied information about the air they breathe, the food they eat and the harmful effects of medicinal drugs. There are countless examples. Relatives of soldiers meeting accidental deaths, mistreated hospital patients, victims of Gulf war syndrome and pursuers of justice on various fronts have all met the wall of official silence.

Beyond the state lie powerful forces with their own interests in a government that can keep a secret (see chapter 19). When junior health minister Edwina Currie revealed in December 1988 the danger of salmonella in egg production, she angered the National Farmers' Union and was forced to resign. In 1993 it emerged that the government was holding back the names of five brands of soft drink known to have levels of patulin, a carcinogenic toxin, above the World Health Organization's safety level. To Maurice Frankel, director of the Campaign for Freedom of Information, this was another example of government succumbing to 'the unbearable temptation to work problems out in secret with industry' (*Guardian*, 11 Feb. 1993). Richard Lacey (1997), a scientist who worked strenuously to highlight the BSE threat but met with opposition from powerful farming and supermarket interests, was to dub the Ministry of Agriculture 'The Ministry of Truth', in evocation of Orwell's visionary nightmare of official deception, *Nineteen Eighty-Four*.

There is no shortage of some kinds of information. The civil service is a giant information-processing plant, producing each week thousands of memos, answers to parliamentary questions, **white** and **green papers**, and streams of data on the state of society, the economy and the international situation *ad infinitum*. The creaking shelves of 'Government Publications' in any university library present precipitous mountain faces and today a seeker after information can go to the government websites and download further voluminous official details at the click of a mouse. Yet all this can be seen as part of a legitimation process masking the true level of official secrecy.

Official Secrets Acts

Having enacted them in 1889, 1911, 1920, 1939 and 1989, Britain has been extremely good at passing Official Secrets Acts. The most restrictive element in this corpus was for long the infamous Section 2 of the 1911 Act, which made it a criminal offence for *any* Crown servant to disclose without authorization *any* information learned

It is an official secret if it's in an official file.
Sir Martin Furnival Jones (one-time head of MI5), quoted in C. Aubrey, *Who's Watching You?* (1981: 19)

at work. It was also an offence to receive such information and the claim that disclosure was in the **public interest** was no defence. Ironically, the 'public interest' is the basis upon which government itself justifies withholding information. Moreover, in the Ponting case, concerning the leaking of information on the sinking of the Argentine warship *General Belgrano* during the Falklands war, the judge, following an earlier House of Lords judgment in *Chandler* v. *DPP* (1962), ruled that the public interest could only be defined by the government, thereby opening the door to political interpretation. The jury was not impressed and surprised many by acquitting Ponting.

Section 2 was a 'catch-all' provision or a blunderbuss: one could theoretically be imprisoned for disclosing the type of biscuits consumed with the fabled civil servant tea. Originally intended as a form of press censorship, it was rushed through a Parliament fearing war with Germany. In 1971 it was reviewed by the Franks Committee, which declared it 'a mess' (Franks 1972: para. 88). Yet for those wishing to keep things under wraps the 'mess' was extremely useful. Thus Sarah Tisdall, a Foreign Office clerk, was sentenced to six months' imprisonment in March 1984 for leaking to the *Guardian* information on the arrival of US Cruise missiles in Britain. As in the Ponting case, the prosecution appeared merely to be revenge for political embarrassment.

The 1989 Official Secrets Act finally laid to rest the infamous Section 2 but did little to open Whitehall's filing cabinets. No past or present employee of the security services could disclose anything about their work and there was no public-interest defence. Those charged under the old system would still have been prosecuted. Thus, in the 2001 Shayler case, where a former MI5 officer leaked information to a Sunday newspaper, the Court of Appeal in September 2001 rejected his defence of public interest.

Beyond Official Secrets Acts

Secrecy is the essence of government.
Attributed to Conservative MP Enoch Powell (1912–98)

The wall of secrecy has involved more than official secrets acts. The Franks Committee reported sixty-one statutes criminalizing the disclosure of information but none punishing unnecessary secrecy. In addition, the thirty-year rule laid down in the Public Records Act consigns forty categories of government papers to the state vaults and the period during which they gather dust may be extended at the discretion of the Lord Chancellor. Another restrictive tool reached the front pages in the arms-to-Iraq affair, when Public Interest Immunity Certificates (PIICs) were issued to prevent the release of documents embarrassing to the government, even though they were vital to the defendants in the Matrix Churchill trial.

"What rankles is that, after years as a civil servant, one has never been trusted enough to be put in a position from where, if one wished, one could have passed on state secrets."

Reproduced by permission of Punch

Official secrecy and the media

In the case of defence matters, there is an additional means of controlling reporting. Introduced in 1912 after the 1911 Official Secrets Act, the D-Notices system (later the Defence Advisory Notices system) was an alternative to formal censorship, based on voluntary restriction. **DA-Notices** are issued by a Defence, Press and Broadcasting Committee, comprising representatives of the media and senior officials. For example, after the 9/11 attacks in 2001, editors and broadcasters were asked to 'minimize speculation' about any forthcoming military action. However, this gentleman's club system can appear something of an Edwardian anachronism in the face of modern terrorism and the rise of the internet.

A further government control over journalists is the lobby system, which gives selected journalists access to ministers. However, they can be pressured to report what ministers want to say; this is dictation rather than journalism. Those stepping out of line can have their membership removed. New Labour made it even easier for awkward journalists to be avoided and the art of 'news management' to be practised (see O'Toole 2006). Sometimes a more accurate account of events may be gleaned from maverick publications such as *Private Eye* and *Red Pepper*, or some of a growing number of leaking websites.

A la recherche du temps perdu: *political memoirs*

Political memoirs rarely threaten security yet the attempts to suppress them have been reminiscent of *Carry On* films, the goal usually being to avoid embarrassment

What I wanted to do was to show Wilson that we'd got him and that we wanted him to resign.

Peter Wright, referring to a secret MI5 file on Harold Wilson, in a TV interview, reported in the *Guardian* (14 Oct. 1988)

in high places. Probably the most celebrated of these were the diaries of Richard Crossman (1975–7), published posthumously from his taped account of his experiences as a minister in the Wilson government. Whitehall tried in vain to prevent publication and during the debate a further secret was revealed – the existence of unwritten 'guidelines' on memoirs, ruling out various subjects such as cabinet discussions and civil service advice. This involved the cabinet secretary inspecting proposed memoirs. Despite objections, Crossman's account surfaced and broke the gentlemanly convention that politicians would not impugn officials (Barberis 1996: 264). (It also inspired the *Yes Minister* TV series.)

The *Spycatcher* case represents the apogee of memoirs furores, the government literally pursuing its prey to the antipodes. Here security was involved because author Peter Wright had worked for MI5. However, the absurdity arose from the book's free circulation throughout the capitals of the western world. In another case, former head of MI5 Stella Rimington produced *Open Secret*, which was something of a paean to MI5, but the one-time insider found herself out in the cold. She was to report her 'stiff bollocking' from Cabinet Secretary Sir Richard Wilson (*Observer*, 9 Sept. 2001).

Yet the floodgates have been opened and guidelines can be breached. By the 1990s, memoirs, often conveniently packaged for the party conference season and newspaper serialization, had become big business. Peter Hennessy spoke of 'duel by memoir' as participants sought to give their version of events. Blair's press secretary Alastair Campbell produced his diaries in two forms, the first censored but the second a more informative version. Alan Clark's uninhibited revelations, not all of them strictly political, raised many eyebrows in 1993. Like Clark, Labour's Chris Mullin never rose to great ministerial heights, yet his *View from the Foothills* offered a new perspective in which some found a comparable lack of inhibition.

However, with a few notable exceptions, the accounts tend to be self-congratulatory. John Major's worthy autobiographical tome could have been enlivened with some mention of colleague Edwina Currie. Tony Blair produced *My Journey* and, not to be outdone by her husband, Cherie Blair brought out *Speaking for Myself*, with revelations about sex, money, royalty and New Labour. A memoir by former SAS chief Sir Peter de la Billière was followed by a flood of bestsellers from former troopers and military leaders. David Cameron was able to taunt Labour by placing *Back from the Brink*, the vengeful account of ex-chancellor Alistair Darling, detailing his relations with PM Gordon Brown, beside the dispatch box during Prime Minister's Questions. While there is a general feeling that material damaging to the public interest should not be featured in the media, the question arises as to who should make that judgement. The debate received a detailed exposition from the Commons Public Administration Select Committee (2006), published as *Whitehall Confidential?*

Access through Parliament

> *Anthony Wright:* Did ministers behave in ways that ministers ought constitutionally not to have behaved?
>
> *Sir Richard Scott:* I have said so, yes.
>
> *Anthony Wright:* Was Parliament denied information that Parliament constitutionally ought to have been provided with?
>
> *Sir Richard Scott:* I think so, yes.
>
> Sir Richard Scott answering Labour MP Anthony Wright before the House of Commons Public Service Committee (HC 313–111, 1995/6, paras 378–80)

Parliament, with its powers of scrutiny, could be expected to be in a position to demand information. The Ombudsman system, the development of the select committees and the use of parliamentary questions, particularly those requesting detailed written answers, can contribute to greater openness. However, armed with their Osmotherly rules (see p. 452), mandarins have kept their lips as well locked as their filing cabinets in the face of scrutiny committees. In its section on ministerial accountability, the *Scott Report* on the arms-to-Iraq affair cited seven examples of ministers withholding information. Parliament could compel disclosure through its power to punish for contempt, but this is impeded by party discipline.

A right to know: towards a Freedom of Information Act

The state's right to conceal can be balanced against a people's right to know. After the second world war, the UN declared the latter 'a fundamental human right'. Denmark, Sweden, Norway, France, Holland, Australia, Canada, Finland, New Zealand and the USA all passed laws giving a presumptive right of access to government-held information. Those wishing to withhold it must make their case in the courts (see Birkinshaw 1991). Calls for a British **Freedom of Information Act** came from libertarian groups such as the Campaign for Freedom of Information (established in 1984) and Charter88 (now Unlock Democracy). Yet governments fought shy and private members' bills introduced in 1978, 1981, 1984 and 1992 all floundered.

There was some progress but it was slow. The 1977 *Croham Directive* aimed to encourage departments to publish the background information for major policy studies. The Citizen's Charter initiatives of 1991 also made available some limited information on public services. In 1992, details of cabinet committees were finally released, followed by *Questions of Procedure for Ministers* (now the *Ministerial*

Code). In 1993, prompted by judicial criticism over the Kirk Sancto case (a soldier's accidental death), an 'Open Government' initiative was unveiled (Cabinet Office 1993). This included a code of practice to be policed by the ombudsman but contained many exemptions. People were offered information as consumers of services rather than as citizens (Raab 1994).

A breakthrough came in 1998 with the incorporation of the European Convention on Human Rights. Article 10 promised new rights to citizens and a white paper, *Your Right to Know*, had appeared in December 1997. This proposed an independent information commissioner with powers to compel official release and a new criminal offence of evading disclosure or destroying records. However, when a Freedom of Information Act duly entered the statute book in November 2000 it proved a considerably watered-down version of the white paper (figure 17.5). It occasioned a backbench revolt as well as the condemnation of the Commons Public Administration Committee.

A principal point at issue was a draconian list of exemptions. Some were classified as absolute, barring disclosure in certain categories such as security, court records, parliamentary privilege and material provided in confidence. Qualified exemptions were

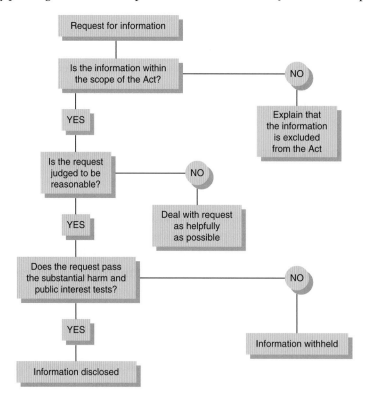

Figure 17.5 A simplified view of how an application under the Freedom of Information Act is processed

those subject to a public interest test. Although the information commissioner could order disclosure on such grounds, ministers retained a veto. A growing breed of government spin doctors, practising the dark arts of news management, promised additional difficulties (O'Toole 2006: 69–81). Frustrated at every turn, Elizabeth France, the first information commissioner, announced her decision in 2002 not to seek reappointment. Yet despite the criticism, the Act was to cause considerable discomfort to officials and politicians as journalists began to dig for information, including that on MPs' expenses. It was described by Tony Blair as 'the worst mistake of my career'.

A right to tell: towards a whistleblower's charter

When public servants feel a government is compromising the public's right to know, what are they to do? In the USA a code of ethics enjoins officials to put loyalty to country above that to persons, party or government. The British 'good chap' theory of government denied any need for such checks but, from the 1980s, confidence began to wilt as affairs such as those of Ponting, Tisdall, Westland and Matrix Churchill highlighted the ethical dilemmas facing civil servants. The First Division Association (FDA) pressed for a US-style code and government finally complied in January 1995, allowing any official faced with a crisis of conscience to appeal to a civil service commissioner. Sir Michael Bett was appointed to the position and by mid-1996 the FDA was pursuing several 'serious incidents' of allegedly improper ministerial conduct (*Financial Times*, 26 June 1996).

Yet critics remained unsatisfied, calling for statutory protection (Birkinshaw 1997). Lord Nolan argued in his first report on standards that public servants should have a right to voice their concerns anonymously. Finally the Public Interest Disclosure Act (the 'whistleblowers' charter') became law in July 1998. Designed to protect all employees speaking out about wrongs carried out by their employers, it enabled them to claim compensation at an industrial tribunal if penalized.

> **Public dis-information**
> According to the *Sunday Telegraph* (2 April 1989), government spending on advertising was planned to increase by twice the rate of inflation from £109 million in 1988/9 to over £120 million in 1989/90. Civil servants complained that they were encouraged to 'expound half-truths, produce dodgy material and leak in the Government's interest'.

A web of information

However, the twenty-first century sees an entirely new informational environment. The burgeoning multi-platform social media not only offer would-be whistleblowers more effective and safer channels, they open the door to the indiscriminate dissemination of information, ideas and conspiracy theories. Operating under the name of Guido Fawkes, Paul Stains was able to publish information and video footage that 'they do not want you to see'. The WikiLeaks website, founded in 2006 to aid whistleblowers and information-leakers, was to strike fear into officials' hearts around the world, releasing many thousands of documents that were meant to be secret. Governments can seek to act in defence but, when sites are attacked, there are hundreds prepared to take its place. As a new environment evolves, the very idea of secrecy becomes a chimera and poses new problems for governance. Informational anarchy offers an opportunity for a better informed citizenry but also poses threats. In March 1994, minister William Waldegrave, defending the government position in the arms-for-Iraq affair, claimed that it was at times proper to lie to Parliament. Indeed, many would agree that some information is better kept secret if government is to function effectively.

Power in Whitehall: Obedient Servants?

It is obvious that technically the large modern state is absolutely dependent upon a bureaucratic basis. The larger the state . . . the more unconditionally this is the case.

Max Weber,
Economy and Society, Vol. II (1978 edn: 971)

The liberal constitution portrays politicians as being in charge in Whitehall; otherwise the whole edifice of democracy becomes a sham. Yet around the turn of the century German sociologist Max Weber, a liberal troubled by the decline of liberal culture, noted an inexorable trend in developed states towards a dependence on bureaucrats. Fearing a body politic trussed in red-tape, he outlined a theoretical *ideal-type* bureaucracy recruited on merit, bound by impersonal rules and playing defined roles which resulted in a politically neutral, disciplined hierarchy under the control of the elected government. Apologists for the British system see in the civil service much of this model and Weber himself was one of its admirers.

The assumption behind the idea of an obedient bureaucracy is that there is a clear distinction between politics (**policy-making**) and administration (**policy implementation**). The **politics–administration dichotomy** underlies much writing on public bureaucracy and was enunciated in 1887 by Woodrow Wilson, who was concerned about corruption in American public life. Yet the distinction is untenable in practice. In the first place, policy can only be made in the knowledge of how it will be implemented. Secondly, no public servant implements policy like a robot; all instructions must be interpreted in the light of particular circumstances. In other words, the policy is being modified. Finally, in their advisory relationships with ministers, the mandarins exert considerable influence at the epicentre of the policy-making process.

Individual ministerial responsibility

Lying at the very heart of liberal democratic theory, the doctrine of **ministerial responsibility** articulates the relationship between minister and department. Because they are elected, it is ministers alone who are *responsible* to the outside world (through Parliament) for departmental actions. Various corollaries follow: civil servants should not themselves speak publicly, they must remain anonymous and, when praise or blame is apportioned, it must fall on the minister who should, in cases of serious error, resign. In the words of the House of Commons Treasury and Civil Service Committee (1994: para. 133): 'Ministerial preparedness to resign when ministerial responsibility for failure has been established lies at the very heart of an effective system of parliamentary accountability.' A shining example of this was the resignation of Sir Thomas Dugdale in the Crichel Down affair (see p. 704), in which officials had behaved improperly. However, this took place in 1954 and belongs to constitutional history.

Despite its detailed exposition, the convention is largely illusory. Mandarins are increasingly to be found addressing the media, their roles overtly politicized and even their names becoming well known. Cabinet Secretary Sir Robert Armstrong found his a household word during the *Spycatcher* affair, while his successor, Sir Robin Butler, hit the headlines variously: approving a £4,700 payment towards Chancellor Norman Lamont's legal costs for evicting a sex therapist from his London home, appearing before the Scott Inquiry and even featuring on the BBC's *Desert Island Discs*. Not only named, they can also be blamed. In the Westland affair, Collette Bowe enjoyed an unsought hour of notoriety, her anonymity broken by Leon Brittan in attempting to protect himself (Birkinshaw 1988: ch. 4). In 1972, the governor of Holloway Prison was publicly rebuked by the Home Secretary for taking prisoner Myra Hindley for a walk and in September 1998 the BSE inquiry named and blamed senior civil servant Elizabeth Attridge for advising John Gummer to reject scientific advice to establish a computer base for tracking cows.

Decentralizing blame

The agencification of the civil service had profound consequences for ministerial responsibility, promising a loss of accountability (Rhodes 1994). Although ministers had discretion, as for example when in May 1998 Home Secretary Jack Straw announced his willingness to answer prison questions, MPs generally found themselves frustrated by ministers refusing to take various questions on the grounds that they were no longer responsible. In 1993–4 widespread criticism of the Child Support Agency resulted in the resignation not of a minister but of its chief executive. Even greater controversy arose over the Prison Service Agency (PSA) as riots, breakouts and problems over IRA prisoners led to buck-passing. The 1995

> *My husband has saved your service from being torn to pieces.*
> Lady Dugdale, to head of the civil service Sir Edward Bridges after her husband's resignation. Quoted in letter from Dugdale's principal private secretary, to the *Daily Telegraph* (20 May 1998)

Learmont Report on the Parkhurst Prison breakout chronicled 'mind-numbing bureaucratic incompetence' (*The Times*, 18 Oct. 1995). Home Secretary Michael Howard, claiming the matter to be 'operational' and therefore not within his responsibility, promptly sacked PSA head Derek Lewis, who protested that he was being scapegoated after his operational independence was undermined (*Guardian*, 18 Oct. 1995). In September 1997 Robin Butler, as cabinet secretary and head of the civil service, at an Economic and Social Research Council conference, added his own voice to a concern that agencification 'obscures and blunts the democratic accountability of ministers' (*Financial Times*, 25 Sept. 1997). More recently, in 2011 the UK Border Agency, under pressure to reduce queues, was found to be letting hundreds of thousands of people into Britain without proper checks. Resisting calls for her resignation, Home Secretary Theresa May argued that the agency's head, Brodie Clark, had defied her instructions. Although strenuously denying the allegation, it was he who was forced to resign.

Loath to go

The resignation aspect of ministerial responsibility appears more honoured in the breach than the observance. Ministers are loath to atone by accepting the loaded pistol. In the Maze Prison breakout case, Northern Ireland Secretary James Prior sweated it out, securing the resignation of the prison governor instead. When Lord Carrington took the honourable way out after the Foreign Office failed to foresee the Falklands crisis, he appeared a relic of another age. Indeed, he would be an exception in any age; Finer's (1956) classic study of cases dating from the mid-nineteenth century shows how rarely the convention has been honoured.

Moreover, by the 1990s it appeared that ministers did not go, even if *they themselves* were culpable. There are many examples. After 'Black Wednesday' in September 1992 (see pp. 565–6) Chancellor Norman Lamont continued his stewardship of the economy. In the Malaysian Pergau Dam scandal a select committee investigation revealed that Foreign Secretary Douglas Hurd had ignored civil service advice. A politician of the old school, Hurd considered his position but in the end did not go. No heads rolled after the Scott Inquiry into the Matrix Churchill affair, despite direct criticism of Attorney General Sir Nicholas Lyell, whose actions could have sent innocent men to jail.

For politicians, the question of resignation appears to be determined by political expediency, not constitutional imperative. Generally those who go do so not for accountability issues or policy failures, but for sexual peccadillos or personal impropriety, often as victims of tabloid reporting. An early casualty of the 2010 coalition was Liberal Democrat David Laws, obliged to resign for apparently fraudulent expenses claims resulting from attempts to conceal his homosexuality.

Where policy or administrative failings are exposed, an ability to 'tough it out' (sometimes at the expense of civil servants or advisers) becomes a mark of government virility. Thatcher, Major, Blair and Cameron all stood by colleagues against calls for resignation during a period in which ministerial frankness before Parliament came seriously into question. Transport Secretary Stephen Byers hung on for a long time, despite worsening rail chaos, before being hounded out by the media in May 2002. Sometimes a sacrificial victim is required. When some 1,000 prisoners recommended for deportation walked free in 2000 because of administrative failings, Home Secretary Charles Clarke resisted calls for resignation but was effectively sacked by the Prime Minister. A notable case of prime ministerial support came over Rupert Murdoch's News Corporation bid to gain full control of satellite broadcaster BSkyB. The issue became embroiled with the phone-hacking scandal and in May 2012 the Leveson Inquiry revealed emails and texts from Culture Secretary Jeremy Hunt and his adviser Adam Smith, showing him to have been biased in favour of the bid. Despite furious calls for his resignation and the expressed concern of Deputy Prime Minister Nick Clegg, Hunt remained in office with the full support of Cameron (although Smith went).

Mandarins and ministers: 'Yes Minister'?

What of the relationship between mandarins and their political masters? Are they the compliant instruments of Her Majesty's Government? Some agree that they are. Attlee is a widely quoted apologist, always finding them 'perfectly loyal . . . That's the civil service tradition, a great tradition. They carry out the policy of any given government' (Williams 1969: 79). In evidence to the House of Commons Expenditure Committee (1977: para. 1877), Edward Heath avowed that in his experience civil servants were definitely all 'under ministerial control', while Harold Wilson declared that any minister unable to master his civil servants 'ought to go' (para. 1924).

'Yes Minister, but . . .'

Yet there is reason to question the compliant civil servant thesis since they have numerous advantages over ministers:

- highly educated, long experienced and street (or corridor) wise to the ways of Whitehall;
- with access to information and the ability to control its flow to the ministerial desk;
- well connected with powerful outside interests impinging on the departmental portfolio;
- armed with detailed historical knowledge of departmental policy;
- more numerous than ministers and able to collude informally and in committees (of which there are hundreds) within and across departmental boundaries;

Now at last I was a Minister in charge of an important Department and I could take decisions [and] lay down the law.
Richard Crossman's diary entry on becoming Minister of Housing and Local Government, *Diaries of a Cabinet Minister* (1976: 293)

- with security of tenure;
- from the confident classes who assume a right to rule.

By comparison, ministers are not experts, are subject to cabinet reshuffles and electoral rejection, and sometimes lack the educational advantages of officials. Moreover, even if blessed with the wisdom of Solomon and the strength of Hercules, the width of a departmental ambit means that no minister (or ministerial team) can possibly be aware of everything going on. Civil servants are thus indispensable: they give advice, draft answers to parliamentary questions, write speeches, arrange meetings, prepare memos and reports and generally organize ministers' lives.

It is not surprising, therefore, that an alternative body of evidence comes not from government publications or officially sanctioned memoirs but from exposés. Crossman's *Diaries* reveal how, from an initial state of euphoria, he was to suffer enervating battles with permanent secretary Dame Evelyn Sharp. Other chroniclers (Benn, Castle, Hattersley) give equally frank insights into bureaucratic power. There are also civil servants who have come out of the bureaucratic closet. Brian Sedgemore, first a mandarin and then an MP, was uniquely qualified to illuminate the private world of public policy. From him we learn of the

> ... arrogant and subtle way in which they dealt with ministers ... developing departmental policies which weak ministers could call their own, using delaying tactics, skilfully suborning powers of patronage that belonged to ministers. (Sedgemore 1980: 26)

For Kellner and Crowther-Hunt (1980) the mandarins were nothing less than 'Britain's ruling class'. Through these sources we enter a world making that of Sir Humphrey Appleby and Jim Hacker seem rather plausible. A House of Commons Expenditure Committee report (1977: para. 137) confirmed that 'some departments have firmly held policy views . . . When they are changed, the department will often try and reinstate its own policies through . . . the erosion of the minister's political will'. In practice the relationship between ministers and civil servants cannot be generalized. Personalities and circumstances vary and the relationship can take many forms.

Politicizing Whitehall? Neutrality under threat

The left had long doubted civil service neutrality, Harold Laski arguing that it only appeared neutral because the political system never threw up radical governments of the left. However, concern also comes from the right, which sees the service having a politically pinkish hue. The administration of the welfare state gives civil servants a vested interest in its maintenance and expansion. The result has been that many critics have argued that the service is becoming **politicized**, with neutrality under threat. While there can be no comparison with the US system, where an incoming president sweeps out thousands of officials in order to install a completely new team, significant changes have occurred.

Appointment: one of us?

> The Civil Service is slowly being destroyed. Unless the Government changes course, we'll go right back to the 19th-century days of nepotism, corruption and incompetence.
>
> John Sheldon (General Secretary of the National Union of Civil and Public Servants), quoted in the *Independent* (7 Nov. 1994)

Although the Northcote–Trevelyan reforms had removed the power of appointment from politicians, Margaret Thatcher took an unprecedented interest in senior appointments (Theakston 1995: 28). Her question as to whether appointees were 'one of us' became emblematic. Prudent careerists recognized that 'if you can't beat 'em', there remained only one sensible thing to do. Ex-mandarin Lord Bancroft noted the rise in the Whitehall 'grovel count' (*Guardian*, 12 Nov. 1985) and government defector Emma Nicholson (1996: 196), veteran of three ministries, noted in her memoirs how 'permanent secretaries can now lose their jobs so that a ministerial favourite can be brought in'.

Civil servants were even found doctoring figures by 'redefining' unemployment and directly falsifying returns (*Guardian*, 29 March 1997). In the Scott Inquiry they confessed to drafting inaccurate, misleading and 'clearly wrong' ministerial replies. In 1994, the *Observer* (24 April) reported the Cabinet Secretary advising departments to avoid anything controversial until after the local and European elections. In a civil service action paper produced in July 2012, Cabinet Office minister Francis Maude announced plans to allow ministers a role in the annual appraisal of civil servants which would affect their grade and bonuses.

Advising ministers

The use of **ministerial advisers** is another way of countering civil service influence. Paid as temporary civil servants, political appointees have loyalties to particular ministers. Seen as 'outsiders', they encountered a wall of impeccably polite Whitehall intransigence. Only during the heat of two world wars did such advisers make any impression and they were quickly demobbed once normal service resumed. Economist Thomas (later Lord) Balogh, brought in by Wilson in 1964, wrote that he was effectively frozen out. In 1970, Edward Heath tried to introduce businessmen but they encountered cold pin-striped shoulders. The 1974 Labour government permitted cabinet ministers two advisers each but their experiences were also frustrating.

To give spurious intellectual justification to the Secretary of State's political prejudices.
Maurice Preston's mock job description as adviser to Labour minister Roy Hattersley, quoted in Hattersley (1996: 169)

The black art of spin

It is now a very good day to get anything out we want to bury.

Notorious email to civil servants by special adviser Jo Moore (11 Sept. 2001)

However, from the 1980s the climate changed. With stronger support from the government some advisers became as well known as the politicians they served. The new breed soon began to put pressure on civil servants and the FDA made official protests that even junior ministers were rejecting official advice, sometimes adding emphasis with the 'F word' (McKie 1994). The privatization programme even saw government turning outside the service to commercial consultants such as Price Waterhouse, their work seeing the light of day in the form of government white papers (Ward 1993). This could be seen as the privatization of policy formation. The New Labour government welcomed much of the remodelled Whitehall architecture. By June 1997 there were fifty-three advisers, an increase on the Conservatives' thirty-eight.

These developments arouse fears that the high ethical standards associated with the British civil service are becoming compromised. In a battle between the government and Mayor of London Ken Livingstone over the London Underground, an official in the Department of Transport, Local Government and the Regions (DTLGR) was moved by adviser Jo Moore for refusing to take part in a campaign to slur Livingstone's transport expert Bob Kiley. David Cameron's choice of former *News of the World* editor Andy Coulson as his communications guru was highly criticized at the time and led to considerable embarrassment associated with the phone-hacking scandal of 2012.

The consolidation of the approach is seen in the exalted titles given to many of the special advisers; in the 2010 coalition both Prime Minister and Deputy Prime Minister appointed 'Chiefs of Staff'.

When governments change

The permanence feature of the civil service is based upon neutrality. A rise in the proportion of the politically committed officials could reach a level where 'the policy commitments of its senior figures will have made it unacceptable to the main alternative government' (Bogdanor 2001: 12). The eighteen-year tenure of the Thatcher–Major governments raised this question. Some claimed that the Rolls-Royce neutrality was still intact. Cabinet Secretary Robin Butler declared: 'If my position wasn't acceptable to an incoming government that would weaken the tradition of impartiality' (Williamson 1995). In the event, the coming of New Labour posed few problems since, in line with Laski's argument, the system had not thrown up a radically left-wing government. In the Major government's eventide one ex-mandarin observed:

> No one at the moment . . . is going to waste time putting up a paper on trade union rights . . . But all a Labour minister will have to do is ask for a full range of options and they'll get them (Timmins and Kampfner 1997).

The problem is less acute in the case of the advisers since they can expect to be paid off at the end of a government's term of office. Upon victory they can of course come back to their desks after a few weeks spent campaigning for the party.

Plus ça Change: Room at the Top

In the opening decades of the twenty-first century Britain's civil service appeared to stand at a crossroads with a questioning of the three shibboleths of permanence, neutrality and anonymity. More formal institutionalization of developments were promised in 2012 by the coalition government, Cabinet Office minister Francis Maude criticizing what he saw as the 'passive resistance' of civil servants to government policies. Research was to be commissioned into government systems (including New Zealand, France, Australia and the USA) where a 'spoils system' operates, in which senior officials resign with the fall of a government, to be replaced with those chosen by its successor.

However, in a constitution moulded through evolution rather than revolution, the idea that the machinery at the heart of the state can be 'reinvented' invites caution. Throughout the decades of challenge and uncertainty the mandarinate survived. Despite accepting that some top appointments are open to national competition, the service continues to 'grow its own timber'. Employing the reasoning of rational choice theory, Dunleavy (1991; see also Dowding 1995) presents a 'bureau-shaping model' where rational senior officials will shape their own bureaux as small agencies, removed from the actual delivery of policy and insulated from the chill winds of cuts. As journalist Andrew Marr noted, the mandarins' interests came to coincide with those of anti-statist politicians (*Independent*, 14 July 1994). The Northcote–Trevelyan model survived two world wars, the Keynesian revolution and the resurgence of neoliberalism. It remains a formidable limb of an entrenched Establishment and the time to write its obituary has not yet arrived.

Key points

- The civil service is part of the executive arm of government.
- The modern service was born in the mid-nineteenth century, when the bourgeoisie gained control of the state.
- The modern structure consists of central government departments and many agencies with varying degrees of autonomy.
- In addition to agencies there are official bodies deliberately placed at arm's length from democracy (quangos).

- Civil servants are said in liberal-democratic theory to be permanent, neutral and anonymous. All these features can be critically questioned.

- Studies have demonstrated how social divisions, established in the nineteenth century, have been broadly maintained.

- Whitehall has for long been characterized by secrecy.

- Senior civil servants play a significant role in the policy process and the extent of their influence occasions a major area of debate.

Review your understanding of the following terms and concepts

agencification
arm's-length
  administration
bureaucracy
bureaucratic power
civil servant
Freedom of Information
  Act

mandarin
meritocracy
ministerial adviser
ministerial responsibility
official secrecy
patronage
policy implementation

politics–administration
  dichotomy
rational choice theory
public interest
quango
Senior Civil Service
specialist and generalist

Questions for discussion and debate

Consider these propositions and be prepared to present the cases for and against. Try to produce debating propositions of your own.

1 The world of Whitehall is a village, with many features of village life.

2 Civil servants should be on tap, but never on top.

3 Individual ministerial responsibility is a dead convention.

4 The Northcote–Trevelyan report institutionalized elitism.

5 Agencification undermines democratic accountability and control.

6 The quango will never die.

7 Ministerial advisers are a problem, not a solution.

8   A civil service should reflect the demographic profile of a country.

9   Without secrecy government cannot function.

10   Permanence, anonymity and neutrality are outmoded principles in public administration.

Further reading

Barberis, P. (ed.) (1996) *The Whitehall Reader*.
Short readings from academics, politicians and officials, giving various angles on debates, both current and perennial.

Burnham, J. and Pyper, R. (2008) *Britain's Modernised Civil Service*.
Scholarly in-depth analysis and with a lively appreciation of the politics of bureaucracy.

Chapman R. and Hunt, M. (eds) (2006) *Open Government in a Theoretical and Practical Context*.
Collection of insightful essays by academics and practitioners.

Crossman, R. H. S. (1975–7) *Diaries of a Cabinet Minister*.
Published posthumously, this frank account forced the establishment door a little further open (and inspired *Yes Minister* TV sitcom).

Elcock, H. (1991) *Change and Decay: Public Administration in the 1990s*.
Sustained critique of the quest for efficiency, effectiveness and economy in the public domain. Latter half contains extracts from key sources.

Flinders, M. and Smith, M. (eds) (1999) *Quangos, Accountability and Reform: the Politics of Quasi-government*.
Outlines the case for the quango.

Fry, G. K. (1995) *Policy and Management in the British Civil Service*.
Lively analysis of civil service reform, giving a scholarly summary of basic information, and with a critical edge.

Hazell, R. *et al.* (2010) *The Impact of the Freedom of Information Act on Central Government in the UK: Does FOI Work?*
Detailed analysis of the operation of the 2001 FOI Act, posing a range of key questions relating to Whitehall culture. Based on interviews with a wide cross-section of civil servants.

Hennessy, P. (2001) *Whitehall*, 2nd edn.

Revised edition of a classic study, showing how the grey men of Whitehall must be of central interest to political scientists.

Hoskyns, J. (2000) *Just in Time: Inside the Thatcher Revolution.*
Raging attack on the alleged obstructionism, negativity and complacency of the Whitehall mandarins by one of Thatcher's managerial evangelists.

Mallalieu, J. P. W. (1941) *Passed to You, Please.*
A short early polemic against overweening officialdom, with a penetrating introduction by Harold Laski.

Osborne, D. and Gaebler, I. (1992) *Reinventing Government.*
Work by US authors inspiring (or justifying) much British civil service reform.

Rhodes, R. A. W. (ed.) (2000) *Transforming British Government, Volume 1: Changing Institutions; Volume 2: Changing Roles and Relationships.*
Monumental and definitive product of a five-year ESRC study to map the changing contours of the UK central state.

Rhodes, R. A. W. and Weller, P. (eds) (2001) *The Changing World of Top Officials: Mandarins or Valets.*
Illuminating comparative analysis puts the Whitehall mandarins in a wider context.

Rogers, A. (1997) *Secrecy and Power in the British State.*
Argues that state secrecy perpetuates elite rule.

Skelcher, C. (1998) *Appointed State: Quasi-governmental Organizations and Democracy.*
Places a microscope on the closed world of quangos, where decisions are taken behind closed doors without accountability to citizens.

Theakston, K. (1995) *The Civil Service since 1945.*
Masterly account of the evolving civil service, demonstrating the mandarins' ability to thwart the reformers much of the time.

Theakston, K. (1999) *Leadership in Whitehall.*
Very readable portraits of nine 'Sir Humphreys' of Whitehall. Notes how they work and how times changed during the twentieth century.

Tonge, J. (2000) *The New Civil Service.*
Explores the changing character of the civil service from the 1980s.

Weir, S. and Hall, W. (eds) (1994) *Ego Trip: Extra-Governmental Organisations in the United Kingdom and their Accountability.*
Articles on the quango threat.

For reading around the subject and some light relief

E. M. Forster, *A Passage to India.*
A study of English manners, arrogance and racism in the Indian Civil Service.

Jonathan Lynn and Anthony Jay, *The Complete Yes Minister.*
Edited version of the TV series (also on DVD).

Simon Petherick, *The Essential Civil Servant.*
Entertaining quotations about civil servants and their world.

William Shakespeare, *Measure for Measure.*
Corrupting effects of high office as a state official uses power to seek sexual favours.

Giacomo Puccini, *Tosca.*
As above, but in operatic form.

C. P. Snow, *Corridors of Power.*
While some find passion in action and sex, Snow finds it in the ambitions and memos of the men in pin-striped suits. Title added a term to the English language.

On the net

http://www.ukonline.gov.uk
The starting point for a vast amount of government information, with links to all departments and agencies, but beware of those spin doctors (see pp. 253–4).

http://www.civil-service.gov.uk/index
There's no shortage of information about the civil service, from statistics to career opportunities.

CHAPTER 18

GETTING AND SPENDING: THE POLITICS OF PUBLIC EXPENDITURE

Contents

It is impossible to understand politics without appreciating the financial dimension. Much of the controversy around who gets what, when and how comes down to questions of money. The Chancellor of the Exchequer, the keeper of the nation's purse, is the second most powerful cabinet figure and the prime minister is formally titled First Lord of the Treasury. This chapter has four main sections. After examining the nature of public expenditure and its associated institutions, we consider the processes involved, including the fixing of public spending levels, the raising of money and the public accounting process. Next we note how public expenditure has been used as an instrument of economic management within the capitalist economy. The final section assesses the extent to which the approach to public expenditure can be seen as a factor contributing to Britain's post-war pattern of economic performance.

The Nature of Public Expenditure

No man is an Island, entire of itself; every man is a piece of the Continent, a part of the main.
John Donne
(1572–1631; poet),
'Devotions' (1624)

At its simplest, **public expenditure** is the money used by the agencies of the state in its multifarious operations, from waging war to emptying the nation's dustbins. Its absolute level is beyond intuitive grasp – total government spending for 2011 was in the region of £691 billion; almost 40 per cent of gross domestic product (GDP – the total annual output of the economy). This is around £10,000 for every person in the country. The lion's share is raised through taxation, supplemented with borrowing and trading enterprises. Since 1994 the government has also sponsored a national lottery to raise money for sport, the arts and charities, though this is run by Camelot, a private, profit-taking company, rather than the state (making it unique within Europe). Thus the state draws money from society, passes it from one agency to another, and returns it to society as services, benefits and grants in a complex pattern of financial flows (figure 18.1).

Public expenditure can also be thought of more philosophically as an expression of community – one of the most important factors in our survival. A polity is cemented by public expenditure: ensuring national security, preserving its culture and guaranteeing social rights through welfare policies. The collective nature of our psyche is denied by *individualists*, who object if the richer are taxed to assist the poorer. Margaret Thatcher even asserted that 'there is no such thing as society' (see Kingdom 1992). From this stems much heated political debate concerning relative

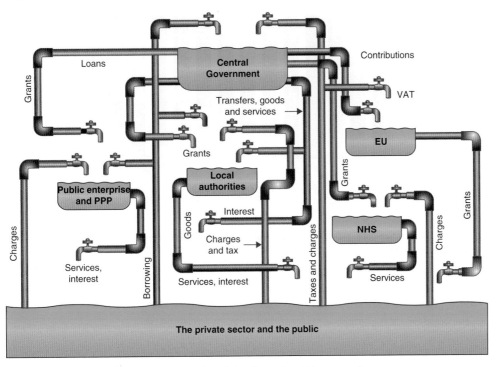

Figure 18.1 A simplified representation of the flow of public expenditure

priorities (figure 18.2). Although centring on technical, dry-sounding processes, this leads to decisions affecting the quality of all our lives.

Trends in public expenditure

Public expenditure grew inexorably throughout the twentieth century, a ratchet effect ensuring that gains during emergencies were never fully relinquished afterwards. Until the first world war it had stood at around 15 per cent of national income, but by 1918 it had climbed to over 50 per cent, stabilizing at around 25 per cent through the 1920s and 1930s. The second world war exerted further pressure, driving it up to 75 per cent, and it subsequently settled at around 35 per cent from 1950 until the mid-1960s. At this point further dramatic growth occurred, both in real terms and as a percentage of GDP, peaking in 1975 at 48 per cent, a time of economic crisis when the IMF demanded cuts (see pp. 563–4). By the late 1980s it had fallen, to stabilize around 40 per cent, where it has remained.

War is not the only reason for the upward trend. The New Liberal government reforms at the beginning of the twentieth century and the 1942 Beveridge Report (the

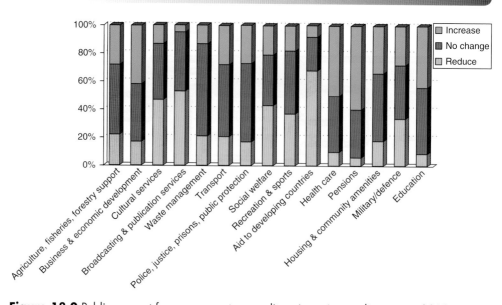

Figure 18.2 Public support for government expenditure in various policy areas, 2013

Source: Data from UK Public Opinion Monitor, 15th survey (Jan/Feb. 2013)

blueprint for the post-war welfare state) opened up a widening range of entitlements. Children were to remain longer at school, with more going on to university, and increasing longevity resulted in more pensioners. Demands on the NHS were to rise with medical advances as well as increased popular expectations of the service. On top of these factors, political parties have promised more and better services in their quest to maximize their share of the vote. There was also the new orthodoxy of Keynesian economics, which made government borrowing more acceptable (see p. 562).

The institutions

Although expenditure concerns all aspects of government, its control lies with two of the most powerful state institutions – the Treasury and the Bank of England.

The Treasury

Let me issue and control a nation's money and I care not who writes the laws.

Mayer Amschel Rothschild (1744–1812), founder of the House of Rothschild

Originally the Keeper of the Royal Purse, Her Majesty's Treasury stands closest to power, both geographically and functionally. Controlling almost every sinew of the body politic, its permanent secretary exerts a dominant presence in Whitehall. The political head, the Chancellor of the Exchequer, lives as the prime minister's neighbour at No. 11 Downing Street. There is often an uneasy relationship between them; while a prime minister may want to see increased services, a chancellor may want to curb expensive ambitions. Nigel Lawson resigned when he felt his advice was not being heeded by Thatcher. The chancellor is often a rival for the top position. In a period prior to Gordon Brown supplanting Tony Blair, the atmosphere at the centre of government was regularly described by journalists as toxic.

Notwithstanding its overweening importance, the Treasury is a small and intimate department of just under a thousand staff, its ambience creating a tightly knit community. An aroma of politics pervades each committee meeting and each informal exchange in the fabled corridors of power. Personal relationships constitute key channels of communication; trust between colleagues is cemented over long acquaintance and counterpoised with mistrust and suspicion of outsiders. Within this village, orthodoxies emerge as unchallengeable wisdom, contributing to a 'Treasury view' – a set of attitudes towards policy and the proper medicine for this or that malady – which will tend to influence all decision-making in Whitehall. Despite the enhanced importance of the Cabinet Office, the Treasury has managed to retain much of its hegemony, able to go beyond conventional economic management to exert a profound influence on policy in areas such as social security, education and health (see Deakin and Parry 2000).

Who are those with such dominance? Working in various sections specializing in the spending of particular departments, they are the 'Treasury men', a very special breed. Although their work sounds technical, they have been by tradition dilettantes *par excellence*, hand-picked from the very cream of civil service applicants, often with no prior specialized knowledge of economics, accounting, or any of the policy areas in which public money is spent. Even within the Treasury the average time spent in any particular policy area is but a fleeting two years, so that they have been 'exposed to little danger of losing their amateur status' (Heclo and Wildavsky 1974: 65). Apologists will argue that the reason the Treasury men can move so lightly between policy areas is their renowned Rolls-Royce minds; they have been the exotic orchids of the Whitehall hothouse, traditionally cultivated in the fertile soil of Oxbridge.

The Bank of England

The Treasury often works in collusion with another formidable institution which, although not part of the civil service, lies at the heart of the governing establishment. Nationalized in 1946, the Bank of England remains formally autonomous, nestling away from Whitehall as 'The Old Lady of Threadneedle Street' in the bosom of the historic square mile forming the City of London. Its appearance as a veritable palace, served by pink-coated flunkeys, is appropriate, for in the political life of the country its role is indeed regal.

This is the government's bank, holding its account (the Consolidated Fund) and with a prime responsibility for implementing fiscal policy. On the domestic front it acts as the government's agent, managing the note issue and the national debt. In international matters it is similarly close to government, dealing in foreign currencies and maintaining the value of the pound, buying and selling gold, and

The good Treasury man is an able amateur. . . He relies on ability to argue, to find internal contradictions, to pick out flaws in arguments whose substance he has not fully mastered and whose subtleties he can only be dimly aware of.
Heclo and Wildavsky (1974: 60)

engaging in international discussions on financial and trade policy. It also stands at the centre of the nation's financial community. As the central bank it is the bank of banks, holding the cash reserves of the clearing banks, providing facilities that an ordinary customer might expect from a High Street bank and acting as a channel of communication between them and the Treasury.

Yet despite its overwhelming importance to the nation, the Bank has never been a passive servant of government; on the contrary, it has often appeared the master, effectively shaping policy through its advice. It can even be seen as a pressure group, using its relationship with the Treasury on behalf of the banking sector against industrial capital and pressing its preference for high interest rates. In addition, the legendary secrecy of the British state is here amplified by the claims of necessary confidentiality, keeping out any prying eyes from Parliament, the media and even the government. Generally, what is known about the Bank is what it wants to be known, information being purveyed through its own carefully edited publications. Some light was allowed in when, in April 1994, Chancellor Kenneth Clarke agreed to the publication of the minutes of his monthly meetings with Governor Sir Edward George. These revealed considerable tension between the two, with the Chancellor resisting interest rate rises.

Given this enormous power, one must ask who is in control and whether they are likely to be responsive to the needs of society. The Bank is formally under a Court, comprising the governor, two deputy governors and nine non-executive directors. Members are drawn from the world of high finance but include one trade union representative. Criticized as outdated, it was reformed by the New Labour government through the 2009 Banking Act, which involved reducing its size from nineteen to twelve. However, critics remained unsatisfied with the Court's accountability and, in January 2012, the Treasury Select Committee called for 'a proper Board – fit for the twenty-first century'.

The governor is a key figure, even grander than the head of the Treasury, moving in the world of the most powerful, feted by millionaire capitalists, delivering speeches declaiming his views and theories, conferring with government and in times of crisis exerting a domineering presence. Despite the dignity surrounding the office, the position is profoundly political. The Wilson government learned very soon of this power. In its first year of office, being unpopular with the financial sector, it suffered in the face of malicious speculation against the pound, and Lord Cromer demanded that the government, notwithstanding its manifesto commitments, make all-round expenditure cuts. Wilson (1974: 62) records:

> In January 1965 . . . I told him that Government expenditure was committed far ahead; schools which were being built, roads . . . were part-way to completion . . .Was it his view, I asked him, that we should cut them off half-finished . . . The question was difficult for him, but he answered, 'Yes'.

When Gordon Brown acquired the keys to No. 11 in 1997, some major changes were made, giving the Bank a crucial new responsibility: while the chancellor would set inflation targets, interest rates would be determined by the Bank on the basis of expert assessment rather than political expediency. Meeting monthly and taking decisions by majority vote in the Bank's committee room, overlooked by a portrait of Sir Montagu Norman (a legendary but eccentric governor from 1920 to 1944), a nine-person Monetary Policy Committee led by the governor makes the decisions, which are also scrutinized by the Treasury Select Committee. There was, however, a political advantage in the Bank's independence: it would relieve chancellors of the responsibility. A further responsibility came in early 2013, as part of a reform set in train by the financial crisis. The coalition government gave the Bank additional powers to regulate the other banks to ensure that distance was kept between the functions of speculation and the safe keeping of customers' deposits.

Parliament

We saw in chapter 14 how public expenditure was the key to increased parliamentary control over the executive. The sovereign's crown was hollow without funds, and as Parliament became the effective payer of the piper it sought to call the royal tune. By the time of Elizabeth I the convention that the Commons had pre-eminence in financial matters had become established. This became official with the passing of resolutions in 1671 and 1678, after attempts by the Lords to breach the convention, and was consolidated in the Glorious Revolution of 1688. Further political controversy arose in 1909 when the Lords rejected New Liberal Chancellor Lloyd George's 'People's Budget'. This crisis resulted in further reductions in the powers of the upper house.

Other important reforms date from the 1780s, under the stimulus of Pitt, and were intended to simplify public accounting and strengthen parliamentary control. Of particular significance was the creation of the Consolidated Fund in 1787, amalgamating a complex muddle of accounts into one, into which all state revenue would flow and from which all expenditure would be drawn. This is in effect the government's bank account and is lodged with the Bank of England.

The rise of the new industrial bourgeoisie brought a new ethic to public expenditure. When the early capitalists acquired wealth, they did not use it extravagantly like the merchants and landowners of old but, like Dickens's Ebenezer Scrooge, tended towards frugality. In this way they could invest in yet more capital and amass wealth quite beyond their needs for personal survival. The cumulative effect was to consolidate the position of the capitalists and their families, who formed an increasingly dominant class. The importance of this was stressed by sociologist Max Weber, who attributed it in large measure to religion – to Protestantism and Calvinistic puritanism. The Protestant work ethic, in Weber's view, explained

The public be damned. I am working for my shareholders.
William Henry Vanderbilt (1821–85; US millionaire railway owner), refusing to answer a reporter asking questions on behalf of the public

> [The capitalist bourgeoisie] has accomplished wonders far surpassing Egyptian pyramids, Roman aqueducts, and Gothic cathedrals . . . It draws all nations into civilisation . . . has created enormous cities . . . rescued a considerable part of the population from the idiocy of rural life . . . and . . . has created more massive and more colossal productive forces than have all previous generations together.
>
> Karl Marx, *The Communist Manifesto* (1848: ch. 1)

the ascendancy of capitalism in Western Europe by adding religious zeal to the lure of profit. This parsimony was to inform the approach to public expenditure. The prime goal was to become that of Victorian prudence – a *balanced budget* as advocated by Mr Micawber in Charles Dickens's novel *David Copperfield*:

> Annual income twenty pounds, annual expenditure nineteen nineteen six, result happiness. Annual income twenty pounds, annual expenditure twenty pounds ought and six, result misery.

Against this background, the key figure in a series of rigorous reforms was Gladstone who, as chancellor, determined that government finance should be as tightly controlled by the bourgeois paymasters as were their own prudently managed businesses. The aim was to evolve a system that would tax capitalists' profits as little as possible, taking just enough to keep open the trade routes and contain the potentially unruly masses at home. The system was conceived in terms of an annual cycle that would balance expenditure and taxation.

Today the Commons is nominally in control of public finance, including spending, taxation and auditing, although as we will discover, much of this control is fictitious.

The purposes of public expenditure

Intuition suggests that the purpose of state expenditure is, like that of a household, to finance its activities, by providing services and paying benefits (see figure 18.3, p. 556). It is sometimes forgotten that in the latter case the state is not actually spending money, it is redistributing it from one section of the population to another as transfer payments (table 18.1). The spending will be done by those receiving benefits, so the state is not actually removing money from the private economy. Indeed, it can be said to be increasing it because the poor will have a higher propensity to spend it than the rich.

There is yet another purpose which is less self-evident and has no analogy with family budgeting. The colossal scale of state finance means that government is able to use its taxation and spending muscle to influence the economy in what is termed

Table 18.1 Income redistribution through taxation and benefits, 2010–11 (averages per household in each category)

	Poorest 20% of households	Richest 20% of households
Original income	£5,100	£81,500
Cash Benefits	+£7,040	+£2,115
Income tax, national insurance and council tax	–£1,271	–£19,727
Indirect taxes	–£3,365	–£8,339
Value of benefits in kind (NHS, education, etc.)	+£7,749	+£5,826
Final 'income'	£15,253	£61,375

Source: Data from Office for National Statistics, *Statistical Bulletin* (June 2012).

fiscal policy. When post-war governments have made their getting and spending decisions, economic objectives have been as much in their mind as the services they wish to fund. The following sections consider these two purposes in more detail.

Paying for the State

In figure 18.1 (p. 547) a number of taps interrupt the financial flows, and a key question considers whose hands are turning these. The issue has been at the heart of British constitutional history and remains at the epicentre of modern political debate.

The Gladstonian cycle

> It is the mark of a chicken-hearted chancellor when he shrinks from upholding economy in detail . . . He is not worth his salt if he is not ready to save what are meant by candle-ends and cheese-parings in the cause of the country.
>
> W. E. Gladstone, quoted in F. W. Hirst, *Gladstone as Financier and Economist* (1931)

The modern system of public finance is largely a nineteenth-century invention, fashioned by the industrial bourgeoisie as part of its greater creation – the liberal-democratic state set in the capitalist economy. Through Gladstone's reforms

Parliament was (nominally) given the kind of control over the economy that a Victorian husband would want over his family, overseeing three basic housekeeping functions:

1. granting of prior approval to planned expenditure (the estimates process);
2. considering the ways and means of raising the sum required (the budgetary process);
3. checking that all past expenditure had been conducted in a proper manner (the accounting process).

Prior approval: who gets what, when, how in Whitehall?

Supply procedure of the House of Commons: flogging a dead mouse?

In prehistoric times there might have been some [parliamentary] control over the expenditure but there certainly has not been in my parliamentary experience.

Arthur Balfour (Conservative PM) in 1905, quoted in Heclo and Wildavsky (1974: 242)

In constitutional theory the Crown asks for Supply and the House considers whether to grant the amount requested or allow only a reduced level; it would never gratuitously offer to increase it. Today of course the Crown means the government ministers. The position suited the parsimonious founders of the liberal state, and eighteenth- and nineteenth-century reforms saw the examination of the Estimates (of the year's expenditure) consuming much parliamentary time, with each departmental vote being moved separately and amendments to reduce even small items. Between 1858 and 1872 the Estimates were reduced seventeen times. Yet despite talk of a golden age this period was tantalizingly brief, the process soon becoming little more than ritual. Government majorities could generally override all opposition and debates were used not to scrutinize the Estimates but to criticize policy. Governments ceased to care which Estimates were debated and allowed the choice of topic to pass to the opposition.

Attempts to strengthen the Commons' role included the creation of an Estimates Committee in 1912 (replaced with a Select Committee on Expenditure in 1970). Following the 1961 Plowden Report, a Public Expenditure Survey (PES) process, aiming to consider expenditure over a longer term, was instigated. However, the reforms were not inaccurately described in the House as 'flogging a dead mouse' (Heclo and Wildavsky 1974: 199–251). The Procedure Committee decided that evolved practice represented the wishes of the Commons and in the early 1980s Supply Days became Opposition Days, with three days reserved for discussion of the Estimates with topics selected by the Liaison Committee.

Does this mean that departmental spending decisions escape the ears, eyes and teeth of any constitutional watchdog? The answer is 'No'. A key instrument in the eighteenth- and nineteenth-century system was the Treasury, which became accountable to the Commons for all departmental expenditure. At first its authority increased hand in hand with that of Parliament but, as the latter waned, the

Treasury star rose; by the mid-nineteenth century it was no longer the junior partner.

Whitehall wars: blood on the carpet

Beneath the charm and courtesy of the Whitehall 'village' there is, as in Agatha Christie's St Mary Mead, an undercurrent of gossip, competition, mistrust and sublimated violence. 'Who gets what' is the purpose of the interdepartmental battle, and allocating funds is 'the most pervasive and informative operation of government' (Heclo and Wildavsky 1974: xii).

A process of negotiation has entailed a protracted series of 'bilaterals' between each department and the Treasury, having more in common with a north African souk than a rational decision-making process; yet the outcome is nothing less than the policy of Her Majesty's Government. The bilateral nature of the encounters is very significant, enabling the Treasury to 'divide and rule', and there is often blood on the carpet as mandarins and ministers fight their corners. Often it is in the interests of departments to develop relationships and networks with each other and with interests in the outside world, which can improve their bargaining power (Smith et. al 1993). Much of the haggling is done by the chancellor's second in command, the Chief Secretary to the Treasury. A glimpse into this taut world was offered in 1994 by the leaking of a letter from Chief Secretary Michael Portillo to Michael Heseltine, President of the Board of Trade, strongly attacking his spending (*Guardian*, 30 July 1994). Arbitration comes from a powerful cabinet committee on Public Services and Expenditure (PSX), sometimes called a 'star chamber', containing one-third of the Cabinet.

Treasury power increased under Gordon Brown, who enjoyed the moniker 'Iron Chancellor' for his stern dealing. In 1998 he introduced his Comprehensive Spending Review (CSR), by which he hoped to end the annual infighting. Less of an innovation compared with the PES regime than government propaganda claimed, this set Departmental Expenditure Limits (DEL) – plans rigidly fixed for three years ahead. The results of the CSRs are announced in the July of the appropriate year; the first came in 1998, covering the period 1999/2000–2001/2. Yet the reforms could not be expected to eliminate competition. Indeed, the prize was now the bigger one of a three-year financial commitment. In the run-up to the first review, Brown was reportedly incensed by Foreign Secretary Robin Cook's unwillingness to make savings to enable more spending on education and welfare (*Sunday Times*, 24 May 1998). It is this role of allocating funds that gives chancellors control over much government activity, making them such formidable rivals to prime ministers. When George Osborne took over in 2010 the coalition mantra was of 'the deficit we inherited' and the pressure was to make cuts across most departments.

The budgetary process: who pays what, when, how?

The second operation in the control cycle entails raising the money – the **budgetary process** – through various forms of taxation (see figure 18.3). Constitutionally the government's right to tax must be renewed by Parliament annually; this is why the chancellor presents the budget. Taxation may be direct or indirect.

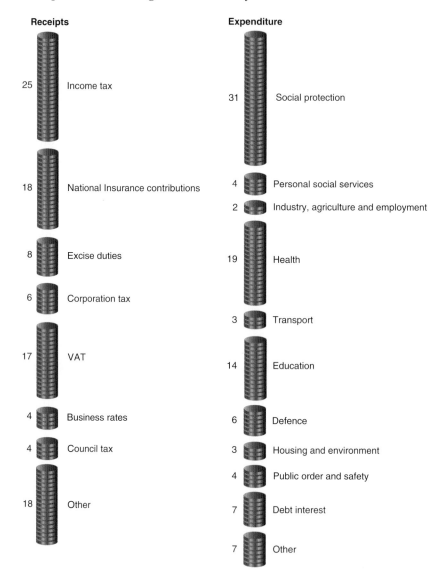

Figure 18.3 Getting and spending: government receipts and expenditure 2013/14 (pence in every pound)

Source: Data from Budget 2013 documents on HM Treasury website: www.gov.uk/hm-treasury

- *Direct taxation* falls upon individuals or organizations. This includes inheritance tax (on assets left after death), capital gains tax (on profits made in selling certain assets) and corporation tax (on company profits). Most important is income tax. Introduced in 1799 as a temporary measure to fund war against France, it has become a keystone of the system, a rise of lp in the rate netting some £1.6 billion a year. Direct taxation can be used to redistribute income in the manner of Robin Hood; when a greater proportion is taken from the income of a rich person than a poor one the system is termed 'progressive'. National Insurance contributions are also effectively a direct tax, which means the true income tax rate is higher (and less progressive) than it appears.
- *Indirect taxation* is tied to goods and services and includes excise duties levied on items such as alcohol, tobacco and petrol. VAT falls across a wide range and is the best known (part of the take goes to the EU). Although rates on commodities can vary (some are zero-rated), they fall equally on all, regardless of means, and are therefore 'regressive'. Thus a move from direct to indirect taxation favours the rich.

Although the bulk of taxation is levied by Westminster, the Scottish Assembly has limited powers, as do local authorities. In the latter case there has been much central interference through capping and reform (see chapter 20). The community charge ('poll tax'), though direct, was mainly regressive, but its replacement, the council tax, being tied to property values, has a more progressive character. The national lottery (figure 18.4) is not a tax (although the odds against winning have led some to declare it a tax on stupidity!). The proceeds going to 'good causes' count as general government revenue, available to reduce public borrowing (see below) and finance capital projects. The 1997 Labour government began using some of this for certain items of NHS expenditure.

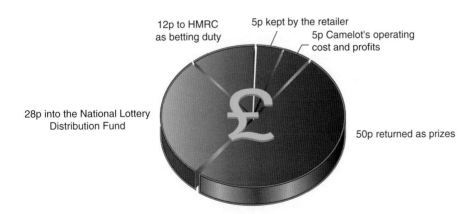

Figure 18.4 Where each pound spent on a lottery ticket goes

The budget

Deep in the bowels of the Treasury the budget, the process of determining how the expenditure will be met, is prepared over the course of the financial year by high-powered committees. Although working below the level of the public eye, the door is opened to thousands of interest groups. The proposals are embodied in the Finance Bill and the chancellor, with the aid of a private secretary and various experts, drafts the budget speech – the focal point of Budget Day. Since 1993 the speech has covered both expenditure and revenue-raising proposals, but it is the latter which excite most media and public attention. Although the constitution decrees that the executive cannot tax without parliamentary approval, today this is automatic. However, days of debate follow as the Finance Bill proceeds upon a ritualistic legislative voyage, when the shadow chancellor, leader of the opposition and various pundits will examine the small print and voice their criticisms.

What's yours?
Convention permits chancellors alcoholic refreshment during their budget speech, a privilege not extended to other MPs. Gladstone sustained himself during his epic long speeches with sherry and beaten egg, Denis Healey drank brandy, Sir Geoffrey Howe took a gin and tonic, Nigel Lawson a mixture of wine and Malvern water but austere Scots Gordon Brown and Alistair Darling chose mineral water, as did George Osborne.

Ostensibly, the reason for budget secrecy was market sensitivity. In 1947, Hugh Dalton inadvertently divulged information to a lobby journalist on his way to deliver his budget and later resigned. When a substantial part of the 1996 budget was leaked to the *Daily Mirror*, editor Piers Morgan felt unable to publish. However, the traditional period of *purdah*, when chancellors retreated behind a veil of silence, has been largely abandoned. Indeed, in an age of media manipulation, eve-of-budget leaks were to become almost *de rigueur*. Under Gordon Brown the veils of secrecy fell away with pre-budget interviews and speeches to business leaders. The coalition Cabinet proved the most leaky ever, giving Labour's Ed Miliband the opportunity to sharpen his rhetorical dagger for the great day.

The budget and politics

Beyond the raising of funds, taxation is used for a variety of politically motivated purposes, including redistributing income, curbing pollution, influencing behaviour (e.g. reducing smoking or car use), and offering election bribes. Conservatives have proclaimed themselves to be the party of low taxation while Labour has endured a tax-and-spend reputation. The eighteen years of Conservative government from 1979 were partly sustained by judicious pre-election budgets promising tax cuts. Yet overall taxes did not fall. In 1978/9, the year before Thatcher took office, tax revenue was 34 per cent of GDP; in 1994/5 it stood at 36 per cent. However, there had been a significant shift from income tax to indirect taxation. In an attempt to change its image, New Labour fought the 1997 election promising no tax rises; one of its leading figures, Clare Short, was sternly reprimanded for suggesting that people like her should actually pay more. Only the Liberal Democrats have ever promised to increase income tax. In the 2002 budget, Labour effectively broke its self-denying ordinance by stealth, raising national insurance contributions to fund a massive increase in NHS spending.

Budget bites

In a media era chancellors have often adorned their budgets with titles.

Nigel Lawson (1983–9)
1987 A Budget for Success
1988 A Tax Reform Budget
John Major (1989–90)
1990 A Budget for Savers
Norman Lamont (1990–3)
1992 A Budget for Recovery
1993 (March) A Budget for Sustained Recovery and a Budget for Jobs
Kenneth Clarke (1993–7)
1993 (November) The Budget of a Responsible Government
1994 A Budget for Jobs
1996 A Budget for Lasting Prosperity

Gordon Brown (1997–2007)
1997 (July) Equipping Britain for Our Long-term Future
1998 (March) New Ambitions for Britain
1999 Building a Fairer Society
2000 Prudent with a Purpose: Working for a Stronger and Fairer Britain
2001 Investing for the Long Term
2002 The Strength to Make Long-term Decisions: Investing in an Enterprising, Fairer Britain
Alistair Darling (2007–10)
2010 Securing the Recovery
George Osborne (2010–
2010 A Budget for Growth

Following the 2010 general election a new body was created by the coalition government. Ostensibly its role was to provide independent economic forecasts in connection with the budget. While the Treasury would remain responsible for economic forecasting, the Office for Budget Responsibility (OBR) would assess the extent to which government policy would be likely to meet targets. However, the independence of the new body was soon to come into question, its declarations and forecasts seen by some as politically biased.

Calling the executive to account

Finally there is the accounting process, checking that the money has been used as Parliament formally agreed. In 1861 Gladstone established one of Parliament's most effective scrutiny instruments, the Public Accounts Committee (PAC). Its membership of around fifteen specialist MPs reflects party balance in the House but the chair is always taken by a prominent member of the opposition.

Since 1866 it has been assisted by a unique constitutional figure, the Comptroller and Auditor General (C&AG), a servant of Parliament with the twin tasks of regulating the release of funds from the Consolidated Fund and auditing the departmental books. In 1983, the C&AG's department became the National Audit Office (NAO), its remit extended beyond Whitehall to other public bodies, while local government was supervised by the Audit Commission. The latter faced uncertainty as the 2010 coalition government announced its planned abolition.

> ### No medals for competence
> The chaos which has emerged over the security contract was predictable and undermines confidence in those responsible for managing the Games.
>
> No credible explanation has been given for an astonishing twelve-fold hike in management costs, from £10 million to £125 million.
>
> Comments from Margaret Hodge MP, Chair of the Public Accounts Committee, on the release of its report on preparations for the London 2012 Olympic Games
> (19 July 2012)

Each year the C&AG and his staff of around 700 audit hundreds of accounts covering over £500 billion. Any department or organization which has its accounts 'qualified' by the NAO may be investigated by the PAC, which has the power to call ministers and civil servants to explain themselves. It has claimed many scalps. Headlines were prompted in September 1993 when it criticized the royal family for lavish spending of £20 million of taxpayers' money on royal palaces. Twenty years later it announced its intention to launch a further investigation into royal finances. In March 2012 the NAO reported that a seven-year efficiency plan, undertaken by the Department for Transport, had cost £129 million more to set up and run than it had saved and PAC chair Margaret Hodge castigated the department for this overspend. Reports can go well beyond state institutions. In 2013 Starbucks, Goldman Sachs and Amazon were all shamed for their tax avoidance practices.

Problems with the audit

The PAC has the advantage of enjoying the goodwill of the Treasury, its parsimonious concerns making it more accommodating to requests for information than is customary towards select committees. However, it would be a mistake to conclude that the watchdogs are unfettered. The contracting out of many services to the private sector and the creation of thousands of quangos creates a zone of public expenditure which the NAO cannot reach. In addition, the Audit Commission lost the right to monitor opted-out schools, which appoint their own auditors. Moreover, wasteful turf wars are fought between the NAO and the Audit Commission, with the former auditing the Metropolitan Police and the Department of Health, for example, while the latter looks at local police authorities and NHS trusts.

The NAO itself comes in for criticism. It has appeared somewhat old-fashioned in style, public finance expert Tony Travers arguing that the regime should resemble that of the rail regulator and should not be afraid to court public controversy (*Public Finance*, 19 Nov. 1999). The PAC has complained that it is too chummy with departments, never publishing a criticism without first obtaining Whitehall approval. A Channel 4 *Dispatches* exposé (24 Sept. 2007), presented by journalist Peter Oborne, confirmed this close relationship; informants spoke of departments using delaying tactics to prevent critical information emerging, and even bullying NAO staff. Although Parliament's position was somewhat strengthened by being given a voice in the appointment of the C&AG, all have been former mandarins and, although they consult the PAC, the choice of inquiries is entirely theirs. In 1992 the C&AG persuaded the PAC chairman to suppress an NAO inquiry into allegations of bribes to secure a £20-billion Al Yamamah arms deal with Saudi Arabia, leaving committee members furious. Hence, the PAC often has to rely on whistleblowers and journalists for evidence of wrongdoing. Only after a series of parliamentary questions did the NAO begin to investigate the Pergau Dam affair, four years after the event.

Managing Capitalism

This second function of public expenditure entails the state using its power to tax, borrow and spend on an enormous scale to influence the nation's economy. This has not always been the intention of government, but it was to become central after the second world war, as governments accepted a responsibility to promote economic growth and high levels of employment.

The national economy is the totality of a myriad of purchases, sales, borrowings, investments, decisions, promises and contracts that people make in their daily and corporate lives. To the classical liberal economists (see p. 32) it was a delicate mechanism that governments should leave well alone under a doctrine known as *laissez-faire*. Expenditure on welfare, for example, would disturb the balance by reducing people's incentive to work and (through taxation) would eat into the profits needed to fuel enterprise. Hence public expenditure was seen as a necessary evil to be limited at all times.

Despite an embryonic welfare state, this cheeseparing approach survived into the twentieth century, the inter-war years sometimes being called a golden age of Treasury control. Economic depression resulting from the failures of the capitalist economy enabled it to practise a firm **monetarist** policy (controlling **inflation** by limiting the quantity of money in the economy) in the belief that industry and world trade could only flourish if there was confidence that the currency would hold its value. Yet the depression persisted, threatening the state's legitimacy. The classical economists had argued that unemployment would automatically correct itself by precipitating a fall in wages, which would restore the demand for labour. However, although wages fell, unemployment persisted. With the spectre of the Russian revolution and the 1926 General Strike, Marx's prophecies of inevitable crisis, culminating in the collapse of capitalism, gained ominous plausibility.

Rescuing capitalism: the coming of Keynes

Capitalism is the astounding belief that the most wickedest of men will do the most wickedest of things for the greatest good of everyone.
Attributed to John Maynard Keynes

However, an alternative diagnosis and prescription was offered by economist John Maynard Keynes, appearing like a knight in armour as the saviour of capitalism. In his *General Theory* (1936) he argued that, contrary to the Gladstonian view, **macroeconomic** budgeting for the state was not the same as the microeconomic budgeting of firms or households. Constantly aiming for a balanced budget was inappropriate and potentially harmful to the economy and employment.

Keynes refuted the classical economists' view that the free market would automatically eliminate unemployment. Left to itself it could reach a point of equilibrium (where aggregate supply equalled aggregate demand) *below* full capacity, thereby creating unemployment. The economy rested upon the fragile flower of confidence; falling wages, far from restoring full employment, would have the opposite effect. Less could be bought, less would need to be made, would-be entrepreneurs would lack the confidence to invest in new projects and, in a downward spiral, more jobs would disappear. The slumps of the inter-war years seemed ample verification of the theory.

The solution was for the state to step in where private investors feared to tread, with government using public expenditure to increase the level of aggregate demand (**demand management**) by spending money on public works such as roads and hospitals. The effect would be to stimulate demand throughout the economy, with more roads requiring more materials, machinery and so on, in a multiplier effect. Of course, if the government financed its expenditure by increasing taxation there might be no increase in aggregate demand because citizens' expenditure would fall. However, it could be financed by borrowing from those citizens with savings who were afraid to invest, creating a *budget deficit*. Alternatively, in times of prosperity a *budget surplus* could be created by reducing expenditure while raising taxes, to repay the national debt. This strategy had the momentous implication that the hallowed goal of the *balanced budget* would no longer be sacrosanct.

Although Keynes was scorned, the experience of the war years seemed to confirm his analysis. Massive government expenditure on arms virtually erased unemployment. There was also an enormous increase in direct government intervention in various walks of life. In the dark days of war, politicians made a raft of welfare state promises encapsulated in the 1942 Beveridge Report.

The years of plenty: the Treasury loses its grip

Hence the post-war decades saw a **long boom** of western capitalism with public expenditure used for the quite new purpose of managing the national economy: stabilizing the trade cycle and maintaining full employment. In addition, key industries (railways, coal, utility companies) were brought into state control through **nationalization**. In this **mixed economy** forceful spending ministers were able to push through costly programmes with no necessary fiscal implications. Moreover, in the expanded welfare state, people did not appear to mind paying more taxes. It seemed that the boom would last for ever; the capitalist economy could be permanently protected from its own propensity to crisis. Although Britain was still a capitalist country, the market was no longer forbidden territory to the state and the nineteenth-century Treasury ideals were rendered anachronistic.

The principle of economic management was further advanced in 1961 with the establishment by a Conservative government of a National Economic Development Council (NEDC – known as Neddy). A consultative body embracing labour, capital and government, this was a timid entry into the area of **economic planning** and corporatism (see pp. 596–7). In 1964, the Wilson Labour government created a purpose-built Department of Economic Affairs (DEA) to usurp the Treasury's role and work with Neddy.

The restoration of the Treasury

However, the long boom was not to be one without end. Inflation reached an alarming 24.7 per cent in 1975, but unemployment, defying the Phillips Curve (which postulated an inverse relationship between the two), continued upward. The state appeared unable to service its existing debts and the concerted call from the IMF, the City, the financial markets, the governor of the Bank of England and the media pundits was for a return to the Victorian principles (Keegan 1984: 88). The cry came echoing back from Whitehall, where the Treasury stood like a rock emerging glistening beneath the retreating Keynesian tide.

Labour Chancellor Denis Healey was obliged to turn humiliatingly to the IMF for large-scale loan support. It came with strings attached; he was forced to exert further controls over the money supply, cut public spending, trim public borrowing and raise interest rates (which reached a record 15.5 per cent). The 'hidden hand' of Adam Smith began to push up his creaking tombstone. In 1976 Labour Prime Minister James Callaghan measured up the corpse of Keynesianism for the Treasury undertakers in his fateful declaration to the Labour conference: 'We cannot now, if we ever could, spend our way out of a recession'. Monetarism was on the agenda before Thatcherism became a word in the economic lexicon.

Public expenditure under Thatcher: the end of Keynes

Selling the family silver.
Former prime minister Harold Macmillan (Lord Stockton) on privatization, House of Lords speech (1986)

When Margaret Thatcher took up residence in Downing Street, Treasury control in the Victorian sense experienced its rebirth. Despite the years of plenty, and the global nature of the crisis, the view was that Keynesianism had failed. While Labour had reluctantly relinquished the economic reins, the New Right government dropped them with relish as it 'rolled back' the state. Collectivist tendencies gave way to individualism, nationalized industries were **privatized** (with control over them passed to newly created **regulatory bodies**), balancing the books became the key budgetary consideration and public expenditure was again to be regarded as a necessary evil. In the Treasury, Keynesians were hunted like medieval witches, prudent young bureaucrats quickly deciding that they had really been closet monetarists all the time (Ponting 1986: 102).

Applying monetarism

The policy differed from that prescribed by monetarist guru Milton Friedman. He argued that the level of public expenditure and taxation did not have an important effect on the economy; the key was to control the rate of increase in **money supply**. However, the Thatcherite agenda also had moral and social goals, including a particular determination to reduce union power and cut welfare-state dependency. The initial strategy had two broad thrusts: controlling the money supply and, preferring the advice of Polonius in *Hamlet* that 'borrowing dulls the edge of husbandry' to that of Keynes, reducing the **public sector borrowing requirement (PSBR)**. The PSBR could be seen as increasing money supply and causing inflation. Moreover, money borrowed by government was not available to the private sector where, contrary to Keynes's view, it would be used more productively.

Yet monetarism did not work as promised and by 1985 Chancellor Nigel Lawson had effectively abandoned it. Paradoxically, public expenditure rose each year throughout the 1980s as cuts in infrastructure spending and services were counterbalanced by increased welfare, health and social security costs resulting from increased unemployment (figure 18.5) and poverty (Mullard 1997: 272). Income

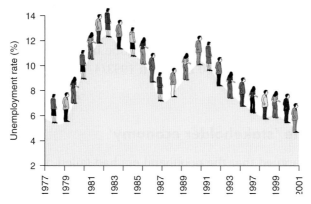

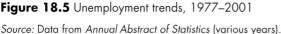

Figure 18.5 Unemployment trends, 1977–2001

Source: Data from *Annual Abstract of Statistics* (various years).

support for the unemployed dwarfed all other categories, reaching almost £45 billion in 1987/8. The balance of payments plunged into deficit from mid-1987 as a weakened productive base at home sucked in imports. By 1989, Britain was running its largest ever trade deficit.

'Wednesday's child is full of woe'

Throughout the Thatcher years a time-bomb had been ticking in the form of the drive towards European economic and monetary union. Although Britain had remained outside the exchange rate mechanism (ERM), from the mid-1980s Chancellor Nigel Lawson had pursued a policy of 'shadowing' the deutschmark in a kind of DIY ERM membership. Unneighbourly tension between 10 and 11 Downing Street led in October 1989 to Lawson's resignation over Thatcher's refusal to sack economic adviser Alan Walters, who declared the European monetary system 'half-baked'. Finally Thatcher conceded that sterling would enter when 'the time was ripe'. The 'right time' arrived under the new chancellor John Major, in October 1990, the eve of the Conservative Party conference. With hindsight the time was to prove quite wrong; Britain was heading towards recession and the pound entered at an unsustainably high level. Efforts to hold sterling's value (including high interest rates) proved harmful to the economy. An atmosphere of fear and panic drove Conservative MPs to the astonishing butchering of their leader, already weakened by her poll tax policy. Ironically, her replacement was the very man who had taken Britain into the ERM. Tumultuous events were to follow.

Selling of overvalued sterling by foreign-exchange speculators saw the Bank of England frantically buying in an effort to protect its ERM position. The doomed rescue operation cost some £18 billion and the government's economic strategy

The major tenet of free market economics – that unregulated markets will of their own accord find unimprovable results for all participants – is now proved to be nonsense.
Will Hutton (neo-Keynesian economist), *The State We're In* (1996: 237)

was entirely discredited. On 16 September 1992 Britain made an ignomini-ous withdrawal from the ERM, a day to enter political demonology as 'Black Wednesday'. The PSBR, which had actually gone into a surplus of £15 billion in 1988/9, sank into a deficit of £50 billion in 1993/4, forcing tax increases at high political cost.

Labour and the 'stakeholder economy'

Neo-Keynesians argued that the neoliberal era had failed. It had elevated selfish-ness and distorted business priorities, with companies aiming to grow not by increasing investment, innovating or expanding markets, but by swallowing up rivals. The greed of shareholders forced companies to put short-term returns above growth. The weakening of the unions, creating a 'flexible' labour market, had created a vast wasteland of part-time and temporary employment without worker protection (Hutton 1996: 327). Critics pointed to rising levels of income inequality. All had taken place against a fiscal background in which less weight was placed on direct taxation (figure 18.6).

Labour rhetoric in opposition echoed much of the critique and Tony Blair began to postulate a 'third way' between unfettered *laissez-faire* and socialism. He spoke of a 'stakeholder society' in which the business and financial communities accept obligations towards employees and society, as well as to shareholders. Upon coming to office in 1997 New Labour quickly reversed the EU Social Chapter opt-out, estab-lished a minimum wage and breathed new life into a number of corporatist-style bodies. In passing responsibility for setting interest rates to the Bank of England Chancellor Gordon Brown vowed that, by removing the temptation of governments to use the rate for electoral advantage, he would end the cycles of 'boom and bust' that had plagued the economy.

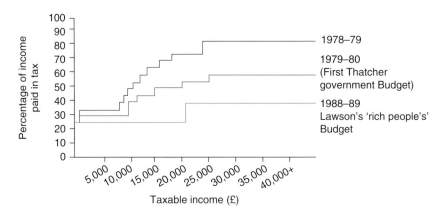

Figure 18.6 The changing income tax profile during the 1980s

> **A reverse Midas touch?**
> In a controversial move, between 1999 and 2002, Gordon Brown sold 395
> tonnes of the country's gold when the price stood at a 20-year low. Probably
> believing that, in an anticipated era free of boom and bust, rampant global
> inflation would be a thing of the past, he favoured assets that would earn their
> keep by generating interest payments.

Keen to appear respectable in the eyes of the City, policy soon revealed much
continuity with that of the immediate past. On capital expenditure, the government
breathed new life into Major's private finance initiative, and there was to be no re-
nationalization, no change in the balance between direct and indirect taxation, and
a pledge to stick to Conservative spending targets for the next two years. Widening
inequality was no longer seen as a problem. A 'Welfare-to-Work' scheme aimed to
promote a work ethic. Thatcher's claim to have killed socialism in Britain appeared,
in the eyes of some commentators, to have some credibility.

> **Public service, private profit**
> **Public–private partnerships** are a way of involving private business in the
> business of the state. The most common form is the **private finance initiative**
> (PFI), launched by the Conservatives in 1992 and much favoured by New
> Labour. Rather than the state borrowing for the building and maintenance of
> capital projects (schools, hospitals, prisons and roads), this is undertaken by
> private contractors who build and lease the facilities to the state. However, the
> end result can be an even heavier burden on the taxpayer (see Wilson and
> Game 2011: 164). The private sector cannot borrow as cheaply as the state
> and the companies also require a profit. It was estimated, for example, that
> the total cost to the NHS of a PFI to build and maintain a hospital could run to
> £900 million (£30 million a year for thirty years), while the traditional borrowing
> option would have cost £180 million (Cohen 1999).

Black Wednesday had demonstrated that government economic policy was at the
mercy of the global economy. Three particular events were to underline this hard
reality: 9/11, crisis in the eurozone and a global credit crunch.

11 September 2001

Prior to that fateful day, the global economy has seen the end of the hi-tech dream
with crashing dot-com shares, rising oil prices and interest rate increases. Hence
9/11 made what was already a precarious situation even worse, and Gordon
Brown faced a stern test. A MORI poll showed economic optimism at its lowest
level since the recession of 1980 (*The Times*, 27 Sept. 2001). Yet while City analysts
feared the worst, figures published in early 2002 by the Office for National Statistics

demonstrated that the economy had managed to defy the sharpest downturn in the world outlook in twenty years. In what could be seen as a sea change in British politics, Brown had gone some way to making Labour a party that industry could trust. Some believed his 'end to boom and bust' mantra. However, the cost of success was growing mistrust from the political left, including the trade unions.

A single European currency: a fistful of euros

Brown's five economic tests

1 Would joining create better conditions for firms making long-term decisions to invest in the United Kingdom?
2 How would adopting the single currency affect our financial services?
3 Are business cycles and economic structures sufficiently compatible for Britain and other EU members to live comfortably with euro interest rates on a permanent basis?
4 If problems emerge, is there sufficient flexibility to deal with them?
5 Will joining help to promote higher growth, stability and a lasting increase in jobs?

Another economic test was posed by the EU policy to establish a single currency. Acceptance of this would place considerable limitations on any government's ability to manage the national economy. While Blair was positive, his chancellor remained cautious, and set five economic tests that should be met before the government would hold a referendum and recommend a 'Yes' vote. When eleven of the EU partners formally adopted the euro on 2 May 1998, he argued that his tests had not been met and Britain stayed resolutely out. As events unfolded, not even Brown's sternest critics could say he had made the wrong decision as the eurozone was sucked into a global crisis that blighted the opening of the twenty-first century.

Global credit crunch

The greatest shock to Labour's economic management was to come in the banking crisis beginning in 2007. The complex movements of the financial markets during this heated period are beyond the scope of this book, but no student of politics can ignore this prime example of the power of global forces to impinge upon a country's domestic policies.

   Described as a credit crunch, it was essentially a severe shortage of money or credit, which made it difficult for capitalist economies to function. Most analysts linked the crisis to the way in which US banks had advanced massive loans to those with poor credit histories in what was euphemistically termed a 'sub-prime mortgage market'. The liberalization in financial markets had seen the separation between investment banks and depository banks vanish. Yet with new risk

I believe that banking institutions are more dangerous to our liberties than standing armies.
Attributed to Thomas Jefferson (US President, 1801–9)

Coming in to talk together: queues of investors outside a London branch of Northern Rock trying to withdraw their savings in September 2007

introduced into banking, governments had not adjusted their regulatory practices, and credit rating agencies and investors failed to recognize the new dangers. In an attempt to shield themselves from the results of their follies the bankers bundled their 'toxic' loans, bonds and assets into complex portfolios that few really understood (Collateralized Debt Obligations – CDOs), which could be sold on internationally to other banks and investors. As the crisis spread, banks became unwilling to lend to each other, and the rate at which they would do so (the Libor rate) rose. (In 2012 it was revealed that from 2005 to 2009 a number of banks, including Barclays, were illegally manipulating the rate to conceal their vulnerability.)

The crisis enveloped the world in a catastrophic domino effect, with sharp downturns in stock markets and the collapse of giant financial institutions. A totemic event came in September 2008 when, in the USA, the mighty Lehman Brothers became the first major bank to file for bankruptcy protection. As credit tightened key businesses began to fail, causing a general decline in economic activity, with national economies suffering a loss of productivity and rising unemployment. Economists spoke of a global recession reminiscent of that of the 1930s. With its extensive global economic commitments Britain could not escape. In August 2008 Chancellor Alistair Darling alarmed his colleagues and the country with a declaration that the economy

I can calculate the movement of the stars, but not the madness of men.
Sir Isaac Newton (1642–1727; physicist), after losing £20,000 of his savings in the 1720 financial crisis, the South Sea Bubble

faced its worst crisis for sixty years, with a downturn more 'profound and long-lasting' than most had feared. By January 2009, as fourth-quarter GDP fell by 1.5 per cent, compared to the previous three months, the UK officially entered a recession.

Political fury was directed at those responsible. In May 2009 the Treasury Select Committee declared that bankers had made 'an astonishing mess' of the financial system, with effects that would be felt for generations. Economic summits were greeted with violent popular demonstrations. A worldwide Occupy movement spread from Wall Street to cities around the world, with a prolonged encampment in 2012 outside St Paul's, nestling close to the financial capital of the City of London (see p. 581).

With the markets unable to correct themselves, governments were compelled to act. In April 2009 Britain hosted a G20 summit in London, in which Gordon Brown played a leading role. Central banks were urged to respond with unprecedented levels of fiscal stimulus, monetary expansion (quantitative easing) and institutional bailouts. In Britain the government launched a rescue package for the banking sector with eye-watering amounts of taxpayers' money in what was effectively a massive nationalization. The three giants, the Royal Bank of Scotland, Lloyds TSB and HBOS, were major recipients. The scale of the bailout was reported variously, but the Governor of the Bank of England (2009) estimated it as almost £1 trillion (close to two-thirds of the annual output of the entire economy).

Praise for Brown and Darling's initiatives came from various international sources, including winner of the Nobel Prize for economics Paul Krugman. Other countries, including Germany, France and the USA, followed the example, with the partial nationalization of banks and state guarantees for inter-bank loans. However, plaudits were less evident at home. Although banking services had been saved, the natural result was a burgeoning national debt, with only Iceland and Greece more indebted than Britain (table 18.2). Opposition parties sought, with some success, to depict the debt incurred in the rescue as testimony to domestic mismanagement rather part of a global crisis.

Never in the field of financial endeavour has so much money been owed by so few to so many.

Mervyn King (Governor of the Bank of England) on the UK bank bailout, quoted in *Moneyfacts* (21 Oct. 2009)

Table 18.2 National debt as a percentage of GDP, 2010

Country	Debt	Country	Debt
Iceland	15.7	France	8.2
Greece	12.7	Japan	7.4
Britain	12.6	Portugal	6.7
Ireland	12.2	Canada	4.8
USA	11.2	Australia	4.0
Spain	9.6	Germany	3.2

Source: Data from *Daily Telegraph* (19 Feb 2010).

The crisis has had major implications for economic and political thinking as well as for practical politics. For some commentators it had fatally discredited the neo-liberal consumerist paradigm that had assumed ascendancy from the late 1970s. In a state of general confusion and bewilderment debate centred variously upon a dysfunctional banking system, national debt, the decline of business, the inequalities in society and a growing mistrust of the political class (see Preston 2011).

Although it is likely that there would have only been marginal differences in the policies the parties would have enacted (all were pledged to reduce the deficit), their rhetoric was of Keynesianism versus the free market. While Labour argued for state expenditure to stimulate economic activity, the Conservatives argued for an era of austerity and public expenditure cuts. With no party securing an overall majority in the 2010 general election, the Conservatives, in coalition with their new Liberal Democratic partners, embarked upon a severe austerity package in the hope the free market would lead to economic revival. The austerity measures, with cuts in education and welfare spending began to define the political agenda.

Public Expenditure and Long-term Economic Decline

Britain has experienced a prolonged period of relative economic decline since the pomp of its nineteenth-century imperial splendour. Chapter 5 examined this in terms of its orientation towards the wider globalizing economy. However, modern Keynesian thinking regards the economy as a government responsibility. Beyond the exogenous factors are endogenous ones, and various hypotheses are advanced by left and right. Here we consider how far the patterns and traditions of public expenditure management in Britain have in themselves contributed, identifying three likely suspects:

- the institutional setting;
- the competitive pattern of Whitehall decision-making;
- a failure to incorporate key economic interests into the process.

The institutional setting: Victorian institutions in a Keynesian landscape

The two key institutions associated with public finance – the Treasury and the Bank of England – have, for critics, lain at the heart of the Britain's problems. Their dominance has meant that nineteenth-century values have lingered like the smell of stale tobacco smoke in the redecorated constitution of the post-war era. Both could be but poor instruments for Keynesianism, placing a 'dead hand' on public expenditure in general, with little thought for industry, employment,

> **The pound in your pocket**
> From now on the pound is worth 14 per cent or so less in terms of other currencies. It does not mean, of course, that the pound here in Britain, in your pocket or purse or in your bank, has been devalued.
>
> Harold Wilson's speech after devaluation of the pound (20 Nov. 1967)

the wider economy or the welfare state. Whatever the economic problem – falling pound, rising pound, balance of payments crisis, inflation or unemployment – the response was invariably a deflationary package. The result was a series of what were termed 'stop–go' policies. When the economy expanded, imports were sucked in, the trade deficit widened and the Bank of England would step in to buy sterling with foreign currency in order to maintain its value as an international reserve currency. As the foreign currency reserves fell, deflation would be introduced (a 'stop' period) to reduce imports. However, this caused unemployment, calling for the economy to be stimulated (a 'go' period) and the cycle would begin again. As a result, the post-war Keynesian period could be described as 'the revolution that never was' (Hutton 1986). Although Gordon Brown claimed to have ended boom and bust, borrowing ran out of control and there was no boom during which to repay the debt.

Competitive decision-making in Whitehall

You never have debates about ethics or morals here, just about saving money.
Patrice Claude (London correspondent of *Le Monde*), quoted in the *Observer* (11 March 2001)

Linked with the dominance of the Treasury and Bank has been the Whitehall method of reaching spending decisions. Despite formally accepting the Keynesian package, the Treasury missed its historic opportunity to become an economic coordinator. Reforms did not eliminate competitive infighting and the Treasury persisted in trying to reduce expenditure, regardless of the merits of individual policies. New Labour's comprehensive spending reviews and talk of 'joined-up government' did little to remove the ethos. In this respect, British government has compared unfavourably with the French, where the Commissariat General du Plan aims to coordinate departments in line with an overall economic policy.

Failure to incorporate key economic interests into policy-making

This same ethos prevented the successful implantation of institutions designed to bring together the key interests: finance, industry and labour (see chapter 19).

Remaining arm's-length quangos, Neddy and some sector-specific 'little Neddies' were never well integrated into the machinery and the Cinderella Department of Economic Affairs was killed off by the ugly sisters, the Treasury and Bank. An Industrial Reorganization Corporation and National Enterprise Board, lacking both powers and funds, were unsuccessful in the late 1960s and 1970s respectively. Further failure came with incomes policy, union antagonism costing Labour the 1979 general election. Under Thatcher the declared policy was to end economic consultation.

While New Labour began to speak of forging a new consensus in a 'stakeholder society', the weakened trade unions reacted with suspicion. They were particularly alarmed when, at the March 2002 Barcelona summit, Blair aligned himself against the rest with two of Europe's most right-wing leaders, Silvio Berlusconi of Italy and Spanish prime minister José Maria Aznar. The three became known as 'the BAB axis' as they called for economic deregulation and opposed employee protection laws. Industrial relations were bleakly reflected when TUC General Secretary John Monks accused Blair of being 'bloody stupid' (*Guardian*, 16 March 2002). This continued to resonate for the 2010 coalition, with its austerity package, which saw a government at loggerheads with the trade unions and frustrated by the bailed-out banks unwilling to lend to business. Economist Will Hutton (1996: 298) has stressed the need for a deep cultural change in which not only do labour and capital work together but the financial community sees itself as 'a servant of business rather than as its master', with banks and their customers showing more commitment to the success of industry and less hunger for dividends, accepting lower rates of return on investments and allowing longer terms for repaying loans.

The hands-off state

All these factors lead to the conclusion that British governments have not used their financial role in the best interests of the economy at large. The persistence of liberal values has meant that, from the time of the Liberal social programme of 1906–14, governments have been willing to help the losers in a capitalist economy with welfare measures but have remained unwilling to interfere with the freedom of businesses to pursue their self-interest. As noted by David Marquand (1988: 121–3), Britain declined to become a 'developmental' state like the more dynamic post-war economies. The result is a state that has always been subservient to the market order, never open enough to engage in purposeful dialogue with industry, never coordinated enough to plan, and never autonomous enough to manage.

The British state is so imbued with the liberal philosophy. . . that sustained, coherent, and disinterested arbitration and sponsorship of the economy is extremely difficult, if not impossible.
Will Hutton, *The Revolution that Never Was* (1986: 196)

Key points

- Few political questions can be addressed without attention to the financial dimension.

- Public expenditure is money spent by the state, its scale is enormous and most is raised by taxation.

- Public expenditure is also an expression of community life; paying taxes can be seen as a duty of citizenship.

- Only Parliament can levy taxes; this is the basis for its historic rise in power.

- The system of public finance established under Gladstone in the nineteenth century reflected *laissez-faire* economic thinking.

- This was largely concerned with parsimony rather than state welfare policies.

- The Chancellor of the Exchequer is the keeper of the nation's purse.

- Her Majesty's Treasury, the Bank of England and the Commons preside over a system of financial controls.

- Because of its great magnitude, public expenditure influences the national economy.

- This allows governments to intervene in pursuit of social goals (Keynesianism).

- Governments have vacillated between Keynesian and *laissez-faire* approaches towards the economy.

- In retrospect some argue that Keynesianism has never been fully practised.

- The 'credit crunch', becoming apparent in 2008, demonstrated the power of the global economy to influence government policy.

Review your understanding of the following terms and concepts

'Black Wednesday'

C&AG

capitalism

Consolidated Fund

credit crunch

demand management

direct taxation

fiscal policy

indirect taxation

inflation

Keynesianism

laissez-faire

macroeconomics

monetarism

money supply

prior approval

privatization

progressive taxation

Public Accounts
    Committee

regressive taxation

stakeholder society

transfer payments

Questions for discussion and debate

Consider these propositions and be prepared to present the cases for and against. Try to produce debating propositions of your own.

1   Public expenditure is a good which binds a community.

2   The Gladstonian cycle of financial control was designed for a bygone age.

3   In its getting and spending, government strangles a capitalist economy.

4   Parliament has no control over public finance.

5   Keynes did not undermine capitalism, he saved it.

6   The 'dead hand' of the Treasury should be shaken.

7   Any shift from direct to indirect taxation is an attack on the poor.

8   Governments should heed the advice of Polonius that 'borrowing dulls the edge of husbandry'.

9   The belief that a national economy can be managed is a delusion.

10 Global financial interests are more powerful than governments.

Further reading

Some of the reading for chapter 5 is also relevant here.

Cahill, K. (2001) *Who Owns Britain?*
Asserts that a conspiracy to keep the land in the hands of the chosen few is a prime cause of Britain's poor economic performance.

Dow, C. (2012) *Inside the Bank of England: Memoirs of Christopher Dow, Chief Economist 1973–84.*
Covers a difficult time for the UK economy and addresses many of the debates which re-emerged in the financial crisis of 2007–8.

Friedman, M. and R. (1985) *The Tyranny of the Status Quo.*
Collaboration between the influential monetarist guru and his wife laments the failure of the Thatcher regime to control money supply in the manner prescribed.

Gamble, A. (1994) *Britain in Decline*, 4th edn.
Traces various explanations for decline, stressing the importance of global influences.

Grant, W. (1993) *The Politics of Economic Policy.*
Accessible and wide-ranging account of forces shaping economic policy.

Heclo, H. and Wildavsky, A. (1974) *The Private Government of Public Money.*
A unique book of remaining relevance, showing those involved in public finance as real people.

Holt, R. (2001) *Second Amongst Equals: Chancellors of the Exchequer and the British Economy.*
Lively account of post-war economic policy, with a penetrating examination of the performance and capabilities of twenty holders of this powerful office.

Hutton, W. (1996) *The State We're In.*
In the traditions of Keynes and J. K. Galbraith, a sustained critique of the 'universal imposition of the market principle and decay of our political system'. Contains a comprehensive reform agenda.

Hutton, W. (2011) *Them and Us: Changing Britain – Why we Need a Fair Society.*
In the light of the credit crunch, argues that reconstructing the financial system is more than a technical question. The moral issue of fairness within capitalism must be addressed.

Keegan, W. (1984) *Mrs Thatcher's Economic Experiment.*
Written by an economic journalist, this account contains the flavour of the real-world politics lying behind all expenditure policy.

Marquand, D. (1988) *The Unprincipled Society.*
Erudite yet accessible critique of Britain's failure to manage its economy.

Mullard, M. (1993) *The Politics of Public Expenditure.*
Examines the political climate in which public expenditure decisions are made.

Preston, P. W. (2011) *England after the Great Recession.*
Examines the political and cultural consequences of the financial crisis.

Thain, C. and Wright, M. (1995) *The Treasury and Whitehall: The Planning and Control of Public Expenditure 1976–1993.*
Monumental study explaining the structures and political forces underlying this key aspect of politics.

For reading around the subject and some light relief

Hilaire Belloc, *Pongo and the Bull.*
The power of money and the moneyed classes.

Brassed Off and *The Full Monty.*
Films/DVDs with moving accounts of social consequences of deindustrialization, which is seen as politically motivated.

Sebastian Faulks, *A Week in December.*
A view of the amorality of financiers, plus various other dysfunctional features of modern life.

David Hare, *The Power of Yes.*
Play performed at the National Theatre, steering through the complexities of the credit crunch and expressing mounting anger at the self-delusion and incompetence of the world of finance.

Lucy Prebble, *Enron.*
A dramatic re-creation of the collapse of this once-powerful US financial institution. Too close to home for the Americans, its Broadway run lasted only a month.

Tim Renton, *Hostage to Fortune.*
An ex-Conservative minister imagines intrigue in Threadneedle Street. Chancellor of the Exchequer and governor of the Bank of England plot the downfall of prime minister.

Joseph Stiglitz, *Freefall: Free Markets and the Sinking of the Global Economy.*
Former World Bank chief economist did not share the belief in unfettered
markets that set off the financial crisis and believes the banks are not
the ones to fix things: 'we called in the plumbers who installed the
plumbing'.

Anthony Trollope *The Way We Live Now.*
Perhaps no longer 'now' (first published in 1875), but this examination of
corruption within the world of finance politics remains relevant.

H. G. Wells, *Tono-Bungay.*
Biting comment on an entrepreneurial society with nothing of value to sell.

Tom Wolfe, *The Bonfire of the Vanities.*
Satire on the US world of capitalist high finance and its penetrating social
implications.

On the net

http://www.hm-treasury.gov.uk
The Treasury's home page provides links to a wealth of information on all aspects
of public expenditure, the budgetary process and the state of the economy, in
addition to details of the institution itself.

http://budgetresponsibility.independent.gov.uk
This site explains the role of the government-created, but independent, Office
for Budget Responsibility in providing authoritative analysis of the UK's public
finances.

http://www.bankofengland.co.uk
The Bank of England home page will lead you to information on the Bank's history,
organization and role, and an extensive range of economic and financial statistics.
There is even a section entitled 'Funny Bank Stories'.

Both the Treasury and Bank of England sites will also lead you to information on
the euro.

http://www.publicfinance.co.uk/
The Chartered Institute of Public Finance and Accountancy offers lively analysis
from expert bloggers on all aspects public finance.

CHAPTER 19

THE POLITICS OF INFLUENCE: WHO GETS WHAT, WHEN, HOW?

Contents

In this chapter we move beyond both the formal institutions of government and the overtly political structures to uncover the more shadowy forces in politics – the powers behind the throne. Where 'real power' lies is the greatest conundrum of the study of politics. We find repeatedly that the apparent puppet-masters are themselves dangling on yet further strings stretching away out of our sight in an infinite regression. The chapter falls into three main sections. The first introduces the concept of group politics and defines the types of groups to be discussed. The next identifies major theoretical approaches to this study, analysing the theories of pluralism and corporatism. We also consider a neoliberal view that the group approach distorts the political process. Finally we go beyond the group approach to examine elitist and Marxist views of power in society.

A country run by a bunch of criminal lunatics with Tony Blair as a hired Christian thug.
Harold Pinter (1930–2008; British playwright), describing the USA in speech at Hyde Park (15 Feb. 2003)

In September 2004 astonished tourists admiring Buckingham Palace could hardly believe their eyes when they witnessed the figure of the fabled Batman ascending the stately porticos. It required a helicopter, a crane, a crash mat and a police officer clad in harness and helmet to apprehend the caped crusader, whose mission was the rights of fathers. In the previous year a mass demonstration on 15 February was recorded in the 2004 *Guinness Book of Records* as the largest in human history. Millions surged through the streets of central London and other British cities, with around one million assembled in Hyde Park to listen to an 'A-List' of celebrity speakers, including the Rev. Jesse Jackson, Tariq Ali, Harold Pinter, Ken Livingstone, Vanessa Redgrave, Bianca Jagger and Tony Benn, bemoaning the invasion of Iraq. On Sunday 22 September 2002, London worshipers and shoppers were disturbed by the sounds of hunting horns, shrieking whistles and wailing bagpipes as a 450,000-strong 'Countryside March' wound its way to Downing Street, pledged to save the 'British country way of life', particularly the hunting of foxes.

In September 2010 an 'Occupy Wall Street' protest set up camp in Manhattan to denounce what was seen as 'corporate greed' in a movement that spread to cities in over eighty other countries. Several thousand protesters gathered outside St Paul's Cathedral, remaining to set up a tented encampment on the cathedral steps, to be addressed by Julian Assange, founder of the controversial WikiLeaks website. In November of the same year some 50,000 students, pupils and university lecturers descended upon London, demonstrating against university tuition fees. Protesters were reported to have broken into Conservative Party headquarters,

Occupy: protesters on the steps of St Paul's, 2012

smashing through the windows chanting 'Die Tory scum'. Deputy Prime Minister Nick Clegg was also a target, subjected to faeces posted through the letter box of his family home. Almost daily the news media report on the activities of marchers, eco-warriors, demonstrators and hurlers of eggs at the high and mighty. Yet away from the glare of the media spotlight chauffeur-driven cars draw up in Whitehall, enabling businessmen and financiers to quietly enter the departments of state and meet with officials. Beyond Whitehall, from London clubs to country houses and even luxury yachts, the great and the good can dine and indulge in private discussions about government and what they want from it.

Although the constitution makes no provision for activities such as these, they are events in politics. To some they are the very heartbeat of politics. It is clear that our study of power and policy-making does not end with constitutions and institutions of government.

Get up, stand up. Stand up for your rights. Get up, stand up. Never give up the fight.
Bob Marley (1945–81; popular singer), *Get up, stand up* (1973)

The Group Approach

Once a parliament has been elected the formal involvement of citizens in politics ends. MPs return joyfully to Westminster, a government is formed, the ballot boxes are stacked away in town hall vaults, and returning officers and vote counters return to their desks. To be sure, a government will take cognizance of public opinion during its term of office, may even form focus groups to test ideas, but such consideration places the population in a position of passivity and can hardly be dignified as participation. Representative democracy does not formally allow people to make policy; it merely permits them to choose between elite policy-makers. However, in practice the process of shaping government policy is not confined to elections, it continues through a complex process of action, negotiation and compromise with a wide range of interests, all of which share some degree of power.

This is the group theory of politics. A key founding figure in group theory was Arthur Bentley, an American economist who realized the limitations of studying policy only in terms of institutions and office-holders. For Bentley, the process of government was essentially about the activities of organized groups; his major work, first published in 1908, averred compellingly that 'when the groups are stated, everything is stated' (1967: 208).

Definitions

The groups in question appear in many guises, raising various definitional issues.

Interest groups and pressure groups

Although essentially different, these two terms are often used synonymously. An **interest group** is an association with a shared interest or concern, while a **pressure group** is one actively attempting to *influence* government. The latter term carries sinister connotations of factions seeking to subvert the democratic process and was probably coined by US journalists as a term of abuse. Some modern writers (particularly those in the pluralist tradition – see below) tend to favour the more anodyne 'interest group'.

Groups and individuals

The reasonable man adapts himself to the world: the unreasonable one persists in trying to adapt the world to himself. Therefore all progress depends on the unreasonable man.
George Bernard Shaw, Man and Superman (1903)

The logic of the group approach is to downgrade the role of individuals. This makes sense in that one vote is likely to have less influence than a group campaign. However, it obscures the fact that groups often have dominant leaderships, reflecting Michels's iron law of oligarchy. Prominent MP Frank Field, for example, first came to public attention as a founder of the Child Poverty Action Group. In the opening decade of the twenty-first century, Liberty, the civil liberties group, was personified in its director Shami Chakrabarti, pop singer Bob Geldof was highly visible in the movement to end global poverty, while the name of Peter Tatchell was virtually synonymous with gay-rights organization OutRage. Groups linked to the economy often throw up particularly powerful figures. Leaders of the CBI and Institute of Directors, as well as a variety of industrial and trade union figures, feature in the national news as visibly as ministers. Thus, groups do not eliminate personality politics; they can actually fuel it by adding to an individual's political weight. Leadership can sometimes lead to Parliament, as in the cases of Field and Chakrabarti's predecessor at Liberty, Patricia Hewitt. The National Union of Students also provides a stream of parliamentary figures.

Pressure groups and parties

Definitions usually stress a fundamental distinction between groups and parties.
- Unlike parties, pressure groups do not seek to enter government, they wish only to influence policy.
- Groups have only a limited range of policy interests; parties are usually concerned with the entire government remit. This distinction is sometimes expressed in terms of functions; groups *articulate* interests and parties *aggregate* them.
- Parties tend to be located along the ideological spectrum but pressure groups may forge links at many points and seek access to governments of any complexion.

Although useful, this distinction breaks down. The differences should be seen in terms of tendencies rather than clear orientations. We saw in chapter 12 that the Labour and Conservative parties have historically been wedded to particular interests. Some pressure groups do indeed fight elections: environmentalists as the Greens, anti-abortionists as the Pro-life party and Eurosceptics as UKIP. Some also aggregate interests as peak organizations (see below), while the Real World Coalition formed a rainbow alliance of over thirty of the UK's leading environmental campaigning organizations (see Jacobs 1996).

Typology

An important dichotomy distinguishes groups on the basis of the interest they fight for. Although the nomenclature varies, the distinction is fundamental.

Promotional groups

The policy goal of **promotional groups** is beyond self-interest and they are sometimes called *cause groups*. Thus, for example, the Royal Society for the Prevention of Cruelty to Children, the Society for the Protection of the Unborn Child and, say, the National Anti-Vivisection Society fight for those unable to defend themselves. Others pursue ideological or moral goals: Liberty is concerned with civil rights while Greenpeace fights for the planet. Generally speaking, membership is open to any concerned individual and they may attract zealots. Thus, members of Mediawatch expose themselves to long television vigils in their mission to purify the airwaves of sex and violence.

Sectional groups

Individual self-interest is the motive for much economic and political activity and this is reflected through **sectional groups**. Sometimes called economic groups, membership is generally restricted to those sharing the interest. Trade unions are a notable example. On the employers' side, there are business associations reflecting various sectors, and even multinational firms. Both unions and employers' associations combine into **peak organizations** – the Trades Union Congress (TUC), the Institute of Directors and the Confederation of British Industry (CBI) – to press their collective demands.

Another category comprises professional associations such as the British Medical Association (BMA) and the Law Society. Sectional interests are not only economic: Stonewall is concerned with the rights of homosexuals, while the diversity of feminist groups consists mainly of women. Many do not devote all their time to politics. The Automobile Association, for example, serves its members in a wide variety of ways, only becoming politically active when motorists' interests are threatened.

The promotional/sectional distinction is blurred in practice with some promotional groups, such as the Howard League for Penal Reform, concerned largely with a sectional interest and some sectional groups often claiming to pursue wider goals for society (health, education, justice, and so on).

The policy bazaar: bargaining with power

Generally governments are not unwilling to talk with groups. This is partly because the groups themselves can have powerful bargaining counters in terms of expertise and veto power.

Expertise

Many groups provide expertise in particular fields – farming, medicine, nature conservation, to name but three – and the state bureaucracy is generally deficient in specialisms. When new problems arise it is likely that voluntary organizations will be first to respond. Thus, as AIDS began its fateful march through the population, the Terrence Higgins Trust clearly understood the problem better than the mandarins. Businessmen know how to promote trade, Sustrans can map out the best cycle routes, and so on. Indeed, where expertise is not brought in the result can be policy failure, as with the poll tax, or the introduction of attainment-testing in schools.

Veto power

The NHS needs doctors, education must have teachers and only farmers can implement agricultural policy. If the London tube drivers strike, the whole city is affected; if teachers do not turn up for work, repercussions reverberate throughout society. A group's leverage increases in proportion to its monopoly status. The 1971 Industrial Relations Act failed owing to trade union unwillingness to play ball. When the NHS was created, threats of non-cooperation from the BMA forced major concessions from Aneurin Bevan, the responsible minister. Of course circumstances can change. The National Union of Mineworkers (NUM) appeared mighty when its strike unnerved the Heath government in 1974, but during the 1980s its monopoly status was broken by the formation (with government encouragement) of an alternative union.

Talking to power: channels of access

To articulate their views to government groups require channels of access. These range from influencing the public at large to direct talks with decision-makers. Beyond the domestic institutions there is also the path to the EU.

The public

In a democracy a favourable climate of public opinion is in a group's interest and there are numerous ways to achieve this. The director of the Child Poverty Action

Street politics?

Group declared 'coverage in the media is our main strategy' (Whiteley and Winyard 1984: 35). The press is critically important, though less helpful to groups of the left. Some major left-wing demonstrations may even go unreported. Power over public opinion can be a function of wealth. Rich interests may enlist the services of the advertising industry – the professional persuaders – to reach parts of the national subconscious that others cannot reach. In the early 1990s the nuclear industry assiduously massaged its public image, its infamous Windscale site became Sellafield and costly TV commercials enticed the public onto guided tours. Less well-endowed groups are usually obliged to adopt more robust tactics with marches and demonstrations.

Parliament

Groups may launch onslaughts with mass demonstrations outside the Palace of Westminster and MPs may be lobbied, besieged in their constituencies or deluged with persuasive mail and email. Some will be sympathetic to particular groups; deaf MP Jack Ashley campaigned with fervour on behalf of the disabled, David Alton pursued the anti-abortionist cause and Chris Bryant and Ben Bradshaw support the rights of gays. Groups try to cultivate long-term relationships with MPs and peers, even appointing them to honorary positions in their associations. The relationship can be symbiotic, a reputation for specialist knowledge serving as a basis for catching the Speaker's eye and impressing the whips. The general showpiece debates on issues chosen by the front benches afford limited opportunities for influence, but the committee stage of legislation can be more useful; proposed amendments, even if defeated, gain valuable publicity. Private members' bills provide a unique (though limited and expensive) opportunity to promote a cause; Friends of the Earth and the Green Party both played a significant part in the early drafting of the 1997 Road Traffic Reduction Bill. Publicity can also be gained through Early Day Motions. The upper house is also not exempt from attention; its function of 'tidying up' bills affords a chance for one last-ditch stand.

It is sometimes argued that promotional groups are more interested in Parliament than are the economic giants, but this is far from true. Indeed, it is possible to view the Houses as *functional* chambers where the members sit as representatives not of constituencies but of corporate interests. Wealthy interests also avail themselves of the services of the professional lobbyist, which can sometimes open a door to less honourable behaviour on the part of MPs (see p. 420).

Parties

The orthodoxy that groups will seek friends anywhere in the ideological landscape is questionable in certain cases. The ideology of many promotional groups gives a

Don't let the buggers get you down.

Inscription on watch given by Michael Mates MP to fugitive businessman Asil Nadir, upon whose behalf he had lobbied partisan leaning. Welfare groups like Shelter expect more from a leftish party while business interests and the law-and-order lobby traditionally expect a better crack of the whip from the right. As seen in chapter 12, the traditional Siamese pairings of labour and capital with the two major parties raises controversial questions. However, it takes two to tango and the parties themselves will attempt to court interest groups by tailoring their manifestos to their needs. In this way New Labour danced towards the business interests in the 1990s and Cameron's Conservatives courted a diversity of interests normally seen as left wing.

The government

Direct lines to ministers at the heart of state power might seem the most promising of all channels. Such meetings are a formal part of government and compliance with the Freedom of Information Act leads some departments to publish regular lists of ministers' meetings with outside interests. There can also be less formal encounters. When in government both main parties have proved there was no such thing as a free lunch by creating variously named dining clubs (membership fee around £10,000), offering businessmen the opportunity to meet ministers at lunches, receptions and private functions, while super dining clubs (around £100,000) opened the door to the prime minister and senior cabinet colleagues. In 2011 the coalition government moved to institutionalize further relationships with business interests, including multinational companies. In a 'buddy' system, planned to expand to some eighty corporations, each one would enjoy privileged access to a particular ministerial buddy. Using telephone calls, emails and meetings with officials, all would take place beneath the radar of official registers.

> *Things will open up for anybody willing to donate £250,000 a year.* Conservative Party treasurer offering opportunities to dine with government members, caught by *Sunday Times* journalists posing as wealthy businessmen in 2012

The more powerful (or more passionate) groups can *demand* meetings with ministers. Even under Thatcher, when consultation styles came to resemble that of Greta Garbo, the presidents of the royal colleges of surgeons, physicians, and obstetricians and gynaecologists demanded a summit meeting over NHS policy in 1988. Again, when the 1988 Local Government Bill (Clause 28) banned the 'promotion' of homosexuality by local authorities, distinguished actor Ian McKellen called for a meeting with the arts minister. In 2011 the End Violence Against Women Coalition, and other groups, demanded a meeting with Justice Secretary Kenneth Clarke over his remarks concerning categories of rape.

Yet although their clients often long to pass through the door of Number Ten, lobbyists advise against such close encounters. Their value is largely symbolic – ritualistic exchanges unlikely to result in policy. One weakness is the incitement of media interest. Bernie Ecclestone's much reported *tête-à-tête* with Tony Blair in 1997 may have brought home the bacon for Formula One racing but there was considerable embarrassment for both. A tributary of the government channel involves the growing number of ministerial advisers. As a Labour adviser, Ed Balls at the Treasury was known to the public well before he became an MP, and under Cameron, Steve Hilton assumed a key role until leaving in 2012.

Whitehall

Demonstrations may catch the headlines and lunches with ministers carry kudos, but it is dealings with the Whitehall mandarins that often prove the most potent sources of influence. It is here that the bargaining counters of the groups are most valued and where the symbiosis of mutual need is most apparent. Consultation can shape the content of official publications, including the green and white papers that set out policy. This influence is greatest because it is conducted below the level of public awareness. The village of Whitehall does not encourage sightseers and those welcomed to tea may rest assured that the curtains will remain drawn; the genteel residents will not betray their secrets even to Commons select committees (see p. 452). The group–mandarin duet sings even more *sotto voce* in the making of statutory instruments, where discussion concerns small but significant details of actual legislation.

The European Union

The EU, drawing on corporatist continental traditions, sees employers and unions as 'social partners', an approach institutionalized through the ECOSOC (see p. 183). This offers a further focus for British pressure groups, and an ear sometimes more receptive than that of their own government. Many hundreds of groups lobby at Brussels over issues such as trade, agriculture, food, commerce and the service industries. They sometimes form transnational alliances. As the flow of directives from the Commission increases, more and more associations are drawn into the web. Interests go beyond the industrial to include human rights, children, consumer protection and the environment.

Groups may approach the institutions directly or try to influence the national government's stance at Brussels. This indirect route is the more popular. Yet there are risks; the government may be forced to let a group down by making concessions in the Council. Groups choosing the direct line may talk to the European Parliament and ECOSOC, but the key access point is the Commission – not the commissioners themselves but the 'Eurocrats' operating within the dense committee network. However, the grave danger of lobbyist involvement with unelected institutions was thrown into stark relief in the March 1999 report of the 'Committee of the Wise', which led to the Commission's resignation (see p. 181). Amongst this catalogue of bureaucratic shame were accounts of the corrupt awarding of contracts and even suspicions of Mafia involvement.

The access professionals – the lobbyists

The process of seeking access was to become a growth industry. The 1980s saw the rise of commercial lobbying firms, existing for the express purpose of approaching officials, MPs and ministers on behalf of clients, some even advertising in *Dod's Parliamentary Companion*. Most leading public relations companies now have a branch specializing in political lobbying, setting up meetings with officials, lunches with ministers and lavish receptions.

However, this is an area of politics where scandal and rumours of scandal permeate the air. **Lobbyists** seeking influence in the Whitehall–Westminster complex require knowledge of the terrain, which is why the firms actually began to employ MPs, so that instead of being lobbied they would do the job themselves. Despite popular concern, the Commons Select Committee on Members' Interests was slow to adjust its rules; MPs were not required to record payments received, give details of their own shareholdings or name the interests represented. Allegations of venality at the heart of government began to circulate during the 1990s. A definitive moment came when two Conservative MPs were trapped by *Sunday Times* journalists posing as businessmen offering £1,000 for a parliamentary question. A 'cash for questions' scandal hit the headlines, resulting in the resignation of one junior minister, Tim Smith, and the sacking of another, Neil Hamilton. The establishment of the Register of Members' Interests did little to discourage developments and the Major government was to descend into a miasma of sleaze.

It is not only MPs who are involved. This world offers lucrative opportunities to the army of ministerial advisers who, upon leaving their government employment, have a deep familiarity with the labyrinthine corridors of power. An official register of firms and their clients (set up at the request of Sir Gordon Downey, Parliamentary Commissioner for Standards) reveals the exodus to the world of influence, almost all major lobbying companies employing them. Interests represented included arms dealing, the tobacco industry and genetic engineering.

Moreover, the political staffers are not the only ones to make their expertise available. The companies are also keen to employ ex-ministers, who have been even closer to the heart of power. In March 2010 Channel 4's *Dispatches* programme broadcast a sting operation in which *Sunday Times* journalists posed as lobbyists seeking recruits. Viewers were able to witness Labour ex-ministers Stephen Byers, Patricia Hewitt and Geoff Hoon enthusiastically presenting their CVs. Byers boasted of secret deals with ministers and claimed influence over major policies. Describing himself as a 'cab for hire' he placed his fare at some £5,000 per day. The three were suspended from the PLP. However, in May 2010 Hoon reportedly took on a top job with defence firm AgustaWestland, which the press reported had secured a £1.7-billion contract while he was defence secretary, and for which no other firms

We all know how it works. The lunches, the hospitality, the quiet word in your ear, the ex-ministers and ex-advisers for hire, helping big business to get its way.

David Cameron, speech before the 2010 general election

were invited to bid (*Daily Mail*, 18 May 2011). There was also to be embarrassment for 'another place' in a cash-for-policy disgrace, when four Labour peers were trapped by *Sunday Times* reporters posing as representatives of a fictitious Chinese company. They appeared willing to seek to actually change the law (on the business rate) for cash.

Ex-ministers and officials wishing to do private work within two years of retirement must seek approval and are barred from lobbying the British government for one or two years after their departure. However, the vetting process is desultory. In January 2009 the Commons Public Administration Committee recommended a statutory register of lobbying companies. However, the preference has been for self-regulation of the industry and the 'revolving door' between Westminster/Whitehall and the corporate world continues to turn. The anti-corruption organization, Transparency International, calls for reform.

The persistence of the problem was underlined in October 2011 when a scandal arose even before a minister had retired. Conservative Defence Secretary Liam Fox was forced to resign after it was revealed that he had allowed close friend Adam Werritty to accompany him on official foreign visits to high-level meetings. Werritty had been funded by defence companies and an Israeli lobbyist who stood to gain from decisions made.

Friends in high places: insiders and outsiders

Access to the citadels of power is clearly not equal. The insider/outsider dichotomy postulated by Wyn Grant (2004) provides a robust theoretical framework for considering pressure group activity. Pioneering British studies, such as those of the BMA (Eckstein 1960), the CBI (Grant and Marsh 1977) and the National Farmers Union (NFU) (Self and Storing 1962) (as well as the majority of smaller case studies and various symposia on the subject) concentrated on groups that are largely successful, respectable and legitimate. These can be described as **insider groups**, enjoying the access advantages described above. Relationships here can be relaxed and informal, extending beyond tea and sympathy in Whitehall to G&Ts in the exclusive clubs and restaurants of London, and even to weekends in country houses, where the high can meet the mighty.

Needless to say, such a warm embrace is not extended to all. Some groups will not find such a sympathetic ear and their demands may need to be voiced in raucous demonstrations or on the cold picket lines. These are the **outsiders**. Sometimes, groups will resort to what is described, somewhat imprecisely, as direct action – essentially behaviour going beyond negotiation or voicing demands to causing havoc through disruptive behaviour.

In practice the insider/outsider dichotomy is not clear-cut; there is a multiplicity of intermediate positions. The location of a group along a notional insider–outsider spectrum is determined by factors such as the following.

- *Public esteem*. The BMA has always gained mightily from the natural veneration that society accords healers. On the other hand, groups espousing causes such as, say, the legalization of cannabis, can be safely snubbed by a government ever conscious that it will be judged by the company it keeps.

- *Media support*. The public approval a group receives is mightily influenced by its media coverage. As argued in chapter 9, this largely favours the political right.

- *Stage of development*. New groups often start as outsiders, sometimes resorting to 'non-responsible' behaviour. However, insider status may well be the ultimate goal. By the end of the 1990s the anti-roads lobby was beginning to come in from the cold as gridlocked motorways fulfilled its prophecies.

- *Ideology*. Where group and government ideologies merge the relationship will be close. Where they diverge it is likely that neither will wish to be seen holding hands with the other. By choosing to remain outside a group avoids any moral burdens of self-restraint.

- *Social positioning*. It helps to know the right people. The middle classes are generally better placed, the representatives of some groups resembling civil servant clones. Sharing norms, values and interests, they will not only speak the same language, they will do so with the same accent.

- *Wealth*. Money can talk in many accents. Wealthy associations such as the CBI or NFU, and popular charities, can spend much on entertaining, lobbying and public relations.

- *Economic leverage*. Large corporations are too important to the economy to be ignored.

Changes of government mean that groups in favour will vary, but for the most part the insider groups will be those close to the heart of the Establishment. The coalition government's 'buddy' system reinforces this impression. There can also be insiders and outsiders at EU level. From its inception, the idea of a federal Europe has offered a tantalizing glimpse of new forms of power to banks, international financiers and multinationals. Today every major company has offices in Brussels.

Theorizing Group Politics

Clearly the politics of influence takes us beyond constitutional theory and different theoretical perspectives are required. These focus more closely on the heart of the power structure within the polity.

The concern about the government's buddy system was always that policy would end up skewed towards narrow corporate interests, rather than the public good.
John Sauven (executive director, Greenpeace) quoted in the *Guardian* (19 Jan. 2013)

Pluralism

Much orthodox British study in the liberal-democratic tradition subscribes to a generally **pluralist** view of politics. The operation of groups is believed to remedy some shortcomings in representative government, including the following.

- A single vote can hardly be said to constitute participation.
- The principle of 'one person, one vote' fails to recognize the variation in the intensity with which views are held.
- People are denied influence between elections.
- Manifesto promises can be broken mid-term.
- Minority voices are generally unheeded.

The modern variant of the theory of pluralism is largely a US import deriving from Bentley. Although he saw group activity as a necessary and inescapable feature of *any* political system, subsequent thinkers developed the theory as a hallmark of liberal democracy. It was not merely a *description* of the way things were, but a prescription of how they *ought* to be. Robert Dahl wrote extensively on the theory in the USA. Coining the term **polyarchy**, he regarded it as no less than a completely new theory of popular sovereignty in which groups help to exert the checks and balances so central to the US constitution (Dahl 1956). In Britain, interest in pluralism, which had been present since the rise of the trade unions (exercising thinkers like Cole, Tawney, Russell, Laski and the Webbs), was reinforced by American commentators on the British scene, such as Samuel Beer (1965), and entered into the mainstream liberal-democratic orthodoxy.

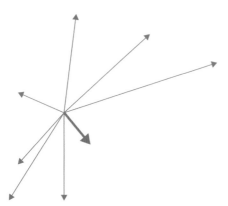

Figure 19.1 A vector diagram

Note: The lines represent the magnitudes and directions of forces acting at a point. They produce a resultant (the bold arrow) which is the sum of their directions and magnitudes; thus every force is taken equally into account. This is analogous to a pure theory of pluralism.

The tenets of pluralism

This benign system, complementing representative democracy, may be portrayed as follows.

- The right to join groups is a mark of a free society.
- Groups provide a more effective means of participation than elections.
- Public policy is the outcome of group forces acting against each other. Thus the system tends towards a state of equilibrium, with all forces having some effect on the outcome (figure 19.1).
- The point where the forces act is the government, which is an impartial referee, its role the balancing of group pressures.
- No single group will dominate because, as in Newton's law of motion, for every force there is an equal and opposite to counterbalance it; the roads lobby will generate an anti-roads lobby, and so on.

- Competition will not threaten the integrity of society because each individual tends to belong to several groups; a loss on one front will be balanced by gains elsewhere.
- The larger the group the more influence it will have, thereby maintaining the majoritarian principle while not silencing minorities.
- People with intense feelings on an issue will tend to exert more pressure than the apathetic, thereby countering the insensitivity in the one-person-one-vote principle.
- Those with a common interest, but not organized, will be accommodated because the government will regard them as *latent groups* ready to mobilize.
- Policies, as the product of bargaining and compromise, will tend to be moderate, fair to all, and conducive to social stability. Pluralist Charles Lindblom (1959) noted how a process of 'partisan mutual adjustment' resulted in **incrementalism** – small policy changes rather than great unsettling leaps.

This of course is an abstract model; the idea of government as a cypher or mere referee is unrealistic and was specifically rejected by Beer (1956) in the heyday of the theory in the mid-1950s. However, a weak role for government is necessary to the theory. Thus when the mighty Shell did a U-turn in 1996 over the disposal of the Brent Spar oil platform following action by Greenpeace, the government, although voicing disapproval, was little more than a bit player in a drama where two multinational organizations competed for public support. Lively (1978: 191) suggested two interpretations of the government role: the *arbiter* model (government with enough power to ensure that the groups play by the rules) and the *arena* model (government as one of the participants in the game).

Policy communities and networks

> When I was at the [Health Education Council] . . . the Ministry of Agriculture was in there like a ton of bricks acting virtually as a lobby for the [farmers].
>
> Dr David Player (former Director General of the Health Education Council), quoted in the *Independent* (17 Dec. 1988)

Neopluralists give a more practical picture of the arena in which the groups bargain. In each policy area ministers, civil servants, professional lobbyists and groups in mutual dependencies (figure 19.2) form what are termed variously 'policy communities', **'sub-governments'** or **'policy networks'**. While the network image can be accommodated within other theoretical perspectives (Smith 1993: 74), it is mainly applied by those of a pluralist leaning. The communities are highly fluid, actors entering and exiting as issues change. Although in some respects

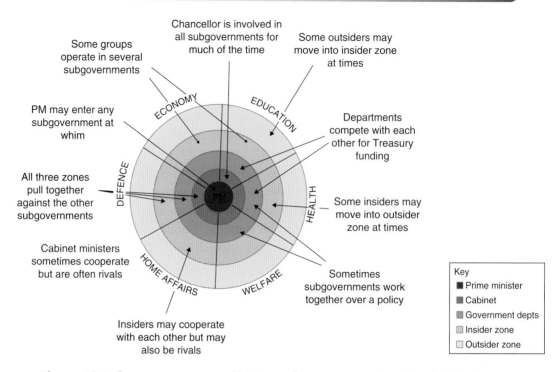

Figure 19.2 The pressure group world in terms of policy communities (simplified view)

members may be rivals, they also work together against other policy communities in pursuit of a greater share of public resources (see Richardson and Jordan 1979; Rhodes and Marsh 1992). Communities themselves may intersect (Grant and MacNamara 1995). Over the BSE crisis communities around the Ministry of Agriculture, Fisheries and Food and the Ministry of Health presented a united front with the British beef interests (Winter 1996: 60–1). Networks also form at EU level through vertical alliances comprising national ministries, European Parliament committees, Eurocrats, politicians and professional lobbyists, as well as the pressure groups themselves.

Evaluating pluralism

Few would quarrel with pluralism's stress on the role of groups in politics. However, their uniqueness to liberal democracy is questionable; they can form under totalitarian regimes. Indeed, they can be seen as *undermining* democracy; Rousseau believed factions subverted the General Will. They can also be internally undemocratic, with unelected leaders whose views may be at variance with those of members. Moreover, the largest groups are not necessarily the winners, tightly knit

With all its defects, [pluralism] does nevertheless provide a high probability that any active and legitimate group will make itself heard effectively at some stage in the process of decision.

Robert Dahl, *A Preface to Democratic Theory* (1956: 150)

associations (the City, the BMA) often having a degree of influence entirely out of proportion to their democratic weight, while groups with vast memberships – teachers, nurses and miners – have suffered successive defeats.

Does pluralism make might right?

> Our country, like every modern state, needs profound democratic reforms. It needs political and ideological pluralism, a mixed economy and protection of human rights and the opening up of society.
>
> Attributed to Andrei Sakharov (1921–89; Soviet nuclear physicist, dissident, human rights activist and Nobel Prize winner)

Critics allege that group activity does not result in equity. Like the Ancient Greek Thrasymachus, pluralism allows that 'might is right'. For long the anti-roads protesters proved little match for a roads lobby of hauliers, engineers, motorway caterers and the bankers behind them. In his farewell address, President Eisenhower famously warned of the menacing growth in America of a 'military–industrial complex' actually threatening the sovereignty of government. Dahl and Lindblom (1976) came to accept in their later work that group politics does not take place on a level playing field. However, preserving the normative aspect of the theory, they argued that a democratic constitution should aim to counter the power of capitalist interests by maximizing group participation and listening to the weak as well as the strong (see Dahl 1985). Of course, this idea of weak government fits snugly within the liberal suspicion of the state. As a kind of political *laissez-faire* it removes moral responsibility from the state for outcomes; you cannot accuse the referee if you lose the game. This culture can induce the losers to blame themselves for their fate.

Questioning the logic of group action

A further criticism of group theory doubts whether groups are as natural as Bentley asserted or as desirable as pluralists claim. By applying the methods of classical economic theory to political analysis, public choice theory attempts to explain political decisions (public choices) in terms of self-interested actors. Olson (1968) suggested that rational individuals will not become active in a group merely because it is fighting for a collective interest that they share. They can do just as well by sitting back and letting others do the work. In the school choir it is easy enough to open the mouth soundlessly and enjoy the free meal after the concert. This is the problem of the 'free-rider'.

This, for Olson, is the explanation of the success of the capitalist interests: 'the multitude of workers, consumers . . . and so on are organized only in special circumstances, but business interests (corporations, banks, the City) are organized as a general rule' (Olson 1968: 143). Groups in the first category must develop strategies for recruiting and retaining members. They must offer **selective incentives** (insurance, free T-shirts, etc.), or use coercion such as a closed-shop arrangement or intimidation. Being artificial, they lack cohesion and remain essentially weak. This can also explain the failure of workers to unite for revolution in the way prophesied by Marx. An alternative interpretation of group politics – corporatism – gives a much stronger role to government.

Corporatism

Corporatism is an approach to government with long European antecedents and became interesting to British scholars during the 1970s as the limitations of pluralist explanations were exposed. Under corporatism government works in deliberate collusion with certain major interests. The system can entail a functional assembly in which members represent not geographical constituencies but interests within society. Corporatism is identified with the fascism of the 1930s (see p. 67) and this unpleasant aftertaste is expunged by the term **neocorporatism**. Philippe Schmitter (1974) distinguished two forms – *state corporatism* and *societal corporatism* – the latter arising naturally within a society and, unlike the former, *not* a feature of oppressive government. For some, a neocorporatist style of government is the answer to the wasteful competition generated by pluralism. It can appear as a great cure-all for national problems, engendering a classless camaraderie allegedly seen in times of war.

The tenets of corporatism

Societal corporatism is the variant to be found in modern liberal democracies and has the following characteristics.

- Politics is seen in terms of groups but they are cooperative rather than competitive.
- Government is not a passive referee; it decides who shall be invited into the consultations and has clear views on policy.
- Groups may even be created by government to represent interests it wishes to work with.
- The interests included tend to be capital and labour, the result being **tripartism**, a *pas de trois* of government, trade unions and employers.
- Those included tend to monopolize the right to represent their interest.
- Sometimes groups join together as peak organizations to facilitate consultation.
- Corporatist institutions can be created to supplement the formal constitution.
- The relationship is reciprocal: not only do groups influence policy, government can influence groups, forcing them to modify their demands and gaining their cooperation.

Evaluating corporatism

This form of corporatism is essentially a consensus-era product. This *ménage à trois* proved most fragile when it could be most valuable – in economic crisis. Under these circumstances:

- unions are liable to opt out once the benefits of full employment are no longer available to compensate for the concessions to capital;
- employers become disenchanted with rules and constraints as profits fall;
- militants on both sides favour confrontation rather than cooperation;
- large firms and unions prefer dealing directly with government rather than through corporatist institutions;
- radical governments of the right find the corporatist embrace inhibiting.

I have no doubt that the civil service is a state within a state to an extent that the trade union movement could never aspire to be.
Barbara Castle (1910–2002; Labour minister), *Mandarin Power*, quoted in Barberis (1996)

The Pattern of Post-war Group Politics

A climate of corporatism

Group participation in Britain has shown both pluralist and corporatist tendencies, the latter most evident in economic policy, including agriculture. In the early twentieth century government encouraged the institutionalization of bodies representing labour and capital as a means of securing state legitimacy. An attempt to set up a National Industrial Conference was made in 1919 and subsequently there were efforts to create a 'Parliament of Industry'. The second world war saw a coalition government increasing its control over various aspects of life, including the economy, the health services and agricultural production, with certain key groups drawn into the state embrace.

This continued into the opening years of the post-war Keynesian era when the management of the economy became a central government responsibility. The nationalization of certain industries, the establishment of the NHS and the expansion of the welfare state increased the need for government to work with various sectional groups involving business, commerce, finance and the unions. Some of these enjoyed close relationships with relevant government departments as policy communities. Their importance in the delivery of government policy gave them powerful bargaining counters. The gain for government was industrial peace, for business interests it was wage restraint and the unions enjoyed full employment and rights to free collective bargaining. The population at large benefited from a growing welfare state. During this period promotional groups played only a limited role.

From the 1960s the state showed more clearly corporatist tendencies with the establishment of consultative institutions. Relative economic decline gave governments added reason to intervene. Union and business representatives were brought together in a number of tripartite institutions to shape economic policy. Most significant was the National Economic Development Council (Neddy) formed in 1961. The unions came together as a peak organization under the Trades Union Congress (TUC – founded in 1867) and, with government encouragement, a number of business associations formed the Confederation of British Industries (CBI) in 1965. Journalists spoke of 'beer and sandwiches' at Number Ten. In the mid-1970s, the Manpower Services Commission, the Health and Safety Commission, and the Advisory, Conciliation and Arbitration Service (ACAS) further institutionalized tripartism. In addition, hundreds of **advisory** and **consultative bodies** concerned with particular industrial sectors and policy areas mushroomed. Various policies reflected a corporatist flavour, particularly over prices and incomes. The strength of the corporatist hold was shown when Edward Heath tried to reverse the trend but was forced into the infamous 'U-turn' for which he would be memorably castigated by his successor. He was to tell the Conservative conference that unions and employers should 'share with the government the benefits and obligations of running the economy' (Kavanagh and Morris 1994: 61). The 'social contract' of the 1975–8 Labour government increased the voice of labour and capital in many domestic policies. But the corporatist tendencies were not restricted to the interests of capital and labour; in social policy certain groups, such as the BMA and the National Union of Teachers, were welcomed onto advisory and consultative bodies.

The drift from corporatism

However, corporatism in the UK was never the full-blown variety. Its decay came in the face of economic crisis. Heath's confrontation with the miners was a defining moment and the collapse of the 'social contract' showed that Labour had lost its trump card – trade union cooperation. The 1978/9 'winter of discontent' became emblematic of 'what was wrong with Britain'. Coming to power in 1979, the Conservative government spoke a rhetoric of the 'enemy within' rather than of partnership. New Right thinking saw group involvement as the problem rather than the solution and it became demonized with talk of 'government overload', 'hyper-pluralism' and **'pluralist stagnation'**. The high steel railings erected across Downing Street were symbolic of a government distancing itself from many outside interests. There followed bitter confrontations with the steelworkers in 1980, the railwaymen in 1982 and, most dramatically of all, the miners in 1984–5. A series of Acts weakened the unions; by the end of Thatcher's reign their political role had virtually disappeared (Marsh 1992: ch. 4). Figure 19.3 chronicles the decline.

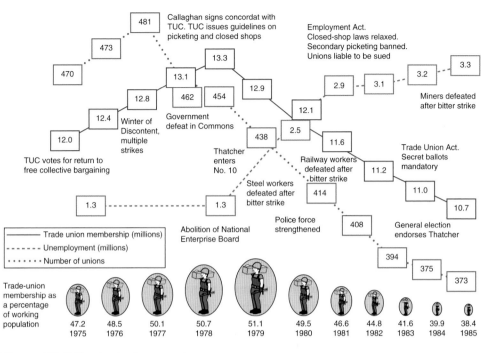

Figure 19.3 The death of corporatism

Source: Data from *Social Trends* (1988: tables 4.19 and 11.8).

With deep symbolism Neddy was abolished in early 1993, its responsibilities passing to the Department of Trade and Industry. Consultation was conspicuously lacking in a number of important policy areas, from pit closures to police pay and conditions. The most dramatic failure was the poll tax; conceived with zero consultation, the outcome extracted a heavy toll on the government and the Prime Minister herself (see Butler et al. 1994). Yet not all groups had been excluded. Various right-wing interests, including the Institute of Directors, insurance companies, merchant banks, oil companies, the roads lobby, the farming interests, estate agents and the City, which provided financial information and advice over the privatization programme, worked closely with government and benefited from the policies. Various public–private partnership schemes further extended the involvement of private business in the business of government. There was also much consultation with New Right think-tanks and private consultants, particularly over the privatization launches. Many routine Whitehall negotiations between various trade associations and middle-ranking or junior civil servants had continued on a routine basis (Grant 2000: 3) and some of the post-war machinery survived. Under John Major the *dirigiste* Michael Heseltine became President of the Board of Trade.

New Labour: new partnerships?

New Labour had made strenuous efforts to gain the approval of business and financial interest groups. Its 1996 annual conference marked a new style, with champagne receptions and working breakfasts between business leaders and leading party figures. Stands were erected by such powerful interests as the Institute of Directors, BA, the British Bankers' Association, Lloyds, and even defence contractors. There was to be a fundamental revamping of the relationship with the unions. The mantra of 'fairness not favours' ruled out any return to the 1970s; the talk was of a 'new social partnership'. It was one that the 'new unionists' – those sympathetic to 'New Labour', including TUC leader John Monks – were prepared to accept.

With no reincarnation of Neddy, government was to remain firmly in the driving seat, supervising a range of advisory groups, such as the Low Pay Commission, embracing not only the CBI and TUC but other players considered central to economic success. For traditional unionists, the partnership appeared to be shifting them to outsider status, while offering much to business and finance. Encouraged by the Social Chapter and the globalizing economy, the unions looked more to Brussels, often strengthening cross-national links (Farnham 1996: 597).

Challenging orthodoxy

Beyond consultative patterns over economic issues there were developments on other fronts. Denied the traditional channels to government institutions, cause groups turn to alternative avenues of access. Orthodox political analysis had suggested that raucous group behaviour was a sign of weakness rather than strength, a case of 'not waving but drowning'. Certainly the activities of groups such as the miners in the 1980s, or more recently animal rights campaigners (who, amongst other things, attacked the managing director of Huntingdon Life Sciences with baseball bats), have met with failure. The huge 2010 protests against student fees also made little impression on the coalition government.

Yet some events have challenged this orthodoxy. From the suffragette movement to the women peace campaigners at Greenham Common, major advances have been made by more direct forms of action by outsider groups. In the van was the Campaign for Nuclear Disarmament (CND), formed in 1957 in response to threats posed by the cold war, with its high-profile marches. There is also the new wave of assertive feminism as well as hundreds of groups concerned variously with the environment, child welfare, child poverty, animal welfare, cruel sports, capital punishment, abortion and homosexuality. Such action became more prominent as the neoliberal agenda gained a hold during the 1980s. A significant point was reached with the campaign against the poll tax. Despite its raucous nature, it was successful, suggesting a Leviathan lying dormant in the generally inert masses.

Shortly after, Heseltine's 1992 pit closure programme was derailed by large-scale demonstrations. A campaign waged by the parents of the children shot in the Dunblane massacre of 1996 resulted in the banning of hand-guns. The environment became a particular focus for action. The movement rapidly grew from the 1992 Twyford Down protests to include a range of groups campaigning in areas such as climate change, road building, airports and forestry. Some groups, such as Friends of the Earth, Climate Action, Plane Stupid and Greenpeace, amassed large memberships. Amidst increasing disruption people not only took to the streets, environmentalists risked death on the high seas, critical-mass cyclists risked rage on the roads, and anti-motorway and airport-runway demonstrators took to the trees and tunnels.

THANKS TO ALL THOSE WHO HELPED US DO OUR WORK IN 1998

Shell for deciding to recycle the Brent Spar at last.

John Prescott for agreeing not to dump any oil installations in the ocean.

Japan for becoming the 26th nation to ratify the Antarctic Treaty.

Michael Meacher for agreeing to ban toxic and radioactive discharges from the sea by 2020.

EU fisheries ministers for banning 'wall of death' driftnets.

Peter Mandelson for not putting PVC on the Millennium Dome roof.

. . . OK, so we had to run campaigns against some of them first – but thanks anyway.

Extract from front cover of Greenpeace, *Annual Review 1998*

Of particular interest to analysts was that fact that direct action was not confined to those who might have been classed as outsiders. Funding for a disruptive Countryside Alliance came from some of Britain's biggest companies, the Duke of Westminster and even America's shooting and hunting lobby (*Independent*, 26 Feb. 1998). September 2000 saw direct action on the motorways by farmers and road hauliers that was to force concessions on fuel tax. The significance of these developments was not just that insider groups were becoming more active but that the tactics of large-scale disruption (or its threat) could yield results.

The coalition government of 2010 did not have to wait long to feel the heat of the new politics; campaigns secured U-turns on various fronts, including NHS reforms, the sale of Forestry Commission land and the proposed English Baccalaureate in education.

Pluralism in question

Pressure group politics is an integral part of the policy-making process in Britain. The theory of pluralism, in the sense of allowing the free formation of groups and their right to seek avenues of access to the powerful, can explain much. However, although never highly developed, there are also corporatist elements, in the sense of institutionalizing the involvement of certain groups. Some important interests, particularly the City, have remained outside the corporatist institutions, and even those included have never entirely eschewed competitive behaviour, often making self-interested decisions which were bad for the economy as a whole (Marquand 1988: 121–3).

For Middlemas (1979: 371–85) the system showed a 'corporate bias', reflecting a *desire* on the part of government to insulate itself from pluralism in order to best meet the needs of capitalist interests. Cawson and Saunders developed a 'dual state thesis', suggesting that economic issues tend to be settled in a closed corporatist style affording much power to capitalist interests, while those broadly concerning welfare emerge from a more open pluralist process (Cawson 1986: ch. 7). However, the economic implication of welfare blurs this distinction. Under New Labour and the 2010 coalition Treasury demands, rather than social considerations, shaped much welfare policy.

However, the ability of any form of group politics to deliver a fair society is questionable. The politics of influence takes place in a murky area of the constitution with secrecy, covert consultation and scandals. Critics see this world like an exclusive golf club, fine for members but not for those beyond the fairways. Trade unions sometimes enter this exclusive world but, while enjoying the corporatist embrace, the expectation is that they will suspend their *raison d'être* and hold down wages. Whether corporatist or pluralist, some interests come out winners and some losers. It is necessary to open yet another door in the labyrinthine world of influence and go beyond the group approach.

Beyond the Group Approach

Some interests appear more advantaged than others. Is this but a symptom of a more fundamental architecture of power? To search for the explanation, we must address fundamental questions about the structure of society. Two broad perspectives that help to illuminate this are the **Marxist** and the **elitist**.

Marxist perspectives

For Marx, the key driving force in politics was a struggle not between groups but between classes (see pp. 91–3). The Marxist perspective argues that, under capitalism, the state always operates in the interests of the owners and controllers of capital. Today economic globalization means that this class is transnational and its power within any single state is amplified (see chapter 5). There are, however, contrasting schools of thought with conflicting views on how this domination is effected. At one extreme, the state may be said to be controlled through the con-spiratorial activities of the capitalist class – an instrumental perspective. At the other extreme, the structural perspective holds that the state is compelled to act in favour of the business and financial interests by virtue of the logic of capitalism.

The instrumental perspective

The view of the state as an instrument of a ruling class is a feature of classical Marxist analysis and Marx's description of the government as a 'committee for managing the common affairs of the bourgeoisie' is regularly cited. The **instrumental perspective** can be supported in many ways, beginning with the manner in which, during the nineteenth century, the rising bourgeoisie reformed the state machinery. Since then the senior civil service, armed forces, judiciary, and so on have largely recruited from the same establishment soil that nurtures the financiers and business leaders. Antonio Gramsci saw a ruling class using these key positions to shape the dominant ideology so that the masses would be content and not threaten the revolution predicted by Marx. The penetration and funding of the Conservative Party (and New Labour) and the ability of a right-wing press to deliver sympathetic governments are further instruments of domination. Ministers and civil servants may themselves take up company directorships upon retirement and the extensive use of patronage offers yet further ways to strengthen the influence of the business and financial communities. Labour's victory in 1997 came only after systematic courtship of capitalist interests and a loosening of its union ties (see chapter 13).

History is at once freedom and necessity.
Antonio Gramsci,
Prison Notebooks
(1929–35)

> There is a high degree of homogeneity among the members of the dominant class . . . They constantly cross each other's paths in an incessant round of meetings, lunches, dinners, functions, and ceremonies, and as members of boards, commissions, councils, committees and institutions of the most varied kind.
>
> Ralph Miliband (1924–94; Marxist scholar), *Capitalist Democracy in Britain* (1984: 7)

Contrary to the pluralist argument that political and economic competition between groups limits their power, there is evidence of coherence, if not collusion, within the capitalist class. This is promoted by intermarriage and various methods of excluding outsiders, including private education, freemasonry and even accents. At the head of Britain's largest companies are the directors, often sitting on the boards of several companies. These directors also sit on each other's remuneration committees which determine the rewards for their stewardship.

The fusion of finance and industry produces an 'inner circle' of finance capitalists at the heart of the state, dominating the top levels of the major cohesion-promoting institutions: the Association of Chambers of Commerce, the Institute of Directors, the British Institute of Management and the CBI. Useem (1984) argued that world recession from the 1970s saw the political activity of big business intensify, with the inner circle representing a City view on behalf of the whole financial and business community on key matters of economic policy. The Thatcherite 'big bang' transformed the City, an influx of foreign capital extending links to a global financial community, and New Labour continued the New Right policy of deregulation.

Egg on the face of power
On 24 December 1988 the *Independent* revealed that the boards of the large food and poultry feed manufacturers, producing most of the eggs sold in British supermarkets, included a number of ex-cabinet ministers and top civil servants (Sir Peter Carey, permanent secretary at the DTI, 1976–83; John Biffen, former leader of the Commons and a senior Conservative MP; and former cabinet secretary Lord Hunt). Another big feed supplier had donated nearly £10,000 to Conservative funds in the 1987 election year. The government agreed to compensate egg producers for lost sales during the salmonella scare. The person responsible for alerting the public (Edwina Currie) disappeared from the ministerial firmament.

The structural perspective

However, although it may capture a deep truth about the *essence* of the state under capitalism, the committee metaphor should not be taken literally. The idea that a class consciously makes the state an entirely compliant instrument is open to question. Indeed, it can be argued that the very existence of state institutions (Parliament, the executive, bureaucracies, and so on) promises some degree of autonomy because these develop interests of their own. This is part of the public choice theorists' explanation for the expansion of social democracy, producing a large empire-building bureaucracy. Many public servants have a firm ideological commitment, regularly voting Labour. In the twilight of the Major government one Conservative minister remarked ruefully that, while some top mandarins might pose problems for Labour, the grades below 'all read the *Guardian* or the *Independent*' (Timmins and Kampfner 1997).

Some writers suggest that liberal democratic states can actually be highly insensitive to the needs of capital. Crouch (1979: 27) argued that 'two of the most remarkable facts . . . are, first, the extent to which the ruling class mistrust the state and try to limit its activities, and second, the relative responsiveness of the polity . . . to working class demands'. Certainly the Thatcher, New Labour and coalition governments all acted to minimize the state sector in various ways. However, the **structural** perspective argues that the state must perform certain functions if the capitalist economy is to survive. It must protect profitability and facilitate private capital accumulation since it depends on this prosperity for its tax income. This interpretation was advanced by the Marxist scholar Nicos Poulantzas (1973), who conducted a long-running debate with Ralph Miliband. In this view, far from appearing as an instrument of the capitalist class, the state must be able to show a degree of real autonomy in order to:

- provide services (health care, education, roads, judicial services and so on) that it is unprofitable for capitalists to provide;
- promote homogeneity within the capitalist class to prevent it destroying itself through competition;
- ensure political stability through welfare spending;
- maintain law and order and protect property;
- legitimate the system by promoting an ideology espousing inequality.

The instrumental model is *voluntaristic*, allowing individuals choice in their behaviour, while the structural one is *deterministic*, seeing them as puppets or role-players. In the latter case politicians are driven by the imperatives of capitalism as the actor playing Hamlet is driven by Shakespeare's script. Although both perspectives can be seen in Marx, the French philosopher Althusser (1969) believed the structural to be the more important. In real-world states we find elements of both; people have some choice but they are constrained by the system.

Welfare statism

It can be argued that the post-war rise of social democracy, with a wide range of policies designed to ease the conditions of the working class, undermines the Marxist thesis of upper-class domination. Yet this may be countered with an argument that the **welfare state** serves the interests of capital by socializing the costs of production, furnishing a body of healthy and reasonably well-educated workers and maintaining social harmony through legitimation. Moreover, if the economy runs out of steam, a fiscal crisis arises as the tax-borne cost of welfare erodes profitability (see O'Connor 1973); when this occurs, the capitalist interests will rein in the welfare state. This appeared to happen with the collapse of the long boom in the mid-1970s when doctors, for example, once insiders, found themselves on the outside as NHS budgets were squeezed in the interests of tax cuts. The New Labour government continued the squeeze, Blair proclaiming an end to the 'something for nothing culture' at the time of the 1998 Queen's Speech. When Chancellor Gordon

Brown announced increased expenditure for health and education in 2002, the press hailed the move as 'Gordon's Gamble'. The 2010 coalition government, taking office in the era of the great credit crunch, imposed wide-ranging welfare cuts as part of its austerity package, while seeking to stimulate business by cutting the top rate of tax from 50 to 45 per cent.

Elite theory

Sometimes termed 'scientific elitism', this approach was pioneered at the beginning of the twentieth century by a school of Italian thinkers now regarded as the classical elitists – Mosca, Pareto and Michels. It was partly a reaction against Marxism. It is also at odds with the pluralistic view of countervailing powers within society. The elitists agreed with Marx that the institutions of liberal democracy did not work in the way claimed by apologists; the masses tended to be dominated by the few, who ruled in their own interest. However, they did not see the economic base of society as the sole cause; the processes, inevitable and ineluctable like laws of nature, were present in all forms of society. The talented in all walks of life would inevitably come out on top and, having done so, would preserve their supremacy by collusion with each other. This elite power is cumulative, new generations coming along and finding silver spoons in their mouths. The elite gains control of the state by dominating the parties, securing the elective offices and monopolizing key official positions; it becomes a ruling class.

For some thinkers **elitism** is not only natural, it is desirable. Key positions are held by those best fitted for them. However, to critics the ever-present danger is that the elite rules in its own interest rather than that of the whole society. Elite theory was rejuvenated in the 1950s by those sceptical of pluralism. Floyd Hunter's famous (1953) study argued that a small coherent corps of wealthy people dominated both the social and political life in a US city, while C. Wright Mills argued that the pluralist belief in automatically balancing forces was more 'ideological hope than factual description' (1959: 126n).

Many chapters in this book suggest that, with its aristocracy and monarchy, public schools, Oxbridge institutions, exclusive London clubs, freemasonry and so on, Britain's social culture is replete with elitist features. This is both symbolized and reinforced in the unique and elaborate honours system. Titles continue

> When democracies have gained a certain state of development, they undergo a gradual transformation, adopting the aristocratic spirit, and in many cases also the aristocratic forms, against which at the outset they struggled so fiercely.
>
> Robert Michels, *Political Parties* (1911)

to be inherited by those in the upper classes, while life peerages can enhance elite power with seats in Parliament for those of talent and achievement. The elite structure has been maintained while permitting some 'short-range' mobility (see Giddens 1973), and has kept most in the class into which they were born. A study by *The Economist* (19 Dec. 1992) revealed that, despite meritocratic rhetoric from the grocer's daughter and circus performer's son who became prime ministers, the education and social background of the top hundred people had changed very little. Two-thirds of the group had been to private schools and over half to Oxbridge. Only one woman had made it into the group without going to Oxbridge – Elizabeth II! Half of David Cameron's 2010 Cabinet of twenty-three had been privately educated, fourteen were Oxbridge graduates and many were millionaires (see p. 471).

Managerialism

It has been argued in one version of elite theory that a **managerial** revolution has swept through the capitalist system, undermining the Marxist analysis of power. Old-style capitalists have been displaced by a diverse body of anonymous share-holders, allowing control of capital to pass to a new managerial class of meritocrats, well educated but of lower social origins and without the same close identification with those controlling the state (see Burnham 1942). Certainly such a class exists. At its peak are the directors of FTSE 100 companies. Although owning little, if any, of the capital they control they are able to enjoy huge remuneration packages (cover-ing salary, benefits and bonuses). To this category were added the directors of the privatized utilities, for whom the term 'Fat Cats' was generated.

In response, Marxists deny that power *has* passed to neutral meritocrats, assert-ing that it remains with the old dominant class, although the latter has undergone an internal transformation. In the first place, although a new ladder of **meritocracy** may exist, it is also open to the sons and daughters of the upper class, and they still have the best chance of ascending. Moreover, the positions of meritocrats remain insecure; they can easily land upon the head of a snake and slither down to square one. Again, the meritocrats operate largely at the level of middle management,

---

Do you suppose that you and half a dozen amateurs like you, sitting in a row in that foolish gabble shop, can govern Undershaft and Lazarus? No my friend: you will do what pays us. You will make war when it suits us, and keep peace when it doesn't . . . When I want to keep my dividends up you will discover that my want is a national need.

Andrew Undershaft (wealthy industrialist), addressing his MP son-in-law in Bernard Shaw's *Major Barbara* (1907)

leaving the traditional elite members, with power based on ownership of property (and shares), in the boardrooms and in strategic control. Between the 1850s and the 1970s (when Britain was transformed into a social democracy) the proportion of chairmen of major companies with upper-class backgrounds remained stable at around 66 per cent (Stanworth and Giddens 1974). In addition, the old upper class is sufficiently permeable to absorb outstanding aspirants from the lower strata who cultivate upper-class mores, use private elite educational establishments for their children, and can become *'plus royaux que le roi'*.

In addition to managerial power is that wielded by finance capitalists, moving in the world driven not by commodities and production but by banks, ledgers and the 'bottom line'. Holding multiple directorships, they unify the business system. Their strength is enhanced beyond measure through economic globalization, deregulation of finance and the formation of the mighty TNCs (see chapter 5). Even during the global financial crisis in the first decades of the twenty-first century, for which bankers shared much culpability, the government appeared unable to control them.

Bureaucracy

For the bureaucrat, the world is a mere object to be manipulated by him.

Karl Marx, *Critique of Hegel's Philosophy of Right* (1843)

Another arm of the elite can be the public bureaucracy. Sociologist Max Weber argued that the complexity of the modern state was such that it must fall under a 'dictatorship of the official'. However, it might be thought that class domination could be countered by a bureaucracy using its power to safeguard the public interest. Yet, as seen in chapter 18, civil service recruitment and socialization processes can harmonize with establishment interests. Upon becoming cabinet secretary in 1988, Sir Robin Butler was immediately proposed for membership of the Athenaeum, Brooks's and the Oxford and Cambridge – exclusive clubs that enable the great to meet the good (Paxman 1991: 313).

Cui Bono? Who Gets the Loot?

Explanations of power in society range from the most benign version of pluralism to elitism and class domination. All tend to devalue the role of the democratically elected government, representing an important corrective to the accounts that see formal institutions as the beginning and end of political life. Power is a complex mystery. One way to solve it is to use the technique of Hercule Poirot and see who gets the loot – to repeat the question posed at the beginning of this book: who gets what, when, how? Such a question focuses our attention on the level of equality in the distribution of life's benefits. While some degree of inequality can be a driver of enterprise, at a more extreme level it can be seen as socially corrosive (see Wilkinson and Pickett 2010).

Although from the late 1970s the corporatist institutions became overgrown with creepers, and for many the path to Whitehall gathered moss, Lawson's 1988 budget placed the loot in the wallets and handbags of the wealthy at the expense of the rest. The growth of inequality could be seen as 'one of the most striking achievements of the Conservative years' (Moran 1999: 201). The Labour government which took office in 1997 inherited levels of poverty and inequality unprecedented in post-war history.

However, New Labour had learned the lesson that socialism in a capitalist economy meant life in opposition. If the capitalist interests at home and abroad needed a sign, the government gave it in pledging to stick to the Conservatives' spending targets for the next two years. The party claimed it had made a new pact with the people; for critics it was a Faustian pact with capital. By the dying days of the regime, with Gordon Brown as prime minister, Britain was reported as being a more unequal country than at any time since modern records began in the early 1960s. Figures from the Department for Work and Pensions revealed that the three years following the 2005 general election saw the incomes of the poor falling while those of the wealthy rose (Elliott and Curtis 2009). Under the 2010 coalition, in the midst of a monumental sovereign debt crisis, with the economy suffering negligible growth, public spending cuts, wage cuts and rising unemployment, an October 2011 report by Incomes Data Services into the remuneration of directors of FTSE 100 companies (covering salary, benefits and bonuses) revealed a 49 per cent increase, and an average income of £2.7 million per annum. Chief executives were receiving £3.8 million. Union leaders called for reforms. The social divide depicted as the 30/30/40 society by economist Will Hutton in 1996 was still very much in evidence (see p. 209).

This is another shining example of how the elite greedy pigs who run our top companies behave.
Paul Kenny (general secretary of the GMB union) on directors' remuneration packages, quoted in the *Yorkshire Post* (28 Oct. 2011)

What of government policies? Nothing represents communal welfare so clearly as public health, yet with powerful lobbies associated with areas as varied as agriculture, convenience foods, tobacco, drugs manufacture and the environment, many issues have arisen (egg production, railways neglect, pesticide use, pollution, road congestion and tobacco advertising) in which governments have appeared slow to defend the public interest. The case of BSE placed the issue in sharp focus. Evidence presented to the inquiry in April 1998 showed that regulations to prevent the catastrophe could have been put in place in the mid-1970s but had been thwarted by lobbying from rendering firms (*Guardian*, 30 April 1998). The Southwood Committee set up to investigate refrained from recommending a ban on the use of cattle offal in food, not for scientific reasons but because they felt politically it was a 'no-goer' with the Ministry for Agriculture, Fisheries and Food (Winter 1996: 163). In broader terms, governments have tended to respond to the City preference for short-term dividends and capital gains, free international capital flows, stable exchange rates and tight monetary controls.

In the shadowy world of power, policy is made in many ways. Government is but one player within a complex network. Sometimes mass opinion can sway a government, sometimes election promises are honoured, sometimes pluralistic bargaining takes place. Feminists and environmentalists, for example, have certainly secured victories. However, the argument that the most important areas are under elite domination (as C. Wright Mills concluded for the USA) is compelling. The pattern of economic power moulds the space in which politics is enacted. The struggles of those representing the poor and underprivileged resemble that of Sisyphus, whose mythological torment is forever to push a great boulder to the top of a hill, from which it will invariably roll down again.

Key points

- The process of making government policy involves many actors beyond the formal institutions of government.

- The politics of influence takes place behind the formal scenery of the constitution; it is largely the domain of organized interests which form pressure groups.

- Promotional groups advance broad principles while sectional groups protect their members.

- Groups have bargaining counters in the form of resources that governments need.

- Points of access to the political system include public opinion, Parliament, political parties, the executive, the bureaucracy and the institutions of the EU.

- Not all groups enjoy equal access to the state institutions.

- Two principal theories explaining group politics are pluralism and corporatism, although there are a number of variants of each.

- Elitists and Marxists look for even deeper sources of power within the polity.

- The question 'who gets what, when, how?' can help us trace the location of power in society.

Review your understanding of the following terms and concepts

corporatism	outsider group	promotional group
determinism	pluralism	ruling class
elitism	pluralist stagnation	sectional group
insider group	policy community	structural power
instrumental power	policy network	sub-government
interest aggregation	polyarchy	voluntarism
interest group	pressure group	

Questions for discussion and debate

Consider these propositions and be prepared to present the cases for and against. Try to produce debating propositions of your own.

1 Pressure groups rather than government institutions are the real makers of public policy.

2 Pressure groups are a natural part of the liberal-democratic state.

3 Loud public campaigns reveal impotence rather than strength.

4 Governments should not be neutral referees in a society of competing interests.

5 Pressure groups are 'serpents that strangle efficient government'.

6 Pluralism allows that 'might is right'.

7 Public policy is made by a small elite.

8 Under capitalism, government is but 'a committee for managing the affairs of the bourgeoisie'.

9 All theories of political power conclude that democratic governments are essentially weak.

10 Direct action is the most effective means of political participation for ordinary people today.

Further reading

Baggott, R. (1995) *Pressure Groups Today.*
A clearly written introductory text.

Bentley, A. E. (1967) *The Process of Government* (first published 1908).
Classic text on the group approach.

Bottomore, T. (1964) *Elites in Society.*
Still a good introduction to elite theory.

Dorling, D. (2011) *Injustice: Why Social Inequality Persists.*
A sustained critique of elitism within Britain.

Grant, W. (1995) *Pressure Groups, Politics and Democracy,* 2nd edn.
A comprehensive introduction, including group activity at the EU level.

Hilton, M., McKay, J., Crowson, N. and Mouhot, J. (2013) *The Politics of Expertise: How NGOs Shaped Modern Britain.*
Argues that leaders of cause groups have become skilful operators in modern politics, using expertise to influence government and changing the nature of grassroots activism.

Hobson, D. (1999) *The National Wealth: Who Gets What in Britain.*
A *tour de force* exploring the relationship between money, status and power from the Norman Conquest to New Labour.

Jordan, G. (1991) *The Commercial Lobbyists: Politics for Profit in Britain.*
Authoritative account of the rise of professional lobbying.

Lehmbruch, G. and Schmitter, P. (eds) (1982) *Patterns of Corporatist Policy-Making.*
Comparative insight with some seminal contributions.

Mazey, S. and Richardson, J. (1993) *Lobbying in the European Community.*
Examines the new access point for pressure-group activity.

Miliband, R. (1984) *Capitalist Democracy in Britain.*
A classic neomarxist perspective on power in society.

Murray, G. and Scott, J. (eds) (2012) *Financial Elites and Transnational Business: Who Rules the World?*
Team of writers places the issue of elitism in a global context.

Norton, P. (ed.) (1999) *Parliaments and Pressure Groups in Western Europe.*
International team of scholars examines the effect on parliaments of their interactions with pressure groups.

Olson, M. (1982) *The Rise and Decline of Nations.*
The politics of influence from a public choice theorist. Argues social stability leads to the emergence of powerful special-interest lobbies

Sampson, A. (2004) *Who Runs this Place?*
Argues that while political institutions appear to embrace drastic reforms, they merely build facades behind which the real rulers wield power.

Scott, J. (1991) *Who Rules Britain?*
Asks if there is still a ruling class in Britain. Traces industrial and financial dynasties and answers 'Yes'.

Scott, J. (1997) *Corporate Business and Capitalist Classes.*
Focuses on the issues of ownership, control and class formation under capitalism.

Watts, D. (2007) *Pressure Groups.*
Insights into British pressure groups in the European Union and the devolved legislatures.

For reading around the subject and some light relief

Ben Elton, *Gridlock.*
Comic novel about the nightmarish power of the roads lobby.

Chris Mullin, *A Very British Coup* (also a TV drama).
Written by outspoken MP. Working class, left-wing Labour leader is elected prime minister only to be discredited by newspaper magnate with allies within British civil service and MI5. (Pure fantasy of course.)

Jeremy Paxman, *Friends in High Places.*
Britain's most acerbic inquisitor of the high and mighty.

Frederic Raphael, *The Glittering Prizes.*
A nostalgic view of a privileged world where success comes as of right to scions of the Establishment.

George Bernard Shaw, *Major Barbara.*
Explores with humour and insight government–industry relations, exposing greed and hypocrisy.

On the net

http://www.cbi.org.uk
http://www.tuc.org.uk
The sites of the peak organizations representing employers and labour, respectively, in their negotiations with government.

With its anarchic nature, the internet is a natural medium for many thousands of groups, from the mainstream to the more outlandish. Beyond the normal websites, many can be located via Facebook and Twitter. Seek out those that interest you.

http://oneworld.org/home
One World is an international NGO campaigning for global justice and using new media to help the world's poor improve their lives.

http://www.greenpeace.org.uk/
Greenpeace is one of the world's main environmental organizations, willing to take extreme measures in 'saving the world'.

http://www.fathers-4-justice.org/
With its eye-catching stunts, this outsider group appears to be a student favourite.

www.countryside-alliance.org
The Countryside Alliance promotes the interests of country folk (as well as the killing of creatures!).

PART IV

THE OUTER REACHES OF THE STATE: WORLDS BEYOND WHITEHALL

The media construction of British politics is generally centralist in orientation; it is around the precincts of Westminster and Whitehall that the heat of policy-making is generated. However, when we refocus through a wider-angle lens we find certain institutions which, while responsible for much state policy, operate with varying degrees of freedom from the central institutions of government. Chapter 20 reminds us that the United Kingdom has not always been united and from 1997 began to become less so. From 1997 a centrifugal constitutional force began to draw the nations apart, reducing the central hold of Westminster and pointing towards some degree of federalism. There is also a pattern of local government, an area of political life that is actually closer to most people's lives than the world of Westminster that so preoccupies the national mass media. Yet despite the democratic value of local government, we find in Chapter 21 that its freedom from the centre is more questionable than the term 'local' implies. Next we consider the judiciary, where separation from the executive and legislature is a central constitutional requirement: the separation of powers. We must ask how impartial and independent the judges are today. Finally we turn to a part of the state machinery with the dangerous power to use force against its citizens: the police and security services. The distancing of the agencies of law and order from the arm of the politicians is necessary to prevent the emergence of a police state. We find that policing throws up major challenges to the modern state.

CHAPTER 20

TERRITORIAL POLITICS: A DISUNITED KINGDOM?

Contents

The constitution has for long been seen as unitary, binding England, Wales, Scotland and Northern Ireland into a single state under the Westminster Parliament as the United Kingdom. Yet although formally established in 1800 with the parliamentary union of Great Britain and Ireland, this kingdom has become something of a constitutional curate's egg – united only 'in parts'. By 1997 a centrifugal process of gathering momentum was creating a constitution with clearly federal features. Recognition of these territorial movements is essential to an understanding of the dynamics of contemporary British politics. This chapter begins by examining Scotland and Wales where, after chafing against the English bit, their peoples voted in 1997 for devolution. Next we turn to the regions of England which, while undifferentiated in political terms, have their own identities. Finally we examine the territorial struggle which, with extreme violence and bitter enmities, placed UK politics in the world headlines for decades: the vexed question of Northern Ireland.

Unity and Devolution

Political scientists once tended to see the British electorate as essentially homogeneous, divided mainly by class but, as chapter 8 revealed, there are greater complexities in the social fabric. The post-war era saw the reopening of an historic schism, reminding politicians in London that the kingdom, though united, comprised four nations. Elections began to reveal a process of division, with territories pursuing different agendas, sometimes through different political parties. Paradoxically this mood of **separatism** appeared to heighten under a highly centralizing government from 1979.

The so-called British Empire is in reality an English Empire, in which Ireland, Scotland and Wales formed the original colonies.

F. A. Ridley, in *Socialist Leader* (Feb. 1948)

Beyond the ballot box there is an increasingly visible economic divide (figure 20.1). The 1980s and 1990s saw massive deindustrialization in northern England as heavy industry and textiles declined, while the collapse of mining devastated communities around the pits. Post-war economic modernization had narrowed the gap between Western Europe's richer and poorer states, but wide differences in living

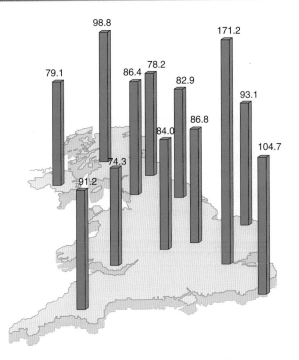

Figure 20.1 National and regional disparities in per capita GDP within the UK, 2009, with the UK average taken as 100

Source: Data from Office for National Statistics, *Statistical Bulletin* (8 Dec. 2010: 4).

standards remained at regional level and these were greatest in the UK. A 1996 study by the economic forecasting organization, the Henley Centre, found per capita income in the south-east to be 20 per cent higher than in the rest of Britain. Those in this favoured garden of England were also likely to be better qualified, to live longer and to do so in larger homes (see Wagstyl 1996). The growing regional divide was compounded by an historical sense of cultural subjugation at the Celtic fringes. These strains on the integrity of the UK were to result in tectonic constitutional shifts in 1998.

For centuries unity was seen by the English political class as essential for security. They needed to capitalize on the insular position provided by nature and remove both the possibility of challenge from within and the establishment of bases for challenge from overseas. Unity was achieved variously by the conquest and political union of the four nations.

Scots, Wha Hae: Scotland

The Scots, unlike the Welsh and Irish, were never forcibly subdued, unity coming politically with the succession of James VI of Scotland to the English throne in 1603. The 1707 Act of Union established a common parliament but protected certain Scottish institutions, including the legal system, the education system, local government and the Presbyterian church. More recently, much public administration came under the Scottish Office at Edinburgh and a secretary of state for Scotland sat in the Cabinet. At Westminster a Scottish Grand Committee examined Scottish issues, but since its composition was supposed to reflect party balance, Scotland's mainly Labour MPs were joined by a leavening of English Conservatives.

A nationalist movement, represented by the Scottish National Party (SNP), was founded in 1928, a Scottish Labour Party was established in 1976, and there was also a separate Scottish press (broadsheet and tabloid). The early 1970s saw a resurgence of nationalism with the discovery of North Sea oil. Seen by the government as a UK asset, many Scots believed the revenues rightfully belonged to Scotland. In 1974 the SNP won eleven seats in the Westminster Parliament with 30 per cent of the Scottish vote. The Labour government held a referendum on **devolution** in 1979 but, when voters shuffled to the polls amidst snow and hail, the hurdle of 40 per cent of the eligible electorate saying 'Yes' proved too high. Under Heath the Conservatives had supported devolution but Thatcher returned to hard-line unionism, which Major maintained. Yet ironically, it was Thatcher's poll tax, visited upon Scotland one year earlier than England, that hardened support for a break from Westminster.

Within two months of taking office in 1997 the Labour government had published white papers on devolution to a Scottish parliament and a Welsh assembly (Senedd). Arousing unprecedented interest, *Scotland's Parliament* sold 500 copies within two hours of going on sale at one Glasgow bookshop (Webster and Bowditch 1997). This foreshadowed the biggest change in the link to the rest of Britain for nearly 300 years.

'Yes, Yes'

The referendum combined two questions: one on a parliament and one on tax–varying powers. On 11 September 1997 (the 700th anniversary of William Wallace's victory over the English at the Battle of Stirling Bridge) the Scots voted decisively 'Yes, Yes'.

The Parliament

The Scottish Parliament in Edinburgh gained primary legislative powers in all areas previously administered by the Scottish Office and a right to vary the basic

Devolution in action: the chamber of the Scottish Parliament

level of income tax by up to 3p. Matters reserved for Westminster under the devolution settlement included foreign policy, defence, central economic affairs, social security and the constitution (in theory preventing Scotland from granting itself independence). The Scottish Executive (effectively the Cabinet) is headed by a First Minister.

The 'new politics' of coalition

In its willingness to adopt partial proportional representation (PR), in the form of the additional member (d'Hondt) system (see p. 285) to elect the 129 Members of the Scottish Parliament (MSPs), Labour sacrificed its historic advantage in Scotland. Under first-past-the-post it would have gained a comfortable overall majority, with the Liberal Democrats as the main opposition and the Conservatives entirely wiped out. Labour claimed high motives for its decision, but it was anticipated that the system had the added advantage of making it unlikely that the SNP would ever gain power on its own, should the political sands shift that way. The Liberal Democrats were naturally happy with a system that promised them a taste of power; following

Table 20.1 The first Scottish Parliament election results, 1999 (no. of MSPs)			
Party	**Constituency**	**List**	**Total**
Labour	53	3	56
SNP	7	28	35
Conservative	0	18	18
Liberal Democrat	12	5	17
Scottish Socialist	0	1	1
Green	0	1	1
Independent Labour	1	0	1
TOTAL	73	56	129

the 1999 election (table 20.1), they found themselves in a coalition with Labour. Scottish Labour leader Donald Dewar, who became First Minister with Liberal Democrat leader Jim Wallace as his deputy, welcomed this as the 'new politics' promised by devolution.

Life had changed for the SNP. From being a small but effective guerrilla band at Westminster, its members were required to become a serious opposition. However, the party's *raison d'être* was constitutional rather than day-to-day policy and it initially appeared ineffectual (Bradbury and Mitchell 2001: 261). Under the coalition, the Scottish Parliament began to find its voice. The Liberal Democrats gained a compromise over the abolition of student fees and in January 2001 they again cheered and punched air as Scottish Labour conceded free universal personal care for the elderly.

From devolution to independence?

In 2009 Lord Calman's Commission on Scottish Devolution delivered a largely positive assessment of a decade of devolved government north of the border:

> The first conclusion we have reached is that devolution has been a real success. The last 10 years have shown that not only is it possible to have a Scottish Parliament inside the UK, but that it works well in practice. . . . The Scottish Parliament has embedded itself in both the constitution of the United Kingdom and the consciousness of Scottish people. It is here to stay. (Commission on Scottish Devolution 2009)

Though problems remained – not least issues of representation articulated in the West Lothian question and inequalities in public funding arising under the Barnett Formula – it was clear that devolution had permeated Scottish political culture.

The West Lothian question

A devolution conundrum was first raised by MP Tam Dalyell when representing that constituency: should Scottish MPs at Westminster be permitted to debate policy for England, while English MPs are excluded from the Scottish Parliament? Again, should Scotland maintain its existing over-representation at Westminster? This was a sobering question for Labour, since without its tartan contingent its Westminster ranks would be depleted. Although there were no proposals to modify the role of Scottish MPs at Westminster, the Scotland Act promised to end their over-representation. The boundary review which came into force ahead of the 2005 general election reduced the number of Scottish MPs at Westminster from 72 to 59.

Although Calman's recommendations were relatively modest – focusing largely on devolving control of some indirect taxes and offering the Scottish Parliament the opportunity to legislate in reserved areas with the consent of the UK Parliament – they were broadly welcomed by the main parties at Westminster.

The Barnett Formula

Introduced in 1978, the Barnett Formula sought to ensure that any change in expenditure in one of the nations that comprise the UK should have a knock-on effect for the others, in proportion to their respective populations. Whilst this mechanism should, in time, bring per capita public central government funding in the various nations into line (the so-called 'Barnett Squeeze'), significant disparities remain (see Table 20.2). Crucially, Scotland is said to benefit by receiving funds in respect of services that the Scottish Parliament has chosen not to finance through its own taxation.

Table 20.2 Index of per capita public funding, 2001–2009 (UK average = 100)

Year	England	Wales	Scotland	N. Ireland
2001–2	96	112	119	132
2002–3	96	113	118	133
2003–4	97	113	117	126
2004–5	97	111	114	126
2005–6	97	111	117	124
2006–7	97	112	118	123
2007–8	97	111	118	125
2008–9	97	111	116	122

Source: Data from House of Lords Select Committee on the Barnett Formula (2009: 16).

What few commentators would have anticipated at the time, however, was that the additional member system, adopted with the express purpose of preventing single-party majority government, would deliver that very thing in 2011 and, moreover, that the SNP, a party committed to full independence for Scotland, would be the beneficiary, with leader Alex Salmond becoming first minister. The dramatic outcome was that, in January 2012, the Scottish government announced its intention to hold a referendum in the autumn of 2014 asking the question 'Should Scotland be an independent country?' Alex Salmond signed an agreement with David Cameron to establish the legal framework for the move and it was formally announced that the historic vote would take place on 18 September 2014.

Hen Wlad Fy Nhadau: Wales

Wales was yoked to England in 1282 following its conquest by Edward I. The Tudors consolidated this subjugation, banning the Welsh language in administration. Industrialization assisted the colonizing impact, with massive English immigration into the South Wales coalfields and steelworks, leaving north and mid-Wales as custodians of the remnants of a national culture. The principality was brought under the English legal, health and education systems, the domination underlined when the 1870 Education Act banned the Welsh language for teaching in the newly emerging state schools.

Plaid Cymru (literally, the Party of Wales) was founded in 1925 to preserve the Welsh cultural heritage but discontent led to more overtly political ambitions and a call for self-government. Campaigning led the Labour government to hold a referendum in 1979 but, with deep English penetration, many non-Welsh speakers feared second-class citizenship in an independent Wales; devolution was decisively rejected. Some distinctiveness was provided for the principality through a Welsh Secretary of State, a Welsh Office (a Whitehall outpost at Cardiff), a Welsh Grand Committee of Welsh MPs and a Select Committee on Welsh Affairs at Westminster. However, Conservative MPs were always heavily outnumbered in Wales (disappearing completely in 1997) and under a Conservative government a quangocracy of Conservative placemen and a succession of (English) Welsh secretaries prompted a renewed desire for independence. Other factors added to disenchantment. With 43 per cent of the population working in the public sector, Thatcher's privatization agenda hit Wales disproportionately, while the Welsh Development Agency's success in attracting inward investment from the EU and beyond suggested possibilities of an independent existence within a global context (see Jones 1997).

Upon returning to office in 1997, Labour's white paper promised *A Voice for Wales*. A referendum on Thursday 18 September 1997 provided one of the most nerve-wracking electoral outcomes of modern politics. In the small hours of Friday morning Wales's 'No' voters might have felt they could retire contentedly to bed with the might of Cardiff, the principality's capital, declaring against a Welsh assembly. However, in the final minutes came the voice of Carmarthenshire in south-west Wales, shifting the mathematical sands to a timid 'Yes'. Yet despite the slender margin, the swing from 1979 of 30 per cent was greater than in Scotland and the government acted as if the result were unequivocal.

The Senedd

Comprising sixty members elected by AMS, the National Assembly for Wales, the Senedd, assumed the responsibilities of the Secretary of State for Wales, though certain areas (foreign affairs, defence, social security and macroeconomic policy) were reserved for Westminster. It is led by an Executive Committee comprising the leaders of a range of subject committees and chaired by a First Minister, elected by the Senedd. The committees were given prominence, with a policy-deliberation role as well as the more traditional one of scrutinizing the executive. With no ability to vary tax or pass primary legislation, the Senedd's powers fell well below those of the Scottish Parliament. However, it inherited a substantial budget (£7 billion in 1997), and was expected to derive some influence through implementing Westminster legislation.

As the main architect of Welsh devolution, the decision of Labour Welsh Secretary Ron Davies to follow the Scots with PR (against the wishes of the Welsh Labour Party) was partly to appease the Liberal Democrats and Plaid Cymru. Acrimony over central interference led many to abstain or switch parties, with the result that, in a territory where it had appeared invincible, Labour failed to secure an overall majority (table 20.3). Elected as First Minister, Blairite Alun Michael rebuffed a Liberal Democrat coalition offer, choosing to establish a minority administration. Presiding over an all-Labour Executive Committee with an even gender balance, he managed to govern by striking judicious deals with the opposition parties. Yet his tendency to ignore local opinion led critics to view him as a Welsh Secretary from

Table 20.3 The first Senedd election results, 1999

Party	Constituency	List	Total
Labour	27	1	28
Plaid Cymru	9	8	17
Conservative	1	8	9
Liberal Democrat	3	3	6
TOTAL	40	20	60

London: a no-confidence vote forced his resignation in February 2000 and he was replaced by the more charismatic Rhodri Morgan.

Marriage of convenience: coalition politics

Morgan opted for a formal coalition with the Liberal Democrats, judging that the vote-by-vote process needed by the minority administration made long-term planning impossible. Many Labour and Liberal Democrat members were unhappy about this marriage of convenience. Initially marginalized, Plaid Cymru and the Conservatives waited for the fault lines in the coalition to show. Plaid ultimately entered coalition with Labour in the wake of the 2007 Assembly elections, where the party was placed second in terms of seats won (fifteeen). This coalition survived until the 2011 elections, in which Labour secured enough seats to allow a return to single-party government.

Although in principle opposing any dilution of the union, the Conservatives had come round to a pragmatic acceptance under William Hague, but Welsh political elites remained unenthusiastic. Plaid Cymru looked to complete independence in the context of Europe, while the Liberal Democrats had consistently argued for tax-varying powers similar to those held by the Scottish Parliament.

The impact of devolution on life in Wales was something of a 'slow-burn'. Ordinary people could see little change in their day-to-day lives. Though the positions on university top-up fees and prescription charges provoked considerable coverage in the mainstream press, the Senedd was still seeking its role and cast envious eyes on the powers of its Scottish counterpart.

Towards parity with Scotland?

Increasing support for devolution resulted in a number of significant changes by 2011, many of which drew on the findings of the 2004 Richard Commission. First, the 2006 Government of Wales Act created a Welsh Assembly Government, an executive body distinct from the National Assembly (the legislature). Though many commentators saw this as an essentially symbolic act, it served to create an institutional structure in Wales that at least appeared to mirror that in Scotland.

Secondly, and perhaps of greater note, a referendum in March 2011 led to the Assembly assuming primary legislative powers over a range of areas where it had previously enjoyed only secondary legislative (or administrative) authority. Although the 35 per cent turnout led some to question the result, the margin of victory (with 64 per cent voting 'Yes') provided a far clearer mandate for reform than that provided by the 1997 devolution referendum.

A Forgotten Nation: English Regionalism

For the English, the conflict of citizenship within a multinational state goes largely unfelt; indeed, 'English' and 'British' are often taken as synonymous. While Whitehall has practised administrative decentralization and governments have created many ad hoc regional bodies to provide services such as gas, water and health care, calls for regional government have evoked little popular enthusiasm. However, Labour had appeared interested in reform and legislation in 1998 empowered the Secretary of State for the Environment, Transport and the Regions to establish Regional Development Agencies (RDAs) and designate voluntary regional chambers, comprising representatives of local authorities and other interests, to which they would be accountable. Local people would be given the opportunity to make the chambers directly elected after a further general election.

An additional impetus for **regionalism** came from the EU social and economic programmes and the Maastricht Treaty made provision for an advisory Committee of the Regions. The Association of County Councils argued that regional groupings of local authorities increased their effectiveness in preparing EU funding bids. Many authorities combined regionally or sub-regionally, even forging continental partnerships. Some formed regional consortia with industry and labour organizations, the northern region making the earliest advances. However, without genuine regional government, England could be seen to be at a disadvantage within the EU. Wales and Scotland had already established Brussels offices for lobbying purposes, while the EU had bases in Belfast, Cardiff and Edinburgh.

In 2002 a white paper, *Your Region, Your Choice*, proposed creating new regional elected assemblies of 25–35 members to which the existing RDAs would be accountable. Largely funded by a central government grant, they would be able to raise additional revenue through the council tax. Campaigners were optimistic but public support was uneven. A BBC poll in March 2002 showed that the main support was confined to the West Midlands, the north-east, the north-west and Yorkshire and Humberside. Moreover, almost half those polled believed that the assemblies would be 'a talking shop for politicians and a waste of money'. Another dampener came from regional business communities, fearing control over economic strategy being transferred into the hands of laymen. Hence, in sharp contrast to the purpose and speed with which devolution was rolled out in Scotland and Wales, New Labour's ambitions for elected regional assemblies in England collapsed. The plan to hold a series of regional referendums was shelved after voters in the first of these, held in the north-east in 2004, delivered a decisive 'No'.

An English question?

However, while there was little support for regionalism, some voices began to call for 'English devolution', with the creation of an English Parliament with 'English votes for English laws'. Such feelings were prompted by perceived inequalities in services that resulted from devolution (such as prescription charges and university top-up fees). Perhaps England needed to find its own political voice. An 'English Question' could be said to be emerging and devolution could not be complete, or the settlement stable, until this had been addressed. The English might not remain content with no separate representation or political voice (see Hazell 2006). Yet initially there appeared little public demand for the creation of yet another tier of government (see Ormston and Curtice 2010). Only in Cornwall, with Mebyon Kernow, a Cornish separatist movement campaigning for self-government and boasting a flag and a language, did there appear to be a chance of a meaningful transfer of power.

A Terrible Beauty: Northern Ireland

With its grim chronology of violence, Ireland has mocked claims to unity. The problem of Northern Ireland has seemed an incomprehensible religious conflict, explained in terms of the 'hot-headedness' of the red-headed men, disdainfully contrasted with the secular rationality of the English, who have long avoided religious war. This is wrong; the problem is a cocktail of racism, apartheid, imperialism, class domination, violent resistance and brooding memories of ancestral cruelty and injustice – it is a political issue. Perhaps more than any other, the Irish problem has roots deeply embedded in a long and bitter history.

The seeds of discontent

Thus you have a starving population, an absentee aristocracy, and an alien Church, and in addition the weakest executive in the world. That is the Irish Question.
Benjamin Disraeli (Conservative leader), Commons speech (16 Feb. 1844)

Although uncomfortably close to England, Ireland remained stubbornly separated by the Irish Sea, hindering English domination. Conquest was finally completed by the Tudors, though the Irish, like the aborigines of the New World, resented subjugation on their own soil. In the English civil wars they saw their chance by favouring the Royalist cause but in the aftermath incurred terrible English wrath in the form of re-conquest, first by Cromwell and later by the Protestant William of Orange (in the famous Battle of the Boyne in 1690). Relegated to the status of second-class citizens in their own country, Irish Catholics were barred from state office and the professions, denied landownership rights and forced to live in a squalor unparalleled in Europe. Land in the south was confiscated by the English, who remained comfortably at home as absentee landlords, extracting crippling rents. In the north, where resistance was fiercer, domination required settler colonization. A Scottish Presbyterian landowning class emerged around Belfast, ruling the natives and dependent upon English mainland support. Rebellions were put down with extreme severity, the troops given full licence to torture, maim and kill. The Catholics rose in 1798 only to be cut down in the battle of Vinegar Hill. The Act of Union of 1800, in which the Irish parliament was swallowed up by Westminster, was adorned with manacles rather than wedding rings.

The industrial revolution reinforced the division. In the north the Protestants shared in English prosperity while subjugating the Catholics. In contrast, the south was excluded from the process of industrialization; it was more useful as a granary to feed workers on the mainland, even when the Irish were themselves starving. The suffering was compounded in 1845 and 1846 when a serious potato blight removed the means of sustenance for some four million people. England did little to help, around a million people died and over two million crossed the Atlantic, taking with them a cargo of festering resentment.

The Home Rule Bills

For most Irish people, the concept of a United Kingdom was farcical, a fact realized in his later years by the great Liberal politician W. E. Gladstone, who determined with some fervour to right what he saw as wrong (Bentley 1984: 245). His first Home Rule Bill of 1886 was defeated in the Commons and his second fell in the House of Lords in 1893. Events surrounding a third bill were dramatic, revealing naked class hatred. Although the Liberals had become convinced home-rulers, there were other matters to occupy them when they returned to government in 1906, including bitter battles with the suffragettes and the House of Lords. Losing their overall majority in 1910, they became dependent upon support from Irish MPs, and to win this Prime Minister Asquith pledged himself to another Home Rule Bill. Although this passed through the Commons in 1912, the Conservatives regarded Irish MPs as inferior in status and not entitled to vote on constitutional issues (Cross 1963: 123–4). It became apparent that they considered themselves, and the class they represented, to be above the constitution. As Conservative opposition leader Balfour had declared in 1906: 'The great Unionist party should still control, whether in power or whether in opposition, the destinies of this great Empire' (Blake 1985: 190). In the Lords the Conservatives defeated the bill, thereby delaying it until 1914. This allowed the Protestants of the north to arm as the Ulster Volunteers under the fanatical leadership of Edward Carson, while Conservatives on the mainland contemplated a *coup d'état*. Conservative leader Bonar Law (himself of Ulster descent) told a crowd outside Blenheim Palace:

There are things stronger than parliamentary majorities . . . I can imagine no length of resistance to which Ulster can go in which I should not be prepared to support them. (Cross 1963: 177)

The Easter Rising

> I have passed with a nod of the head
> Or polite meaningless words . . .
> All changed, changed utterly:
> A terrible beauty is born.
>
>   W. B. Yeats (1865–1939; Irish poet), 'Easter, 1916'

The impending holocaust was eclipsed in June 1914 by the assassination of Archduke Franz Ferdinand of Austria-Hungary. The bill was passed but placed in cold storage for the duration of the first world war. Yet Irish activists, mistrusting the English, sought German help and, on Easter Sunday 1916, declared a republic. This was put down harshly, the English toasting their triumph with the blood of martyrs through executions and imprisonments. Roger Casement, a British consul in Germany who had enlisted enemy assistance, was hanged for high treason and his standing undermined by the circulation of diaries revealing his homosexuality.

In the post-war general election Sinn Féin (the republican party) gained an overwhelming victory in Ireland and those elected refused to enter Westminster, establishing an independent Irish parliament at Dublin, the Dáil. Renewing the republic of Easter 1916, they appointed a president, Eamon de Valera, and government. At the same time an Irish Republican Army (IRA) formed under Michael Collins, to which the British responded in 1920 with measures that Asquith said 'would disgrace the blackest annals of the lowest despotism in Europe' (Taylor 1965: 155). The infamous Black and Tans, chosen for their penchant for violence, were recruited to assist the Royal Ulster Constabulary (RUC) in a reign of terror.

Partition

After much tortuous negotiation, Prime Minister Lloyd George and the Irish politicians signed a compromise treaty based on **partition** on 6 December 1921, giving birth to the Irish Free State (Eire). The twenty-six counties of the south received dominion status on the Canadian model and six of the nine counties of Ulster remained as a UK province, with an elected bicameral assembly (at Stormont) and an executive exercising certain devolved powers. The fact that Ulster had far more autonomy than Wales or Scotland reflected hopes that it would eventually decide to reunite under Dublin. The arrangement was to leave the Ulster Catholics as second-class citizens, living in ghettos in the poorest housing, doing the most unpleasant jobs and receiving the worst education. Between 1920 and 1922 'ethnic cleansing' took place on an epic scale; Catholic relief agencies estimated that some 23,000 Catholics were driven out of Belfast alone (Hennessy 1997: 11). Constituency boundaries were also gerrymandered to ensure Protestant dominance. For the south, the 'solution' had come not as a result of statesmanship but through violence and bloodshed, leaving a fermenting sense of grievance; 1949 saw Eire's departure from the Commonwealth.

Belfast from the 1960s: the killing streets

Although the settlement contained the germs of further violence, the Irish question ceased to be a scourge of British politicians as republicanism gave way to a less confrontational nationalism. However, economic decline was to fan the embers of discontent in the north. With heavy dependence on industries in irrevocable decline (shipbuilding and textiles) producing unemployment higher than in the rest of the UK, Prime Minister Terence O'Neill attempted to attract new industries and sought closer involvement with the south.

As a new generation of Catholics grew into political awareness, inspired by the international civil rights movements of the 1960s, the Protestants became alarmed and a reaction set in, partly under the demagogic influence of the Reverend Ian Paisley. The B-Specials, an auxiliary unit of the RUC, attacked civil rights demonstrators, leading to a retaliatory rejuvenation of the IRA, which had effectively disarmed. Again the politics of Northern Ireland was to open as a running sore on the British body politic. The divisions were not only reflected in ideological battles, they were overlain with the machinery of violence and death. Rather than conventional parties, the participants were religious groupings with constitutional aspirations and sometimes paramilitary connections. With marches and violence, their politics were often of the street rather than the debating chamber.

The two leading Protestant/unionist parties were the Official Unionists and Paisley's more working-class and fundamentalist Democratic Unionist Party (DUP). They also mobilized through organizations such as the Orange Order and the Apprentice Boys of Derry, engaging in political symbolism through provocative parades and marches. Protestant paramilitary organizations included the Ulster Volunteers, splintering into the Ulster Defence Association and the Ulster Freedom Force. In addition, the RUC was Protestant dominated and itself used unusual and extremely violent methods. The Catholic/nationalist cause was represented by the Social Democratic and Labour Party (SDLP), favouring constitutional methods, and Sinn Féin (the political wing of the IRA). The IRA splintered from the 1970s, into the more extreme Irish National Liberation Army (INLA), the Provisional IRA, and latterly the Real IRA.

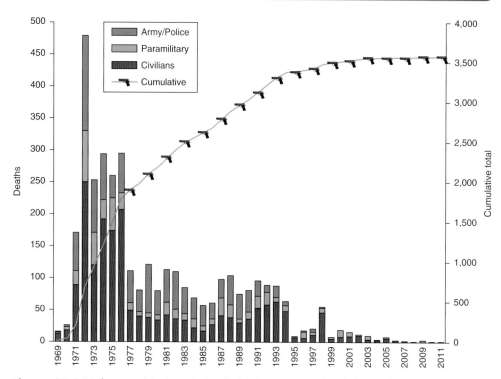

Figure 20.2 Violence in Northern Ireland: deaths associated with the civil disturbances, 1969–2011

Source: Data from the CAIN project website (http://cain.ulst.ac.uk).

What a God-awful country. Get me a whisky and soda.
Reginald Maudling (Home Secretary, 1970–2) to an official upon his return from a visit to Belfast

In this ferment non-sectarian politics had little place and the mainland parties did not seek a serious presence. However, the Ulster Unionists had historic links with the Conservatives, generally supporting them at Westminster. In 1970 a non-sectarian Alliance Party formed, with links with the Social Democrats, though its broad position was to maintain the mainland connection. A new player entered the game in 1969 when, following a request from the RUC, backed by militant civil rights leader Bernadette Devlin (Hattersley 1996: 77), the British government took the fateful decision to send in the army to restore the peace. From initially welcoming the move, Catholics were to develop a feeling of menacing harassment and the pattern of violence began an unremitting escalation (see figure 20.2).

Developments were to see the powers of state repression increase, hardening Catholic and world sympathy for the IRA. Internment without trial was introduced in August 1971 and on 20 January 1972 British troops fired on civil rights demonstrators, leaving thirteen dead. Television brought the violence into living rooms on the mainland, entering the inventory of grim anniversaries as 'Bloody Sunday'. In March 1972 the Heath government assumed *direct rule* over the province. The gerrymandered constituencies had meant that Stormont remained under an indelible Protestant majority, offering no voice to the Catholics. It was suspended and a Northern Ireland Office was created under a secretary of state, a poisoned chalice for any British politician. In 1974 the violence arrived on the mainland with devastating bombing in pubs in Guildford and Birmingham. In response the Prevention of Terrorism Act was rushed through Parliament, outlawing the IRA and further extending police powers. Special (Diplock) courts were created in Ulster which dispensed with juries to avoid their intimidation. To add to the tension harsh treatment of prisoners was to be condemned by the European Court of Human Rights.

Evidence that the RUC had adopted a 'shoot-to-kill' policy in 1982 occasioned the notorious Stalker affair, in which a British police officer heading an inquiry into the matter was impeded in his investigations, subjected to character assassination and suspended from duty in May 1986, just days before he was to travel to Belfast to interview RUC chief Sir John Hermon. In 1984, an IRA bomb exploded in the Brighton hotel housing leading members of the Conservative Party (including Margaret Thatcher) attending their annual conference. As the violence escalated, the feared British SAS became involved, shooting eight IRA men and a civilian at Loughall, County Tyrone, in 1987 and, on 6 March 1988, to an echo of excited public celebrity, gunning down three alleged would-be bombers in Gibraltar. No bomb was ever found and the European Court of Human Rights ruled that unreasonable force had been used, a judgment seen by Downing Street as 'defying common sense' (*The Times*, 28 Sept. 1995).

Seeking a political solution

Paradoxically, although wanting to end the bloodshed, British governments refused to talk; Sinn Féin remained a pariah party. Ministers empowered themselves to exclude named individuals from the mainland, including the party's leader Gerry Adams. In 1988 its access to the British media was denied (though broadcasters made a mockery of this by using actors to speak their words).

Clearly any return to the Stormont model, with gerrymandered constituencies and no voice for the Catholic minority, could not work. Moreover, the shifting demographic sands had seen, during the 1980s and 1990s, a steady rise in the nationalist vote, reflecting an increase in the Catholic population. UK governments recognized the need to break the stranglehold with some form of **consociationalism** (see O'Leary 1989) and a **power-sharing executive** permitting Catholic involvement.

The Anglo-Irish Agreement

An alternative political solution was seen in a forum that would permit the Irish Republic some involvement in Ulster's affairs. This was attempted in the

I can only say that it would turn my stomach.
Prime Minister John Major, House of Commons (1 Nov. 1993), in response to suggestion by left-wing MP Dennis Skinner that the government talk with Gerry Adams and the Provisional IRA

Anglo-Irish Agreement, signed in November 1985 by Thatcher and Irish premier Dr Garret FitzGerald. To Unionists, this was the thin end of a republican wedge. Paradoxically, Sinn Féin opposed the Agreement on the grounds that it condoned partition.

The Downing Street Declaration

With the departure of Thatcher the Anglo-Irish Agreement was suspended and fresh talks initiated. These proceeded uneasily, but in 1993 John Major and Irish prime minister Albert Reynolds signed the historic Downing Street Declaration, asserting the right of the peoples of north and south to unite should they ever so wish, and denying any British government strategic interest in Northern Ireland. Most controversially, it offered a place at the negotiating table to Sinn Féin on the condition that it renounce violence. An IRA ceasefire was declared on 31 August 1994 and Protestant paramilitaries responded with a similar renunciation. A changing climate was apparent when it was revealed that secret talks had been taking place between the British government and the IRA. In February 1995 a Framework Document outlined a consociational democracy (see Lijphart 1996). This entailed an assembly elected by PR exercising devolved powers, **cross-border bodies** to consider joint issues such as tourism, and the involvement of all parties in both north and south, including Sinn Féin. Popular support would be ascertained through a referendum.

Unionists remained suspicious, and a series of disastrous by-elections left Major's government increasingly dependent upon their support in Westminster. He began holding up progress by demanding that the IRA hand in its weapons – a gesture of surrender. A stalemate developed that continued until 7.01 p.m. on 18 February 1996, when the seventeen-month ceasefire came to an end as a bomb rocked London's Docklands. A widespread pattern of IRA bombs and bomb scares in the run-up to the 1997 general election left Major with no peace memorial.

The Good Friday Agreement

Tony Blair's first official journey as prime minister was to Ulster, where he declared that 'the settlement train would leave with or without Sinn Féin', who were invited into renewed talks, subject to a ceasefire (*Financial Times*, 26 June 1997). He pledged to put new proposals to the people in a referendum. There would be negotiations on decommissioning weapons and a Parades Commission to regulate marches. In the summer of 1997, a number of parades by Protestant Orangemen through Catholic areas were abandoned and Northern Ireland Secretary Mo Mowlam persuaded the IRA to instigate a second ceasefire. Although Ian Paisley denounced it as a 'total surrender', all-party talks began. Mo Mowlam, the first woman to play such a central role, proved exceptionally tenacious, even entering the Maze Prison to talk with convicted terrorists.

> **The violence behind the violence**
> A Catholic teenager frustrated at not being able to go to a Chinese restaurant at the end of his own street in a Protestant area finally cracked and went for a takeaway. He was stabbed in the eye with a screwdriver. One of thousands of sectarian incidents in Northern Ireland remaining unreported amid the greater atrocities; reported in the *Guardian* (11 April 1998).

Another key player entering the stage was US President Bill Clinton. From its initial nationalist sympathies, the USA began to assume the role of an honest broker. Senator George Mitchell, who chaired the peace talks, was a Catholic with Irish grandparents, but he trod carefully through the minefield. In November 1995, Clinton himself visited Belfast and Dublin. After tortuous negotiations, often extending into the small hours, a potentially ground-breaking sixty-seven-page agreement emerged on Good Friday, 10 April 1998. The proposals, to be put to referendums in north and south, included the following:

1. a Northern Ireland Assembly of 108 elected by PR, with legislative powers and a power-sharing executive;
2. a North–South Ministerial Council to consider issues such as cross-border cooperation;
3. the Irish government to renounce constitutional claims to Northern Ireland and Westminster to replace the Government of Ireland Act;
4. a Council of the Isles comprising members from the north and south of Ireland and the Scottish and Welsh assemblies.

There were also to be releases of prisoners coupled with a decommissioning of arms.

The referendums

Tensions mounted in the days before voting, the situation aggravated by the release of terrorists on both sides. However, Blair made the vote a highly personalized affair and opposition party leaders John Major and Paddy Ashdown weighed in to signal cross-party support. At a pop concert featuring Irish band U2 from the south and Ash, a group with Protestant backgrounds from the north, Unionist leader David Trimble (with his teenage daughter) and SDLP leader John Hume symbolically shook hands. The referendums showed resounding support for the Agreement. With the 81 per cent turnout in the north exceeding expectations, 677,000 voted 'Yes' and 275,000 'No'. In constituency terms, seventeen were for and only one against. However, the greatest support was from Catholics, a *Sunday Times*/Coopers and Lybrand exit poll revealing 96 per cent of them voting 'Yes' compared with 55 per cent of Protestants. In the Republic, a turnout of 56 per cent showed 94 per cent support for relinquishing claims to the north.

My daddy's saying yes. But my mummy's a Christian.
Protestant barmaid on the eve of the May 1998 referendum, quoted in the *Sunday Times* (24 May 1998)

Table 20.4 Seats in the Northern Ireland Assembly, June 1998					
Party	**Seats**	**Party**	**Seats**	**Party**	**Seats**
Unionist		**Nationalist**		**Other**	
Ulster Unionist	28	SDLP	24	Alliance	6
DUP	20	Sinn Féin	18	Women's Coalition	2
UK Unionist	5				
Independent Unionist	3				
Popular Unionist	2				

The Assembly

The next vote was the election to the Assembly, taking place by STV in June 1998, in eighteen constituencies. However, the referendum had not succeeded in quelling opposition; Ian Paisley's DUP and the UK Unionists stood only in order to secure enough seats to wreck the Assembly. In the event, some 75 per cent of voters supported a party favouring the Agreement. Fringe parties, including the Women's Coalition, which had campaigned for peace, made some gains (table 20.4). Trimble's Ulster Unionists won a majority and the Unionist dissidents failed to win enough seats to prevent the Assembly electing him as First Minister. His deputy was the Catholic Seamus Mallon. The power-sharing principle ruled out single-party governance. Elected by the Assembly rather than chosen by Trimble, the executive was a coalition of the four main parties: three seats each for the Ulster Unionists and SDLP and two each for Sinn Féin and the DUP. This was a system intended to surmount the almost insurmountable: to forge a consensus amongst politicians more hostile towards each other than would be expected in any system where normal politics prevailed.

Fears that the peace process might unravel were ever-present. The Protestant Orangemen appeared intent upon defying a Parades Commission ban on their march through the Catholic Garvaghy Road. Banner-waving and clad in their bowler hats and regalia, they faced the RUC in military-style riot gear across trenches and barbed wire. The pendulum of violence would swing both ways and in August 1998 twenty-nine people were killed and many more injured by a bomb planted in Omagh by the self-styled Real IRA.

Although devolution eventually came on 1 December 1999, the following years saw the spirit of the Agreement shrouded by atrocities that shocked the world. Negotiations with the body set up to supervise arms decommissioning were protracted and tortuous. In the 2001 UK general election the battle lines appeared to harden as extremists on both sides made gains at Westminster. With his position within his party weakened, in July 2001 Trimble resorted to desperate measures by resigning as First Minister. With the peace process on a knife edge, the British and Irish governments set out a package of measures aiming to deliver the Good Friday Agreement. This identified four outstanding issues:

1. reforming the police in line with recommendations made in the 1999 Patton report;
2. normalizing security arrangements;
3. stabilizing the newly created institutions;
4. decommissioning weapons.

> The leadership of the Ulster Volunteer Force and Red Hand Commandos – in their own time and their own space – will give whatever answer to the question of whether they will or will not reciprocate.
>
> David Ervine of the Progressive Unionists in response to the IRA's 2001 decommissioning offer

Acting under heavy pressure from its political wing and the USA, the IRA finally announced a scheme agreed with the decommissioning body to put weapons 'completely and verifiably beyond use'. Trimble welcomed 'the day we were told would never happen', and the UK government responded swiftly on 'normalization', scaling back on military bases. Yet optimism, never high, was lowered further in October 2002, when police officers raided the Sinn Féin offices at Stormont and homes in north and west Belfast. The object was to seize electronic files in response to suspicions of IRA spying within the Northern Ireland Office. The result was some arrests and the Assembly was suspended for the fourth time since devolution. Although notionally still in office, its members were reduced to spectators in a province effectively being governed directly from Westminster.

Not until October 2006, with the publication of a 'road-map' agreement jointly by the British and Irish governments, did progress seem possible. An historic meeting of the then DUP leader Ian Paisley (hitherto dubbed 'Dr No' in the popular press) and Sinn Féin leader Gerry Adams led to the restoration of power-sharing in May 2007. Although the sight of the two long-time adversaries smiling and apparently relaxed in one another's company in itself represented a seismic shift in the political landscape, the formation of a functioning DUP–Sinn Féin executive was truly ground-breaking. Paisley became First Minister, with the Sinn Féin deputy leader Martin McGuinness, a former IRA commander, taking on the role of Deputy First Minister.

On 28 June 2012, at an arts festival in Belfast's Lyric Theatre, Queen Elizabeth II, in the year of her golden jubilee, met and shook hands with Martin McGuinness. The meeting was described as historic but, with no live footage available to the public and the nearby roads closed and guarded by flak-jacketed police, few could be entirely certain that lasting peace had come. Within days, the media were reporting stone-throwing, fighting and police action in the streets when, on 12 July, in a continuation of the provocative marching practice, republican and unionist marches clashed. Five months later, in December 2012, the decision of Belfast City Council to designate just eighteen days each year when the Union flag would be flown over the City Hall (it had previously been flown every day since the building opened in 1906) provoked a loyalist backlash that persisted for months, with violent protests and bomb threats. In January 2013, the BBC reported that the cost of policing the demonstrations in the first month alone was in excess of £7 million.

Policing the troubles

Policing, a long-standing bone of contention, was also subject to reform. The Protestant-dominated RUC, which had existed since the partition of 1921, had lost over 300 members to terrorist attacks, with thousands more injured. Yet its own tactics since the early 1960s had shown astonishing levels of violence and brutality, occasioning thousands of complaints. In 1999 the Patton report had called for an equal balance of Catholic and Protestant recruits and the renouncing of the force's very name. Some attempt to sugar the pill was made later that year in collectively honouring the force with the George Cross. The symbolic break with the past came on 3 November 2000 when the RUC became the Police Service of Northern Ireland (PSNI – selected in preference to Northern Ireland Police Service for fear of its abbreviation to Nips) and the first recruits, selected on a 50:50 basis, began intensive training. The Police Authority was replaced by a Policing Board, ten members being drawn from the UUP, DUP and the SDLP (Sinn Féin refused to take seats) and the remaining nine, including the chairman, appointed on a non-political basis.

Thereafter, progress on policing Northern Ireland, though slow, was sure, though it was hardly propitious that the new force's first investigation was into an unseemly brawl in Stormont's Great Hall between leading politicians, which marred David Trimble's re-election as First Minister. The PSNI began to recruit more officers from the Catholic community and, in 2010, agreement was reached for the transfer of control from Westminster.

But if the focus remains on the past, the past will become the future, and that is something no one can desire.
Report of the International Decommissioning Body (the Mitchell Commission) (22 Jan. 1996: para. 16)

A time to forget

Optimists hoped that the time had come to forget the troubled past. Yet there was much to forget: deaths of hunger strikers, 'Bloody Sunday', 3,500 lost lives and 40,000 wounded over the previous thirty years (see figure 20.2). One in four of those voting in the 1998 referendum could claim to have known someone who had been

A time to forget? Some 2000 murals have been painted in Northern Ireland to celebrate, commemorate and exasperate

killed. The ancestral voices speak from even greater distance, regularly rekindled by ceremonies and marches to mark bitter anniversaries such as the Battle of the Boyne, the Siege of Londonderry and the Easter Rising.

Quasi-Federalism or a Nation of Nations?

In the days of empire, world dominance forged a British identity and helped unify the kingdom, but with decolonization this cement began to crumble. Hence, an era that had witnessed the end of empire also saw a questioning of the bond between the four nations of the UK, confronting the state with increasingly demanding problems of **territorial management**. The 1997 Labour government (with Liberal Democrat approval) saw the solution in devolution, aiming to preserve the union by releasing a safety valve upon a pent-up nationalistic fervour. The new settlements were intended to offer stability and opportunities for 'new politics' reflecting constructive harmony rather than the adversarial style of Westminster. In contrast, some Conservatives could see in devolution the thin end of a wedge that would ultimately fracture the union.

New Labour's devolution programme in fact saw the UK transformed into something of a half-way house between a unitary state and one that was truly federal. Bogdanor (2009) and others have used the term 'quasi-federalism' to characterize these arrangements, recognizing that whilst the Westminster Parliament remained legally sovereign, possessing the authority to recall devolved powers, the newly created institutions operated with a significant degree of political autonomy in many areas. This quasi-federalism, partially entrenched through the referendums, moved further with the granting of primary legislative powers to Wales.

However, it is inaccurate to simply apply the term 'quasi-federalism' to the overall settlement that emerged as a result of the devolution programme. In reality, we have seen the emergence of a unique 'nation of nations', with both quasi-federal and confederal elements, the latter including the British–Irish Council (Bogdanor 2009: 287).

New politics – dull politics?

Elected by PR, the new assemblies certainly gave more opportunities to minority parties (including the Conservatives, whose numbers had been almost eliminated outside England) and coalition administrations became the norm rather than the exception. In addition, positive discrimination in candidate selection brought in more women (table 20.5). Greater use of committees offered new opportunities for members to be involved in shaping policy. There was even hope that a new ethos would spread to Westminster.

Table 20.5 Gender balance in the Scottish Parliament and Welsh Assembly, 2011

Party	Scottish Parliament		Welsh Assembly	
	Men	Women	Men	Women
Labour	20	17	15	15
Conservative	9	6	10	4
Liberal Democrat	4	1	3	2
SNP	50	18	–	–
Plaid Cymru	–	–	7	4
Green	1	1	0	0
Independent	0	1	0	0
Presiding Officer	0	1	–	–
TOTAL	84	45	35	25

Yet new politics posed new questions. There was the possibility that constructive harmony would exorcize all passion from politics. Rhodri Morgan (2000) himself argued that committee work lacked the sense of theatre that stirred public interest. Indeed, there remained doubts whether assembly members or voters, conditioned by adversarial politics and first-past-the-post, were ready for consensual politics. Coalitions did not end party fighting and often increased tensions within parties, an experience mirrored at Westminster in the wake of an inconclusive 2010 general election. PR also gave more representation to the political extremes including, in the case of Northern Ireland, those who initially appeared to have little desire to see the system work. Here coalition was not optional, it was built into the power-sharing architecture. While the Liberal Democrats and Labour may sometimes have been uncomfortable bedfellows in Scotland and Wales, the four-partner Stormont executive placed a constitutional duvet over a ménage of those who were historically the most bitter of enemies. Debates over questions such as health or education could melt into insignificance beside the passionate issue of the constitutional settlement itself.

Westminster may lack the appetite for an entirely new kind of politics; New Labour formed a centralizing government and devolution was introduced not to weaken the union but to bolster it in the face of burgeoning separatism. The relationship between London and the capitals remained uncertain, with the potential for turf wars. There were still secretaries of state for Wales and Scotland, officials continued to be members of the home civil service and the new assemblies soon found themselves at loggerheads with Westminster (Nicholson 2001).

Federal drift

Federal leanings
Constitutionally, devolution does not of itself mean federalism. It is, by definition, created by the act of a superior body, devolving some of its own powers and responsibilities to a subordinate one; these could be revoked at any time. In a federal system, such as the USA, the centre and regions stand constitutionally equal, with the distribution of powers and responsibilities set out in a written constitution.

Despite its aspirations, the devolution settlements may not represent points of constitutional stability, for in all cases further ambitions remain. For nationalists in Northern Ireland the goal remains a united republic, while many Unionists still crave the *status quo ante*. For the SNP the long-term objective is full independence; Scottish founder of the Adam Smith Institute, Madsen Pirie, anticipated this would occur within a decade of devolution (Groom 1997), a prophecy that may prove wrong only in its timescale. In Wales, where devolution initially offered the most limited gains, there was the more modest aspiration to the same powers as the Scottish Parliament, an outcome achieved, in part, through the 2011 referendum.

Enthusiasm for the union may even wilt in England. During sporting events such as football's World Cup many supporters rediscover the red cross of St George, which is painted on faces, waved in foreign stadiums and flown over English pubs. In addition, there have been renewed calls for an English parliament and devolution to the English regions. Uneven development had seen economic prosperity and political power concentrated in the south-east, leaving much of the country demanding the same kind of self-determination as Wales and Scotland. The centrifugal drift is enhanced by EU membership, which can undermine the role of the nation-state while emphasizing the regions. The presence of several small EU states, including the Irish Republic, makes a separate Scotland and Wales look viable. Moreover, the Good Friday Agreement, in conceding the right of Ulster to secede from the UK, weakens the case for denying the same rights to Wales and Scotland. Chapter 5 revealed the limitations of nation-state autonomy in a globalized economy; this chapter has exposed the challenge from within. Multinational states look increasingly like ill-adapted dinosaurs, vulnerable to legitimacy crises and rising nationalism. In the UK citizens begin to wonder how united the kingdom is and how united it should remain.

Key points

- The UK is a multinational state, a 'nation of nations', vulnerable to legitimacy crises and requiring territorial management.

- The English political class traditionally saw unity of the British Isles as essential for security, accomplishing this by conquest.

- Increasing disenchantment produced nationalist movements in Scotland and Wales, leading to devolution following referendums.

- Three attempts to grant home rule for Ireland proved unsuccessful.

- The compromise of partition established the Irish Free State (Eire) while Ulster remained as a UK province.

- In Ulster the Catholics were treated as second-class citizens.

- The Irish question flared up again in the 1960s, with serious levels of violence and leading to direct rule from Westminster.

- The Good Friday Agreement led to a new assembly exercising devolved powers in 1998 but violence continued until power-sharing in 2007 offered greater stability.

- Yet with continuing violence in Northern Ireland and a referendum on Scottish independence, few could conclude that problems of territorial management were solved.

Review your understanding of the following terms and concepts

Anglo-Irish Agreement	nationalism	SDLP
Barnett Formula	Orange Order	Senedd
consociationalism	partition	separatism
devolution	Plaid Cymru	Sinn Féin
DUP	power-sharing executive	SNP
federalism	quasi-federalism	Ulster unionism
home rule	regional assemblies	West Lothian question
IRA	RUC	

Questions for discussion and debate

Consider these propositions and be prepared to present the cases for and against. Try to produce debating propositions of your own.

1   Scottish and Welsh nationalism are essentially different.

2   The 'new politics' of devolution bears a striking resemblance to the old politics.

3   The Conservative Party must always oppose devolution.

4   The establishment of a single-party SNP government in Scotland transforms the independence debate.

5   The post-war conflict in Northern Ireland cannot be understood without an historical perspective.

6   A power-sharing executive in Northern Ireland can leave all unsatisfied.

7   It is time for devolution for England.

8 The 'West Lothian question' is one without answer.

9 The 'Irish problem' has not yet been solved.

10 The kingdom cannot remain united in the contemporary world.

Further reading

Aughey, A. (2001) *Nationalism, Devolution and the Challenge to the United Kingdom State.*
Examines the threatened concept of 'Britishness' and finds it alive if not entirely well.

Bogdanor, V. (2001) *Devolution in the United Kingdom.*
Measured analysis places developments in an historical context, from Gladstone's espousal of Home Rule in 1886 up to 1998.

Bogdanor, V. (2009) *The New British Constitution.*
Chapter 4 provides a clear and concise overview of the changing relationship between the UK's constituent parts. Addresses the concept of quasi-federalism within the UK.

Hazell, R. (ed.) (2006) *The English Question.*
In the light of devolution, will the English be content without their own assembly?

Kearney, H. (2006) *The British Isles: A History of Four Nations.*
Emphasizes how an understanding of the present requires an historical perspective encompassing more than just English history.

Keating, M. and Loughlin, J. (1997) *The Political Economy of the Regions.*
International study of regionalism, with chapters on the EU, Wales, Scotland and the English regions.

MacDonald, M. (1986) *Children of Wrath: Political Violence in Northern Ireland.*
Argues that the colonization of Ireland created a problem that could not be resolved.

Marr, A. (1992) *The Battle for Scotland.*
Explains the 'Scottish question'.

McEvoy, J. (2008) *The Politics of Northern Ireland.*
A clear and concise potted history of the north, with helpful analysis throughout.

McGarry, J. and O'Leary, B. (1997) *Explaining Northern Ireland: Broken Images.*
Excellent analysis of the political complexities of the contemporary Irish situation.

Mitchell, J. (2012) *Devolution in the United Kingdom.*
Highlights the importance of the English dimension in the debate on territorial politics. Argues that the UK should be understood as a state of distinct unions, each with its own trajectory.

Pilkington, C. (2002) *Devolution in Britain Today.*
Provides a full historical background and considers the relative success of devolution in each nation.

Trench, A. (ed.) (2008) *The State of the Nations 2008: Into the Third Term of Devolution in the UK.*
The last in a long-running series assessing the progress of UK devolution.

For reading around the subject and some light relief

Braveheart.
DVD/film saga of thirteenth-century Scottish revolt against English tyranny.

The Crying Game.
Award-winning DVD/film set amidst the contemporary violence over Northern Ireland.

Douglas Hurd, *Image in the Water.*
A narrow victory makes Labour dependent on its Scottish MPs. Tory Opposition leader wants to eject Scotland from the UK. A beleaguered prime minister announces a referendum in favour of the Union and UK membership of the EU. Fiction from distinguished former foreign secretary, ahead of its time!

Mario Vargas Llosa, *The Dream of the Celt.*
Powerful historical narrative. It is the summer of 1916 and republican Roger Casement awaits the hangman in Pentonville Prison after the disastrous Easter Rising. His petition for clemency is threatened by the leaking of his secret life as a homosexual.

Michael Collins.
DVD/film about the Irish civil war.

Michael Shea, *State of the Nation.*
Set in a Scotland in deep economic crisis after four years of independence. Sinister TNC moves in to take advantage.

Stella Rimington, *Present Danger*.
Thriller from the ex-director general of MI5. MI5 officer Liz Carlyle is posted to Northern Ireland and soon discovers that the peace process is dangerously precarious.

Simon Thirsk, *Not Quite White*.
Jon Bull is sent by Westminster to Wales's last remaining Welsh-speaking town to see why all attempts to bring it into the twenty-first century have failed. Explores complex tensions when English colonialism and Welsh nationalism meet.

On the net

http://www.assemblywales.org/
The Senedd's site explains its structure, working and history.

http://www.scottish.parliament.uk/index.aspx
The 'How it all happens' link explains how the parliament works, how MSPs are elected, and how legislation is made.

http://www.niassembly.gov.uk/
Click 'About the assembly' for details of the structures and processes of the Northern Ireland Assembly. As with the Scottish site, there is also video coverage of assembly proceedings.

http://www.plaidcymru.org/
http://www.snp.org.uk/
The sites for the Welsh and Scottish nationalists.

http://www.parliament.uk/topics/Regional-assemblies.htm
Links to a variety of parliamentary material on regional assemblies.

CHAPTER 21

THE GRASS ROOTS OF DEMOCRACY: LOCAL GOVERNMENT

Contents

> *The media construction tends to see in Westminster, Whitehall and the Cabinet the holy trinity of political life, but this places the political thermometer too near the radiator of London. Throughout history it is in local rather than central government that ordinary people have encountered much of the reality of the state. A vast range of important services (including roads, law and order, education, water supply, housing, hospitals and social security) were pioneered here. This is also a level of government where many ordinary people can experience democracy at first hand by electing, or being elected to, local councils. This chapter first charts the evolution of our modern system of local government. Next we discuss the local political system, identifying the principal actors in the municipal drama. We also consider what local authorities actually do, discuss the question of management and leadership and look at the crucial area of finance. We conclude by addressing the controversial question of central–local relations.*

Local Government, Democracy and Local Governance

As the self-government of sub-national territorial units of the state, some form of **local government** is found in virtually all developed polities as a complement to central government. It is generally seen as a sign of a healthy democracy – a constitutional separation of powers. Indeed, eliminating local government is generally taken as a symptom of totalitarianism; it was an early casualty of Hitler's rise in Germany. Modern local government has the following characteristics:

Strong democracy requires two important elements: popular participation at the local level; and popular participation at the national level.

House of Commons Communities and Local Government Committee, 6th Report (2009: Para 2)

- locally elected representatives who form the council;
- power to levy taxes;
- clearly delineated territorial boundaries;
- large permanent bureaucracies;
- responsibility for a wide range of services;
- a legal *persona* as a **body corporate** – the **local authority** in the name of which all activities are carried out.

When we speak of **local politics** we go beyond formal structures to the complex processes of settling differences and reaching compromises over community issues that can take place in the streets as well as in the town hall. It involves local elections, parties, pressure groups, media and local opinion. It can also involve a world of intrigue and power struggles between politicians and bureaucrats within the debating chambers and corridors of town halls.

The term **local governance** draws attention to the fact that the elected local authorities forming the main focus of this chapter are by no means the only providers of local services. There is a wider range of bodies operating locally, including various quangos, voluntary societies and private organizations working in partnership (or sometimes competition) with the elected authority.

Evolution

The spirit of local democracy

Local government has a long history and from the first there has been a tension between the centre and the locality. Its evolution saw a twin-track development, with two traditions – localist and centralist – that continue to colour modern debate.

- The *localist tradition*. At the time of the Roman occupation towns were established for retired soldiers, and some of their names remain. *Londinium* was established some seven years after the invasion of AD 43. The break-up of the Roman empire and invasions by Anglo-Saxons and Vikings ensured that communities in Britain were self-governing, power lying with the ownership of land (see Chandler 2007: 1). **Parish** government developed around the manor houses, where landowners established churches for their dependent communities, and as the manor declined, parish councils assumed the governing role. Also part of the localism tradition were guilds, developing from the twelfth century as associations of craftsmen and merchants. Their interests lay in orderly, well-conducted town life and they lent a strong dynamic to civic administration; guild halls often became in effect town halls.
- The *centralist tradition* arose from the ruling needs of royal authority. The key territorial unit was the **county**. Kings would impose local agents, sheriffs and Knights of the Peace, who became Justices of the Peace (JPs), to collect taxes, recruit soldiers, keep order and dispense justice.

By the mid-eighteenth century local government was a patchwork counterpane. It had evolved into a two-tier system, with counties containing parishes of various sizes and status, operating under the eyes of the JPs and local landed interests, and **boroughs** (often controlled by the guilds) with royal charters granting them independence from county jurisdiction.

The industrial revolution: a municipal revolution

The social upheavals of industrialization destroyed this pattern as massive urbanization drew people from the countryside to spawn huge teeming communities around the factories, the like of which had never been seen before. This did not necessarily happen in those market boroughs where municipal institutions were well established. Often sleepy rural hamlets were traumatized by a range of social and economic problems quite beyond the administrative capacity of the *ancien régime* of squirearchy and JP. Housing was hastily erected with little thought for comfort or sewerage. The new urban areas were characterized by disease, poverty, crime and threats to public order. Over all, the spectre of the French Revolution and its aftermath haunted the bourgeoisie, leaving them in a state of perpetual fear of the Frankenstein's monster they had created – the vast new social force identified by Marx, the urban working class.

The initial response was necessarily localist. The capitalists required a strong passive workforce, good roads, public health, public transport, a degree of education, street lighting and law and order. This was accomplished by a range of ad hoc bodies: boards of leading citizens (sometimes elected), responsible variously for services such as the poor law, burial, gaols, asylums, sanitation, water supply, roads, street lighting, hospitals, civic improvement and education.

Municipal reform

> The truth, Sir, is that we have a chaos as regards authorities, a chaos as regards rates, and a worse chaos than all as regards areas.
>
> G. J. Goschen, House of Commons speech introducing bills to reform local government (3 April 1871)

Following the Reform Act of 1832, which increased the power of the Liberals, a number of official inquiries were conducted into the state of the municipal institutions. The Elizabethan poor law was reformed in 1834 to reflect Benthamite 'less eligibility' principles. An inquiry into local government was deeply critical of administration by the old landed classes and the 1835 Municipal Corporations Act modernized the system with prudent accounting, elections and a widening remit of efficient services.

Later Local Government Acts (1888 and 1894) created a complex system, including counties sharing responsibilities with their constituent districts and

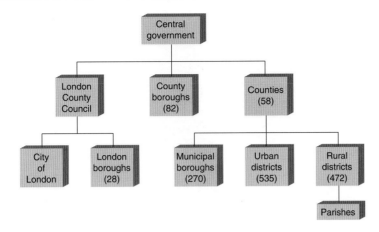

Figure 21.1 The local government structure in England and Wales at the end of the nineteenth century

Note: Actual numbers varied slightly.

county boroughs, which stood apart from the counties in which they were located and were responsible for all their services (figure 21.1). The 1888 Act met the unique needs of the huge London conurbation with an entirely new administrative county, under a London County Council (LCC) (figure 21.2), embracing a second tier of metropolitan boroughs and three county boroughs. It was, as Redlich and Hirst stated in a classic work of 1903, 'a system . . . condemned by logic . . . [but] approved by experience' (1970: 115).

> The County Councils are likely to prove stronger and more exacting than local sanitary authorities have been, though here it must be recollected that manufacturers who find it convenient to pour their refuse into the nearest rivers will be very apt to seek a place on the County Councils.
>
> Leading article in *The Times* on the prospects for the new county councils
> (23 Oct. 1888)

As the modern pattern became established, the responsibilities of the ad hoc bodies and voluntary societies were gradually absorbed (not without resistance and infighting). The new authorities also bought out various utility companies (water, tramways, electricity and gas). With municipal schools, hospitals, bath-houses, parks, improved roads and pavements, libraries, museums, art galleries and even public conveniences, the late nineteenth century can be seen as the high point of local government. The energy of capitalism was harnessed with municipal endeavour. Joseph Chamberlain was able to build a national reputation through his modernization of the city of Birmingham. The economic elite were also the

Municipal pomp: Manchester Town Hall

political leaders; Gothic town halls, the cathedrals of the age, testify to the importance placed by the Victorian capitalists upon their municipalities and, indeed, upon themselves.

Into the twentieth century: reappraising the pattern

Although the nineteenth-century boundary pattern reflected the prevailing patterns of life, with no mechanism to accommodate subsequent demographic movements, it remained in a Victorian time warp. As the twentieth century progressed, railways, trunk roads, aeroplanes, telecommunications, radio and television enlarged the territory in which people lived their daily lives. Traditional heavy industries that urbanization had served went into decline and the urban–rural dichotomy was blurred as towns increasingly interacted with their hinterlands.

The problems of London were the most acute; the LCC area and surrounding counties had experienced enormous population growth, imposing heavy housing demand and traffic congestion. Following the 1957 Herbert report the LCC area was enlarged from 75,000 to 510,000 acres, absorbing parts of Kent, Surrey and Essex, and the whole of Middlesex (figure 21.2). The newly staked territory was to be

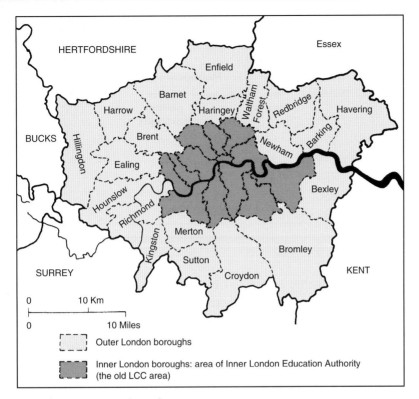

HERTFORDSHIRE

Essex

Enfield

Barnet

Harrow

Haringey

Waltham Forest

Redbridge

Havering

BUCKS

Hillingdon

Brent

Newham

Barking

Ealing

Hounslow

Richmond

Kingston

Merton

Bexley

Bromley

Sutton

Croydon

KENT

SURREY

0   10 Km

0   10 Miles

Outer London boroughs

Inner London boroughs: area of Inner London Education Authority (the old LCC area)

Figure 21.2 The Greater London reforms

divided into thirty-two boroughs (plus the City of London), with functions shared between two tiers. In 1963 a new Greater London Council (GLC) emerged, which took over the London Passenger Transport Executive.

For the rest of the country the 1972 Local Government Act preserved the two-tier principle, resisting calls for a pattern of single-tier all-purpose authorities. Six new metropolitan boroughs were created in major conurbations on the GLC model. However, these eventually became locked in a political battle with the Thatcher government and, along with the GLC, they were abolished in 1986, their functions absorbed by their districts as unitary authorities. London became unique in the world as a major capital city without a strategic authority.

Calls for more unitary authorities continued, although they met with resistance. After further piecemeal reforms the local government map had settled by 1998 at 34 counties, divided into 238 districts, and 46 new unitary authorities (table 21.1). Scotland and Wales had moved to a completely unitary system. The government claimed that under the **unitary system** services would be closer to citizens. However, with fewer councils, cutting the number of councillors by almost a third, this was difficult to sustain. The exercise was criticized for its lack of rationality

Table 21.1 The decline in the number of local authorities between 1994 and 1998

Year	England					Scotland	Wales	NI	Total
	Non-metropolitan			Metropolitan					
	Counties	Districts	New unitaries	London[a]	Metro-politan boroughs				
1994	39	296	0	33	36	65	45	26	540
1995	38	294	1	33	36	65	45	26	538
1996	35	274	14	33	36	32	22	26	472
1997	35	260	27	33	36	32	22	26	471
1998	34	238	46	33	36	32	22	26	467

[a] Including City of London.

(Stoker 1993: 4) and some suspected a government smoke-screen obscuring a fundamental weakening of local democracy (Leach 1998: 35).

Full circle

In London the wheel of reform moved to complete a circle when, on 7 May 1998, the Labour government held a referendum on the creation of a new elected strategic top-tier authority for the Greater London area, effectively restoring the GLC and, even more radically, introducing an **elected mayor**. The issue was not seen as particularly controversial (it was supported by the three main political parties) and although the people voted 'Yes', turnout was distinctly underwhelming. The new regimen brought Ken Livingstone, deposed leader of the GLC, back to the helm as the first elected mayor. In its Local Government Act of 2000 the Labour government sought to induce other authorities to adopt this style of leadership, but with only limited success (see p. 665).

The Local Political Environment

Each local authority is a miniature political system populated by elected politicians, bureaucracies, electorates, parties and interest groups.

The council

Councils are composed of locally elected councillors. There are some 20,000 in England and Wales, in over 400 local authorities. Although (unlike MPs) they are unpaid they receive allowances and expenses. The size of a council varies to reflect the size of the populations served: in 2012 Sheffield had 84 councillors and Birmingham 120. Sitting like local parliaments, councils are formally the linchpins of local politics. Full meetings in the council chamber usually take place once a month although, like Parliament, any idea that this is a decision-making body is a myth. There are sometimes coalitions but many councils split along party lines, with disciplined Westminster-style voting. The internal power structure can vary but certain leading councillors increasingly dominate, reducing most members to backbencher status. In a minority of cases, leadership lies with an elected mayor, a development encouraged by central government.

Choosing councillors: local elections

Local elections are of great constitutional significance. Unlike any other state actors outside Westminster, councillors can claim legitimacy. In England and Wales they are elected by first-past-the-post to serve four-year terms representing wards, each of which usually returns three members. Counties, London boroughs, some unitary and shire districts and all parishes have whole-council elections every four years. Metropolitan districts, some unitary authorities and some shire districts elect one-third of the council each time, with three elections in every four-year cycle.

Local electoral behaviour

This can betray the centralism within British politics, with voters often casting a judgement on central government. Because national governments are usually at their lowest ebb in mid-term, local elections tend to show a swing to the opposition parties. Hence, the long period of Conservative government in the 1980s and 1990s subjected the party to a painful near-death by a thousand cuts at local elections, with heavy losses (often to the Liberal Democrats) in their traditional south-eastern heartlands. However, when Labour took the Westminster reins it too began to receive maulings in local elections, until even the BNP was stealing council seats. During a period of perennial opposition the Liberal Democrats could regularly benefit, but in coalition from 2010 they began to pay the price of power, which proved particularly heavy.

Turnout

A mush-discussed issue is relatively low turnout (often below 40 per cent), the lowest of all EU countries. By contrast, in many other EU countries turnout is in the region of 60 per cent, while in Denmark, Sweden, Austria, Spain and Italy it is between 70 and 80 per cent. In none of these countries in voting compulsory. Those favouring centralism invariably take low turnout as evidence that people do not

The strength of free peoples resides in the local community. Local institutions are to liberty what primary schools are to science.

Alexis de Tocqueville (1805–59; French writer and politician), *Democracy in America* (1839)

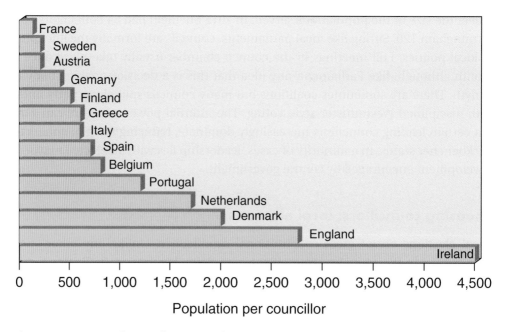

Figure 21.3 Ratio of councillors to population in selected European countries

Source: Data from Wilson and Game (2011: 275).

value local democracy. However, in many cases one party enjoys so entrenched a position that a rational person might not bother to vote. In urban areas Labour have traditionally dominated, while the Conservatives have had green boots securely planted in the mud of the shires. Lack of publicity, a rise in local quangos (the 'new magistracy') and central domination also help to explain low turnouts. A further factor is the relatively large size of ward populations (figure 21.3), making councillors more distant from electors. Rallings and Thrasher (1994) concluded that factors helping to increase turnout included a close contest, elections by thirds, single-member wards, small ward populations and middle-class social profiles. However, these effects were very small, suggesting that more deep-seated causes were at work.

High turnout is generally seen as a sign of a healthy democracy and various suggestions to improve it are canvassed, such as the following:

- mobile polling stations located at places of work, colleges, hospitals, supermarkets, railway stations and other places where people congregate;
- electronic voting;
- weekend polling;
- postal voting;
- proportional representation.

Since the 2002 elections authorities have continued to experiment with new forms of voting, often electronic methods. The reform most likely to prove most significant, however, would be the introduction of PR, which would produce more close contests (see Rallings and Thrasher 1994). This is used for elections to the Greater London Assembly and the devolved assemblies, for local government in Scotland and Northern Ireland and for European Parliament elections (see chapters 6 and 20). The supplementary vote system is used in the election of mayors. However, central government has shown little enthusiasm for PR in the election of English councillors (Wilson and Game 2011: 257).

Beyond the ballot box

It is also possible to increase popular interest through various other forms of participation, including:

- citizens' juries, bringing together groups of twelve to sixteen selected as representative of the community to consider an issue in depth (usually over several days);
- focus groups of approximately twelve to twenty people brought together to give in-depth responses to a particular question;
- deliberative opinion polls involving debate on an issue prior to voting;
- standing citizens' panels providing a stable sample, statistically representative of the population, to act as sounding boards;
- area-based neighbourhood committees;
- user-group forums;
- tenants' and residents' groups;
- referendums;
- public question times at council meetings;
- interactive technology using the internet to inform and ascertain people's views on particular issues.

Political parties

Although local government is dominated by parties, they have received little attention. In 2005, a policy paper published by the Office of the Deputy Prime Minister on *Vibrant Local Leadership* made scant reference to them. An exception was the Widdicombe Committee (1986), which noted high levels of party dominance in the town halls but regarded this with disapproval. Although independents have long existed, opponents of party politics often evoke a mythical age when independents supposedly ran councils. Yet in the nineteenth century Liberals and Conservatives fought for control over ad hoc boards and boroughs. However, it was Labour, without the advantages of wealth and position, that needed the weapon of formal organization. Its rise first occurred at local level and was deeply feared, the old adversaries sometimes forming anti-Labour alliances, and behaving like Tweedledum and Tweedledee when confronted by a

> monstrous crow
> As black as a tar–barrel,
> Which frightened both the heroes so,
> They quite forgot their quarrel.

> (Lewis Carroll, *Through the Looking Glass*: ch. 4)

Local national parties

Today the term 'local party' is something of a misnomer. Although some are genuinely local, most are effectively branches of national parties, the same army of canvassers tramping the streets for both local and parliamentary elections. The relationship between national organizations of the three major parties and their local troops varies (see Leach 2006: ch. 2), but three centralizing implications apply.

- There is an ideological identification between national and local politics.
- Local politicians often look to the national party for inspiration and guidance.
- National leaders expect to dominate, even suspending the membership of councillors of whom they disapprove.

Local parties can sometimes be ideologically more extreme than their national counterparts. In the 1980s, a tough breed of New Right councillors seemed intent on outdoing their leaders in neoliberalism, while local socialism moved further to the left than the PLP. Blairites kept a watchful eye and were fully prepared to suspend those seriously 'off message'. Liberal Democrat parties tend to be less ideologically focused and more pragmatic, varying from area to area according to conditions.

Party animals

The impact of parties on local politics can be examined at two levels. Within the community they can act as catalysts, mobilizing electorates, educating the public, stimulating interest in issues, improving accountability, aggregating and articulating interests, recruiting members and promoting citizen participation. Within the town halls the language is often of control and discipline. Such domination, particularly in urban areas, has increased, becoming manifest in a number of ways.

- *Party groups.* The local government equivalents of parliamentary parties, groups can meet behind closed doors to plan strategy.
- *Council committees.* These generally reflect the balance in the council chamber.
- *Committee chairs.* The majority party can monopolize these influential positions.
- *Local 'cabinets'.* Senior councillors from the majority party can form a cabinet.
- *Council leaders.* The majority party leader can become the council leader.
- *Elected mayors.* Although candidates may stand as independents, there is a

strong likelihood that they will be party figures. (Of fourteen elected mayors in post in 2011, two were Liberal Democrats, three Conservatives, four Labour and one an English Democrat; only four were independents.)

- *Political appointments.* Officers and advisers can be chosen with sympathetic views.

The establishment of the Widdicombe Committee on the Conduct of Local Authority Business was prompted by concern over what was seen as excessive party politicization. It reported in 1986, with legislation following in 1989, which limited party dominance in certain ways by extending the rights of minority parties and restricting the use of political advisers.

No overall control

Coalitions are not uncommon in local politics. The rise of the Liberal Democrats saw an increase in the number of 'hung councils' with no one party in overall control. After the May 2010 local elections, 125 of the 355 English councils were run by coalitions or parties that could not command a majority. Sometimes a formal coalition between two or more parties will see committee chairs shared and even cross-party agreement on policy. However, in most cases the largest party takes the lead, holding the chairs but making policy concessions to other parties. In a minority of cases no effective power-sharing arrangement is found and the result is prolonged wrangling (see Leach and Stewart 1992).

Local interest groups

In several respects local interest-group behaviour resembles that at national level. Although only a small proportion may be active at any time, the potential is enormous; as long ago as the 1970s Newton (1976: 38) identified over 4,000 organizations in Birmingham alone, which Maloney *et al.* (2000) found to have risen by a third by the end of the century. The rise of single-issue politics from the 1980s has added to the number. In addition, the reduction in the traditional service delivery functions of local authorities during the 1980s led to the greater involvement of groups from the voluntary sector (see Wilson and Game 2011: ch. 18). Groups seek channels of access to officers, leading councillors, backbench councillors and local opinion and it is possible to speak of local insider and outsider groups, although the dichotomy is not rigid (Stoker 1991: ch. 5).

Insiders

This category includes chambers of commerce, companies, professional bodies and sometimes trade unions. Saunders (1980) showed councillors of the London borough of Croydon hand in glove with private business interests in facilitating the commercial development of the town centre, confirming Dearlove's findings in Kensington and Chelsea (1973). Here we find local corporatism of the 'gin-and-tonic' kind. However, councils are not always captured exclusively by capitalist interests. In Sheffield, for example, the local trade unions, through the Trades and Labour Council, for long enjoyed a close relationship with councillors (see Hampton 1970).

From the late 1970s the insider category was also enlarged as many authorities took on an increased commitment to consultation with service users (Stoker 1991: 125–8). Left-wing authorities would even provide funding for voluntary and cause groups. The Labour government encouraged this with its 1998 Compact on Relations between Government and the Voluntary Community Sector in England, aiming to encourage partnerships in providing services (Wilson and Game 2011: 358–62). As head of the 2010 coalition David Cameron spoke of a 'big society', looking to voluntary organizations to work with, or even supplant, the state in providing services. Yet ironically, the wish to protest as outsiders became greater as the big society came up against severe funding cuts.

Outsiders

Movements representing squatters, gays, lesbians, ethnic minorities, one-parent families and dispossessed sections of society can sometimes be drawn into partnership but at other times excluded. The international 'Occupy' movement in 2011, with protesters setting up disruptive encampments in many cities, could elicit little sympathy from Conservative councils. Similarly, groups concerned with environmental issues have often encountered the cold face of officialdom. Even citizens' groups can be excluded in favour of establishment interests in areas such as housing (see Dunleavy 1981).

The extent to which local groups play a part in policy-making is also conditioned by the central–local government relationship. Sometimes it is better for a group to turn its attention to Westminster or even Brussels. As Cockburn's study of Lambeth noted, to local capitalist interests, 'deals that matter most over taxation and employment policy, grants and control, are deals done at Westminster and Whitehall' (1977: 45).

'Yes Councillor': municipal mandarins

The view of the expert can become too narrow. Professional enthusiasm can carry the expert beyond the bounds of good judgement, and 'Bumbledom' can be a real danger. . . The control of the expert by the amateur representing his fellow citizens is the key to the whole of our system of government.

Report of the Royal Commission on Local Government in Greater London, 1957–60,
Cmnd 1194 (1960)

Local government employs thousands of people, from members of various professions to staff working as cleaners. However, as in the case of civil servants, our interest lies in the officials at the top of the bureaucratic hierarchy. These are permanent employees and their role raises the Weberian warning of the dictatorship of the official. Formally, councillors make policies that officers implement, but in practice matters are more complex. Councillors are essentially laypeople while officers are professionals, with all the tricks of a poor man's Sir Humphrey Appleby. Indeed, the bureaucratic threat can be greater than that in Whitehall. Ministers are full-time politicians while most councillors are part-timers. Moreover, unlike many civil servants, the top administrators are not *generalists* but qualified *specialists*, their authority reinforced by professional associations. Local bureaucrats can also gain authority through formal and informal networks with Whitehall and even with Brussels.

There can be an underlying class dimension. Officials are generally middle class and much of their work entails informal consultation with local elites, where they 'believe that they are behaving quite properly and [do] . . . not see that they are consulting a minority opinion' (Hill 1974: 87). Some have been accused of resenting working-class councillors (Henney 1984: 321–41). The status of the senior officials was to rise with the move towards a more private-sector style of management. To the fury of the group Taxpayers Alliance, the chief executive of Essex County Council was found to be receiving a basic salary of £230,000 in 2009, to which bonuses were also added. Andrea Hill, chief executive of neighbouring Suffolk County Council, had to be content with £220,000. There is also a new career path that can lead them to Whitehall positions. In 2011 Sir Bob Kerslake, one-time chief executive in Sheffield, became head of the civil service. As in other parts of the state, there is a degree of male domination, although women's particular managerial skills have been increasingly recognized (see Maddock 1993). By 2010 around one-fifth of chief executives were women.

> *A boys' room culture still exists and sometimes there'll be jokes of a sexual nature and calling women tarts. I'm surprised it still exists*
>
> Unnamed female chief executive, quoted in Local Government Chronicle (22 Oct. 2009)

What Does Local Government Do?

Local democracy is meaningless if it is not linked with important services. Parish government today is of little more significance than maypole dances performed on village greens. Yet if it had important functions, it would, as in France, be a central feature of communal life. Although interesting the Webbs in the 1920s, few studies of local government have stressed the political importance of its functions.

In the provision of services local authorities are by no means entirely free. For long they were subject to the legal doctrine of **ultra vires** (beyond the power), meaning that, however well intentioned, they could not exceed those powers given to them by Parliament. An action that may be legal for an individual (say, giving children free ice-cream) would not be allowed unless Parliament so decreed. This was changed in the 2011 Localism Act, which gave authorities a 'general power of competence', allowing them greater freedom in providing services. It also promised more freedom in planning. Communities minister Andrew Stunell asserted on the website of the Department for Communities and Local Government that 'new rights and powers coming into force will begin to put communities firmly back in control of their own destiny, and reverse a 100 years of government centralisation'.

Classifying functions

Local authorities are *multi-functional*, to be distinguished from *ad hoc* single-purpose bodies. They have been able to provide most state services required by ordinary people from womb to tomb, which may be broadly classified as follows:
- *protective* – fire and police services, consumer protection;
- *environmental* – roads, transport, planning, refuse collection and recycling;
- *personal* – schools, social services, housing;
- *recreational* – parks, sports facilities, theatres, art galleries, libraries;
- *commercial* – markets, restaurants, transport;
- *promotional* – employment creation, tourism, economic regeneration;
- *regulatory* – implementing regulations and monitoring standards (national and European).

Who does what? Allocating functions within the state

> When you have provided the proper constitution of local authority you must provide that the local authority must have sufficient powers; and that it gets these powers by diminishing the excessive and exaggerated powers that have been heaped on the central authorities in London.
>
> Lord Salisbury (Conservative prime minister) speaking on the creation of the LCC (1888), quoted in K. Young and P. L. Garside, *Metropolitan London* (1982)

Is there any clear rationale explaining the division of functions between local and central government? There are few theories to underpin such a discussion. A basic premise of any rational explanation must be that services where local knowledge, local participation and sensitivity to the popular will are important should be provided locally. This is in line with the subsidiarity principle which is frequently applied to the distribution of functions between the EU institutions and member states. However, other rational arguments can dictate otherwise.

- *Equality*. From a socialist perspective, it would be unfair if, for example, the social services in one area were better than those in another. This demands central administration to ensure equality.
- *Efficiency*. Some services are better (and more economically) administered over wider areas. Indeed, over the years several functions pioneered by local government have been transferred to central government or regional boards.

Beyond rationality comes politics and it is in this realm that the issue is often settled. Central government may use its power to shape the allocation of functions to its own advantage.

Local Governance: Beyond the Ballot Box

A 'new magistracy'?

As elected councils began to lose responsibilities to non-elected bodies, the term 'new magistracy' was coined by John Stewart (1992, 1995), in evocation of a bygone age when local bigwigs had ruled the towns and cities through *ad hoc* boards. The 'new magistracy' emerged in three principal ways:

- local authority appointees were removed from boards upon which they had previously sat;
- local government functions were transferred to appointed quangos;
- bodies were allowed to opt out of local authority control.

By the late 1990s local authorities had ceased to make appointments to health authorities or the family health service agencies running the GP services. Self-governing trusts had been created to run hospitals and community health care services. Housing associations had to a considerable extent taken over public housing, while Housing Action Trusts and Urban Development Corporations had assumed many urban development functions. Training and Enterprise Councils were responsible for many educational and economic development matters. Grant-maintained schools, sixth-form colleges, colleges of further education and what were once the polytechnics had come under appointed boards, financed by nationally appointed funding bodies. Control of the police had been lost to new police authorities (see chapter 22). By 1997 there were over 5,000 local quangos but only 445 local authorities.

What kind of people form this unelected magistracy? Estimated at around 66,000, they were to outnumber councillors by three to one (Hall and Weir 1996). They are not strongly representative of the populations served, tending to come from local business communities. Politically many claim to be independent but there are sometimes allegations: 'patronage . . . as well as the desire by the government to see greater private sector involvement, all contribute to the possibility of one set of political interests predominating' (Skelcher and Davies 1996: 20). Despite reform, the emphasis has continued to be on working in partnership with private-sector agencies rather than returning hands-on functions to local government (Chandler 2007: 296).

The enabling authority: government by contract

The fact that local government is responsible for a service does not necessarily mean it should deliver it; responsibility may be '**contracted out**' to the private or voluntary sectors. Such a practice was by no means new but, following the 1988 Local Government Act, it became a principal goal of central government policy, with compulsory competitive tendering (CCT) required for an ever-widening range of functions, from refuse collection to professional, legal and accounting responsibilities. Sharing the same ideological roots as privatization, the policy was strongly advocated by right-wing think-tanks. Local responses varied with political disposition, but in virtually all authorities the culture was changed (Audit Commission 1993).

In addition, they were encouraged to extend the Private Finance Initiative (PFI – see p. 567) into areas such as school building and maintenance. There were also concerns that the search for profit would lower the quality of services and increase the risks of fraud and corruption (Doig 1995: 104). A number of scandals arose over the use of PFIs as costs rose, and by 2011 the National Audit Office was urging government to find alternatives when planning major projects.

Management and Leadership: the Dilemma of Local Democracy

In general we suffer from too much government – especially local government.
Norman Tebbit (Conservative MP), *Unfinished Business* (1993)

How is a local authority to be organized? It is expected to be a vehicle for the political participation of ordinary citizens but it controls an enterprise dwarfing many commercial undertakings. The quest to marry the two antagonistic objectives has formed a key area of post-war debate. The traditional organization of a local authority entailed departments for different services headed by chief officers responsible to committees of elected councillors. Critics alleged this to be cumbersome and lacking central direction. The reports of the Maud (1967) and Bains (1972) committees recommended concentrating power in a small board or policy committee of senior councillors. However, while authorities tried various experiments, councillors in general resisted the loss of power this kind of **corporate management** model implied for most of them. In the changed climate of the 1980s 'New Public Management' became a recognizable international movement, which suggested that mere tinkering with the age-old machinery would not suffice (Hambleton 1996: 94). The concept of the enabling authority changed the municipal culture, calling more for lawyers and accountants than councillors. Indeed, Conservative minister Nicholas Ridley (1988) envisaged them meeting only a few times a year.

We can't go on meeting like this: cabinets and elected mayors

In September 1990 the Audit Commission published *We Can't Go On Meeting Like This*, its punning title condemning labyrinthine committee structures that were ill equipped for speedy decision-making. Environment Secretary Michael Heseltine continued the debate, advocating local cabinets and appointed council managers or directly elected US-style mayors (see Elcock 1995). New Labour maintained the momentum, their 1998 white paper (DETR 1998) foreshadowing the 2000 Local Government Act. This required all 494 councils to separate councillors' decision-making and representational roles. They were given three leadership options (figure 21.4):

- a directly elected executive mayor who appoints a cabinet from among councillors;
- a leader, elected by the council, who then appoints a cabinet;
- a directly elected mayor working in tandem with a full-time manager appointed by the council.

Councils choosing elected mayors would need public support through referendums, and local people could themselves demand such a referendum.

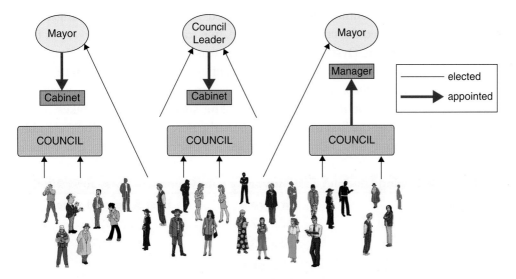

Figure 21.4 Local government management structure: the different systems compared

Turn again Livingstone, Lord Mayor of London

The Greater London area, without a strategic authority since the GLC's abolition, was seen as a particularly suitable launch-pad for a mayoral system. After much speculation, the model emerged. Elected by the supplementary vote system, the mayor would work with three or four deputies and a bureaucracy of around 250 (much smaller than the 25,000 serving the old GLC). With an annual budget of some £3.3 billion, he/she would set policy objectives to be approved by a twenty-five-member Greater London Assembly (GLA). This would be elected by the additional member system, with fourteen chosen by FPTP and eleven from London-wide party lists. The mayor's responsibilities were to include public transport, the fire service, strategic planning, trunk roads, traffic management, the ambulance service and the arts. In addition, responsibility for the Metropolitan Police Force was to be inherited from the home secretary. With a salary in excess of £100,000 per annum, the expectation was that formidable personalities would be attracted to the new position. In the event, eleven candidates featured on the ballot paper, with all the main parties represented.

However, political skulduggery accompanied the nomination process. The Conservative front runner, Lord (Jeffrey) Archer, was discredited during his campaign (eventually finding himself imprisoned for a different matter). In the Labour Party, Tony Blair went to extreme lengths to prevent Ken Livingstone's selection as the party's candidate. Buoyed by his high standing in the polls, Livingstone declared the system corrupt, promptly standing as an independent and savouring success in May 2000 (table 21.2). He was re-elected in 2004 but defeated in 2008 and 2012 by the no less colourful character of Conservative Boris Johnson.

In a controversial tenure, and with a limited range of powers, Livingstone's achievements included the congestion charge, free transport for under-18s in full-time education and the Oyster card system. He was also instrumental in London's successful bid for the Olympic Games and dealt effectively with the aftermath of the 7/7 terrorist attack of 2005. However, his proposal to introduce a cycle hire scheme for the capital was to fructify under the name of his successor as 'Boris bikes'.

At the same time as the first mayoral election, the new Greater London Assembly was elected. Labour and Conservatives gained nine seats each, the Liberal

Table 21.2 Electing London's first Mayor by supplementary vote, June 2000		
Candidate	**First vote**	**First & second vote**
Ken Livingstone (Ind)	667,877	776,427
Steven Norris (Con)	464,434	564,137
Frank Dobson (Lab)	223,884	
Susan Kramer (Lib Dem)	203,452	

Democrats four, with three going to the Greens. In the case of the latter two parties, all seats were gained as 'additional members', demonstrating the advantage of PR to small parties.

Beyond London

Given that all authorities were obliged to adopt one of the options by June 2002, the vast majority favoured that of a leader elected by the council, supported by a cabinet. These usually came from the majority party and most authorities operated a collective style of decision-making. This disappointed the Blair government, which tried to induce a more prime ministerial style of leadership. Under the cabinet system the role of 'backbench' councillors is downgraded. They form specialist committees with the role of scrutinizing cabinet policy. They are also left with constituency work. Some critics see the divide between the policy and constituency roles as artificial, others doubt whether speedy decisions are better decisions. However, the coalition's 2011 Localism Act did allow councils to consider moving to a more traditional committee system of decision making, if they wished.

The elected mayor system was the one favoured by the government, but was not to prove widely popular. While a few authorities had adopted it by 2002, far more were rejecting the idea. The dignity of the new office was not enhanced in Hartlepool, where the winning candidate, by an overwhelming majority, was a man in a monkey suit (the mascot of Hartlepool United). By 2009, 37 of the 152 major authorities had put the question to their electorates, with only 12 saying 'yes'. In May 2012 the coalition government compelled eleven of the largest cities to hold referendums but it was only the people of Bristol who voted for such a system.

Finance: Who Pays the Piper?

The world of local government finance is mysterious and arcane but its study provides an important key to understanding relationships with the centre. Local expenditure is by definition public expenditure and any central government will take great interest in it. The scale (some £169 billion for the UK in fiscal year 2014, amounting to around 25 per cent of government total managed expenditure) is huge, and the services traditionally provided tend to be labour-intensive, with no easy routes to savings (figure 21.5). Gross expenditure falls into two categories.

- *Capital expenditure* covers items of lasting value (land, schools and major items of equipment).
- *Revenue expenditure* is incurred in the running of services (e.g. payments to contractors, wages) and non-current expenditure (e.g. loan charges).

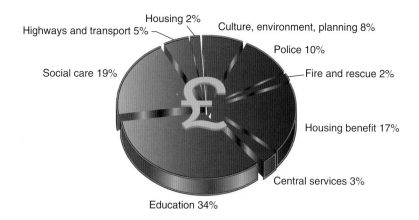

Figure 21.5 Local government net current expenditure, 2012–2013

Source: Dept. of Communities and Local Government, Statistical Release (31 July 2013).

Revenue income comes from three principal sources: fees and charges, local taxation and grants from central government, including the redistributed business rate. For capital expenditure, money can be borrowed. Revenue expenditure far exceeds that on capital, a difference that has widened under pressure to make cuts. Each source has been made subject to increasing central control.

Fees and charges

Local authorities have always charged for certain services. In the nineteenth century, they were able to raise large amounts from water, electricity, gas, roads and public transport, but nationalization reduced these opportunities. There is room for political debate over the issue. Early Labour Party ideology tended to oppose charging, seeing local government as a vehicle for municipal socialism. However, several services afford opportunities for charging and authorities are now free to use their own initiative on what to charge for. They can of course set charges below cost to encourage take-up, link them to age or ability to pay, or use them to deter use (e.g. parking, in order to discourage car use). London's congestion charge, for example, is intended to incentivize people to use public transport.

The hand of the centre

At first sight it might appear that central government has little interest in local charges. However, if a service is offered below cost a subsidy is required from some other source – ultimately taxpayers. The Thatcher government introduced **deregulation** and commercial pricing; public transport fares and housing rents were raised and the 1989 Local Government and Housing Act gave the centre the right to designate further areas for charging, while excluding education, policing and fire.

Local taxation

In both political and constitutional terms local taxation has been by far the most significant element of local government income, the essential guarantee of local autonomy. It was to prove a site of fierce controversy and political action. The original instrument was through rates (introduced in 1601 to finance the poor law), a tax with liability based on the occupation of domestic and non-domestic property. Broadly speaking, the more desirable a property, the higher the rate. The system came increasingly under criticism, accused of being:

- regressive;
- a disincentive to property improvement;
- lacking buoyancy (not rising automatically with inflation);
- insufficient in yield.

Moreover, it seemed fiendishly designed to penalize the middle classes, with over 50 per cent of adults in lower income groups benefiting from rebate schemes.

The hand of the centre

Controversy began when, in 1984, the Thatcher government gave itself the power to limit what authorities could raise through rates – rate-capping. This reduced the

"We're in Band C!"

burden on middle-class taxpayers. The government then went further, replacing the rates with a 'community charge'. This fell equally on most adults, with the intention of making councils accountable to most of the people for their spending. It was quickly dubbed a '**poll tax**'. An earlier poll tax had led to the Peasants Revolt of 1381 but in 1990 it was the masses revolting, with stormy and sometimes violent scenes outside council chambers. The poll tax helped to bring down Margaret Thatcher and, on April Fool's Day 1993, it followed her off the stage. Its successor, the council tax, returned to property values and slipped into place relatively quietly (see Keen and Travers 1994).

Central grants

With an unparalleled fundraising capability through income and sales taxes, as well as other forms of duty, central government commands the heights of the taxation system. Local government has increasingly been obliged to rely upon some of this revenue being passed back in the form of grants. Central grants can also help to redistribute the nation's wealth in favour of the poorer areas, through a process of equalization. There are in principle two types of grants.

- *Specific grants*: these are for particular services (housing, education, police, etc.), usually with the centre contributing a given percentage of expenditure incurred. Restricting expenditure to a particular function is sometimes termed 'ring-fencing'.
- *General grants*: currently known as the Revenue Support Grant (RSG), this supplements a local authority's general income.

The total amount given by central government to local government constitutes Aggregate External Finance (AEF). This stood at some £72 million in 2012/13.

The hand of the centre

A specific grant gives central government more control. It can persuade authorities to follow certain policies and compensate them for taking on extra burdens such as housing asylum-seekers. General grants allow more local discretion. The balance between the two has seesawed over time, usually reflecting the political advantage of the party in control at Westminster. The 2010 coalition, as part of its localism agenda, removed ring-fencing from most grants, leaving only education, public health and policing with specific grants. However, this helped remove central government from the firing line as the draconian cuts of some 26 per cent in grant funding that its deficit-reduction policy demanded began to bite.

Redistributed business rate

Unlike the domestic rate, the non-domestic rate (collected from businesses) did not disappear with the poll-tax reform. Previously it had been collected by local authorities as part of their income. Reformed as the Uniform Business Rate, the money was paid into a central pool, to be distributed on the same basis as the RSG – effectively a further central grant. However, the coalition government announced that from 2013 local authorities would again be allowed to retain a proportion of the money collected locally.

Borrowing

Like individuals and organizations, local authorities can borrow and they do so for the same kinds of reasons. If we cannot afford a holiday in Disneyland we do not go, but when we purchase a car or a house, we borrow because there is a tangible asset to act as collateral. Thus, local authorities generally only borrow for *capital expenditure* (schools, houses, machines and the like). Borrowing has the additional advantage of spreading costs over the successive generations, who will benefit from the facility.

The hand of the centre

However, authorities do not have complete freedom. Before 1981 they required central loan sanction. Originally this was to ensure prudence but in the post-war era it became an instrument of economic management. The 1980 Local Government, Planning and Land Act introduced a general power for the centre to set ceilings on capital expenditure. Central government has also favoured recourse to the Private Finance Initiative (PFI), whereby private contractors build and maintain a facility, 'renting' it to the authority (see p. 567).

Auditing the books

Sleaze is not confined to the Palace of Westminster. Revelations of the Poulson affair in the 1970s exposed the corrupt awarding of contracts and *Private Eye* has for long logged a shameful catalogue of 'Rotten Boroughs'. A number of characteristics leave local government open to corruption. Single-party rule produces local oligarchs who may make the authority their fiefdom, doing favours to themselves and their friends. Attendance allowances can be claimed for token appearances at meetings, the awarding of contracts offers temptations of bribery, and 'fact-finding' can become junketing in sunny climes or even the fleshpots of the world (Doig 1995: 104).

Hence, like other organizations, local authorities must submit their accounts for annual audit. Originally this aimed to ensure good accounting practice, prevent corruption, and identify *ultra vires* expenditure. In 1983 the system was toughened up with the creation of the Audit Commission (see p. 560). It soon claimed some notable scalps. In 1993 Lambeth Council was accused of fraud and malpractice, including over £20 million of unauthorized highways expenditure. In 1994 a damning report came from District Auditor John Magill concerning Westminster Council under Dame Shirley Porter. Officers and members were accused of 'wilful misconduct' and gerrymandering through the sale of council houses (*Guardian*, 26 March 1997). In 2002, the 'Donnygate' scandal saw the former chair of Doncaster Council's planning committee jailed for four years after receiving a £160,000 farmhouse for pushing through a housing development application for a property developer. The town's elected mayor, Ray Stockhill, received a two-year suspended sentence for accepting payments of over £30,000 from the same source.

Following the Widdicombe report and recommendations from the Nolan Committee, the 2000 Local Government Act made provision for a code of ethics to be drawn up in consultation with the Local Government Association. This was to be adopted by all authorities, with alleged breaches investigated by a Standards Agency and councillors and officers were to face suspension if found in breach of the code.

Local Government in a Centralist State

> Local government can be a tool for achieving socialist change. This has been submerged in parliamentary, centralist views of progress.
>
> David Blunkett (as leader of Sheffield City Council), interviewed in M. Boddy and C. Fudge, *Local Socialism: The Way Ahead* (1984)

It will be apparent from the foregoing discussion that the hand of central government is ever present in the work of local authorities. While British citizens may feel this is the natural state of affairs, as the Commons Select Committee on Communities and Local Government Committee pointed out (2009: paras 29–38), it is not so in most other comparable European countries. Central domination is but another feature of Britain's uncodified constitution. We have seen that control over finance gives power, but there are also other instruments available to the centre.

On a day-to-day basis administrative control comes through a regular stream of instructions and circulars landing on the desks of local officials to instruct, advise and threaten. Parliamentary supremacy means that all legislation comes from the centre and laws can be made or amended to ensure that local authorities act in the way desired. Local government owes its very existence to legislation and this existence is frail, as was seen when the government abolished the troublesome metropolitan counties and the GLC. In addition, the actions of an authority can be subject to judicial review. The intergovernmental relationship can be dragged into the courts as, for example, when Lord Denning ruled against the GLC's 1981 'Fares Fair' policy. The Widdicombe Committee (1986: ch. 3, para. 49) reminded councillors that the fact that a local authority is elected 'may lend political authority to its actions within the law . . . but does not provide a mandate to act outside or above the law. Its continued existence . . . depends on the contribution it can make to good government.' However, the 'law' is anything the central government wishes to drive through Parliament, and 'good government' can be whatever the Cabinet or prime minister approve of.

A steady erosion of local autonomy by central government has been a persistent post-war trend that was to be accelerated in the 1980s. The outcome was fierce central–local battles as many left-wing authorities tried to resist central cuts. The state of tension was renewed by the level of expenditure cuts demanded by the 2010 coalition government

> The fundamental idea of Centralisation is, distrust. It puts no Faith in Man; believes not in Hope, nor in the everlastingness of truth; and treats charity as an idle word. Its synonyms are, irresponsible control; meddling interference; and arbitrary taxation.
>
> J. Toulmin Smith, *Local Self-Government and Centralization* (1851)

Analysing central–local intergovernmental relations

The analysis of central–local relations is central to the study of local government. In essence it is a political relationship in which the interests of the parties can vary. A number of theoretical models have sought to explain the relationship.

- **Agency**. The idea that local government should be an agency of the centre, with little will of its own, is essentially the Benthamite position, justified on grounds of efficiency rather than democracy. From the 1930s, W. A. Robson (1966) lamented the loss of the latter. Writing in the 1990s, King (1993: 196) could still employ the agency terminology, likening the central–local relationship to that between government and its Next Steps agencies.
- **Stewardship**. Chandler (2009) modifies the agency perspective to see local authority in the position of the steward, responsible for an area and with significant discretion but no real independent power.

- **Partnership**. In the early 1970s, scholars refuted the agency model by noting that differences in per capita spending on particular services (education, housing, social services) between authorities demonstrated local autonomy (Boaden 1971; Davies 1972). It was argued that central and local government existed together in a largely harmonious social democratic partnership.
- **Power-dependence**. Rhodes (1981) stressed that local authorities, like other organizations and pressure groups, engage in a pluralistic bargaining process with the centre. In this they have significant resources (expertise, organization, information) and there is no reason to believe that the wishes of the centre must always prevail. This was underlined throughout the 1980s as the centre was repeatedly forced to pass new legislation following successive failures to impose its will. However, John (1994a), after studying council house sales, argued that this model ignored central government's capacity to learn and ultimately dominate. Hogwood (1997: 715) noted that a government's duration in office is a key factor in its ability to control. Thus, a long period of Conservative rule concluding with the Major years, saw an effective marginalizing of local government (see Kingdom 1999: 27–45).
- **Dual state**. The neo-Marxist 'dual-state thesis' (Saunders 1984: 24) depicts central government as a closed system of corporate decision-making (concerned with collective investment) and local government as relatively open (concerned with collective consumption – welfare). In a capitalist society the interests of capital come first.
- **Marxist**. A Marxist view portrays local authorities as subject to a greater power – not central government but the forces of wealth and capital (see Cockburn 1977). The history of local government can be read as a series of responses to the needs of the capitalist economy (see Castells 1977). Under conditions of fiscal crisis, when government tax revenue fails to match expenditure (see O'Connor 1973), central governments will seek cuts and agencies responsible for welfare provision, predominantly local authorities, will suffer. This became a compelling argument in the light of the policy of the coalition government after 2010.

The wider network

The model of a single central–local relationship is simplistic. The real world of local governance is messy and bewilderingly complex, with relationships varying from one authority to another and arising around different policy areas and issues within networks of interested parties (see Rhodes 1988). Thus, for example, the poll tax issue would engage one network, local management of schools another. Voluntary societies, environmentalists, private-sector providers and large business interests move on and off the stage in an ever-changing policy drama. Moreover, the relationship is not static over time. In the immediate post-war years the vocabulary of partnership seemed appropriate, while later decades were characterized by antagonism and mistrust.

EU membership introduces further complexity. Authorities can lobby at Brussels, arguing the case for *subsidiarity* to reclaim responsibilities (thereby hoisting the British government – the leading advocate of the principle – with its own petard). Indeed, the European Commission successfully brought an enforcement action against the UK government for failing to implement a directive protecting workers in conditions of compulsory competitive tendering (preventing them being rehired at a cheaper rate) (Woodhouse 1995: 413). Authorities have not themselves responded uniformly to European opportunities; some have created special EU units, some have even established a lobbying presence in Brussels, sometimes in consortia, while others have remained minimalist (see John 1994b). With devolution for Scotland and Wales and a greater regional focus in other EU countries, EU membership could set the cat amongst the central–local pigeons, strengthening calls for English regionalism (see p. 627).

Local Democracy: a Future in Question

> It is but a small proportion of the public business of a country which can be well done, or safely attempted, by the central authorities; . . . the legislative portion at least of the governing body busies itself far too much with local affairs.
>
> J. S. Mill, *On Representative Government* (1861)

Throughout the 1980s and 1990s there was a feeling that local democracy in Britain was in crisis, perhaps near extinction. Indeed, according to John Major's former adviser, Baroness Hogg, ministers had seriously considered abolishing it altogether in 1990 (*Observer*, 14 July 1996). In a March 1998 pamphlet, published by the Institute for Public Policy Research, Tony Blair warned local government: 'If you are unwilling or unable to work the modern agenda then government will have to look to other partners to take on your role'. With fast-food chains operating Education Action Zones there could be little doubt who the new partners would be.

Other voices expressed support for local government. In 1993 the public service union UNISON and the local authority associations established a Commission for Local Democracy, including representatives from the major parties, local officials and academics. Chaired by former editor of *The Times*, Simon Jenkins, it made over forty proposals, broadly claiming more freedom from central control (Commission for Local Democracy 1995). In June 1997, the government signed the EU Charter of Local Self-Government, and a series of consultation papers spoke the language of democratic renewal, ethics and finance.

Under the Conservative–Liberal Democrat coalition David Cameron's 'big society' mantra took policy form in the 2011 'Localism Act'. However, this spoke of empowering local communities rather than local government, with rights for others to bid to provide services. This placed greater reliance on voluntary organizations, the National Council for Voluntary Organisations warning that volunteers must not be overstretched or exploited. UNISON feared further privatization, opening a door not to communities but to multinational corporations. Moreover, with the greater freedom came the poisoned chalice of managing funding cuts of some 26 per cent. Hence, while the Localism Act appeared to offer reformers much that they desired, debate was by no means dead.

Key points

- Local government is the self-government of territorial units of the state.

- Local governance refers to a broader set of processes and institutions that shape communal life.

- Britain has a long history of local government, combining localist and centralist traditions.

- Industrialization produced the modern system of local government.

- The importance of local government is determined by what it is allowed to do.

- Today a number of local services are provided by unelected quangos – a 'new magistracy'.

- Modern local government is essentially political, involving parties and interest groups.

- Local councils operate in the shadow of central government, not least because of its financial importance.

- The 1980s saw bitter central–local confrontations, with some dramatic revamping in terms of management style and functions.

- The coalition government's Localism Act relaxed some central controls over local authorities, but at a time of severe funding cuts.

Review your understanding of the following terms and concepts

central–local relations
centralism
community charge (poll tax)
corporate management
council
council officer
council leader
council tax

county
county borough
elected mayor
enabling authority
local governance
metropolitan county
parish
rate-capping
rates

Revenue Support Grant
shire county
single-tier system
specific grant
uniform business rate
ultra vires
unitary system

Questions for discussion and debate

Consider these propositions and be prepared to present the cases for and against. Try to produce debating propositions of your own.

1   The modern system of local government is a product of the industrial revolution.

2   Low electoral turnouts show that people care little for local democracy.

3   Party politics has no place in local government.

4   Officials must inevitably dominate councillors.

5   Britain needs a system of unitary authorities.

6   The 'enabling authority' disables local democracy.

7   The directly elected mayor has no place in British political culture.

8   Local government without central control would be a charter for extremists.

9   To be meaningful local authorities must have important functions.

10   The only curb on local taxation levels should be the view of the community.

Further reading

Local libraries contain much information on local government in the area. This can furnish material for local projects.

Chandler, J. (2007) *Explaining Local Government: Local Governance in Britain since 1800*.
Excellent account of the evolving system, charting a process of increasing centralization.

Chandler, J. (2009) *Local Government Today*.
Encompasses changes to the structure and function of the system since 2000, including developments flowing from the 2007 Local Government Act.

Checkland, S. G. and E. O. A. (eds) (1974) *The Poor Law Report of 1834*.
Unique insight into the utilitarian and moralistic outlook that was central to industrialization.

Commission for Local Democracy (1995) *Taking Charge: The Rebirth of Local Democracy, Final Report*.
Details an extensive and thought-provoking reform agenda covering local government and quangocracy.

Dunleavy, P. J. (1980) *Urban Political Analysis*.
Lively and provocative, though introducing some highly sophisticated analysis. Not for beginners.

Rhodes, R. (1992) *Beyond Westminster and Whitehall: The Sub-central Government of Britain*.
Clear exposition of the power-dependence approach and much else.

Stewart, J. (2000) *The Nature of British Local Government*.
A stimulating mix of anecdotal evidence and systematic research, illuminated by history and contemporary developments.

Stoker, G. (ed.) (2000) *The New Politics of Local Governance*.
Authoritative essays edited by scholar with a keen interest in reform.

Stoker, G. (2003) *Transforming Local Governance: From Thatcherism to New Labour*.
Authoritative and systematic assessment of the changing nature of local governance in Britain, with a well-developed conceptual framework.

Wilson, D. and Game, C. (2011) *Local Government in the United Kingdom*, 5th edn.
Authors argue that cricket is only boring to those who do not understand it, and suggest local government is the same. They prove their point with an engaging text.

For reading around the subject and some light relief

Roy Hattersley, A *Yorkshire Boyhood*.
Labour ex-politician recounts his local government years.

Winifred Holtby, *South Riding*.
Few novels take county government as their background, but here by-laws and drainage are entwined with the passions of ordinary people.

J. K. Rowling, *The Casual Vacancy*.
An empty seat on the Pagford parish council becomes the catalyst for town warfare in an election fraught with passion, duplicity and unexpected revelations. But no wizardry!

On the net

https://www.gov.uk/government/organisations/
department-for-communities-and-local-government
The Department for Communities and Local Government provides statistics and facts, but also some 'spin' on its policies.

http://www.lgiu.org.uk/
The Local Government Information Unit is a good starting point for independent information and analysis and links to the local authorities' own sites. Check your own to find out what your elected representatives have been doing; you may even be able to read the minutes of council meetings.

http://www.info4local.gov.uk
This website is one way local government learns about central government initiatives, but it's useful for students too.

http://www.local.gov.uk/
Much of the Local Government Association's website is open to the public as well as to its members (councillors and officers). In addition to a wide range of news and up-to-date statistics, it covers local government relations with central government and other organizations.

CHAPTER 22

TRIALS AND ERRORS: JUSTICE AND POLITICS

Contents

In this chapter we turn to the institutions applying the laws that emerge from the political process. We begin by mapping the institutional stage upon which legal dramas are enacted: the system of courts. Next we examine the dramatis personae *– the lawyers and judges – and place a critical lens upon the constitutional principle of judicial impartiality. The fourth section examines the role of judges in the political process and finally we consider certain special institutions concerned with administrative justice, the protection of citizens from the state itself. In each section we shall find that the dignified world of wig and gown is not so far removed from the undignified world of politics that decides who gets what, when and how.*

Many books on politics say little, if anything, about judges, courts and the administration of justice. This is because the law is supposed to be above politics and the judges, like high priests, to be outside party, class and faction. They are expected to dispense justice to weak and powerful, rich and poor, without fear or favour. However, we shall find that the judicial process and those working within it are by no means insulated from the controversies and vicissitudes of political life.

Of all our constitutional institutions, none is as august and dignified as those associated with the administration of justice. Judges deck themselves in the regalia of another age as necessarily as plumbers wear boiler-suits, and the most venerable members of the judiciary, until very recently, sat in the House of Lords. In court, judges expect impeccable courtesy and deference (indeed, failure to display this can be punished as contempt), enshrined in archaic forms of language. When Lord Chief Justice Taylor tried to abolish wigs in 1996, he was met with obdurate opposition from barristers addicted to 'pantomime flummery' (Robertson 1997). Although most judges did stop wearing wigs in 2008, barristers continued to wear them when robed. Yet pageantry and splendour has a purpose: it is intended to bestow upon the system an aura of power, wisdom and integrity. Through these legal custodians the principle of the rule of law is manifested. This is the orthodox view; in this chapter we put it to the test.

Judgement must always be passed with complete solemnity – because it's such rot. Suppose a judge throws a woman into clink for having stolen a corncake for her child. And he isn't wearing his robes. . . . then the sentence he passes is a disgrace and the law is violated. It would be easier for a judge's robe and a judge's hat to pass sentence than for a man without all that paraphernalia.

Azdak in Bertolt Brecht's *The Caucasian Chalk Circle* (1948)

The Legal System

The administration of justice was traditionally shared by the Lord Chancellor's Department, responsible for administering the courts and appointing judges, and part of the Home Office. Under John Smith the Labour Party was committed to amalgamating these into a single Ministry of Justice and, although this was dropped from the 1997 manifesto, it was finally achieved in 2007 in the wake of the 2005 Constitutional Reform Act.

The courts

The structure of the courts in England and Wales is hierarchical (figure 22.1); superior courts check the actions of those below through a process of appeal. The organization reflects a fundamental dichotomy between **civil jurisdiction** (citizen versus citizen using such laws as tort and contract) and **criminal jurisdiction** (state versus citizen, as in crimes such as burglary or murder).

Civil jurisdiction

Minor cases begin in county courts, presided over by itinerant circuit judges, while more serious ones are heard in the High Court. Appeals go on to a Court of Appeal (Civil Division) and thence, upon further appeal, to the Supreme Court, the highest court in the land.

Criminal jurisdiction

Minor criminal cases are tried summarily (without a jury) in a magistrate's court. For serious criminal cases the magistrate's court conducts committal proceedings,

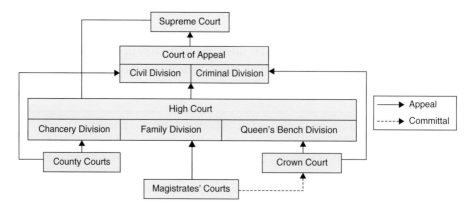

Figure 22.1 The courts in England and Wales

which merely decide whether there is a case to answer. If there is, it will go to a Crown Court to be tried before a jury and presided over by a High Court judge or circuit judge. Appeals from the Crown Court may be taken to the High Court (on a point of law) or the Court of Appeal (Criminal Division), and thence to the Supreme Court.

The European dimension

To the domestic system must be added two European courts.

The European Court of Human Rights

The European Convention on Human Rights (ECHR) was signed by a number of European countries in 1950. Alleged breaches are investigated by the European Commission on Human Rights and cases appear before the Court. The ECHR itself was not incorporated into domestic law until the 1998 Human Rights Act. This increased the potential for controversy by making the courts more political. A decision not to incorporate it into EU treaties means that it does not have the same legal status as European law, but it remains a potent tool in the hands of judges – whether sitting on the bench in UK courts or at Strasbourg. This can be seen, for example, in the case of the former imam Abu Qatada al-Filistini, a Jordanian Islamist with alleged links to al-Qaeda who had entered the UK on a forged passport in 1993. Imprisoned without trial for the best part of a decade under anti-terror laws, he was finally released on bail in February 2012, after the Court ruled that he could not be deported for trial in Jordan, where evidence against him might have been obtained by means of torture (in violation of the right to a fair trial guaranteed under Article 6 of the ECHR). Only after a tortuous process was he finally deported in 2013, after Jordan had agreed a treaty with the UK guaranteeing fair trials.

The European Court of Justice (ECJ)

As the importance of the EU increases in the lives of states and citizens so does its court – the European Court of Justice (ECJ, see p. 182). All UK courts must take notice of ECJ decisions and lower courts may look to it for definitive rulings on the meaning of European law and treaties.

Access to the law

A prerequisite of a just legal system is that all have equal access. Yet in practice critics have argued that this is by no means the case; lawyers' clientele has remained predominantly middle class (Zander 1969). Curious reasons are advanced for this.

- *Cost.* Lawyers' fees, protected by the monopolistic practices of the Law Society, mean that access to the legal system does not come cheap. For many it is better to suffer a wrong than risk an expensive lawsuit.
- *Legal expertise.* It has been in the nature of the legal profession to take a greater interest in the problems of the wealthy than the poor. The intricacies of business and commerce tend to preoccupy the legal mind, to the exclusion of problems with landlords, local authorities and social security agencies.
- *The nature of the law.* The law has placed its greatest emphasis on the management and protection of property.
- *Class.* The upper-middle-class image of the profession is itself a deterrent. A yawning gulf exists between working-class people and the popular image of the smooth-talking, self-confident lawyer. Fear of embarrassment, of appearing foolish, tends to keep many ordinary people away from the intimidating consulting room.

Attempts have been made to improve access. First, there is a system of *legal aid*, whereby the state gives financial assistance to litigants. Introduced in the 1949 Legal Aid and Advice Act, it represented a significant development, both for the law and for democracy. Generally aid depends upon income and the merits of the case. However, it is subject to abuse both by wealthy individuals finding a technical means to qualify and by 'fat cat' barristers claiming huge fees. In 2010 it was reported that the number of barristers earning more than £100,000 per annum in legal aid fees had risen to nearly 1000 in the previous year, with the top ten earning close to £7 million between them (*Daily Telegraph*, 22 March 2010).

The 1980s saw a great rise in the number of claimants. The government attempted to ease the cost to the state by reducing eligibility. The 1988 Legal Aid Act transferred administration from the Law Society to a new quango, the Legal Aid Board. In 1995 the system was cash-limited and solicitors and advice agencies were to compete for contracts to hold legal aid budgets. The government also moved to exclude personal injury cases, extending the 'no win, no fee' principle throughout civil proceedings and involving the private insurance market. To critics this compromised the government's professed commitment to human rights without achieving the stated goal of bringing the cost of legal aid under control. By 2012 the legal aid bill was running at more than £2 billion annually (*Guardian*, 9 Jan. 2012). In an effort to reduce it, the coalition government further tightened the eligibility criteria in the 2012 Legal Aid, Sentencing and Punishment of Offenders Act, widely criticized as denying justice to the poorest and most vulnerable.

The *Dramatis Personae*

The courts are rather like churches – nothing without the people inside them. Control is jealously guarded by a veritable priesthood of curates, vicars, bishops – even, until very recently, an archbishop in the form of the Lord Chancellor. The law, perhaps the oldest and most venerable of the professions, saw its heyday under the Victorians. The capitalist bourgeoisie based their claim to wealth, prestige and power on property and needed lawyers to secure these. The reform of the law along Benthamite lines, through Acts of Parliament, was the basis for establishing the new order, and the huge increase in private and public legislation made Parliament an earthly paradise for the great Victorian lawyers. The natural partners of the capitalists, like them the lawyers were hard-working, generally became immensely wealthy and registered this with a profound sense of their own dignity and importance. As the Lord Chancellor sang in Gilbert and Sullivan's *Iolanthe*:

> The Law is the true embodiment
> Of everything that's excellent.
> It has no kind of fault or flaw
> And I, my lords, embody the law.

Respect for the law became, in practice, a veneration of lawyers that endures to this day.

In the administration of justice lawyers fall into three categories: solicitors, barristers and the judiciary. Although entwined together with dense legal bindweed, they have long practised a strict division of labour. While not entirely unique to Britain, the system is relatively unusual and not much admired by lawyers from other countries.

> The Lawyer is exclusively occupied with the details of predatory fraud either in achieving or in checking chicanery, and success in the profession is therefore accepted as marking a large endowment of that barbarian astuteness which has always commanded men's respect and fear.
>
> Thorstein Veblen (1857–1929; American social scientist), *The Theory of the Leisure Class* (1899)

Solicitors

Solicitors can be employed in various contexts, including national and local government, but they mainly practise privately, usually in partnerships, dealing directly with the public. They are collectively represented by their 'trade union', the Law

I dined at my Lord Chancellor's, where three Sergeants at law told their stories, how long they had detained their clients in tedious processes by tricks.
John Evelyn (1620–1706), *Diary* (26 Nov. 1686)

Society, which has enjoyed considerable influence as an 'insider' pressure group *par excellence*. Although they may work very closely with clients, perhaps understanding every nuance of their cases, they were by convention prohibited from appearing in a superior court, having to instruct a barrister, their superior in the legal pecking order.

In 1989 the Lord Chancellor, Lord Mackay of Clashfern, unveiled three green papers proposing reforms of the profession which placed some very lively cats among the legal pigeons. The goal was to introduce free-market disciplines into the cloistered world of wig and gown: breaking the barristers' advocacy monopoly, and allowing lawyers to take cases on a US-style 'no win, no fee' basis, to advertise their services and to publish fees. The most innovative feature of the resulting Courts and Legal Services Act 1990 that followed was the right of audience for lawyers provided they had gained a certificate of advocacy. However, barristers could expect to maintain their hegemony in the rarefied atmosphere of the upper courts. The 2007 Legal Services Act went further, offering consumers easier redress against those providing legal services and encouraging competition within the market.

Barristers

Known collectively as 'the Bar', barristers are far less numerous than solicitors and, despite their superior status, are dependent on the latter for business. They may advance to a higher grade by 'taking silk', when they are formally appointed a Queen's Counsel (QC) by the monarch, having been informed of the recommendations of the Queen's Counsel selection panel by the Justice Secretary. At the apex stand two political appointees: the *Attorney General* (the government's attorney) and the *Solicitor General for England* (the government's solicitor). (The Scottish legal system functions separately from that in England and Wales, with a *Solicitor General for Scotland*.) A number of barristers have gone on to become MPs, their allegiance going predominantly to the Conservative Party or Labour's right (such as Clement Attlee, John Smith and Tony Blair).

As a group, barristers remain socially insulated, over half operating in the hothouse of London in one of the four great Inns of Court, marked by much tradition. They are richly remunerated. Lord Falconer QC had to be persuaded to leave a £500,000-a-year commercial practice to become Blair's Solicitor General in 1997 (*The Times*, 27 June 1997); by comparison, even in 2010, the highest-paid member of the judiciary, the Lord Chief Justice, received a salary of just £239,845. In 2011, Conservative MP Stewart Jackson argued that it was 'inappropriate' for 500 barristers to earn more annually than the prime ministerial salary of £142,500 (*Daily Mail*, 2 July 2011).

Controlling the profession through the General Council of the Bar and a Bar Secretariat, the Inns of Court have an ancient lineage, being well established by the fifteenth century. They were originally concerned with training barristers through

A client is fain to hire a lawyer to keep from the injury of other lawyers – as Christians that travel in Turkey are forced to hire janissaries, to protect them from the insolencies of other Turks.

Samuel Butler (1612–80; English satirist), *Prose Observations* lectures and 'arguments', and successful students would duly be 'called to the Bar'. This training gradually declined until, by the early nineteenth century, the call was a formality, the student being merely required to pay an appropriate fee and symbolize attendance for twelve terms by consuming a prescribed number of dinners. Nineteenth-century reforms added to wealth and gastronomic capacity a requirement to pass examinations.

The organization continued to reflect that of the ancient Oxbridge colleges. Traditionally, the Bar has been no place for a woman; in 1995, they accounted for only 16 per cent of the pool of suitable candidates for silk, 8.5 per cent of applicants and only 5.8 per cent of QCs appointed (*Independent*, 27 June 1996). Attempts at reform saw female applicants becoming disproportionately successful after 2000, but the numbers of women applying to take silk remain low. Whereas 66 per cent of the forty-one female applicants were successful in 2010–11, taking twenty-seven of the 120 posts available, women accounted for just 19.5 per cent of all applicants (QCA Press Release 2011).

The judiciary

For historical reasons it is mainly from the Bar that judges have been chosen. This has an important implication for the legal system because judicial office is seen as

Working clothes: undeterred by the rain, Supreme Court judges walk to Parliament in full regalia

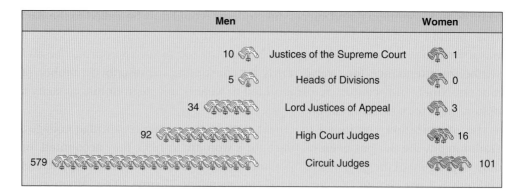

Figure 22.2 The judicial hierarchy, 2010

Note: One Supreme Court seat was vacant at the time of publication.

Source: Data from Ministry of Justice (2010: supplementary table S6.09).

legal business rather than as an aspect of public service. It helps to legitimate the law by reinforcing the impression of independence. In the sense that appointment is seen as promotion (although one which the richest barristers will spurn), the judiciary may be regarded as the top of the legal hierarchy (figure 22.2).

Appointments were traditionally made by the Lord Chancellor, based on secret 'soundings' or 'consultations' among existing judges and senior lawyers. Reformers argued for an independent appointments commission, staffed with lay people as well as representatives from both sides of the legal profession. Following a raft of proposals from the Labour government in 2003, major reform finally materialized in the form of the Constitutional Reform Act 2005. This brought significant change to the upper echelons of the judiciary: replacing the Appellate Committee of the House of Lords with a new UK Supreme Court; creating a more independent system of appointments to this highest court (figure 22.3); establishing a new Judicial Appointments Commission to oversee other senior judicial appointments; and reforming the position of Lord Chancellor to make the Lord Chief Justice head of the judiciary.

Magistrates

At the bottom of the judicial hierarchy are the unpaid magistrates sitting in the local courts as Justices of the Peace (JPs), most of whom are not lawyers (they are advised by clerks who are qualified lawyers). In large cities there are also stipendiary (professionally qualified and paid) magistrates. JPs were key figures in local government until the municipal reforms following industrialization swept them from centre stage. They retained a legal role, which was increased with responsibility for

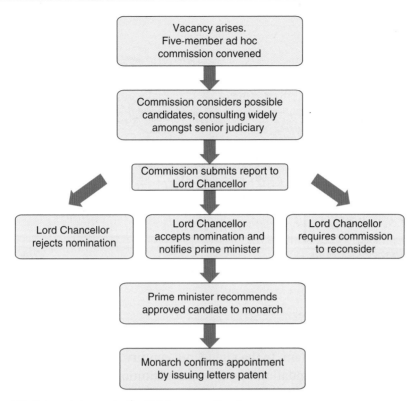

Figure 22.3 Appointments to the UK Supreme Court

Note: Prospective Supreme Court justices must have held high judicial office for two years or have been a qualifying legal practitioner for 15 years. The appointment commission comprises the president and deputy president of the Supreme Court, one member of the Judicial Appointments Commission (JAC), one member of the Judicial Appointments Board for Scotland, and one member of the Northern Ireland Judicial Appointments Commission.

juvenile cases after 1908. Despite some reforms the system remains elitist. Formal appointment is by the Lord Chancellor acting on the advice of local committees. Technically anyone can become a magistrate, but critics have seen the process in the hands of local oligarchies within political parties, chambers of commerce and the freemasons.

Twelve men good and true: the jury

Although we have introduced the highest and most mighty we have not encompassed the full judicial *dramatis personae* until we consider the twelve ordinary people forming the **jury**. These are mainly used in serious criminal cases and their job is to determine innocence or guilt. They are directed by the judge, who will also pass sentence. Selected randomly from the population, juries are without doubt the

"The jury will ignore that last remark..."

Reproduced by permission of *Punch*

most democratic aspect of the legal system – perhaps the most democratic aspect of the whole political system. In the eighteenth century Lord Camden stated: 'trial by jury is indeed the foundation of our free constitution; take that away and the whole fabric will soon moulder into dust' (quoted in Jackson 1960). Here ordinary citizens are allowed to speak so authoritatively that the most lofty in the land must heed their words. It was a jury that acquitted Clive Ponting of charges of treason, against the direction of the judge.

However, juries live under threat. The police in particular find them tiresome, conducting an unceasing campaign for their abolition or limitation. In response the Labour government introduced the 1967 Criminal Justice Act, which allowed majority verdicts rather than unanimity. In December 2000, the New Labour government attempted to curb the right to trial by jury by reintroducing the Criminal Justice (Mode of Trial) Bill. Magistrates would decide whether to try cases themselves or send them to the Crown Court to be heard before a judge and jury. This prompted vehement opposition in the Lords, including from Labour peers such as Helena Kennedy QC, who argued strongly against removing this long-established and fundamental right. In January 2002, after a prolonged barrage of criticism from lawyers, Labour peers and civil liberties groups, Home Secretary David Blunkett jettisoned the plan. The demise of the jury system would constitute a grave threat to democracy. An example came in Northern Ireland where fears of intimidation led, in 1973, to juries being dispensed with in certain terrorism cases. In these 'Diplock courts' convictions were often based on confessions obtained during long hours of police interrogation, where allegations of ill-treatment were subsequently proved.

Radical lawyer Michael Mansfield (1997) has argued that far from being contracted, the system should be extended, with all crimes eligible for jury trial. The 2001 Auld Report made some recommendations for improving the system, with juries being provided with written summaries of cases and lists of issues that needed to be decided. It also recommended making it more difficult for professional people to evade jury service, which had resulted in a preponderance of working class or unemployed representation and tabloid reports of jurors celebrating 'over a pint' with the defendants after their acquittal (Gibb 1988). The 2003 Criminal Justice Act reduced grounds for exemption but also identified new circumstances under which a trial could dispense with a jury in cases of serious fraud and where there was a risk of jury tampering. This issue was highlighted in February 2013 when, in the trial of Vicky Pryce, wife of disgraced minister Chris Huhne, the judge dismissed the jury over the quality of the questions they asked him and ordered a re-trial.

Questions of Independence and Impartiality

Justice requires that judges act with both independence and impartiality. These are not the same; the first means freedom from outside influence and the second, freedom from bias. Whilst the absence of judicial independence will inevitably undermine impartiality, a fully independent judiciary will not necessarily be free from bias.

Judicial independence

Judicial independence is the principle that those holding judicial office should be able to dispense justice free from political influence. This is part of the constitutional doctrine of the separation of powers. Judicial independence is protected in a number of ways. First, judges enjoy considerable security of tenure, their continuance in office being limited only by the requirement to retire at the age of seventy-five. It is extraordinarily uncommon for judges to be suspended or removed from office and those few who have suffered this fate have invariably faced sanction as a result of physical incapacity, prolonged incompetence or some serious impropriety. Secondly, the salaries of judges are met directly from the Consolidated Fund, effectively placing their remuneration beyond the day-to-day control of politicians. Thirdly, the *sub judice* rules generally prevent politicians, the media and others from seeking to influence the courts by speaking about a case whilst legal proceedings are ongoing.

The changes heralded by the 2005 Constitutional Reform Act, in terms of affording the new Supreme Court physical and operational independence from other branches of central government, reducing the role of the Lord Chancellor (once a standing denial of the separation of powers) and creating a more independent appointments process in respect of all senior judicial posts, have further enhanced judicial independence. However, institutional independence does not remove the possibility of political interference. For example, in dealing with those arrested over the violence seen in British cities in the summer of 2012, David Cameron urged magistrates and judges to impose tough sentences and they duly obliged. The issue assumed greater salience as a result of the 1998 Human Rights Act (see p. 703).

Judicial impartiality

The issue of **judicial impartiality** evokes sociological questions. The iconic statue above the Central Criminal Court (the Old Bailey) shows Justice blindfolded, not knowing who sits on the balance she holds. Judges favour neither rich nor poor, neither right nor left. This picture of judicial impartiality is essential to the legitimation of liberal-democratic government. Judges must appear to stand above the confused *mêlée* of classes, parties and interests. To address this we must consider the judges themselves.

Who are the judges? Social characteristics

The British judiciary has for long been tied by silken threads of class to the Establishment, one important condition until recently having been success as a barrister. The career path traditionally ensured that judges would be relatively old and predominantly male, and the likelihood that their faces would be white was as certain as that their wigs would be so. In 1994 a less secretive process was introduced for appointments below High Court level, with open advertisements in newspapers. Yet despite protestations from Lord Chancellor Lord Mackay that the 'old boy network' no longer operated, figures released by his department in 1995 revealed that 80 per cent of Lords of Appeal, Heads of Division, Lords Justices of Appeal and High Court judges had Oxbridge backgrounds, as had over 50 per cent of middle-ranking circuit judges. Only amongst the lower-ranking district judges was social composition more mixed. Yet even here 12 per cent had travelled by the Oxbridge route. In May 1995 Sir Thomas Legg, permanent secretary in the Lord Chancellor's Department, told the Commons Home Affairs Committee: 'it is not the function of the professional judiciary to be representative of the community'.

By 2000, there were still no black or Asian judges on the High Court bench. However, with Labour's relatively reformist Derry Irvine as Lord Chancellor, there was a slow but steady increase in both ethnic minorities and women; between 1998 and 2001, the proportion of women in the judiciary as a whole increased from 10 to 14 per cent (Lord Chancellor's Department 2001b). Of particular significance was the elevation of Lady Justice Butler-Sloss to head the Family Division. However, by 2011 there was still a long way to go, particularly at the highest levels. Although women held 14,540 of the 28,607 magistrate posts in 2010 (Ministry of Justice 2011a: 185), they only accounted for 20 of the 161 posts in the senior judiciary – Justices of the Supreme Court, Heads of Division, Lord Justices of Appeal and High Court judges (Ministry of Justice 2010: 60). In terms of ethnicity, 4.2 per cent of the judiciary declared themselves to be from a black and minority ethnic (BME) background in 2011 (up from 3.9 per cent in 2010). However, just 4 of the 161 senior level judges in post in April 2011 were from a BME background, with 123 from a white background and 34 having no recorded ethnicity (Ministry of Justice 2011b: 78).

This soil does not nourish radical saplings. From the beginning, selection is by their seniors, who fashion the clay in their own image before administering the breath of life. When those from less propitious backgrounds receive the call – and there is evidence of a widening entry to the Inns of Court School of Law (Bar Council 1989: 51), they are unlikely to make any impression on the impassive face of tradition. Characteristically motivated by social aspiration, with little desire to challenge the status quo, they will already have been subject to a battery of socializing pressures and will make sure they join the right clubs and say the right things with the right accents. One club has appeared particularly attractive: the freemasons, a shadowy organization involving strange rites, secret handshakes and rolled-up trouser-legs. Rumours regularly circulate that membership interferes with judicial impartiality and in 1997 Home Secretary Jack Straw announced that all new recruits to the criminal justice system should declare their membership, existing members being invited to sign a voluntary register. Judicial hostility was palpable, with even the Lord Chancellor in full cry.

Interest affiliation

Judges may be associated with interest groups and political movements. Judicial affiliations were brought to public attention in 2000 in the case of exiled Chilean dictator General Pinochet. Lord Hoffmann, one of the Law Lords hearing his appeal against extradition, was found to be closely linked with Amnesty International. The House of Lords was forced to hear the case again, thus opening the door to a surge of challenges on similar grounds (Woodhouse 2001: 223). The media began taking an interest in the potential for judicial bias, highlighting, for example, the religious backgrounds of judges involved in a case concerning the separation of Siamese twins against their parents' wishes in 2000.

Judges, Politics and the Law

The principle of the separation of powers would exclude judges from the making of laws and debating policy. However, in the real world the judiciary dips more than a toe into the murky process. Before the 2005 Constitutional Reform Act, this was institutionalized in the constitutionally anomalous position of its head, the Lord Chancellor (p. 95). A number of holders of the office, such as the Conservative Lord Hailsham and Labour's Lord Irvine, were well known as political figures and the Attorney General and Solicitor General continue to be political appointees. In the former office, Lord Goldsmith's advice over the legality of the 2003 invasion of Iraq placed him at the epicentre of political controversy. Beyond this formal proximity to power there are other ways in which judges enter the world of politics.

Legislative influence

Evolving the common law

British common law is no more than a body of past judgments, a great coral reef of wisdom from successive ages. In trials lawyers will delve into the records to find *precedents* to guide current decisions. This **case law** is continually evolving. Where two or more cases appear to have been resolved differently, or where social conditions have changed, the judge will exercise discretion and so create a further precedent. In a BBC Radio 4 series in 2012, Helena Kennedy QC made the case that the common law was a significant factor in the development of capitalist interests.

Interpreting statute law

Statute law is made by Parliament and takes precedence over the common law. However, this does not rule out the creative role of the judiciary. No Act of Parliament can take into account all the circumstances of any particular case and invariably some interpretation, or *statutory construction*, is required. Although judges try to reflect the legislators' intentions, they do not always succeed. For example, the Law Lords decided that the race relations legislation (intended to outlaw discrimination generally) did not apply to private clubs. Again, much legislation invokes the concept of 'reasonableness' in determining standards of acceptable behaviour, which in practice means what *judges* regard as reasonable. Moreover, where loopholes exist in legislation (which they often do), judges can show great ingenuity in inserting their own policy judgements. In 2011, in the controversy over super-injunctions, judges were accused of making laws beyond

The Common Law of England has been laboriously built about a mythical figure – the figure of the 'reasonable man'.

A. P. Herbert (1890–1971; British writer and politician), *Uncommon Law* (1935)

the authority of Parliament by creating a privacy law on the basis of Article 8 of the ECHR.

The Law Commission

This quango, composed entirely of lawyers, is responsible for revising the law. Its role is defined formally as technical and non-political, concerned with clarifying obscure language, repealing obsolete statutes, and consolidating and codifying masses of complicated statute or common law. However, it can make major recommendations with more than a cosmetic impact. For example, the controversial 1986 Public Order Act incorporated most of the recommendations of a report made by the commission three years earlier. The 2009 Law Commission Act strengthened the commission by requiring the Lord Chancellor to explain to Parliament the reasons why any of its proposals might have been rejected.

Review of legislation

In many countries (including the USA and France) judges are responsible for reviewing legislation in the light of the constitution. The doctrine of parliamentary supremacy has rendered **judicial review** abhorrent to the British constitution. However, membership of the EU increased the scope for judicial activism in a process of 'constitution creep' (Thompson 1997: 186). Indeed, judges appeared to be ahead of politicians in recognizing their responsibility to review domestic legislation in the light of EU law. The powers to suspend an Act were revealed in the *Factortame* case (see p. 98). EU law can also be a basis for judicial review. The Equal Opportunities Commission (EOC) claimed that, in denying certain rights to those working less than eight hours a week, the 1978 Employment Protection Act conflicted with EU law. The House of Lords found for the EOC. EU membership also liberalized judicial attitudes towards statutory interpretation. The courts now refer to *Hansard* in determining the intention behind legislation. Originally prohibited, this first became necessary to establish whether national law was *intended* to comply with EU law, and it has since been extended to all cases of ambiguity. In addition, the 1998 Human Rights Act requires ministers introducing bills to show whether they comply with the ECHR. Provisions in breach must be debated. A Human Rights Committee of both houses considers such issues. If the judges consider an Act to be in conflict with the Convention they may issue a 'declaration of incompatibility' – in effect referring it to the committee for a rethink.

Review of executive actions

While unable to strike down legislation, judges have had the power to quash executive actions when challenged in the courts. This can produce a quasi-political

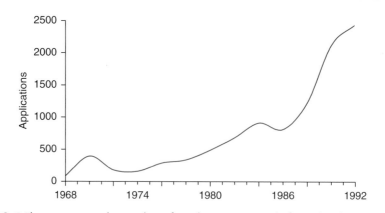

Figure 22.4 The increase in the number of applications to apply for judicial review of administrative action, 1968–1992

Source: Data from Butler and Butler (1994: 318).

check since, in reality, it may be dissatisfaction with the legislation itself that produces the action. Traditionally, judges had been content to confine such review to the principle of *ultra vires*, where officials have taken action beyond their legal powers. Where they brought in other considerations (reasonableness or fairness), they did so only on the basis of legislative intent, thereby respecting parliamentary sovereignty. Calls for judicial review were to rise sharply from the mid-1980s (figure 22.4) as individuals and groups became more aware of a growth in executive power and judges became more willing to consider the spirit as well as the letter of the law. Mr Justice Laws asserted that political controversy should not be grounds for believing a decision to be outside the courts' jurisdiction (Woodhouse 1995: 405–6).

Judicial activism

In the great debates of the day judges are by no means shrinking violets. When delivering judgments their exegesis will often pass comment on various matters of social concern, such as the role of the family, discipline in schools, moral standards, and so on. They can even take off their wigs and gowns and enter the political fray directly, sometimes by confronting politicians. Restrictions on judicial pronouncements came in the form of the Kilmuir guidelines laid down in 1955, though observance of these has varied with Lord Chancellors and they were relaxed by Lord Mackay in 1988. Judges even began to discuss issues over lunchtime sandwiches with journalists (see Dyer 1995). Lord Chief Justice Taylor gave regular press conferences and speeches, including the BBC Dimbleby Lecture, in which he attacked the government's handling of the criminal justice system.

Flattering invitations

Governments can also invite judges into the political realm in various ways. Legislation can be drawn up that asks them to adjudicate in controversial social matters, as in Edward Heath's short-lived (1971) Industrial Relations Court. Restrictive union legislation during the 1980s also brought judges into some bitter political struggles. In addition, leading members of the judiciary are frequently asked to head inquiries into controversial questions. Reports such as Scarman (race relations), Nolan (sleaze), Taylor (the Hillsborough disaster), Hutton (the death of David Kelly) and Leveson (phone-hacking) make their authors household names. This places them in the front line of controversy and open to political attack as, for example, when Lord Howe publicly denounced Sir Richard Scott's inquiry into the Matrix Churchill affair.

Justice in Action

A criticism of judges in general is that their social backgrounds lead to a tendency to act in a broadly conservative manner. However, in certain areas they have become more liberal, increasingly coming into conflict with governments. This has been largely around the application of the 1998 Human Rights Act, and often with reference to terrorism.

Cultural influences and bias

Class

Generally judges have been found to be more lenient towards members of the professions than towards the working class or the unemployed. Prudent solicitors recognize this when advising clients to wear a conventional middle-class uniform in court. This is not to deny that there are liberal judges (Lord Justice Woolf, for example, expressed publicly his desire for reform), but they tend to stand out as the exception. Radical lawyers campaigning for the rights of the disadvantaged and wrongly imprisoned, such as Helena Kennedy, Anthony Lestor and Michael Mansfield, point to inequity. In large cities, law centres financed by charities and local authorities have been established to combat bias, directing legal attention away from business and property matters to concerns affecting ordinary people, such as welfare, consumer affairs and employment.

Framing Eve

The male domination of the legal profession and judiciary is manifest in the way women are treated. Sexism is institutionalized into the law itself as well as its practice. Until the late nineteenth century, marriage meant that a woman surrendered all separate legal and property rights and until very recently wives could not be raped by their husbands, who enjoyed contractual rights to sex upon demand. Helena Kennedy, one of the few women QCs, found herself in a world of sexist innuendo and jokes about prostitutes and rape cases. To her, journalist Andrew Neil's libel action against a newspaper that had suggested he had consorted with a prostitute resembled a 'stag party', with amusing definitions of terms such as 'bimbo' (Kennedy 1992: 141–2). Judges have regularly displayed excessive leniency in rape cases, the women said to have been 'asking for it'.

Although far fewer women commit crimes than men, it is often said that, like Eve, they lie behind them. They can receive harsher sentences than men because, as many are mothers, community service is considered less suitable. Indeed, 45 per cent of women released to the supervision of the Probation Service have fewer than two convictions, compared with just 29 per cent of men (Ministry of Justice 2010: supplementary table S5.08).

Compensation for rape is particularly difficult. In the case of a man who had become more sexually violent following brain damage in a road accident, two women whom he had brutally assaulted (forcing one to strip, trussing her up 'like a chicken', raping and stabbing her) received just £7,080 and £10,480 in compensation. Although sentenced to life imprisonment, the man later received £45,750 in compensation for the car accident (Kennedy 1992: 28). The British Crime Survey reported that in the period 2006/7 fewer than one in a hundred rape cases led to a conviction.

Prosecuting Counsel: And you say she consented?

Defendant: I didn't say she consented.

PC: Did she agree?

D: She didn't agree.

PC: Having said no at first, she just gave in?

D: She enjoyed it.

Judge: The enjoyment wiped out her initial resistance – is that what you are saying?

D: Yes.

From a trial at the Old Bailey, reported by Sue Lees in *New Statesman* (December 1989)

Black justice

Judges will hotly deny that decisions are influenced by racial factors. However, Ministry of Justice (2011b: 11) statistics reveal that while black people constituted just 2.7 per cent of the population aged ten or over in 2009, they constituted 13.7 per cent of the prison population. Although social deprivation must account for some of this there are other factors. Kennedy (1992: 162) reports research by probation services showing that black defendants were more likely to receive immediate custodial or suspended sentences, a conclusion reinforced by more recent research published by the Ministry of Justice (2011b: 17). Though conviction rates for indictable offences in 2010 were higher for white offenders (81 per cent) than for black (74 per cent) or Asian groups (77 per cent), the average custodial sentences given to those convicted saw this pattern reversed, with those in the black ethnic group averaging 20.8 months, Asians 19.9 months and whites 14.9 months.

Political and moral views

Political leanings

Prima facie the evidence has suggested a natural bias of the judiciary towards the right. It has appeared that Labour governments have been more likely 'to act in ways which offend the judicial sense of rightness, the judicial sense of where the public interest lies' (Griffith 1981: 236–7). However, as we shall see below, from the mid-1980s reforms to the legal profession and government policies towards crime, sentencing and punishment soured relations with the Conservative Party and contributed to increased judicial political activism.

Moral issues

Members of sexual minorities, prostitutes, holders of unorthodox views, squatters, student protesters and so on can all expect rough justice. According to gay rights campaigner Peter Tatchell, men having consensual sex with males over sixteen in the early 1990s – before the 2000 Sexual Offences (Amendment) Act equalized the age of consent – were five times more likely to be prosecuted than those having sex with girls under sixteen and three times less likely to walk away with just a caution.

The judiciary and the police

The judiciary has generally supported the police in areas such as questioning, seizure, obtaining 'confessions', conduct of identification parades, and telephone tapping, when legal powers have been exceeded. It is generally recognized by the Director of Public Prosecutions, in deciding whether or not to proceed against

NUPKINS'S JUSTICE.

Learned Magistrate :—" HEAR THE EVIDENCE FOR THE DEFENCE? NONSENSE! I WON'T HEAR A WORD OF IT !
WHAT'S THE USE?——I COULD NOT THINK OF DOUBTING A POLICEMAN'S WORD."

Source: Mary Evans Picture Library

the police, that it is exceedingly difficult to secure a conviction. Even the five-year inquiry under retired High Court judge Sir John May into the wrongful imprisonment of the Guildford Four on the basis of false confessions was only mildly critical of the police. Helena Kennedy (1992: 6) has reported how criminal lawyers will present cases on the assumption that 'the judges will always prefer the police account unless the defence case is overwhelming'. However, the 2012 inquiry into the Hillsborough disaster revealed the police to be capable of lying.

Justice and rights

Property rights versus civil rights

The rise of the bourgeoisie was dependent upon property rights. These are legally vested in individuals through contracts and leases. Their protection has been a prime focus for the judiciary.

Workers' rights

From their inception trade unions were opposed by judges. In the nineteenth century, when a series of Combination Acts sought to restrict their growth, the judiciary assisted the process through statutory interpretation and common-law decisions. Indeed, towards the end of the century it was necessary to curb judicial anti-unionism with legislation. Hence the 1875 Conspiracy and Protection of Property Act effectively legalized strikes and the 1906 Trade Disputes Act reversed the notorious Taff Vale judgment. In 1913, further judicial zeal was curbed with the Trade Union Act to reverse the 1910 Osborne judgment, which had prevented the fledgling Labour Party from using union funds. Legislation during the 1980s was designed to push more industrial relations issues into the courts, which were not slow to respond, interpreting it in a way that cut union protection to a minimum (Marsh 1992: 109). The miners', printers' and seamen's unions all suffered from large-scale sequestration of funds under court orders.

Central–local relations

In this political minefield the courts have frequently been friendly to the right, as a number of *causes célèbres* show. In the 1976 *Tameside* case a newly elected Conservative council cancelled a plan for comprehensive education prepared by its Labour predecessor. The Labour Secretary of State intervened under powers in the 1944 Education Act but the House of Lords supported the council on the grounds of a local mandate for its actions. However, in the 'Fares Fair' case, although the High Court upheld the Labour-controlled GLC's right to reduce London Transport fares, the Appeal Court ruled that the statutory duty to provide 'economic' transport ruled out the policy.

Security

In matters of national security the judiciary has appeared willing to disregard most other considerations in siding with the state. In the *Hosenball* case (1977), an American journalist was ordered to be deported by Merlyn Rees, the Labour home secretary, for obtaining for publication material said to be harmful to UK security. Lord Denning, in dismissing an appeal, said, 'when the state is in danger . . . even the rules of natural justice had to take second place' (*The Times*, 30 March 1977). In IRA cases, judicial enthusiasm to convict resulted in serious miscarriages of justice, such as the cases of the Guildford Four, the Maguire family and the Birmingham Six. However, the 1998 Human Rights Act was to see judges more critical of anti-terror measures introduced in the wake of the 9/11 and 7/7 atrocities.

A changing climate: open conflict with government

Tabloid justice
If you can't do the time, don't do the crime.
Conservative Home Secretary Michael Howard's 'prison works' conference soundbite (1993)

In 1990, crime rates reached the highest level since records began in 1851 (*Criminal Statistics* 1993). In September 1991 Archbishop of Canterbury George Carey declared that 'human wrongdoing is inextricably linked to social deprivation, poverty, poor housing and illiteracy'. The government was unwilling to accept that its policies were implicated and blame was placed on judicial liberalism. There were even attacks from the podium at the 1995 Conservative conference, party chairman Brian Mawhinney urging members to write to judges to complain about light sentences.

The government began to meddle with judicial discretion. The 1994 Criminal Justice and Public Order Act contained several controversial measures, including an end to the traditional right of silence. A suspect's refusal to speak could now be cited in court as a suggestion of guilt. Lord Chief Justice Taylor expressed open opposition, arguing that this undermined a cornerstone of British justice: the presumption of innocence. The 1997 Crime (Sentences) Act aimed to deal with 'soft' judges through mandatory prison sentences for certain offenders, the judiciary complaining that the government was taking more notice of the tabloids than the judges, while Blair claimed that the 'biggest miscarriage of justice is when the guilty walk away unpunished'. The 2003 Criminal Justice Act allowed previous convictions of an accused to be 'heard' (cited) in certain cases, restricted trial by jury and permitted exceptions to the double-jeopardy rule. Lawyers were infuriated by the government's tabloid-speak of 'victim justice' rather than criminal justice. In the Lords, former Master of the Rolls Lord Donaldson condemned the lack of trust in the judiciary. Perhaps the only succour for the government was Her Majesty's Opposition, determined to show it too could be as tough as the tabloids demanded. To some extent the House of Lords began to appear as a liberal court and 'soft judges', concerned about harsh sentencing, human rights and the welfare of asylum-seekers, appeared more in tune with radical pressure groups.

Yet much of the judicial opposition was constitutional rather than ideological. Judges may well have felt that so long a period of single-party rule was itself unconstitutional, producing 'arrogance . . . with regard to the law and judicial decisions' (Woodhouse 1996: 424). The battle was for judicial independence. In some cases, as when adjudging Home Secretary Howard to have acted unlawfully in April 1994 (by introducing a scheme for compensating victims of violent crimes without parliamentary approval), the courts could be said to have been protecting Parliament's rights in a way the House appeared no longer able to. Labour's return to office did little to reduce executive–judicial tension.

Even before its incorporation, a greater judicial willingness had emerged to use the ECHR as 'persuasive legal authority'. However, the 1998 Human Rights Act opened up new vistas of activism. Taking effect first in Scotland (being tied to devolution), it resulted in a deluge of challenges (Woodhouse 2001: 226). Within a year of being introduced in England and Wales over 600 cases had come to the High Court and above, many with far-reaching implications (Woodhouse 2002: 254). Several cases were to inflame public controversy, as in that of Abu Qatada al-Filistini (see p. 683), or of Anthony Rice, a convicted sex attacker released during a life sentence on human rights grounds in August 2005, who went on to murder a forty-eight-year-old woman.

While the government spoke of the need for a dialogue over the Act, the judges demurred, Lord Bingham commenting: 'I do not myself see it as the role of judges to engage in a dialogue' (Woodhouse 2002: 254). Labour home secretaries Straw and Blunkett both found themselves in conflict with the judiciary over issues such as freedom of speech, sentencing, juries and treatment of asylum-seekers. Further controversial security issues followed the 7/7 bombings. Where national security is involved, there is a right to derogate (opt out of) ECHR provisions, but judging what constitutes a sufficient threat remains problematic. In the case of *A and others* v. *Secretary of State for the Home Department* (2004) the Law Lords ruled that the indefinite detention of terrorist suspects authorized under the 2001 Anti-terrorism, Crime and Security Act was incompatible with the Human Rights Act. Judges later invoked the Act to question the use of so-called 'control orders' allowed under the 2005 Prevention of Terrorism Act. In February 2013 Home Secretary Theresa May openly attacked judges for ignoring rules made by Parliament that were intended to prevent foreign criminals from evading deportation on the grounds of a right to a family life. The scale of the problem was illustrated by a succession of cases. Mr Justice Blake, the senior immigration judge, openly defied the Home Secretary in a ruling allowing Olufisayo Ogundimu, a former drug dealer with thirty convictions, to remain in Britain despite Home Office attempts to deport him back to

Nigeria, on these grounds (*Daily Telegraph*, 28 February 2013). He had fathered a child and had a baby on the way with another woman. Mrs May promised to introduce new legislation.

Administrative Justice

We have seen how judges are drawn into politics through judicial review of executive actions, where citizens seek **redress of grievance** not from a fellow citizen but from the state itself. This became increasingly likely during the twentieth century, with a burgeoning of the welfare state, an extensive road-building programme, intensified activity by coercive forces such as police and immigration control, and increased regulation of social life in areas ranging from rent control and race relations to gender equality. The process of expansion was further accelerated from the 1980s as reforms associated with the new public management movement reduced ministerial responsibility to Parliament (see Flinders 2001). As Britain became something of a 'contracting state', more and more legal remedies were sought in areas previously seen as the province of politics.

Some countries deal with this through separate systems of courts and a body of **administrative law** such as the French *droit administratif*. However, in Britain most of the relevant law is in the form of general statutes and a haphazard body of common law. This is supplemented by a system of administrative tribunals and public inquiries and the office of ombudsman.

Administrative tribunals

Although taking multifarious forms, **administrative tribunals** (table 22.1) are generally bodies adjudicating in various categories of cases where a citizen feels aggrieved by some action of a government official or fellow citizen (employer or landlord). Traditionally, they offered the advantages of speed, informality and expertise. Most were, and remain, standing bodies, concerned with areas such

> ### The Crichel Down affair
> This famous 1954 case highlighted the issue of minister–civil servant relationships. It concerned the restoration of land previously requisitioned by the government for military purposes. Although the former owners wished to regain possession, Ministry of Agriculture officials thwarted them with underhand tactics. The owners, well-connected members of the upper-middle class, were able to fight for their rights and after a public inquiry the officials were severely censured and minister Sir Thomas Dugdale resigned.

Table 22.1 Tribunals receiving more than 1000 cases, 2010–2011

Tribunal	No. of cases		
	2008–9	**2009–10**	**2010–11**
Social Security and Child Support	242,800	339,200	418,500
Employment	151,000	236,100	218,100
First Tier Tribunal (Immigration and Asylum)	188,700	159,800	136,800
Mental Health	22,500	25,200	25,900
Tax First Tier	N/A	10,400	8,900
Upper Tribunal (Administrative Appeals Chamber)	4,800	3,700	4,100
Asylum Support	2,000	3,100	4,100
Special Educational Needs and Disability	3,100	3,400	3,400
Criminal Injuries Compensation	2,500	3,800	2,700
War Pensions and Armed Forces Compensation	2,500	2,600	2,200
Employment Appeal	1,800	2,000	2,000
Adjudicator to HM Land Registry	1,800	2,000	1,300
Lands	1,100	1,100	750
VAT and Duties	5,400	N/A	N/A
TOTAL	631,900	793,900	831,000

Source: Data from Ministry of Justice (2011c: 22).

as rents, social security, pensions, benefits, immigration, housing and the NHS, though others arise on an ad hoc basis for particular cases. For most of their history tribunals hardly constituted a system, more a motley counterpane, defying precise enumeration. Some were so closely woven into the state fabric that it was difficult to discover whether they were tribunals or merely committees. The 2001 Leggatt Report (see below) found seventy different tribunal systems in England and Wales, employing 3,500 people and hearing around a million cases a year. Dissatisfaction following the Crichel Down affair led to the establishment in 1954 of the Franks Committee on Administrative Tribunals and Inquiries.

Some reform followed: proceedings became public unless personal privacy was involved, limited appeals machinery was introduced (appellate tribunals and the courts) and some legal representation permitted. In 1958 a Council on Tribunals was created as a watchdog appointed by the Lord Chancellor. However, its pleas for more powers went unheeded by bureaucrats keen to cocoon themselves against the winds of change. In May 2000, acknowledging the haphazard nature of the system, the Lord Chancellor set up a review under retired appeal court judge

Sir Andrew Leggatt. Reporting in August 2001, Leggatt saw the main problem as lack of independence from government departments. He proposed a single system covering a wide range of tribunals (including employment, tax, social security and immigration) under the Lord Chancellor. More fundamental change followed with the 2007 Tribunals, Courts and Enforcement Act. A new unified structure saw them divided into First Tier and Upper Tier and a Senior President of Tribunals was appointed to preside over the new system.

Public inquiries

Government and officials have another alternative to the courts in the **public inquiry**, particularly in cases of collective grievance over issues such as planning and state acquisition of land. Hearings, sometimes dragging on for years, are conducted before interested parties and voluminous reports issued. The 1957 Franks Report led to more stringency in their operation; the reports are now published and reasons given for recommendations. Although not bound by the recommendations, ministers tend to follow them, which is not surprising, since the inspectors tend to be from the heavenly list of the great and the good, chosen as a 'safe pair of hands'.

As with tribunals, bureaucrats have often seen these exercises as administrative operations, but the siting of airports, nuclear power stations and motorways affects the quality of people's lives and incites intense feeling. Large-scale public hearings, such as that considering Heathrow Airport's fifth terminal, attract considerable media attention and involve pressure groups, local authorities and private companies. However, the general feeling of those who attend is often one of impotence before a bland wall of polite bureaucratic intransigence. Where protesters give vent to their feelings, they may be removed by the inspector's ever-present henchmen in blue. As a result there is an increased tendency for protesters to ignore this avenue and resort to direct action (see chapter 19).

The ombudsmen

A 1961 report by the British section of Justice, the legal reform group, recommended introducing an **ombudsman system** based on the Scandinavian model – a troubleshooter to investigate citizens' complaints about **maladministration** (Whyatt 1961). The idea was received frostily by both officials and government.

A very British ombudsman

Although the Labour government proved more sympathetic to the idea, the position created in 1967 was so locked into existing institutions that it was but a pale shadow of the Nordic model. Even the term 'ombudsman' (people's friend) was translated through Whitehallspeak into 'Parliamentary Commissioner for Administration' (PCA), who was to be a servant not of the people but of Parliament. All complaints were to be made through an MP. When Justice assessed the impact of the new institution in 1977, the report's title, *Our Fettered Ombudsman*, betrayed its conclusion (Widdicombe 1977); Britain's PCA was shackled by heavy chains forged by the unharmonious blacksmiths of Whitehall. The system was guardedly extended to the NHS, local government and the devolved assemblies. In 2010–11 the Parliamentary and Health Service Ombudsman received 23,667 enquiries but conducted only 403 formal investigations. In the same year the Local Government Ombudsman recorded 21,840 complaints and enquiries, with over 11,000 sent for investigation.

Ombudsmen or ombudsmice?

> I remain concerned at the length of time that it takes departments and agencies both to respond to the statement of complaint which is the precursor of an investigation and to agree to redress when investigation by my office has disclosed injustice resulting from maladministration.
>
> *Report of the Parliamentary Commissioner for Administration, 2001–2002*

Designed for a deferential and secretive polity, these are very British ombudsmen. They remain on the sidelines of political life, with limited autonomy and jurisdiction; relatively few know of the system and few use it. Little confidence could be gained when New Labour's Jack Straw became the first minister to refuse a demand by the ombudsman for the release of information under the 'Open Government' code. And in May 2002, the Home Office and Cabinet Office were accused of obstructive behaviour in response to a request for papers relating to the Hinduja case. There is no doubt that some wrongs have been righted but, to critics, the value of the ombudsmen sometimes appears more in protecting bureaucracy than citizens. While there is scope for improvement, however, few could disagree that the office, initially foreign to British culture, has withstood the 'test of time' (see Kirkham 2007).

The Citizen's Charter: freedom, equality and fraternity – or your money back

Citizens' rights were supposed to be further augmented with the issue by the Cabinet Office (1991) of *The Citizen's Charter*. It was soon followed by numerous glossy progeny covering specific services (patients, passengers, parents), setting performance targets. Hailed as John Major's 'big idea', this laid down standards for various services, allowing the public to complain, and in some cases receive compensation, much as they might in a department store. However, critics have seen the charters as fig leaves to conceal falling standards; they were hardly substitutes for redress offered through Parliament or the courts (see Kingdom 1996). In 1995 the 'cones hotline', a 'Charterline' established in 1993 to hear complaints from motorists, was scrapped for lack of calls. In 2008 the Public Administration Select Committee argued for 'public service guarantees' to empower service users by setting out clear entitlements.

Towards an administrative court

Using its powers to review administrative actions, the judiciary has found all departments vulnerable. In a much-publicized scandal the Foreign Secretary was castigated in the Pergau Dam affair, the Transport Secretary was found to have been at fault over night-flying restrictions at Heathrow, Gatwick and Stansted, and the Department of Health was in trouble over availability of beds. The December 1992 decision to close thirty-one pits, with 30,000 job losses (to make the industry more attractive for privatization), was outlawed. However, the department proving most susceptible has been the Home Office, with a long-running series of clashes over asylum, prisoners' rights, sentencing policy, the handling of miscarriages of justice (the Guildford Four, the Birmingham Six, the Broadwater Three, Judith Ward, Stefan Kiszko, the Taylor sisters) and victims' compensation. However, despite many high-profile cases, judicial review remains discretionary, striking intermittently and unpredictably and leading some to doubt whether it can be regarded as meaningful control over government (see Rawlings 1986). Moreover, being expensive it is unavailable to many individuals and groups.

In 1971 Justice suggested creating a special division of the High Court to provide an avenue to appeal from tribunals on points of law. This would have resembled the prestigious French *Conseil d'Etat*, a supreme administrative tribunal through which ordinary citizens can, at small cost, obtain a wide range of remedies against officialdom. The suggestion met bureaucratic opposition on the grounds that such a court would lack expertise. However, increasing use has been made of the Queen's Bench Division of the High Court in public law cases with specialist judges. This was renamed the Administrative Court (England and Wales), the change coinciding with the coming into force of the Human Rights Act, which was expected to increase the need for it. A leading judge, Mr Justice Scott Baker, was appointed with overall responsibility and the arcane names of its orders were made more user-friendly; thus *mandamus*, compelling an authority to act, became a mandatory order, and *certiorari*, preventing action, became a quashing order.

Law and Politics

It has never been the case that the judiciary is outside politics but, from the early 1980s, their involvement was to become more apparent. While the confrontational style of governments may have contributed to this, there are other salient factors, including a political culture that is less willing to trust its leaders, robust judicial activism, the enlarging presence of the EU in daily life, the Human Rights Act, a greater use of tribunals and inquiries for decision-making, devolution and the 2000 Freedom of Information Act. Should Britain take the final step to a written constitution, the involvement of judges could be expected to increase even further.

However, while many of these developments proceed in the name of freedom and rights, the greater involvement of judges at the expense of the discretionary power of ministers narrows the area under democratic control and accountability; the people do not appoint judges and they cannot remove them. Judicial involvement may be supported by the argument that the law protects the 'public interest'. However, critics from the left may feel that, when judges consider the public interest, the public they have in mind is perhaps more that in the public school than the public convenience. In contrast, critics from the right see judges increasingly pursuing a dangerous 'human rights agenda' that protects the individual rather than the population at large. What is perhaps more certain is that a separation of powers is a constitutional aspiration rather than a description of political reality.

> *If the law suppose that . . . the law is a ass.*
> Mr Bumble in Charles Dickens's *Oliver Twist* (1837–8)

Key points

- Within the British state the legal institutions are the most august and venerated.

- The organization of the courts is hierarchical, with a dichotomy between civil and criminal jurisdiction.

- The European Court of Human Rights and the European Court of Justice are increasingly important in the judicial system.

- The jury system is the only democratic chink in the legal system.

- High costs mean that for many people access to the law is restricted.

- The legal profession grew in importance during the eighteenth and nineteenth centuries as the industrial bourgeoisie sought to safeguard property and wealth.

- Judicial independence is central to a free society.

- Lawyers and judges are generally from the upper-middle classes, predominantly male and white. These factors call into question their impartiality.

- Although the role of judges is formally seen as interpreting and applying the law, in practice they play a quasi-legislative role.

- Britain does not have a special set of administrative law and courts. The vacuum is filled with administrative tribunals, ombudsmen, citizen's charters and the Administrative Court.

- Law and the legal system cannot be regarded as above politics and lawyers are increasingly entering the political sphere.

Review your understanding of the following terms and concepts

administrative law
administrative tribunal
barrister
case law
criminal and civil
  jurisdictions
common law
Constitutional Reform
  Act 2005
declaration of
  incompatibility

European Convention on
  Human Rights (ECHR)
European Court of
  Human Rights
judicial activism
Judicial Appointments
  Commission
judicial impartiality and
  independence
judicial review
jury

legal aid
Lord Chancellor
ombudsman
precedent
public inquiry
Secretary of State for
  Justice
Supreme Court
statute law

Questions for discussion and debate

Consider these propositions and be prepared to present the cases for and against. Try to produce debating propositions of your own.

1 Trial by jury is an essential plank of democracy.

2 British judges shape the law as well as administer it.

3 Judges nurse conservative leanings.

4 Women bringing rape charges in British courts face an uphill battle.

5   Britain has an ombudsmouse rather than an ombudsman.

6   The Human Rights Act undermines the ability of government to protect its citizens.

7   Judge-led public inquiries take minutes and last years.

8   Judges are increasingly pursuing a human rights agenda.

9   Judicial activism is necessary for the prevention of overbearing government.

10   This house gives a black mark to white justice.

Further reading

Bingham, T. (2011) *The Rule of Law*.
Britain's former senior law lord sees the idea of the rule of law as the foundation of modern civilization and more fundamental than that of democracy. Examines its origins and distils its essence.

Bogdanor, V. (2009) *The New British Constitution*.
Chapter 3 provides an excellent and accessible overview of the significance of the 1998 Human Rights Act.

Griffith, J. A. G. (2010) *The Politics of the Judiciary*, 5th edn.
Throws down the gauntlet to those believing in the neutrality or independence of the judiciary. Continues to irritate in establishment circles.

Kennedy, H. (1992) *Eve was Framed*.
Searching, semi-autobiographical polemic by woman barrister criticizing the legal profession, with special emphasis on its sexism.

Lee, S. (1988) *Judging Judges*.
Defends judges against critics of the left.

Loughlin, M. (2000) *Sword and Scales: An Examination of the Relationship between Law and Politics*.
Accessible assessment of the tangled relationships between law and politics. Introduces political scientists to the legal dimensions of a number of central themes of political studies.

Rawls, J. (1999) *A Theory of Justice* (first published 1971).
For those who want to delve into the complexities of this elusive concept, this is the classic work.

Rosenberg, J. (1997) *Trial of Strength*.
Details the battle between ministers and judges over who makes the law.

Thompson, E. P. (2013) *Whigs and Hunters* (first published 1975).
Explores the relationship between the law and economic power.

For reading around the subject and some light relief

Geoffrey Chaucer, 'The Sergeant of the Law' in the *Canterbury Tales*:
> Nowher so bisy a man as he ther nas,
> And yet he semed bisier than he was.

Charles Dickens, *Bleak House*.
Satire on the Court of Chancery. Tells of *Jarndyce v. Jarndyce*, a case which continues interminably for the profit of the lawyers and the ruin of others.

Frances Fyfield, *Deep Sleep*.
One of a number of thrillers featuring prosecutor lawyer Helen West; written by real-life lawyer.

Franz Kafka, *The Trial*.
A nightmare vision of a judicial system. Begins: 'Someone must have slandered Joseph K., because one morning, without his having done anything wrong, he was arrested'.

Sally J. Kenney, *Gender and Justice: Why Women in the Judiciary Really Matter*.
Explores North American and European jurisdictions and courts, demonstrating the value of a gender analysis. Argues for more women and more feminists on the bench.

John Mortimer, *Rumpole of the Bailey*.
Humorous tales by famous playwright/barrister. Also available as DVDs.

David Pannick, *Advocates*.
Thought-provoking and amusing account of the practices and morality of the Bar.

Twelve Angry Men.
Classic film in a jury room, starring Henry Fonda.

On the net

All the British legal institutions have websites offering an accessible account of their roles. In addition, there are countless references to cases and confrontations between judiciary and government which can be accessed through a search engine. Some key official sites are listed here.

http://www.supremecourt.gov.uk/index.html
The Supreme Court website offers information on its role and offers links to various other parts of the legal system

http://www.ombudsman.org.uk/
This site includes the parliamentary and health service ombudsman's annual reports and extensive statistics.

http://www.justice.gov.uk/
The Ministry of Justice is at the heart of the criminal justice system. A vast amount of information is available here, plus links to related sites, such as the Criminal Cases Review Commission, which deals with miscarriages of justice.

http://lawcommission.justice.gov.uk/index.htm
The Law Commission's website includes a vast amount of information about its role in law reform.

http://www.justice.org.uk/
Justice is a major legal reform organization addressing areas such as human rights, criminal justice, the European Union, access to justice and the rule of law.

CHAPTER 23

THE COERCIVE STATE: THE POLITICS OF LAW AND ORDER

Contents

One of the defining characteristics of the state is the right to use violence. Although a necessary power, it is one fraught with danger, evoking fears of a 'police state' or military dictatorship. The world is full of examples of how real this threat is. Clearly debates around issues of law and order must be central to politics. This chapter begins with the evolution of the police service, and its organization and culture. We then focus on its twin functions of fighting crime and maintaining public order, which leads to a consideration of four trends in modern policing – centralization, militarization, politicization and the increasing involvement of the private sector. This is followed by an examination of the crucial question of who guards the guards – the police complaints procedure. We also go beyond the police to consider the more shadowy world of the military and the security services. We conclude by considering the debate over two styles of policing: coercive versus consensual.

Policing the State

There are grounds for believing that policing in the UK is a model for the world. Certainly many men and women in all ranks serve with dedication, tact, and often great bravery. Yet the position they are in is necessarily one of acute political sensitivity. Policing can only enjoy legitimacy in a society that constantly debates its role and evaluates its operation. It is a measure of the success of British policing that a number of associated issues feature openly in modern political debate.

Evolution

Although the history of policing may be traced back to before the Norman Conquest, originating in the principle that a community accepted a joint responsibility for maintaining the peace, like most of the apparatus of the modern state, the police service was largely a nineteenth-century creation of the bourgeoisie. In the dense urban communities, lawlessness could thrive and an ever-present threat of civil unrest was made more terrifying to the propertied class by the spectre of the French Revolution and its terrible aftermath. An early move to strengthen law and order was made in the eighteenth century by Henry Fielding (author of the classic *Tom Jones*), a justice at London's Bow Street Court, who gathered together a group of upper-class vigilantes – the celebrated Bow Street Runners.

Radical agitation in the period 1815–19 saw magistrates bringing in the cavalry to break up a large but peaceful working-class demonstration in Manchester in August 1819. Known as the Peterloo Massacre, it created a scandal and was clearly no way to legitimate the political order. As home secretary, Sir Robert Peel secured a number of important penal reforms, introduced in the 1829 Metropolitan Police Act. This set the model for modern policing: a paid, uniformed, full-time, disciplined and specially trained corps. Consolidated under the 1856 County and Borough Police Act, it became the model for other municipalities which has survived, in its essentials, to the present.

Structure, accountability and control

There are forty-three territorial police services in England and Wales; by the end of 2011 they were employing nearly 140,000 police officers as well as over 70,000 civilians and 15,000 police community support officers (CSOs). Although nominally under local government, reforms in the latter part of the twentieth century are said to have left policing removed from community control. The key figures in the chain of command and accountability had been the local police authority (comprising councillors and other local figures), the chief constable and the home secretary. Parliament has also had a part to play, though a smaller one than might be expected. However, a major change was to come under the coalition government's Police Reform and Social Responsibility Act 2011.

Not only can the chief constable do what he likes, but he can spend all our money doing it.
Gabrielle Cox (Manchester Police Committee chairperson), quoted in the *Guardian* (11 Aug. 1984)

Police and Crime Commissioners

Once exercising considerable control, the role of police authorities had been gradually reduced, so that by 2001 it was mainly limited to consulting the local community about their concerns and priorities, identifying local objectives and setting targets within objectives set by the home secretary. Under the 2011 Act, the roles performed by police authorities in England and Wales were transferred in 2012 to forty-one directly elected **Police and Crime Commissioners** (PCCs). The reform was presented as a way of restoring the lost local accountability of police services. Commissioners were granted the power to:

* hire, fire or suspend chief constables and hold them to account;
* set out a five-year Police and Crime Plan determining local policing priorities, in consultation with the chief constable;
* set the annual force budget (Strickland 2012: 7).

However, the changes served to bring into focus the fundamental question of precisely who might be suitable to 'guard the guards', a theme that we return to later in this chapter. Far from removing politicians, national figures, including former deputy prime minister John Prescott in Humberside, were soon jostling for the position, alongside former chief constables, local councillors and retired colonels. Critics questioned whether former politicians – many still clearly wedded to a partisan agenda – should be permitted to use these new positions to rail against (or acquiesce to) the government of the day. Others questioned the idea of former chief constables holding their successors to account. By the time of the election in November 2012 the issue was overtly political, with the parties themselves fielding candidates. However, the electorate was unenthusiastic, producing an historically low turnout, with one polling station in Newport, Gwent, visited by no voters at all. Many of those who did vote were moved to spoil their ballot papers, arguing that policing should not be politicized in this way. Controversy did not die with the elections. Within weeks the new commissioners were being accused of appointing their friends to lucrative positions as deputies.

The chief constable

In day-to-day policing the key figure is the chief constable who, as a servant of the Crown, was not under the direction of the police authority. Although an annual report has traditionally been presented, this has not been obligatory. One element of local control has been over funding, although this is limited (see below).

The home secretary

The home secretary is in a sense the minister for the police. Although having considerable formal powers, incumbents have often appeared somewhat timid. In the 1980s Douglas Hurd was admired for the way he was able to cultivate 'an appearance of almost deliberate powerlessness when it comes to police operation' (Evans 1986a). When power has been used it has more often been to direct police authorities rather than chief constables. During 1984, when the South Yorkshire authority tried to withhold funds for policing the miners' strike, the Chief Constable sought the support of both the Home Secretary and the Attorney General, the latter applying to the High Court for powers to coerce the authority. However, from the 1990s, both Conservative and Labour home secretaries began to take a stronger line, sometimes incurring the wrath of the police associations.

London's Metropolitan Police Service (the 'Met') differed from the others in that it was the direct responsibility of the home secretary until the 1999 reforms of London government, when it came under a new twenty-three member Metropolitan Police Authority (MPA) and the London mayor. The 2011 Act resulted in the MPA being replaced by the Mayor's Office for Policing and Crime (MOPC). Operational matters remained the responsibility of the Metropolitan Police Commissioner (effectively the chief constable), with the mayor setting the force's annual budget in consultation with the commissioner. The MOPC is monitored by the London Assembly's Police and Crime Panel.

Parliament

Since, as officers of the Crown, the police escape local accountability, it might be thought that they are accountable to Parliament through the home secretary. However, a 'catch 22' situation pertains: the Speaker has ruled that, because police administration lies with police authorities, the home secretary is *not* answerable (*House of Commons Debates* 1958: col. 1259).

Who controls?

> Had the Metropolitan Police been influenced over the past ten years by elected representatives . . . many of the mistakes would have been avoided and its reputation would stand far higher.
>
> Roy Hattersley (shadow home secretary), quoted in J. Benyon (ed.), *Scarman and After* (1984: 108)

The lack of direct political accountability in policing in England and Wales has traditionally been defended on the grounds that it insulates the police from politicians and prevents the rise of a **police state**. However, it can be argued that evils are more likely in the absence of democratic accountability. We explore this later in the chapter.

Culture and the Policing Function

Policing entails two broad functions – fighting crime and maintaining public order. Both require considerable discretion and the way this is exercised shapes society, making policing an essentially political role. Hence it is important to study the ideas and attitudes informing actions – the **police culture**.

Police culture

Policing is an all-consuming occupation and can create an incestuous professional community. Socializing in the community being policed is obviously difficult, officers often spending their leisure hours with each other, reinforcing attitudes and creating strong pressure to conform (a so-called 'canteen culture'). This culture is secretive, as is shown in a tendency to join the freemasons; in 1988 the *Sunday Times* acquired a list of no fewer than a hundred senior Scotland Yard officers who were active members. There were believed to be some 5,000 masons in the Metropolitan

Reading isn't an occupation we encourage among police officers. We try to keep the paperwork down to a minimum.

Joe Orton (1933–67; British dramatist), *Loot* (1965)

"Look, this is damn silly if we're both masons."

force alone and allegations circulated that membership enhanced promotion prospects, influenced investigations and led to cover-ups (Chittenden 1988). Although the Home Affairs Select Committee concluded in March 1997 that the problem was exaggerated, serious public concern led Home Secretary Jack Straw to follow their recommendation that new recruits to the police, probation and prison services, as well as judges, should register freemason membership. In spite of this requirement, however, many serving officers remain members of lodges. Indeed, it was reported that leading police officers had formed a new lodge, 'Sine Favore' (*Daily Telegraph*, 20 Aug. 2011).

Characteristically, the police are associated with certain attitudes towards race, gender, class and ideology.

Race

A traditional reluctance to employ black people, and their disinclination to apply, reinforces white police culture. Attracting increasing attention since the 1970s, it is one of the major problems of policing today. Research by the Policy Studies Institute in the 1980s found the casual manner in which racist language was used its most telling feature. West Indians were regularly referred to as 'nigger', 'sooty', 'coon', 'spade',

I freely admit that I hate, loath and despise niggers . . . I don't let that affect my job though.
Police officer quoted in D. Smith and J. Gray, *Police and People in London* (1985: 403)

'monkey' and 'spook', while Asians were invariably 'Pakis', regardless of origins. These norms led officers who did not think of themselves as racists to use the terms (Smith and Gray 1985: 390–3). The Police Complaints Authority's 1993 annual report recorded 172 complaints of racism, but in only a single case were charges recommended.

Colour blindness?

Sergeant: Now then, Savage, I want to talk to you about some charges that you have been bringing in lately. I think that perhaps you're being a little overzealous. Some of these cases are plain stupid: walking on the cracks in the pavement, walking in a loud shirt in a built-up area during the hours of darkness and walking around with an offensive wife. In short, Savage, in the space of one month you've brought 117 ridiculous, trumped-up and ludicrous charges

Constable Savage: Yes, sir.

Sergeant: Against the *same* man, Savage – a Mr Winston Kudogo of 55 Mercer Road. Savage, why do you keep arresting this man?

Constable Savage: He's a villain, sir. And a jailbird.

Sergeant: I know he's a jailbird, Savage. He's down in the cells now. We are holding him on a charge of possession of curly black hair and thick lips. Savage, would I be correct in assuming that Mr Kudogo is a coloured gentleman?

Constable Savage: Well, I can't say I've ever noticed, sir.

From BBC TV's *Not the Nine O'Clock News* (1979)

Such attitudes have helped to precipitate racial disturbances. The 1986 Broadwater Farm riots in Tottenham, during which a policeman was brutally murdered, illustrated the intensity of feeling. Subsequent research revealed that 75 per cent of young blacks perceived the police as being unjust towards them; as many as 67 per cent of young whites agreed (Lea et al. 1986). A particularly notable case was that of Mark Duggan, a 29-year-old black man, shot on 4 August 2011 in north-east London by police attempting to arrest him on suspicion of planning an attack and possessing a handgun. A furious protest over his death led to widespread rioting, looting and arson in many parts of London and other major cities.

A major *cause célèbre* was the 1997 Stephen Lawrence case, in which five white youths were accused of murdering a black student. The Met failed to convict and displayed a profound lack of sympathy towards the Lawrence family. During the public inquiry that followed under Sir William Macpherson, Home Office expert Paul Pugh declared police racial awareness training to have been a waste of money. While apologizing for the way the case had been handled, Metropolitan

> We've got a young lad in there, he's dead, we don't know who he is and we'd like to clarify that point. If he's not your son, all well and good, but we need to know and I'm sure you'd like to know too.
>
> Senior police officer to Stephen Lawrence's parents, quoted in the *Independent*
> (8 April 1998)

Commissioner Paul Condon resisted calls for resignation, and no officer faced disciplinary charges, all leaving with pension rights fully intact.

With its suggestion of institutional racism, the 1999 Macpherson Report was probably the most trenchant recognition of the problem ever published. The same year, a report from Her Majesty's Inspector of Constabulary declared racism to be endemic throughout Britain's police forces and noted a failure to recruit and retain black officers. Despite the inclusion of specific provisions relating to the police in the 2000 Race Relations (Amendment) Act, the Police Complaints Authority – replaced by the Independent Police Complaints Commission (IPCC) in 2004 – noted a threefold increase in racial complaints between 1998/9 and 2000/1.

In 2003, undercover filming amongst police recruits for a BBC investigative programme, *The Secret Policeman*, destroyed any illusion that racism had been eliminated from the ranks of the service. Ten years after the Stephen Lawrence inquiry a report by the Equality and Human Rights Commission (2009) found some progress had been made in employing ethnic minority officers, but observed: 'There are still racist police officers and there are still policies and practices that raise serious concerns about their impact on ethnic minority people.' Specialist crime units remained 'closed shops' to ethnic minorities.

In 2010/11 there were 1,471 complaints against forces in England and Wales on the grounds of discriminatory behaviour (the bulk of which was race related). For the Metropolitan Police race relations remains a particular issue. In April 2012, the IPCC announced that it would 'increase its level of scrutiny' over how Scotland Yard handled complaints relating to alleged racial discrimination (*Guardian*, 17 April 2012).

Gender

The police ethos is overtly masculine, similar to that found in other predominantly male preserves like the army or rugby clubs (the police field formidable teams, sometimes including internationals). Women have experienced great difficulty in developing their careers, constituting only a small – albeit increasing – proportion of the service (see table 23.1), and conversation and jokes mock women colleagues ('plonks'). Smith and Gray (1985: 373), choosing a deliberately mild example, report

Table 23.1 Women police officers: percentage of police officers in post by gender, 2005–2010 (full-time equivalents)

	2005/06	2006/07	2007/08	2008/09	2009/10
Women	22.3 (9.3)	23.3 (10.1)	24.2 (11.1)	25.1 (12.0)	25.7 (13.0)
Men	77.7 (90.7)	76.7 (89.9)	75.8 (88.9)	74.9 (88.0)	74.3 (87.0)
TOTAL	141,523	141,892	141,859	143,770	143,734
	(1,689)	(1,662)	(1,699)	(1,713)	(1,725)

Note: Figures for senior police offers in parentheses.

Source: Data from Ministry of Justice (2010: tables 6.01 and 6.02).

an older constable enthusing over the practice whereby new WPCs were always 'stamped on the bare bum' with the official rubber stamp.

In February 1993 the Home Office released a report by academic researchers on sex discrimination in the police service, disclosing that nearly all policewomen experienced sexual harassment, ranging from 'groping' to rape. Women were also twice as likely as men to take sick leave because of frustration over career development (*Guardian*, 12 Feb. 1993). Alison Halford, who rose to become one of Britain's senior-most policewomen, brought a celebrated case to the Equal Opportunities Commission after being rejected for promotion to deputy chief constable nine times while less-qualified men advanced. The service responded by bringing disciplinary charges against her. Both cases were dropped and a financial settlement was accepted by Halford; her subsequent book title summed up her career – *No Way up the Greasy Pole* (1993).

However, 1995 saw Britain's first woman chief constable when Pauline Clare was appointed to head the Lancashire force. By 2012 there were six women at this level (five permanent, one temporary) (Berman 2012a). The proportion of women officers rose significantly during the first decade of the twenty-first century; accounting for just 18 per cent of all officers in 2002, the figure had risen to nearly 26 per cent by 2010 (table 23.1), with the percentage of senior positions held by women also increasing.

Although changes were taking place, for reformers the pace was tortuously slow and problems remained. The Equality and Human Rights Commission reported the account of a black officer applying for a job as a race and diversity trainer with one of the country's largest police forces in which the equality chief referred to a secretary in the following terms: 'Look at the t**s on her – I'd s*** her over the desk' (Whitehead 2009). In a headline-catching case in 2010, a tribunal awarded PC Barbara Lynford £273,000 after finding that Sussex police discrimination caused her to become mentally ill and unable to work. The tribunal accepted that, in a firearms unit at Gatwick airport in 2003, she suffered a 'working environment . . .

You haven't got a wooden leg, have you? Then you'd have the full set.
Remark from a head of equality and diversity training on learning that a black officer was gay, reported to the Equality and Human Rights Commission; quoted in Whitehead (2009)

characterised by an attitude to women which was disrespectful'; she was repeatedly abused and sworn at, with lewd remarks made about her (Dodd 2010).

An absence of women in the service is a question not merely of unequal opportunities; it has deep operational and political implications. The non-consensual pattern of policing (see below), which can actually incite violence, is a product of the macho culture. Attitudes towards women in general are similarly sexist. A particular problem arises with rape. In the first place, victims are loath to report it, and those that do so (about one in four) have been subject to humiliating scepticism (Benn et al. 1983). The Greenham Common demonstrations, where women stepped outside traditional structures of protest to express a particularly female view of the arms race, widened awareness of the problem with a huge number of arrests for trivial offences, intimidating dawn raids, many injuries, sexual harassment, strip searching and photographing.

Class

The police stand in a curious position socially; approved of by the middle classes, whose property and privileges they work to protect, they have traditionally recruited from the working class (Reiner 1982). Yet paradoxically this is the class they appear to oppress. In the Met, officers divided the citizenry into two broad categories – 'slag' or 'rubbish' and 'respectable people' – defined largely in terms of social class (Smith and Gray 1985: 434). The class basis is not surprising, because the job can be variously onerous, boring and dangerous. Hence the police are among the most oppressed of the working class, suffering from an alarming rise in stress-related illnesses, with a significant number of retirements being on medical grounds. From the 1970s relations with the Conservatives began to come under stress with a series of cost-cutting and managerial reforms (see below). This reached a critical point under the coalition government of 2010–15. There was also resentment over perceived snobbery towards the service, as seen in the so-called 'plebgate' affair involving bicycle-riding chief whip Andrew Mitchell.

Political complexion

Although officially neutral, the police service appears to be right wing, many designating themselves Conservative. Indeed, the National Front, in its heyday, experienced little difficulty in seducing 'chief constables and even the Home Office into providing the movement with the necessary facilities for its public campaigns' (Walvin 1984: 142). Police culture exerts a constant socializing effect. As recruits work their way up, the pressure is to conform, to become more macho, more racist and more right wing. Indeed, higher-class recruits may even affect lower-class accents (Smith and Gray 1985: 435). The successful officer will not usually be one who stands out against prevailing norms, and those in positions of authority will tend to promote in their own image. However, the culture affects the pattern of policing in both fighting crime and maintaining public order. Of course violent demonstrations and rowdy strikes are generally promoting left-wing interests so that the act of policing can appear to be supporting the political right.

Fighting crime

The image of the police treating all equally is open to question. Police culture tends to favour the white and the wealthy and offences relating to property dominate crime statistics (table 23.2). The weight of police suspicion bears most heavily on the lower sections of the working class (unskilled workers, the unemployed and the young), who are more likely to be treated with contempt and abuse. Researchers listened to an officer, not considered unusual at that time, addressing a boy in the absence of his parents:

> 'You're a fucking little cunt aren't you? You've been at it again haven't you, you little bastard? . . . I'm going to nail your fucking hide to the wall'. (Smith and Gray 1985: 420)

It is unlikely that a member of one of the professions would be addressed in such terms. The evidence is that black people, particularly Afro-Caribbeans, are far more

Table 23.2 Fighting crime: recorded crime and detection rates in England and Wales, 2011–2012

Offence	Recorded crimes	Sanction detections[a]	Sanction detection rate (%)
Violence against the person	762,515	331,725	43.5
Sexual offences	53,665	16,124	30.0
Robbery	74,690	15,427	20.7
Burglary	501,053	64,988	13.0
Offences against vehicles	417,444	44,864	10.7
Other theft offences	1,105,117	233,984	21.2
Fraud and forgery	141,241	30,996	21.9
Criminal damage	631,221	85,193	13.5
Drug offences	229,103	211,513	92.3
Other offences	60,263	41,113	68.2
TOTAL	3,976,312	1,075,927	27.1

[a] Detection where the offender receives a formal sanction (e.g. being charged or summonsed, cautioned, reprimanded or given a final warning).

Source: Data from *Home Office Statistical Bulletin 08/12: Crimes detected in England and Wales 2011/12* (table 2a).

likely than others to be stopped, and even arrested, on the grounds of intuition. In 2009/10, for example, just 67.2 per cent of those stopped and searched were white (despite this group constituting 88.6 per cent of the population) (*Home Office Statistical Bulletin* 07/11: table 2d). Yet the popular view that blacks are more prone to commit violent crime is not borne out by the statistics.

Various areas have caused concern, including brutality, false confessions and the decision to prosecute.

Police brutality

The macho style has resulted in a harrowing catalogue of cases. For example, in 1969 in Leeds, David Oluwale, a Nigerian, was singled out for 'special treatment' in which he was urinated on, beaten severely and his body abandoned in the country-side; in an ensuing cover-up notebooks were doctored. In August 1993 Joy Gardner died of suffocation after police taped over her mouth when attempting to deport her. The three police officers charged with her manslaughter were subsequently acquitted. While most deaths in custody are not specifically related to police treat-ment – resulting instead from natural causes, drug misuse or injuries sustained prior to arrest – the trend during the 1990s was disturbing. Yet, with forty-nine such deaths in 1998/99 and thirty-one in 1999/00, the opening decade of the twenty-first century appeared to reveal a downward trend, with just fifteen individuals dying in custody in 2008/09 (Independent Police Complaints Commission 2010: table 2.1). However, a joint investigation by BBC Radio 4's *File on 4* and the Bureau of Investigative Journalism in January 2012 found that official figures understated the number dying in custody after being restrained by police. Of eighty-six people who died in such circumstances between 1998/9 and 2008/9, only sixteen were categorized by the IPCC as being directly 'restraint-related'.

False confessions and miscarriages of justice

Formal protection for suspects was based on the famous though ill-understood Judges' Rules, permitting the right to silence and access to a solicitor or friend. These did not carry statutory force, were applied capriciously and were subject to abuse. In addition, 'confessions' extracted by police officers appeared to reflect the talents of Agatha Christie rather than Sherlock Holmes. A major *cause célèbre* was the *Confait* case: three boys convicted of murder and arson on the basis of false con-fessions after a male homosexual had been found dead in his blazing home in April 1972. This led in 1977 to a Royal Commission on Criminal Procedure, set up against police wishes, which reported in 1981.

The resultant Police and Criminal Evidence Act 1984 (PACE) made provision for restricting police power: all interviews were to be taped, suspects were to be given the right to have a solicitor present and confessions were to be unforced and only used as evidence if taped. Yet in reality little changed; indeed, suspects were arrested more often, detention was authorized as a matter of routine, the law on interrogation remained unclear, the right to legal advice proved difficult to enforce and the taping of interviews was easily evaded. Police could also pressurize suspects (see Sanders and Young 1995). The Act actually *increased* police powers.

Public concern about miscarriages of justice continued to hit the headlines. In 1989, the West Midlands serious crime squad was suspended, pending an inquiry, after a series of trials collapsed amidst allegations of fabricated evidence. Officers from the squad had been involved in the controversial conviction of the 'Birmingham Six', imprisoned for the pub bombings of November 1974. In January 1990 the 'Guildford Four', convicted on the basis of false confessions for the pub bombings of October 1974, walked free. In 1997, the 'Bridgewater Three' were released after being imprisoned for the murder of newspaper boy Carl Bridgewater on the basis of improper methods by Staffordshire police.

In 1991 a Royal Commission on Criminal Justice was established 'to examine the effectiveness of the criminal justice system in England and Wales in securing the conviction of those guilty of criminal offences *and the acquittal of those who are innocent*' (emphasis added). However, it simply recommended fine tuning, suggesting no fundamental reforms and offering 'little comfort to those now languishing in jails for crimes they did not commit, convicted on the basis of confessions they did not want to make' (Sanders and Young 1995: 140). Concern led to the 1995 Criminal Appeal Act, establishing the Criminal Cases Review Commission. However, with its chair a freemason and its membership heavily weighted towards the prosecuting authorities, its independence appeared questionable (see Mansfield 1997). Although the Commission claimed by 2010 to have had a hand in the quashing of more than 300 convictions, this total could be said to have been 'statistically enhanced': first, by the practice of counting each individual affected by an outcome in a particular case as a separate success; secondly, by the way in which cases resulting in a change in conviction type (for example, a murder conviction being reduced to manslaughter) were classed as 'wins'; and thirdly, by the inclusion of those cases where the original conviction was upheld but the sentence was varied. Bob Woffinden (2010) argued that the Commission has also been prone to focus on trivial cases, whilst failing to deliver the kinds of landmark rulings widely anticipated at the time of its creation.

The decision to prosecute

Arrest does not in itself mean that a criminal prosecution will follow and traditionally the police enjoyed discretion over this decision. Dissatisfaction led in 1986 to the creation for England and Wales of a Crown Prosecution Service (CPS), under a Director of Public Prosecutions (DPP). Many problems dogged the new service, including inadequate funding, police scepticism, some very expensive trials ending in acquittals, such as those of three footballers accused of taking bribes (two trials and the police investigation costing £12 million), and a failure to prosecute police officers accused of offences. Of the eight most serious cases of deaths in police custody between 1990 and 1995, only two resulted in prosecution. The relatives' support group, Inquest, argued that 'the perception is that the police are above the law and that those deaths are not taken seriously' (*Guardian*, 5 Oct. 1996). In 1998 its director, Dame Barbara Mills, retired after High Court criticism for repeatedly failing to bring prosecutions over deaths in police custody. Her poisoned chalice was taken up by David Calvert-Smith QC. So uncomfortable was the position that he was even to feature in BBC Radio 4's *On the Ropes*!

There were numerous cases of failure to convict and the CPS was accused variously of delaying, failing to provide prosecuting lawyers with the right documents and failing to disclose evidence. By 2002 the rate of acquittals, which had stood at around 32 per cent in the 1980s, had reached 68 per cent (O'Reilly and Robbins 2002). Outrage followed the case of Damilola Taylor, a 10-year-old boy murdered on his way home from Peckham library. With suggestions of pressure from politicians after the fiasco of the Stephen Lawrence trial, the police and DPP brought a case against four boys with very little evidence to convict. They were acquitted in April 2002 and, amidst mounting concern, the DPP was asked by Attorney General Lord Goldsmith to review the CPS. It was not until 2006, at the end of a third trial, that two men were finally convicted of the crime they had committed as boys.

New initiatives

A variety of measures to improve crime-fighting were unveiled in a 2001 white paper, *Policing a New Century*, including a non-emergency telephone number (rather like NHS Direct), attempts to increase recruitment levels by lifting a ban on foreigners, and recruiting thousands of uniformed police community support officers (PCSOs) to deal with low-level anti-social behaviour. By September 2011 there were 15,469 PCSOs (*Home Office Statistical Bulletin* 03/12: 7), with at least one force (South Yorkshire) suggesting that they might replace all warranted police officers (or 'bobbies') on the beat with PCSOs or 'plastic policemen' (*Daily Telegraph*, 13 April 2012). Despite these measures, by 2012 crime rates were still stubbornly high (see table 23.2) and the fear of crime had also risen markedly. The British Crime Survey reported that around 60 per cent of those surveyed thought that crime had risen in the 'last few years' – in spite of the fact that the incidence of some major categories, such as violence against the person, had actually fallen (*Home Office Statistical Bulletin* 10/11: 23).

Maintaining public order

Despite the increase in powers (under the 1984 Act), the police record in crime-fighting is questionable. The prolonged failure to catch the 'Yorkshire Ripper' in the 1980s provided bizarre evidence of ineptitude. However, in the second of their functions they can appear more effective. Maintaining **public order** is a more overtly political function. Indeed, the police can sometimes be cast as instruments of government policy. They often act as if they are protecting not public order but the state itself, working through the Counter Terrorism Command (successor to the Special Branch) and in liaison with MI6. It is here that some of the worst police violence has been seen.

In making public order decisions police culture leads officers to feel little empathy with the people who march in support of causes such as anti-fascism, gay rights, CND, Irish republicanism or environmentalism. They can see such people as unpatriotic enemies, expressing views such as: 'It's the scum of the earth. Why should we protect that?' (Smith and Gray 1985: 436). Legislation also tends to support police action. In the early 1980s powers rested mainly on the 1936 Public Order Act. This was replaced by the 1986 Public Order Act, which was intended to legitimize many powers already assumed without authorization. The 1994 Criminal Justice and Public Order Act contained a number of new measures roundly criticized by civil liberties groups. Powers to stop and search were increased and police were enabled to restrict travellers, squatters, protesters and those attending 'raves'. A new offence of 'aggravated trespass' made trespass a criminal rather than a civil offence, giving the police the right to act against those demonstrating against, say, new roads, airport runways or foxhunting.

> *Criminality and thuggery masquerading as political protest.*
> Home Secretary Jack Straw on the anti-capitalism May Day protests (House of Commons, 2 May 2000)

The change of government in 1997 did little to stop the momentum. In 1998 Labour's Jack Straw unveiled his Crime and Disorder Bill, which promised night-time curfews for children and special parenting classes. His rhetoric proclaimed 'a zero-tolerance strategy'. It was certainly the strategy adopted at the state visit of Chinese premier Jiang Zemin in October 1999, when peaceful demonstrators had flags and banners ripped from their hands and Chinese secret police mingled with the Met. Following widespread condemnation and a High Court challenge by the Free Tibet Campaign, the Met conceded that its officers had acted unlawfully. However, strong-arm tactics continued to be in evidence at demonstrations – as seen in the policing of the protests against increased university top-up fees and government cuts in 2010.

The acquittal of the officer convicted by an inquest jury of the manslaughter of Ian Tomlinson, a newspaper seller unwittingly caught up in the 2009 G20 protests, did little to quell what appeared to be a deteriorating relationship between the police and the public. Filming had shown the officer using a baton to strike

Tomlinson and push him to the ground; he died shortly afterwards. It was revealed during the trial that the Met had repeatedly tried to conceal records showing that the officer had been regularly accused of excessive force throughout his career, including claims that he punched, throttled, kneed and unlawfully arrested people.

Making the punishment fit the crime: penal policy

> My object all sublime,
> I shall achieve in time,
> To let the punishment fit the crime,
> The punishment fit the crime.
>
> W. S. Gilbert and Arthur Sullivan, *The Mikado* (Act 2)

The treatment of convicted criminals is a major cause for debate, with two polar extremes: a tough retributive approach that can even include death (capital punishment), or punishment as a means of rehabilitation. Those arguing the latter case characterize prisons as 'universities of crime', with some 60 per cent of their 'graduates' reoffending within two years. In 2011 it was reported that 59 per cent of those given a prison sentence of less than twelve months reoffended within a year, compared to 51 per cent of those given community sentences (*Guardian*, 10 May 2011).

[It is] right that we are tough on crime and tough on the causes of crime.
Tony Blair, party leadership acceptance speech (21 July 1994)

For most of the twentieth century home secretaries aimed to limit or reduce the prison population. However, Conservative Michael Howard reversed the thinking with his 'prison works' mantra. An October 1993 promise to expand the prison building programme was followed in September 1995 with plans for Britain's first 'boot camp' for young offenders. The 1997 Crime (Sentences) Act established mandatory prison terms, including 'life' for anyone aged eighteen or over convicted for a second time of a serious violent or sexual crime.

New Labour, keen to refute any accusations of being 'soft on crime', generally supported these policies, and its own Crime and Disorder Act 1998 toughened up the treatment of young offenders. They would be forced to make reparations to their victims and the principle of *doli incapax* (presuming that children under fourteen cannot distinguish between right and wrong) was abolished. It also included plans for the early release of minor offenders, with the extension of electronic tagging and community-service orders as alternatives to prison. The public appeared to approve of the tough line, British Social Attitudes Surveys indicating considerable support for greater police powers and stiffer sentencing, as well as firmer discipline in home and school (see Tarling and Dowds 1998). In 2011, when

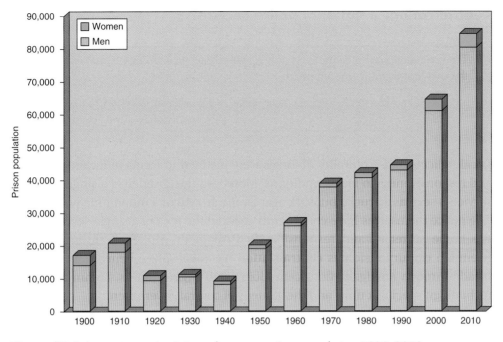

Figure 23.1 A punitive society? Annual average prison population 1900–2010

Source: Data from Berman (2012b: table A).

Conservative Justice Secretary Ken Clarke sought to break away from the punitive 'arms race' engaged in by his Labour and Conservative predecessors with a package of measures designed to reduce the prison population by some 6,000, he encountered a tabloid-fuelled tsunami of opposition which swept along David Cameron, Nick Clegg and even Ed Miliband, leaving his policy in tatters. Demoted to the post of minister without portfolio in the following reshuffle, the veteran politician was indeed a minister without policy.

Whether or not prison works, Britain's rate of imprisonment is one of the highest in Europe. Between 1980 and 2010 the average prison population doubled (figure 23.1); it continued its inexorable rise, reaching 88,179 in December 2011 and leaving Home Office statisticians struggling.

Trends in Modern Policing

Traditionally, the British police service was decentralized, non-militaristic and apolitical. This remains the official picture but, like so much of the constitution, the formal face can mask reality.

Centralization: a national police service?

> The combination of a centralized police system and an unwritten constitution is the stuff that dictators dream about.
>
> John Alderson (retired chief constable and academic), *A New Cromwell: The Centralization of the Police* (1994)

Local policing and a plurality of forces were justified in terms of local democracy and responsiveness to local conditions. Moreover, the absence of a single national service is seen as a crucial bulwark against the growth of a monolithic police state. The police themselves have consistently resisted the idea of a single service under the home secretary and responsible to Parliament. However, throughout the twentieth century insidious **centralization** has taken place beneath a pluralistic facade through amalgamation, centralized staff organizations, communications technology, specialist units and the strategy of central government.

Amalgamation

I am inclined to the view that we are witnessing a move, perhaps unintended, for national control of the police by central government.

Sir John Smith (ACPO President), speech (4 Feb. 1994)

A royal commission reviewing the constitutional position of the police argued in 1962 that a single force would be more efficient and offer a clear line of accountability. Although the 1964 Police Act stopped short of unification, it increased the home secretary's power to effect amalgamations and strengthened the system of central inspection. Governments did promote amalgamations and the 1972 Local Government Act created some joint forces (such as Thames Valley and West Mercia). A 1993 white paper questioned whether forty-three separate organizations made 'the most effective use of resources available for policing' (Home Office 1993: 41–2).

Centralized staff associations

De facto centralization of the police service has occurred through the development of national associations. Important among these is the Police Federation, a kind of union representing all officers up to the rank of chief inspector (officially the police cannot join a union). It speaks for members in negotiations with government and through public pronouncements as if for a single force. The ability of the Federation to unify its members was demonstrated in May 2012, when over 30,000 officers marched through London to demonstrate against budget cuts and proposed reforms of the service.

Of even greater significance is the Association of Chief Police Officers (ACPO), representing senior officers, including chief constables. ACPO does more than speak for its members, it coordinates policing nationally, particularly through the

National Reporting Centre (NRC), which liaises with the Home Office (which part funds ACPO) and MI5. ACPO also operates the Mutual Aid Coordination Centre set up by the 1964 Police Act, whereby police may be deployed anywhere in the country like a national force. The system was particularly visible during the 1984/5 miners' strike, when convoys of blue minibuses became a familiar sight on the M1.

Advanced communications technology

Forces now operate sophisticated computer and electronic communications systems. These assist in the collection and collation of vast quantities of data for national records, offering 'precise and rapid central control' (Campbell 1980: 65). Since 1969 the Police National Computer Unit at Hendon has controlled a complex communications network of almost a thousand terminals located throughout the country. By 2009 the system contained around 10 million personal records and processed close to 200 million information 'transactions' each year. The 9/11 attack in 2001 opened the doors to increased surveillance, with particular attention to electronic communication and electronic movements of money internationally.

Specialist units

Further centralization comes from the development of specialist CID squads, including regional crime squads, the National Drugs Intelligence Unit and the Serious Fraud Office. In addition, there are the specialist squads of the Metropolitan force such as the Special Branch (now subsumed into the Counter Terrorism Command or SO15), concerned with national security and working with MI5, and the Royalty Protection branch (SO14). Even the Crown Prosecution Service can be seen as part of a centralizing tendency.

Central government strategy

Finally, there is the role of central government. Whitehall's ability to influence policing is by no means new; it has been part of a 'hidden constitution' since the early twentieth century, particularly in class disputes (see Morgan 1987). The policing of the miners' strikes of the 1980s provided a number of telling insights. Strategy was coordinated by a high-powered cabinet committee (Misc. 101) chaired by Thatcher and including leading ministers and a representative of the armed forces. It received regular reports from the NRC. The Cabinet Office also played a part, by word of mouth to mask a link between the Coal Board and police (Boateng 1985: 239).

The 1994 Police and Magistrates Court Act aimed to increase Home Office control. Ex-chief constable-turned-academic, John Alderson (1994), saw the legislation creating Britain's first 'Minister of Police'. Senior officers were placed on fixed-term contracts renewed by the home secretary, putting them under pressure to act in a manner likely to gain ministerial approval. Ian Oliver, chief constable of Grampian, who voiced objections, was effectively sacked in 1998. Police authorities began to complain of excessive interference with the shortlists for their independent members (*Police Review*, 18 Nov. 1994).

Central government also sidelined local government in crime prevention. Programmes such as Safer Cities, Crime Concern, Inner City Task Forces, Neighbourhood Watch and schemes for Citizen Patrols were developed by the Home Office and other central departments. Where they looked for local involvement, the preference was for the business community (see Loveday 1994). Home Secretary David Blunkett's 2001 white paper, *Policing a New Century*, envisaged further centralization, with provision for home secretaries to overrule chief constables and send in 'hit squads' to run 'failing' forces. The creation of directly elected Police and Crime Commissioners was another centrally driven initiative which reduced local government influence.

Towards a British 'FBI'

The tragedy of the Police State is that it always regards all opposition as a crime, and there are no degrees.
Lord Vansittart (1881–1957; British diplomat), House of Lords speech (June 1947)

In July 1989, Metropolitan Police Commissioner Peter Imbert, in a lecture to the Police Federation, called for an even tighter degree of central control through the creation of a single, national detective force along the lines of the US Federal Bureau of Investigation (FBI). Comprising police, customs officers, lawyers, accountants, computer experts and immigration officers, the new body would be centrally funded, responsible to Parliament through the home secretary and with access to a national computerized intelligence system. Local forces would exist alongside but be required to yield some of their sovereignty. A move in this direction was seen in the 1997 Police Act, which made provision for a National Crime Squad for England and Wales. Launched in April 1998, it became the Serious Organised Crime Agency in April 2006.

With such centralizing forces at work, why does government resist the formation of a single police service? Critics argue that its formal fragmentation serves as a convenient fiction to permit a *de facto* centralization which can evade accountability to Parliament.

Militarization

The economic problems of the 1970s saw waves of unrest, with much 'goodwill' between the police and people breaking down. Demonstrations and strikes met new styles of **militarization**, with marching in troops, charges, visors, CS gas, and intimidatory tactics such as the rhythmic beating of riot shields. Forces now have arsenals of rubber bullets, riot shields, water cannon and armoured vehicles.

Bobbies on the beat? Police officers with automatic weapons patrol the Mall during the Queen's Diamond Jubilee in June 2012

Figures released by the Home Office in June 2011 showed that the police had been authorized to use firearms 18,556 times in the year ending 31 March 2010. Once officers are armed, mistakes can be fatal. In 2012 Inquest recorded fifty-four civilian fatalities resulting from police shooting between 1990 and 2012 (twenty-one by the Met). The Mark Duggan shooting in August 2011 precipitated a week of riots and looting that was said to have played a part in at least five deaths and more than £200-million worth of damage.

A third force?

In some countries there exists within the coercive apparatus of the state a third force, poised between the police and the military. This avoids using the military to quell civil disturbance, while protecting police relationships with citizens. However, the hallmark of such forces is extreme violence. In France, for example, the Compagnie Républicaine de Sécurité is feared; in the Paris riots of 1968 it injured 1,500 in a single night. Britain has traditionally eschewed such a force but today we are witnessing the appearance of **paramilitary** units.

In the early 1970s, establishment fears of left-wing movements led to the creation of a National Security Committee, to prepare for nothing less than an internal attack on the state (Bunyan 1977: 293). In 2010 a National Security Council was established, based in the Cabinet Office. Meeting weekly and chaired by the Prime Minister, it also includes senior ministers, with the Chief of the Defence Staff and heads of intelligence agencies attending when required.

There was also the Special Patrol Group (SPG), established in London by the Labour government in the 1960s to combat crime and given a paramilitary remit while remaining formally within the Met. It was replaced in 1987 by the Territorial Support Group. The SPG's existence remained largely unknown until the India House incident in 1973 when, in a religious protest, two Pakistanis from Bradford invaded the Indian High Commission and were shot dead by SPG guards. The Blair Peach affair in April 1979 brought home the extent to which the SPG operated in a realm above the law. Peach, one of the objectors to a National Front demonstration (held with extreme provocation in the largely black area of Southall), was struck on the head with a rubber cosh filled with lead (an unauthorized weapon) by an SPG officer. Before long he was dead. The events following this had all the characteristics of a cover-up and no prosecutions were made (Rollo 1980: 165).

> His tongue was stuck to his upper jaw, and the upper part of his head was all red as if he was bleeding inside.
>
> Local resident who attempted to administer aid to Blair Peach, quoted in J. Rollo, 'The Special Patrol Group', in P. Hain (ed.), *Policing the Police* (1980: 158)

Today most forces have special groups known variously as mobile support units, armed response units, special operations units and tactical aid groups, some of which have themselves been involved in *causes célèbres*. Firearms units, sometimes known as Trojan patrols, resemble the US 'Swat Squads', with black fireproof overalls, body armour and military-style helmets. In 2001 it was reported that some had quietly armed themselves with the Heckler & Koch G36K, a high-velocity military assault rifle used by German special forces and capable of piercing body armour (Robbins and Clark 2001). In addition they can use stun-guns (Tasers), which deliver an electric shock, causing uncontrollable muscle contractions. The legitimacy of such units was enhanced by the terrorist threat in the post 9/11 climate. Today gaily coloured holiday-makers find themselves mingling with menacingly armed figures at Britain's airports.

Politicization

Although formally outside politics, it has already been shown that policing has political consequences. Where there is inequality, the police must constantly seek to restrain the 'have-nots' from threatening the 'haves' and it is not surprising that they have felt an affinity with the political right. However, involvement in politics goes beyond this to an overt presence as a political pressure group.

Publicity campaigning

Although the Police Federation and ACPO are statutorily restricted, they have broken out of this straitjacket to become mouthpieces of collective police views. Unlike the civil service, the police do not subscribe to a Trappist school of public relations; they have argued against light sentences, juries, community policing and a suspect's right to silence. They have also made strong moral judgements about schools, drugs, parents, the church, industrial relations and homosexuality.

The politicization was never better illustrated than when the Police Federation actually launched a Law and Order Campaign in 1975. The movement arose over frustration that 'soft' groups were having a liberalizing effect on the law, policing and penal policy. Their campaign copied the methods of other pressure groups, with public speaking engagements, feeding the media and lobbying. The Federation announced in February 1978 its intention to make law and order an issue in the forthcoming general election, even sponsoring large newspaper advertisements. More recently, the coalition government's cuts to policing levels showed the police behaving like a trade union when, in May 2012, over 30,000 off-duty officers took part in a protest march through the streets of London. The growing sense of politicization was demonstrated in March 2013 when the Federation held a ballot to end the bar on industrial action. This showed an 81 per cent majority of those voting to be in favour. However, with only 42 per cent of members voting, this was not enough to move forward.

Police superstars

Leading police figures have sought to project themselves as national celebrities. In particular, Metropolitan commissioners have found a unique platform. Notable was Sir Robert Mark, brought in by the libertarian home secretary Roy Jenkins in 1967 to clear up internal corruption. He soon revealed a fiercely anti-libertarian stance on many social issues (Kettle 1980: 13). In 1973 he was invited to deliver the prestigious BBC Dimbleby Lecture, giving him the largest audience any policeman had ever had. This has been seen as the coming of age of politically assertive policing in Britain. Other senior officers have also enjoyed celebrity. James Anderton, chief constable of Greater Manchester, was particularly prominent during the 1980s, proclaiming that AIDS sufferers and drug addicts dwelt in 'a cess-pit of their own making', though he was eventually restrained after proclaiming that he was guided by 'voices'. In the 1990s Ray Mallon, as a detective superintendent in the Cleveland force, earned the moniker 'Robocop' for his public advocacy of zero-tolerance policing. In 2002 he completed his mutation into a politician when he became Middlesbrough's first directly elected mayor. Met Commissioner Paul

Condon caused an outcry in July 1995 by stating that most London muggings were committed by young black males. A particularly political commissioner was Sir Ian Blair, who also gave the Dimbleby Lecture, in which he called for a debate on policing methods in a changed society. He was later forced to resign over the killing of Jean Charles de Menezes in the aftermath of the 7/7 bombings.

The politics of confrontation

Senior officers have enjoyed direct links with Whitehall and the police service has been seen as a pressure group enjoying insider status. Whenever there is a proposal for a change in the law relating to criminal or judicial procedure, or whenever there is a *cause célèbre* involving the police, a well-maintained network springs into life.

However, when differences become irreconcilable corporatism is replaced with confrontation. This was increasingly the case from the early 1980s, as both main parties tried to introduce the kind of radical reforms that were being implemented in other parts of the public sector. The key issue was crime rates; despite substantial increases in expenditure on fighting crime, these continued to rise (figure 23.2) (*Home Office Statistical Bulletin* 19/96). Abandoning the 'adulation

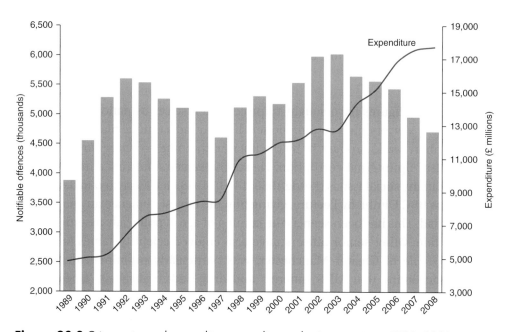

Figure 23.2 Crime rates and expenditure on police and prison services, 1989–2008

Source: Data from *Social Trends, Annual Abstract of Statistics*, House of Commons Library Research Papers (various years), Home Office recorded crime statistics, Mills et al. (2010a,b).

towards the police demonstrated by Mrs Thatcher' (Loveday 1996: 23), the Major government alleged inefficiency and sought to 'destabilise established police interests'.

The hostile atmosphere continued under New Labour. As home secretary, Jack Straw endured booing and jeering at Police Federation conferences, and his successor, David Blunkett, was soon reminded of the negotiating weight of both the Federation and ACPO. Condemning Blunkett's reform package on pay and conditions, they voted 10:1 to reject it. They even began to consider using the Human Rights Act to overturn a 1919 ban on strike action. In April 2002 Blunkett announced a climbdown in the face of ACPO opposition. In 2012 Conservative Home Secretary Theresa May's relationship with the police was described as toxic as she sought to impose cuts to pay and pensions, reduce the police budget and remove some 16,000 officers from the streets.

> *This man is a bully. Police officers deal with bullies on a daily basis; they don't scare us, we take them on.*
> Glen Smyth (Metropolitan Police Federation Chair), speaking of David Blunkett on the BBC news (24 Feb. 2002)

Helping the police with inquiries: suspicious customers

In his Dimbleby Lecture Sir Ian Blair discussed the problems of modern policing and spoke of the declining influence of agencies of community cohesion, including churches, trade unions, tenants' associations and voluntary clubs. He also noted the disappearance of various agents of social enforcement, such as park-keepers, caretakers and bus conductors. Many would applaud the idea of community spirit but the question arises over how far non-policing agencies should go in a democracy.

DIY crime fighting

The rise (and perceived rise) in crime rates led, during the 1980s and 1990s, to calls for citizens to become more active in crime prevention and even detection. Home Secretary Michael Howard called on citizens to 'walk with a purpose'. They were encouraged by 'crime-busting' television programmes, often relaying footage from a steady accretion of CCTV cameras on urban buildings. Domestic alarms became almost as ubiquitous as television aerials and the Neighbourhood Watch movement saw thousands of suburban community groups coming together to keep a watchful eye over their cars, houses and garden gnomes. To critics this is not far removed from vigilantism. The danger of DIY policing is of a lynch-mob mentality, as seen in the vigilante attacks on a number of innocent victims (including a paediatrician) mistaken for one of the forty-nine paedophiles identified by the *News of the World* in 2000. However, the courts often find against over-zealous amateur law enforcers. In August 1999, Norfolk farmer Tony Martin was convicted of murder (later reduced to manslaughter) for shooting dead a burglar; he served a three-year prison sentence.

Privatization

While suspects are not yet seriously referred to as 'customers', private-sector involvement in policing has been encouraged. The 1980s saw considerable expansion of the private security industry, with militaristically uniformed guards patrolling industrial sites, shopping malls, car parks and even residential areas. War in Iraq and Afghanistan saw a global boom in private security companies, often manned by ex-military personnel. Security firms sometimes work in conjunction with the police and by 1997 the £2-billion-a-year industry of some 8,000 firms with 170,000 employees was dwarfing the state police service. When firms such as Group Four (later renamed G4S) took over the transport of prisoners, embarrassing escapes led satirists to comment on Thatcher's desire to set the people free! Some employees are ex-police officers but others have been convicted criminals and have themselves been responsible for an estimated 2,000 crimes a year (*Evening Standard*, 15 July 1997). Concern led to regulation and since 2003 this has come from a quango, the Security Industry Authority.

From 1993 major privatizations were also seen in the prison service, with contracts awarded to build and run new prisons. Home Secretary Jack Straw endured boos and cries of 'rubbish' at the 1998 Prison Officers' Association conference when, despite his earlier opposition, he declared himself a 'convert' to the idea (*Independent*, 20 May 1998). The Adam Smith Institute has envisaged a future in which the state police operate in competition with private-sector agencies.

Problems with the use of private companies were highlighted with a series of fiascos concerning security for the 2012 London Olympic Games. There were allegations of illegal immigrants being employed, of inadequate training and of the police being forced to step in when guards failed to turn up or were found asleep at their posts. Most headline catching was the failure of G4S, awarded a £284-million contract, to recruit sufficient staff for the job. The Ministry of Defence was called upon to provide 3,500 extra troops, many just back from gruelling service in Afghanistan.

Private-sector managerialism

The time is ripe for taking on the boys and girls in blue.
The Sheehy report (1993)

A critical report compiled by businessman Sir Patrick Sheehy (1993) aimed to introduce private-sector-style management into the police service. It spoke of 'cosy relationships' where recruits could expect a job for life, with little by way of performance management or appraisal. The service was also top heavy with senior grades. The reform proposals provoked outspoken condemnation from the police associations, with 20,000 officers congregating in an unprecedented protest rally in July 1993. Home Secretary Michael Howard agreed to drop certain key recommendations, including performance-related pay, short fixed-term contracts and a higher age for full retirement pension entitlements. However, the management culture of the service was changed, with increased paperwork at all levels.

Quis Custodiet Ipsos Custodes? Who Guards the Guards?

Being deliberately subject to only weak democratic oversight, modern policing raises the age-old question articulated by the Latin satirist Juvenal in the first century AD: who will guard the guards themselves?

The complaints procedure

> If one of the boys working for me got himself into trouble, I would get all of us together and I would literally script him out of it. I would write all the parts out and if we followed them closely we couldn't be defeated.
>
> Metropolitan Police sergeant quoted in Smith and Gray (1985: 355)

During the 1970s investigations into allegations of police brutality and deaths in police custody left victims' families unsatisfied. The 1976 Police Act established a quango, the Police Complaints Board (PCB), a lay body with a limited supervisory role over the process. However, the investigation remained in police hands. Following serious race and anti-police riots in Brixton, Lord Scarman's report (1981: para. 4.2) cited the absence of an independent **police complaints procedure** as one of five crucial factors contributing to the breakdown of police–community relations. The 1984 Police and Criminal Evidence Act established a three-tiered approach, adding independent supervision of police investigations into serious cases by a Police Complaints Authority (PCA), which replaced the PCB. Although the reform fell short of truly independent investigation, the response of the Police Federation in its 1989 annual conference was a vote of no confidence in the PCA, which officers accused of siding with complainants.

In 2004 the PCA was replaced by an Independent Police Complaints Commission (IPCC). A non-departmental public body, the IPCC was to oversee the whole of the police complaints system, investigating the most serious complaints, such as deaths in police custody and shootings, and hearing appeals from citizens about the way a complaint had been dealt with by a local force. Critics continued to question whether this new quango would be able to deal with the police tradition of sticking together when under attack.

Despite a steady increase in complaints since 2000 (figure 23.3), the number formally investigated and upheld remained very low (just 12 per cent in 2011/12) and an increasing number of dissatisfied complainants have appealed to the IPCC,

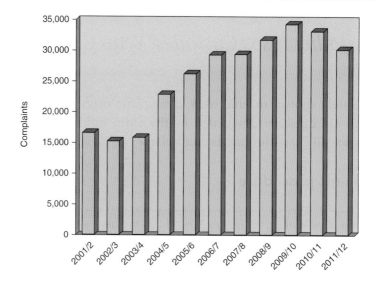

Figure 23.3 Complaints about the police, 2001/2–2011/12 (number of complaint cases recorded)

Note: Includes complaints about British Transport Police from 2006/7.

Source: Data from Independent Police Complaints Commission (2012: table 1).

over one-third of which were upheld in 2011/12 (Independent Police Complaints Commission 2012: 1). However, an increasing proportion were resolved informally. Although dismissals may result, this can be avoided by officers retiring or resigning before proceedings have been completed. Figures obtained by Channel 4 News under the Freedom of Information Act in 2012 revealed that whilst only five police officers were dismissed for racist behaviour between 1999 and 2012, a further seven were forced to resign, 293 were disciplined and 749 (513 of these in the Met) were referred to the IPCC.

Beyond the Blue Horizon

It is not only through the police service that the state exerts its coercive power. Although less overt than they have been in Northern Ireland, there are other fingers on the iron hand which can operate on the home front, including the military and the security services.

The military

Ostensibly states have a military arm to defend themselves from invasion or to subjugate other states. During the imperialist era Britain's military was a feared world power. In two hellish world wars it became even more central, but with the post-war dismantling of empire it was anticipated that the men on horseback would retire to their barracks. However, they were to seek a role rather nearer home to confront 'the enemy within'.

Who controls?

Control of the military is vested formally in government ministers responsible to Parliament, which grants its funds. The modern history of political control dates from the creation of the Committee of Imperial Defence in 1902, after the Boer war. During the second world war this was replaced by the War Cabinet and a Ministry of Defence established. In 1964 the three service departments were amalgamated under the Secretary of State for Defence and a Defence Council.

The service chiefs are, like civil servants, heavily involved in decision-making. Sometimes appearing as the more arrogant of the British upper class, they take it hard if politicians resist their 'advice'. Here is another corporatist enclave where the select influence the destiny of the nation away from the prying eyes of democracy. Parliament and the full Cabinet have very little hold on the reins; thus defence spending reached astronomical heights as the twentieth century drew to a close (figure 23.4) and the arms industry grew fat. Talk of a post-cold-war peace dividend proved overly optimistic as new flashpoints emerged and the threat posed by globalized terrorist groups became apparent to all.

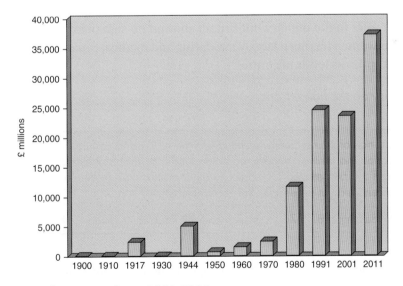

Figure 23.4 Defence expenditure, 1900–2011

Source: Data from Butler and Butler (1994: 393–5); *Annual Abstract of Statistics* (2001: table 4.2; *UK Defence Statistics* (2012: table 1.1).

Who are the military?

The majority of those marching to venues like the Somme were from the working class but the people who matter in the military, the top brass, follow very much in the traditions of British elitism, with members of the royal family still continuing to hold high military rank. Before the rise of the industrial bourgeoisie, commissions in the army and navy were reserved for the sons of the aristocracy and wealth was needed for their purchase and for subsequent promotion. However, the worldwide policing necessary to protect free trade made the bourgeoisie more than a little concerned and a modernization programme placed the military in the hands of the new elite. The social prestige is such that retired officers retain their titles like honours, even having them engraved on their tombstones.

The British army probably has a worse record of racism than any other state institution, remaining largely untouched by the post-1970s anti-discriminatory laws. In 1997 only 1 per cent of military personnel came from ethnic minorities, compared with more than 5 per cent of the civil service (*Financial Times*, 14 Oct. 1997). Prince Charles himself expressed concern at the milk-white complexions of his royal guards. Although the headline figure rose steadily to 6.6 per cent by October 2009, concerns remained. However, given the traditional role of the army in subduing foreign enemies, a racist culture is not entirely surprising.

Warfare is traditionally a male activity and the few women wishing to fight were often obliged to cross-dress. In 2012 there were 76,694 women in the army, representing 13.6 per cent of the total. In January 2013 the USA lifted its ban on women in combat roles in the military but Britain showed no sign of following suit. Hence the role for women has been largely in a caring and medical capacity. Women do not enter the top-brass levels of control.

The military on the home front

> There is no horror, no cruelty, sacrilege, or perjury, no imposture, no infamous transaction, no cynical robbery, no bold plunder or shabby betrayal that has not been . . . perpetrated . . . under no other pretext than those elastic words, so convenient and yet so terrible: 'for reasons of state'.
>
> Mikhail Bakunin (1814–76; Russian anarchist), *Rousseau's Theory of the State* (1873)

The military in any state contains a fearsome potential for violence. Most *coups d'état* are military-backed and it is not unusual for a state to direct such power on its own citizens. In Britain today, governments can make 'reasonable' use of troops in riotous situations. In the confrontation with the miners there were rumours of soldiers in police uniforms, distinguishable by the absence of a number. Perhaps the most telling post-war use of the army in civil situations has been in Northern Ireland from 1969 (see chapter 20).

Overt military involvement in civil affairs can be conducted by a special elite corps – the Special Air Service (SAS) – which first caught the public imagination in 1980 when, under the eyes of television cameras, it daringly ended a siege of the Iranian Embassy. It also operated under cover in Northern Ireland, where codes permitted extra military freedoms, buttressed by special emergency powers granted by Parliament.

Although conventions restrict the use of troops in mainland Britain, there is nothing to prevent these changing. The royal prerogative means that in a state of emergency troops can be used in any way at all. The post 9/11 terrorist threat strengthened the rationale for such deployment. In February 2003 Prime Minister Tony Blair authorized the use of troops in various sites around the country, including the deployment of 450 soldiers and 1,000 extra police officers to patrol Heathrow airport. In 2011 there was widespread support for the idea that troops might be deployed on the streets of major cities to quell the riots that had swept the country in the wake of the police shooting of Mark Duggan (see p. 721).

The security services: the 'cloak and dagger' of the state

Courses on British government often ignore the **security services**, not because such matters should not be discussed in front of children but because they are things that nobody is supposed to talk about. Here we meet agencies operating below the level of public accountability and consciousness. People have some vague notion from the novels of authors such as John le Carré and Ian Fleming that they exist, but these are often chauvinistic fantasies about superhuman figures like James Bond.

The services are not new. The Home Office, with an historic responsibility for state security, has maintained an ad hoc network of spies and informers, partnering the industrial capitalism rising in the eighteenth century (Bunyan 1977: 153). They comprise a number of agencies.

- The *Special Branch* of the Met (subsumed in 2006 into the Counter Terrorism Command) was created in 1883 to be concerned mainly with criminal offences against the state and subversive organizations. It was always heavily involved with Irish affairs. The emphasis is on intelligence gathering and 'watching', with 'political policing' (Bunyan 1977: ch. 3).
- *MI5* was established in 1909 to root out subversive activity at home. Today it works closely with the Counter Terrorism Command, calling on police powers (of arrest and so on) when required.

- *MI6, the Secret Intelligence Service,* is concerned with organizing espionage overseas. In 1919 it 'poured in agents and several million pounds in a vain effort to subvert the [Russian] revolution' (Bunyan 1977: 155).
- The *Government Communications Headquarters (GCHQ)* at Cheltenham is concerned with worldwide electronic surveillance.
- *Defence Intelligence* of the Ministry of Defence (previously known as the Defence Intelligence Staff) oversees the work of the intelligence staffs of the armed services.
- The ordinary *police service* (liberally interpreting its public order function) is increasingly concerned with matters of security.

Although separate organizations, they work together at various levels, coordinated by Scotland Yard (Campbell 1980: 116). The paranoid secrecy of the state is never more tight-lipped than here, serving not merely to safeguard Britain's secrets from potential enemies, but to conceal the fact that the agencies can sail extremely close to the wind. When joining MI5, Peter Wright (1987: 31) was told that it could not be part of Whitehall because its work 'very often involved transgressing propriety or the law'.

The British government long fostered the idea that the security services did not actually exist: the Head of MI6 in 1956 (and former head of MI5), Sir Dick Goldsmith

"None of you knows each other, I trust."

Reproduced by permission of *Punch*

White, was officially listed as Deputy Under Secretary at the Foreign Office and Superintending Under Secretary of the Library and Records Department (Bunyan 1977: 189–90). However, a surprising break with tradition came in 1991 with the appointment of Stella Rimington as head of MI5; not only was she a woman but she was named. In July 1993 MI5 published a booklet on the security service, revealing some 2,000 people operating in its secretive world. However, when Rimington decided to publish her own memoirs (2001), describing the vetting process as 'Kafkaesque', she fell from grace.

The class factor

Unlike the police service, the security services remain very much a bastion of the lordly amateur male establishment world of John Buchan, even to the extent, according to Peter Wright (1987: 36), of closing down MI5 once a year for the Lord's test match, where they have an unofficially reserved patch in the Lord's Tavern. The girls managing the files, the 'Registry Queens', were said to be debutantes recruited from the aristocracy, perhaps the best vetting of all. Recruitment has traditionally been conducted on an informal basis and most members (including the spies) have come from the public school–Oxbridge hothouse. However, the terrorist threat of the late 1990s led to some expansion of the recruitment pool, with adverts in newspapers and on the London tube for drivers, linguists, surveillance officers and technology experts. Adverts also appeared in women's changing rooms in health clubs.

What are the buggers up to?

In protecting the state from subversion and espionage the activities of the security services are potentially infinite in their variety. After the first world war, fear of communism saw working-class activists harassed and even imprisoned. The National Unemployed Workers' Movement was kept under constant surveillance by the Special Branch, its leaders eventually arrested and its documents confiscated. One notorious act concerned the Zinoviev letter.

In the soft-focus days of the 1960s, when the Beatles, Mary Quant and student uprisings seemed to symbolize a new era, and Harold Wilson appeared to be making Labour a natural party of government, members of the Establishment talked long into the night of *coups* to prevent the drift. In this Orwellian scenario those feeling under threat could hardly complain to the Prime Minister, who believed he too was under surveillance (see Knightley 1986).

The definition of **subversion** must have a considerable bearing on whom the security services fix their attentions upon, and it was a Labour home secretary who threw the gates open. The definition given by Lord Denning in his 1963 report on the Profumo scandal was contemplating 'the overthrow of the government by unlawful

> **The Zinoviev letter**
> This letter was reputedly uncovered during the 1924 general election campaign. Apparently sent by Gregory Zinoviev, president of the Communist International, to a prominent member of the British Communist Party, it urged armed revolution. The resulting paranoia effectively ruined Labour's election chances. A middle-man named Thurn, who received £7,500 from the Conservative Party, touted the letter around and ensured its publication in the *Daily Mail*. Its authenticity was never proved and it appears to have been the product of a dirty tricks operation involving 'members of M16 and MI5, the top personnel at the Foreign Office, and the Tory party' (Bunyan 1977: 159).

means'. However, in 1978, Merlyn Rees dispensed with 'unlawful'. This gave the green light to the security services (Kettle 1980: 52–3), allowing them to turn inward on the body politic like a virus, investigating left-wing politicians, trade unionists and anyone expressing an unorthodox political opinion. In 1990, Colin Wallace claimed that, as an army public relations officer in the 1970s, he had been involved in MI5 operations ('Clockwork Orange') to smear British politicians (*Observer*, 4 Feb. 1990).

> 'There are also certain matters of personal conduct which could quite possibly leave you open to blackmail.'
> *Shit!!* . . .
> I thought about it for a little while. They must have been bugging my phone. There was no other explanation. And for ages.
>
> MP Alan Clark on meeting with Cabinet Secretary Sir Robert Armstrong, shortly after becoming a minister, *Diaries* (24 June 1983)

Diana, to her dying day, thought it was MI5 on behalf of the establishment at the height of the 'wars of the Wales' who bugged her and were responsible for the Squidgy tapes.
Anthony Holden, 'Royal Blues', in *Red Pepper* (Oct. 1997)

The collection and collation of information can lift government to Kafkaesque levels. The ending of the cold war left MI5, like the writers of spy thrillers, casting around for a *raison d'être*, but by 1993 some 70 per cent of its resources were devoted to 'counter-terrorism'. An unprecedented bank of data was built up, focusing on leaders of groups like CND, Greenpeace, the trade unions, schools and universities, hospitals, the theatre and the media. In August 1997, former MI5 officer David Shayler disclosed in a newspaper article that the service still held a file on Home Secretary Jack Straw (president of the National Union of Students in 1969), and ministers Peter Mandelson and Harriet Harman. In 1998 Straw himself opened a window of light, but did little to allay fears, by revealing that MI5 currently held nearly half a million files (*The Times*, 30 July 1998).

In February 1993 Channel 4's *Dispatches* programme showed extraordinary levels of surveillance of those protesting against a motorway through Twyford Down, with police, private security firms and even a detective agency, and names faxed to the Department of Transport. John Alderson saw MI5 police involvement in security as the acorn of a police state (*Red Pepper*, April 1996). The unmasking, in 2010, of Mark Kennedy (aka Mark Stone), an officer in the National Public Order Intelligence Unit, demonstrated the lengths to which the police were prepared to go. Kennedy had infiltrated numerous environmental pressure groups during his seven-year operation, even entering into long-term sexual relationships as a means of preserving his cover.

The increased activity was supported by legislation. Even before 9/11 there had already been significant changes in response to the fear of terrorism. The 2000 Terrorism Act replaced the Prevention of Terrorism Act and the Northern Ireland Emergency Provisions Act (both of which required annual renewal) with a permanent UK-wide measure. This included a new definition of terrorism. Previously the use of violence for political ends, it became the use or threat, for the purpose of advancing a political, religious or ideological cause, of action that involves serious violence against any person or property, endangers the life of any person or creates a serious risk to the health or safety of the public or a section of the public.

In addition to promoting renewed vigilance and calls for increased funding for MI6, the new definition opened the door to the introduction of a draconian catalogue of measures on the home front. The 2000 Regulation of Investigatory Powers Act paved the way for the creation of a surveillance society; the 2001 Anti-Terrorism, Crime and Security Act sanctioned the indefinite detention of foreign terror suspects without charge or trial; the 2002 Proceeds of Crime Act allowed for the confiscation of assets without trial; the 2005 Prevention of Terrorism Act replaced indefinite detention of foreign terror suspects with control orders; the 2006 Terrorism Act criminalized a wide range of activities seen as encouraging or glorifying terrorism; and the 2008 Counter-Terrorism Act extended the period for which terrorist suspects could be detained without charge from twenty-eight to forty-two days. Although the formation of the coalition government in May 2010 signalled the end of plans for the introduction of a nationwide biometric ID-card scheme, the new government extended control in other areas. The Draft Communications Bill heralded in the 2012 Queen's Speech, for example, sought to massively extend the power of the police and security services to collect data on private electronic communications such as emails and text messages.

Who watches the watchers?

Dissatisfaction with the current state of affairs led in 1989 to a Security Services Act; for the first time, official recognition was given to the existence of MI5 (though not of MI6) and a tribunal was created to hear complaints. In addition, a commissioner (a Law Lord) would oversee warrants for bugging and entering and make an annual report to Parliament, though this could be edited by the prime minister.

The club of ex-Home Secretaries is, in my view, one of the worst features of British public life: they all compliment each other. . . but nobody believes [they] are really kept informed by the security services.
Tony Benn, *Diaries* (1991: 587)

A report from the Commons Home Affairs Committee (1993) noted that, while all the country's closest allies had independent oversight of their security services, Britain's operated beyond the realm of parliamentary scrutiny. Among elected politicians, only the prime minister is formally in the know, but even this is doubtful. The British tradition of the neutral civil service has created a situation in which 'Ministers, and Prime Ministers, increasingly become putty, on questions of "security", in their senior adviser's hands' (Thompson 1980: 157). When David Shayler blew the whistle on what he saw as MI5 inefficiency and bungling, he came under investigation for suspected breach of the Official Secrets Act, leading to his prosecution (*Guardian*, 30 July 2003).

The Coercive State and the Community

It would of course be absurd to expect policing and other forms of state coercion to operate without force and violence; this is why they are created. While it is not the only cause of disharmony, capitalism, with its tendency towards inequality, needs a strong state (see Gamble 1988). Hence the emergence of the modern police service was tied to the industrial revolution. Yet the service managed to develop an ethos of community spirit linked with the gradual assimilation of the working class into the system, reaching a peak in the post-war corporatist decades. Dixon of Dock Green, a caring 'bobby' featuring in a long-running television series, did not seem grossly at variance with reality.

Yet the neoliberal right, 'enemy-within' rhetoric of the late 1970s did not point to **consensus policing**. Thatcher recognized the key role that would be given to the police in her economic and industrial relations policies, promising in her 1979 manifesto to 'spend more on fighting crime even while we economize elsewhere'. Since then, fear of terrorism and increasing social inequality have strengthened the case for strong policing.

Community policing

Against the trend came the Scarman Report, following the Brixton riots of 1981, which saw the roots of crime, riots and public disorder in the social environment. It aroused considerable public and official interest, with recommendations favouring **community policing** including:

- new recruitment procedures to screen out racism and sexism and encourage more black people and women to apply;
- outlawing of discriminatory practices;
- increased community consultation;
- reduction in police discretionary powers;
- increased accountability by means of lay visitors to police stations.

PC Attila Rees, ox-broad, barge-booted, stamping out of Handcuff House in a heavy beef-red huff, black-browed under his damp helmet . . . lumbering down towards the strand to see that the sea is still there.

Dylan Thomas (1914–53; poet), Under Milk Wood (1954)

One of the most prominent advocates of community policing was John Alderson (a former barrister) who, as chief constable of Devon and Cornwall, sought to concern *every* officer with community relations. However, in the neoliberal environment the approach could not flourish. Consistently opposed by the Police Federation, he finally left the service for an academic post. In his Dimbleby Lecture Met Commissioner Sir Ian Blair also expanded on the theme, although he too was forced out of office. However, with six women chief constables in post by 2012, there was the possibility of a further change in attitudes. Sara Thornton, a career policewoman and advocate of neighbourhood policing, who had studied Philosophy and Politics at Durham University, was appointed to the post of chief constable of Thames Valley in 2007, after more than twenty years' service. Moreover, reports regularly reveal a majority preferring the friendly 'bobby on the beat' to the 'Sweeney' image of fast cars and tough policing. With surveys showing fear of crime higher than justified by the reality, and many afraid to go out at night or travel by public transport, the case for community policing is compelling.

The long arm of the law

Yet hurdles stand in the way of a return to a community approach. Reports such as those from Scarman and Macpherson do not recognize all the problems. They ignore fundamental contradictions between the community approach and the features of modern policing, including increased centralization, militarization and the incorporation of the security forces. They also fail to emphasize democratic control through elected councils as the way to local accountability. Without this, community policing can become community control (Gordon 1984: 56). Reform to policing since the 1990s appears to have created a situation in which the 'long arm of the law' remains at an 'arm's length' from the democratic state.

> *I never saw any of them again except the cops. No way has yet been invented to say goodbye to them.*
> Philip Marlowe, in Raymond Chandler's *The Long Goodbye* (1954)

Key points

- Every state assumes a right to use physical force and coercion. Liberal democracy is no exception; a free market requires a strong state.

- However, policing is not formally under the control of politicians.

- This does not mean that policing is outside politics.

- The UK does not have one single police force; separate forces service different regions.

- These were traditionally run by police authorities, with local government representation.

- Directly elected Police and Crime Commissioners replaced these in 2012.
- The modern police service in Britain was a creature of the industrial revolution.
- Previously policing was undertaken by volunteers.
- There are various areas of debate over policing, including sexism, racism and brutality.
- From the 1970s British policing became increasingly centralized, militarized and politicized.
- Through ACPO the police can resemble a national force, but without direct responsibility to Parliament.
- The police complaints process was enhanced by the creation of the IPCC in 2004.
- The military and security services play a covert policing role.
- Community or neighbourhood policing provides an alternative to coercive policing.

Review your understanding of the following terms and concepts

Association of Chief
  Police Officers (ACPO)
canteen culture
chief constable
community policing
consensus policing
Counter Terrorism
  Command
Crown Prosecution
  Service

Independent Police
  Complaints
  Commission (IPCC)
Judges' Rules
'Met'
MI5 and MI6
militarization
paramilitary unit
Police and Crime
  Commissioner

police authority
Police Complaints
  Authority (PCA)
Police Federation
police state
public order
security services
Special Patrol Group
  (SPG)
subversion

Questions for discussion and debate

Consider these propositions and be prepared to present the cases for and against. Try to produce debating propositions of your own.

1   The modern police service is a product of the industrial revolution.
2   Elected Police and Crime Commissioners bring politics into policing.
3   Britain needs a national police service.
4   Institutional racism is a meaningless term.
5   The home secretary cannot be a minister for policing.
6   The police complaints procedures should be independent.
7   Community policing is an impractical ideal.
8   Prison works.
9   Police influence over government policy is essential for effective policing.
10   Policing is no job for a woman.

Further reading

Cowley, R. (2011) *A History of the British Police*.
From the shire reeve of Alfred the Great to 'Blunkett's Bobbies' (PCSOs), a comprehensive account of the British police force and also mention of the Irish policing system.

Emsley. C. (2010) *The Great British Bobby: A History of British Policing from 1829 to the Present*.
Traces the development of Britain's forces of law and order from the earliest watchmen and constables of the pre-modern period to the police service of today, candidly but with affection for the tradition.

Gregory, J. and Lees, S. (1999) *Policing Sexual Assault*.
A detailed account of police practice in the UK in response to sexual assault. Notes

that when the number of rape cases had almost trebled, the proportion of cases resulting in a conviction had dropped from 24 to 8.6 per cent.

Halford, A. (1993) *No Way up the Greasy Pole.*
Inside account of sexism in the police service by its most celebrated victim.

Knightley, P. (1986) *The Second Oldest Profession: Spies and Spying in the Twentieth Century.*
Specialist journalist's account of a field too boggy for most academics.

Leishman, F., Loveday, B. and Savage, S. (2000) *Core Issues in Policing.*
Team of authorities cover a comprehensive range of contemporary policing issues, including accountability, policy-making and the effect of the media.

Newburn, I. (2003) *Crime and Criminal Justice Policy*, 2nd edn.
All aspects clearly presented in historical context.

Ramsay, A. (2008) *Girl in Blue: How One Woman Survived Fourteen Years in the Police Force.*
Anne Ramsay's account of fourteen years as a WPC and detective in Scotland before leaving with post-traumatic stress disorder. 'It was such a male-dominated environment. I was treated like a piece of meat . . . . If you didn't respond to the advances of an officer, you were a lesbian.'

Reiner, R. (2010) *The Politics of the Police*, 4th edn.
Explores the highly charged debates that surround policing, including the various controversies and developments that have led to a change in the public's opinion.

Reiner R. (2011) *Policing, Popular Culture and Political Economy.*
Collection of Reiner's significant articles across four decades.

Rimington, S. (2001) *Open Secret: The Autobiography of the Former Director-General of MI5.*
Some fascinating details on MI5's journey into the twenty-first century, but not as many as some MPs would have wished.

Rowe, M. (2004) *Policing, Race and Racism.*
Assesses the impact of the Lawrence Inquiry and the Macpherson Report. Argues that the police response to race issues raised fundamental issues about the relation of policing to society as a whole.

Smith, D. J. and Gray, J. (1985) *Police and People in London.*
An in-depth study of the Met at work in the 1980s.

Urban, M. (1997) *UK Eyes Alpha: The Inside Story of British Intelligence.*
BBC journalist reports wide range of interviews with those involved. Title is the security term for highly sensitive intelligence.

For reading around the subject and some light relief

There is no shortage of novels, films and TV series about spies, cops and robbers. While enjoying the excitement, remain alert to the political dimensions of the state's right to use force against citizens.

Bertolt Brecht, *The Threepenny Opera*.
Satirical musical play on the relationship between capitalism and law and order.

Robert Harris, *Enigma*.
Tense novel of code-breaking and spying based on second-world-war events.

Stephen Knight, *The Brotherhood*.
An exposé of freemasonry in Britain in the higher reaches of the Establishment, including MI5, judiciary and police.

John le Carré, *The Spy Who Came in From the Cold*.
Modern classic depicting a secret world of spying and treachery.

Ian McEwan, *Sweet Tooth*.
Set during the 1970s, exposes the human side of MI5 as Cambridge graduate Serena Frome is forced to abandon the first rule of espionage – trust no one.

Chris Mullin, *A Very British Coup*.
Ex-steel worker Harry Perkins has led Labour to a stunning victory with a radical manifesto as MI5, the city and the press barons plan to destroy him. (The Channel 4 TV series, *The Secret State*, was based on the novel.)

G. F. Newman, *Law and Order*.
A powerful and realistic TV drama series exploring police–Establishment relations (available on DVD).

Lynda La Plante, *Prime Suspect*.
TV series showing in dramatic form some of the problems facing women in the police service (available on DVD).

Stella Rimington, *At Risk*.
Better than the autobiography, said some reviewers. MI5 intelligence officer Liz Carlyle must deal with an impending terrorist crisis while suffering a patronizing sexist attitude from her MI6 partner. Former director general of MI5 would know all about both problems.

On the net

https://www.gov.uk/government/organisations/home-office
The Home Office site is a good starting point for many of the issues dealt with in this chapter.

https://www.gov.uk/government/organisations/ministry-of-defence
The Ministry of Defence can play a (sometimes controversial) role in home security.

https://www.gov.uk/government/organisations/the-security-service-mi5
Once so secretive that its very existence was denied, the security service now has its own section of the gov.uk website.

CHAPTER 24

A POLICY-MAKING PROCESS: THINKING HOLISTICALLY

In this final chapter we remind ourselves that the political system is an organic whole in which the various parts considered in the previous chapter interact in the formation of public policy. To appreciate this we need to take a holistic perspective.

The final outcome of all political activity is public policy: the decisions about who gets what, when and how. Although it is common to speak of a policy-making process, this is not the kind of process that might be outlined in a book on management theory in which decision-makers assemble data and arrive at a rational conclusion. Public policy emerges from an infinitely complex set of interactions involving elements detailed in every chapter in this book. Governments are deeply enmeshed in a dense biomass of political life, and politics is a process involving not merely the institutions of state but also those of the economy and civil society, and subject to a range of influences emanating from the global context. Political energy issues from multifarious sources, including differences in ideology, wealth, education, employment status, class, gender, race, geographical location, and so on. Moreover, the process embraces institutions well beyond the formal Westminster–Whitehall terrain, encompassing the judiciary, the police, the military, the secret services, trade unions, private firms and thousands of pressure groups espousing numerous causes. Yet despite this seamless cohesion, the previous chapters have been characterized by distinct focuses. There are two principal reasons for this.

- *Verisimilitude.* The world of government and politics really is to some extent formally compartmentalized through the organizational structures of the state. Thus, for example, the judiciary is distinct from the civil service, Parliament is distinct from local government, parties differ from pressure groups, and so on. We saw in chapter 4 that this division is actually part of the constitution; the division of authority is seen as a protection from tyrannical government.
- *Political analysis.* In scientific study it is usual to split up, compartmentalize and classify; this helps us to make sense of the complexity of the world. Thus, for example, actors will split a play up into its scenes, acts and dialogues in the process of mastering it and the biologist will dissect plants and animals, even to the level of their DNA.

However, ultimately the actors will want to rebuild the play in its entirety to reveal its dramatic intent. We must take a **holistic** or **synoptic** perspective of the whole in order to understand the role of each part in the making of policy. To take another analogy, a football team is something qualitatively different from the eleven individuals who comprise it. To assess its likely success we need to understand how these individuals work together. There are various ways of conceiving politics in holistic terms. Here we introduce two closely related perspectives that underlie much study and debate: the organic and the systemic.

Organic theories of the state

A long-prevailing view of the state has pictured it as a living organism (often using the imagery of the human body), with its various organs fulfilling particular functions but bound together in mutual dependence. This goes back to the Ancient Greeks, but a particular version flourished in the nineteenth century amongst a school of biological political theorists. The notion of the organism was not merely metaphor; the state was believed to be a life form, capable of birth, life, disease and death. They also spoke of the state's adaptation to its environment through a slow process of evolution in which some organs became more important and others (like the human appendix) withered away.

States, like men, have their growth, their manhood, their decrepitude, their decay.
Walter Savage Landor (1775–1864; English writer), *Imaginary Conversations* (1824–9)

Functionalism

The organic view was to underlie an approach to the study of society and the state termed **functionalism**. This argued that state structures and institutions must, like the organs of the body, perform certain necessary functions (respiration, reproduction, digestion and so on) for it to survive. The approach was applied by influential anthropologists like A. R. Radcliffe-Brown (1881–1955) and Bronislaw Malinowski (1884–1942) to explain and compare primitive societies where formal institutions did not exist. Thus while a society might not have a western-style parliament, it would necessarily require the function of making rules.

A function only has meaning in terms of the whole and, by the same reasoning, if an institution acts in a way that is harmful to the whole it is, like a disease in an organism, dysfunctional. The sociologists Talcott Parsons (1902–79) and Robert Merton (1910–2003) adapted the anthropologists' ideas more specifically to industrialized societies, revealing that even here it is possible to ask questions based on functional analysis. Thus we may enquire whether an institution really fulfils the function it is supposed to (does Parliament really make laws?), or whether those functions are fulfilled elsewhere (the civil service, the Cabinet, and so on). It can be seen that questions such as these, which seek to look behind the institutional facade, arise throughout this book. Organic and functionalist thinking also has ideological implications. It leads to a Burkean form of conservatism that institutions should be allowed to grow naturally and not be tampered with – a veneration of the status quo.

Systems theory and the political system

The organic view demanded a degree of metaphysical faith and fell out of favour. However, it was replaced with the idea of the **political system**. Although the term is often used loosely to denote little more than 'where politics takes place', the concept is essentially holistic. Systems theory was pioneered by the biologist Ludwig von Bertallanfy, who stressed that 'each part depends not only on conditions within itself, but also . . . on conditions within the *whole* of which it is part' (1952: xix). The concept was introduced into political science by the American scholar David Easton, who entitled a seminal work *The Political System*, on the holistic premise that 'the phenomena of politics tend to cohere and to be mutually related' (1953: 97).

The systems approach advanced thinking by adding to the organic view a mechanical one. The **system** differs fundamentally from the organism in that it does not evolve under some internal dynamic of its own; it is conceived as a machine *designed* by human hand to fulfil a particular purpose. Thus a car is designed to transport us; it will never seek to place its own interest before its rider as might a horse (an organic system). Perceived in this way the state becomes something that can be *changed* on the basis of *reason* – an enlightenment belief. Bentham and the philosophical radicals saw the state as a constitutional Lego set to be constructed at will. We have seen throughout this book how the rising bourgeoisie, acting under the ideology of liberalism, made prolific use of the idea of deliberate change, to the extent of sculpting the modern British liberal-democratic state.

Policy networks

The network image is yet another way of seeing policy-making in holistic terms (Smith 1993: 74). The essence of this approach is a focus on how a large range of actors and institutions are linked together in relationships of power and dependence. Policy communities form from shifting combinations of ministers, private interests, individuals and bureaucracies, where there is no single centre of power (see Richardson and Jordan 1979; Rhodes and Marsh 1992; Grant and MacNamara 1995). The net becomes even wider with the governance perspective, increasingly used by scholars (see Pierre and Stoker 2000). This emphasizes the concept of multi-level governance (Smith 1997), noting layers of governance and quasi-governance at international, provincial, regional and local levels. It extends to relations between bodies such as NATO, the World Bank and the EU, and the transnational corporations and NGOs operating above the level of nation-states and engaging in complex processes of negotiation, bargaining, exchange and compromise across an unlimited political space.

A holistic study strategy

If the study of public policy-making is perceived holistically, one is drawn to conceptualize the parts of the political system in terms of their relationships to the whole and to each other. This can open the door to levels of understanding far deeper than that gained from compartmentalized knowledge. We realize that the behaviour of one element cannot be fully explained without understanding its relationship with all the other elements. Some lessons on holistic thinking come from science in general and particularly from meteorology, where it is crucially necessary to take a global perspective. The range of influences that shape our weather are so complex that, even with computers capable of performing hundreds of millions of calculations a second (the present state of the art), it will always be impossible to include every causal factor; hence we will never be able to predict our weather with complete accuracy. Scientists speak of the 'butterfly effect' wherein a small flapping of wings may set in motion a chain of events that will alter the course of a storm on the other side of the globe. Policy emerges from such causal chains. Clinton's election in the USA may have contributed to the election of Blair in Britain, producing the New Labour agenda. Ill-advised bank loans in the USA precipitated financial crisis in Britain, widespread demonstrations, violence and the coalition austerity package. The complexity of the policy-making process also means that much of what happens as a result of government decisions are so often lamented as 'unintended consequences'.

Review your understanding of the following terms and concepts

functionalism	organic view of the state	political system
governance	policy network	synoptic perspective
holistic perspective	policy-making process	systems theory

Further reading

Dorey, P. (2005) *Policy Making in Britain: An Introduction.*
Comprehensive example of the policy-making approach to the analysis of British government.

Easton, D. (first published 1965) *A Systems Analysis of Political Life.*
Classic exposition of systems theory as applied to political science.

Hill, M. (2012) *The Public Policy Process*, 6th edn.
Well-established text clearly detailing the relationship between theoretical and practical aspects of policy-making. Notes how different policy issues can be made by different policy processes.

John, P. (2012) *Analysing Public Policy*, 2nd edn.
Clearly explains the most common and widely used frameworks for the study of public policy-making.

Parsons, W. (1996) *Public Policy: An Introduction to the Theory and Practice of Policy Analysis.*
Accessible introduction to the policy studies approach using interdisciplinary and comparative methods. Covers agenda formation, policy-making, implementation and evaluation.

Runciman, W. G. (ed.) (2004) *Hutton and Butler: Lifting the Lid on the Workings of Power.*
Essays offering insights into a major policy event: the invasion of Iraq. Looks at the Hutton and Butler reports to consider the most intimate workings of government. A distinguished group of scholars and practitioners probe the realities of decision-making at the highest levels of government.

For reading around the subject and some light relief

Despite the complexities, the muddling through and dysfunctionalities in the process of forming public policy, the nightmare visions that writers sometimes entertain are usually imaginings of how things might be without a democratic policy-making process. Indeed, in the contemporary world some nightmare scenarios really do exist.

Ray Bradbury, *Fahrenheit 451.*
A world in which people are rendered incapable of fighting for their rights because the burning of books leaves them unable to think politically.

Anthony Burgess, *A Clockwork Orange.*
An alarming vision of a future dominated by technology, violence and authoritarian government.

William Golding, *Lord of the Flies.*
Group of boys marooned on a coral island expect fun but endure nightmare without government.

Aldous Huxley, *Brave New World*.
A fable set in the seventh century AF (after Ford), where life is subjugated by science, all under World Controller Mustapha Mond. In *Brave New World Revisited*, Huxley believes his prophecies are already (1958) coming frighteningly true.

George Orwell, *Nineteen Eighty-Four*.
A nightmare of totalitarianism with 'newspeak' and 'doublethink', where war is peace, freedom is slavery and ignorance is strength.

George Orwell, *Animal Farm*.
Pigs rule.

Chronology of Events

427BC	Birth of Plato.
384BC	Birth of Aristotle.
1066	Norman Conquest.
1086	Domesday Book.
1154	Henry II first Plantagenet English king.
1170	Thomas Becket murdered.
1215	Magna Carta.
1258	Simon de Montfort forces reforms on Henry III.
1265	De Montfort's Parliament; defeat and death of de Montfort.
1284	Edward I completes conquest of Wales.
1290	Edward I begins conquest of Scotland.
1295	Edward I's 'Model Parliament'.
1314	Robert the Bruce secures Scottish independence.
1327	Edward II deposed and murdered.
1338	Hundred Years War begins.
1362	English becomes official language in Parliament and courts.
1381	Peasants' Revolt.
1399	Richard II deposed by Henry IV.
1400	Welsh revolt under Owen Glendower.
1415	Battle of Agincourt.
1450	Jack Cade's rebellion against Henry VI.
1453	Final English defeat and end of Hundred Years War.
1455	Wars of the Roses begin.
1476	Caxton sets up printing press.
1485	Battle of Bosworth Field; Tudor dynasty begins.
1493	Vasco da Gama finds sea route to India.
1515	Thomas Wolsey becomes Lord Chancellor and Cardinal.
1517	Martin Luther begins Reformation.
1534	Act of Supremacy; Henry VIII takes control of Church in England.
1535	Thomas More executed.
1536	Anne Boleyn executed.
1558	Elizabeth I becomes Queen.
1577	Drake begins circumnavigation.
1588	Spanish Armada defeated.
1600	English East India Company founded.
1601	Elizabethan Poor Law; rates introduced.
1603	Irish revolts suppressed. Death of Elizabeth I; accession of James VI of Scotland as James I of England.
1605	Gunpowder plot.
1611	English and Scottish Protestants settle in Ulster.
1620	Pilgrim Fathers settle in New England.
1628	Petition of Right to Charles I by Commons.
1629	Charles I tries to rule without Parliament.
1635	John Hampden refuses to pay ship money.

1642	Charles I attempts to arrest five members of Parliament. Outbreak of civil war.		Hanoverian succession.
1644	Battle of Marston Moor. North lost to Charles I. Royalist campaign in Scotland.	1707	Act of Union of English and Scottish Parliaments.
1645	New Model Army formed. Royalist army crushed at Naseby.	1714	Death of Queen Anne; accession of Elector of Hanover as George I. Riot Act enables magistrates to call in military to quell civil disorder.
1646	Charles I surrenders to Scots.	1715	Septennial Act; Parliament prolongs its life from three to seven years.

1642   Charles I attempts to arrest five members of Parliament. Outbreak of civil war.

1644   Battle of Marston Moor. North lost to Charles I. Royalist campaign in Scotland.

1645   New Model Army formed. Royalist army crushed at Naseby.

1646   Charles I surrenders to Scots.

1647   Charles I handed over to Parliament, seized by army, flees to Carisbrooke Castle.

1648   Second civil war; New Model Army defeats Scots and Royalists.

1649   Charles I executed; England governed as republic under Cromwell. England suppresses Ireland.

1651   Cromwell becomes supreme in all Britain after Battle of Worcester. First English Navigation Acts. Thomas Hobbes publishes *Leviathan*.

1655   English take Jamaica.

1658   Cromwell dissolves Rump Parliament, becomes Lord Protector.

1660   Restoration of monarchy; Charles II returns from exile.

1665   Great Plague of London.

1666   Great Fire of London.

1681   Charles II tries to rule without Parliament; establishes Oxford Parliament.

1685   Monmouth's rebellion crushed by James II at Sedgemoor.

1688   William of Orange lands with army in England; flight of James II. The 'Glorious Revolution'.

1689   Bill of Rights limits monarchy.

1690   Locke's *Two Treatises on Government*. Battle of the Boyne; William crushes Irish.

1693   National Debt begun.

1694   Bank of England founded.

1701   Act of Settlement establishes Hanoverian succession.

1707   Act of Union of English and Scottish Parliaments.

1714   Death of Queen Anne; accession of Elector of Hanover as George I. Riot Act enables magistrates to call in military to quell civil disorder.

1715   Septennial Act; Parliament prolongs its life from three to seven years.

1720   'South Sea' bubble.

1721   Robert Walpole seen as first prime minister.

1733   John Kay invents flying shuttle. Jethro Tull advocates new agricultural technology.

1742   Walpole falls.

1748   Montesquieu publishes *L'Esprit des Lois*.

1757   Pitt as Secretary of State is main force in British government. Clive conquers Bengal.

1759   Canal age begins.

1760   Beginning of 100-year period termed 'industrial revolution'.

1763   First British empire at its height.

1764   John Wilkes expelled from Commons.

1769   Richard Arkwright invents water frame for spinning.

1770   James Cook discovers New South Wales.

1774   Warren Hastings appointed first Governor General of India.

1776   American Declaration of Independence. Adam Smith's *Wealth of Nations*.

1783   Treaty of Versailles; American independence recognized. Pitt the Younger becomes PM.

1784   Last appearance of monarch in Cabinet.

1785   Cartwright invents power loom.

1787   American Constitution drafted. Consolidated Fund established.

Creation of Royal Ulster Constabulary.

1789 Washington first US President. French Revolution begins with storming of Bastille (14 July). Bentham's *Introduction to the Principles of Morals and Legislation*.

1792 Denmark first country to prohibit slave trade. France becomes republic.

1851 Great Exhibition.

1798 Battle of Vinegar Hill.

1800 Parliamentary union of Great Britain and Ireland.

1804 Napoleon Bonaparte becomes French Emperor.

1805 Battle of Trafalgar; victory and death of Nelson.

1807 Slave trade abolished in British empire. Napoleon in control of all Europe. Britain blockaded by continent.

1811 Luddite riots against new machinery.

1812 Napoleon retreats from Moscow.

1814 Napoleon abdicates; Louis XVIII King of France.

1815 Napoleon escapes from Elba. Battle of Waterloo. Corn Law protects British agricultural interests at expense of commerce.

1819 'Peterloo Massacre'.

1823 USA announces 'Monroe Doctrine'.

1824 Repeal of Combination Acts legalizes trade unions.

1829 Metropolitan Police formed.

1832 First Reform Bill.

1833 First British Factory Act. First government grant for education.

1834 Poor Law Amendment Act. 'Tolpuddle Martyrs' transported to discourage working-class association.

1835 Municipal Corporations Act. Peel's 'Tamworth Manifesto'.

1836 Chartist movement formed.

1837 Queen Victoria's accession.

1839 Anti-Corn-Law League formed.

1842 Chartists present second Charter.

1845 Irish potato famine.

1846 Corn Laws repealed; Peel resigns; Conservatives split; Disraeli becomes leader.

1848 Revolutionary movement throughout Europe. French Republic proclaimed. Marx and Engels produce *Communist Manifesto*.

1854 Crimean war; France and England declare war against Russia. Much British bureaucratic incompetence exposed; Northcote–Trevelyan Report.

1855 Crimean war ends.

1856 Bessemer process invented.

1858 British Crown assumes sovereignty over India.

1859 Darwin's *Origin of the Species*. J. S. Mill's *On Liberty*.

1861 American civil war begins. J. S. Mill's *Considerations on Representative Government*. Public Accounts Committee established.

1864 First Socialist International.

1865 American civil war ends.

1866 Office of Comptroller and Auditor General established.

1867 Second Great Reform Bill. Bagehot's *The English Constitution*. Vol. 1 of Marx's *Capital*.

1868 Disraeli succeeds Lord Derby as PM; later defeated by Gladstone in general election.

1870 Forster's Education Act sets up school boards.

1872 Secret ballot introduced.

1874 General election; Disraeli succeeds Gladstone as PM.

1880 Gladstone returned as PM.

1883 National insurance introduced in

Germany. Special Branch of Met. established.

1884 Third Parliamentary Reform Bill. Fabian Society founded.

1885 Dicey's *Law and the Constitution*.

1886 First Irish Home Rule Bill defeated in Commons. Unionist defectors from Liberals join Conservatives.

1888 County Councils Act.

1889 Second Socialist International. Great strike at London Docks. First Official Secrets Act.

1890 Parnell ruined by divorce case.

1893 Second Irish Home Rule Bill rejected in Lords. Independent Labour Party formed.

1894 Manchester Ship Canal opens. Gladstone resigns.

1899 Boer war starts.

1900 Labour Party formed. 'Khaki election'.

1901 Queen Victoria dies. Taff Vale judgment.

1902 Boer war ends. Committee of Imperial Defence established.

1903 First flight of heavier-than-air machine at Kitty Hawk, USA. Emmeline Pankhurst forms Women's Social and Political Union.

1905 Liberal landslide; first Labour MPs.

1906 Suffragette activism. Trades Disputes Act reverses Taff Vale judgment.

1908 Asquith becomes PM.

1909 Old-age state pension scheme introduced. Lords reject 'People's Budget'. Henry Ford begins manufacturing cheap motor cars. MI5 established.

1910 Edward VII's death; accession of George V. Labour exchanges established. Liberals battle with House of Lords, win two general elections, but become dependent upon Irish MPs. Osborne judgment.

1911 Parliament Act reduces Lords' power. MPs to be paid. National Insurance introduced. Second Official Secrets Act passed with notorious Section 2.

1912 Third Irish Home Rule Bill. *Titanic* disaster.

1913 'Cat and Mouse Act'.

1914 Archduke Ferdinand assassinated; war in Europe. Britain declares war on Germany. Coalition government formed. Irish Bill passed but put in cold storage.

1916 Lloyd George becomes PM. New coalition reduces role of Liberals. Easter uprising in Ireland. Battle of the Somme; 420,000 British soldiers killed ('lions led by donkeys').

1917 USA declares war on Germany. Russia proclaimed a republic; Bolshevik revolution. Balfour Declaration.

1918 Armistice signed. Women given vote. 'Coupon Election'. Sinn Féin MPs win majority of Irish seats but set up own Parliament (Dáil). Michael Collins forms IRA. New Labour Party constitution.

1919 Versailles Treaty. League of Nations established (Germany excluded).

1920 Black and Tans sent into Ireland.

1921 Irish settlement; Irish Free State set up; Ulster to remain in UK.

1922 1922 Committee formed. Coalition ends. Conservatives win general election. First woman takes seat in Commons.

1923 Baldwin dissolves Parliament over tariff reform. General election makes Labour second-largest party; rules for ten months with Liberal support.

1924   Liberals withdraw support over Campbell case. Zinoviev letter affair. Conservatives return triumphantly to office.

1925   Winston Churchill puts Britain back on gold standard. Drastic cuts in wages and industrial unrest.

1926   General strike.

1928   Equal Franchise Act; voting age for women lowered to 21.

1929   Labour wins election as largest single party for first time. Second Labour government under MacDonald. Liberal decline becomes inevitable. Wall Street crash. BBC established.

1931   Economic depression; Cabinet split over public expenditure cuts. MacDonald resigns. Surprise coalition under MacDonald overwhelmingly endorsed by electorate. Henderson becomes Labour leader.

1932   Lansbury becomes Labour leader.

1933   Hitler appointed Chancellor by Hindenburg and begins to gain iron control in Germany.

1934   Hitler becomes dictator. Foundation of NCCL.

1935   Baldwin succeeds MacDonald as PM. Attlee becomes Labour leader. Conservatives win election.

1936   Spanish civil war breaks out. Public Order Act. Keynes's *General Theory of Employment, Interest and Money*. BBC TV begins.

1937   Chamberlain forms coalition.

1938   Germany annexes Austria. British navy mobilized. Chamberlain signs Munich Agreement with Hitler.

1939   Britain recognizes Franco government in Spain; civil war ends. Conscription introduced. Germany invades Poland. Britain declares war on Germany. Third Official Secrets Act.

1940   Labour joins coalition; Churchill forms National Government. Army evacuated from Dunkirk. Italy declares war on Britain and France. Germans capture Paris. Battle of Britain. Attlee recognized as deputy PM.

1941   Japanese attack Pearl Harbor.

1942   Beveridge Report.

1943   Mussolini overthrown. Italian Fascist Party dissolved.

1944   D-Day invasion of Europe. Paris liberated. Bretton Woods Agreement; IMF and World Bank established. Great Education Act.

1945   Mussolini and mistress shot by Italian partisans. Suicide of Hitler and mistress. End of war against Germany (2 May). UN Charter signed. Landslide Labour victory; Attlee becomes PM. Britain begins to create modern welfare state. Atomic bomb against Japan. Russia declares war against Japan. Japan surrenders. Lend Lease terminated. Nuremberg Trials. UN formed. Attlee takes decision that Britain will manufacture atomic bombs.

1946   USA eventually approves loan to Britain.

1947   Nationalization of mines. Marshall Aid plan begins. India and Pakistan become dominions. Marriage of Princess Elizabeth.

1948   End of British mandate for Palestine; partition into Jewish and Arab states. NHS established. Electricity nationalized. Republic of Ireland Bill signed.

1949   Parliament Act reduces Lords' power. NATO formed after Russians blockade Berlin. Gas nationalized.

1950 Rebuilt House of Commons opens. Labour secures narrow election victory.

1951 Resignation of Bevan over NHS charges. Attlee dissolves Parliament. Labour defeated in election, despite receiving most votes; Churchill becomes PM.

1952 George VI's death.

1953 Elizabeth II's coronation; ceremony televised. Steel de-nationalized.

1954 Crichel Down case. Food rationing ends.

1955 Churchill resigns as PM; succeeded by Eden. Conservative general election victory. Independent TV begins. Gaitskell succeeds Attlee as Labour leader.

1956 Britain's first atomic power station opens at Calder Hall. Suez crisis. Anthony Crosland publishes *The Future of Socialism*.

1957 Eden resigns as PM; replaced by Macmillan.

1958 EEC treaty comes into force. CND launched under Bertrand Russell. Life Peerage Act. First women peers in House of Lords.

1959 Conservatives' third successive election victory.

1960 Macmillan's 'wind of change' speech; Conservatives form Monday Club. Plowden Report on public expenditure. Kennedy elected US president. Momentous Labour conference; Gaitskell makes 'fight, fight, and fight again' vow.

1961 Justice Report, *The Citizen and the Administration*. NEDC established.

1962 Cuban missile crisis. 'Beeching axe' reduces British Rail network. Macmillan's 'Night of the Long Knives'. First post-war Immigration Act.

1963 British application to join EEC rejected. Harold Wilson Labour leader after Gaitskell's death. Profumo scandal. Peerage Act enables peers to renounce hereditary titles. Macmillan resigns as PM; succeeded by Sir Alec Douglas-Home. Kennedy assassinated.

1964 Nelson Mandela sentenced to life imprisonment in South Africa. Labour gains narrow general election victory; Wilson becomes PM. Police Act limits local control of police forces.

1965 Douglas-Home resigns; Heath elected Conservative leader under new procedure. Death penalty abolished. Prices and Incomes Board created.

1966 Election increases Labour majority to almost 100. Sir Edmund Compton becomes first ombudsman.

1967 Jo Grimond resigns as Liberal leader; replaced by Jeremy Thorpe. Britain makes another failed application to join EEC. *Rookes* v. *Barnard* judgment attacks right to strike.

1968 NHS prescription charges re-introduced. Enoch Powell's 'Rivers of Blood' speech. Fulton Report on civil service.

1969 British army units to be deployed in N. Ireland. Voting age lowered to 18. Government seeks TUC voluntary agreement to curb unofficial strikes. Redcliffe-Maud Report on local government.

1970 Heath gains surprise election victory. Third application to join EEC. Army uses rubber bullets in N. Ireland.

1971 Currency decimalized. Immigration Act reduces status of Commonwealth immigrants to that of aliens. Both Houses of Parliament vote to join EEC. US balance of trade slides into deficit with major consequences for world capitalism.

1972 'Bloody Sunday' in Londonderry. Increased IRA bombing. Direct Westminster rule over N. Ireland introduced. Power crisis; state of emergency and power cuts. Local Government Act to reorganize system.

1973 Britain, Ireland and Denmark join EEC. VAT introduced. Heath U-turns on economic policy. N. Ireland referendum strongly supports retaining link with Britain. First sitting of new Ulster Assembly collapses in chaos. Diplock Courts introduced in terrorist cases. Arab–Israeli war; oil prices quadruple. Fuel conservation measures include three-day week.

1974 End of direct rule in N. Ireland. Parliament debates energy crisis. Miners' strike. Heath calls election to decide 'who governs'; no clear result; Labour becomes minority government. Second election in October returns Labour (majority three). Ulster Assembly collapses; direct rule resumed. IRA bombings in Guildford and Birmingham pubs and in London.

1975 Margaret Thatcher defeats Heath to become Conservative leader. Referendum on remaining in EEC; 2 to 1 majority 'Yes'. First live broadcast of Commons. Unemployment exceeds 1 million.

1976 Wilson's unexpected resignation; Callaghan becomes PM. David Steel elected Liberal leader. Lord Hailsham expounds 'elective dictatorship' thesis. Blunt spy scandal. Police Complaints Board established. PM announces death of Keynesianism: 'we cannot spend our way out of recession'.

1977 Government loses absolute majority. Lib–Lab pact established.

1978 Regular broadcasting of parliamentary proceedings begins. IRA bombing in British cities. IMF Articles redrawn to mark end of Bretton Woods Agreement. Public-sector strikes bring 'Winter of Discontent'.

1979 Scottish and Welsh referendums reject devolution proposals. Government defeated on no-confidence motion; PM announces general election. Thatcher becomes first woman PM. Earl Mountbatten and others killed by IRA bomb on boat in Sligo. New system of Commons select committees introduced.

1980 Zimbabwe becomes independent with Robert Mugabe as PM. National Front and Anti-Nazi League clashes at Lewisham. Bombings and violence in Ulster mark ten years of internment. Callaghan retires as Labour leader; replaced by Foot. Reagan becomes US president.

1981 Labour leadership election method changed to give unions and constituencies a say. 'Gang of Four' establish Council for Social Democracy; SDP formed. Rupert Murdoch buys *The Times*. IRA hunger strikes; death of Bobby Sands. SDP alliance with Liberals. Extensive public expenditure cuts.

Inner-city riots and confrontations with police. Marriage of Prince Charles to Lady Diana Spencer. OPEC unify oil price structure. Anglo-Irish summit agrees on Intergovernmental Council; Ian Paisley promises to make province ungovernable. Scarman Report on Brixton riots. Arthur Scargill elected NUM leader. British Nationality Act closes door to non-whites.

1982   Unemployment reaches 3 million; Thatcher's popularity at all-time low. Falklands war; Carrington resigns as Foreign Secretary. Thatcher's popularity soars. Roy Jenkins becomes SDP leader. IRA bombs in Hyde Park and Regent's Park; eleven killed. Greenham Common anti-nuclear protest begins.

1983   'Falklands election' gives Conservatives 144 majority. Jenkins resigns as SDP leader; succeeded by David Owen. Public expenditure cuts of £500 million. Thirty-eight IRA prisoners escape from Maze prison; governor resigns. Kinnock replaces Foot as Labour leader. First US Cruise missiles arrive at Greenham Common. Audit Commission established.

1984   Trade union membership banned at GCHQ. Miners' strike begins. Sarah Tisdall jailed for leaking documents about Cruise missiles. Eighteen councils rate-capped. Clive Ponting charged under Official Secrets Act. Police Complaints Authority replaces Police Complaints Board. IRA bomb in Brighton hotel housing Conservative leaders for party conference. BT privatized; massive profits on first day's trading.

1985   House of Lords televised live. Oxford refuses Thatcher honorary degree. Ponting acquitted. Miners drift back to work after failure of talks. Violent rioting in Brixton and Broadwater Farm. Anglo-Irish Agreement; mass resignation of Ulster Unionist MPs. Westland affair begins. Church of England *Faith in the City* report. White Paper 'Completing the Internal Market' published.

1986   Heseltine resigns from Cabinet criticizing Thatcher style. Brittan resigns over Westland affair. GLC and metropolitan counties abolished. *The Independent* launched. 'Big Bang' in City. *Spycatcher* case. British Gas privatized. US air attack on Libya from British bases. Crown Prosecution Service comes into operation. EC Single European Act.

1987   BA privatization. Moscow talks between Thatcher and Gorbachev signal thawing of cold war. Thatcher's third successive general election triumph.

1988   Thatcher becomes longest-serving PM of century. Budget reduces top-rate tax to 40 per cent (lowest in Europe); £2,000 million of tax cuts go to wealthiest. Imports rising faster than exports; fuelled by consumer credit boom. Ibbs report. Trade deficit rises to record £2,150 million. Inflation begins upward spiral. Poll tax bill receives royal assent after stormy passage. SDP and Liberals form Social and Liberal Democrats; Paddy Ashdown emerges as leader. European Commission President Jacques Delors declares that 1992 single market will mean workers' rights and social reform. Thatcher resists calls for Britain to join EMS in Bruges speech. Legislation replaces Section 2 of Official Secrets Act. Broadcasting Standards Authority set up. British Steel privatized. Media interviews with Sinn Fein banned. Charter88 formed. Lockerbie air disaster (flight Pan Am 103).

1989 Ayatollah Khomeini's *fatwa* on Salman Rushdie. Conservative losses in European elections; Greens gain 15 per cent of votes but no seats. Televising of Commons begins. Chancellor Lawson's dramatic resignation; John Major replaces him. Berlin Wall comes down.

1990 Nelson Mandela released from prison. 'Guildford Four' released. Cold war ends; dramatic changes in Eastern Europe. Anti-poll-tax demonstrations. Labour's popularity higher than ever (24 per cent). Iraq invades Kuwait; US and British troops sent. Interest rates rise in attempt to control inflation. Geoffrey Howe's devastating resignation speech triggers Conservative leadership contest; John Major emerges as leader and PM.

1991 Gulf war. IRA bombs in London. Woolf Report into prison riots. Electricity privatization. 'Birmingham Six' freed by Court of Appeal. N. Ireland talks begin. Citizen's Charter launched.

1992 Maastricht Treaty signed. Unexpected Conservative general election victory. Intensification of IRA bombing campaign on British mainland, especially London. Betty Boothroyd first woman Speaker. Kinnock resigns; John Smith elected Labour leader. 3000th death in N. Ireland since 1969. UK leaves ERM on 'Black Wednesday'. Separation of Prince and Princess of Wales. Queen's *'annus horribilis'*. Treaty on European Union signed (Maastricht).

1993 Single European Market comes into force. Inflation lowest for 25 years; unemployment 3 million. Britain ratifies Maastricht Treaty. BNP wins council seat in Isle of Dogs. Labour agrees to OMOV for candidate selection. Major calls for 'back to basics'. Anglo-Irish 'Downing Street Declaration'.

1994 Free vote reduces homosexual age of consent to 18. Ordination of women priests approved. UK accepts modified rules on QMV in enlarged EU. Rail privatization. Channel tunnel opens. Prince of Wales admits adultery. *Sunday Times* raises 'cash for questions' scandal. Jacques Santer succeeds Delors as EC president. John Smith dies. Blair elected Labour leader. IRA ceasefire. Nolan Committee established. National Lottery launched. Whip withdrawn from eight Conservative Eurosceptic rebels; Government dependent on Ulster Unionists.

1995 Austria, Finland and Sweden join EU. MPs suspended over 'cash-for-questions'. 'Whipless Tories' reinstated. Labour revise Clause Four. Joint framework document on N. Ireland. First direct talks between British government and Sinn Féin for 23 years. First report of Nolan Committee. Harold Wilson dies. Major throws down gauntlet over party leadership. MPs agree to reveal outside earnings. Princess of Wales gives frank TV interview. Conservative majority falls to three as Emma Nicholson defects to Lib Dems.

1996 Labour's all-women shortlists ruled illegal. Gerry Adams meets Bill Clinton. Canary Wharf bomb ends IRA ceasefire. Scott Report on 'arms-for-Iraq' affair. N. Ireland peace talks boycotted by most participants. Dunblane massacre. Conservative majority down to one, following by-election. Former US Senator George Mitchell to chair N. Ireland peace talks; Sinn Féin excluded. Manchester bomb injures nearly 200. Prince and Princess of Wales divorce. Labour and Lib Dems announce joint talks on constitutional reform. By-election eliminates government's majority.

1997 Major secures Ulster Unionist support by promising a N. Ireland Grand Committee. Public criticism of police failure to achieve convictions in Stephen Lawrence killing. Worldwide ban on UK beef exports following BSE crisis. Major calls general election, heralding longest-ever campaign. Labour election landslide; 10.6 per cent swing but lowest turnout since 1935. Conservatives wiped out in Scotland and Wales. Major resigns leadership. Number of women MPs and Lib Dems doubles. Blair youngest PM since 1812; five women in first Cabinet. Bank of England given power to set interest rates. UK signs up to EU Social Chapter. William Hague elected Conservative leader. Brown's first budget maintains overall Conservative spending plans. N. Ireland Secretary Mo Mowlam invites Sinn Féin to multi-party talks. Death of Diana, Princess of Wales provokes unprecedented public grief. Scottish and Welsh referendums approve devolution proposals. Blair holds historic meetings with Gerry Adams. Formula One tobacco sponsorship controversy. Kyoto climate summit.

> **By-elections**: *Wirral South* (Lab gain from Con); *Uxbridge* (Con hold); *Paisley South* (Lab hold); *Beckenham* (Con hold); *Winchester* (LD gain from Con)
>
> **Deaths**: *Iain Mills MP* (Meriden, Con); *Martin Redmond MP* (Don Valley, Lab); *Sir Michael Shersby MP* (Uxbridge, Con); *Gordon McMaster MP* (Paisley South, Lab); *Diana, Princess of Wales*
>
> **Major Public Acts**: Confiscation of Alcohol (Young Persons); Firearms (Amendment); Knives; Protection from Harassment; Sex Offenders; Special Immigration Appeals Commission

1998 Blair announces fresh inquiry into Bloody Sunday. Countryside March against foxhunting ban. European Commission rules eleven countries eligible to join single currency. EU begins entry negotiations with five former East European countries. France and Britain ratify nuclear test ban treaty. Controversy surrounds arms shipments to Sierra Leone. Birmingham G8 summit calls for further trade liberalization. Referendums back Good Friday Agreement. N. Ireland Assembly inaugural meeting; David Trimble chosen as First Minister; violence continues; Omagh bomb kills 29. Lords defeat Euro-elections bill five times. Welsh Secretary Ron Davies resigns after Clapham Common incident. Mandelson 'outed' as homosexual. Neill Report proposes reforming rules governing party financing and campaigns. Jenkins Report on electoral reform recommends AV+. Met Commissioner Sir Paul Condon apologizes at Lawrence inquiry but denies institutional racism. BSE inquiry reveals serious shortcomings in governance. Conservative leader in Lords (Cranborne) sacked over secret deal with Labour over Lords reform. Prince Charles's 50th birthday party hosted by Camilla Parker-Bowles. Royal assent for Human Rights Act. Joint Lab–Lib Dem cabinet committee sees remit broadened. Mandelson resigns from Cabinet over undeclared loan from colleague Geoffrey Robinson (who also resigns).

> **Deaths**: *Enoch Powell*, former MP (Con, later Ulster Unionist) and Health Secretary
>
> **Major Public Acts**: Bank of England; Crime and Disorder; Data Protection; Government of Wales; Greater London Authority (Referendum); Human Rights; National Minimum Wage; Northern Ireland; Registration of Political Parties; Scotland

1999 Euro introduced in eleven EU countries. NHS crisis following winter flu epidemic. Paddy Ashdown announces retirement. Free vote in Commons reduces age of homosexual consent to 16. Damning Foreign Affairs Select Committee report on arms-to-Sierra Leone affair; scandal over select committee leaks to ministers. In line with ECHR, death penalty abolished for any offence. Alun Michael narrowly defeats Rhodri Morgan for Welsh Labour leadership. Macpherson Report on Stephen Lawrence inquiry alleges institutional racism in Met. European Commission resign *en bloc* following corruption report. After failure of negotiations, NATO begins bombing Yugoslavia on humanitarian grounds, its first ever attack on a sovereign state.

Prominent human rights lawyer Rosemary Nelson murdered by Loyalist Red Hand Defenders in Northern Ireland. National minimum wage comes into force. Four members of IRAs Balcombe Street gang released from prison as confidence-building measure for Sinn Féin. First elections to Scottish and Welsh assemblies. Lords support government-backed amendment allowing 92 hereditary peers to remain for interim period. David Steel and Lord Elis-Thomas elected presiding officers for Scottish and Welsh assemblies respectively. Biggest revolt of Labour MPs since taking power sees 67 opposing welfare reforms. Labour losses in first UK European Parliament elections held under PR.

Tony Benn announces retirement as MP. Scottish Parliament formally opened by Queen. Crime statistics suggest police reluctance to combat suspected black criminality following Macpherson Report.

Charles Kennedy elected Lib Dem leader. Greenham Common Peace Group disbands after 18 years. Patton Report on RUC; force is subsequently awarded George Medal for gallantry. Lord Archer secures nomination as Conservative candidate for London mayor, but later withdraws after losing whip over providing false alibi in libel case. Paddington train crash (31 dead; 244 injured) prompts criticism of rail privatization.

Cabinet reshuffle: Mandelson returns to replace Mo Mowlam as N. Ireland Secretary. House of Lords gives third reading to Lords reform bill. Australian referendum rejects republicanism. N. Ireland talks reconvened at Stormont; IRA begin decommissioning weapons. Michael Portillo returns to Parliament (Kensington and Chelsea by-election victory). N. Ireland Assembly confirms appointment of ten-member executive to work under Trimble. Ban on homosexuals in armed forces lifted, in line with ECHR ruling. ECHR rules that Bulger killers had not received fair trials. Inaugural meeting of Council of the Isles. Shaun Woodward defects to Labour following sacking from shadow cabinet. Kenneth Clarke and John Major attack Hague's 'move to the right'. New Year's honours list contains record number of names but government plan to mark millennium with 2000 thwarted by two refusals.

By-elections: *Leeds Central* (Lab hold); *Eddisbury* (Con hold); *Hamilton South* (Lab hold); *Wigan* (Lab hold); *Kensington & Chelsea* (Con hold)

Deaths: *Derek Fatchett MP* (Leeds Central, Lab); *Roger Stott MP* (Wigan, Lab); *Alan Clark MP* (Kensington & Chelsea, Con); *Screaming Lord Sutch*, leader of Monster Raving Loony Party

Major Public Acts: Employment Relations; European Parliamentary Elections; Greater London Authority; House of Lords; Welfare Reform and Pensions

2000   Neill Committee recommends new methods for dealing with corruption amongst MPs. Wakeham Report on Lords reform. Lord Archer expelled from Conservative Party. John Major's retirement as MP. Ken Livingstone successfully stands as independent in London mayoral election but is suspended from Labour Party. Civil list frozen until 2011. Cherie Blair gives birth to son, Leo; Blair takes 14 days' paternity leave. Betty Boothroyd resigns as Speaker. House of Lords defies Commons over repeal of Section 28. Direct rule imposed on N. Ireland for 108 days. Scottish Parliament repeals Section 28. Queen Mother celebrates 100th birthday. Fuel protests: militant hauliers and farmers bring country to virtual standstill. Lords reject bill restricting right to trial by jury. Michael Martin controversially elected new Commons Speaker. Edward Heath announces retirement as MP. Labour–Lib Dem coalition established in Welsh Assembly. HRA comes into force. Met makes compensation payment of £320,000 to parents of Stephen Lawrence. Communications white paper proposes new umbrella regulatory authority (OFCOM). President Clinton visits N. Ireland to revive faltering peace process.

By-elections: *Ceredigion* (Plaid Cymru hold); *Romsey* (LD gain (from Con); *Tottenham* (Lab hold); *Glasgow, Anniesland* (Lab hold); *Preston* (Lab hold); *West Bromwich West* (Lab gain from Speaker); *Falkirk West* (Lab hold)

Deaths: *Michael Colvin MP* (Romsey, Con); *Bernie Grant MP* (Tottenham, Lab); *Clifford Forsythe MP* (South Antrim, Ulster Unionist); *Donald Coggan*, former Archbishop of Canterbury (1974–80); *Robert Runcie*, former Archbishop of Canterbury (1980–91); *Robin Day*, broadcaster; *Audrey Wise MP* (Preston, Lab); *Donald Dewar MP* (Glasgow Anniesland, Lab), First Minister of Scotland

Major Public Acts: Financial Services and Markets; Freedom of Information (FOIA); Local Government; Political Parties, Elections and Referendums (PPERA); Regulation of Investigatory Powers; Representation of the People; Transport

2001 Mandelson resigns (again) over Hinduja passport affair; Scottish executive agrees to free care for elderly after Lib Dem pressure in coalition. Blair advances N. Ireland peace process. Electoral Commission created by PPERA (2000). Blair's first meeting with US President Bush at Camp David. Commons agrees future Speakers will be elected by secret ballot. David Shayler prosecuted under Official Secrets legislation; denied defence under ECHR. Decennial UK census. Labour landslide victory in general election, but turnout lowest since 1918. Queen's Speech demonstrates government commitment to substantial private-sector role in state services. Hague resigns as Conservative leader; Iain Duncan Smith elected to succeed. Three nights of race riots by Asian youths in Oldham; worst since 1985; NF and BNP involved. Further race riots in several northern towns. Anti-capitalist demonstrations in London see 65 arrests. Amidst some public outrage Parole Board orders release of Bulger killers. Rioting in Belfast injures forty police officers. David Trimble formally resigns as First Minister of N. Ireland Assembly after IRA fail to decommission arms. Terrorist attacks on Pentagon and World Trade Center (9/11). Furore over 'good day to bury bad news' email message by 'spin doctor' Jo Moore. Anti-terrorism Bill rushed through Commons; enacted with modification by Lords. Blair sets up war cabinet to supervise action in Afghanistan. Scottish Parliament bans foxhunting.

Opposition to proposal for largely appointed second chamber in long-awaited Lords reform white paper. Baroness Shirley Williams becomes Lib Dem leader in Lords. Trimble re-elected as N. Ireland First Minister despite rebellion in own party. RUC renamed Police Service of Northern Ireland. Labour MP Paul Marsden defects to Lib Dems, alleging bullying by whips.

By-elections: *Ipswich* (Lab hold)

Deaths: *Quintin Hogg* (Baron Hailsham of St Marylebone – 'Lord

Hailsham'), Conservative peer, former Lord Chancellor, Secretary of State for Education and Science, Leader of Lords and party chairman; *Jamie Cann MP* (Ipswich, Lab); *Mary Whitehouse*, campaigner for decency on television; *Sir Raymond Powell MP* (Ogmore, Lab)

Major Public Acts: Anti-terrorism, Crime and Security; Human Reproductive Cloning; Special Educational Needs and Disability

2002   Enron scandal in USA spreads to UK with both main parties having accepted financial aid from company. Suspected Islamic activists detained in police swoops. Keith Vaz suspended from Commons following standards commissioner investigation. Labour vacates Millbank headquarters owing to expense. Budget brings big spending increases on health and education. Paul Boateng becomes first black cabinet member in reshuffle. Local elections see advances for BNP in north. First mayoral elections held in seven authorities. Lords reform plans abandoned after fierce opposition.

Home Secretary David Blunkett withdraws controversial draft order (snooper's charter) giving public bodies access to telephone and internet records. Queen's Golden Jubilee celebrations judged a success. Disappointing outcome from UN Johannesburg summit on sustainable development. Edwina Currie reveals affair with John Major. Police raid Stormont offices of Sinn Féin on suspicion of espionage. Stormont suspended for fourth time since devolution.

Modernization of Commons ends unsocial hours and allows bills to 'roll over'. UN weapons inspectors allowed into Iraq. President Bush remains sceptical.

By-elections: *Ogmore* (Lab hold)
Deaths: *Princess Margaret*, sister of Queen Elizabeth II; *Queen Elizabeth, the Queen Mother*; *Myra Hindley*, Moors murderer
Major Public Acts: Education; European Parliamentary Elections; Nationality, Immigration and Asylum; Police Reform; Proceeds of Crime; Sex Discrimination (Election Candidates); Tobacco Advertising and Promotion

2003   US court imposes life sentence on 'shoe bomber', Richard Reid. Opposition to threatened UK military action in Iraq sees over 1 million gathering to protest in London. UN Security Council fails to pass resolution authorizing further use of military force against Iraq but US and UK governments decide to invade. Blair convinces MPs of need of action. Robin Cook, Leader of Commons, resigns from Cabinet in order to voice his opposition. Ba'athist regime collapses; Saddam Hussein goes into hiding, only to be captured some weeks later. Doubts emerge over documentary evidence used to support claim that Saddam was stockpiling weapons of mass destruction (WMD). Controversy over government's 'dodgy dossier'. Suicide of weapons expert David Kelly after questioning by Commons Foreign Affairs Select Committee. Ken Livingstone introduces congestion charge across central London. Russian President Vladimir Putin makes state visit to Britain; first leader to do so since Tsar Alexander II. Iain Duncan Smith stands down as Conservative Party leader after losing 'vote of confidence' by 1922 Committee. Michael Howard assumes leadership.

By-elections: *Brent East* (LD gain from Lab)

Deaths: *Roy Jenkins*, Lib Dem peer, former SDP leader, President of European Commission, former Labour MP (Glasgow Hillhead), home secretary and Chancellor of Exchequer; *George Younger*, Conservative peer, former MP (Ayr), Secretary of State for Defence and Secretary of State for Scotland

Major Public Acts: Anti-social Behaviour; Criminal Justice; European Parliament (Representation); Extradition; Local Government; Regional Assemblies (Preparations)

2004 Hutton report on death of David Kelly upholds original verdict of suicide, but fails to silence conspiracy theorists; attacks BBC for its handling of story. BBC Director General, Greg Dyke, journalist Andrew Gilligan and several other senior BBC figures resign. Fathers 4 Justice protesters in Commons shower Tony Blair with purple flour during PMQs. European Parliament elections produce 12 UKIP MEPs. London Mayor Ken Livingstone returned for second term. Butler report criticizes quality of government intelligence on WMD. Peter Mandelson appointed UK European Commissioner. Tony Blair confirms intention to step down at some point in next parliament. David Blunkett resigns as home secretary following accusations that he sought to speed up visa application of nanny employed by his former lover. Insurgency continues in Iraq.

By-elections: *Birmingham Hodge Hill* (Lab hold); *Leicester South* (LD gain from Lab)

Deaths: *Hugh Jenkins*, former Labour MP and chair of CND; *Jim Marshall MP* (Leicester South, Lab); *Paul Foot*, left-wing journalist; *Anthony Meyer*, former Conservative MP who challenged Margaret Thatcher for leadership of party in 1989

Major Public Acts: Asylum and Immigration (Treatment of Claimants, etc.); Children; Civil Contingencies; Civil Partnership; Domestic Violence, Crime and Victims; Higher Education; Hunting

2005 Freedom of Information Act (2000) comes into force. Doubts emerge over IRA's commitment to arms decommissioning. Hunting Act comes into force. Prevention of Terrorism Act ends indefinite detention of foreign terrorist suspects, whilst introducing 'control orders'. Constitutional Reform Act paves way for UK Supreme Court and more independent and transparent judicial appointments process. Prince Charles marries Camilla Parker-Bowles: she is to be known as HRH Duchess of Cornwall. General election sees Labour Party returned for historic third consecutive term – though with much reduced majority (65). Ulster Unionist Leader David Trimble resigns, having lost his

Westminster seat. Bob Geldof's Live 8 concerts. UK-hosted G8 summit in Scotland is accompanied by demonstrations coordinated by Make Poverty History campaign. UK wins race to host 2012 Olympics.

July 7 (7/7): five suicide bombers target transport network in London, killing 52. Brazilian Jean Charles de Menezes shot dead by police, having been mistaken for a terrorist. Islamist preacher Omar Bakri Mohammed prevented from re-entering UK. Commission on Decommissioning announces that IRA's weapons have been 'put beyond use'. Race riots in Birmingham. Government defeated in attempt to allow terrorist suspects to be detained for 90 days without trial. David Cameron succeeds Michael Howard as Conservative leader.

By-elections: *Cheadle* (LD hold); *Livingston* (Lab hold)

Deaths: *James Callaghan*, former Labour Party leader and PM (1976–9); *Sir Edward Heath*, former Conservative Party leader and PM (1970–4); *John Tyndall*, former leader of National Front and BNP founder; *Robin Cook MP* (Livingston, Lab), former foreign secretary, Lord President of Council and Leader of Commons; *Mo Mowlam*, former Labour MP and Secretary of State for Northern Ireland

Major Public Acts: Constitutional Reform; Disability Discrimination; Education; Inquiries; Prevention of Terrorism; Serious Organised Crime and Police

2006 Lib Dem leader Charles Kennedy resigns amid allegations of excessive drinking. Sir Menzies Campbell succeeds him, defeating Chris Huhne. Queen celebrates 80th birthday. Welsh Assembly (Senedd) opens. Local elections see major losses for Labour. In cabinet reshuffle Margaret Beckett becomes first woman foreign secretary. British citizens evacuated from Lebanon following clashes between Israeli forces and Hizbollah. Stern Review on climate change published. Saddam Hussein found guilty of crimes against humanity and hanged.

By-elections: *Dunfermline & West Fife* (LD gain from Lab); *Bleanau Gwent* (Ind hold); *Bromley & Chislehurst* (Con hold)

Deaths: *Merlyn Rees*, former Labour home secretary; *Rachel Squire MP* (Dunfermline & West Fife, Lab); *Tony Banks*, Labour peer, former MP and Minister for Sport; *John Profumo*, former Conservative MP and Secretary of State for War, resigned in wake of Profumo scandal in 1963; *Peter Law MP* (Blaenau Gwent, Ind); *Eric Forth MP* (Bromley & Chislehurst, Con); *Ted Grant*, left-wing politician and founder of Militant Tendency; *Saddam Hussein*, former President of Iraq

Major Public Acts: Climate Change and Sustainable Energy; Equality; Government of Wales; Identity Cards; Immigration, Asylum and Nationality; Legislative and Regulatory Reform; Northern Ireland; Northern Ireland (St Andrews Agreement); Racial and Religious Hatred; Terrorism

2007 Concern following spate of prison escapes. Tony Blair questioned by police over 'cash for honours' affair.

Al-Qaeda threaten to kidnap Prince Harry during his deployment in Afghanistan. Climate Change Bill is published. Basic rate of income tax cut from 22 to 20%; 10% rate abolished – provoking anger on Labour backbenches. Lisbon Treaty signed, DUP leader Ian Paisley and Sinn Féin leader Gerry Adams meet to discuss possibility of restoring devolved government in N. Ireland. SNP forms minority administration in Scotland after elections. Labour and Plaid Cymru form coalition in Wales. A new power-sharing executive is established in N. Ireland. New Ministry of Justice takes on remaining responsibilities of Department for Constitutional Affairs, and some from Home Office.

Tony Blair stands down as PM (and as MP). Gordon Brown assumes Labour leadership unopposed. Jacqui Smith becomes first female home secretary. Islamist terrorists attack Glasgow Airport. Ban on smoking in all enclosed public spaces comes into force in England. Rumours circulate that Brown is planning snap election, to capitalize on good poll ratings. Sir Menzies Campbell resigns as Lib Dem leader. Vince Cable praised for his performance as acting leader but does not stand for role permanently. Nick Clegg narrowly defeats Chris Huhne in contest. Conservatives enjoy post-conference bounce in polls. Gordon Brown is accused of losing his nerve in failing to call general election. High speed rail-link between London and Channel Tunnel finally comes into service.

By-elections: *Ealing Southall* (Lab hold); *Sedgefield* (Lab hold)
Deaths: *David Ervine*, Progressive Unionist Party leader; *Francis Cockfield* (Baron Cockfield), former Conservative minister and European Commissioner; *Piara Khabra MP* (Ealing Southall, Lab); *Anita Roddick*, Body Shop founder and political campaigner
Major Public Acts: Corporate Manslaughter and Corporate Homicide; Forced Marriage (Civil Protection); Greater London Authority; Income Tax; Statistics and Registration Service; Sustainable Communities; Tribunals, Courts and Enforcement; UK Borders; Welfare Reform

2008 Peter Hain resigns as Secretary of State for Work and Pensions over donations scandal linked to his failed bid to become Labour Party deputy leader. Derek Conway (Con) suspended from Commons for ten days over monies paid to his son from parliamentary expenses. Mohamed Al Fayed gives evidence to inquiry into death of his son, Dodi, and Diana, Princess of Wales, alleging they were victims of murder plot by royal family. Conservative Boris Johnson defeats Ken Livingstone in London mayoral election. BNP wins its first seat on Greater London Assembly. Fears of impending crisis in banking sector fuelled by government's decision to nationalize Northern Rock. Support for Labour falls sharply in economic crisis. Government announces £500-billion bailout plan for banking sector.

By-elections: *Crewe & Nantwich* (Con gain from Lab); *Henley* (Con

hold); *Haltemprice & Howden* (Con hold); *Glasgow East* (SNP gain from Lab): *Glenrothes* (Lab hold)
Deaths: *Gwyneth Dunwoody MP* (Crewe & Nantwich, Lab), Chair of Transport Select Committee; *Charles Wheeler*, journalist and political commentator; *John MacDougall MP* (Glenrothes, Lab); *Harold Pinter*, playwright and anti-war campaigner
Major Public Acts: Banking (Special Provisions); Climate Change; Counter-Terrorism; Criminal Justice and Immigration; Education and Skills; European Union (Amendment); Human Fertilisation and Embryology; Pensions; Planning

2009 Woolworths stores close their doors for last time. Government announces £20 billion of loan guarantees for small and medium-sized businesses and backs construction of third runway at Heathrow. Lloyds TSB takes over HBOS as banking crisis deepens. Government takes major stake in struggling Royal Bank of Scotland. Unemployment nears 2 million. In Scotland, SNP's budget is revised by Scottish Parliament. Lloyds Group's share price plummets and government takes controlling stake. Retail Price Index falls to 0%. Protests in London to coincide with G20 summit. New 50% top rate of income tax announced.

Joanna Lumley's campaign to win residency rights for former Ghurkhas results in rare Commons defeat for government. Britain hands over city of Basra to US forces, marking end of UK military operation in Iraq. *Daily Telegraph* starts publishing leaked details of MPs' expenses, resulting in scandal and resignation of Speaker Michael Martin. He is replaced by Conservative MP John Bercow. Labour suffer further major losses in local elections. Election of two BNP candidates to European Parliament prompts BBC to invite leader, Nick Griffin, to join panel on flagship *Question Time* programme. Unemployment at around 2.5 million. Ali Mohmed al-Megrahi, convicted of bringing down Pan Am flight 103 over Lockerbie in 1988, released from prison on compassionate grounds. *Sun* switches allegiance to Conservatives. New UK Supreme Court opens for business. Sir Thomas Legg publishes official audit of MPs' expenses, many required to pay back significant sums. Total number of servicemen killed in Afghanistan since 2001 tops 200. EU Lisbon Treaty signed.
By-elections: *Norwich North* (Con gain (from Lab); *Glasgow North East* (Lab gain from Speaker)
Deaths: *Sir Clement Freud*, former Liberal MP, broadcaster and writer; *Edward ('Eddie') George* (Baron George), former Governor of Bank of England; *Jack Jones*, former leader of Transport and General Workers Union; *David Taylor MP* (NW Leicestershire, Lab)
Major Public Acts: Banking; Borders, Citizenship and Immigration; Coroners and Justice; Parliamentary Standards; Policing and Crime; Welfare Reform

2010 Alastair Campbell defends 'dodgy dossier' before Chilcot inquiry into British involvement in invasion of Iraq. Former PM Tony Blair questioned some weeks later. Control of policing finally devolved to N. Ireland Executive following negotiations between DUP and Sinn Féin. Gordon Brown dissolves Parliament. In live televised election debates between leaders of the three main UK parties Lib Dem leader Nick Clegg generally seen as 'winner'. General election produces hung parliament – first since February 1974 election. Conservatives and Lib Dems enter into talks over coalition. Final agreement includes commitment for referendum on introduction of AV system. David Cameron becomes PM with Nick Clegg as Deputy; Lib Dems gain five seats in Cabinet. Caroline Lucas, leader of UK Green Party, becomes first Green MP. Coalition's emergency budget sees VAT increase from 17.5 to 20% from 2011; personal income tax allowance increased. Coalition suffers its first 'man overboard' with resignation of David Laws, Chief Secretary to the Treasury, over expenses scandal. Ed Miliband confirmed as new Labour leader, beating older brother David. Tony Blair's memoirs, *A Journey*, reveal scale of rift between him and Chancellor Gordon Brown. The long-running Saville inquiry into Bloody Sunday finds that shooting of 27 civilians by British Army in Northern Ireland in 1972 was unjustified. Equality Act comes into effect, prohibiting discrimination on the grounds of race, gender, disability, belief, age and sexual orientation. Uprisings begin in Tunisia in what becomes known as Arab Spring.

Deaths: *Michael Foot*, former Labour MP and party leader (1980–3), cabinet minister in the 1970s; *Ashok Kumar MP* (Middlesbrough South & East Cleveland, Lab); *Lord Peter Walker*, former Conservative MP and cabinet member, founder of Tory Reform Group; *James ('Jimmy') Reid*, leading Scottish trade unionist; *Sir Cyril Smith*, long-serving former Liberal (later Lib Dem) MP for Rochdale; *James Pickles*, high-profile judge and, later, tabloid columnist

Major Public Acts: Academies; Digital Economy; Energy; Equality; Financial Services; Identity Documents; Sustainable Communities Act 2007 (Amendment); Terrorist Asset-Freezing (Temporary Provisions)

2011 MPs David Chaytor, Eric Illsley, Elliot Morley and Jim Devine sentenced in expenses scandal. One-time Met officer Mark Kennedy exposed as an *agent provocateur*, infiltrating environmental pressure groups. Andy Coulson, David Cameron's Communications Director and former *News of the World* editor, resigns in phone-hacking scandal. House of Commons votes 234:22 in defiance of ECHR granting prisoners right to vote. Referendum in Wales sees voters approve plan for more power to Welsh Assembly. As Arab Spring develops, British, American and French air forces launch attacks on ground targets in Libya in support of UN Security Council Resolution 1973, which protects civilian populated areas. NATO-orchestrated military campaign continues until October, when

Libyan leader Muammar Gaddafi is shot dead by rebels near Sirte.

Mass protests in London over planned cuts in public spending and increases in student fees. Run-up to referendum on electoral reform exposes some cracks in coalition but voters reject AV. Devolved elections held on same day see SNP secure majority at Holyrood. Labour take half the seats in Welsh Assembly, establishing single-party administration. Sinn Féin and DUP are big winners in N. Ireland Assembly elections. In English local elections Labour make gains at Lib Dems' expense. Queen Elizabeth II becomes Britain's second longest-serving monarch (after Queen Victoria). June sees hundreds of thousands of public sector workers strike over planned changes to their final salary pension schemes. *News of the World* falls victim to phone-hacking scandal with final edition published on 10 July. UK economy enjoys second consecutive quarter of modest growth. Downing Street launches its e-petitions website.

Rioting and looting spread across England following police shooting of Mark Duggan. Parliament is recalled. The PM's prerogative to fix date of general election surrendered with passage of Fixed Term Parliaments Act. Liam Fox forced to resign as Defence Secretary for breaking *Ministerial Code*. Protesters affiliated to global Occupy movement force closure of St Paul's Cathedral for first time since second world war; Chancellor and Dean of St Paul's resign amidst ongoing protests. Unemployment continues to rise, hitting 2.6 million. Youth unemployment hits 1 million for first time since mid-1980s. OECD warns of possibility of double-dip recession for UK and eurozone. Public sector workers strike again over proposed pension changes. Leveson inquiry into press standards opens. David Cameron effectively 'vetoes' an EU treaty designed to stabilize euro, resulting in short-lived bounce in polls for Conservatives.

By-elections: *Oldham & East Saddleworth* (Lab hold); *Barnsley Central* (Lab gain from Ind); *Leicester South* (Lab hold); *Belfast West* (Sinn Féin hold); *Inverclyde* (Lab hold); *Feltham & Heston* (Lab hold)

Deaths: *Phil Gallie MP* (Conservative & Unionist, and MSP); *Henry Leach*, Admiral of the Fleet; *Charles Choules*, last surviving first world war combatant; *David Cairns MP* (Inverclyde, Lab); *Brian Haw*, anti-war protester; *Philip Gould*, key New Labour strategist and pollster; *Alan Keen MP* (Feltham & Heston, Lab); *Christopher Hitchens*, controversial journalist and author

Major Public Acts: Budget Responsibility and National Audit; Education; Fixed-term Parliaments; Parliamentary Voting System and Constituencies; Police Reform and Social Responsibility; Terrorism Prevention and Investigation Measures

2012 Gary Dobson (36) and David Norris (35) convicted of racially aggravated murder after third trial over killing of Stephen Lawrence in 1993. SNP-controlled Scottish government announces plans for referendum over independence in 2014. UK government debt is said to have broken through £1 trillion for first time, with economy shrinking once more. Lib Dem Energy Secretary Chris Huhne resigns after CPS charges him over allegations concerning evading penalty points relating to driving offence. Unemployment hits 2.7 million in March (17-year high). UK officially back in recession. Conservative Party co-treasurer Peter Cruddas resigns, having been filmed appearing to offer access to PM in return for donations; 'cash for access' scandal follows. Local elections see SNP winning most councillors in Scotland, whilst Labour make further gains in England and Wales. Boris Johnson elected for second consecutive term as London mayor, narrowly defeating Ken Livingstone, who announces retirement from front-line politics. Olympic flame arrives in Cornwall and travels length and breadth of UK. In his testimony to Leveson inquiry into press standards, Cameron admits to 19 meetings with Rebekah Brooks, 15 with James Murdoch and 10 with Rupert Murdoch whilst in opposition. Barclays Bank's £290-million fine for trying to fix Libor (inter-bank lending rate) prompts departure of chief executive, Bob Diamond. The 2012 London Olympics (27 July–12 August) are widely seen as focus for national unity as economy continues in doldrums.

Damning report into 1989 Hillsborough disaster prompts government to establish an independent investigation into police. Edinburgh Agreement, signed by David Cameron and Scottish First Minister Alex Salmond, sets scene for 2014 referendum on Scottish independence. First elections for police and crime commissioners in England and Wales fail to capture public's imagination, with around 15% turnout. Leveson inquiry recommends establishment of an independent regulatory body, operating within statutory framework.

Cracks in the coalition revealed as the House of Lords Reform Bill, favoured by the Lib Dems, lost because of Conservative opposition. In response, Nick Clegg vows to oppose changes proposed in the Sixth Periodic Review of constituencies, which favours the Conservatives.

By-elections: *Bradford West* (Respect gain from Lab); *Manchester Central* (Lab hold); *Corby* (Lab gain from Con); *Cardiff South & Penarth* (Lab hold); *Croydon North* (Lab hold); *Middlesbrough* (Lab hold); *Rotherham* (Lab hold)

Deaths: *Norman St John-Stevas*, former Conservative MP and Leader of the House; *Edward Short* (Baron Glenamara), former Labour MP and deputy leader; *Marsha Singh*, former MP (Bradford West, Lab); *Sir Rhodes Boyson*, educator, author and former Conservative MP; *Malcolm Wicks MP* (Croydon North, Lab); *Eric Hobsbawm*, Marxist historian; *William Rees-Mogg* (Baron Rees-Mogg), former editor of *The Times* (1967–81) and life peer

Major Public Acts: Financial Services; Health and Social Care; Domestic

Violence, Crime and Victims; Legal
Aid, Sentencing and Punishment of
Offenders; Protection of Freedoms;
Scotland; Welfare Reform

2013 Amendment to Boundary Changes
Bill tabled by Labour and Lib Dem
peers carried to postpone changes
until 2018. UK loses triple-A credit
rating. Chris Huhne and former
wife, Vicky Pryce, jailed for eight
months for perverting the course
of justice. Cross-party talks on
implementation of Leveson Report
break down without agreement.
Scottish independence referendum
calendared for 18 September 2014.
David Miliband resigns as an MP,
fearing his continued involvement
in British politics a 'distraction'
to his brother. Kent Police and
Crime Commissioner, Ann Barnes,
appoints Paris Brown (17) as
the first youth police and crime
commissioner. Brown steps down
six days later in the wake of ill-
advised Tweets. Death and funeral
of Margaret Thatcher in April evokes
mixed reaction but is seen to have
marked the end of an era. Street
parties break out in a number of
cities; the Wizard of Oz song 'Ding
Dong! The Witch is Dead' reaches
number two in the charts. Funeral
resembles that given to royalty.
Eastleigh by-election, triggered
by resignation of Chris Huhne.
Lib Dems hold seat, though with
reduced majority. To alarm of other
parties, UKIP comes second with
greatly increased share of the vote;
subsequently increase share of vote
in local elections. UKIP successes
place Cameron under increasing
pressure from Eurosceptic wing
of his party, with some calls for his
replacement as leader. In response,
the Conservatives publish a draft
European Union (Referendum) Bill,
offering the prospect of an 'in–out'
referendum by 2017. Drummer
Lee Rigby, a serving British soldier,
attacked and butchered to death in
a 'home-grown' Islamist terrorist
attack conducted in broad daylight
in Woolwich. Islamist cleric Abu
Qatada finally deported to Jordan
to face terror charges. The Marriage
(Same Sex Couples) Act passes into
law, legalising gay marriage. Duchess
of Cambridge gives birth to a son,
George, who becomes third in line to
the throne. Violent scenes in Belfast
as sectarian rioting returns. Shock
government defeat (by 272 to 285) in
emergency motion on involvement
in possible US-led military action
against the Assad regime in Syria

By- elections: *Eastleigh* (LD hold);
Mid-Ulster (Sinn Féin hold); *South
Shields* (Lab hold)

Deaths: *Jimmy Halliday*, former SNP
leader (1956-1960); *Bruce Millan*,
former Labour MP (1959–88) and
Secretary of State for Scotland
(1976–9); *Margaret Thatcher*, former
Conservative leader (1975–90) and
PM (1979–90); *John Gilbert*, former
Labour MP (1970–97) and Minister
for Transport (1975–6); *Peter Fraser*,
former Scottish MP (Conservative,
1979–87), Solicitor General for
Scotland (1982–9) and Lord Advocate
(1989–92); *Alan Whicker*, renowned
television broadcaster and journalist

Major Public Acts: Crime and
Courts; Electoral Registration and
Administration; Marriage (Same Sex
Couples); Succession to the Crown

Glossary

Words in **bold** type within entries refer to terms or concepts found elsewhere in the Glossary. Remember to consult the Index to locate more information and for terms (especially institutions and organizations) not included here.

absolute majority   A majority greater than 50 per cent.

abstention   Deliberate non-voting.

accountability   Answerability to a higher authority (the people, in a **democracy**).

Act of Parliament   Law passed by Parliament.

administrative law   Concerned with cases between the citizen and the state.

administrative tribunal   Deals with citizens' grievances against the state.

adversarial politics   Description of British **two-party system**, seeing it based on argument rather than compromise between parties.

advisory body   Set up by government to conduct an inquiry and come up with recommendations.

anarchy   Society without government.

anthropocentrism   Seeing human life as the principal criterion of value.

aristocracy   Government by an enlightened elite.

arm's length administration   Quasi-autonomous agencies running various state services with little government interference.

art of the possible   Classic aphorism used to define politics, drawing attention to compromising and wheeling and dealing evident in real world.

authoritative allocation of values   Definition of politics. May be contrasted with **market** allocation in that allocation is on the basis of political authority, rather than ability to pay.

authority   Form of **power** distinguished by the fact that it is accepted by those over whom it is held.

autonomy   Self-determination; usually of a state.

behaviouralism   Approach to social sciences, including political science, taking only observable phenomena as its data.

bill   The form in which legislation is introduced into Parliament (when passed it becomes an **Act**).

Bill of Rights   Constitutional document guaranteeing citizens' rights.

bipartisan   Consisting of two parties.

block vote   Large number of votes tied together and cast at one go; a controversial feature of the Labour Party conference.

body corporate   Organization with a persona in law (e.g. local authority).

borough   Historic **local government** area based on a town which had gained a royal charter entitling it to certain freedoms.

bourgeoisie   French term for town-dweller appropriated by Marx to denote a capital-owning social **class** spawned by the industrial revolution; to Marx, the ruling class.

broadsheet   Quality newspaper.

budgetary process   Method whereby government determines its annual expenditure and sources of income.

bureaucracy   Strictly speaking, rule by officials. Weber argued that the growth of **socialism** would result in such rule. Used without pejorative connotations to denote a large hierarchical organization.

by-election   Election held following death or retirement of sitting member.

Cabinet   Group of leading ministers heading the government.

cabinet government   Government by a team rather than a single ruler; *see also* **collective responsibility**.

Cabinet Secretariat   Special part of **civil service** responsible for servicing the Cabinet and its committees; can be influential in policy.

Cabinet Secretary   Head of **Cabinet Secretariat** (and of civil service).

cadre party   Party in Parliament consisting of MPs; may or may not have a mass membership outside Parliament.

capitalism   Mode of production in which private individuals, rather than the state, own materials necessary to produce what society needs for its survival.

case law   Law resulting from previous judicial decisions (precedent).

central–local relations   Relationship between central government and its territorially based agencies; most often in connection with **local government**.

centralization   Central government's dominance over other state agencies.

ceremonial   Ostentatious aspects of government, usually with little importance for decision-making, but often crucial for **legitimation**.

Chartism   Working-class organization founded in 1836, demanding universal male suffrage without property qualification.

citizen   Member of a **state**, with rights and obligations.

citizens' assembly   A body of citizens representing a geographical area coming together to debate local issues.

citizens' jury   A small group of citizens brought together to give an opinion on a government proposal.

city-state   Political unit about which most Ancient Greek political thought was written; very small and not comparable with complex modern **nation-states**.

civic culture   Political culture in which people have confidence in, and will cooperate with, government.

civil jurisdiction   Pertaining to that part of the legal system concerned with cases involving one citizen against another.

civil rights   Rights accruing to individuals as **citizens** which may not be infringed by other citizens or by the state.

civil service   The central government **bureaucracy**.

civil society   That part of social life outside the control of the state.

class   Section of population sharing a common social status; almost invariably associated with socioeconomic factors. Usually divided into upper, middle and lower. In Marxist terms, seen as a dichotomy arising from the position of individuals in the productive process; *see also* **bourgeoisie** and **proletariat**.

coalition Parties working together as a government.

cold war State of East–West tension beginning after the second world war.

collective responsibility Constitutional convention reflecting the idea of **cabinet government**; entails various things including the idea that ministers participate in collective **policy-making**.

collectivism Sees the collectivity, rather than the individual, as the essential human unit.

colonialism Form of domination of one state over another associated with **imperialism**; may be established after military conquest or economic penetration of a weak economy (**neocolonialism**).

common law Law formed on the basis of precedents set in previous cases; reflects the accumulated wisdom of the past rather than legislation.

communism **Ideology** of equality and the common ownership of property.

community policing Form of policing in which the force becomes deeply involved in community affairs to establish mutual trust.

comparative advantage Economic theory underpinning the philosophy of **free trade** associated with Adam Smith, arguing that if each nation produces that which it does most efficiently, the world will maximize its wealth.

consensus Harmony between possibly opposed factions. The era of consensus politics in Britain (late 1940s–mid-1970s) saw Labour and Conservatives in agreement over a wide range of policies.

consensus policing Policing based on gaining the consent and cooperation of those policed rather than force.

conservatism View of politics, society and the constitution that is suspicious of radical change. Has deep intellectual antecedents; associated particularly with Edmund Burke and the ideology of the Conservative Party.

consociationalism Two or more communities living harmoniously in the same state (as in Belgium).

constituency Territorial electoral division (e.g. Glasgow Hillhead). Can also denote the nature of a politician's support (e.g. 'small businessmen are the natural constituency of the Conservative Party').

constitution Set of rules, customs and conventions defining the composition and powers of state institutions and regulating their relationships to each other and to private **citizens**; unwritten constitutions do not exist as a single document but in the form of custom and practice and various laws.

constitutional amendment Formal change to the **constitution**.

constitutional convention Regularly observed practices regarded as part of the **constitution**.

constitutional government Government constrained by rules and procedures laid down in the **constitution**; contrasted with arbitrary government.

constitutional monarchy Political system in which a **monarchy** is so constrained by the **constitution** that it plays no part in decision-making.

consultative body Set up by government to bring together interested parties for policy discussions.

consumer voting model Voting behaviour model seeing voters as shoppers in a political market-place, choosing parties on the basis of their shop windows (**manifestos**, etc.).

contracting-out **Privatization** of work previously done by the state, often enforced, as in CCT (compulsory competitive tendering in local government) and market-testing (civil service).

core executive The complex network of people, relationships, structures and procedures around the **Cabinet**.

corporate management Form of management urged upon **local government** which seeks to unify control of its services under a single chief executive.

corporatism Theory of **pressure group** activity in which the government incorporates certain groups into the **policy-making** process.

county Top-tier **local authority** with ancient lineage.

criminal jurisdiction Pertaining to the criminal law in which the crimes are against the state rather than against a particular person.

cross-bencher Member of House of Lords disdaining allegiance to any party.

cross-border body Body set up to consider certain policy areas across national boundaries (e.g. N. Ireland and Eire).

cross-class voting Phenomenon whereby individuals belonging to one social class vote for a party ostensibly supporting the interests of another.

DA-notice system Voluntary code whereby the press restrains itself from publishing material on defence which officials want kept secret.

de facto In actuality.

de jure According to law.

deference Belief amongst citizens that they should not play much part in government; they are happy to leave things to those whom they believe to be superior.

delegated legislation Laws made by **bureaucrats** with power delegated by Parliament.

demand management Keynesian principle whereby government uses its financial influence in the economy to manipulate the level of aggregate demand to maintain full employment.

democracy Rule by all **citizens** in a community.

democratic deficit Absence of popular control and **accountability**; term frequently used of EU institutions.

demos Greek word for the people as a collectivity (hence **democracy**).

deregulation Removal by the state of controls tending to protect state services from competition (e.g. local authority transport services).

détente Reduction of tension between states; used particularly of East–West relations during the **cold war**.

determinism Doctrine that everything that happens does so because of other forces; downgrades human free choice (**voluntarism**) as a factor explaining events.

devolution State authority passed down from a higher level of government to sub-national areas; *see also* **federalism**.

dignified and **efficient elements** Distinction between those elements of a **constitution** which have no direct impact on **policy-making** and those which do; does not mean that the dignified elements are unimportant.

direct democracy Form of **democracy** in which **citizens** actually take part in making decisions; almost impossible in the real world.

early day motion Parliamentary instrument whereby MPs can signal concern over an issue.

ecocentrism Placing nature in general before human life as a criterion of value.

economic and monetary union (EMU) The linking of economies and currencies of a number of states; a major project of the EU.

economic planning Government intervention in the economy to achieve certain future goals, such as full employment, economic growth, balance of payments; opposed by **monetarists**.

elected mayor Politician elected by all citizens in a local government area to lead the authority.

election campaign Efforts made by **political parties** in the run-up to an election to win voters' support.

electoral college A group of electors acting on behalf of a larger body.

electoral quota Number of votes a candidate requires to be elected under certain systems of **proportional representation**.

electoral swing Calculation measuring the percentage shift of party support across the country; may or may not be uniform.

electoral volatility Condition in which the electorate cannot be relied upon to vote regularly for the same party.

elitism Body of thought on power in society which sees as inevitable the formation of elites which will consolidate their positions, collude with each other and control government in their own interests.

embourgeoisement Process whereby members of the working class acquire middle-class habits and characteristics.

endogenous explanation Explaining national political events solely in terms of factors internal to the country.

Enlightenment Seventeenth-century European intellectual movement which saw a flowering of science and faith in rational thought and progress in social and political life.

entrenchment Often used of **constitutions** to denote provisions that

cannot be changed by the normal process of law-making; absent in the UK.

environmentalism Ideology derived from ecology aiming to prevent human despoilation of life forms.

Establishment Imprecise term used for a narrow, upper-middle-class elite with much power in society.

Euroscepticism Opposition to European **federalism**.

exchange rate Value of one currency in terms of that of another country.

Exchange Rate Mechanism (ERM) A system of fixing currencies against each other on the way to complete **economic and monetary union**.

executive That part of an organization responsible for policy-making; in politics usually with reference to the **government**, or; more narrowly, the **Cabinet**; *see also* **core executive**.

executive agency Civil service body created to administer functions hived off from the main body of the civil service (often referred to in the UK as Next Steps agencies).

exogenous explanation Explanation of national political events based on external factors.

Fabianism Approach to social and political reform advocated by the Fabian Society, stressing small incremental advances rather than revolution.

faction Segment within a party; usually considered more hard-edged than a **tendency**.

false consciousness Errors of perception concerning one's self-interest; may explain why working-class people support the Conservatives.

fascism **Ideology** espousing nationalism, militarism and demagoguery.

federalism Process whereby states voluntarily pool their **sovereignty**, thereby creating a higher level of government.

feminism   Ideology supporting equal rights for women.

fiscal policy   Taxation policy; may be used in pursuit of various objectives (e.g. full employment or pollution control).

floating voter   Member of electorate who easily changes party allegiance.

franchise   The right to vote in elections.

free press   Doctrine that newspapers should be free to print what they like without government direction or censorship.

free trade   Free flow of goods in international trade, unimpeded by tariff barriers; has fuelled much political controversy.

Freedom of Information Act   Legislation giving citizens a legal 'right to know' much of what happens in government.

functionalism   Body of theory looking primarily at the way institutions and practices contribute to the working of a social or political system; may be contrasted with an institutional approach.

Gemeinschaft and **Gesellschaft**   German terms meaning community (based on bonds of affection, kinship, etc.) and association (based on contract), respectively.

General Will   A shared feeling/view amongst people, beyond self-interest, of their common good; central to Rousseau's thinking.

generalist   Civil servant with no special or professional skill; often holding a high position within the British service.

global capitalism   Modern, hi-tech, multinational **capitalist** economy unconstrained by national boundaries.

globalization   Growing interdependence of individuals, countries and regions of the world.

'Golden Age' of Parliament   Period approximately between the 1832 and 1867 Reform Acts when Parliament appeared to have the power to bring down governments; ended by the rise of party discipline.

governance   The act of governing, whether by a formal **government** of elected ministers and officials or by other holders of power such as the IMF. With inter-state groupings, such as the EU, we can speak of multi-level governance.

government   (1) The process of ruling a community; (2) an elite group formally recognized as being in control of the community.

green paper   Government document to stimulate public debate; *see also* **white paper**.

Hansard   Official record of parliamentary proceedings.

hegemony   Rule or domination, often of one state over others; used by neo-Marxists of a **class** dominating society by holding leading positions in various walks of life.

hereditary peer   Member of House of Lords by right of inheritance of title.

hidden hand   Used by Adam Smith and neoliberal economists to account for the order which comes out of an unregulated **market**.

historical materialism   Marx's 'scientific' theory of history, which sees it shaped by the means of production.

hiving off   Chopping off pieces of public **bureaucracy** to form semi-autonomous executive agencies responsible for some clearly defined block of work.

holism   Theory stressing the *whole* of the object of study rather than the parts.

ideology   Political doctrine claiming to give a universally applicable theory of people and society from which may be derived a programme of political action.

imperialism   Extension of the **hegemony** of one country by conquest (military or economic) and imposed rule over others.

incrementalism   Theory of government decision-making holding that radical steps are impossible or undesirable.

individualism   Doctrine seeing the individual as the prime unit in morality and politics; underlies the theories of classical economists in which individuals pursue their own self-interest.

industrial revolution   Period between 1760 and 1860 (approximately) based on multiple innovations in production methods and technologies; revolutionary in the social transformation it induced.

inflation   General rise in prices throughout the economy; often measured by the Retail Price Index (RPI).

inner cabinet   Unofficial **Cabinet** consisting of the PM and a few chosen members of the government.

insider group   **Pressure group** with a close (sometimes secretive) relationship with government.

institutional racism   Entrenched practices reflecting **racist** attitudes, such as discrimination in job appointments or immigration procedures.

instrumental explanation   An interpretation of politics seeing the state as an instrument of some greater power behind the throne; in **Marxism**, this is the **bourgeoisie**.

interest aggregation   Bringing interests together to construct a body sufficiently large (party or group) to have political clout.

interest group   Association of people with some common concern; *see also* **pressure group**.

intergovernmentalism   An intergovernmental relationship in which governments work together while retaining their national **sovereignty**; contrast with **supranationalism**.

international association   Association formed across nations such as NATO and the United Nations Organization.

Iron Curtain   Powerful image employed by the West to describe the separation between the communist East European bloc and the capitalist West during the **cold war**.

iron law of oligarchy   Sociological 'law' postulated by Michels stating that in any **political party** a small elite would eventually gain control.

jingoism   Chauvinistic militarism (from an anti-Russian music-hall song of 1878).

judicial impartiality   Constitutional principle that judges are impartial with regard to the interests within society.

judicial independence   The principle that judges cannot be influenced by the executive or legislature in reaching decisions; *see also* **separation of powers**.

judicial review   A process in which the **judiciary** is able to review legislation and actions of the **executive** in terms of their constitutionality.

judiciary   The body of judges.

jury   Part of judicial system; highly democratic in that the jury is selected at random, so does not include power-seekers in the way electoral politics does. Used by the Greeks not only for legal decisions.

Keynesianism   Economic theory arguing that the free **market**, left to itself, will not automatically work for the benefit of all. Consequently the state must intervene to achieve desirable social ends, particularly full employment.

laissez-faire   Slogan adopted by classical

economists; the state should keep out of the private **capitalist** economy.

legislative process Series of stages by which a **bill** becomes an **Act**; entails passage through Parliament.

legislature Institution formally charged with making laws – Parliament.

legitimacy Quality of being popularly accepted as rightful and just.

legitimation Actions and processes designed to secure **legitimacy**; may entail deception.

Leviathan Huge sea monster – Hobbes's term for the all-powerful ruler.

liberal democracy Form of **democracy** placing stress upon the idea of individual freedom and a *limited* role for government; linked with idea of **market** economy.

liberalism **Ideology** seeing minimum government and individual freedom as its prime virtues; attractive to **capitalism** by permitting the operation of the free **market**.

life peer Member of House of Lords, ennobled for life but not able to pass the title down.

limited government Government restrained from arbitrary rule; accomplished variously by **rule of law, separation of powers**, or a **constitution**.

lobby (verb) To seek the ear of a member of government; (noun) (cap.) The 'club' of parliamentary correspondents who receive unattributable briefings from government.

lobbyist One practised in the art and craft of dealing with MPs and ministers on behalf of pressure groups.

local authority Body responsible for delivering **local government** services; comprises a workforce, a **bureaucracy** and an elected council.

local governance Broadly, the function of various locally based public bodies, elected *and* unelected.

local government Self-government by the people of some subnational territorial unit within the state through an elected council.

local politics Party and **pressure-group** activity, demonstrating, bargaining, and lobbying taking place within a unit of **local government**.

long boom Period from the end of the second world war to the beginning of the 1970s when the developed **capitalist** countries enjoyed rising standards of living and a great rise in material wealth.

machinery of government Institutions through which government works; **civil service** departments, **local authorities**, etc.

macroeconomic policy Policy concerning the aggregate performance of the national economy.

maladministration Bad administration causing inconvenience or suffering.

managerialism Approach to government in which the public sector tries to ape private-sector methods; tends to reduce elected politicians' authority.

mandarin Term used to describe members of the upper echelons of the **civil service**. Originally used of officials in imperial China.

mandate Approval for a set of policies gained by a party elected to office on the basis of a **manifesto**.

manifesto Set of policy promises made by the parties to entice electors.

market Key mechanism (based on price) in classical economic theory; it is said to work as if controlled by a **hidden hand** to achieve optimum allocation of the resources in society.

Marxism Body of thought with many strands deriving from the ideas of Marx;

sees the private ownership of materials needed for production as the key to explaining society and politics.

mass party **Political party** organized throughout the country with thousands of members.

MEP Member of the European Parliament.

mercantilism Economic doctrine favoured in the sixteenth and seventeenth centuries. Argued that a country should seek to export as much as possible, while restricting imports. Did not suit the **capitalists** of the **industrial revolution**, who favoured **free trade**.

meritocracy Literally, rule by the most able; more colloquially, refers to a system (educational or social) where promotion is based on merit, usually measured by examination performance.

militarization Used of police to refer to greater use of defensive and offensive weapons and militaristic tactics.

mind politics Term used in this book to denote an arena of political activity concerned with influencing what people think, rather than allocating values.

ministerial adviser Expert from outside the **civil service** who advises ministers on policy; may adopt openly partisan stance and is not welcomed by the **bureaucrats**.

ministerial responsibility Doctrine declaring that the minister in a government department is the only one who should be questioned, praised and blamed. May be expected to resign where extreme shortcomings are revealed (e.g. Lord Carrington over the Falklands war).

minority government Government by a party without an **absolute majority**, relying on support from other parties.

mixed economy One in which **capitalism** is modified so that some of the productive capital in society is owned by the people (e.g. Britain before the **privatization** programme).

mob rule The downside of **democracy**; term used by opponents of democracy.

monarchy Rule by a single person; usually hereditary.

monetarism Economic doctrine holding that governments should do little in the economy, being content to control the rate at which the quantity of money in circulation rises. Everything else is then said to take care of itself through the **market**.

money supply Quantity of money in the economy, believed to be causally linked with **inflation**.

multi-media mogul Owner of newspaper and broadcasting empires; often global in scope.

multi-member constituency Electoral district returning more than one candidate; a prerequisite of **proportional representation**.

multi-party system **Political system** in which three or more parties contest elections and gain seats in the assembly. Often associated with coalition government.

multipolarity Describes the fragmented world after the breakdown of the bipolar East–West stand-off known as the **cold war**.

nation-state The state as understood today; to be contrasted with the **city-states** of Ancient Greece.

nationalism Ideological attachment to the nation and its interests.

nationalization State acquisition of private property or a business within its territory.

natural law System of law deriving from human nature, rather than invented by reason; an idea present in political thought from the time of the Ancient

Greeks. The great Roman statesman Cicero (106–43 BC) spoke of 'right reason – which is in accordance with nature, and is unchangeable and eternal' (*Republic*: III, 22).

natural rights Rights (say to life or property) that some philosophers believe to come from nature rather than from government.

Nazism Variant of fascist ideology promoted in Germany by the National Socialist Party in the 1930s.

neocolonialism Form of domination characteristic of the post-war era in which **capitalists** from the developed world effectively dominate the less-developed economies through **multinational corporations**.

neocorporatism Used to distinguish the practice of post-war **corporatism** from the pre-war **fascist** variant.

neoliberalism **Ideology** aiming to replace **social democracy** by returning to *laissez-faire* principles; *see also* New **Right** and **Thatcherism**.

neopluralism A theoretical approach that gives a critical acceptance to traditional **pluralism** and also recognizes overarching forms of power such as that of capital.

New Right Term for a resurgence of anti-social-democratic thought; in many ways restating the free-market ideas of the nineteenth-century economists.

new world order Term used by President George Bush (senior) to denote the post-**cold-war** world based on **capitalism**.

news management The practice of politicians and their press secretaries of attempting to influence the reporting of politics; *see also* **spin doctor**.

non-aligned world Group of nations professing neutrality during the **cold war**.

north–south divide Political gulf between the north and south of Britain emerging from the late 1970s.

official censorship Government restriction on what people can see, hear or read.

official secrecy The keeping of state secrets; justified on the grounds of national security.

oligarchy Oppressive rule by a small group.

ombudsman Common term for **citizens'** trouble-shooter (e.g. the Parliamentary Commissioner for Administration) who investigates complaints of **maladministration**.

opinion poll Survey of public opinion on some issue by use of sampling techniques.

organic system **System** that has grown naturally rather than having been designed by people.

outsider group **Pressure group** that government is unwilling to listen to.

paramilitary Militaristic methods and equipment used by non-military organizations (e.g. Special Patrol Group).

parish One of the oldest units of **local government**; very small and based on the area around the church.

parliamentary privilege Set of privileges accorded to MPs; supposed to enable them to perform better as representatives, without fear of, say, libel.

parliamentary questions (PQs) Questions from MPs to members of the government on a rota system during **Question Time**.

parliamentary sovereignty Belief that Parliament is the supreme source of **sovereignty** in the **constitution**. Dicey believed this to be the only morally defensible version of sovereignty in a **democracy**.

partisan dealignment Tendency of voters to break away from stable (especially class-based) identification with a **political party**.

partisanship   Political bias, as in newspaper reporting and editorial comment.

partition   Political division of a country; as in Ireland.

party conference   Usually the highly publicized annual meeting of all elements of the mass party organization.

party discipline   MPs' obedience to their party leadership.

party identification   Used by psephologists to describe voters who always vote for the same party regardless.

party list   Feature in **proportional representation** electoral systems; displays the candidates of a party, sometimes in order of preference.

party system   Usually defined in terms of the number of parties taking part in the political fray.

patriarchy   Society in which men dominate women.

patronage   Making appointments on the basis of favour rather than electoral choice or expertise.

peak organization   Umbrella organization formed by the association of a number of **pressure groups** (e.g. the TUC).

peer group   Body of individuals equal in some significant respect (age, rank, status, etc.).

pluralism   Theory of politics seeing **pressure groups** as central to the political process; generally holds their effect to be benign and democratic.

pluralist stagnation   Right-wing explanation for Britain's post-war economic failure, claiming that too many **pressure groups** were being permitted to voice their demands.

police and crime commissioner   Elected official taking over the role of police authorities (from 2012) to oversee chief constable, determine priorities and set budgets.

police complaints procedure   System for handling complaints against the police.

police culture   Characteristic set of attitudes held by the police.

police state   Totalitarian state where police are under control of the government.

Policy Cabinet   A small **Cabinet** of about five, the members of which are concerned with the whole area of government policy, rather than being responsible for specific departments; has never really been tried in Britain.

policy implementation   Carrying out government policy; formally the task of the **bureaucracy**.

policy-making   Essential act of government in the modern state. The extent to which government is free to make policy is a matter of debate.

policy network   Loosely knit and changing complex of interest groups, politicians and officials brought together, sometimes in harmony, sometimes in conflict, over policy issues.

polis   Ancient Greek term for city.

political culture   Set of ideas and attitudes held towards the **political system**.

political party   Group formed for the purpose of gaining political office, usually through winning elections.

political philosophy   Generalized answers to fundamental questions such as the nature of justice.

political science   May loosely be used to denote the study of politics generally, or more rigorously to indicate the application of scientific method.

political socialization   Social process through which individuals develop an awareness of political values, norms and processes; continues throughout life.

political system   A whole consisting of institutions of **government** and the society they serve, a concept stressing the **holistic** nature of politics; no part can be properly understood without reference to its place in the whole.

political theory   Theories about political institutions, law, **constitutions**, **democracy**, etc.

political thought   Corpus of theories whereby people have sought to explain political behaviour, values, and mechanisms and institutions of **political systems**.

politicization   Process whereby an institution may become actively involved in politics (e.g. the **civil service** and police).

politics–administration dichotomy   Long-standing distinction between making policy and carrying it out; underlies **separation of powers** between **executive** and **legislature**.

polity   The political organization of a state.

poll tax   Tax placed on all citizens equally, regardless of ability to pay; imposed in 1381 (causing Peasants' Revolt) and as community charge in late 1980s.

polyarchy   Robert Dahl's term for a form of **pluralism** seeing in groups a more effective balance of power than in the **constitution**.

populism   Form of **government** supposed to enshrine the will of the people. Some political leaders have an instinctively populist appeal. Presidents, where directly elected, may claim populist mandate.

positive law   Law believed to have been made by applying human reason rather than by some metaphysical power such as God; *see also* **natural law**.

postmodernism   A vaguely defined stage beyond the modernism of the **Enlightenment**.

power   Key concept in the study and practice of politics; the ability to achieve some desired effect regardless of opposition. May take many forms.

power-sharing executive   An **executive** formed to reflect both majority and minority interests.

preferential voting   System that permits voters to indicate alternative preferences.

presidential government   System of government by one person, usually elected directly by the people.

press baron   **Capitalist** owner of large-circulation newspapers; today empires extend into the media and entertainments industry, hence **media mogul**.

pressure group   Association wishing to influence government policy.

primary election   Election to choose the candidates; held before the real election.

private finance initiative (PFI)   Means of financing state capital projects (e.g. school buildings) by 'renting' them from private-sector providers; used as an alternative to borrowing.

private member's bill   **Bill** introduced into Parliament by an MP in their personal capacity rather than by the government; rarely gets onto the statute book.

privatization   Transfer of state-owned assets into private hands.

proletariat   Marx's term for the working class.

promotional group   **Pressure group** concerned with promoting an ideal rather than the self-interest of its members (e.g. RSPCA).

proportional representation   Electoral system intended to create an assembly that accurately reflects the level of support for the parties in the country.

psephology   Study of elections and electoral behaviour.

Public Bill committee Committee of MPs considering **bills** during their process through Parliament (the committee stage).

public choice theory Theory seeking to explain and analyse politics on the basis of the **individualist** premises of classical economics.

public expenditure Expenditure by the state, including redistribution through transfer payments.

public inquiry Official inquiry into some matter of public concern.

public interest Vague term meaning the collective interest of society. What is, or is not, in the public interest is often a matter of judgement. In the Ponting case, the judge denied the right of a citizen to make up his own mind on the matter, declaring that only the government could decide.

public order Well-regulated civic life.

public–private partnership (PPP) Means of providing a public service through involvement of the private sector.

public sector borrowing requirement (PSBR) Amount of money government wishes to borrow in any year.

qualified majority voting Voting in which more than a simple majority is required for success.

quango Quasi-Autonomous Non-Government Organization.

Queen's Speech Great day in the **ceremonial** calendar of British politics, marking the annual opening of Parliament and outlining the government's proposed programme for the year.

Question Time One-hour period in the parliamentary timetable when MPs address questions to ministers.

racism Attribution of characteristics of superiority and inferiority to members of particular races.

rational decision-making Making a decision on the basis of reason rather than self-interest, political advantage or prejudice.

rationalism Faith in reason, as opposed to religion or superstition.

redress of grievance Means taken to right a wrong (often inflicted by the state on a citizen).

referendum Popular vote on a particular issue rather than to choose a representative; being used increasingly in Britain.

regionalism Giving political power to geographical regions of the state; *see also* **devolution**.

regulatory body Instead of providing a service, government creates bodies to monitor and control those that do; **privatization** led to a great increase.

representative government Form of government in which a minority acts on behalf of the rest of the population.

republic State in which supreme power rests with the people; contrasted with **monarchy**.

royal prerogative Set of special privileges enjoyed exclusively by the monarch since medieval times; today many of the most important are effectively held by the PM.

rule of law Constitutional doctrine that the ultimate source of **authority** in the state is the law; kings and governments are themselves subject to it.

sectional group Pressure group composed of members of society from some sectional interest.

sectoral cleavage An alternative to **class** as an explanation of voting behaviour.

security services State agencies concerned with espionage (MI5 and MI6).

select committee Committee of MPs established to undertake some particular task on behalf of Parliament and scrutinize the **executive**.

selective incentive   Inducement made by a **pressure group** or **political party** to recruit and retain members.

separation of powers   Constitutional doctrine in which the various functions of **government** (rule-making, rule execution and judging) are placed with separate institutions in order to check each other and prevent despotism.

separatism   Desire to be governed as a separate state; *see also* **devolution**.

sexism   Attitudes falsely ascribing certain attributes to one sex, usually to justify inequality.

Shadow Cabinet   Opposition frontbench team.

simple plurality   Electoral system in which the successful candidates are those with the most votes in each **constituency** (i.e. the first past the post or 'winner takes all'); contrast with **proportional representation**.

single currency   The result of a joining together of currencies of different states, as in the creation of the euro.

single-party system   **Political system** in which one party dominates; under totalitarian regimes may actually eliminate its rivals by force.

sleaze   Term increasingly used to describe corrupt or dubious behaviour by politicians.

social class *see* **class**.

social Darwinism   Applying the principle of the survival of the fittest to social development; opposed to government intervention in society.

social democracy   Ideology of moderate **socialism**, mixed economy, welfare state, etc.

socialism   Egalitarian **ideology** under which the state actively cares for citizens.

Reformist socialism aims to achieve this by reform of liberal institutions rather than violent confrontation (*see also* **Fabianism**); revolutionary socialism aims to overthrow capitalism by force.

sovereignty   Concept of the ultimate source of **power** within the state.

'special relationship'   Britain's view of its relationship with the USA.

spin doctor   Politician's aide concerned with **news management**.

spoils system   System of **patronage** in which election victors distribute offices to those who have assisted them.

sponsorship   Relationship of MPs to various non-party organizations (e.g. some Labour MPs are sponsored by trade unions).

state   In simple terms, a sovereign community, within a defined territory.

state of nature   A condition imagined by some philosophers (Hobbes, Locke, Rousseau) as a basis for determining what the role of **government** should be.

statute   Laws made by Parliament.

structural explanation   Explanation of political behaviour seeing it as determined by the structure in which it takes place (e.g. the **capitalist** economy).

subgovernment   Community formed by those concerned with policy in a certain area (**insider pressure groups, civil service**, the specialist press, ministers, etc.); sometimes termed a policy community.

subsidiarity   Principle that the powers of different levels of government should always be placed as low (i.e. as close to the people) as is compatible with efficiency.

subversion   Attempt to overthrow the government by unlawful means.

suffragette   Woman active in the cause of women's voting rights.

supranational association international organization in which member states surrender sovereignty to the greater authority. Mainly used of the EU.

synopticity Taking an analytical perspective that sees all aspects of politics as belonging to a larger whole.

system Set of elements interacting together to constitute a larger whole.

tabloid Popular newspapers; also called 'redtops' or 'the gutter press'.

tactical voting Behaviour designed to keep out a disliked candidate by supporting the rival most likely to defeat him or her.

tendency Used in politics to designate sections within parties (e.g. Militant Tendency).

territorial management Government role in balancing the **devolutionary** claims of different regions.

Thatcherism **Neoliberalism** as espoused by Margaret Thatcher.

theocracy Government by religious leaders acting on behalf of a divine being.

think-tank Body of intellectuals set up privately or by government to consider public policy issues.

'third way' **Ideological** position espoused by New Labour (and others) claiming to be between **social democracy** and **neoliberalism**.

transnational corporation Private company operating in the global economy and not located within any particular country.

tripartism Form of **corporatism** developed in Britain in the immediate post-war decades involving government, employers and unions.

two-party system **Political system in** which two equal parties monopolize in terms of votes and parliamentary seats.

tyranny Oppressive rule.

ultra vires Legal principle restraining public bodies within a framework of powers prescribed by the **sovereign** body.

underclass Disadvantaged class developing during the 1980s (unemployed, ethnic minorities, etc.).

unitary system **Local government** areal structure without subdivisions.

utilitarianism Moral philosophy preached by Bentham, J. S. Mill and others; sees the maximization of utility (happiness) as the basis for all law, morality, political institutions and right behaviour.

variable geometry Term used to describe a process whereby groups of members move towards integration at differing speeds (applied to EU).

violence, state Legitimate use of force against citizens (e.g. by police).

voluntarism View that humans control their own actions, rather than acting as the system forces them to do.

welfare statism A social democratic kind of ideology.

West Lothian question Term used to describe the problem of Scottish MPs being able to vote on certain English matters at Westminster while English MPs cannot vote on issues coming before the Scottish Parliament.

whip MP charged with maintaining **party discipline** in Parliament.

white paper Document published by government to outline and explain its policy; *see also* **green paper**.

world economy The idea that all countries are interlocked through trade.

xenophobia Fear (and often hatred) of foreigners.

Bibliography

Abrahams, M. (1958) 'Class distinctions in Britain', in *The Future of the Welfare State*, London, Conservative Political Centre.

Adonis, A. and Pollard, S. (1997) *A Class Act: The Myth of Britain's Classless Society*, London, Hamish Hamilton.

Alder, J. (2011) *Constitutional and Administrative Law*, 8th edn, Basingtoke, Palgrave Macmillan.

Alderson, J. (1994) *A New Cromwell: The Centralisation of the Police*, London, Charter 88.

Aldridge, H. et al. (2011) *Monitoring Poverty and Social Exclusion*, York, Joseph Rowntree Foundation.

Almandras, S. (2011) *Protection of Freedoms Bill: Bill 146 of 2010–2011*, London, House of Commons Library Research Paper 11/20.

Almond, G. A. and Verba, S. (1963) *The Civic Culture*, Princeton, NJ, Princeton University Press (reprinted 1989).

Almond, G. A. and Verba, S. (eds) (1980) *The Civic Culture Revisited*, Boston, MA, Little Brown.

Althusser, L. (1969) *For Marx* (transl. B. Brewster), Harmondsworth, Penguin.

Amery, L. S. (1947) *Thoughts on the Constitution*, London, Oxford University Press.

Amis, M. (2007) 'The age of horrorism', *Observer* (10 Sept. 2006).

Arblaster, A. (1984) *The Rise and Decline of Western Liberalism*, Oxford, Blackwell.

Archer, C. (2008) *The European Union*, Abingdon, Routledge.

Arneil, B. (1999) *Politics and Feminism*, Oxford, Blackwell.

Atkinson, W., Roberts, S. and Savage, M. (eds) (2012) *Class Inequality in Austerity Britain*, Basingstoke, Palgrave Macmillan.

Audit Commission (1990) *We Can't Go On Meeting Like This*, Abingdon, Audit Commission Publications.

Audit Commission (1993) *Realising the Benefits of Competition: The Client Role for Contracted Services*, London, HMSO.

Auerbach, M. M. (1959) *The Conservative Illusion*, New York, Columbia University Press.

Aughey, A. (2001) *Nationalism, Devolution and the Challenge to the United Kingdom State*, London, Pluto.

Auld, R. (chair) (2001) *Review of the Criminal Courts of England and Wales*, London, Stationery Office.

Axford, B. (1995) *The Global System: Economics, Politics and Culture*, Cambridge, Polity.

Bache, I. and George, S. (eds) (2006) *Politics in the European Union*, 2nd edn, Oxford, Oxford University Press.

Bache, I. and Jordan, A. (eds) (2008) *The Europeanization of British Politics*, Basingstoke, Palgrave Macmillan.

Bagehot, W. (1963) *The English Constitution*, London, Fontana (first published 1867).

Baggott, R. (1995) *Pressure Groups Today*, Manchester, Manchester University Press.

Bains, M. A. (chair) (1972) *The New Local Authorities: Management and Structure*, London, HMSO.

Baker, D. and Fountain, I. (1996) 'Eton gent or Essex man? The Conservative parliamentary elite', in Ludlam and Smith (eds), pp. 86–97.

Baldwin, N. (2005) *Parliament in the 21st Century*, London, Politico's.

Balogh, T. (1968) 'The apotheosis of the dilettante: the establishment of mandarins', in Thomas, H. (ed.), *Crisis in the Civil Service*, London, Anthony Blond.

Banton, M. (1985) *Promoting Racial Harmony*, Cambridge, Cambridge University Press.

Bar Council (1989) *Quality of Justice: The Bar's Response*, London, Bar Council.

Barberis, P. (ed.) (1996) *The Whitehall Reader*, Buckingham, Open University Press.

Barker, R. (1994) *Politics, Peoples and Government*, Basingstoke, Macmillan.

Barnett, S. and Gaber, I. (2001) *Westminster Tales: The Twentieth Century Crisis in Political Journalism*, London, Continuum.

Barrell, R., FitzGerald, J. and Riley, R. (2007) *EU Enlargement and Migration: Assessing the Macroeconomic Impacts*, NIESR Discussion Paper No. 292.

Barron, J., Crawley, G. and Wood, T. (1991) *Councillors in Crisis*, Basingstoke, Macmillan.

Bartle, J. and Griffiths, D. (eds) (2001) *Political Communications Transformed: From Morrison to Mandelson*, Basingstoke, Palgrave Macmillan.

Bauman, Z. (2000) *Community: Seeking Safety in an Insecure World*, Cambridge, Polity.

Baxter, J. and Koffman, L. (eds) (1985) *Police, the Constitution and the Community*, Abingdon, Professional Books.

Beer, S. H. (1956) 'Pressure groups and parties in Britain', *American Political Science Review*, 50(1), 1–23.

Beer, S. H. (1965) *Modern British Politics*, London, Faber.

Bell, D. (1960) *The End of Ideology*, Glencoe, IL, Free Press.

Bellamy, R. and Castiglione, D. (1996) 'Introduction: constitutions and politics', *Political Studies*, 44, 413–16.

Benn, M. et al. (1983) *The Rape Controversy*, London, National Council for Civil Liberties.

Benn, T. (1979) *Arguments for Socialism*, Harmondsworth, Penguin.

Bentley, A. F. (1967) *The Process of Government*, Cambridge, MA, Harvard University Press (first published 1908).

Bentley, M. (1984) *Politics Without Democracy, 1815–1914*, London, Fontana.

Bergg, D. (2004) 'Taking a horse to water? Delivering public service broadcasting in a digital universe', in Tambini, D. and Cowling, J. (eds), *From Public Service Broadcasting to Public Service Communications*, London, Institute for Public Policy Research.

Berlin, I. (1970) 'Two concepts of liberty', in Berlin, I., *Four Essays on Liberty*, Oxford, Oxford University Press.

Berman, G. (2012a) *Police Service Strength*, London, House of Commons Library, Standard Note SN00634.

Berman, G. (2012b) *Prison Population Statistics*, London, House of Commons Library, Standard Note SN/SG/4334.

Bernstein, E. (1961) *Evolutionary Socialism*, New York, Random House.

Beveridge, W. (chair) (1942) *Social Insurance and Allied Services*, Cmd 6404, London, HMSO.

Bhavnani, K. K. and R. (1985) 'Racism and resistance in Britain', in Coates et al. (eds), pp. 147–59.

Bingham, T. (2011) *The Rule of Law*, Harmondsworth, Penguin.

Birkinshaw, P. (1988) *Freedom of Information: The Law, The Practice and the Ideal*, London, Weidenfeld and Nicolson.

Birkinshaw, P. (1991) *Reforming the Secret State*, Buckingham, Open University Press.

Birkinshaw, P. (1997) 'Freedom of information', *Parliamentary Affairs*, 50(1) 164–81.

Black, E. (2000) 'MPs rebel over paper votes', *Sunday Times* (24 Dec.).

Blair, A. (2005) *The European Union Since 1945*, Harlow, Pearson.

Blake, R. (1985) *The Conservative Party from Peel to Thatcher*, London, Fontana.

Blick, A. and Jones, G. (2010) *Premiership: The Development, Nature and Power of the Office of the British Prime Minister*, Exeter, Imprint Academic.

Boaden, N. (1971) *Urban Policy Making*, Cambridge, Cambridge University Press.

Boateng, P. (1985) 'Crisis in accountability', in Baxter and Koffman (eds), pp. 237–45.

Bochel, H. (ed.) (2011) *The Conservative Party and Social Policy*, Bristol, Policy Press.

Bogdanor, V. (1996a) 'The monarchy and the constitution', *Parliamentary Affairs*, 49(3), 407–22.

Bogdanor, V. (1996b) *Politics and the Constitution: Essays on British Government*, Aldershot, Dartmouth.

Bogdanor, V. (1997) *The Monarchy and the Constitution*, Oxford, Oxford University Press.

Bogdanor, V. (2001) *Devolution in the United Kingdom*, Oxford, Oxford University Press.

Bogdanor, V. (2009) *The New British Constitution*, Oxford, Hart.

Bogdanor, V. (ed.) (2010) *From New Jerusalem to New Labour: British Prime Ministers from Attlee to Blair*, Basingstoke, Palgrave Macmillan.

Bogdanor, V. (2011) *The Coalition and the Constitution*, Oxford, Hart.

Borisyuk, G., Johnson, R., Rallings, C., and Thrasher, M. (2010) 'Parliamentary constituency boundary reviews and electoral bias: how important are variations in constituency size?', *Parliamentary Affairs*, 63(1),4–21.

Bottomore, T. (1964) *Elites in Society*, Harmondsworth, Penguin.

Bower, T. (1988) *Maxwell: The Outsider*, London, Aurum Press.

Bradbury, J. and Mitchell, J. (2001) 'Devolution: new policies for old?', *Parliamentary Affairs*, 54, 257–75.

Brand, J. (1992) *British Parliamentary Parties: Policy and Power*, Oxford, Oxford University Press.

Briscoe, S. (2006) *Britain in Numbers*, London, Politico's.

Bronstein, J. and Harris, A. (2012) *Empire, State, and Society: Britain since 1830*, Chichester, Wiley-Blackwell.

Brown, G. (1972) *In My Way*, London, Gollancz.

Bruce, S. (2012) *Politics and Religion in the United Kingdom*, Abingdon, Routledge.

Bruce-Gardyne, J. (1984) *Mrs Thatcher's First Administration*, London, Macmillan.

Bunyan, A. (1977) *The History and Practice of the Political Police in Britain*, London, Quartet.

Burch, M. and Holliday, I. (1996) *The British Cabinet System*, Hemel Hempstead, Prentice Hall/Harvester Wheatsheaf.

Burke, E. (1782) *Reform of Representation in the House of Commons*, in *Works* (1861, vol. VI), London, Bohn.

Burke, J. (2001) 'No more cool Britannia for Europe's leper', *Observer* (11 March).

Burleigh, M. (2005) *Earthly Powers: Religion and Politics in Europe from the French Revolution to the Great War*, London, HarperCollins.

Burleigh, M. (2006) *Sacred Causes*, London, HarperCollins.

Burley, A. and Mattli, W. (1993) 'Europe before the Court: a political theory of legal integration', *International Organization*, 47 (Winter), 41–76.

Burnham, J. (1942) *The Managerial Revolution*, London, Putnam.

Burnham, J. and Pyper, R. (2008) *Britain's Modernised Civil Service*, Basingstoke, Palgrave Macmillan.

Butler, D. (1960) 'The paradox of party difference', *American Behavioural Scientist*, 4(3).

Butler, D. (1995) *British General Elections since 1945*, Oxford, Blackwell.

Butler, D. and Butler, G. (1994) *British Political Facts, 1900–1994*, Basingstoke, Macmillan.

Butler, D. and Butler, G. (2010) *British Political Facts*, 10th edn, Basingstoke, Palgrave Macmillan.

Butler, D. and Kavanagh, D. (eds) (1992) *The British General Election of 1992*, Basingstoke, Macmillan.

Butler, D. and Kavanagh, D. (eds) (1997) *The British General Election of 1997*, Basingstoke, Macmillan.

Butler, D. and Kavanagh, D. (2002) *The British General Election of 2001*, Basingstoke, Palgrave Macmillan.

Butler, D. and Stokes, D. (1969) *Political Change in Britain*, London, Macmillan.

Butler, M. (1986) *Europe: More than a Continent*, London, Heinemann.

Cabinet Office (1991) *The Citizen's Charter: Raising the Standard*, Cm 1599, London, HMSO.

Cabinet Office (1993) *Open Government*, Cm 2290, London, HMSO.

Cabinet Office (1999a) *Bringing in and Bringing on Talent*, London, Stationery Office.

Cabinet Office (1999b) *Modernising Government*, Cm 4310, London, Stationery Office.

Cahanum, S. (1997) 'Finishing school: Asian girls in the British educational system', in Giddens, A., *Sociology: Introductory Readings*, Cambridge, Polity, pp. 344–7.

Cahill, K. (2001) *Who Owns Britain: The Hidden Facts Behind Landownership in the UK and Ireland*, Edinburgh, Canongate Books.

Callaghan, J. (1987) *Time and Chance*, London, Collins.

Callaghan, J. (1997) *Great Power Complex*, London, Pluto.

Campbell, D. (1980) 'Society under surveillance', in Hain et al. (eds), pp. 65–150.

Cannadine, D. (1999) *The Decline and Fall of the British Aristocracy*, London, Picador.

Carey, S. and Burton, J. (2004) 'The influence of the press in shaping public opinion towards the EU in Britain', *Political Studies*, 52(3), 623–40.

Carr-Brown, J. (2001) 'No. 10 spins its own news on Pravda.com', *Sunday Times* (18 Feb.).

Carson, R. (1962) *Silent Spring*, New York, Houghton Mifflin.

Carter, J. (2006) *Our Endangered Values: America's Moral Crisis*, New York, Simon & Schuster.

Castells, M. (1977) *The Urban Question*, London, Edward Arnold.

Cawson, A. (1986) *Corporatism and Political Theory*, Oxford, Basil Blackwell.

Cecil, H. (1912) *Conservatism*, London, Thornton Butterworth.

Chandler, J. A. (2007) *Explaining Local Government: Local Governance in Britain since 1800*, Manchester, Manchester University Press.

Chandler, J. A. (2009) *Local Government Today*, 4th edn, Manchester, Manchester University Press.

Chapman R. and Hunt, M. (eds) (2006) *Open Government in a Theoretical and Practical Context*, Aldershot, Ashgate.

Charmley, J. (1998) 'The Conservative defeat: an historical perspective', *Political Quarterly*, 69(2), 118–25.

Checkland, S. G. and E. O. A. (eds) (1974) *The Poor Law Report of 1834*, Harmondsworth, Penguin.

Childs, S. (2009) *Women and British Party Politics: Descriptive, Substantive and Symbolic Representation*, Abingdon, Routledge.

Childs, S. and Webb, P. (2011) *Sex, Gender and the Conservative Party: From Iron Lady to Kitten Heels*, Basingstoke, Palgrave Macmillan.

Chittenden, M. (1988) 'Freemasonry "rife" among top police', *Sunday Times* (10 April).

Chomsky, N. (1997) *World Orders, Old and New*, London, Pluto.

Chrimes, S. B. (1967) *English Constitutional History*, 4th edn, London, Oxford University Press.

Clark, A. (2012) *Political Parties in the UK*, Basingstoke, Palgrave Macmillan.

Clifford, P. and Heath, A. (1994) 'The election campaign', in Heath et al. (eds), pp. 7–23.

Coates, D., Johnson, G. and Bush, R. (eds) (1985) *A Socialist Anatomy of Britain*, Cambridge, Polity.

Cockburn, C. (1977) *The Local State*, London, Pluto Press.

Cockerell, M., Hennessy, P. and Walker, P. (1984) *Sources Close to the Prime Minister: Inside the Hidden World of the News Manipulators*, London, Macmillan.

Coen, D. and Richardson, J. (2009) *Lobbying the European Union: Institutions, Actors, and Issues*, Oxford, Oxford University Press.

Cohen, N. (1999) 'How Britain mortgaged the future', *New Statesman* (18 Oct.), 25–7.

Coleman, S. (2001) 'Online campaigning', *Parliamentary Affairs*, 54, 679–88.

Collings, D. and Seldon, A. (2001) 'Conservatives in opposition', *Parliamentary Affairs*, 54, 624–37.

Commission for Local Democracy (1995) *Taking Charge: The Rebirth of Local Democracy, Final Report*, London, Municipal Journal.

Commission on Scottish Devolution (2009) *Serving Scotland Better: Scotland and the United Kingdom in the 21st Century. An Executive Summary of the Final Report*, Edinburgh, Commission on Scottish Devolution.

Cornford, F. M. (ed. and translator) (1941) *The Republic of Plato*, Oxford, Clarendon Press.

Council on Environmental Quality (1980) *Global 2000 Report*, Washington, DC, US Government Printing Office.

Cowley, P. (1999) 'The absence of war? New Labour in parliament', *British Elections & Parties Review*, 9(1), 154–70.

Cowley, P. (2001) 'The Commons: Mr Blair's lapdog?' *Parliamentary Affairs*, 54, 815–28.

Cowley, P. (2005) *The Rebels: How Blair Mislaid his Majority*, London, Politico's.

Cowley, R. (2011) *A History of the British Police*, Stroud, History Press.

Cracknell, D. (2001) 'United they're damned', *Sunday Times* (23 Dec.).

Cracknell, R., McGuiness, F. and Rhodes, C. (2011) *General Election 2010*, London, House of Commons Library, Research Paper 10/36.

Crewe, I. (1983) 'Representation and ethnic minorities in Britain', in Glazer, N. and Young, K. (eds) *Ethnic Pluralism and Public Policy: Achieving Equality in the United States and Britain*, London, Heinemann.

Crewe, I. (1986) 'On the death and resurrection of class voting: some comments on *How Britain Votes*', *Political Studies*, 34(4), 620–38.

Crewe, I. (1988) 'Has the electorate become Thatcherite?', in Skidelsky, R. (ed.) *Thatcherism*, London, Chatto and Windus.

Crewe, I. (1993) 'Voting and the electorate', in Dunleavy et al. (eds), pp. 92–122.

Crewe, I. (1997) 'The opinion polls: confidence restored?' *Parliamentary Affairs*, 50(4), 569–85.

Crick, B. (1964) *In Defence of Politics*, Harmondsworth, Penguin (5th edn, London, Continuum, 2000).

Crick, B. (1987) *Socialism*, Buckingham, Open University Press.

Criddle, B. (1997) 'MPs and candidates', in Butler and Kavanagh (eds), pp. 186–209.

Criddle, B. (2010) 'More diverse yet more uniform: MPs and candidates', in Kavanagh and Cowley (eds), pp. 306–49.

Crosland, A. (1956) *The Future of Socialism*, London, Jonathan Cape.

Cross, C. (1963) *The Liberals in Power 1905–1914*, London, Pall Mall Press.

Crossman, R. H. S. (1963) 'Introduction', in Bagehot, W., *The English Constitution*, London, Fontana.

Crossman, R. H. S. (1975–7) *Diaries of a Cabinet Minister*, 3 vols, London, Jonathan Cape.

Crouch, C. (1979) *State and Economy in Contemporary Capitalism*, London, Croom Helm.

Curran, J. and Seaton, J. (2009) *Power Without Responsibility: The Press, Broadcasting and the Internet in Britain*, 7th edn.

Curtice, J. (1997) 'Anatomy of a non-landslide', *Politics Review*, 7(1), 2–8.

Curtice, J. (2001) 'So much command of the Commons, so little over the electorate', *Independent* (9 June).

Curtice, J. (2010) 'So what went wrong with the electoral system? The 2010 election result and the debate about electoral reform', *Parliamentary Affairs*, 63(4), 623–38.

Curtice, J. and Steed, M. (1987) 'Analysis', in Butler and Kavanagh (eds), pp. 316–62.

Curtice, J. and Steed, M. (1992) 'Appendix: the results analysed', in Butler and Kavanagh (eds), pp. 322–62.

Dahl, R. (1956) *A Preface to Democratic Theory*, Chicago, IL, University of Chicago Press.

Dahl, R. (1985) *A Preface to Economic Democracy*, Cambridge, Polity.

Dahl, R. and Lindblom, C. E. (1976) *Politics, Economics and Welfare*, New York, Harper.

Dangerfield, G. (1936) *The Strange Death of Liberal England*, London, Constable.

Davidson, S. (2009) *Quantifying the Changing Age Structure of the British Electorate 2005–2025: Researching the Age Demographics of the New Parliamentary Constituencies*, Leicester, De Montfort University.

Davies, B. (1972) *Variations in Children's Services among British Urban Authorities*, London, Bell.

Dawkins, R. (2006) *The God Delusion*, London, Transworld.

Deacon, D., Goldin, P. and Billig, M. (2001) 'Press and broadcasting: "real issues" and real coverage', *Parliamentary Affairs*, 54, 666–78.

Deakin, N. and Parry, R. (2000) *The Treasury and Social Policy: The Contest for Control of Welfare Policy*, Basingstoke, Macmillan.

Deane, P. (1963) *The First Industrial Revolution*, Cambridge, Cambridge University Press.

Dearlove, J. (1973) *The Politics of Policy in Local Government*, London, Cambridge University Press.

Denemark, D. (1996) 'Thinking ahead to mixed-member proportional representation', *Party Politics*, 2(3), 409–20.

Denver, D. (1998) 'The British electorate in the 1990s', *West European Politics*, 21(1), 197–217.

Denver, D., Carman, C. and Johns, R. (2012) *Elections and Voters in Britain*, 3rd edn, Basingstoke, Palgrave Macmillan.

Denver, D., Norris, P., Broughton, D. and Rallings, C. (eds) (1993) *British Elections and Parties Yearbook, 1993*, Hemel Hempstead, Harvester Wheatsheaf.

Department of Communities and Local Government (2011) *Race, Religion and Equalities: A Report on the 2009–10 Citizenship Survey*, London, DCLG.

Department of the Environment, Transport and the Regions (1998) *Modern Local Government: In Touch With the People*, London, Stationery Office.

Devine, F. (1997) *Social Class in America and Britain*, Edinburgh, Edinburgh University Press.

Dicey, A. V. (1959) *An Introduction to the Study of the Law of the Constitution*, 10th edn, London, Macmillan (first published 1885).

Dodd, V. (2010) 'Firearms policewoman wins record damages in sexism case', *Guardian* (18 June).

Doig, A. (1984) 'Public service and private gain', *Public Money*, 4(3).

Doig, A. (1995) 'Continuing cause for concern? Probity in local government', *Local Government Studies*, 21(1), 99–114.

Dorey, P. (1995) *British Politics since 1945*, Oxford, Blackwell.

Dorey, P. (2005) *Policy Making in Britain: An Introduction*, London, Sage.

Dorey, P. and Kelso, A. (2011) *House of Lords Reform Since 1911: Must the Lords Go?* Basingstoke, Palgrave Macmillan.

Dorling, D. (2011) *Injustice: Why Social Inequality Persists*, Bristol, Policy Press.

Dow, C. (2012) *Inside the Bank of England: Memoirs of Christopher Dow, Chief Economist 1973–74*, Basingstoke, Palgrave Macmillan.

Dowding, K. (1995) *The Civil Service*, London, Routledge.

Downs, A. (1957) *An Economic Theory of Democracy*, New York, Harper and Row.

Draper, D. (1997) *Blair's 100 Days*, London, Faber.

Driver, S. (2011) *Understanding British Party Politics*, Cambridge, Polity.

Driver, S. and Martell, L (1988) *New Labour: Politics after Thatcherism*, Cambridge, Polity.

Duff, A. (1997) *The Treaty of Amsterdam*, London, The Federal Trust.

Dunleavy, P. (1980) *Urban Political Analysis*, London, Macmillan.

Dunleavy, P. (1981) *The Politics of Mass Housing in Britain: Corporate Power and Professional Influence in the Welfare State*, Oxford, Clarendon Press.

Dunleavy, P. (1991) *Democracy, Bureaucracy and Public Choice*, Hemel Hempstead, Harvester Wheatsheaf.

Dunleavy, P. (1993) 'The political parties', in Dunleavy et al., pp. 123–53.

Dunleavy, P. and Husbands, C. T. (1985) *British Democracy at the Crossroads: Voting and Party Competition in the 1980s*, London, George Allen & Unwin.

Dunleavy, P. and Rhodes, R. A. W. (1990) 'Core executive studies in Britain', *Public Administration*, 68(1), 3–28.

Dunleavy, P., Gamble, A., Holliday, I. and

Peele, G. (1993) *Developments in British Politics 4*, Basingstoke, Macmillan.

Dunleavy, P., Margetts, H., O'Duffy, B. and Weir, S. (1997) *Making Votes Count*, Democratic Audit Paper 11, Colchester, University of Essex, Democratic Audit.

Dunleavy, P., Gamble, A., Holliday, I. and Peele, G. (2000) *Developments in British Politics 6*, Basingstoke, Macmillan.

Dunleavy, P., Margetts, H., Smith, T. and Weir, S. (2001) 'Constitutional reform, New Labour and public trust in government', *Parliamentary Affairs*, 54, 405–24.

Dunleavy, P., Margetts, H., Smith, T. and Weir, S. (2005) *Voices of the People: Popular Attitudes to Democratic Renewal in Britain*, revised edn, London, Politico's.

Durham University (2000) *Who Runs the North East Now?* Durham, Durham University.

Duverger, M. (1966) *The Idea of Politics*, Indianapolis, Bobbs-Merrill.

Dyer, C. (1995) 'And the verdict m'lud?', *Guardian* (7 April).

Easton, D. (1953) *The Political System*, New York, Knopf.

Easton, D. and Dennis, J. (1969) *Children and the Political System: Origins of Political Legitimacy*, New York, McGraw-Hill.

Eckstein, H. (1960) *Pressure Group Politics*, London, George Allen & Unwin.

Ecologist (1992) 'Whose common future?' special issue of *The Ecologist*, 22(4).

Elcock, H. (1991) *Change and Decay: Public Administration in the 1990s*, Harlow, Longman.

Elcock, H. (1995) 'Leading people: some issues of local government leadership in Britain and America', *Local Government Studies*, 21(4), 546–67.

Eldridge, J. (ed.) (1993) *Getting the Message: News, Truth and Power*, London, Routledge.

Electoral Commission (2001) *Election 2001: The Official Results*, London, Politico's.

Electoral Commission (2005) *Black and Minority Ethnic Survey*, London, Electoral Commission.

Electoral Commission (2010) *Report on the Administration of the 2010 UK General Election*, London, Electoral Commission.

Electoral Reform Society (2010) *The UK General Election 2010 In Depth*, London, Electoral Reform Society.

Elliott, L. and Curtis, P. (2009) 'UK's income gap widest since 60s', *Guardian* (8 May).

Elshtain, J. B. (1981) *Public Man, Private Woman*, Princeton, NJ, Princeton University Press.

Emsley. C. (2010) *The Great British Bobby: A History of British Policing from 1829 to the Present*, London, Quercus.

Equality and Human Rights Commission (2009) *Police and Racism: What has been Achieved Ten Years after the Stephen Lawrence Inquiry Report?* London, EHRC.

Evans, G. (1993) 'Class conflict and inequality', in Jowell, R. et al., *International Social Attitudes: The 10th British Social Attitudes Report*, Aldershot, Dartmouth, pp. 123–41.

Evans, P. (1986a) 'Police are all too often a target of those frustrated by society', *The Times* (10 Nov.).

Evans, P. (1986b) 'The low profile policy', *The Times* (11 Nov.).

Ewing, K. D. and Gearty, C. A. (1990) *Freedom under Thatcher: Civil Liberties in Modern Britain*, Oxford, Clarendon Press.

Eysenck, H. J. (1951) 'Primary social attitudes', *British Journal of Sociology*, 2, 198–209.

Farnham, D. (1996) 'New Labour, the new unions and the new labour market', *Parliamentary Affairs*, 49(4), 584–98.

Farrar, M., Robinson, S., Valli, Y. and

Wetherly, P. (eds) (2012) *Islam in the West*, Basingstoke, Palgrave Macmillan.

Farrell, D. (2011) *Electoral Systems: A Comparative Introduction*, 2nd edn, Basingstoke, Palgrave Macmillan.

Faucher-King, F. (2005) *Changing Parties: An Anthropology of Political Party Conferences*, Basingstoke, Palgrave Macmillan.

Finer, S. E. (1956) 'The individual responsibility of ministers', *Public Administration*, 34, 377–96.

Finer, S. E. (ed.) (1975) *Adversarial Politics and Electoral Reform*, London, Anthony Wigram.

Fisher, J. (1997) 'Donations to political parties', *Parliamentary Affairs*, 50(2), 235–45.

Fisher, J. and Wlezien, C. (eds) (2011) *The UK General Election of 2010: Explaining the Outcome*, Abingdon, Routledge.

Flinders, M. (2001) 'Mechanisms of judicial accountability on British central government', *Parliamentary Affairs*, 54, 54–71.

Flinders, M. (2013) *Defending Politics: Why Democracy Matters in the 21st Century*, Oxford, Oxford University Press.

Flinders, M. and Smith, M. (eds) (1999) *Quangos, Accountability and Reform: The Politics of Quasi-Government*, London, Macmillan.

Foley, M. (2000) *The British Presidency*, Manchester, Manchester University Press.

Franks, O. (1957) *Report of the Committee on Administrative Tribunals and Inquiries*, Cmnd 218, London, HMSO.

Franks, O. (1972) *Departmental Committee on Section 2 of the Official Secrets Act 1911*, Cmnd 5104, London, HMSO.

Fraser, A. (2013) *Perilous Question: the Drama of the Great Reform Bill 1832*, London, Weidenfeld & Nicolson.

Friedman, M. and R. (1985) *The Tyranny of the Status Quo*, Harmondsworth, Penguin.

Fry, G. K. (1995) *Policy and Management in the British Civil Service*, Hemel Hempstead, Prentice Hall/Harvester Wheatsheaf.

Fryer, P. (1988) *Black People in the British Empire*, London, Pluto.

Fukuyama, F. (1992) *The End of History and the Last Man*, London, Hamish Hamilton.

Fulton, Lord (1968) *The Civil Service, Vol. 1: Report of the Committee*, Cmnd 3638, London, HMSO.

Galbraith, J. K. (1993) *The Culture of Contentment*, Harmondsworth, Penguin.

Gallup (1976) 'Voting behaviour in Britain, 1945–1974', in Rose, R. (ed.), *Studies in British Politics*, 3rd edn, Basingstoke, Macmillan.

Gamble, A. (1981) *An Introduction to Modern Social and Political Thought*, Basingstoke, Macmillan.

Gamble, A. (1988) *The Free Economy and the Strong State*, Basingstoke, Macmillan.

Gamble, A. (1990) *Britain in Decline*, 3rd edn, Basingstoke, Macmillan.

Gamble, A. (1994) *Britain in Decline*, 4th edn, Basingstoke, Palgrave Macmillan.

Gamble, A. (2000) *Politics and Fate*, Cambridge, Polity.

Gamble, A. (2003) *Between Europe and America: The Future of British Politics*, Basingstoke, Palgrave Macmillan.

Garner, R. and Kelly, R. (1998) *British Political Parties Today*, Manchester, Manchester University Press.

Gavin, N. T. (1996) 'Class voting and the Labour Party in Britain', *Electoral Studies*, 15(3), 311–26.

Geddes, A. and Tonge, J. (2010) *Britain Votes 2010*, Oxford, Oxford University Press.

George, S. (1991) *The Debt Boomerang*, London, Pluto.

George, S. (1994) *An Awkward Partner: Britain in the European Community*, 2nd edn, Oxford, Oxford University Press.

Gerrard, J. (2011) *The Clegg Coup: Britain's First Coalition Government Since Lloyd George*, London, Gibson Square.

Gibb, F. (1988) 'Justice by lottery?', *The Times* (25 Oct.).

Gibson, R., Nixon, G. and Ward, S. (2003) *Political Parties and the Internet*, Abingdon, Routledge.

Giddens, A. (1979) *The Class Structure of the Advanced Societies*, 2nd edn, London, Hutchinson.

Giddens, A. (1990) *The Consequences of Modernity*, Cambridge, Polity.

Giddens, A. (1998) *The Third Way: The Renewal of Social Democracy*, Cambridge, Polity.

Giddens, A. (2001) *Sociology*, 4th edn, Cambridge, Polity.

Giddens, A. and Sutton, P. W. (2010) *Sociology: Introductory Readings*, Cambridge, Polity.

Giddens, A. and Sutton, P. W. (2013) *Sociology*, 7th edn, Cambridge, Polity.

Giles, J. (2008) 'Born that way', *New Scientist* (2 Feb.).

Gladden, E. N. (1967) *Civil Services of the United Kingdom*, London, Frank Cass.

Glasgow University Media Group (1976) *Bad News*, (1980) *More Bad News*, (1982) *Really Bad News*, London, Routledge and Kegan Paul.

Goldthorpe, J. (1982) 'On the service class: its formation and future', in Giddens, A. and MacKenzie, G. (eds), *Social Class and the Division of Labour: Essays in Honour of Ilya Neustadt*, Cambridge, Cambridge University Press.

Goldthorpe, J. (1987) *Social Mobility and Class Structure in Modern Britain*, 2nd edn, Oxford, Clarendon Press.

Goodin, R. (1992) *Green Political Theory*, Cambridge, Polity.

Goodman, A., Johnson, P. and Webb, S. (1997) *Income Inequality in the UK*, Oxford, Oxford University Press.

Goodwin, B. (2007) *Using Political Ideas*, Chichester, Wiley.

Goodwin, M. (2011) *New British Fascism: Rise of the British National Party*, Abingdon, Routledge.

Gordon, P. (1984) 'Community policing: towards the local police state', *Critical Social Policy*, 4(1), 39–58.

Gordon, P. and Klug, F. (1986) *New Right, New Racism*, London, Searchlight Publications.

Governor of the Bank of England (2009) http://moneyfacts.co.uk/news/economy/boe-governor-size-of-bank-bail-out-breathtaking/ (accessed 18/03/2012).

Grahl, J. and Teague, P. (1990) *1992: The Big Market*, London, Lawrence and Wishart.

Gramsci, A. (1971) *Selections from Prison Notebooks*, London, Lawrence and Wishart.

Grant, M. (2009) *The UK Parliament*, Edinburgh, Edinburgh University Press.

Grant, W. (1987) *Business and Politics*, London, Macmillan.

Grant, W. (1993) *The Politics of Economic Policy*, Hemel Hempstead, Harvester Wheatsheaf.

Grant, W. (1995) *Pressure Groups, Politics and Democracy*, 2nd edn, Hemel Hempstead, Harvester Wheatsheaf.

Grant, W. (2000) *Pressure Groups and British Politics*, Basingstoke, Macmillan.

Grant, W. (2004) 'Pressure politics: the changing world of pressure groups', *Parliamentary Affairs*, 57(2), 408–19.

Grant, W. and MacNamara, A. (1995) 'When policy communities intersect: the case of agriculture and banking', *Political Studies*, 43(3), 509–15.

Grant, W. and Marsh, D. (1977) *The CBI*, London, Hodder and Stoughton.

Gray, J. (1995) *Enlightenment's Wake: Politics and Culture at the Close of the Modern Age*, London, Routledge.

Gray, J. (1998) *False Dawn: The Utopia of the Global Free Market*, London, Granta (revised edn 1999 entitled *False Dawn: The Delusions of Global Capitalism*).

Gray, J. (2003) *Al Qaeda and What it Means to be Modern*, London, Faber.

Greer, G. (1970) *The Female Eunuch*, London, MacGibbon & Kee.

Gregory, J. and Lees, S. (1999) *Policing Sexual Assault*, London, Routledge.

Grice, A. (1997) 'Don't mention the party', *Sunday Times* (23 March).

Griffith, J. A. G. (1981) *The Politics of the Judiciary*, London, Fontana.

Griffith, J. A. G. (1991) *The Politics of the Judiciary*, 4th edn, London, Fontana (5th edn 1994).

Griffiths, S. and Hickson, K. (eds) (2009) *British Party Politics and Ideology After New Labour*, Basingstoke, Palgrave Macmillan.

Groom, I. (1997) 'If at first you don't succeed', *Financial Times* (11 Sept.).

Hailsham, Lord (1978) *The Dilemma of Democracy*, London, Collins.

Hale, T. and Held, D. (2011) *Handbook of Transnational Governance: Institutions and Innovations*, Cambridge, Polity.

Halford, A. (1993) *No Way Up the Greasy Pole*, London, Constable.

Hall, K. (ed.) (2005) *The Oxford Companion to the Supreme Court of the United States*, Oxford, Oxford University Press.

Hall, W. and Weir, S. (1996) *The Untouchables: Power and Accountability in the Quango State*, Colchester, University of Essex, Democratic Audit and London, Charter88.

Hambleton, R. (1996) 'Reinventing local government: lessons from the USA', *Local Government Studies*, 22(1), 93–112.

Hampsher-Monk, I. (1987) *The Political Philosophy of Edmund Burke*, Harlow, Longman.

Hampton, W. (1970) *Democracy and Community*, London, Oxford University Press.

Hanley, D. (2007) *Beyond the Nation State: Parties in the Era of European Integration*, Basingstoke, Palgrave Macmillan.

Harden, I. and Lewis, N. (1986) *The Noble Lie*, London, Hutchinson.

Harrison, M. (1985) *TV News: Whose Bias?*, Hermitage, Policy Journals.

Harrison, M. (1987) 'Broadcasting', in Butler and Kavanagh (eds), pp. 139–62.

Harrison, M. (1992) 'Politics on the air', in Butler and Kavanagh (eds), pp. 155–79.

Harrop, M. and Scammell, M. (1992) 'The tabloid war', in Butler and Kavanagh (eds), pp. 180–210.

Harvey, D. (1989) *The Condition of Postmodernity*, Oxford, Blackwell.

Hattersley, R. (1996) *Who Goes Home? Scenes from Political Life*, London, Little, Brown.

Hay, C. (2007) *Why we Hate Politics*, Cambridge, Polity.

Hayek, F. von (1976) *The Road to Serfdom*, London, Routledge (first published 1944).

Hayward, J. (ed.) (2008) *Leaderless Europe*, Oxford, Oxford University Press.

Hazell, R. (ed.) (2006) *The English Question*, Manchester, Manchester University Press.

Hazell, R. (ed.) (2008) *Constitutional Futures Revisited: Britain's Constitution to 2020*, Basingstoke, Palgrave Macmillan.

Hazell, R., Worthy, B. and Glover, M. (2010) *The Impact of the Freedom of Information Act on Central Government in the UK: Does FOI Work?* Basingstoke, Palgrave Macmillan.

Hearn, W. E (1867) *The Government of England*, London, Longmans.

Heath, A. and Park, A. (1998) 'Thatcher's children?' in Jowell et al., pp. 1–22.

Heath, A., Jowell, R. and Curtice, J. (1987)

'Trendless fluctuation: a reply to Crewe', *Political Studies*, 35(2), 256–77.

Heclo, H. and Wildavsky, A. (1974) *The Private Government of Public Money*, London, Macmillan.

Held, D. (1987) *Models of Democracy*, Cambridge, Polity.

Held, D. (1989) 'The decline of the nation state' in Hall, S. and Jacques, M. (eds), *New Times*, London, Lawrence and Wishart, pp. 191–204.

Held, D. and Kaya, A. (eds) (2006) *Global Inequality: Patterns and Explanations*, Cambridge, Polity.

Held, D. and McGrew, A. (eds) (2007) *Globalization Theory: Approaches and Controversies*, Cambridge, Polity.

Held, D., McGrew, A., Goldblatt, D. and Perraton, J. (1999) *Global Transformations*, Cambridge, Polity.

Helm, T. and Jones, G. (2006) 'Conservatives' success story stalls', *Daily Telegraph* (27 Dec.).

Hennessy, P. (1985) 'The megaphone theory of "Yes Minister"', *Listener* (19 and 26 Dec.).

Hennessy, P. (1986) *Cabinet*, Oxford, Basil Blackwell.

Hennessy, P. (1992) *Never Again: Britain 1945–1951*, London, Jonathan Cape.

Hennessy, P. (1994) 'The throne behind the power', *The Economist* (24 Dec.).

Hennessy, P. (1995) *The Hidden Wiring: Unearthing the British Constitution*, London, Cassell.

Hennessy, P. (1998) 'The Blair style of government', *Government and Opposition*, 33(1) 3–20.

Hennessy, P. (2000) *The Prime Minister: The Office and its Holders Since 1945*, London, Allen Lane.

Hennessy, P. (2001) *Whitehall*, 2nd edn, London, Pimlico.

Hennessy, T. (1997) *A History of Northern Ireland 1920–1996*, Basingstoke, Macmillan.

Henney, A. (1984) *Inside Local Government: a Case for Radical Reform*, London, Sinclair Browne.

Heppell, T. and Seawright, D. (eds) (2012) *Cameron and the Conservatives: The Transition to Coalition Government*, Basingstoke, Palgrave Macmillan.

Hertz, N. (2002) *The Silent Takeover: Global Capitalism and the Death of Democracy*, London, Simon and Schuster.

Hewart, Lord (1929) *The New Despotism*, London, Ernest Benn.

Heywood, A. (2012) *Political Ideologies: An introduction*, 5th edn, Basingstoke, Palgrave Macmillan.

Hill, D. (1974) *Democratic Theory and Local Government*, London, George Allen & Unwin.

Hill, M. (2012) *The Public Policy Process*, 6th edn, Harlow, Pearson.

Hills, J. (1981) 'Britain', in Lovenduski, J. and Hills, J. (eds), *The Politics of the Second Electorate: Women and Public Participation*, London, Routledge and Kegan Paul, pp. 8–32.

Hilton, M., McKay, J., Crowson, N. and Mouhot, J. (2013) *The Politics of Expertise: How NGOs Shaped Modern Britain*, Oxford, Oxford University Press.

Himmelweit, H., Humphreys, P. and Jaeger, M. (1985) *How Voters Decide*, Milton Keynes, Open University Press.

Hirst, P. and Thompson, G. (1966) *Globalization in Question*, Cambridge, Polity.

Hitchens, C. (2007) *God is Not Great*, London, Atlantic Books.

Hitler, A. (1969) *Mein Kampf*, London, Hutchinson (first published 1925).

Hobbes, T. (1985) *Leviathan* (ed. C. B. Macpherson), Harmondsworth, Penguin (first published 1651).

Hobolt, S. B. (2009) *Europe in Question: Referendums on European Integration*, Oxford, Oxford University Press.

Hobsbawm, E. (1990) *Nations and Nationalism since 1780*, Cambridge, Cambridge University Press.

Hobsbawm, E. (1995) *Age of Extremes*, London, Abacus.

Hobson, D. (1999) *The National Wealth: Who Gets What in Britain*, London, HarperCollins.

Hoggart, R. (1958) *The Uses of Literacy*, Harmondsworth, Penguin.

Hogwood, B. W. (1997) 'The machinery of government, 1979–97', *Political Studies*, 45(4), 704–15.

Holden, A. (1997) 'Royal blues', *Red Pepper* (Oct.).

Hollingsworth, M. (1986) *The Press and Discontent: A Question of Censorship*, London, Pluto.

Hollingsworth, M. (1997) 'Get out of this one, Mr Spin', *Observer Review* (16 Feb.).

Holme, R. and Elliot, M. (eds) (1988) *1688–1988: Time for a New Constitution*, London, Macmillan.

Holt, R. (2001) *Second Amongst Equals: Chancellors of the Exchequer and the British Economy*, Exeter, Imprint Academic.

Home, Lord (1976) *The Way the Wind Blows*, London, Collins.

Home Office (1993) *Police Reform: A Police Service for the Twenty-first Century*, Cm 2281, London, HMSO.

Hood Phillips, O. (1987) *Constitutional and Administrative Law*, 7th edn, London, Sweet and Maxwell.

Hoskyns, J. (1984) 'Conservatism is not enough', *Political Quarterly*, 55(1), 3–16.

Hoskyns, J. (2000) *Just in Time: Inside the Thatcher Revolution*, London, Aurum Press.

House of Commons Communities and Local Government Committee (2009) *The Balance of Power: Central and Local Government*, HC 33-I, Session 2008/9, London, Stationery Office.

House of Commons Expenditure Committee (1977) *The Civil Service: Eleventh Report and Volumes of Evidence, 1976/7, Vols. I–III*, HC 535, London, HMSO.

House of Commons Home Affairs Committee (1993) *Accountability of the Security Service*, HC 270, Session 1992/3, London, HMSO.

House of Commons Public Administration Select Committee (2006) *Whitehall Confidential? The Publication of Political Memoirs*, HC 689-I, Session 2005/6, London, Stationery Office.

House of Commons Public Administration Select Committee (2008) *From Citizen's Charter to Public Service Guarantees: Entitlements to Public Services*, HC 411, Session 2007/8, London, Stationery Office.

House of Commons Select Committee on Defence (1982) *The Handling of Press and Public Information During the Falklands Conflict: First Report*, HC 17–1, London, HMSO.

House of Commons Treasury and Civil Service Committee (1994) *The Role of the Civil Service*, HC 27-I, Session 1993/4, London, HMSO.

House of Lords Select Committee on the Barnett Formula (2009) *The Barnett Formula: First Report of Session 2008–09, Report with Evidence*, London, Stationery Office.

Hume, D. (1882) 'That politics may be reduced to a science', reprinted in Dahl, R. and Neubauer, D. E. (1968) *Readings in Modern Political Analysis*, Englewood Cliffs, NJ, Prentice Hall.

Humphrys, J. (2001) 'Don't blame me, minister, if the voters are losing faith', *Sunday Times* (24 Dec.).

Hunter, F. (1953) *Community Power Structure*, Chapel Hill, NC, University of North Carolina Press.

Huntington, S. (1996) *The Clash of Civilizations and the Remaking of World Order*, New York, Simon and Schuster.

Hutton, W. (1986) *The Revolution that Never Was*, London, Longman.

Hutton, W. (1996) *The State We're In*, London, Vintage.

Hutton, W. (1998) 'What is Power?', *Observer* (1 Nov.).

Hutton, W. (2002) *The World We're In*, London, Little Brown.

Hutton, W. (2011) *Them and Us: Changing Britain – Why we Need a Fair Society*, London, Little Brown.

Independent Police Complaints Commission (2010) *Deaths in or Following Police Custody: An Examination of the Cases 1998/99–2008/09*, Manchester, IPCC.

Independent Police Complaints Commission (2012) *Police Complaints: Statistics for England and Wales, 2012*, London, IPCC.

Ingham, B. (1991) *Kill the Messenger*, London, Fontana.

Ipsos Mori (2006) *Ethnic Minority Voters and Non-Voters at the 2005 British General Election*, London, Ipsos Mori.

Jackson, N. and Lilleker, D. (2009) 'MPs and E-representation: Me MySpace and I'. *British Politics*, 4(2), 236–64.

Jackson, R. M. (1960) *The Machinery of Justice in England*, Cambridge, Cambridge University Press.

Jacobs, M. (1996) *The Politics of the Real World*, London, Earthscan.

Jacques, M. (2009) *When China Rules the World*, London, Allen Lane.

Jaggar, A. (1983) *Feminist Politics and Human Nature*, Brighton, Harvester.

Jeffrey, B. (2009) Speech at Civil Service Live conference, http://network.civilservicelive.com/pg/pages/view/263498/.

Jeffreys, S. (2011) *Man's Dominion: The Rise of Religion and the Eclipse of Women's Rights*, Abingdon, Routledge.

Jenkins, S. (2006) *Thatcher and Sons*, London, Allen Lane.

Jennings, I. (1959) *Cabinet Government*, 3rd edn, Cambridge, Cambridge University Press.

Jennings, I. (1966) *The British Constitution*, 5th edn, Cambridge, Cambridge University Press.

John, P. (1994a) 'Central–local government relations in the 1980s and 1990s: towards a policy learning approach', *Local Government Studies*, 20(3), 412–36.

John, P. (1994b) *The Europeanisation of British Local Government: New Management Strategies*, York, Joseph Rowntree Foundation.

John, P. (2012) *Analysing Public Policy*, 2nd edn, Abingdon, Routledge.

Johnson, R. W. (1985) *The Politics of Recession*, London, Macmillan.

Johnston, R. J. and Pattie, C. J. (1996) 'The strength of party identification among the British electorate', *Electoral Studies*, 15(3), 295–309.

Johnston, R. J. and Pattie, C. J. (1997) 'Towards an understanding of turnout in British general elections', *Parliamentary Affairs*, 50(2), 280–91.

Johnston, R. J., Pattie, C. J. and Allsopp, J. G. (1988) *A Nation Dividing? The Electoral Map of Great Britain 1979–87*, Harlow, Longman.

Johnston, R. J., Pattie, C. J., Rossiter, D., Dorling, D., Tunstall, H. and McAllister, I. (1998) 'Anatomy of a Labour landslide: the constituency system and the 1997 general election', *Parliamentary Affairs*, 50(2), 131–48.

Johnston, R., Pattie, C. J., Dorling, D. and Rossiter, D. (2001) *From Votes to Seats: The Operation of the British Electoral System since 1945*, Manchester, Manchester University Press.

Jones, B. (1997) 'Wales: a developing political economy', in Keating and Loughlin (eds).

Jones, G. W. (1983) 'Prime ministers' departments really do create problems: a rejoinder to Patrick Weller', *Public Administration*, 61(1), 79–84.

Jones, T. (2011) *The Revival of British Liberalism: From Grimond to Clegg*, Basingstoke, Palgrave Macmillan.

Jordan, G. (1991) *The Commercial Lobbyists: Politics for Profit in Britain*, Aberdeen, Aberdeen University Press.

Joseph Rowntree Reform Trust (2010) *State of the Nation Survey 2010*, York, Joseph Rowntree Reform Trust.

Jowell, J. and Oliver, D. (eds) (2011) *The Changing Constitution*, 7th edn, Oxford, Oxford University Press.

Jowell, R., Curtice, J., Park, A., Brook, L., Thompson, K. and Bryan, C. (1998) *British Social Attitudes: The 14th Report. The End of Conservative Values?* Aldershot, Ashgate.

Kampfner, J. (2003) *Blair's Wars*, New York, Free Press.

Kanazawa, S. (1998) 'A possible solution to the paradox of voter turnout', *Journal of Politics*, 60(4), 974–95.

Kavanagh, D. (1980) 'Political culture in Britain: the decline of the civic culture', in Almond and Verba (eds).

Kavanagh, D. (1995) *Election Campaigning: The New Marketing of Politics*, Oxford, Blackwell.

Kavanagh, D. (1996) 'British party conferences and the political rhetoric of the 1990s', *Government and Opposition*, 31(1), 27–44.

Kavanagh, D. (1997) 'The Labour campaign', *Parliamentary Affairs*, 50(4), 533–41.

Kavanagh, D. and Butler, D. (2005) *The British General Election of 2005*, Basingstoke, Palgrave Macmillan.

Kavanagh, D. and Cowley, P. (eds) (2010) *The British General Election of 2010*, Basingstoke, Palgrave Macmillan.

Kavanagh, D. and Morris, P. (1994) *Consensus Politics: from Attlee to Major*, Chichester, Wiley.

Kavanagh, D. and Seldon, A. (2000) *The Powers Behind the Prime Minister: The Hidden Influence of Number Ten*, London, HarperCollins.

Kearney, H. (1990) *The British Isles: A History of Four Nations*, Cambridge, Cambridge University Press.

Keating, M. and Loughlin, J. (eds) (1997) *The Political Economy of Regionalism*, London, Frank Cass.

Keegan, W. (1984) *Mrs Thatcher's Economic Experiment*, Harmondsworth, Penguin.

Keen, P. and Travers, T. (1994) *Implementing the Council Tax*, York, Joseph Rowntree Foundation.

Kellner, P. and Crowther-Hunt, Lord (1980) *The Civil Servants: An Enquiry into Britain's Ruling Class*, London, Macdonald.

Kennedy, H. (1992) *Eve was Framed*, London, Chatto and Windus.

Kenny, M. and Smith, M. J. (1997) '(Mis)understanding Blair', *Political Quarterly*, 68(3) 220–30.

Kettell, S. (2006) *Dirty Politics: New Labour, British Democracy and the Invasion of Iraq*, London, Zed Books.

Kettle, M. (1980) 'The politics of policing and the policing of politics', in Hain et al. (eds), pp. 9–64.

Keynes, J. M. (1936) *General Theory of Employment, Interest and Money*, London, Macmillan.

King, A. (2001) *Does the United Kingdom Still Have a Constitution?* London, Sweet and Maxwell.

King, D. (1993) 'Government beyond Whitehall', in Dunleavy et al. (eds), pp. 194–218.

Kingdom, J. (1992) *No Such Thing as Society*, Buckingham, Open University Press.

Kingdom, J. (1996) 'Citizen or state consumer: a fistful of charters', in Chandler, J. A. (ed.), *The Citizen's Charter*, Aldershot, Dartmouth, pp. 7–23.

Kingdom, J. (1999) 'Centralisation and fragmentation: John Major and the reform of local government', in Dorey, P. (ed.), *The Major Premiership*, Basingstoke, Macmillan, pp. 45–67.

Kirchheimer, O. (1966) 'The transformation of West European Party Systems', in LaPalombara, J. and Weiner, M. (eds), *Political Parties and Political Development*, Princeton, NJ, Princeton University Press, pp. 177–200.

Kirkham, R. (2007) *The Parliamentary Ombudsman: Withstanding the Test of Time*, London, The Stationery Office.

Klare, M. T. (1992) 'US military policy in the post-cold-war era', in Miliband, R. and Panitch, L. (eds), *New World Order: Socialist Register 1992*, London, Merlin, pp. 131–42.

Klug, F. (1997) 'Can human rights fill Britain's morality gap?' *Political Quarterly*, 68(2), 143–52.

Klug, F. (2000) *Values for a Godless Age: The Story of the United Kingdom's New Bill of Rights*, Harmondsworth, Penguin.

Klug, F., Starmer, K. and Weir, S. (1996) 'Civil liberties and the parliamentary watchdog: the passage of the Criminal Justice and Public Order Act 1994', *Parliamentary Affairs*, 49(4), 536–49.

Knightley, P. (1986) *The Second Oldest Profession: The Spy as Bureaucrat, Patriot, Fantasist and Whore*, London, André Deutsch.

Krøløkke, C. and Sørensen, A. S. (2006). 'Three waves of feminism: from suffragettes to girls', in Krøløkke, C. and Sørensen, A. S., *Gender Communication Theories and Analyses*, Thousand Oaks, CA, Sage, pp. 1–24.

Kuhn, R. (2007) *Politics and the Media in Britain*, Basingstoke, Palgrave Macmillan.

Lacey, R. (1997) 'Ministry of Agriculture: Ministry of Truth', *Political Quarterly*, 68(3), 245–54.

Lasswell, H. D. (1936) *Politics: Who Gets What, When, How?*, New York, McGraw Hill (reprinted 1958).

Lasswell, H. D. and Kaplan, A. (1950) *Power and Society*, New Haven, CT, Yale University Press.

Lawrence, D. H. (1950) 'Nottingham and the mining country', in *Selected Essays*, Harmondsworth, Penguin.

Lawson, N. (2006) 'The sweet irony of Tony Blair brought down by the excesses of Thatcherism', *Independent* (18 April).

Lawson, N. (2008) *An Appeal to Reason: A Cool Look at Global Warming*, London, Duckworth.

Lea, J. et al. (1986) 'The fear and loathing at Broadwater Farm', *Guardian* (4 June).

Leach, R. (1998) 'Local government reorganisation RIP?' *Political Quarterly*, 69(1), 31–40.

Leach, R. (2009) *Political Ideology in Britain*, 2nd edn, Basingstoke, Palgrave Macmillan.

Leach, S. (2006) *The Changing Role of Local Politics in Britain*, Bristol, Policy Press.

Leach, S. and Stewart, J. (1992) *The Politics of Hung Authorities*, Basingstoke, Macmillan.

Lee, S. (1988) *Judging Judges*, London, Faber and Faber.

Lee, S. and Beech, M. (eds) (2011) *The Cameron–Clegg Government: Coalition Politics in an Age of Austerity*, Basingstoke, Palgrave Macmillan.

Leftwich, A. (1984) *What is Politics? The Activity and its Study*, Cambridge, Polity.

Lehmbruch, G. and Schmitter, P. (eds) (1982) *Patterns of Corporatist Policy-Making*, London, Sage.

Leishman, F., Loveday, B. and Savage, S. (2000) *Core Issues in Policing*, 2nd edn, Harlow, Longman.

Lent, A. and Sowemimo, M. (1996) 'Remaking the opposition?', in Ludlam and Smith (eds), pp. 121–42.

Lijphart, A. (1994) *Electoral Systems and Party Systems: A Study of Twenty-Seven Democracies 1945–1990*, Oxford, Oxford University Press.

Lijphart, A. (1996) 'The Framework proposal for Northern Ireland and the theory of power sharing', *Government and Opposition*, 31(3), 267–74.

Lindblom, C. E. (1959) 'The science of muddling through', *Public Administration Review*, 19, 79–88.

Lively, J. (1978) 'Pluralism and consensus', in Birnbaum, P., Lively, J. and Parry, G. (eds), *Democracy, Consensus and Social Contract*, London, Sage.

Lockwood, D. (1966) 'Sources of variation in working class images of society', *Sociological Review*, 14, 249–67.

Lodge, J. (ed.) (1993) *The European Community and the Challenge of the Future*, London, Pinter.

Lord Chancellor's Department (2001a) *The House of Lords: Completing the Reform*, Cm 5291, London, Stationery Office.

Lord Chancellor's Department (2001b) *Judicial Appointments in England and Wales: The Appointment of Lawyers to the Professional Judiciary*, London, Stationery Office.

Loughlin, M. (2000) *Sword and Scales: An Examination of the Relationship Between Law and Politics*, Oxford, Hart.

Louis, W. R. and Bull, H. (eds) (1986) *The Special Relationship: Anglo-American Relations Since 1945*, Oxford, Oxford University Press.

Loveday, B. (1994) 'The competing role of central and local agencies in crime prevention strategies', *Local Government Studies*, 20(3), 361–73.

Loveday, B. (1996) 'Business as usual? The new police authorities and the Police and Magistrates' Courts Act', *Local Government Studies*, 22(2), 22–39.

Lovelock, J. E. (1979) *Gaia: A New Look At Life on Earth*, Oxford, Oxford University Press.

Lovenduski, J. (1996) 'Sex, gender and British politics', *Parliamentary Affairs*, 49(1) 1–16.

Lovenduski, J. (1997) 'Gender politics: a breakthrough for women', *Parliamentary Affairs*, 50(4), 708–19.

Lovenduski, J. and Norris, P. (1994) 'Labour and the unions: after the Brighton conference', *Government and Opposition*, 29(3), 201–17.

Lovenduski, J. and Norris, P. (eds) (1996) *Women in Politics*, Oxford, Oxford University Press.

Lovenduski, J. and Randall, V. (1993) *Contemporary Feminist Politics*, Oxford, Oxford University Press.

Lowe, P. and Goyder, J. (eds) (1983) *Environmental Groups in Politics*, London, Allen and Unwin.

Ludlam, S. and Smith, M. (eds) (1996) *Contemporary British Conservatism*, Basingstoke, Macmillan.

Ludlam, S. and Smith. M. (eds) (2001) *New Labour in Government*, Basingstoke, Palgrave Macmillan.

Ludlam, S. and Smith. M. (eds) (2003)

Governing as New Labour, Basingstoke, Palgrave Macmillan.

MacAskill, E. (2005) 'George Bush: "God told me to end the tyranny in Iraq"', *Guardian* (7 Oct.).

MacDonald, M. (1986) *Children of Wrath: Political Violence in Northern Ireland*, Cambridge, Polity.

MacGillivray, A. (2006) *A Brief History of Globalization*, London, Constable and Robinson.

MacIver, D. (ed.) (1996) *The Liberal Democrats*, Hemel Hempstead, Prentice Hall Harvester.

Mackenzie, W. J. M. (1969) *Politics and Social Science*, Harmondsworth, Penguin.

Maddock, S. (1993) 'Barriers to women are barriers to local government', *Local Government Studies*, 19(3), 341–50.

Magee, B. (1973) *Popper*, London, Fontana/Collins.

Magnus, P. (1963) *Gladstone*, London, Murray.

Mair, L. (1970) *Primitive Government*, Harmondsworth, Penguin.

Mallalieu, J. P. W. (1941) *Passed to You, Please*, London, Victor Gollancz.

Malony, W., Smith, G. and Stoker, G. (2000) 'Social capital and urban governance', *Political Studies*, 48(4), 802–20.

Mandelson, P. and Liddle, R. (1996) *The Blair Phenomenon: Can New Labour Deliver?* London, Faber.

Manent, P. (2006) *A World Without Politics? A Defence of the Nation-State*, Princeton NJ, Princeton University Press.

Mansfield, M. (1997) 'Justice for all', *Red Pepper* (April).

Marquand, D. (1988) *The Unprincipled Society*, London, Fontana.

Marr, A. (1992) *The Battle for Scotland*, Harmondsworth, Penguin.

Marsh, D. (1992) *The New Politics of British Trade Unionism*, Basingstoke, Macmillan.

Marsh, D. and Stoker, G. (2010) *Theory and Methods of Political Science*, 3rd edn, Basingstoke, Palgrave Macmillan.

Marwick, A. (1982) *British Society Since 1945*, Harmondsworth, Penguin.

Maud, Sir J. (chairman) (1967) *Management of Local Government*, London, HMSO.

Mazey, S. and Richardson, J. (1993) *Lobbying in the European Community*, Oxford, Oxford University Press.

McAlpine, A. (1997) *Once a Jolly Bagman*, London, Weidenfeld and Nicholson.

McCann, D. (2010) *The Political Economy of the European Union*, Cambridge, Polity.

McCormack, M. (ed.) (2007) *Public Men: Masculinity and Politics in Modern Britain*, Basingstoke, Palgrave Macmillan.

McEvoy, J. (2008) *The Politics of Northern Ireland*, Edinburgh, Edinburgh University Press.

McGarry, J. and O'Leary, B (1997) *Explaining Northern Ireland: Broken Images*, Oxford, Blackwell.

McGuinness, F. and Clements, R. (2012) *Membership of UK Political Parties*, London, House of Commons Library Standard Note SN/SG 5125.

McKenzie, R. (1967) *British Political Parties*, 2nd rev. edn, London, Heinemann.

McKie, D. (1994) 'Uncivil servants sign off', *Guardian* (23 April).

McLean, I. (2012) *What's Wrong with the British Constitution?*, 2nd edn, Oxford, Oxford University Press.

McNair, B. (2000) *Journalism and Democracy*, London, Routledge.

Meadows, D. H., Meadows, D. L., Randers, J. and Behrens, W. III (1972) *The Limits to Growth*, London, Earth Island.

Mellows-Facer, A., Cracknell, R. and Lightbown, S. (2009) *European Parliament Elections 2009*, London, House of Commons Library Research Paper 09/53.

Meredith, S. (2008) *Labours Old and New:*

The Parliamentary Right of the British Labour Party 1970–79 and the Roots of New Labour, Manchester, Manchester University Press.

Michels, R. (1962) *Political Parties*, New York, Collier (first published 1911).

Middlemas, K. (1979) *Politics in Industrial Society*, London, André Deutsch.

Miliband, R. (1961) *Parliamentary Socialism*, London, Merlin.

Miliband, R. (1984) *Capitalist Democracy in Britain*, Oxford, Oxford University Press.

Miller, W. (1991) *Media and Voters*, Oxford, Clarendon Press.

Mills, C. W. (1959) *The Power Elite*, New York, Oxford University Press.

Mills, H., Silvestri, A. and Grimshaw, R. (2010a) *Police Expenditure, 1999–2009*, London, Centre for Crime and Justice Studies.

Mills, H., Silvestri, A. and Grimshaw, R. (2010b) *Prison and Probation Expenditure, 1999–2009*, London, Centre for Crime and Justice Studies.

Milne, A. (1988) *DG: Memoirs of a British Broadcaster*, London, Hodder and Stoughton.

Milward, A. S. (1979) 'Fascism and the economy', in Laqueur, W. (ed.), *Fascism: A Reader's Guide*, Harmondsworth, Pelican, pp. 409–53.

Ministry of Justice (2010) *Statistics on Women and the Criminal Justice System*, London, Ministry of Justice.

Ministry of Justice (2011a) *Judicial and Court Statistics 2010*, London, Ministry of Justice.

Ministry of Justice (2011b) *Statistics on Race and the Criminal Justice System 2010*, London, Ministry of Justice.

Ministry of Justice (2011c) *Annual Tribunal Statistics 2010–2011*, London, Ministry of Justice.

Minkin, L. (1980) *The Labour Party Conference*, Manchester, Manchester University Press.

Mitchell, A. (1994) 'Backbench influence: a personal view', *Parliamentary Affairs*, 47(4), 687–704.

Mitchell, J. (2012) *Devolution in the United Kingdom*, Manchester, Manchester University Press.

Monbiot, G. (2002) Global democracy: a parliament for the planet. *New Internationalist*, no. 342 (Jan./Feb.), 12–14.

Moore, C. (2013) *Margaret Thatcher; the Authorised Biography, Vol. 1: Not for Turning*, London, Allen Lane.

Moran, M. (1999) 'Estates, classes and interests', in Holliday, I., Gamble, A., and Parry, G. (eds), *Fundamental of British Politics*, Basingstoke, Macmillan.

Morgan, J. (1987) *Conflict and Order: The Police and Labour Disputes in England and Wales 1900–1939*, Oxford, Clarendon Press.

Morgan, R. (2000) *Variable Geometry UK*, Cardiff, Institute of Welsh Affairs, Discussion Paper 13.

Morley, J. (1903) *Life of William Ewart Gladstone, Vol. I*, London, Macmillan.

Mugham, A. (2002) *Media and the Presidentialisation of Parliamentary Elections*, Basingstoke, Palgrave.

Mullard, M. (1993) *The Politics of Public Expenditure*, London, Routledge.

Mullard, M. (1997) 'The politics of public expenditure control: a problem of politics or language games', *Political Quarterly*, 68(3), 266–75.

Muller, W. D. (1977) *The Kept Men*, Hassocks, Harvester.

Murray, C. (1990) *The Emerging British Underclass*, London, Institute of Economic Affairs.

Murray, G. and Scott, J. (eds) (2012) *Financial Elites and Transnational Business: Who Rules the World?*, Cheltenham, Edward Elgar.

Naurin, D. and Wallace, H. (2008) *Unveiling the Council of the European Union: Games Governments Play in Brussels*, Basingstoke, Palgrave Macmillan.

Newburn, T. (2003) *Crime and Criminal Justice Policy*, 2nd edn, Harlow, Pearson.

Newton, K. (1976) *Second City Politics*, Oxford, Clarendon Press.

Newton, K. (1986) 'Mass media', in Drucker, H. et al. (eds) *Developments in British Politics 2*, London, Macmillan, pp. 313–28.

Newton, K. (1993) 'Economic voting in the 1992 general election', in Denver et al. (eds), pp. 158–76.

Newton, K. (1998) 'Politics and the news media: mobilisation or political malaise?' in Jowell et al., pp. 151–68.

Nicholson, E. (1996) *Secret Society*, London, Indigo.

Nicholson, M. (2001) 'Labour MSPs forced to cave in on free care', *Financial Times* (26 Jan.).

Niskanen, W. A. (1973) *Bureaucracy: Servant or Master?*, London, Institute of Economic Affairs.

Nolan, Lord (chair) (1995) *First Report of the Committee on Standards in Public Life*, Cm 2850-I, London, HMSO.

Norris, P. (1993) 'The gender–generation gap', in Denver et al. (eds), pp. 129–42.

Norris, P. (1996a) *Electoral Change Since 1945*, Oxford, Blackwell.

Norris, P. (1996b) 'The Nolan Committee: financial interests and constituency service', *Government and Opposition*, 31(4), 441–8.

Norris, P. (1996c) 'Women politicians: transforming Westminster', *Parliamentary Affairs*, 49(1), 89–102.

Norris, P. (ed.) (2001) *Britain Votes 2001*, Oxford, Oxford University Press.

Norris, P. and Lovenduski, J. (1994) *Political Recruitment: Gender, Race and Class in the British Parliament*, Cambridge, Cambridge University Press.

Norris, P. and Wlezien, C. (2005) *Britain Votes 2005*, Oxford, Oxford University Press.

Norton, P. (1978) *Conservative Dissidents: Dissent Within the Conservative Party 1970–74*, London, Temple Smith.

Norton, P. (1993a) 'The Conservative Party from Thatcher to Major', in King et al., pp. 29–69.

Norton, P. (1993b) *Does Parliament Matter?* Hemel Hempstead, Harvester Wheatsheaf.

Norton, P. (1994) 'The growth of the constituency role of the MP', *Parliamentary Affairs*, 47(4), 705–20.

Norton, P. (ed.) (1996) *The Conservative Party*, Hemel Hempstead, Prentice Hall Harvester.

Norton, P. (ed.) (1999) *Parliaments and Pressure Groups in Western Europe*, London, Routledge.

Norton, P. (2003) 'Governing alone', *Parliamentary Affairs*, 56, 543–59.

Norton, P. (2005) *Parliament in British Politics*, Basingstoke, Palgrave Macmillan.

Norton, P. and Aughey, A. (1981) *Conservatives and Conservatism*, London, Temple Smith.

Nozick, R. (1974) *Anarchy, State and Utopia*, New York, Basic Books.

Nugent, N. (2010) *The Government and Politics of the European Union*, Basingstoke, Palgrave Macmillan.

Oakeshott, M. (1962) *Rationalism in Politics and Other Essays*, London, Methuen.

O'Connor, J. (1973) *The Fiscal Crisis of the State*, New York, St Martin's Press.

O'Donnell, G. (ed.) (2010) *The Cabinet Manual: A Guide to Laws, Conventions and Rules on the Operation of Government*, London, Cabinet Office.

O'Leary, B. (1989) 'The limits to coercive consociationalism in Northern Ireland', *Political Studies*, 37, 562–88.

Olson, M. (1968) *The Logic of Collective Action*, New York, Schocken.

Olson, M. (1982) *The Rise and Decline of Nations*, New Haven, CT, Yale University Press.

O'Reilly, J. and Robbins, T. (2002) 'Bandit country UK: why criminals win', *Observer* (10 March).

Ormston, R. and Curtice, J. (2010), 'Resentment or contentment? Attitudes towards the union ten years on', in Park, A., Curtice, J., Clery, E. and Bryson, C. (eds) *British Social Attitudes: the 27th Report*, London, Sage.

Osborne, D. and Gaebler, T. (1992) *Reinventing Government*, Reading, MA, Addison-Wesley.

Ostrogorski, M. (1902) *Democracy and the Organisation of Political Parties*, London, Macmillan.

O'Toole, B. (2006) 'Freedom with or freedom of information: the role of "special advisers in British central government"', in Chapman and Hunt (eds), pp. 69–82.

Owen, D. (2008) *In Sickness and in Power*, London, Methuen.

Paley, W. (1842) *Works*, London, Bohn (first published 1785).

Parkin, S. (1988) 'Green strategy', in F. Dodds (ed.), *Into the 21st Century: An Agenda for Political Realignment*, Basingstoke, Green Print.

Parris, M. (1996) *Scorn*, Harmondsworth, Penguin.

Parsons, W. (1996) *Public Policy: An Introduction to the Theory and Practice of Policy Analysis*, Cheltenham, Edward Elgar.

Pateman, C. (1983) 'Feminism and democracy', in Duncan, G. (ed.), *Democratic Theory and Practice*, Cambridge, Cambridge University Press.

Pattie, C. J. and Johnston, R. J. (1996) 'Paying their way: local associations, the constituency quota scheme and Conservative Party finance', *Political Studies*, 44, 921–35.

Pattie, C. J., Johnston, R. and Fieldhouse, E. (1993) '*Plus ça change*? The changing electoral geography of Britain, 1979–1992', in Denver et al. (eds), pp. 85–99.

Pattie, C. J., Fieldhouse, E. and Johnston, R. J. (1994) 'The price of conscience', *British Journal of Political Science*, 24, 359–80.

Paul, K. (1997) *Whitewashing Britain: Race and Citizenship in the Postwar Era*, Ithaca, NY and London, Cornell University Press.

Paxman, J. (1991) *Friends in High Places*, London, Penguin.

Peele, G. (1991) *British Party Politics: Competing for Power in the 1990s*, Hemel Hempstead, Philip Allan.

Pelling, H. and Reid, A. J. (2005) *A Short History of the Labour Party*, 12th edn, Basingstoke, Macmillan.

Perkins, A. (2001) 'Blair: first among equals?' *Guardian* (6 Oct.).

Pienaar, J. (1988) 'A cabinet exile reflects on the cravings of power', *Independent* (15 Sept.).

Pierre, J. and Stoker, G. (2000) 'Towards multi-level governance', in Dunleavy et. al. (eds), pp. 29–46.

Pilger, J. (1998) *Hidden Agendas*, London, Vintage.

Pilkington, C. (2002) *Devolution in Britain Today*, Manchester, Manchester University Press.

Pinto-Duschinsky, M. (1997) 'Tory troops are in worse state than feared', *The Times* (6 June).

Plowden, W. (1994) *Ministers and Mandarins*, London, Institute for Public Policy Research.

Ponting, C. (1986) *Whitehall: Tragedy and Farce*, London, Hamish Hamilton.

Popper, K. R. (1962) *The Open Society and its Enemies: Vol. 2: Hegel and Marx*, London, Routledge & Kegan Paul.

Poulantzas, N. (1973) *Political Power and Social Classes*, London, New Left Books.

Preston, P. (1997) 'Party free or parti pris?' *Observer* (2 March).

Preston, P. W. (2011) *England after the Great Recession*, Basingstoke, Palgrave Macmillan.

Putnam, R. (2000) *Bowling Alone*, New York, Simon & Schuster.

Quinn, T. (2012) *Electing and Ejecting Party Leaders in Britain*, Basingstoke, Palgrave Macmillan.

Raab, C. D. (1994) 'Open government: policy information and information policy', *Political Quarterly*, 65(3), 340–7.

Rallings, C. and Thrasher, M. (1994) *Explaining Electoral Turnout: a Secondary Analysis of Local Election Statistics*, London, HMSO.

Ramsay, A. (2008) *Girl in Blue: How One Woman Survived Fourteen Years in the Police Force*, Basingstoke, Palgrave Macmillan.

Randall, V. (1982) *Women and Politics*, Basingstoke, Macmillan.

Rawlings, H. F. (1986) 'Judicial review and the "control of government"', *Public Administration*, 64(2), 142–3.

Rawls, J. (1999) *A Theory of Justice*, Cambridge, MA, Harvard University Press (first published 1971).

Rawnsley, A. (2001) 'Good, bad and ugly', *Observer* (11 March).

Redlich, J. and Hirst, F. W. (1970) *Local Government in England, Vol. II* (ed. Keith-Lucas, B.), London, Macmillan (first published 1903).

Reiner, R. (1982) 'Who are the police?', *Political Quarterly*, 53(2), 469–71.

Reiner, R. (ed.) (1996) *Policing*, Aldershot, Dartmouth.

Reiner, R. (2010) *The Politics of the Police*, 4th edn, Oxford, Oxford University Press.

Reiner, R. (2011) *Policing, Popular Culture and Political Economy*, Farnham, Ashgate.

Rhodes, R. A. W. (1981) *Control and Power in Central–Local Government Relations*, Farnborough, Gower.

Rhodes, R. A. W. (1988) *Beyond Westminster and Whitehall: The Sub-central Government of Britain*, London, George Allen & Unwin.

Rhodes, R. A. W. (1994) 'The hollowing out of the state: the changing nature of the public service in Britain', *Political Quarterly*, 65(2), 138–51.

Rhodes, R. A. W. (ed.) (2000) *Transforming British Government, Volume 1: Changing Institutions, Volume 2: Changing Roles and Relationships*, Basingstoke, Macmillan.

Rhodes, R. A. W. and Dunleavy, P. (1995) *Prime Minister, Cabinet and Core Executive*, Basingstoke, Macmillan.

Rhodes, R. A. W. and Marsh, D. (1992) *Policy Networks in British Government*, Oxford, Oxford University Press.

Rhodes, R. A. W. and Weller, P. (eds) (2001) *The Changing World of Top Officials: Mandarins or Valets*, Buckingham, Open University Press.

Richards, D. (1996) 'Recruitment to the highest grades in the civil service: drawing the curtains open', *Public Administration*, 74(4), 657–77.

Richards, P. G. (1970) *Parliament and Conscience*, London, George Allen & Unwin.

Richardson, J. J. and Jordan, A. G. (1979) *Government under Pressure*, Oxford, Martin Robertson.

Riddell, P. (1996) *Honest Opportunism: The Rise of the Career Politician*, London, Hamish Hamilton.

Riddell, P. (2000) *Parliament under Blair*, London, Politico's.

Riddell, P. (2001) 'New look behind the revolving doors of power', *The Times* (13 June).

Ridley, F. F. and Wilson, D. (1995) *The Quango Debate*, Oxford, Oxford University Press.

Ridley, N. (1988) *The Local Right*, London, Centre for Policy Studies.

Rimington, S. (2001) *Open Secret*, London, Hutchinson.

Robbins, T. and Clark, J. (2001) 'Police buy top assault rifle to tame gunmen', *Sunday Times* (17 June).

Robertson, G. (1997) 'Justice in all fairness', *Guardian* (30 April).

Robson, W. A. (1966) *Local Government in Crisis*, London, George Allen & Unwin.

Rogers, A. (1997) *Secrecy and Power in the British State*, London, Pluto.

Rogers, R. and Walters, R. (2006) *How Parliament Works*, 6th edn, Harlow, Pearson Education.

Rollo, J. (1980) 'The Special Patrol Group', in Hain (ed.), pp. 153–208.

Rose, R. (1964) 'Parties, factions and tendencies in British politics', *Political Studies*, 12(1), 33–46.

Rose, R. (2001) *The Prime Minister in a Shrinking World*, Cambridge, Polity.

Rose, R. and McAllister, I. (1986) *Voters Begin to Choose: From Closed Class to Open Elections*, Beverly Hills, CA, Sage.

Rosenberg, J. (1997) *Trial of Strength*, London, Richard Cohen.

Rousseau, J. J. (1913) *The Social Contract*, London, Dent (first published 1762).

Rowan, D. (1998) 'Meet the new world government', *Guardian* (22 Feb.).

Rowe, M. (2004) *Policing, Race and Racism*, Abingdon, Willan.

Royal Commission on the Distribution of Income and Wealth (1976) *Report No. 3: Higher Incomes from Employment*, London, HMSO.

Runciman, W. G. (2004) *Hutton and Butler: Lifting the Lid on the Workings of Power*, Oxford University Press/British Academy.

Rush, M. (2001) *The Role of the Member of Parliament since 1868*, Oxford, Oxford University Press.

Rush, M. (2005) *Parliament Today*, Manchester, Manchester University Press.

Russell, M. (2001) 'What are second chambers for?' *Parliamentary Affairs*, 54, 442–58.

Ryan, A. (2013) *On Politics: A History of Political Thought from Herodotus to the Present*, London, Allen Lane.

Sabine, G. H. (1963) *A History of Political Theory*, 3rd edn, London, Harrap.

Saggar, S. (1992) *Race and Politics in Britain*, Hemel Hempstead, Harvester Wheatsheaf.

Saggar, S. (2001) 'The race card, again', *Parliamentary Affairs*, 54, 759–74.

Sampson, A. (1992) *The Essential Anatomy of Britain: Democracy in Crisis*, London, Hodder and Stoughton.

Sampson, A. (2004) *Who Runs this Place?* London, John Murray.

Sanders, A. and Young, R. (1995) 'The PACE regime for suspects detained by the police', *Political Quarterly*, 66(2), 126–40.

Sanders, D., Clarke, H., Stewart, M. and Whiteley, P. (2011) 'Simulating the effects of the Alternative Vote in the 2010 UK general election', *Parliamentary Affairs*, 64(1), 5–23.

Saunders, P. (1980) *Urban Politics: A Sociological Interpretation*, Harmondsworth, Penguin.

Saunders, P. (1984) 'Rethinking local politics', in Boddy, M. and Fudge, C. (eds), *Local Socialism: The Way Ahead*, London, Macmillan, pp. 22–48.

Saunders, P. (1995) 'Privatization, share ownership and voting', *British Journal of Political Science*, 25(1), 131–7.

Savage, M. et al. (2013) 'A new model of social class: findings from the BBC's Great British Class Survey experiment', *Sociology*, 47(2), 219–50.

Scammell, M. (1995) *Designer Politics: How Elections are Won*, Basingstoke, Macmillan.

Scammell, M. (2000) 'New media, new politics', in Dunleavy et. al. (eds), pp. 169–184.

Scarman, Lord (1981) *The Brixton Disorders, 10–12 April 1981: Report of an Inquiry*, Cmnd 8427, London, HMSO (reprinted by Penguin 1982).

Schmitter, P. (1974) 'Still the century of corporatism', *Review of Politics*, 36, 85–131.

Schneider, C. J. (2008) *Conflict, Negotiation and European Union Enlargement*, Cambridge, Cambridge University Press.

Scott, J. (1985) 'The British upper class', in Coates et al. (eds), pp. 29–54.

Scott, J. (1991) *Who Rules Britain?* Cambridge, Polity.

Scott, J. (1997). *Corporate Business and Capitalist Classes.* Oxford, Oxford University Press.

Scruton, R. (1980) *The Meaning of Conservatism*, Harmondsworth, Penguin.

Sedgemore, B. (1980) *The Secret Constitution*, London, Hodder and Stoughton.

Seldon, A. and Kavanagh, D. (2005) *The Blair Effect: 2001–5*, Cambridge, Cambridge University Press.

Self, P. and Storing, H. (1962) *The State and the Farmer*, London, George Allen & Unwin.

Seltman, C. (1956) *Women in Antiquity*, London, Pan.

Seyd, P. and Whiteley, P. (1992) *Labour's Grass Roots*, Oxford, Clarendon Press.

Sheehy, P. (1993) *Inquiry into Police Responsibilities and Rewards: Report*, Cm 2280.I, London, HMSO.

Shepherd, J. and Laybourn, K. (2013) *Britain's First Labour Government*, Basingstoke, Palgrave Macmillan.

Sherman, J. (2002) 'Mapping the rise of a new No. 10 powerbase', *The Times* (31 Jan.).

Shore, C. (2000) *Building Europe: The Cultural Politics of European Integration*, London, Routledge.

Simhony, A. (1991) 'On forcing individuals to be free: T. H. Green's liberal theory of positive freedom', *Political Studies*, 39(2), 303–20.

Simon, H. A. (1947) *Administrative Behaviour*, London, Macmillan.

Sivanandan, V. (1981) 'From resistance to rebellion', *Race and Class*, 23 (Autumn).

Skelcher, C. (1998) *Appointed State: Quasi-governmental Organizations and Democracy*, Buckingham, Open University Press.

Skelcher, C. and Davies, H. (1996) 'Understanding the new magistracy: a study of characteristics and attitudes', *Local Government Studies*, 22(2), 8–21.

Smith, A. (1982) *The Wealth of Nations*, Harmondsworth, Penguin (first published 1776).

Smith, A. (1997) 'Studying multi-level governance: examples from French translations of the structural funds', *Public Administration*, 75, 711–29.

Smith, D. J. and Gray, J. (1985) *Police and People in London*, Aldershot, Gower.

Smith, J. (2005) *Reinvigorating European Elections: The Implications of Electing the European Commission*, London, Chatham House.

Smith, M. (1993) *Pressure Power and Policy: State Autonomy and Policy Networks in Britain and the United States*, Hemel Hempstead, Harvester Wheatsheaf.

Smith, M. (1999) *The Core Executive in Britain*, Basingstoke, Macmillan.

Smith, M., Marsh, D. and Richards, D. (1993) 'Central government departments and the policy process', *Public Administration*, 71(4), 567–94.

Solomos, J. (2003) *Race and Racism in Britain*, 3rd edn, Basingstoke, Palgrave Macmillan.

Spretnack, C. and Capra, F. (1986) *Green Politics: The Global Promise*, London, Collins.

Squires, J. and Wickham-Jones, M. (2002) 'Mainstreaming in Westminster and Whitehall: from Labour's Ministry for Women to the Women and Equality Unit', *Parliamentary Affairs*, 55, 57–70.

Stanworth, P. and Giddens, A. (eds) (1974) *Elites and Power in British Society*, Cambridge, Cambridge University Press.

Stanyer, J. (2001) 'The new media and the old: the press, broadcasting and the Internet', *Parliamentary Affairs*, 54, 249–59.

Stewart, J. (1992) 'The rebuilding of public accountability', paper presented at European Policy Forum, December.

Stewart, J. (1995) 'Appointed boards and local government', *Parliamentary Affairs*, 48(2), 226–41.

Stewart, J. (2000) *The Nature of British Local Government*, Basingstoke, Macmillan.

Stiglitz, J. (2002) *Globalization and its Discontents*, New York, Norton.

Stoker, G. (1991) *The Politics of Local Government*, 2nd edn, Basingstoke, Macmillan.

Stoker, G. (1993) 'Introduction: local government reorganisation as a garbage can process', *Local Government Policy Making*, 19(4), 3–5.

Stoker, G. (ed.) (2000) *The New Politics of Local Governance*, Basingstoke, Macmillan.

Stoker, G. (2003) *Transforming Local Governance: From Thatcherism to New Labour*, Basingstoke, Palgrave Macmillan.

Strickland, P. (2012) *Police and Crime Commissioners*, London, House of Commons Library Standard Note SN/HA/6104.

Stuart, C. (ed.) (1975) *The Reith Diaries*, London, Collins.

Studlar, D. T. (1983) 'The ethnic vote 1983: problems of analysis and interpretation', *New Community*, 9(1–2), 92–100.

Sutton Trust (2010) *The Educational Backgrounds of Members of Parliament in 2010*, London, Sutton Trust.

Tarling, R. and Dowds, L. (1998) 'Crime and punishment', in Jowell et al., pp. 197–214.

Taylor, A. J. P. (1965) *English History 1914–1945*, London, Oxford University Press.

Tempest, M. (2002) 'Lords reform architect condemns concessions', *Guardian* (9 Jan.).

Thain, C. and Wright, M. (1995) *The Treasury and Whitehall: The Planning and Control of Public Expenditure 1976–1993*, Oxford, Clarendon Press.

Theakston, K. (1995) *The Civil Service since 1945*, Oxford, Blackwell.

Theakston, K. (1999) *Leadership in Whitehall*, Basingstoke, Macmillan.

Theakston, K. and Fry, G. K. (1989) 'Britain's administrative elite: permanent secretaries 1900–1986', *Public Administration*, 67(2), 129–48.

Thomas, H. (ed.) (1959) *The Establishment*, London, Anthony Blond.

Thompson, B. (1997) 'Conclusion: judges as trouble-shooters', *Parliamentary Affairs*, 50(1), 182–9.

Thompson, E. P. (1975) *Whigs and Hunters*, London, Allen Lane.

Thompson, J. B. (1995) *The Media and Modernity: A Social Theory of the Media*, Cambridge, Polity.

Thranhardt, D. (1995) 'The political uses of xenophobia in England, France and Germany', *Party Politics*, 1(9), 323–45.

Timmins, N. and Kampfner, J. (1997) 'New tricks for old dogs', *Financial Times* (18 March).

Tonge, J. (2000) *The New Civil Service*, Tisbury, Baseline.

Toynbee, P. and Walker, D. (2001) *Did Things Get Better? An Audit of Labour's Successes and Failures*, Harmondsworth, Penguin.

Trench, A. (ed.) (2008) *The State of the Nations 2008: Into the Third Term of Devolution in the UK*, Exeter, Imprint Academic.

Trevor-Roper, H. R. (1981) 'The phenomenon of fascism', in Wolf, S. J. (ed.), *European Fascism in Europe*, London, Methuen, pp. 19–38.

Trollope, A. (1883) *An Autobiography*, London, Blackwood (reissued in Oxford World Classics series, 1999, with editorial introduction).

TV Licensing (2013) *Telescope 2013 Report* (available online via http://www.tvlicensing.co.uk/).

Urban, M. (1997) *UK Eyes Alpha: The Inside Story of British Intelligence*, London, Faber.

Urry, J. (1985) 'The class structure', in Coates et al. (eds).

Urwin, D. (1989) *Western Europe since 1945*, 4th edn, Harlow, Longman.

Urwin, D. (1997) *A Political History of Western Europe since 1945*, Harlow, Addison Wesley Longman.

Useem, M. (1984) *The Inner Circle: Large Corporations and the Rise of Business Political Activity in the US and the UK*, Oxford, Oxford University Press.

Ussher, K. and Walford, I. (2011) *National Treasure*, London, Demos.

Van der Gaag, N. (1995) 'Women: still something to shout about' *New Internationalist*, no. 270 (Aug.), 7–10.

Vidal, J. (1997) *McLibel: Burger Culture on Trial*, Basingstoke, Macmillan.

Vincent, A. (1992) *Modern Political Ideologies*, Oxford, Blackwell.

Von Bertallanfy, L. (1952) *General Systems Theory*, New York, Harper.

Wagstyl, S. (1996) 'Nice work if you can get it', *Financial Times* (18 Dec).

Walker, P. G. (1972) *The Cabinet*, London, Fontana.

Waller, R. and Criddle, B. (1997) *Almanac of British Politics*, London, Routledge.

Walvin, J. (1984) *Passage to Britain*, Harmondsworth, Penguin.

Ward, G. (1993) 'Reforming the public sector: privatisation and the role of advisers', *Political Quarterly*, 94, 298–305.

Wass, Sir D. (1984) *Government and the Governed* (BBC Reith Lectures), London, Routledge and Kegan Paul.

Watts, D. (1997) *Political Communication Today*, Manchester, Manchester University Press.

Watts, D. (2007) *Pressure Groups*, Edinburgh, Edinburgh University Press.

Watts, D. (2008) *The European Union*, Edinburgh, Edinburgh University Press.

Wayne, M. (1998) *Dissident Voices: The Politics of Television and Cultural Change*, London, Pluto.

Weber, M. (1978) *Economy and Society, Vol. II*, Berkeley, CA, University of California Press (first published 1922).

Webster, P. and Bowditch, G. (1997) 'White Paper becomes a best seller', *The Times* (25 July).

Weir, S. and Boyle, K. 1997) 'Human rights in the UK: introduction to the special issue', *Political Quarterly*, 68(2), 128–34.

Weir, S. and Hall, W. (eds) (1994) *Ego Trip: Extra-Governmental Organisations in the United Kingdom and their Accountability*, London, Charter 88 Trust.

Weiss, T. G. and Urquhart, B. (2012) *What's Wrong with the United Nations and How to Fix it*, 2nd edn, Cambridge, Polity.

Wentz, R. E. (1993) *Why People do Bad*

Things in the Name of Religion, Macon, GA, Mercer University Press.

White, M. (2001) 'Why Labour MPs are the new opposition', *Guardian* (7 June).

White, S. (ed.) (2001) *New Labour: The Progressive Future?* Basingstoke, Palgrave Macmillan.

Whitehead, T. (2009) 'Racism and sexism persists in persists in police service', *Daily Telegraph* (11 Jan.).

Whiteley, P. (2011) *Political Participation in Britain: The Decline and Revival of Civic Culture*, Basingstoke, Palgrave Macmillan.

Whiteley, P. and Winyard, S. (1984) 'The origins of the "New Poverty Lobby"', *Public Administration*, 61(1), 32–54.

Whiteley, P., Seyd, P. and Richardson, J. (1994) *True Blues: The Politics of Conservative Party Membership*, Oxford, Clarendon Press.

Whyatt, J. (1961) *The Citizen and the Administration*, London, Justice.

Widdicombe, D. (1977) *Our Fettered Ombudsman*, London, Justice.

Widdicombe, D. (1986) *The Conduct of Local Authority Business*, Cmnd 9797, London, HMSO.

Wilkenson, H. (1995) *No Turning Back: Generations and the Genderquake*, London, Demos.

Wilkinson, R. and Pickett, K. (2010) *The Spirit Level: Why More Equal Societies Almost Always Do Better*, Harmondsworth, Penguin.

Willetts, D. (1996) *Blair's Gurus*, London, Centre for Policy Studies.

Williams, F. (1969) 'A prime minister remembers: the war and post-war memories of the Rt. Hon. Earl Attlee', in King, A. (ed.), *The British Prime Minister*, Basingstoke, Macmillan.

Williamson, N. (1995) 'Civil service ready for Blair, says Sir Robin', *The Times* (20 Nov.).

Wilson, D. and Game, C. (2011) *Local Government in the United Kingdom*, 5th edn,, Basingstoke, Palgrave Macmillan.

Wilson, G. (1994) 'Biology, sex roles, and work', in C. Quest (ed.) *Liberating Women*, London, Institute of Economic Affairs.

Wilson, H. (1974) *The Labour Government 1964–70*, Harmondsworth, Penguin.

Wilson, T. (1966) *The Downfall of the Liberal Party 1914–1935*, London, Collins.

Winter, M. (1996) 'Intersecting departmental responsibilities, administrative confusion and the role of science in government: the case of BSE', *Parliamentary Affairs*, 49(4), 550–65.

Woffinden, B. (2010) 'The Criminal Cases Review Commission has failed', *Guardian* (30 Nov.).

Woodhouse, D. (1995) 'Politicians and the judiciary: a changing relationship', *Parliamentary Affairs*, 48(3) 401–18.

Woodhouse, D. (1996) 'Politicians and the judges: a conflict of interest', *Parliamentary Affairs*, 49(3), 423–40.

Woodhouse, D. (1998) 'The Parliamentary Commissioner for Standards: lessons from the "Cash for Questions" inquiry', *Parliamentary Affairs*, 51(1), 51–61.

Woodhouse, D. (2001) 'The law and politics: more power to the judges – and to the people?' *Parliamentary Affairs*, 54, 223–37.

Woodhouse, D. (2002) 'The law and politics: in the shadow of the Human Rights Act', *Parliamentary Affairs*, 55, 254–70.

Woolf, M. (2010) 'Queen primed for hung parliament', *Sunday Times* (7 Feb.).

Wright, E. O. (1985) *Classes*, London, Verso.

Wright, P. (1987) *Spycatcher*, New York, Viking.

Young, H. (1989) *One of Us*, London, Macmillan.

Young, H. (1998) *This Blessed Plot: Britain and Europe from Churchill to Blair*, Basingstoke, Macmillan.

Zander, M. (1969) 'Who goes to solicitors?', *Law Society's Gazette*, no. 66.

Index

Using the Index: The index draws together references to the myriad people, events and institutions found throughout the text, and also to the concepts underlying the study of politics. You should begin searching by looking up the most specific term possible. Analytical subheadings and cross-references ('see' and 'see also') will guide you to the various aspects of a topic, highlighting interrelationships and reinforcing a holistic approach to the study of politics. Use the **Glossary** for brief definitions and the **Contents** for an overview of the whole book. Note that material in the **Glossary** and **Chronology** is *not* indexed. The index is arranged in word-by-word order, ignoring 'and', 'in', etc.; page numbers in italics refer to illustrations.